MANAGING FOR THE FUTURE

MASSACHUSETTS INSTITUTE OF TECHNOLOGY

ANCONA, KOCHAN, SCULLY, VAN MAANEN, WESTNEY

Organizational Behavior & Processes

South-Western College Publishing

an International Thomson Publishing company I(T)P®

Cincinnati • Albany • Boston • Detroit • Johannesburg • London • Madrid • Melbourne • Mexico City
New York • Pacific Grove • San Francisco • Scottsdale • Singapore • Tokyo • Toronto

Dedicated to those who have inspired us to try to be better students and teachers.

Special dedications to

Professor Jack Barbash
Professor Arthur H. Gladstein
Professor Marius B. Jansen
Professor Joanne Martin
Professor Edgar H. Schein

Publishing Team Director: Dave Shaut
Acquisitions Editor: John R. Szilagyi
Developmental Editor: Jamie Gleich Bryant
Production Editor: Mardell Toomey
Media Technology Editor: Kevin von Gillern
Media Production Editor: Robin Browning
Production House: DPS Associates, Inc.
Internal Design: Michael H. Stratton
Cover Design: Michael H. Stratton
Marketing Manager: Rob Bloom
Manufacturing Coordinator: Sue Kirven

Library of Congress Cataloging-in-Publication Data

Managing for the future : organizational behavior & processes /
    Deborah Ancona . . . [et al.]. -- 2nd ed.
        p.   cm.
    Includes bibliographical references and index.
    ISBN 0-538-87546-1
    1. Personnel management. 2. Organizational change. I. Ancona,
Deborah G. (Deborah Gladstein) II. Title: Organizational behavior &
processes. III. Title: Organizational behavior and processes.
HF5549.M31345 1998
658-dc21   98-48895
                                                     CIP

1 2 3 4 5 6 7 8 9 MZ 6 5 4 3 2 1 0 9 8

Printed in the United States of America

I(T)P®
International Thomson Publishing
South-Western College Publishing is an ITP Company.
The ITP trademark is used under license.

BRIEF TABLE OF CONTENTS

TABLE OF CONTENTS

OVERVIEW OF THE MODULES

This is the second edition of the *Managing for the Future* Modules and it is somewhat different from the first edition. We still focus on changes going on in organizations today and some of the most commonly held visions of what the "organization of the future" will look like. However, with the passage of time, we are more able to separate hype from reality, and to talk about the unintended consequences of the recent era of change in the firm. In this edition we spend a great deal more time laying out the three theoretical lenses—strategic design, political, and cultural—and weaving them throughout the modules. The lenses are used to help analyze organizations and direct managerial action. This edition also places more emphasis on skills and the actions managers need to accomplish to cope effectively with change. As our students have complained about excessive reading, we have now broken the readings down into "core" and "supplemental" so that faculty can choose the length and depth of readings for a given class. Finally, we have organized the modules in four groupings: Analytics, Teams, Organizations, and Skills, reflecting how we teach the course.

The modules and recent changes are the product of our own cross-functional team, composed of the five of us from MIT, and others who have joined us in our endeavors. The MIT set represents the disciplines of anthropology, social psychology, sociology, and industrial relations. We have co-taught the core for the past five years and have updated the teaching materials based on that experience. A number of new faculty, and visitors have taught with us and contributed to our thinking and writing. These include Professors Mitch Abolafia, Stuart Albert, Ella Bell, Paul Carlile, Deborah Kolb, and Amy Segal. We have also gone beyond MIT's borders to recruit scholars from other schools to contribute modules. There are two brand new modules in this edition. The first on "issue selling" is by Professors Susan Ashford and Jane Dutton from the University of Michigan. The second is a "negotiations" module by Professor Deborah Kolb from the Harvard Center on Negotiations and Simmons Center for Gender and Organizations.

The course continues to be molded around the features of the "new" organization: a networked, flat, flexible entity made up of a diverse workforce operating in a global environment. We continue to examine changes in the firm from the strategic design, political, and cultural lenses, but teach these lenses more intensively. These two frameworks compose the "analytic" grouping of modules and form the core structure of the course. We then move on to use the frameworks to analyze and plan managerial action in "teams" and "organizations." When looking at both teams and organizations we include an analysis of the environment to show how context influences structures and processes. Finally, we integrate "skills" sessions throughout the course so that students have a sense of how to manage in the shifting corporate landscape. We continue to stress international issues and cases and links to strategy.

Our aim is not to teach the "correct" way to manage or the "perfect" way to design an organization. There is no one best way. Rather, our aim is to provide a general understanding of possible managerial approaches to particular problems and introduce ways to analyze the various social costs and benefits typically associated with any given approach. Because we exist in a time of considerable tumult and flux, there are many different managerial approaches being advocated. Thus, we include readings from academics, consultants, and the popular press, some of which contradict each other, so that students can debate what the future will look like, what actions are appropriate in various situations, and what is hype versus reality. We also hope that students can become more critical readers of both the business and academic press and more informed users of consultant services.

Students learn in different ways, so our modules include varied teaching media including cases, experiential exercises, readings, teamwork, discussions, papers, projects in real organizations, and videotapes. One of our goals is to get students to be more aware of their own beliefs and actions, to compare these with the conceptual material and their responses in exercises and in class, and perhaps to change the way they think and act as managers. Thus, we want students to learn new theories and models, but also to learn more about themselves now and how they need to develop in the future. Students should leave with a better sense of their learning styles, the roles they take on in teams, and how they respond to new managerial challenges such as downsizing and taking new products to market.

Given our varied goals (including learning theory, applying that theory, examining one's own beliefs and behaviors, and becoming more capable organizational participants), these modules and the course they support require that the professor take on different roles. On some days the professor is a lecturer, on others a case leader. During experiential exercises the professor is a facilitator, while certain team exercises may require that he or she be a coach. Thus, the teacher is not always the "expert," just as the goals of the day are not always to memorize a given set of concepts. While we sometimes found it difficult to teach in new ways, the detailed teaching notes helped us to make the transition a lot easier.

The design of the modules mirrors the way we teach this course. The material is organized as a set of modules that can be used together as a full course, as an addition to an existing course, or individually as one-day seminars or executive education courses. The modules examine current practices in real companies around the world, but also provide concise readings on key up-to-date theoretical contributions. We have fewer readings and examples than most texts, because we have found it more effective to teach less material, but teach it in a way that has students retaining and using the material. Thus, students will not be exposed to all the social-psychological theory of groups, but they will learn skills in creating work teams and some key concepts and models of teams, and they will have to apply those concepts and models to cases, their own behavior in teams, and team diagnosis. In this way learning is not rote memorization, but internalized concepts that can be applied to new situations. A module can be taught in one three-hour session, which facilitates the learning from experiential exercises, in two one-and-a-half hour sessions, or in three one-hour sessions.

While we provide cases, experiential exercises, and conceptual material, we believe that students learn best when they must apply what they have learned in a real situation. Thus, we strongly suggest that the class be broken up into small teams that work together throughout the term and that these teams be given the task of analyzing a real organization or team. Our Module 2A, "Conducting Team Projects," helps to prepare students for a study of a real organization, while Module 3, "Making Teams Work," provides a listing of alternative team assignments as well as materials to help teams work productively and learn about their own team process. Again, these assignments help motivate students to learn the material in the course and help them in the process of making theory useful.

Thus, our specific objectives in this book, and the courses it supports, can be summarized as follows:

1. Introduce students to a framework of the "new" organization and three lenses—strategic design, political, and cultural—from the behavioral sciences that help students to analyze it.

2. Provide opportunities to apply these theories to real organizational and managerial problems.

3. Participate in ongoing work teams in which students can learn about teamwork.

4. Allow students to examine their own behavior and beliefs about organizations, they can contrast them with the theories and observations of others.

5. Encourage students to become critical readers of the business press, the trends it discusses, and the services offered by different organizational consultants.

6. Enable students to be informed and engaged participants in organizational transformation.

Below we provide a quick overview of each module in the book (see Figure I.1) followed by a more in-depth explanation of what each module contains. The introduction ends with some summary statements.

FIGURE I.1 QUICK MODULE OVERVIEW

ANALYTICS

Module 1 The "New" Organization: Taking Action in an Era of Organizational Transformation

- Contrasts emerging new organizational forms with the traditional bureaucratic model.
- Examines features of the "new" organization: networked, flat, flexible, diverse, and global.
- Critiques the new model.
- Includes exercise to get students to talk about organizations in transition from the old to the new model.
- New case that emphasizes the "new" organization as a context in which to take action.

Module 2 Three Lenses on Organizational Analysis and Action

- Introduces three lenses to examine organizations: the strategic design lens, the political lens, and the cultural lens.
- Delves into each lens separately with a new case, role play, and exercise.
- Includes a custom-produced video of events in one organization and an exercise that has students comparing and contrasting the three models.

Module 2A Conducting Team Projects

- Includes detailed instructions for a team project to diagnose a real organization.
- Provides teaching materials for launching the project.

TEAMS

Module 3 Making Teams Work

- Provides a handbook with pragmatic, step-by-step advice to help students create and maintain effective working teams.
- Provides readings that enable a common vocabulary or teams and a model of team effectiveness.
- Includes a survey instrument that can be used for a mid-term evaluation of how well student teams are operating.

Module 4 Diverse Cognitive Styles in Teams

- Provides a diagnostic instrument to assess students' own cognitive styles.
- Includes an experiential exercise to help students understand how their style interacts with those of others.
- Includes readings to elaborate on the concept of cognitive style, its dimensions, and how it can be used, and abused, in organizations.
- Pushes students to apply this framework to their own team behavior.

Module 5 Team Processes

- Concentrates on understanding internal team dynamics, including what can go wrong in teams and how to improve team processes.
- Includes reading on how to observe team dynamics, improve team decision making, and use influence tactics.
- Includes two experiential exercises: a videotape analysis of a team making a decision, and a role play in which teams must design a new product.
- Applies the three lenses to team analysis.

Module 6 Teams in Organizations

- Introduces the "external perspective" of teams—the relationship between a team and its external environment.
- Includes readings on how the organizational context shapes teams, how team members can effectively manage their environment, and key team-organization dynamics.
- Includes a case of a team leader's struggle to work in a difficult environment.
- Includes detailed lecture notes on the "external perspective" of teams.

FIGURE I.2 QUICK MODULE OVERVIEW (CONTINUED)

ORGANIZATIONS

Module 7 Workforce Management: Employment Relationships in Changing Organizations

- Examines changing employment relationships in organizations, including part-time work, temporary workers, and working at home.
- Provides conceptual material that identifies flexibility for employees and flexibility for organizations and how the two forms create contradictions in organization.
- Includes a case illustrating the difficulties of evaluating employees under different employment contracts.
- Includes an experiential exercise that reinforces the personal and human resource consequences of creating a flatter and more flexible organization.

Module 8 Managing Change in Organizations

- Introduces two very different models of organizational change: top-down change and bottom-up change.
- Provides conceptual material that includes a historical perspective on change in the field of organizational behavior.
- Includes an in-depth case on change efforts at Xerox, which allows students to compare and contrast the top-down and bottom-up approaches to change.
- Includes a report on an over-stressed workforce at Xerox and an exercise in which students must develop a change strategy to deal with this issue.

Module 9 Organizational Action in Complex Environments

- Introduces the concept of organizational environment.
- Includes readings on three different perspectives on the organizational environment: the strategic design, political, and cultural perspectives.
- Includes a case examining Roussel-Uclaf, a French company, which lends itself to an analysis of organizational environments in a global market.
- Includes a new case examining Electrolux-Zanussi, a successful merger of a Swedish and Italian firm.

Module 10 Learning Across Borders: Disneyland from California to Paris via Tokyo

- Introduces the concepts of organizational change and cross-border learning.
- Includes conceptual material on corporate and national culture.
- Includes new varied and extensive case materials on Disneyland Paris and allows for a case analysis comparing the Disney experience in France, the U.S., and Japan.

SKILLS

Module 11 Managing Cultural Diversity

- Introduces the bystander perspective on diversity.
- Includes video clips of actual diversity issues at a university.
- Provides instructions for a workshop to learn from the video.

Module 12 Negotiation and Conflict Resolution

- Provides a complete overview of concepts in negotiation.
- Provides a skill-based view of how to negotiate.
- Includes a negotiations exercise developed by Deborah Kolb to do in-class.
- Includes a video to show how others carried out the exercise.

Module 13 Change from Within: Roads to Successful Issue Selling

- Provides a conceptual and practical guide to issue selling in organizations.
- Includes a case to analyze issue selling in the corporate context.
- Includes an exercise so that students can practice issue-selling skills.

THE FOUNDATION FOR THE MODULES

ANALYTICS

MODULE 1—The "New" Organization: Taking Action in an Era of Organizational Transformation

The modules center on a framework for the organization of the future. In this module we examine some of the features that characterize the emerging "new" organizational form—it is networked, flat, flexible, diverse, and global. We contrast this form with its traditional predecessor and discuss the pros and cons of each. We try to separate hype from reality and look at the costs of new organizational designs. For example, the traditional bureaucratic form achieves control and stability while the new form facilitates coordination and rapid adaptation. The traditional bureaucratic form stresses distance and buffering from the external environment while the new form is constantly and tightly linked to other firms, both competitors and allies. We discuss some of the forces that are pushing organizations to adopt new forms and some of the forces that inhibit even those changes that sound so promising. We emphasize that the jury is still out as to what the "new" organization will look like. Finally, we recognize that many organizations are currently in a state of flux—caught between the old and the new and exhibiting features of each. This ongoing situation calls for the analysis of contradictory forces in organizations and makes the understanding of organizational change paramount. A case is used to show the "new" organization as a context in which to take action.

MODULE 2—Three Lenses on Organizational Analysis and Action

We believe that the behavioral sciences provide three powerful lenses with which to understand the movement from the old to the new form: the **strategic design** lens, the **political** lens, and the **cultural** lens. The strategic design lens positions the organization as a goal-directed entity in which an engineering approach can be used to craft an organizational structure and system of rewards, careers, controls, and tasks that "fit" a given environment. The political lens, in contrast, views the organization and its environment as a set of changing interests and coalitions that are in conflict over scarce resources and that negotiate agreements. The result is an organization consisting of multiple stakeholders and existing in a network of political relationships. The cultural lens views the organization as a set of deeply held assumptions that are acquired early in a firm's history and that are passed on through stories, symbols, myths, and socialization procedures. These deeply held assumptions signal to people how to act and react to events around them. They may sabotage major change efforts because "that is simply not the way we do things around here." These three lenses highlight very different aspects of organizational behavior. It is only through an understanding of all three that a complete organizational diagnosis and understanding of change can take place.

These three lenses form the core analytic concepts for the course and their treatment has been greatly expanded. Now there is a case to teach strategic design stressing grouping, linking, and alignment. There is a role play to teach the political perspective, specifically stake-holder analysis, power and influence, and conflict resolution. There is an exercise to hone cultural analysis and a short custom-produced videotape illustrating events in one organization that allows students to apply all three lenses to analysis an action.

MODULE 2A—Conducting Team Projects

This module contains instructions for a team project to diagnose and suggest recommendations in a real organization. The module includes a guide to analysis using the three lenses and also a step-by-step guide to all the steps involved in such a project. These materials can be handed out to students for them to work on by themselves. Alternatively, the module includes materials to teach a class that serves as a project introduction and sendoff. Students learn about using metaphors for organizational analysis and stretch their thinking about intervention within the organizational context.

This module includes an exercise in analyzing a video to understand metaphorical thinking better. The "orchestra" is a common metaphor for team or organizational cooperation with a mix of self-management and distinctive leadership. Students watch a video of an orchestra's preparation for a performance and discuss the metaphorical lessons that can be drawn from it. This exercise prepares them for their own analysis of new organizational forms using metaphors. We have found that students have fun coming up with a variety of creative and instructive metaphors.

TEAMS

There is a large emphasis on teams in the class. Teams can be used within the class framework to carry out an organizational analysis and further train students in using the three lenses. Teams are seen as a key structural element in the "new" organization, and students are expected to improve their team design and management skills in the class. Thus, four modules are devoted to teams and the diversity and negotiations modules can also be adopted to a team orientation.

MODULE 3—Making Teams Work

This module is somewhat unique in that it does not correspond to a class, but rather is a tool to help students work effectively in ongoing teams. This module is most useful in courses that use teams extensively and have major team projects. The module serves two major functions: first, it provides a conceptual introduction to the nature and vocabulary of teams; second, it provides a handbook that helps students to create effective working teams. In addition, the module includes a survey instrument that allows students to do a mid-term evaluation of how well they are operating as a team.

The impetus to include this module is that students often have differing notions of what a team is, when a team should be created, and what different types of teams exist. The conceptual part of the module allows all students to begin the course with a shared vocabulary and shared model of teams and teamwork.

This module is also motivated by the fact that teams often suffer from process problems. Most courses provide conceptual aid, but not pragmatic advice about how to go about setting goals, creating a team structure, defining a team process, and learning to deal with problems over time. The team handbook provides actual steps to follow and barriers to avoid in answering the questions: "Who are we?" "What do we want to accomplish?" "How can we organize ourselves to meet our goals?" "How will we operate?" and "How can we continuously learn and improve?" The survey instrument lets students evaluate how well they have answered these questions, and how they compare with other teams in the class.

MODULE 4—Diverse Cognitive Styles in Teams

Teams create the need to work with a diverse set of other people in a changing set of configurations. This type of structure requires a greater understanding of one's own style, the style of coworkers, and how those styles interact. This module takes students through an assessment of their own cognitive styles, and an experiential exercise to see what that means with regard to interaction with others. This particular diagnostic device is seen not as the "answer" to understanding all interpersonal interaction, but rather as a starting point for assessing similarities and differences between individuals and how to deal with them.

The diagnostic device used for the self-assessment part of this module is similar to the Myers-Briggs instrument. It focuses on an individual's information environment and illuminates a person's preferences in how to take in information and how to make decisions. This approach fits the manager's world of highly interpersonal and informational tasks, high levels of problem solving with others, and the need for fast-paced decision making. Students are encouraged to think about the kinds of activities they enjoy, the ways in which they like to get information, how they see others, and how others may see them.

The experiential exercise calls for students to engage in a problem-solving exercise with a specially configured group. Students then report on how they worked together. Later, when students learn about the nature of the group configuration, they are asked to compare and contrast what it is like to work with similar versus different types of individuals. They also discuss how multiple valid solutions to the same problem can be derived and how people's different preferences for solutions can enhance or inhibit organizational change.

MODULE 5—Team Processes

This module concentrates on internal team dynamics. The focus here is on what can go wrong in teams, how to improve and lead teams, and how to observe ongoing processes, particularly decision making. This module contains conceptual material on how to observe a team and team decision making. If this module is used in the same course as Module 2, then students can also apply the strategic design, political, and cultural diagnostic lenses to team behavior. We also provide a choice of exercises that push students to apply the conceptual material to actual teams in action. One choice is to have students observe and analyze a film of a team making a decision. The second option is to have students engage in an experiential exercise in which they must design and build a product that will compete with products created by the other teams in the class.

The conceptual material examines what to observe in teams, e.g., communication, influence, task and maintenance behaviors, decision making, conflict, atmosphere, and emotional issues. It also covers problems that teams often encounter, such as poor organization, groupthink, and biased information, and how to improve team decision making. A listing of key influence tactics that team members and leaders can use to shape and shift team processes is also included.

Students seem to remember and internalize these concepts most readily when they have to apply them. The film is a wonderful example of the complexity of team decision making, which not only helps to illustrate many team phenomena, but also allows students to try to predict what will happen as the team progresses and to ponder how best to manage the process. The product development task requires students to apply the team concepts to themselves. When engaged in a time-limited task that requires multiple skills, creativity, and coordination, students must evaluate how well their teams allocated roles, made decisions, communicated, and handled conflict.

MODULE 6—Teams in Organizations

While Module 5 concentrates on internal team dynamics, this module concentrates on the relationships between a team and its external environment. The focus here is on how the organizational context influences a team, e.g., the impact of team design, rewards, and supervision; what team members need to do to effectively manage their environment, e.g., obtain resources, influence key stakeholders, and obtain feedback; and how internal dynamics and external boundary management interact. The conceptual material is applied to a case study of a task force run by a recent MBA graduate.

The readings in this module emphasize that in the new organization teams can seldom work in isolation. More often, they must not only manage their internal operations, but also must engage in a complex set of interactions with top management, other teams, multiple functional groups, and even people outside the organization. The readings outline effective strategies for handling these external interactions. Also stressed here is the fact that beyond the hype of the wonders of teams lies the reality that teams are often stressful for individuals, difficult to manage, and not capable of providing all the productivity and satisfaction gains that the popular press has touted.

The case provides a longitudinal look at one team leader's struggle to meet his goals. By examining the design of the team, its early processes, the ways in which outsiders were handled, and the nature of the organizational context, students learn a lot about how to manage and how not to manage a team. The issues of how to design an organization to facilitate effective teamwork can also be emphasized in this module.

ORGANIZATIONS

MODULE 7—Workforce Management: Employment Relationships in Changing Organizations

This module examines the changing employment relationships in organizations that are trying to be flatter and more flexible. It examines the departures from old models of lifelong employment security, the nature of flexible and varied work arrangements, e.g., part-time work, working at home, and the use of temporary workers; the unintentional contradictions that often emerge in using multiple arrangements; and the issues of equity and fairness that these new arrangements create. Key concepts are made very real as students analyze a case in which promotion decisions must be made for employees following very different career paths. Students also participate in an experiential exercise where concurrent downsizing, redeployment, and teamwork create challenges.

The conceptual material presented here identifies two types of flexibility: flexibility for employees and flexibility for organizations. The former involves flexibility about time, space, the division of labor, careers, skills, and assignments as seen in the introduction of flextime, job sharing, telecommuting, nonlinear careers, and multiskilling. Flexibility for organizations means a greater ability to expand and contract the number of employees. Here the workplace has experienced downsizing; the increased use of temporary workers, consultants, and subcontractors; and outsourcing of work to other firms. These two forms of flexibility are, however, often hard to reconcile and create numerous managerial dilemmas.

The case in this module helps to illustrate some of the difficulties of simultaneously evaluating employees with different employment arrangements. As students struggle to determine who should get promoted, personal values and prejudices are often exposed and multiple solutions to the dilemma are examined.

The experiential exercise is one that students seldom forget. As a managerial transformation that looks great on paper is actually implemented, the personal and human resource consequences of creating a flatter and more flexible organization are uncovered. The exercise results in an awareness of the necessity of carefully crafting a transformation plan and the importance of thinking systematically about the sometimes isolated pieces of a transformation.

MODULE 8—Managing Change in Organizations

As organizations struggle to increase productivity and prepare for the next century, they are in the midst of unprecedented change. In this module we follow the extensive changes made by the Xerox corporation as it deals with stiff global competition while managing a worldwide set of operations and trying to create an organization that is responsive to employee needs. The module provides two very different models of change: top-down change and bottom-up change. It examines how both models exist at Xerox and how change is best understood by taking both into account.

The conceptual material that is provided in this module includes a historical perspective of how organizational change has been studied in the field of Organizational Behavior, and maps out the top-down and bottom-up approaches to change. An in-depth case study of Xerox, from both perspectives, is provided. With these materials students can discuss the strengths and weaknesses of the two models of change and which model may be better suited for the organization of the future.

Students are also provided with a report on issues of work and family, and an over-stressed workforce at Xerox. They are asked to develop change strategies for the corporation that deal with these issues in the context of what was learned about previous change efforts.

MODULE 9—Organizational Action in Complex Environments

This module helps to develop an understanding of how to analyze an organization's environment, that is, the "social actors" outside the organization, especially other organizations, that are important for its survival and success. As organizations move to become more networked, flexible, and global, interaction with the external environment increases and becomes even more critical to success. Just as we present three different perspectives on organizations in Module 2, here we present three different but complementary perspectives on the environment: the strategic design, the political, and the cultural perspectives. Any analysis of the organizational environment is made more complex in a global context. Through a case study of a multinational corporation, the intricacies of environmental analysis in a global context are made real.

Each of the three perspectives—the strategic design, the political, and the cultural—contributes a distinctive approach to analyzing the organizational environment. Each provides insights to managers about how to "manage," and the limits of managing, the external environment. The three perspectives are compared and contrasted through an analysis of one of the two cases. The first is Roussel-Uclaf in France in 1988, as it tries to make the decision about marketing RU486. Further insights about organizational environments in a global context are achieved when the analysis moves to Roussel-Uclaf in 1992 as it tries to decide about marketing the drug in the United States market. The second case, Electrolux-Zanussi, examines the core competency of a Swedish firm to acquire and integrate other firms. In this case, the acquisition is an Italian firm. An environmental analysis is needed to fully understand how effective integration takes place. This case is also excellent for teaching organizational change and can be used in conjunction with Modules 8, 10, and 12 to form an organization change section.

MODULE 10—Learning Across Borders: Disneyland from California to Paris Via Tokyo

One of the most difficult aspects of operating in a global context is determining how a particular product or process will fare when transplanted into a rather different and distinctive cultural context. This module provides insights into this particular dilemma by providing an in-depth view of the concept of organizational and national culture, and applying the three lenses to study how one firm shifts in design from one country to another. The module focuses on Disney's theme park operations in France. While France is the main focus of the day, a thorough analysis requires comparisons with the United States and Japanese experiences with their theme parks. Students tend to move easily into case analysis since most are familiar with Disney products and its culture, and most are fascinated by the differential results of the various theme parks.

The Disney case includes input from scholarly papers, consultant reports, and business press accounts. From these readings students can gain a thorough understanding of Disneyland in California and how the strategic design, political, and cultural elements fit together. When moved to different contexts, however, the fit becomes much worse. The analysis focuses on what Disney has learned across borders and what it still needs to learn to survive.

These materials allow students to contrast the Disney experience in France, the U.S., and Japan. Students can then be asked to consult to Disneyland Paris executives as to how to improve their operations. For classes with international students, this module promotes active participation by those students. Time can also be allocated for student presentations. By the end of the module students should understand how to learn and change when shifting natural contexts.

SKILLS

MODULE 11—Managing Cultural Diversity

This is a completely new module and replaces the old module on Managing Cultural Diversity. Here the Bystander perspective is introduced. Students are asked to view videotapes of vignettes of actual occurrences within a business school. These include student-group interviews with recruiters, discussions about teachers' choices of cases, and a professor meeting with a student group. The vignettes are based on actual experiences and the participants represent different genders, races, and nationalities. The vignettes are often repeated with participants acting differently and thus getting different responses to their actions.

Students are asked for their reactions to the vignettes, whether participants and bystanders acted appropriately, and to share these reactions with their classmates. They learn about their responsibilities as bystanders in situations involving unfair treatment, see the result of action and nonaction in these situations, and come to understand their own biases.

MODULE 12—Negotiation and Conflict Resolution

Working in a diverse and changing organization with extensive external contact means greater interpersonal interaction and often greater conflict. In this type of environment negotiation skills are of paramount importance. This module provides a complete overview of the key concepts that managers will need to effectively engage in negotiations. It includes a comprehensive but accessible review of the newest thinking on current negotiation theory and practice.

The role play that is included in the module sets the negotiation in a real-world context where students have to "read" the signals that are given off by various organizational actors, and then decide what to do. The role play can also be set up to explore gender issues in negotiation.

The module includes a video that specifically looks at how people set the stage for negotiations. By contrasting early set ups, people are able to compare and contrast alternative beginnings.

This module can be used in conjunction with the other "skills" modules, or combined with the "teams" or "organizations" modules, or paired with the political lens, or paired with the diversity and cognitive styles modules, as it is a central skill in the new organization.

MODULE 13—Change from Within: Roads to Successful Issue Selling

Like Module 12, this is an entirely new module. Focusing on the best methods to raise both comfortable and charged issues within the firm, we show that today's managers must be prepared to sell ideas both up and down the organization. Six essential issue selling processes are explained in detail: bundling, framing, language, involvement, approach, and timing. From this tactical foundation, we proceed to explore the challenge of selling charged, or "undiscussable," issues in a variety of corporate environments.

The Inex case that is included concentrates on the difficulties of selling a charged issue in an unresponsive organization. Students are asked to map out a tactical strategy for having the issue heard and supported by middle management, and in so doing, discover that an issue is frequently not sold solely on its own merits.

This module fits well with the other skills modules, and it can be combined with Module 8, on organizational change, and Module 9, on organization action, to show different facets of dynamic action in companies.

THE COMPLETE SET OF MODULES

Taken together, these modules cover most topics covered by conventional texts, from perception, interpersonal communication, and cognitive styles, to group process, team performance, and intergroup relations, to organizational environments, change and rewards. (See Figure I.2 for a listing of what topics are covered in each module.) Rather than going through the course topic by topic, however, topics are tied together as they apply to understanding organizations of today and tomorrow, and by the use of the three analytic lenses.

The materials in these modules and our approach to teaching are eclectic. We meld case studies, experiential exercises, theory, and video. We blend our individual preferences for the strategic design, political, or cultural perspective into an appreciation of all three. We try to examine and predict what the "new" organization will look like, while realizing that we cannot be sure. Will organizations be large sets of integrated firms like the Japanese, or will we see lots of smaller, virtual firms that pull together the manufacturing, service, and distribution of other specialized companies? Will we be able to manage our diversity and link across the globe, or fall back to keeping within our own borders? We do not know the answers to these questions, but we do know that it is fun and motivating to think about the form of the future and the skills and capabilities that will be needed when we get there. We hope that our approach and materials work as well for you as they have worked for us.

These modules represent our sense of what works best in the limited time allocated to teach an introductory course in organizational behavior. We will continue to try to update this material and add to it. We also would like to think these modules as a product of the whole field. That is, we encourage you to let us know of changes that you would like to see, or ideas that you have. If you think that you have a module that would fit into the framework of the course and would add to the breath or depth of the material covered, please get in touch with us.

The Foundation for the Modules

FIGURE I.2 TRADITIONAL TOPICS COVERED IN EACH MODEL

Module 1. The "New" Organization

- Structure
- Future Organizational Design
- Organizational Change
- Historical Framework of Organizational Behavior
- Perception
- Organizational Environments
- Globalization

Module 2. Three Lenses on Organizational Analysis and Action

- Perception
- Structure
- Politics
- Power
- Culture
- Design

Module 3. Making Teams Work

- Attitudes and Behavior
- Learning
- Communication
- Interpersonal Relationships
- Leadership
- Diversity
- Group Process
- Group Performance
- Conflict
- Roles and Goals

Module 4. Diverse Cognitive Styles in Teams

- Perception
- Attitudes and Behavior
- Personality
- Individual Decision Making
- Diversity
- Employee Development
- Job Design
- Motivation
- Conflict

Module 5. Team Processes

- Needs, Goals, and Motives
- Communication
- Interpersonal Relations
- Leadership
- Diversity
- Group Process
- Group Decision Making
- Power
- Influence
- Conflict

Module 6. Teams in Organizations

- Personality
- Communication
- Interpersonal Relationships
- Leadership
- Diversity
- Group Process
- Group Decision Making
- Group Performance
- Intergroup Relations
- Power
- Politics
- Conflict

Module 7. Workforce Management

- Stress
- Group Process
- Careers
- Reward Systems
- Future Organizational Designs
- Organizational Change
- Employee Development
- Job Design
- Organizational Structure

Module 8. Managing Change in Organizations

- Power
- Politics
- Negotiations
- Conflict
- Learning
- Diversity
- Intergroup Relations
- Organizational Change

FIGURE I.2 TRADITIONAL TOPICS COVERED IN EACH MODEL (CONTINUED)

Module 9. Organizational Action in Complex Environments

- Perception
- Organizational Learning
- Leadership
- Politics
- Conflict
- Future
- Organizational Design
- Networks

Module 10. Learning Across Borders: Disneyland from California to Paris via Tokyo

- Culture
- Organizational Environments
- Organizational Diagnosis
- Globalization
- Socialization
- Job Design
- Control Systems
- Organizational Effectiveness

Module 11. Managing Cultural Diversity

- Attitudes and Behavior
- Communications
- Diversity
- Group Process
- Power
- Politics
- Conflict
- Culture
- Organizational Change

Module 12. Negotiation and Conflict Resolution

- Power
- Politics
- Negotiations
- Conflict
- Communications
- Interpersonal Relationships
- Diversity
- Relations
- Influence

Module 13. Change from Within: Roads to Successful Issue Selling

- Change
- Issue Selling
- Feedback
- Strategy
- Influence
- Middle Management
- Conflict
- Negotiations

ACKNOWLEDGMENTS

We would like to express our appreciation to colleagues who have taught with us and contributed to our thinking and writing; Mitch Abolafia, Stuart Albert, Ella Bell, Paul Carlile, Deborah Kolb, Amy Segal, Susan Ashford, and Jane Dutton.

ABOUT THE AUTHORS

Deborah Ancona

Deborah Ancona is the Seley Distinguished Professor of Management at the Sloan School of Management at MIT. She received bachelor's and master's degrees in psychology from the University of Pennsylvania, and a Ph.D. in organizational behavior from Columbia University. Prior to joining MIT, she was on the faculty of the Amos Tuck School at Dartmouth College. Professor Ancona's major research interests include group processes, team performance, boundary management, and time and timing in organizations. She has published articles in these areas in *Administrative Science Quarterly, Academy of Management Journal, Organization Science*, and *Group and Organization Studies*.

Thomas A. Kochan

Thomas A. Kochan is the George M. Bunker Professor of Management at the Sloan School of Management at MIT. He received his bachelor's, master's, and Ph.D. degrees in industrial relations from the University of Wisconsin. Prior to joining MIT, he was on the faculty of the School of Industrial and Labor Relations at Cornell University. Professor Kochan's major research interests include industrial relations theory and public policy, human resource strategy and organizational governance, negotiations and conflict-resolution processes, and organizational change and transformation. His recent books include *The Mutual Gains Enterprise* (1994), *Transforming Organizations* (1992), and *The Transformation of American Industrial Relations* (1986). He has also published in *Administrative Science Quarterly, The Academy of Management Journal, Industrial and Labor Relations Review, Industrial Relations, The Quarterly Journal of Economics,* and other journals. He is a past president of the International Industrial Relations Association.

Maureen Scully

Maureen Scully is an assistant professor of industrial relations and organization studies at the Sloan School of Management at MIT. She received a bachelor's degree in social studies from Harvard-Radcliffe, and a master's degree in sociology and a Ph.D. in organizational behavior from Stanford University. Professor Scully's research focuses on injustice and social change in organizations. She has studied how inequality is both legitimated and contested in organizations, how employees perceive merit-based reward systems, how reward systems change during transitions to teamwork, how ethics programs in organizations ramify in unexpected ways, how employee groups use grassroots activism to redress inequalities, and how alternatives to individualistic, merit-based rewards should be created.

John Van Maanen

John Van Maanen is the Erwin Schell Professor of Organization Studies at the Sloan School of Management at MIT. He has been a visiting professor at Yale University, University of Surrey (UK), and INSEAD (France). Professor Van Maanen works in the general area of occupational and organizational sociology. Cultural descriptions figure prominently in his work. He is the author of numerous articles and books including *Essays in Interpersonal Relations, Organizational Careers, Tales of the Field,* and most recently, *Representation in Ethnography.* He currently serves on the editorial boards of *Administrative Science Quarterly, Journal of Contemporary Ethnography,* and *Qualitative Sociology,* and he is a member of the American Sociological Association and the Society for Applied Anthropology.

D. Eleanor Westney

D. Eleanor Westney is the Sloan Fellows Professor of strategy and international management at the Sloan School of Management at MIT. She received her undergraduate education at the University of Toronto and her Ph.D. in sociology from Princeton University. She has focused much of her research on Japanese organizations and is the author of *Imitation and Innovation: The Transfer of Western Organizational Forms to Meiji Japan* (Harvard University Press, 1987). Since joining the Sloan faculty in 1982, she has worked extensively on cross-border management issues and is the editor (with Sumantra Ghoshal) of *Organization Theory and the Multinational Corporation* (Macmillan, 1993). Her current research focuses on the future evolution of the Japanese business system and on the internationalization of R&D.

Deborah M. Kolb

Deborah M. Kolb is Professor of Management at the Simmons College Graduate School of Management and the Director of the Center for Gender in Organizations there. From 1991–1994, Professor Kolb was Executive Director of Program on Negotiation at Harvard Law School. She is currently a Senior Fellow at the Program where she co-directs the Negotiations in the Workplace Program. An authority on gender issues in negotiation, she has also developed curriculum on managerial mediation

15

OVERVIEW

and negotiation in business organizations and a teaching module on gender in negotiations for the National Institute of Dispute Resolution. Deborah Kolb received her Ph.D. from MIT's Sloan School of Management, where her dissertation won the Zannetos Prize for outstanding doctoral scholarship. She has a BA from Vassar College and an MBA from the University of Colorado.

Jane E. Dutton

Jane E. Dutton is the William Russell Kelly Professor of Business Administration at the University of Michigan Business School. Professor Dutton's major research interests are in understanding strategic agenda building in organizations and how people are valued and devalued at work. She teaches MBA, undergraduate, and Ph.D. courses in Organizational Behavior. She has done field work in a variety of organizations, but she is currently focusing on people who work in jobs that are typically devalued (staff, temporary workers, service workers). She has edited many books and published articles in a variety of academic and practitioner journals.

Susan J. Ashford

Susan J. Ashford received her M.S. and Ph.D. in Organizational Behavior from Northwestern University and currently is the Michael and Susan Jandernoa Professor of Organizational Behavior at the University of Michigan Business School. After spending eight years at Dartmouth College's Amos Tuck School, she joined the Michigan faculty in 1991, where her reserach focuses on the ways that individuals are proactive in all facets of their organizational lives. Her work has been published in a variety of outlets including: the *Academy of Management Review, Academy of Management Journal, Journal of Applied Psychology, Organizational Behavior and Human Decision Processes, Research in Organizational Behavior*, and *Strategic Management Journal*, among other outlets. Professor Ashford served on the editorial board for the *Academy of Management Journal* since 1984 (consulting editor, 1990–1993), is currently a board member for the *Academy of Management Review, Organizational Behavior and Human Decision Processes*, and has also reviewed for several other journals.

MASSACHUSETTS INSTITUTE OF TECHNOLOGY

ANCONA, KOCHAN, SCULLY, VAN MAANEN, WESTNEY

MANAGING FOR THE FUTURE

Organizational Behavior & Processes

THE "NEW" ORGANIZATION: TAKING ACTION IN AN ERA OF ORGANIZATIONAL TRANSFORMATION

module 1

CONTENTS

MODULE 1 (M-1)

THE "NEW" ORGANIZATION: TAKING ACTION IN AN ERA OF ORGANIZATIONAL TRANSFORMATION

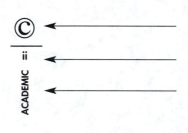

Icon indicates what part you are in, either core Ⓒ or supplemental Ⓢ.

Page number.

Within each part there are sections—Module Overview (OVERVIEW), Academic Perspective (ACADEMIC), Popular Press (PRESS), Case (CASE), Exercise (EXERCISE).

Dedicated to those who have inspired us to try to be better students and teachers.

Special dedications to
Professor Jack Barbash
Professor Arthur H. Gladstein
Professor Marius B. Jansen
Professor Joanne Martin
Professor Edgar H. Schein

Acquisitions Editor: John R. Szilagyi
Developmental Editor: Jamie Gleich Bryant
Production Editor: Mardell Toomey
Production House: DPS Associates, Inc.
Cover Design: Michael H. Stratton
Marketing Manager: Rob Bloom

ISBN: 0-538-87688-3

1 2 3 4 5 6 7 D1 4 3 2 1 0 9 8

Printed in the United States of America

South-Western College Publishing
an International Thomson Publishing company I(T)P®

Cincinnati • Albany • Boston • Detroit • Johannesburg • London • Madrid • Melbourne • Mexico City
New York • Pacific Grove • San Francisco • Scottsdale • Singapore • Tokyo • Toronto

THE "NEW" ORGANIZATION: TAKING ACTION IN AN ERA OF ORGANIZATIONAL TRANSFORMATION

Companies, non-profit institutions, and public-sector organizations today all seem to be demanding that the people they hire and promote be team players, change agents, leaders, entrepreneurs, coaches—all ways of saying that their high-potential employees must understand the "people" side of management and be able to take effective action in the organizations of today and tomorrow. This chorus of demands for organizational skills is rooted in the widespread perception that we are in an era of organizational transformation, when new forms of enterprise are emerging and old forms are changing radically. This module introduces you to the models of organization that dominated management thinking for many years and to those that are emerging today. It describes the major drivers behind their development, provides a sampling of the controversies over the scale and significance of the so-called "new" model, and presents some of the challenges in taking effective action in the "new" organization. In addition, the assignments and the class activities will begin to build your capabilities in experiential learning; that is, learning by reflective analysis of your own experience and that of your classmates, and learning from interactive class exercises.

The module begins with an extended class note on **Changing Organizational Models**, which examines the key features of traditional and emerging models of organization—the "old" model (often called *bureaucracy*) and the "new," which is networked, flat, flexible, diverse, and global. The note points out that the early excitement about the new model, ubiquitous in the business press in the early 1990s, has been replaced by a growing recognition of how difficult it can be to shift to the new forms, and how challenging it can be for those trying to take action in the new work context. It then provides an introduction to some of the individual skills and organizational features required by the new model.

This note is followed by a sampling of comments by leading academics on the new model, some from those who believe that a major organizational transformation is taking place today, and some from those who take a much more skeptical view, but who also differ from each other on what matters about organizational trends in today's society. The purpose of these brief quotations is to hone your own ability to reflect critically on what you read and what you have experienced concerning today's organizations. This is followed by **"The Strategy that Wouldn't Travel,"** a short case study of one manager trying to move an organization from the old to the new model in terms of some of the features of the new organization. As you read this case study, prepare to discuss in class the following questions:

1. What are the features of the new organizational model that this company is trying to develop?

2. What did Karen and her team do that made the changes at the Wichita plant happen? What were the features of the organizational context that helped?

3. What can Karen Jiménez do to take more effective action in the context of the second plant?

The module also includes a reading on the new organization from the business press of the early 1990s, to give you a feel for the excitement and expectations surrounding the model at that time. It is followed by a note on **Reading the Business Press** to provide some perspective on the article, and to encourage you to develop your critical skills as you read popular business journals and the business section of the newspaper.

The module includes a one-page questionnaire, **Mapping your Organization**, which asks you to characterize an organization in which you have worked in terms of how well it fits the model of the new organization. Come to class having filled out that page, and prepared to discuss the following questions:

1. What specific structures or processes in your organization led you to rate it as you did on each of the five features of the new organization?
2. What skills and knowledge were most important for you in working effectively in that organization? What skills do you think were most important for your manager?

ADDITIONAL EXERCISES

You can expand your learning about these issues in several ways. One is to go through current issues of the business press, such as *Business Week, Fortune, Forbes, The Wall Street Journal, The Economist, Management Today, The Asian Wall Street Journal,* and *Asian Business,* and look for stories on individual organizations that are changing or on general trends in management and organization. See how many of the themes from the readings and discussions in Module 1 also loom large in these articles. What is the viewpoint of the story: is it admiring? skeptical of the extent of change? does it focus on successes, or difficulties, or both? On what kind of information sources does it draw?

Another way of learning more about what kinds of changes might be occurring in today's organizations is to talk with your parents about the changes they have seen in their workplaces over the last decade. You might also look more closely at the organization in which you now find yourself—your business school or college—and try to assess the extent to which it is facing some of the same pressures for change, such as changes in technology, pressures to become more efficient, competitive forces toward greater innovation, that are seen as the drivers of the move to the new organization.

Finally, you can draw on more systematic frameworks and analysis through the readings cited in the footnotes for the classnotes, or in articles in recent issues of the more "reader-friendly" management research journals such as the *Harvard Business Review, California Management Review,* and *Sloan Management Review.*

M-1

core

CLASS NOTE: "CHANGING ORGANIZATIONAL MODELS"

In the early and mid-1990s, a rapidly growing stream of articles in the business press proclaimed that a major organizational transformation was taking place in the United States. The organization of the 21st century was already emerging, according to these writers, and it was radically different from what had gone before: it was customer-focused, team-based, networked in alliances with suppliers, customers, and even competitors, flat, flexible and innovative, diverse, and global. Its workforce was empowered and committed; its managers acted as coaches, not bosses; it was a "learning organization," constantly striving to improve and innovate. Organization theorists, some of whom had long predicted that the shift to the "knowledge-based society" would bring about a major change in organizations, provided a more academic perspective on the new era of the "post-modern," "post-bureaucratic," "post-Fordist" organization (see for example Clegg, 1990; Heckscher and Donnellon, 1994; Kaysen, 1996; Capelli et al., 1997).

U.S. corporations were not the only organizations to respond to the drumbeat of organizational change. The Clinton administration picked up the theme of organizational transformation, vowing to "re-invent" government to make it leaner, more responsive, and more flexible. Government organizations from the postal service to the Internal Revenue Service organized teams and task forces, moved to more flexible labor practices, and looked to the corporate world for models of effective new organizational practices. Private non-profit organizations, from public broadcasting to universities, adopted and adapted the language and the models of the "new" organization. And the robust American economy, whose successes in generating employment, growth, and global competitiveness were widely associated with its organizational transformation, legitimated the "cutting-edge" models espoused by American management and organizations in much of the rest of the world.

A survey of Asian business in 1993 portrayed leading companies in Japan, Korea, Taiwan, and Southeast Asia as "becoming less bureaucratic and more customer-focused, decentralising responsibility, motivating staff, continually improving quality, enhancing efficiency, and speeding up decision making . . . exploring management buzz concepts such as 'downsizing' and 'business process re-engineering' that have hitherto seemed irrelevant to Asian companies enjoying double-digit growth" (Selwyn, 1993, pp. 22–23).

The recent crisis in the Asian economies has, if anything, only intensified these efforts. Some European firms such as ABB could convincingly claim to have been leaders rather than followers in the transition to the "new" organizational form, and provided local models of the new organization for other European firms. Business leaders in the so-called "emerging economies" of Latin America, Eastern Europe, and Russia had hopes of "leap-frogging" rapidly from their more traditional organizational forms of family business or state-owned enterprise to the models of the next century. And throughout the world, subsidiaries of U.S. multinational corporations tried, with varying degrees of success, to implement abroad at least some of the changes they were undergoing at home, thereby disseminating at least the rhetoric of the "new" organization.

But by the late 1990s, although few challenged the view that changes in organizational forms were underway, the early sense of excitement and liberation from the "old," stodgy ways of doing things was giving way to a recognition of the enormous challenges involved in the transformation. Not only was it often extraordinarily difficult to shift organizations from the "old" to the "new," but as the "new" became established in some companies, it often proved to have problems and challenges of its own. Working and managing in the old organization may have been boring, constricting, and frustratingly slow, but working and managing in a networked, team-based, flat, flexible, diverse, and global organization often proved to involve long hours, high levels of uncertainty, and rapid personnel turnover that got in the way of developing the networks needed to make the organization work. Stress and burn-out took their toll, and many people quit in search of less stressful work. Involuntary departures also increased, as downsizing became a way of life in many companies, and Americans became accustomed to corporations simultaneously announcing record profits and a program of employee lay-offs and early retirements. The expectations of the 1960s that technological advances would produce a wealthy, leisure society proved to be sadly misplaced: Americans are working longer hours, and individual incomes overall are not rising (although household incomes tended to rise as women joined the labor force). The wage gap between the highest and lowest paid worker in a company has been rising steadily: according to one source, in the last twenty-five years, U.S. CEO salaries have surged from being 35 times that of the entry-level worker to 150 times (Thurow, 1997, p. 405). Analysts are divided on whether these developments are only a temporary by-product of the shift to the new organizational model, or whether they are intrinsically linked to the flat, flexible, networked features of the new organization, whose quest for continued gains in efficiency and productivity entails a continuous re-configuration of its work force.

In other words, the new organization is hard to get to, and often hard to work in when you get there. Moreover, the certainty of the early 1990s that every organization would have to move to *the* new model has given way to a recognition that not only will we see a number of variants of the "new" organization, but that for many organizations the "old" model has proven to have considerable resiliency. We see today some organizations that continue to follow the old model, and many more that exhibit features of the "old" in combination with aspects of the "new." In a recent interview, for example, a manager in a major hotel chain proudly described his company's new team-based, customer-focused organization, and in the next breath revealed that their management experts were training maids in the sixty steps to follow in making a bed, which according to intensive study had proved to be the fastest and most efficient way to make a bed. Such rigidity in standard operating procedures, characteristic of the old organization, can be seen in a wide range of successful organizations today, from McDonald's production of burgers and fries to software developers.

Nevertheless, the model of the new organization has transformed the organizational landscape in which we work and try to take effective action, whether as employees, as managers, as customers, as suppliers, or as citizens and stakeholders struggling to come to terms with the effects of the new organizational forms on our societies and our communities. Business schools are increasingly required to change their curricula to produce managers who can act effectively in organizations that are more team-based, more closely linked to customers and suppliers, flatter, quicker to respond to change, more diverse in the composition of their workforce, and more effective at operating in an increasingly global economy. Organizations in both the private and public sector want managers who have the people skills and the understanding of organizations to help them move towards what many of their leaders see as the organizational model of the twenty-first century. To understand more clearly what this means, we need to examine more closely the key features of the old model and the new.

KEY FEATURES OF THE "OLD" MODEL OF THE ORGANIZATION

The German sociologist Max Weber (1864–1920) was the first to identify systematically a set of features shared by modern large-scale organizations in both the private and the public sectors. For Weber, writing at the turn of the century, the model of "rational-legal bureaucracy" that he developed was the "new" organization of his era, the quintessential modern organizational form. This organizational form provided the base for the expansion in scale and the predictability of the large industrial enterprise and the administrative apparatus of the nation state that were to dominate the organizational landscape of the new twentieth century.

Today, when we take for granted the idea that such different organizations as General Motors, Citibank, UPS, Harvard University, the Army, and state government are fundamentally the same kind of social system and that they can "benchmark" their practices and learn from each other, the concept of an "organization" as a basic category of social systems is hardly surprising. But this recognition is a relatively recent phenomenon, and Max Weber can be seen as its originator, although there was a considerable lag between his identification of the bureaucratic model and its widespread application in the study of organizations. Weber's work was first translated into English in the late 1940s, at a time when the expansion of the social sciences in U.S. universities and the rapid expansion of U.S. industrial enterprise opened up new opportunities for behavioral scientists to pursue research into the behavior of people *in* organizations and the behavior *of* many types of organizations. Weber's model of bureaucracy provided a conceptual framework for generalizing beyond the study of any one particular type of organization. Subsequent generations of organizational theorists expanded Weber's model of "bureaucracy," moving beyond his focus on the organization's internal features to include an analysis of its relationships with its external environment.[1]

The classic model of formal organization (bureaucracy), which in the 1950s and the 1960s defined the "modern" organization, included the following features:

1. Clearly delineated *specialized* individual positions and jobs, with careful and detailed specification of the qualifications required to fill the position, the responsibilities and performance requirements of that position, and the assignment to it of the resources required to do the job

2. A *formal hierarchy* of these positions, with a clear line of authority that set out the powers—and limitations of those powers—for each position or office in a clear and detailed "chain of command" (this feature is why the classic model is often referred to as a "command and control" system)

3. Formal *rules and standard operating procedures* that governed activities, specified in written documents and files (the feature of the "old" organization that has given "bureaucracy" such a negative image as a social system; it too often seems to make following the correct rules and procedures more important than accomplishing the ultimate goals)

4. Set *boundaries* for each department and subunit, and clear boundaries between the organization itself and its environment, with relationships that cross those internal and external boundaries assigned to formal "boundary-spanners"—that is, offices that specialized in handling various elements in the environment and protecting the rest of the organization from "disturbances" from the outside

5. *Standardized* training and training requirements, career paths, and reward systems, based on the development of expertise and creating a predictable and stable *career* for those who fulfilled dutifully the requirements of their positions

In most organizational analyses, the organization's environment was assumed to be a single country. Even in multinational corporations, this assumption was rarely challenged: such companies were usually organized into country subsidiaries responsive to

---

1 For a more detailed but still concise analysis of the emergence of organizational analysis, see W. Richard Scott, 1992, especially Chapter 1.

their local environment, and linked to the rest of the corporation through specified boundary-spanning departments, such as the International Division, or through top-level expatriate managers who served as key boundary-spanners in the multinational system.

The classic model of the organization had many strengths. Its virtues included:

1. *Predictability and Reliability*: The emphasis on following rules and standard procedures that so exasperates the critics of bureaucracy ensured, at its best, that outcomes were predictable and reliable. Organizations as diverse as the traditional local bank branch and IBM in its heyday had, in common with a reputation for being bureaucratic, the ability to offer customers reliable, standard, predictable products and services, every time.

2. *Impartiality*: One of the main reasons for the bureaucratic emphasis on rules, standard procedures, and clearly specified arenas of responsibility was to produce what Max Weber called an "impersonal" system, that did not differentiate its outcomes and procedures according to individual differences or favoritism. This contrast to the family-based enterprise and the personalized state systems of feudalism was long seen as one of the strengths of bureaucracy and one of its peculiarly "modern" characteristics.

3. *Expertise:* The specialization of jobs and positions allowed individuals and departments to deepen their expertise in a particular task, making for levels of experience-based and knowledge-based capabilities that exceeded those of less specialized systems.

4. *Clear Lines of Control:* The hierarchy of offices made it clear who had the authority to make decisions and to receive information on which to base those decisions. In the classic model, information flows up and decisions flow down.

The very strengths of the "old" bureaucratic model can become weaknesses, however, if the environment changes so that these virtues are no longer a source of advantage. Analysts of organizations have long known that not all parts of the organization are equally "bureaucratic:" those parts of the organization that had to be more innovative (like research laboratories, for example) usually exhibited fewer bureaucratic features—much less reliance on rules, less standardization and flatter hierarchies. For many years, a more "organic" and less "mechanical" version of organization was seen as a necessary corrective to the dominant bureaucratic model in certain parts of the organization (such as R&D laboratories, or in new high-growth businesses, for example). But increasingly, as organizations found themselves having to respond to intensifying competition by becoming more innovative in more areas—customer service, continuous improvement in manufacturing, greater diversity of products and services—the virtues of bureaucracy in terms of stability and predictability often came to be seen as liabilities. The Total Quality Management efforts of the 1980s revealed to many organizations that deeply entrenched specializations and internal "walls" between departments could get in the way of the cross-departmental and cross-functional cooperation needed to implement quality initiatives. New information technologies changed the very nature of the "files" and information channels so central to the concept of bureaucracy. And for many companies, international competition and expanding global markets expanded the cross-border dimension of activity beyond the group of specialized "international managers" whose preserve it had been for so long.

Gradually, over the 1980s and into the 1990s, the changes necessary to make organizations work more effectively came to be seen by many managers and management scholars as constituting a new model of organization, whose features contrasted significantly with those long regarded as central to the model of organization.

© 7 ACADEMIC

KEY FEATURES OF THE "NEW" MODEL OF THE ORGANIZATION

The "new" organization can be defined in terms of five complex, interacting features: networked, flat, flexible, diverse, and global. Let us take each in turn, and look more closely at the elements that make up each feature and the factors in the business environment that are widely seen as drivers of the new features.

Networked

U.S. management theory and practice have long emphasized the need for clear lines of individual authority and responsibility for managerial autonomy, and for protecting the organization's core activities from the uncertainties and volatility of its environment. In contrast, the "new" model sees the organization as based on interdependence across individuals, groups and subunits within the organization, and with key elements of its environment. The boundaries of the "new" model are "permeable" or "semipermeable," allowing the much more frequent movement of people and information across them.

Within the organization, this translates into several specific sub-features:

1. Emphasizing teams as fundamental units of activity within each organizational arena of activity, rather than individual jobs
2. Using cross-functional teams that bring together people from different departments or sections of the organization
3. Creating systems for sharing information widely in the organization, horizontally and in both directions vertically (as opposed to the "old" model where information travels up and decisions travel down)

In the organization's relations with its environment, it means:

1. Building close relationships with suppliers, rather than buffering the effects of their behavior (or misbehavior) through inventories and arm's-length contracts and control systems. The "Just-In-Time" delivery systems popularized in the quality movement of the 1980s, for example, mean that suppliers are closely integrated into the manufacturing process, delivering small lots of parts as they are needed for production. This means sharing much more information with suppliers, and developing much higher levels of interdependence with them.
2. Putting people in functional areas such as production and R&D directly in contact with certain customers, rather than relying on specialized boundary-spanning departments like marketing or customer service to mediate between the customer and those parts of the organization that develop and produce products or services
3. Building coalitions to work together with key stakeholders, such as local community groups or government agencies over environmental issues, or with labor unions over the organization of work, rather than adopting a confrontational or defensive posture
4. Building alliances and cooperative networks with other companies, so that another firm may be a "3-C" company—one that is simultaneously a competitor, a customer, and a collaborator or partner

One version of the networked organization is what has been called the "virtual company." This seems close to what in the 1980s was called the "hollow corporation:" that is, a small cluster of managers who contract out all or nearly all of the tasks involved in producing the company's product or service. One example of the "virtual organization" is the independent movie project, where the producer contracts for the duration of the production with the writer, director, actors, camera operators, and so on. Some of the more dramatic scenarios of organizational transformation posit that more and more organizations in the 21st century will be "virtual companies," linking workers, suppliers, and customers around the globe through advanced communications technologies.

There are many complex factors driving the growing recognition of the importance of networks, including the following factors:

1. The availability of new telecommunications and information technologies vastly increases the range of possibilities for connecting people and organizational units across distance and formal organizational boundaries.

2. The competitive need for rapid response to customer needs, changing environments, and demands for innovation means that specialized individual jobs and "islands" of expertise can no longer provide the integration of knowledge needed to create value for customers.

3. The need for increasingly complex and diverse resources to develop and deliver value to customers means that companies can no longer hope to rely wholly on internally-generated resources and capabilities, but must draw on external sources as efficiently and effectively as possible.

4. The "old" model of dealing with a rapidly shifting environment by trying to insulate the core activities of the firm from the sources of change too often meant that a company followed its routines long after they had proved inadequate. Instead, organizations have increasingly found that it is more effective and efficient to deal with volatility (that is, rapid shifts) in the environment by building networks between the source of that volatility (the customer, the supplier, the regulator) and the part of the organization most directly affected by it: for example, by putting product development engineers into direct contact with key customers, or linking suppliers directly into the production process with Just-in-Time inventory systems.

Flat

Perhaps the broadest consensus on the organization of the 21st century (and on what constitutes best practice today) is that the company is much leaner and has far few layers of management than the "old" model. This has meant that many large companies such as IBM and Procter & Gamble have removed several layers of middle management in the past decade. It also means that companies have grown in sales but reduced their number of employees, thereby improving productivity significantly.

But flattening the hierarchy is not simply a matter of reducing layers of management. The "flat" organization is also one that seeks "empowerment" of the operating levels of the organization, pushing decision-making down to the "front line" of the company, so that the unit of the organization responsible for implementing any decision also has the power to make it, or at least participate in making it. This flattening of the hierarchy has been both possible and necessary because of the following factors:

1. Organizations need to respond more rapidly and more flexibly to changes in their markets and technology and to engage their people in continuous improvement of operations, and therefore to eliminate the delays caused by a tall, control-oriented hierarchy.

2. Changes in information technology remove the need for layers of middle managers whose main tasks have centered on organizing and transmitting information, and this allows organizations to monitor activities more quickly and adjust accordingly. This removes the longstanding justification for more hierarchical systems of control—that people at the "front line" of the organization had to be prevented from taking unapproved initiatives that might take weeks or months to correct if they were wrong.

3. Organizations face intense competitive pressures to cut costs. Some attribute these pressures to competition from firms in other countries in an increasingly global economy; others stress instead the intense competition among U.S. firms to increase their appeal to stock analysts and investors by steadily improving their "bottom line," and cutting costs is a proven way of looking good to these constituencies. Fewer managers means a smaller payroll—and firms have finally discovered that getting rid of a manager cuts costs more significantly than getting rid of a low-level employee.

ACADEMIC 9

Flexible

Many companies are finding it difficult to rely on the well-codified but rigid rules, routines, and structures that have been the key characteristics of the models of bureaucracy and formal organization in the past. The great strength of "going by the rules" has been predictability, control, and fairness. Today, however, companies are increasingly called to respond flexibly to diverse needs of employees, customers, and other stakeholders (that is, those who have a "stake" in the survival and success of the organization, including shareholders and local communities), in ways that allow a variety of responses without giving rise to serious accusations of injustice and unfairness. Individuals must turn their hands to whatever activity will help solve a problem or satisfy the customer, without being restrained by formal procedures or job descriptions. Many manufacturing firms, for example, are moving to "flexible production" or "customized mass production" that enable a factory to adjust quickly to a wide variety of changing market demands. Many service firms are emphasizing tailoring their services to the specific needs of particular customers or groups of customers, rather than emphasizing a "one-size-fits-all" approach. Firms must develop systems that encourage innovation and creativity, rather than seeing change as disturbing.

Part of this flexibility is the growing use of temporary structures such as projects, task forces, and informal "communities of practice" that do not affect an individual's formal position or the formal organizational structure, but which allow the speedy reconfiguration of people and resources to address certain problems or play a key linking function. It also involves the use of "temporary" or contingent workers, which links to the "diversity" of the new organization discussed later.

The need for flexibility is seen to be driven by:

1. Intensifying competition, so that capabilities for tailoring products and services to a range of customer needs are increasingly a source of competitive advantage
2. An increasingly diverse labor force, with needs that differ over life cycles as well as across workers
3. An increasingly complex and unpredictable external environment, with which the organization is more and more interdependent, as we saw in the discussion of the externally networked organization

Diverse

The three previous features of the "new" model reinforce the fourth: the need for the new organization to accommodate a diversity of perspectives and approaches, career paths and incentive systems, people and policies within its boundaries, and to respond to an increasingly diverse array of external constituencies and stakeholders. The "old" model, in retrospect, is exemplified by the "organization man" of the 1950s—a male executive, committed to serving the interests of the firm in return for a secure, predictable, and long term career and social identity, and usually with a wife who does not work outside the home—and by a "managing by the rules" approach that treats every employee and every situation by a predefined, standardized set of rules. The new model presents a diverse array of possible career trajectories, including part-time work, home-based "tele-working" (where employees are linked to the office through home computers), different "tracks" that people can choose depending on their interests and family situations, and increasing levels of exits from the firm. It includes an array of people who are in the firm but have a nontraditional relationship to it: full-time contract workers, for example, or former employees hired on as independent consultants. It is open to people from a wide variety of backgrounds and provides avenues for them to let the organization know if older systems of communication and traditional expectations of managers are creating a difficult or stressful work environment.

An organization that values diversity is preferred in today's world because of:

1. The growing diversity of the workforce, in demographic terms (more women working, greater ethnic and international diversity, more people entering and leaving the organization at different points in their lives)
2. A greater need for innovation and creative approaches to solving problems, which are seem to benefit from diverse approaches and viewpoints
3. Growing volatility (that is, unpatterned and unpredictable change) in the business environment
4. Flat, flexible, and networked organizations that are linked closely to other organizations with different systems and cultures, and with customers who have a variety of needs and approaches. Firms often find that in order to flourish in this environment they need to muster comparable diversity internally. Functioning effectively in this environment requires not only an ability to recognize and tolerate diversity but a willingness to value it.

Global

Many companies in the past were international, but not global: that is, they operated in many countries, but they kept operations in each country quite distinct, with little interdependence or interaction across the organizations in different countries. To be "global" means to be involved in interactions across borders.

Relatively few companies are now insulated from international interactions—as suppliers, customers, or competitors are often from outside their home country. Even firms in those industries that remain quite strongly focused on their home market must often deal with competitors from another country and with the need to learn from "best practice" developed outside that market. In consequence, more and more of the networks that characterize the "new" organization stretch across borders. Some of these networks are internal to the company, as the firm extends itself across borders by setting up its own marketing offices or factories outside its home country. Other networks are external: companies build international links with foreign customers and suppliers, expanding their markets by export or by marketing alliances with foreign firms and reducing their costs by finding low-cost sources for parts and subsystems. But more and more, we see that value chains (that is, the steps involved in producing a final product or service), which tended to be located within one country in the "old" model, are crossing borders.

We are also seeing that linking across countries, which used to be the job of specialist international managers, increasingly involves a much greater number of individuals at middle and even lower levels of the company. Blue collar workers go from the American auto plants in which they are employed to the Japanese factories of their parent company to learn core skills. Junior engineers travel internationally to solve problems for customers or to work on international technology development projects. More and more people in the organization are required to develop an international or global way of thinking about their business.

Some of the key factors that underlie the growing importance of the global dimension of the new organization are:

1. Greatly reduced costs of international transportation and communications, such that products and parts can be made in one location and sold at competitive prices in many locations (for example, cars made in Japan and Korea and car parts from Germany and Taiwan are sold throughout the world).
2. The growing equalization across advanced industrial and newly industrializing societies of what Michael Porter calls "advanced factor endowments"—including workforce education levels, technological and managerial capabilities, telecommunications, and transportation infrastructure. This equalization increases the number of firms that can pick up and apply new product or process technologies. Components for consumer

11

ACADEMIC

electronics or telecommunications equipment, for example, are made by companies based in countries all around the world. This both intensifies international competition and increases the range of strategic options that any firm has in purchasing components or finding markets for its products.

3. The "globalization" of markets, as living standards become more similar across countries and as the "consuming class" becomes larger and more oriented to the international market in many countries. Although many markets remain very local and distinctive, others increasingly offer firms the opportunity to expand their markets with only modest tailoring of their product or service.

4. Continuing differences in cost structures across countries, such that firms trying to lower their costs can identify high-capability but lower-cost locations for support activities (such as the growing use by U.S. companies of software engineering centers in India or data-processing centers in Ireland) or for production (such as manufacturing operations in the export processing zones of Asia).

5. The potential for expanding the capabilities of the firm by cross-border learning, especially by building networks into leading markets or centers of technology. Formerly, companies expanded internationally by exploiting the advanced capabilities they had developed in their home markets. Today, however, we see that long-established multinationals from the "Triad" (North America, Japan, and Western Europe) and "new" multinationals from the NICs (Newly Industrializing Countries) are both expanding into the most advanced markets in order to improve (rather than exploit) their competitive advantage. Japanese and European pharmaceutical firms enter the United States to gain biotechnology capabilities, for example; U.S. firms go to Japan to set up business units in advanced display technologies; Samsung, the Korean business group, puts its headquarters for its personal computer business in California.

The model of the networked, flat, flexible, diverse, and global "new" organization that we have presented here and that you will continue to encounter in many of your

---

FIGURE 1.1 SOME CONTRASTING FEATURES OF THE OLD AND NEW MODELS OF ORGANIZATION

Old Model	New Model
Individual position/job as basic unit of organization	Team as basic unit
Relations with environment handled by specialist boundary-spanners	Densely networked with environment
Vertical flows of information	Horizontal and vertical flows of information
Decisions come down, information flows up	Decisions made where information resides
Tall (many layers of management)	Flat (few layers of management)
Emphasis on structures	Emphasis on processes
Emphasis on rules and standard procedures	Emphasis on results and outcomes
Fixed hours	Flexible workday, part-time workers
Career paths upward, linear	Career paths lateral, flexible
Standardized evaluation & reward systems	Customized evaluation & reward systems
Single strong culture with strong expectations of homogeneous behavior	Diversity of viewpoints & behaviors
Ethnocentric mind-set	International/global mind-set
Specialist international managers	Boundary-crossers at all levels
Local value chains	Value chains crossing borders
Environment defined in terms of country of location	Environment seen as global

---

readings about organizations today and in the business press is an "ideal type" in the sense used by Max Weber: a construct or "mental model" that is useful in identifying the key elements of a complex social phenomenon. Few if any real organizations completely embody all the features of the model. Moreover, an "ideal type" is not an "ideal" in the popular sense of being intrinsically good and desirable. Weber's model of bureaucracy was an "ideal type," but Weber himself was far from considering it "ideal"—he referred to the "iron cage" of bureaucracy and worried about its effects on the quality of modern work life. Similarly, the "new" organizational model is an "ideal type" that is useful in analyzing the trends of change in organizations today.

But it is also a model that exerts great pressure on organizations today to think about changing in the direction of becoming more networked, flat, flexible, diverse, and global. There are three reasons for this pressure. One is that this model seems to be more effective and more efficient for organizing certain kinds of economic, political, and social activities in an information-based world. Another is that it has become so widely accepted in today's society that an organization that does not present itself as networked, flat, flexible, diverse, and global runs the risk of being seen as stodgy, old-fashioned, and unattractive to prospective employees and investors. And a third is that many managers and writers regard the features of new model not just as an ideal type but as a set of "ideals"—they believe strongly that organizing by teams, for example, is not just more effective than organizing by individual positions, but that it is *better* in terms of what is good and even morally right in terms of the great wave of history. They believe that flat is better than tall, flexible is better than predictable, diverse is better than homogeneous, and global is better than domestic, regardless of the organization's context. You may choose to believe this as well, but the model of the "new" organization we have presented here does not make this assumption. We want you to understand it as a Weberian "ideal type" that helps you understand and categorize certain aspects of today's organizations. And we would encourage you to question and assess critically the idealization of the new model, even as you wrestle with the challenges of taking effective action in organizations that have adopted—or are in the process of adopting—its elements.

TAKING ACTION IN THE NEW MODEL

These and other features of the "new" organization involve major changes in the roles and careers of individual managers, the kinds of organizational capabilities needed by the organization, and the relationships that the organization has with its environment. For example, the fact that firms are simultaneously calling for high commitment and effort from employees and moving to a flexible workforce requires rethinking the relationship between the individual and the organization. In a flat, networked organization, managers cannot rely on formal authority to accomplish their goals; they must negotiate with other key players, build trust, and work across the boundaries of their assigned roles. Most of the analyses of the new organization agree that it changes the skills that individuals need in order to take action, and changes the kinds of tools that the organization must make available to them.

This is not easy. Rosabeth Kanter has identified a set of contradictory demands that the "new game," as she calls it, is generating for individual managers:

- "Think strategically and invest in the future—but keep the numbers up today.
- Be entrepreneurial and take risks—but don't cost the business anything by failing.
- Continue to do everything you're currently doing even better—and spend more time communicating with employees, serving on teams, and launching new projects.
- Know every detail of your business—but delegate more responsibility to others.
- Become passionately dedicated to 'visions' and fanatically committed to carrying them out—but be flexible, responsive, and able to change direction quickly.

Ⓒ

13

ACADEMIC

- Speak up, be a leader, set the direction—but be participative, listen well, cooperate.
- Throw yourself wholeheartedly into the entrepreneurial game and the long hours it takes—and stay fit.
- Succeed, succeed, succeed—and raise terrific children." (Kanter, 1989, pp. 20–21)

Obviously, taking action in the "new organization" and shifting organizations from the old to the new model both have wide-ranging implications on three levels: for the skills and knowledge of the individual manager, for the capabilities of the organization, and for the organization's relationships with its environment. Let us turn to a brief examination of some of these challenges.

One way to think about what the "new organization" means for the kinds of skills needed by individual managers, the challenges of managing the organization, and the challenges of managing the organization's interactions with its environment is to take each of the five characteristics of the new model and look at its implications for each of these levels. A complete analysis would take a book rather than a short survey. But the following section gives one example for each level and each feature; you yourself can and should think of others. The examples also show how difficult it can be to isolate any one feature of the new organization and discuss it separately from the rest: each feature is related to the others in very important ways, as we shall see.

Networked

For individual managers, the increasing reliance on networks of people linked in teams as a basic building block of the organization means that they must develop their capabilities at *teamwork*—that is, their skills as team *members* as well as team leaders (far more managers are eager to develop their skills at leadership than at membership). Too often we assume that "being a good team player" is a matter of personality. While some people find teams a more congenial setting than others, being a good team member and a good team leader involves a wide range of skills that can be learned and steadily improved. These skills include understanding the dynamics of team interaction and how these are likely to develop over time, developing better observation skills to enable one to see those dynamics at work in the team, and learning how to diagnose team problems.

At the level of the organization, moving to teams requires processes within the organization for putting effective teams together and for setting the conditions under which they can work well. This means developing *team structures* that are clearly understood within the organization and that enable people to assimilate quickly to a new team. This does not mean that an organization can have only one kind of team: it can have several kinds of teams, but action will be most efficient when each type of team has a clear and widely shared model of its structure and process ("If this is a cross-functional team to address quality issues, it means that we have people from each key function, shared formal responsibility, etc.").

At the level of the organization's interactions with its environment, networks with outside organizations involve *alliances* with other organizations. Often these alliances require a delicate balancing of current *cooperation* and potential *competition*, so that an organization needs to develop systems to manage information flows with its "allies" and to maximize its learning from the alliance. Long-term alliances covering many related projects (with a supplier firm, for example, or a key customer) require different systems for management than short-term, single project alliances. Developing and continuously adapting these systems is one of the major challenges of operating in an external alliance network.

Flat

In a flat organization, managers can rely far less on getting things done by simple commands and a reference to the authority of the managers above them. Often they must work with people in departments who report to different bosses, and have a different set of priorities and incentives. In this kind of organization, managers must develop *negotiation skills* that enable them to identify the interests and needs of the people whose cooperation they must have, and to work through to a "win-win" situation in which all those involved are better off because of the cooperation. Again, we too often think that a "good negotiator" is someone with a certain kind of personality. But like teamwork, negotiation skills can—and in the new model of the organization, must—be learned.

A flat organization has fewer opportunities for moving up a career ladder than the old, tall organizational hierarchy. Therefore one of the traditional incentives for good performance—promotion—is much scarcer in the new model. Organizations therefore need to develop new *incentive systems*, and new concepts of *career* that involve more horizontal than vertical movement.

In a flat organization that is also increasingly networked with its environment, relationships with the "outside" are no longer monopolized by a small number of specialized boundary-spanners or by top management. More and more people in the organization are working across its external boundaries—interacting with customers, with suppliers, and with other stakeholders. In this context, it can be difficult to maintain the sense of *boundaries*—of being committed first and foremost to one's own organization, and of being *cooperative* but not *coopted* (that is, not substituting the needs and agendas of the other organization for one's own). The flat organization needs to develop ways of simultaneously maintaining effective cooperative links across the boundaries of the firm and the commitment of the employees to the long-term interests of their own organization.

Flexible

One of the features of the flexible organization is that managers are often working on several projects or teams simultaneously. Developing the skills of *multi-tasking*—of managing one's time and commitments so as to be able to work efficiently at several tasks— can be crucial to survival in the firm.

One of the major challenges in the flexible organization is *workforce management*. In the bureaucratic model, workforce management is, ideally, simply a matter of figuring out which rule applies in a particular case and then applying it. In the flexible organization, a multitude of different practices makes for much more uncertainty. For example, being responsive to the customer can mean that someone from the organization has to travel to that customer and fix a problem. How is that extra time compensated? Can the person take extra time off later? If someone is particularly good at handling this kind of situation, and gets sent out a lot, thereby accumulating extra compensating time off, does that create perceptions of unfairness among others in that person's group? If so, how should they be addressed? If that person is working in a team and is suddenly called away to cope with unexpected customer demands, how can the team cope? In the flexible organization, these issues can be rarely addressed by developing a set of rigid rules. Instead, they require active management, and perhaps, "contingent" rules—that is, rules that apply in certain situations.

In the interactions between the flexible organization and its environment, one of the key management challenges is to maintain *learning*. One of the reasons for becoming more networked with other organizations to keep the organization innovative and responsive to change. This means that the relations with those other organizations must involve systems for capturing what the organization learns from that relationship and sharing it with other parts of the organization for whom it may be relevant. For example, a group of engineers may find in working with one of their suppliers that a certain set of supplier incentives creates serious problems, and they may work out with that supplier a much more effective set. The organization will benefit most from that learning if it can be spread from that particular group to other groups that are working with suppliers, to see if the new approach works better in other settings as well.

Diverse

In an organization with an increasingly diverse workforce and increasingly differentiated teams and sets of activities, managers need to develop better *listening skills* and the capacity for *empathy*; for understanding how something looks and feels to the other person. Listening skills can and must be cultivated. Many managers think that they are being good listeners when instead they are dedicated talkers. Others think they are being empathetic when they ask themselves, "What would I do if I were in this person's position?" when instead they should be asking, "What does this person's position feel like to *him/her*?" In a diverse organization, managers cannot assume that their own background and experience give them the basis for understanding how things are seen by others.

In an organization characterized by diversity, conflicts are inevitable, and if well handled by the organization they can provide opportunities for the organization to become more flexible and more innovative. But this requires *systems for conflict resolution* and an organizational culture that recognizes the inevitability of conflict and believes it can be resolved.

Managing the environment in the diverse organizations involves an increasingly diverse set of *stakeholders*—that is, groups with a stake in the survival and performance of the organization. For U.S. companies, for example, increasingly demanding institutional investors (pension funds, mutual funds) may pull the firm in the direction of emphasizing current returns, while local communities, employees, and unions may pull the firm in very different directions. Environmental groups are employing an array of tactics, from legislation to lawsuits, to influence company policies. As organizations become more international, they increase the range of stakeholders they have, and also increase the potential for contradictory pressures from them. And as organizations become more externally networked, they increase their interdependence with key external stakeholders, including suppliers and customers. Managing the diverse stakeholders of the "new model" is a major organizational challenge.

Global

As more of the activities of the organization stretch across country borders, managers need to develop their skills in *cross-cultural communication*. In many ways these skills build on and even contribute to the skills of listening and empathy that managers need to cultivate to respond to diversity. But cross-cultural communication can often involve specific understanding of the particular context of the organization in other societies. The knowledge required reaches from the minutiae of what constitutes a courteous way to introduce oneself in a business setting to the complexities of how customers and other stakeholders expect to be treated in that country in that particular industry segment.

At the level of the organization, stretching activities across countries involves major challenges in *cross-border integration*, that is, in coordinating activities that are taking place in different locations and in very different contexts. A U.S. company that is producing subassemblies in a subsidiary in Singapore, for example, has to integrate the production schedules of the subsidiary with the final assembly at home, and make sure it has a rapid feedback system to resolve any problems that develop either with the schedule or with the subassembly itself.

Organizations that are operating outside their home country must decide on the extent of *local responsiveness* they want to develop in their activities. For example, many Japanese companies have set up manufacturing plants in the United States. Often they feel that in order to maintain their competitive advantage, they must introduce work systems and practices with which U.S. workers are not familiar; that is, they have not adapted to established work practices. But many of them, to compensate for this, have tried to be more locally responsive to the communities in which their U.S. plants are located, encouraging their executives to get involved with a variety of community activities in which they would never be involved in Japan. Deciding on the degree of local responsiveness to the established organizational patterns of each country is a major challenge for organizations operating across country borders.

As we have seen, the "new" model of the organization can be challenging as a workplace. Moreover, the transition to the "new" model—or even to certain elements of it—is itself often besieged by paradox. Much of the writing in the business press today assumes that the major challenge facing managers is to "get everyone on board" in moving to the new model. Yet more thoughtful analysts have identified some apparent contradictions in the march to the new organization:

1. "Downsizing" and "flattening" the organization, thereby increasing insecurity among employees about whether they have any future with the organization, and at the same time demanding greater effort, commitment, and involvement from employees
2. Moving an organization to a team-oriented empowered organization—but at the top-down command of a strong leader
3. Increasingly recognizing that firms depend on the resources and the dynamism of their environments to build competitive advantage, even as they pursue strategies that are good for the firms but have negative consequences for their environments. Some of those strategies include the move to a smaller but more highly rewarded core of high commitment employees, and a growing auxiliary workforce of part-time and contract employees. This may increase unemployment and lead to an increasingly unequal distribution of income in the society. In other words, there is an implicit tension between the recognition that what is good for the firm may not be good for the system as a whole, and the recognition that the competitiveness of the firm is closely related to the comparative advantage of the economic and social system in which it is embedded.
4. Trying to build the new organizational capabilities of the "new" model in the expectation that this will enable the firm to perform well over the long term, while facing intense competitive pressures for immediate improvement in financial performance

Yet for more and more organizations, the "new" organization is an "ideal" in the popular sense: a model to strive towards, a vision of where the organization is going, and a source of inspiration and motivation (a "rhetorical device"). Taking action in today's organization increasingly demands an understanding of the networked, flat, flexible,

© 17 ACADEMIC

FIGURE 1.2 FRAMEWORK FOR TAKING ACTION IN THE "NEW" ORGANIZATION

Organizational characteristics	Requisites for taking effective action	Individual skills	Organizational features	Managing the environment
• Networked		Teamwork	Team structure	Developing alliances
• Flat		Negotiation	Developing incentive systems	Boundary management
• Flexible		Multi-tasking	Workforce management	Learning
• Diverse		Listening/empathy	Conflict resolution systems	Stakeholder relationships
• Global		Cross-cultural communication	Cross-border integration	Local responsiveness

diverse, and global model and of the kinds of individual skills and organizational capabilities needed to work more effectively in this context.

"This context"—the new model of organization—remains more clearly defined in theory than in practice. One reason is that we are realizing how much variation there is across different versions of the "new," how many different variants of "networked" are possible, for example, and how even a simpler element like "flat" can be manifested in a number of variants of structure and empowerment. The most likely scenario for the twenty-first century is a wide variety of forms of new organizations, which can best be understood as different versions of the basic model. "Diverse" is likely to be a feature not only of the "new" organization itself, but also of the emerging population of networked, flat, flexible, diverse, and global organizations.

REFERENCES

Capelli, Peter, and Laurie Bassi, Harry Katz, David Knoke, Paul Osterman, and Michael Useem. 1997. *Change at Work*. New York: Oxford University Press.

Clegg, S. R. 1990. *Modern Organizations: Organization Studies in the Postmodern World*. London: Sage Publications.

Heckscher, C. and A. Donnellon, eds. 1994. *The Post-Bureaucratic Organization: New Perspectives on Organizational Change*. Thousand Oaks, CA: Sage Publications.

Kanter, Rosabeth Moss. 1989. *When Giants Learn to Dance*. New York: Simon and Schuster.

Kaysen, Carl, ed. 1996. *The American Corporation Today*. New York: Oxford University Press.

Scott, W. Richard. 1992. *Organizations: Rational, Natural, and Open Systems*. Englewood Cliffs, NJ: Prentice-Hall, Third edition.

Selwyn, Michael. 1993. "Radical Departures: Revolutionary Strategies Are Separating Asia's Leaders from the Followers." *Asian Business* (August 1993), pp. 22–25.

Thurow, Lester. 1996. "Almost Everywhere: Surging Inequality and Falling Real Wages." In Carl Kaysen, ed. *The American Corporation Today*. New York: Oxford University Press, pp. 383–412.

A SAMPLING OF ANALYSES OF THE NEW ORGANIZATION

"The typical large business 20 years hence will have fewer than half the levels of management of its counterpart today, and no more than one-third the managers. In its structure, and in its management problems and concerns, it will bear little resemblance to the typical manufacturing company, circa 1950, which our textbooks still consider the norm. Instead it is far more likely to resemble organizations that neither the practicing manager nor the management scholar pays much attention to today: the hospital, the university, the symphony orchestra. For like them, the typical business will be knowledge-based, an organization composed largely of specialists who direct and discipline their own performance through organized feedback from colleagues, customers, and headquarters. For this reason, it will be what I call an information-based organization. Businesses, especially large ones, have little choice but to become information-based. . . . A good deal of work will be done differently in the information-based organization. Traditional departments will serve as guardians of standards, as centers for training and the assignment of specialists; they won't be where the work gets done. That will happen largely in task-focused teams."

Reprinted by permission of *Harvard Business Review*, from "The Coming of the New Organization" by Peter F. Drucker. Jan/Feb 1988. Copyright © 1988 by the President and Fellows of Harvard College; all rights reserved.

"Managerial work is undergoing such enormous and rapid change that many managers are reinventing their profession as they go. With little precedent to guide them, they are watching hierarchy fade away and the clear distinctions of title, task, department, even corporation, blur. Faced with extraordinary levels of complexity and interdependency, they watch traditional sources of power erode and the old motivational tools lose their magic. . . .

Leaders in the new organization do not lack motivational tools, but the tools are different from those of traditional corporate bureaucrats. The new rewards are not based on status but on contribution, and they consist not of regular promotion and automatic pay raises but of excitement about mission and a share of the glory and the gains of success. The new security is not employment security (a guaranteed job no matter what) but employability security—increased value in the internal and external labor markets . . . The new loyalty is not to the boss or to the company but to projects that actualize a mission and offer challenge, growth, and credit for results. . . .

The new managerial work consists of looking outside a defined area of responsibility to sense opportunities and of forming project teams drawn from any relevant sphere to address them. It involves communication and collaboration across functions, across divisions, and across companies whose activities and resources overlap. Thus rank, title, or official charter will be less important factors in success at the new managerial work than having the knowledge, skills, and sensitivity to mobilize people and motivate them to do their best."

Reprinted by permission of *Harvard Business Review*, from "The New Managerial Work" by Rosabeth Moss Kanter. Nov/Dec 1989. Copyright © 1989 by the President and Fellows of Harvard College; all rights reserved.

"By the beginning of the twenty-first century, the organization men (and women) of the 1950s will be gone, and so, too, will many of the attributes that dominated their corporate lives. Upward mobility within a clearly defined job or function, conformity to the cultural and social norms of the top executives, strict lines of demarcation between work and family activities and obligations, geographic transfer and job choice based on one partner's career needs or demands, and loyalty to the corporation may all be part of corporate history. Hourly workers will no longer be able to count on seniority to produce increased wages, fringe benefits, promotion opportunities, and job security. Unions and collective bargaining will find it more difficult to move those with limited education or training into the middle class.

To do well in the corporation of the future, individual employees will need to enter the labor market with a solid technical and analytic educational foundation, gain access on the job to experiences in decision making, problem solving, and teamwork, commit to a lifetime process of learning and updating of one's skills, and organize into collective networks and organizations capable of bargaining and influencing their employers from the workplace up to the strategic levels of corporate decision making.

To be competitive and prosper in this environment, corporations will need to attract high-quality workers, design work systems that fully utilize their skills, encourage employees to stay long enough to appropriate the benefits of training investments, share power and cooperate with workers and their representatives, and release employees into the external labor market with marketable skills. For the overall economy and society to prosper in this new environment will require significant reforms of labor and employment policies that provide the education, training, and social insurance foundations needed to promote labor market mobility and effective negotiations, dispute resolution, and cooperation among stakeholders within and across organizations."

Thomas A. Kochan, "The American Corporation as an Employer: Past, Present, and Future Possibilities" in *The American Corporation Today* edited by Carl Kaysen. Copyright © 1996 by the Alfred P. Sloan Foundation. Used by permission of Oxford University Press, Inc.

"All industries are in a state of flux influenced by a subset of the discontinuities described below.[2]... During the next decade, the critical work of managers who are confronted with these competitive discontinuities will be to:

1. *Create a shared competitive agenda for the entire organization.* This agenda will be shared with employees, current and potential customers, suppliers, collaborators, and investors. The view of the future must be compelling, directional, and motivating. As the organization starts to share an overall competitive agenda, senior managers can afford to decentralize decision making. . . .

2. *Focus on changing the industry dynamics and leveraging the resources of the company.* The goal is to reshape existing industries, as well as to create new ones. In order to accomplish this goal, the organization must focus on resource accumulation and resource leverage more than on resource allocation per se (the current preoccupation of managers). Managers must stretch beyond the resources available to them within their firms to creatively exploit resources that are available from suppliers, partners, competitors, and customers. These then become multipliers of the resources available within the firm.

2 Those discontinuities are: (1) "from cozy to competitive"; (2) "from local to global"; (3) "from 'like me' to 'like who?'" (i.e. the emergence of new competitors); (4) "from clear to indeterminate industry boundaries"; (5) "from stability to volatility"; (6) "from intermediaries to direct access"; (7) "from vertical integration to specialists"; (8) "from a single to a multiple intellectual heritage."

3. *Create a flexible system that can reconfigure resources to address emerging opportunities.* In most firms the organization becomes an impediment to proactive and rapid response to the marketplace. The ability to conserve and redeploy resources rapidly is a critical capacity for the future. this means learning fast, forgetting even faster, becoming boundaryless, and focusing on winning in the marketplace.

4. *Develop a global capacity.* This means that the organization can think and act globally or locally and access customers, suppliers, and talent worldwide. The organization must become a color-blind meritocracy."

From C. K. Prahalad, "The Work of New Age Managers in the Emerging Competitive Landscape" in *The Organization of the Future*, edited by Frances Hesselbein, et al. Copyright © 1997 The Peter F. Drucker Foundation for Nonprofit Management. Reprinted by permission of Jossey-Bass, Inc., Publishers.

AND SOME SKEPTICAL VOICES

"Regardless of when Drucker is writing (and this is not to deny that his work has contained some very valuable insights), the present is always an exciting, challenging time to be contrasted with a stable past. These same stirring announcements of impending change can be found repeated in nearly all of his writings from the 1950s to the present. . . . Every generation believes itself to be on the forefront of a new managerial frontier and posits the coming of a new organization that will revolutionize the way people work and interact. . . . To see these claims about revolutionary newness only in regard to an underlying truth or falsehood is ultimately to miss the point. What is more important to understand is the *rhetorical* nature of management discourse and practice—now and then. To view management from a rhetorical perspective is to recognize that *the way people talk about the world has everything to do with the way the world is ultimately understood and acted in, and that the concept of revolutionary change depends to a great deal on how the world*

is framed by our language. Viewing management in this way is also to realize that the primary concern of managers—as well as other players in the field of management—is, or at least should be, mobilizing action among individuals rather than endless quibbling about 'the way the world really is'."

Robert G. Eccles and Nitin Nohria, with James D. Berkley, *Beyond the Hype: Rediscovering the Essence of Management.* (Harvard Business School Press, 1992), pp. 25, 29.

"Americans often don't know or pay much attention to history. American business writers seem to know even less. Today we are bombarded with breathless descriptions of the virtual organization, the networked organization, and the boundaryless organization. We are told about the 'new employment contract,' a nice way of saying that long-term careers in a single organization are a thing of the past and that we are all contingent workers now. . . . A big problem exists with all of this—namely that the 'new' organizational forms aren't all that new at all. In fact, this was how enterprise was organized more than one hundred years ago. . . . There are several enduring truths about organizations and management. One is the norm of reciprocity, which exists in all nationalities and cultures. We cannot expect dedication and loyalty from employees unless we are willing to make some reciprocal commitment to them. Another truth is the idea of core competence or capability. Contracting out core tasks has often been a recipe for disaster, in the 1890s as well as in the 1990s. This is because contracting out leaves the foundation of competitive success in the open market. A third truth is that to succeed you must understand the basic forces and ideas that shape modern economic life, reject trends if they don't make sense, and never substitute rhetoric for judgment."

From Jeffrey Pfeffer, "Will the Organization of the Future Make the Mistakes of the Past?" in *The Organization of the Future* edited by Frances Hesselbein, et al. Copyright © 1997 The Peter F. Drucker Foundation for Nonprofit Management. Reprinted by permission of Jossey-Bass, Inc., Publishers.

21

PRESS

"One of the first problems faced by advocates of the New Organization is that if its benefits are so obvious, why aren't there far more textbook examples available? . . . Our daily experience is perhaps mostly with organizations that seem to have rationalized their operations in tune with the long established principles of efficiency, predictability, quantification and control including the substitution of non-human for human technologies. Chains of command are obvious and the divisions of labor intense. The exemplar of the service industry seems to be McDonald's, where homogenous products, rigid technologies, standardized work routines, close supervision and highly centralized control systems are clearly in place. To be sure, this is an organizational form that has a few elements of the New Organization in place: an increasingly global presence (i.e., there are now more McDonald's outlets outside the United States than inside), tightly networked to suppliers (i.e. frozen potato vendors) and marketing partners (i.e. the Walt Disney Company), diverse in the social characteristics of its entry-level (but low-paid) workforce and chock full of cross-functional teams and task forces at headquarters. But, in the main, McDonald's looks and feels far closer to the old form of organization based on assembly line production and bureaucratic rules and regulations. The principles of Frederick Taylor's scientific management are alive, well, and thriving at McDonald's. Order and prescribed choice are enforced norms for both customers and employees. On your next visit, try ordering a Big Mac cooked medium rare.

More importantly, such forms of organization seem to be spreading—an imitative process that sociologist George Ritzer calls "the aggressive McDonaldization of society." Going or gone are the idiosyncratic, local family run businesses of the past emphasizing personal, highly differentiated products and services. The look-alike chain stores of the suburban malls drive out the family-owned enterprises of Main Street. Wal–Marts open up and local pharmacies and hardware stores close. Corner gas stations and local garages lose work to AAMCO Transmissions and Midas Muffler and Brake Shops. KinderCare provides a stable of bonded contract babysitters in almost identical facilities located coast to coast. Seven-Elevens and Circle K's replace Mom and Pop markets. Au Bon Pain croissaneries turn up in Paris. Kentucky Fired Chicken[3] outlets appears in Beijing. Drive-in clinics provide McDoctors and McDentists. Century 21 sells real estate from Interchangeable[4] offices across the country (and beyond). None of the organizations embody the supposedly innovative and novel spirit that animates the flat, flexible, networked, diverse, and global characteristics of our rather idealized New Organization yet all are expanding rapidly. If Henry Ford were alive he'd probable be delighted: eating at McDonald's, having his taxes done at H&R Block, servicing his car at Jiffy Lube, buying gifts for his grandchildren at Toys 'R Us and losing weight at Nutri-Systems."

From John Van Maanen, "Coda to the New Organization," Working Paper, 1997. Reprinted by permission of the author.

3 Note: This is not a typo; it is a play on words.

4 Ditto.

THE STRATEGY THAT WOULDN'T TRAVEL

by Michael C. Beers

It was 6:45 p.m. Karen Jiménez was reviewing the notes on her team-based productivity project for what seemed like the hundredth time. In two days, she was scheduled to present a report to the senior management group on the project's progress. She wasn't at all sure what she was going to say.

The project was designed to improve productivity and morale at each plant owned and operated by Acme Minerals Extraction Company. Phase one—implemented in early 1995 at the site in Wichita, Kansas—looked like a stunning success by the middle of 1996. Productivity and morale soared, and operating and maintenance costs decreased significantly. But four months ago, Jiménez tried to duplicate the results at the project's second target—the plant in Lubbock, Texas—and something went wrong. The techniques that had worked so well in Wichita met with only moderate success in Lubbock. Productivity improved marginally and costs went down a bit, but morale actually seemed to deteriorate slightly. Jiménez was stumped.

She tried to "helicopter up" and think about the problem in the broad context of the company's history. A few years ago, Acme had been in bad financial shape, but what had really brought things to a head—and had led to her current dilemma—was a labor relations problem. Acme had a wide variety of labor requirements for its operations. The company used highly sophisticated technology, employing geologists, geophysicists, and engineers on what was referred to as the "brains" side of the business, as well as skilled and semi-skilled labor on the "brawn" side to run the extraction operations. And in the summer of 1994, brains and brawn clashed in an embarrassingly public way. A number of engineers at the Wichita plant locked several union workers out of the offices in 100-degree heat. Although most Acme employees now felt that the incident had been blown out of proportion by the press, the board of directors had used the bad publicity as an excuse to push out an aging chief executive and bring in new blood in the form of Bill Daniels.

The board had asked Daniels to lead the company in part because he came from a prominent management-consulting firm that was noted for its approach to teamwork and change. As it turned out, he had proved a good choice. Daniels was a hands-on, high-energy, charismatic businessman who seemed to enjoy media attention. Within his first year as CEO, he had pretty much righted the floundering company by selling off some unrelated lines of business. He had also created the shared-serviced department—an internal consulting organization providing change management, reengineering, total quality management, and other services—and had tapped Jiménez to head the group. Her first priority, Daniels told her, would be to improve productivity and morale at the company's five extraction sites. None of them were meeting their projections. And

Michael C. Beers is a manager at the Ernst & Young Center for Business Innovation in Boston, Massachusetts, where he researches and consults on organizational behavior and knowledge management.

although Wichita was the only site at which the labor-management conflict was painfully apparent, Daniels and Jiménez both thought that morale needed an all-around boost. Hence the team-based productivity project.

At the time, Jiménez felt up to the task. She had joined Acme in her late twenties with an MBA and a few years at a well-known consulting firm under her belt. She had been at the helm of more than a few successful change efforts. And in the ten years since she joined Acme, she had gained experience in a number of midlevel positions.

With a hardworking team of her own in tow, Jiménez commenced work. First, she decided on a battle plan. For several reasons, Wichita seemed ideal as an inaugural site. Under the former CEO, the site had spent long periods of time on the market. The plant consistently underperformed, and the old regime wanted to be rid of it. Periodically, frustrated by the lack of what he considered serious offers, the former CEO ordered improvement programs, which were always abandoned after a short time. Jiménez believed that the failures of those change programs were predictable: expectations had been unrealistic, there had been little commitment from management, and the improvement-project team members had been given little authority to implement changes. As she considered her mission at Wichita, Jiménez was certain that her new political clout combined with her experience as a consultant would make the project manageable. Moreover, she reasoned that because many previous efforts had failed, her efforts would look doubly good if the project succeeded. If it failed, the situation could be positioned with the proper spin as an intractable set of problems that no one could solve.

The biggest problem at Wichita was clearly that labor and management didn't get along. As a result, costs to maintain the heavy equipment were significantly out of line with those incurred by other operations. Wichita's high fixed costs and razor-thin margins meant that every dollar saved in maintenance was a dollar of profit. While operating costs were high, too, they weren't nearly as high as maintenance costs.

Jiménez set about fixing the labor relations problem. And although things hadn't improved as smoothly or as quickly as she had hoped, Wichita was a great success. The problem was, Daniels had wasted no time in touting the early successes to stakeholders. In fact, not long after the Wichita project had gotten under way, he described it at great length in a speech to the financial Analysts' Society on Wall Street. With characteristic embellishment, he cited the project as a vision for the future of Acme—indeed, he called it *the* organization for the twenty-first century. He all but told the analysts that the Wichita model would soon be rolled out through the entire enterprise.

Jiménez had been furious—and more than a little frightened. She didn't want her feet held to the fire like that; she knew that reproducing Wichita's success might not be possible and that even if it were, it might not be accomplished in a cookie-cutter fashion. In fact, she had tried to let Daniels know of her feelings on more than a few occasions, long before he spouted off to Wall Street. She had met with him and sent him reports, E-mail, and memos. The message, it seemed, had fallen on deaf ears.

Inside Wichita

Jiménez looked at the clock again: it was now 7:30. The $75 million project that could bring Acme in the twenty-first century was listing, she mused, and so was her career. She looked at her computer screen for inspiration, but it was blank. Maybe if she reviewed the success story once more. She opened the file marked "Wichita" and studied the work-process flowchart. The site had been unexceptional in almost every way. There were three functional groups: operations, which consisted of hourly workers who operated and maintained the extraction equipment; "below ground," a group composed of engineers, geologists, and geophysicists who determined where and how to drill for the desired minerals; and "above ground," a group of engineers in charge of cursory refinement and transportation of the minerals. Before the team project had been put in motion, Wichita had shown little coordination or communication among these groups.

Jiménez knew that she had had at least one stroke of good luck in Wichita in the form of David Keller. Keller, a 39-year Acme veteran, had been looking for one last job before he retired, and he wanted it to be in Wichita, where his family had lived for 8 years earlier in his career. He wanted to retire there. Keller was widely respected in the company and Jiménez genuinely liked him. So, with the blessing of Daniels and the other senior managers, she had appointed him project leader.

She smiled as she thought about Keller. He was a Korean War vet who had relocated several times for Acme, serving in just about every possible line and staff position. He joined the company in 1957 and was immediately baptized in the dust and heat of North Africa, where the company had set up operations soon after World War II. Keller was a link to Acme's heady past, when it had thought nothing of clearing Allied land mines planted in the desert in its drive to expand. It struck Jiménez that Keller had joined the company before she was born.

Jiménez thought about the Wichita project's rough spots. One of them had been the institution of a monthly "problem chat," an optional meeting open to all staff to discuss unresolved problems. No one attended the first one. She and Keller sat there nervously, together eating six doughnuts before she called a secretary and had them carted away.

But over time, people began to show up. After about four months, the meetings were well-attended, lively problem-solving discussions that actually produced some improvements. In one case, a maintenance worker explained to a facilities engineer that one of the standard equipment configurations was failing as a result of high levels of heat and sand contamination, resulting in occasional downtime. With Keller mediating, the complaint had been taken well, without the usual friction. The engineer easily fabricated a new configuration more suitable to the conditions, and downtime was virtually eliminated. Such insights were common at the problem chats. Previously, no organizational mechanism had existed for capturing solutions or transferring them to other parts of the operation.

Jiménez and Keller then introduced teams to "select a problem and implement a tailored solution," or SPITS. These were ad-hoc groups made up of members from each of the functional areas. The groups were formed to work on a specific project identified in a problem chat; they were disbanded when the problem was solved. It was the implementation of SPITS teams that led some eight months later to a wholesale reorganization of the Wichita work site. Jiménez believed that SPITS had been a breakthrough that had shown her how to boost productivity and morale—the goal that Daniels had set for her. The program had given cross-functional teams of 12 to 15 people from operations, above ground, and below ground the responsibility and authority to address problems as they occurred without seeking the approval of management.

Jiménez reminded herself that even after SPITS there were still some rocky moments in Wichita. Some engineers resented having to work alongside operations personnel. They told Keller, "These miners don't understand why we do what we do." Likewise, some operations staff balked at having to work with engineers who "knew how to mine only on a computer screen."

But one year into the pilot, things began to hum. People weren't just working together, they were socializing together. At one of the problem chats, an operations worker jokingly suggested that the brains and the brawn duke it out once a week to get rid of the tensions. Keller jumped on the joke and had T-shirts made that said BRAINS AND BRAWN; he then challenged the groups to square off weekly in a softball game. Early into the first game, a 200-pound miner slammed into a thin, wiry engineer at home plate, and Jiménez, watching from the sidelines, was sure that her corporate change plan had just been called out. But the engineer simply dusted himself off, laughing and swearing at the same time. At the next game, the engineer showed up wearing knee and shoulder pads, and Jiménez heard both his colleagues and the operations guys laughing. She knew something had changed. Later that night at a bar, the beer flowed

25

CASE

in massive quantities, but she happily picked up the check. Her BRAINS AND BRAWN shirt now hung on her office wall—a symbol of everything that was wrong and everything that was possible.

Cookie-Cutter Conundrum

Jiménez again came back to the present. She closed the file, got up abruptly, and grabbed her coat. She needed some air and some food and decided to walk the two blocks to the local sandwich joint. She felt a little like an inventor who had just developed a great new invention that is certain to make the company tons of money. "That's great!" and imaginary boss replies. "Now give me another 50 just like it!"

As she walked, she tried to think objectively about the Lubbock site. Lubbock was in better shape than Wichita to begin with, but not by much. Operating costs there were too high, and the plant rarely met its production goals. Acme had considered divesting itself of Lubbock on more than one occasion. When Jiménez initially planned the team-based productivity rollout, she had thought of Lubbock as a beta site; and kinks from Wichita would be worked out there, and then the plan would be rolled out to the rest of the company over a two-year period. The shared-services department didn't have the staff to oversee Wichita's fine-tuning and concentrate on Lubbock as well, so Jiménez assigned only one of her top internal consultants, Jennifer Peterson, and two of Peterson's staff to the Lubbock project. She then engaged Daniels's former consulting firm and assigned Dave Matthews, a vice-president of the firm, on-site responsibility.

Bad news seemed to dog Jiménez at every turn. For example, Keller declined to be a part of the team. Mystified and a little hurt, Jiménez turned up the pressure a bit, hinting that it might look bad for him not to work on the Lubbock site. Keller was resolute.

"Look, Karen," he had said. "I'm 63 years old. My kids are all out of the house. I've relocated ten times for the company, but I plan to retire soon. I don't want to spend the next three years burning myself out traveling all over the country. I'm staying in Wichita. If I have to, I'll take early retirement and walk." Although Jiménez thought he might be bluffing, she couldn't afford to call his hand. Keller had many powerful allies in the company and was viewed as the prototypical Acme man; his latest success with the Wichita turnaround was seen as yet another in a series of impressive achievements. Jiménez knew she couldn't afford to lose his experience and knowledge; if she couldn't get him full time, she would do her best to pick his brain and transfer his knowledge to a project team.

Keller had promised full access to his entire staff; the consultants could interview and brainstorm and strategize all they wanted. Jiménez, Peterson, and Matthews took advantage of that opportunity, but even extensive interviews with Keller and his staff hadn't yielded any truly valuable insights. No matter how carefully Jiménez and her group tried to re-create the circumstances and techniques that had worked so well in Wichita, they made very little progress. The Lubbock employees just didn't seem to react with the same enthusiasm as the Wichita workers had. Because no one was showing up for the problem chats—despite the "selling" of the meetings' benefits by Jiménez, Peterson, and Matthews—attendance was made mandatory. It was true that Jiménez's team had attempted to reduce the cycle time and "total time to investment recovery" of the project, but that goal hadn't seemed unreasonable. Jiménez thought that there would be fewer mistakes in Lubbock and that the project would need less time and fewer resources than Wichita had.

If anything, just the opposite occurred. Problems never encountered on the Wichita project created havoc at Lubbock. One particularly vexing to Jiménez was that the Lubbock workers refused to engage in any of the team-building exercises and events developed for the them by the project team. The softball games that had been played with enthusiasm in Wichita were skipped by the Lubbock crowd until the project team finally offered to spring for food and beer. Even then, there was more eating than playing. I felt like I was bribing prison inmates, Jiménez remembered.

There had been some improvements. The site had begun to meet its weekly goals more consistently and had seen some reduction in operations and maintenance costs. Normally, Jiménez would have been complimented on a job well done, but in the context of what had gone before and what was expected, the improvements weren't enough—and Jiménez knew it.

She returned to her office, still without an answer. Full and generous funding had been approved for team-based productivity project by the steering committee at the personal request of Bill Daniels; this level of funding was not easily come by at Acme. How could she convince him—without looking like a failure—that the project couldn't be rolled out with the speed and grace he envisioned? What's more, it was clear that stalling the implementation would dull some of the project's luster and in all likelihood jeopardize funding. She *did* think that the project would work, given time. But she wasn't exactly sure how. And any waffling might get her crucified by her colleagues.

The meeting with the senior managers was rapidly approaching. What could she say to them?

27

CASE

HARVARD BUSINESS REVIEW (Nov. Dec. 1996) Vol. 74–76, pp. 18–22.

HBR's cases present common managerial dilemmas and offer concrete solutions from experts. As written, they are hypothetical, and the names used are fictitious. We invite you to write to Case Suggestions, *Harvard Business Review*, 60 Harvard Way, Boston, MA 02163, and describe the issues you would like to see addressed.

QUESTIONNAIRE: MAPPING YOUR ORGANIZATION

YOUR ORGANIZATION/COMPANY:

ORG/COMPANY NAME_____

TYPE OF BUSINESS/ACTIVITY _____

APPROXIMATE SIZE (Number of employees)_____

Which of the following statements best describes this organization?

_____ It fits the model of the "new" organization.

_____ It is trying to move toward the model of the "new" organization but still has some features of the old.

_____ It fits the model of the "old" organization, without many signs that it is trying to change.

_____ It seems to be a fairly stable hybrid, combing features of the old and the new.

How would you rate that organization on each of the following five features of the "new" organization?

FLAT:

Very tall				Very flat
1	2	3	4	5

FLEXIBLE:

Very inflexible				Very flexible
1	2	3	4	5

NETWORKED:

Individual as key unit, few horizontal internal links				Teams as basic units, dense horizontal links
1	2	3	4	5

Very limited external links				Very extensive external links
1	2	3	4	5

DIVERSE:

Very homogeneous				Very diverse
1	2	3	4	5

GLOBAL:

Very locally focused				Very international
1	2	3	4	5

C

29

QUESTIONNAIRE

NOTES

(Use this side of the page to make any brief notes on your organization that you wish.)

QUESTIONNAIRE 30

M-1

supplemental

THE SEARCH FOR THE ORGANIZATION OF TOMORROW

by Thomas A. Stewart

Lawrence Bossidy, CEO of Allied-Signal, predicts "organizational revolution" for corporate America. Says David Nadler, president of Delta Consulting Group, who works with the chiefs of AT&T, Corning, and Xerox, among others: "CEOs feel that companies need to be structured in dramatically different ways." In outfits as diverse as Eastman Kodak, Hallmark Cards, and General Electric—even the San Diego Zoo—the search for the organization perfectly designed for the 21st century is going ahead with the urgency of a scavenger hunt.

From many quarters we hear that hierarchical organization must wither away. In this view of the future middle managers have the life expectancy of fruit flies. Those who survive will not be straw bosses but Dutch uncles, dispensing resources and wisdom to an empowered labor force that designs its own jobs. Enabled, to use a trendy term, by information technology and propelled by the need to gain speed and shed unnecessary work, this flat, information-based organization won't look like the Pharaonic pyramid of yore but like—well, like what? Like a symphony orchestra, Peter Drucker suggests. No, a jazz combo, some say. More like a spider web, others offer.

Hamlet: Or like a whale?
Polonius: Very like a whale.

Gee, thanks. But where's my desk? What do I do eight hours a day—or ten, or twelve? Who gives me my annual review? When do we start?

Good questions, which as yet have not had good answers. Says H. James Maxmim, the CEO of Laura Ashley Holdings: "We're just beginning to explore the post-hierarchical organization. We don't know what it looks like yet." Some hints, however, are emerging.

The 21st-century organization arises at the confluence of three streams. One is described by the term "high-involvement workplace," meaning operations with self-managing teams and other devices for empowering employees. Novelties once, these participative mechanisms have proved they can consistently deliver jaw-dropping gains in productivity, quality, and job satisfaction. A second productivity turbocharger is a new emphasis on managing business processes—materials handling, say—rather than functional departments like purchasing and manufacturing. Third is the evolution of information technology to the point where knowledge, accountability, and results can be distributed rapidly anywhere in the organization. The trick is to put them together into a coherent, practical design. Then you have the company yours may become, and the one your sons and daughters will work for.

At the end of this rainbow, say those who have peeked, is a whole kettleful of gold. Advises Bossidy, who until last summer was vice chairman of General Electric: "Look at GE Appliances." In that $5.4-billion-a-year business, redesign has brought with it a $200 million drop in average inventory. McKinsey & Co. principal Douglas Smith, one of the blue-chip consulting firm's experts on organization, figures that a company applying the new principles of organization design can cut its cost base by a third or more. Smith bases his claim on results from companies that have already reorganized parts of their operations: an industrial goods manufacturer that cut costs and raised productivity more than 50%, a financial service company where costs fell 34%, and others.

Results like that come from changing a company in profound ways, not just tinkering with the boxes on an organization chart. For years, Smith says, the basic questions about how best to arrange people and jobs stayed the same: "Do we centralize or decentralize—and where do we stick international?" The answer was never satisfactory. Companies were set up by product, or by customer, or by territory, and then switched when those arrangements stopped working. All that rejiggering missed the point, says Smith: "It mattered only to the top people in the company. Below them you found the same functional, vertical organization. For the 90% of the people who serve customers and make product, all that changed was the boss's name."

No longer. The Kodaks, GEs, and their ilk have first retailored the work people do, then management structures, with startling results. To make sense out of the rush of experimentation, McKinsey's Smith and his colleague Frank Ostroff are polishing a paper that lays out what Ostroff calls "perhaps the first real, fundamentally different, robust alternative" to the functional organization (see Figure 1.3 on page 34). In the months since Ostroff released an early draft to his consulting colleagues, it has proved the document most often requested inside the firm.

There's nothing new about self-managing teams—they were "discovered" 43 years ago at the bottom of a coal mine in Yorkshire by a researcher from the Tavistock Institute of Human Relations in London. Since then, forms of worker self-management have been adopted at countless sites. Marvin Weisbord, an expert on organizational development, notes that all rely on one basic idea: "The people who do the work should have in their hands the means to change to suit the customer."

That means workers should have the incentive and the power to respond to whoever buys their output—at times someone else within their organization—not just whoever cuts their paychecks. Weisbord adds that self-management *typically* delivers 40% increases in output per man-hour.

To see how it's done, skip the blackjack table next time you're in Puerto Rico and pay a visit to Bayamón, outside San Juan, where a new General Electric factory has been running for a year and a half. The place makes arresters, which are surge protectors that guard power stations and transmission lines against lightning strikes.

Bayamón is a godchild of Philip Jarrosiak, manager of human resources for GE's capacitor and power protection operations. Once a minor-league infielder, Jarrosiak joined GE when he was 20, landing an hourly job making aircraft engines in Rutland, Vermont. In the 32 years since, he put himself through college at night and worked his way into management ranks, where he specializes in designing high-performance workplaces at both greenfield and established sites. Bayamón is his newest and, Jarrosiak says, "an opportunity to put in everything I know."

The facility employs 172 hourly workers and just 15 salaried "advisers," plus manager R. Clayton Crum. That's it: three layers, no supervisors, no staff. A conventional plant, Jarrosiak says, would have about twice as many salaried people. Every hourly worker is on a team with ten or so others; they meet weekly. Each team "owns" part of the work—assembly, shipping and receiving, etc. But team members come from all areas of the plant, so that each group has representatives from both upstream and downstream operations. An adviser sits in the back of the room and speaks up only if the team needs help. What vaults Bayamón into the next century is the way it teaches its workers. Says Harvard professor Shoshanna Zuboff, author of In the Age of the Smart Machine: "The 21st-century company has to promote and nurture the capacity to improve and to innovate. That idea has

FIGURE 1.3 A NEW VIEW OF ORGANIZATION

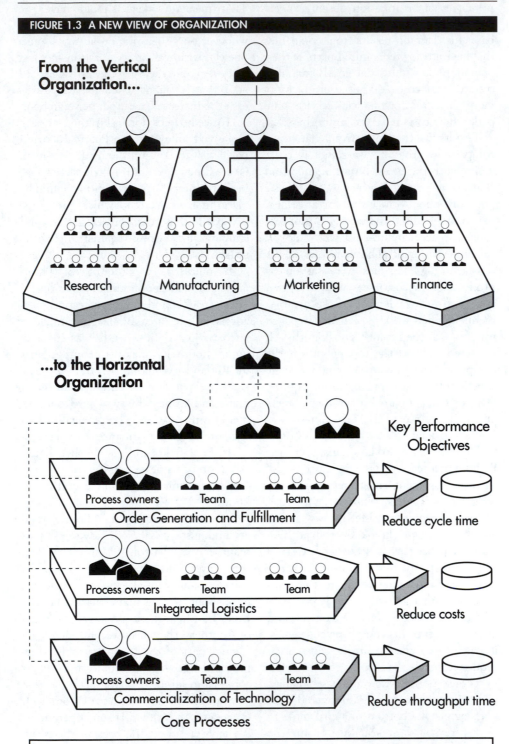

From the Vertical Organization...

Research   Manufacturing   Marketing   Finance

...to the Horizontal Organization

Key Performance Objectives

Process owners   Team   Team
Order Generation and Fulfillment
Reduce cycle time

Process owners   Team   Team
Integrated Logistics
Reduce costs

Process owners   Team   Team
Commercialization of Technology
Reduce throughput time

Core Processes

A new view of organization by McKinsey consultants Frank Ostroff and Doug Smith is meant to help clients hung up by the old template. Says Ostroff: "They needed a clear architecture" to show how a functional pyramid (top) could become a process-oriented, horizontal organization.

radical implications. It means learning becomes the axial principle of organizations. It replaces control as the fundamental job of management."

Bayamón is a perpetual-learning machine. Hourly workers change jobs every six months, rotating through the factory's four main work areas. In six months they'll begin their second circuit of the plant, and everyone on the floor will know his job and how it affects the next person in line. The reward for learning is a triple-scoop compensation plan that pays for skill, knowledge, and business performance. The first time around, workers get a 25-cent-an-hour pay raise at each rotation; thereafter they can nearly double their pay by "declaring a major," so to speak, and learning a skill like machine maintenance or quality control. More pay comes from passing courses in English, business practices, and other subjects. Toss in bonuses—$225 a quarter or more—for meeting plantwide performance goals and having perfect attendance. Promotions and layoffs will be decided by skill level, not seniority. In just a year the work force became 20% more productive than its nearest company equivalent on the mainland, and Jarrosiak predicts productivity will rise 20% more by the end of 1993.

For years plants like Bayamón existed barely connected to the organizations of which they are a part. Some Procter and Gamble factories were worker run as long ago as 1968, a fact concealed from competitors—and sometimes from headquarters. The Gaines pet food plant in Topeka, Kansas, just celebrated 20 years of self-management. For two decades, under three owners—Anderson Clayton, General Foods, and Quaker Oats—Topeka has always placed first when its labor productivity was compared with that of other pet food plants within its company. According to Herman Simon, plant manager for 17 years, higher-ups who saw the numbers vowed never to mess with the plant. But they rarely went away determined to make their other factories over in its image.

Says a frustrated William Buehler, senior vice president at Xerox: "You can see a high-performance factory or office, but it just doesn't spread. I don't know why." One reason is that nervous executives experiment where failure won't be fatal, and thereby contain the gains too. Says Jarrosiak: "I hate pilot programs off in a corner of a plant. You need commitment."

You also need to be able to envision how such operations fit into a large-scale enterprise. Says McKinsey's Ostroff: "Executives know what teams can do. But they need a picture that links the high-performance team to the whole organization and multiplies the gains." It's relatively easy to oversee one of these operations when it's confined within one function, like manufacturing. For self-directed management to spread, a company must lay goals, responsibilities, and measurements across functions. Ostroff argues: "Senior managers need to be able to say `empowerment' and `accountability' in the same sentence."

Business processes—almost sure to become a term you will hear lots of—can form the link between high-performance work teams and the corporation at large. Organizing around processes, as opposed to functions, permits greater self-management and allows companies to dismantle unneeded supervisory structures.

It's a management axiom that crab grass grows in the cracks between departments. Purchasing buys parts cheap, but manufacturing needs them strong. Shipping moves goods in bulk, but sales promised them fast. "I call it Palermo's law," says Richard Palermo, a vice-president for quality and transition at Xerox. "If a problem has been bothering your company and your customers for years and won't yield, that problem is the result of a cross-functional dispute, where nobody has total control of the whole process." And here's Palermo's corollary: People who work in different functions hate each other.

Upon this fratricidal scene, enter the process doctor. Depending on which consulting firm he's coming from, he may describe his work as "reengineering" or "core process redesign" or "process innovation." Michael Hammer, a consultant in Cambridge, Massachusetts, defines, though not exactly lyrically, what the doctor is up to: "Reengineering is the fundamental analysis and radical redesign of business processes to achieve dramatic improvements in critical measures of performance."

Process management differs from managing a function in three ways. First, it uses external objectives. Old-line manufacturing departments, for example, tend to be measured on unit costs, an intradepartmental number that can lead to overlong production runs and stacks of unsold goods. By contrast, an integrated manufacturing and shipping process might be rated by how often it turns over its inventory—a process-wide measurement that reveals how all are working together to keep costs down. Second, in process management employees with different skills are grouped to accomplish a complete piece of work. Mortgage loan officer, title searcher, and credit checker sit and work together, not in series. Third, information moves straight to where it's needed, unfiltered by a hierarchy. If you have a problem with people upstream from you, you deal with them directly, rather than asking your boss to talk to theirs.

Reengineered processes have been in place at Kodak for more than two years. The 1,500 employees who make black and white film—inevitably called Zebras—work not in departments but in what's called "the flow." (Black and white is big business: about $2 billion a year from sales of 7,000 products used in printing, X-rays, even spy satellites.) Headed by Richard Malloy, a 25-member leadership team watches the flow. They measure it with end-of-process tallies like productivity. Within the flow are streams defined by "customers"—Kodak business units—and scored on customer satisfaction measures such as on-time delivery. One stream, for example, is charged with making hundreds of types of film for the Health Sciences Division and works closely with it to schedule production and to develop new products, a Zebra specialty. In the streams most employees work in self-directed teams. A few functions—accounting and human resources—remain outside the streams.

When the flow began in 1989, the black and white film operation was running 15% over budgeted cost, took up to 42 days to fill an order, was late a third of the time, and scored worst in Kodak's morale surveys. Last year the group came in 15% under budget cost, had cut response time in half, was late one time out of 20, and wore the biggest smiles in Rochester, New York. Why? Says Zebra Robert Brookhouse: "When you create a flow and a flow chart, you find where you're wasting time, doing things twice. And because we own our entire process, we can change it."

Organizing around a process seems to yield sterling results as consistently as high-involvement factories do. Privately held Hallmark (1991 sales: $2.9 billion) expects big gains now that Steven Stanton of CSC Index, a Cambridge, Massachusetts, consulting firm, has helped the company reengineer its new-product process. The greeting-card maker lives or dies on new stuff—some 40,000 cards and other items a year, the work of 700 writers, artists, and designers on what Hallmark boasts is the world's largest creative staff. The process of developing a new card had become grotesque; it took two years—longer than the road from Gettysburg to Appomattox Court House. The company was choking on sketches, approvals, cost estimates, and proofs. Says Hallmark's Don Fletcher: "We needed a lot of people just to check items in and out of departments."

Fletcher's title, vice-president for business process redesign, pretty much tells what happened. Starting this spring, about half the staff will be put to work on cards for particular holidays like Valentine's Day or Christmas. The birthday and get-well card folks will follow. A team of artists, writers, lithographers, merchandisers, bean counters, and so on will be assigned to each holiday. Team members are moving from all over a two-million-square-foot office building in Kansas City so they can sit together. Like a canoe on a lake, a card will flow directly from one part of the process to the next within, say, the Mother's Day team;

before, it had to be portaged from one vast department to the next. This should cut cycle time in half, which will not only save money but will also make the company more responsive to changing tastes.

Hallmark hasn't eradicated departments. There will be "centers of excellence" to which workers will return between projects for training and brief, special stints, a bit like homerooms in high school. For now, department heads remain the senior managers of the business. But the head of graphic arts, which makes separations and proofs, has told Fletcher that he hopes the department infrastructure will eventually dissolve in the flow.

That's the right idea, say hard-core process managers. If you reengineer a process, pocket a one-time gain, and return to your desk, says McKinsey's Smith, "the barnacles you scrape off will

just grow back." The way to keep them off, says Hammer, is to obliterate the functions: "In the future, executive positions will not be defined in terms of collections of people, like head of the sales department, but in terms of process, like senior-VP-of-getting-stuff-to-customers, which is sales, shipping, billing. You'll no longer have a box on an organization chart. You'll own part of a process map."

Can a whole company literally lie on its side and organize horizontally, by process? You got it, says Allied-Signal's Bossidy: "Every business has maybe six basic processes. We'll organize around them. The people who run them will be the leaders of the business."

An industrial company might select processes like new-product development, flow of materials (purchasing, receiving, manufacturing), and the order-delivery billing cycle. Into these process flows will

MCKINSEY'S PLAN

It's hot stuff at McKinsey & Co. these days: a ten-point blueprint for a horizontal company prepared by Frank Ostroff and Doug Smith, consultants in the firm's organization-performance group.

1. *Organize primarily around process, not task.* Base performance objectives on customer needs, such as low cost or fast service. Identify the processes that meet (or don't meet) those needs—order generation and fulfillment, say, or new-product development. These processes—not departments, such as sales or manufacturing—become the company's main components.
2. *Flatten the hierarchy by minimizing subdivision of processes.* It's better to arrange teams in parallel, with each doing lots of steps in a process, than to have a series of teams, each doing fewer steps.
3. *Give senior leaders charge of processes and process performance.*
4. *Link performance objectives and evaluation of all activities to customer satisfaction.*
5. *Make teams, not individuals, the focus of organization performance and design.* Individuals acting alone don't have the capacity to continuously improve work flows.
6. *Combine managerial and non-managerial activities as often as possible.* Let workers' teams take on hiring, evaluating, and scheduling.
7. *Emphasize that each employee should develop several competencies.* You need only a few specialists.
8. *Inform and train people on a just-in-time, need-to-perform basis.* Raw numbers go straight to those who need them in their jobs, with no managerial spin, because you have trained front-line workers—salesmen, machinists—how to use them.
9. *Maximize supplier and customer contact with everyone in the organization.* That means field trips and slots on joint problem-solving teams for all employees all the time.
10. *Reward individual skill development and team performance instead of individual performance alone.*

go management teams to tend sub-processes and teams of workers to carry out tasks. Whoever is needed will be there: The materials-flow group might have finance folks but no marketers—but the marketers will be plentiful in the new-product process. There are no departments in Bossidy's 21st-century corporation: "You might have a CEO, but he won't have many people who report to him."

If metallurgists and actuaries are taken out of departments and clumped around processes, what happens to their specialized skills? A minor problem, argues James Champy, CEO of CSC Index: "State-of-the-art knowledge comes from a small group of people. Most people in a function don't contribute expertise. They execute." Put the innovators in a stafflike or lablike group. Create a house Yellow Pages so functional expertise is easy to find even though dispersed. Link experts in a real or electronic network where they can keep each other up to date and can get training and career development help.

"That's okay," says Bossidy. "The engineers can have a club. But they can't work in the same room, and they can't sit at the same table at the company banquet." His vision is somewhat radical, he admits, understating the case. "So corporations will first try to make the matrix work. Boy, that will drive employees and managers nuts."

One trouble with breaking down the walls: In most companies functional and hierarchical walls are load bearing. Remove them and the roof caves in. A big burden they bear is to collect, evaluate, and pass on information. Another is to determine employees' career paths—to define ambition, reward, and sycophancy. In a flat shop of teams and processes, both information flow and careers will have to be different.

Walk around futuristic companies and you see odd sights: suppliers who work in their customers' offices; widely available, easy-to-read charts tracking scrap, on-time delivery, and other data that rivals would kill for; hourly workers logged onto PCs reading their E-mail. They're all part of an effort to put information where it can be used at the moment it's needed. Says Delta Consulting's David Nadler: "In the organization of the future, information technology will be a load-bearing material—as hierarchy is now. You can't have self-management without it." That is, computer networks and the information they carry will help define your corporate structure. Let information flow wherever it's needed, and a horizontal self-managed company is not only possible, it's inescapable.

Building computer highways that can transport cost and other data sideways within a process, as well as vertically to top management, is a step in this direction. Other steps include training that teaches workers how their actions affect overall business performance and measurements that direct tasks at optimum outcomes, such as rewarding salespeople for gross margin, not gross sales.

You have to transport power as well as knowledge. In a hierarchy, rank defines authority: A manager can okay deals up to $50,000, his boss to $100,000, her boss to $250,000 . . . That's obsolete, in Harvard business school professor Quinn Mills's view. The question isn't how high the money gets; it's how high your customer's blood pressure gets. "Does he need an answer immediately? Do you have to be able to be flexible? If so, you have to empower the person who talks to the customer." If you can't entrust such matters to the folks in the field, maybe you should switch places with them. They can have your desk, where the decisions, obviously, are less important.

What happens to the career ladder? CSC Index Chief Executive Champy suggests that law firms, with only three levels of hierarchy—associate, partner, and senior partner—might provide the very model of a modern career path. Says Champy: "A lawyer's career is a progression to more complex work—tougher cases, more important clients. Titles don't change, but everyone knows who has the highest status."

The oldest art in organization design—carving out strategic business units—will still matter in this new world. The goal, as

---

WHAT A ZOO CAN TEACH YOU

The Zoological Society of San Diego has done more than most businesses to transform itself into a 21st-century organization. It deserves to be seen for its management as well as for its spectacular collection of beasts and birds.

With 1,200 year-round employees, $75 million in revenues, and five million visitors a year, the San Diego Zoo and its Wild Animal Park make a sizable outfit whose competitors—among them Walt Disney and Anheuser-Busch, owner of nearby Sea World—are real gorillas. Also, as a world-renowned scientific and conservation organization, the zoo must maintain high technical standards and a Caesar's-wife purity on environmental and other issues.

The zoo is steadily remodeling to show its animals by bioclimatic zone (an African rain forest called Gorilla Tropics, or Tiger River, an Asian jungle environment) rather than by taxonomy (pachyderms, primates). As displays open—three out of ten are finished—they're fundamentally altering the way the zoo is run.

The old zoo was managed through its 50 departments—animal keeping, horticulture, maintenance, food service, fund raising, education, and others. It had all the traits of functional management, says David Glines, head of employee development. Glines started out as a groundsman, responsible for keeping paths clear of trash. If he was tired or rushed, Glines remembers, "Sometimes I'd sweep a cigarette butt under a bush. Then it was the gardener's problem not mine."

The departments are invisible in the redesigned parts of the zoo. Tiger River, for instance, is run by a team of mammal and bird specialists, horticulturists, and maintenance and construction workers. The four-year-old team, led by keeper John Turner, tracks its own budget on a PC that isn't hooked up to the zoo's mainframe. Members are jointly responsible for the display, and it's hard to tell who comes from which department. When the path in front of an aviary needed fixing last autumn, the horticulturist and the construction man did it.

Seven people run Tiger River. When it started there were 11, but as team members learned one another's skills, they decided they didn't need to replace workers who left. (P.S.: They're all Teamsters union members.) Freed from managerial chores now handled by teams, executives can go out and drum up more interest in the zoo.

Any effect on business? Southern California tourism took some hits in 1991—first from the Gulf war, then from the recession—but the San Diego Zoo enjoyed a 20% increase in attendance. Part of the reason is price: At $12 it costs less than half as much to enter the zoo gates as it does to get into Disneyland.

Zoo director Douglas Myers credits employees' sense of ownership. Says he: "I told them recession is coming; we're going to target our marketing on the local area alone, and we're going to ask all our visitors to come back five times—so each time they'd better have more fun than the time before. The employees came through."

Nadler sees it, is to create "enterprises with clear customers, markets, and measures, and few internal boundaries." That means letting sets of customers or customer needs define business units, and grouping into businesses the people and processes necessary to serve them.

That's how Xerox designed its new horizontal organization. Until this year, Xerox was set up in the usual functions—R&D, manufacturing, sales, and the like. The new design creates nine businesses aimed at markets such as small businesses and individuals, office document systems, and engineering systems. Each business will have an income statement and a balance sheet, and an identifiable set of competitors. New manufacturing layouts will permit so-called focused factories dedicated to specific businesses.

Most of the businesses will sell through a new Customer Operations Group, a mingling of sales, shipping, installation, service, and billing, created so customers can keep just one phone number on their Rolodexes. In fact, the businesses will see to Customer Operations—that is, negotiate contracts—so that market forces extend deeply into the company. Teams lead the businesses, whose building blocks are what CEO Paul Allaire calls "microenterprise units": complete work processes or subprocesses. Says Allaire: "We've given everyone in the company a direct line of sight to the customer."

In a functional hierarchy, job descriptions, career paths, and information flow are all geared toward control—of work, workers, and knowledge. Compare that with the evolving 21st-century company, where work is lined up with customers, not toward bosses. Senior executives have charge of the handful of processes that are critical to satisfying customers. Self-directed, the work force does most of the hiring, scheduling, and other managerial tasks that once ate up kazillions in indirect labor costs. The few people left between the executives and the work teams spend their time trying to change the organization, not to control it: They are reaching out to grab a new technology or a new customer, or to respond to a new demand from an old one. Jobs, careers, and knowledge shift constantly.

The boundaries of the company will be fluid too. The growing number of strategic alliances suggests as much. So do the actions of companies like Wal-Mart Stores and Procter & Gamble, which have interwoven their order-and-fulfillment process so that the bells of Wal-Mart's cash registers in effect ring in P&G warehouses, telling them to ship a new box of Tide to replace the one you just bought.

In the view of Harvard economist Robert Reich, the boundaries will become so fluid that corporations will become temporary arrangements among entrepreneurial cadres. Except for high-volume, capital-intensive work, says Reich, "Every big company will be a confederation of small ones. All small organizations will be constantly in the process of linking up into big ones."

That may be more fluidity than most people can accept, at least as long as mortgage applications ask, "How long have you been with your current employer?" But the new flexible organization will be a powerful competitor. Smith finds a metaphor in *Terminator II*, the movie where Arnold Schwarzenegger faces a metal monster that liquifies, then hardens again in a new shape—now a man, now a machine, now a knife. Says Smith: "I call it the *Terminator II* company." How'd you like to have to compete with one of those?

READING THE BUSINESS PRESS

Much of the information about trends in management that you have and will acquire in your life as a manager comes from the business press. It is important to learn how to read this material quickly and critically. You can help enhance these skills by asking the following questions:

What is the "story" that this article is telling? Is the article advocating a certain point of view, or is it balancing different points of view? Does the article have an explicit or an implicit causal model—that is, an assumption about what drivers produce what effects?

What kind of evidence does the article use? If it relies heavily on quotations from "authorities," who are they and how are these sources likely to influence the kind of information the article presents?

The article "The Search for the Organization of Tomorrow" is making a case for believing that a major managerial shift is underway, and has an explicit causal models. It argues strongly that changes in organization and management are necessary, given certain changes in the environment. The "drivers" cited are intensifying international competition and changing information technology.

What evidence does the reading present for a major change in organization and management?

1. Quotes from "authorities," primarily top managers. Note that very few articles in the business press go to multiple sources in the company, and that there is a strong preference for top-level managers. Note too that the article contains many references to consultants and academics.

2. Vivid "mini-cases" that describe the changes in a particular company, usually in terms of one specific dimension of change, and usually in terms of success

3. An explicit causal model

Who are the authorities?

This article draws on a number of key "authorities" to give evidence of the kinds of changes that are underway. Table 1.1 on page 42 presents a "count" of the various people cited. Think how the nature of the sources might color the portrayal of the "new organization." These authorities tend to be people with a strong stake in having the changes viewed as successful. This does not mean that their viewpoint is not useful; it means that the reader must look carefully beyond the specific examples to ask, "What would it take to convince me that the model underlying these stories is valid and useful?"

41

PRESS

TABLE 1.1 *FORTUNE*, "THE SEARCH FOR THE ORGANIZATION OF TOMORROW," MAY 18,1992

Sources/"Authorities"	Number of quotes[5]
Managers	
Lawrence Bossidy, CEO, Allied Signal	5
H. James Maxmin, CEO, Laura Ashley	1
Philip Jarrosiak, Manager HRM, GE's capacitor & power protection operations	2
Herman Simon, plant manager, Gaines	1
William Buehler, Senior V-P, Xerox	1
Richard Palermo, V-P, Xerox	1
Don Fletcher, V-P, Hallmark	1
Paul Allaire, CEO, Xerox	1
Consultants	
David Nadler, Delta Consulting	2
Doug Smith, McKinsey	5
Frank Ostroff	3
Mike Hammer, CSC Index	2
James Champy, CSC Index	2
Academics/Researchers	
Peter Drucker	1
Marvin Weisbrod	1
Shoshanna Zuboff	1
Quinn Mills	1
Robert Reich (pre-Clinton appointment)	1
Workers	
Robert Brookhouse, Kodak "Zebra"	1

5 This number refers not to the specific number of quotations, but to the number of times in the article at which the person's statements or views are cited. The article goes back to some of the sources at several different points in the article.

MANAGING FOR THE FUTURE

MASSACHUSETTS INSTITUTE OF TECHNOLOGY

ANCONA, KOCHAN, SCULLY,
VAN MAANEN, WESTNEY

Organizational Behavior & Processes
Instructor's Module

THREE LENSES ON ORGANIZATIONAL ANALYSIS AND ACTION

module 2

MODULE 2 (M-2)

THREE LENSES ON ORGANIZATIONAL ANALYSIS AND ACTION

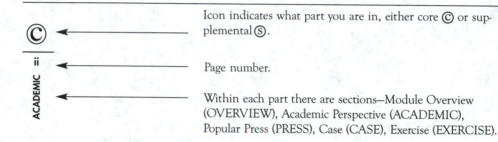

Icon indicates what part you are in, either core Ⓒ or supplemental Ⓢ.

Page number.

Within each part there are sections—Module Overview (OVERVIEW), Academic Perspective (ACADEMIC), Popular Press (PRESS), Case (CASE), Exercise (EXERCISE).

Dedicated to those who have inspired us to try to be better students and teachers. Special dedications to

Professor Jack Barbash
Professor Arthur H. Gladstein
Professor Marius B. Jansen
Professor Joanne Martin
Professor Edgar H. Schein

Acquisitions Editor: John R. Szilagyi
Developmental Editor: Jamie Gleich Bryant
Production Editor: Mardell Toomey
Production House: DPS Associates, Inc.
Cover Design: Michael H. Stratton
Marketing Manager: Rob Bloom

ISBN: 0-538-87689-1

1 2 3 4 5 6 7 D1 4 3 2 1 0 9 8

Printed in the United States of America

South-Western College Publishing
an International Thomson Publishing company I(T)P®

Cincinnati • Albany • Boston • Detroit • Johannesburg • London • Madrid • Melbourne • Mexico City
New York • Pacific Grove • San Francisco • Scottsdale • Singapore • Tokyo • Toronto

CONTENTS

THREE LENSES ON ORGANIZATIONAL ANALYSIS AND ACTION

This module introduces three lenses on organizational analysis and action that have been developed over the years by researchers, teachers, consultants, and practitioners who study and participate in organizations. Ours is a behavioral science perspective that differs from the economic realm of bundles of contracts and utility-maximizing individuals and from the decision modeling realm where all decisions can be programmed. The behavioral science perspective builds on psychology, sociology, political science, and anthropology. From these disciplines we have developed the *strategic design, political,* and *cultural lenses.*

You can think of these as three different lenses that you could put on your mental camera in order to get different views of an organization you are trying to understand and change. Through each lens you will be directed to observe slightly different features, e.g., the structure of the firm, key stakeholders and their interests, or artifacts and assumptions, respectively. Also, each lens focusing on one feature will reveal a different view from the others. An organization chart will represent a system of grouping and linking critical tasks in one lens, a picture of the current power structure and dominant coalition in the second, and a symbol to be interpreted in the third. As a manager taking action, the strategic design lens sets you up as an "organizational architect" improving the fit between the strategy and organization and across organizational components. The political lens casts you as a forger of coalitions and negotiator leveraging varying interests. The cultural lens defines your role as articulating a vision and creating symbols and stories. All need to be done.

The accompanying module, 2A, provides the instructions for applying these three lenses, along with characteristics of the "new" organization, to performing an organizational analysis.

THE STRUCTURE OF THE MODULE

This module is divided into five parts. The first part provides an introduction and motivation for using the three lenses by way of the concept of cognitive schema. The second part introduces the strategic design lens and calls for its application to the ABB case. The third part introduces the political lens and uses the Rosewell role play to practice stakeholder analysis and action. The fourth part provides readings on the cultural lens and provides an exercise that allows students to do a cultural analysis of their own institution. Finally, the fifth part provides a case, Dynacorp, that illustrates how all three lenses can be used to develop a plan for analysis and managerial action.

ADDITIONAL ACTIVITIES

1. Find an article in the business press about a particular organization. Assess whether the article is using (implicitly or explicitly) the strategic design, political, or cultural perspective, or some combination thereof.

For example, the business press in June 1995 was abuzz about the merger between Lotus and IBM. Some articles discussed who would occupy the vice-presidential roles after the merger and which positions might be retained or eliminated (a strategic design perspective). Some articles discussed the interests of employees as both stockholders and knowledge workers with some power to leverage if they threatened to leave (a political perspective). Some articles discussed the implications of mixing such seemingly diverse corporate cultures (a cultural perspective).

2. Write a brief essay explaining which of the three perspectives you are most naturally comfortable with and why.

ADDITIONAL SUGGESTED READINGS

The importance of looking at organizations from multiple perspectives is one of the hallmarks of a behavioral approach to organizations. The behavioral approach recognizes that there are many ways in which individuals make sense of work, numerous ways in which behaviors in organizations can have ramifications, and multiple paths to a variety of organizational outcomes (from job satisfaction to corporate performance). The behavioral approach is therefore different from a more traditionally economic approach to organizations, which has tended to look for one best way to optimize profitability. The following books each present different clusters of approaches to organizational behavior and processes that overlap with or supplement the perspectives presented in this module.

Bolman, Lee G., and Terrence E. Deal. 1991. *Reframing Organizations: Artistry, Choice, and Leadership.* San Francisco: Jossey-Bass.

Morgan, Gareth. 1986. *Images of Organization.* Newbury Park, CA: Sage Publications.

M-2

core

PART 1: INTRODUCTION

In order to solve an organizational problem or take advantage of an organizational opportunity, it is helpful to have a rich understanding of the organization and the issues. A good picture of an organization is useful for probing more thoroughly into the possible nature and sources of the issues and the range of approaches. It is easy to skip this analysis in favor of familiar approaches. People often summarize an organizational problem in a way that suggests there is a singular source, such as, "The main problem we have here is a delay in manufacturing." They leap into that line of inquiry: "OK, let's see what we can do to speed up the manufacturing process." In fact, if they had a richer picture of the organization, they might learn that the problem is elsewhere, perhaps to do with the design/manufacturing interface, or the relationship with suppliers, or the way that overtime compensation is handled. It is helpful to understand that there are many ways to look at an organization and many illuminating features that can be observed. Different individuals will tend to focus on one set of problems or issues over others.

There is an often-told parable about "the three blind men and the elephant" that reminds us of the importance of an individual's viewpoint:

> Three blind men were asked to describe what an elephant is like. One blind man felt the elephant's tail and observed, "An elephant is very much like a piece of rope." The second blind man felt the elephant's side and observed, "An elephant is very much like a wall." The third blind man felt the elephant's trunk and observed, "An elephant is very much like a pipe." Each was right. And each was incomplete and partly misguided.

Our informal diagnoses of organizations, based on bits and pieces of our experiences, are often partly right but somewhat incomplete and misguided. This module presents some more formal and complete models for looking at organizations that have been developed in the social sciences. Of course, none of these models is a complete theory of the world either. Rather, the challenge is for you to understand whether there are certain approaches to organizations that you naturally tend to adopt, whether there are certain potentially useful approaches that you tend to overlook, and whether these can be balanced and integrated to provide a more complete analysis.

This module introduces three classic perspectives on organizations. These three perspectives can be thought of as lenses, each of which presents a distinctive view of the organization. Before reading about how these three perspectives have developed, it is helpful to think about how each of us brings our own personal views to organizations.

OUR PERSONAL "SCHEMAS"

Each of us has certain ways of looking at the world. We have what social psychologists call *schemas,* which we use every day to navigate through complex situations. "A schema is a cognitive structure that represents organized knowledge about a given concept or type of stimulus. A schema contains both the attributes of the concept and the relationship among the attributes" (Fiske and Taylor, 1984, p. 140). Social psychologists developed this idea upon observing that individuals construct their own maps of the social world.

What is Helpful About Schemas?

Schemas help people function in cognitively efficient ways. As certain kinds of situations or data become familiar, it is easier to rely on a tried and true model of how to react than to rethink the situation anew. For example, someone who drives a crowded freeway to work every morning may always jump into the leftmost lane on approaching the toll plaza; that is her schema for dealing with traffic. She hardly has to think about it—she just does it. When she started driving that route, she may have taken different approaches and arrived at this one after trial and error. Even if it isn't the very fastest lane each morning, overall it may reduce stress to have this taken-for-granted strategy, leaving her mind a little freer to focus on the radio news. Schemas give us an approach to repeated situations and free up our minds for other more complex and highly varying activities.

It is particularly helpful to develop schemas about organizations in which we work. This is the essence of becoming an "old hand"—the value of employees with seniority is that they have worked out a number of their own unwritten schemas for how to get things done. (In more formal terms, they have developed specialized human capital or tacit knowledge that makes them particularly valuable and difficult to replace.) Without schemas, every task would be a monumental new project.

> Most organizations provide complex and noisy informational environments in which organizational participants gather information about other individuals and relevant work tasks, which they must then integrate with their own thoughts, feelings, and work behaviors. To manage these multiple information-processing demands, people accomplish many cognitive activities without conscious awareness, attention, or much forethought. In other words people rely on highly structured, pre-existing knowledge systems to interpret their organizational world and generate appropriate behaviors. Such a knowledge system . . . is often called a schema. (Lord and Foti, 1986, pp. 20–21)

This cognitive processing is helpful because it helps individuals find recurring patterns in complex everyday data. But schemas are not meant to be hard and fast rules. Without some conscious examination of them, we might be led astray.

How Do Our Schemas Lead Us Astray?

Schemas Become Outdated   Although our personal schemas may initially seem efficient, they can become outdated. People can be stubbornly attached to their schemas. Schemas need updating. Our schemas derive from our experiences, but over time they can also come to shape our experiences in self-fulfilling ways.

For example, in the past, textbooks included mostly examples of men in professional roles. On the one hand, these pictures were a fairly accurate representation, statistically, of who was most likely to occupy professional roles some years ago. A person with a schema that "you should ask for *Mister* so-and-so if phoning the manager" may have had an accurate, time-saving schema. On the other hand, schemas do not just reflect organizational life, they help to shape it. It has been difficult for women to move into traditionally male professional roles precisely because most people's schemas have not included a picture of women in those roles.

The entrance of women into professional roles may help some people change these particular schemas. And at the same time, changing schemas may make it easier for women to enter professional roles. People who do not update their schemas may find themselves in embarrassing situations, such as the students who asked the woman standing in the department office for some help with photocopying, thinking she must be the secretary, only to discover they had just asked the chair of the department to photocopy their assignments.

© ACADEMIC

5

Schemas Are Resistant to Change   It is both a beauty and a weakness of schemas that they become familiar and difficult to change. Even if we know our old schemas are not perfect—the leftmost lane is not always the fastest moving in the morning commute—sometimes it is easier to stay with them than to experiment; it may be enough to have a schema that works out pretty well on average.

People may especially need to change their schemas in times of organizational change, but may be reluctant to do so. Resistance to organizational change usually does not come from a failure to come up with the right blueprint for future practices. It more often comes from people's reluctance to give up their comfortable old approaches. A familiar refrain in organizations is "But we've *always* done it that way." People may not simply be saying that the old way was wonderful. They may be saying that they had come up with ways of coping with the old system—some schemas for getting around the bugs, the red tape, and the obstacles—so that they could function in the old system without having to reinvent everything every day and get a headache from the stress. A new system requires building new schemas; it takes a lot of energy and thoughtfulness to update old schemas.

Schemas Become Universal Rules   Schemas encourage us to react to types of situations or types of people in certain ways. Because it is difficult to collect additional, thorough data as each situation or person comes along, the universal rules embodied in our schemas save time. They are helpful to overworked people. However, much of organizational life is not universal ("always do X to make a business travel reservation"), but instead is contingent ("do X to make domestic travel arrangements and Y to make international travel arrangements"). What you do depends on some more specific, distinguishing information about the situation.

Consider a busy manager who was stressed about writing performance evaluations for his employees and documenting aspects of their performance. He came up with a simplifying schema to determine who his strongest employees were, a rule of thumb that he thought had been fairly accurate: "The people who are here the latest at night are the best workers." He began to worry, however, that his performance evaluations were demoralizing some excellent workers and praising some less productive workers. His schema was leading him astray. Employees who worked very efficiently and creatively but had families were rarely in the office until late at night. People who chatted and took long lunches during the day or people who had trouble grasping the more complex projects were often still there until late at night. When he saw someone either leave early or stay late, he needed to understand the contingencies that affected their work hours and not to make universal judgments.

Schemas Are Incomplete   We develop schemas in line with our ongoing experiences, but we may miss some important features. Consider the new engineer who observed that the other engineers always spoke loudly and slowly when phoning down to the production floor. This became his schema too—always speak loudly and slowly to production. He inferred that the reason was because the people in production were not too bright. This assumption got him into trouble when he bumped into production people in the hallways and spoke to them loudly and slowly. The information that he was missing was that the engineers spoke loudly and slowly on the phone because the machinery running in the background was very noisy.

As is often the case with schemas, his schema included some implicit causal reasoning about why something was done. Lacking complete information, his schema had faulty causal reasoning and encoded a stereotypical bias that was misguided and left him embarrassed. Schemas can be helpful to us, but it is useful also to be aware of our assumptions and to seek additional richer information about organizational life. Understanding multiple perspectives on organizations helps us become better organizational members, decision makers, and change agents.

BUILDING MORE COMPLETE MODELS

Despite their shortcomings, our personal schemas are pretty good as informal starting points for understanding and coping with how the world works. However, sometimes we would like to look at more formal models and data about how the world works, in order to check our own understandings. Social scientists look for patterns and insights about the social world, drawing on previous research, adding their own hypotheses, and collecting data that challenge, test, or expand their ideas in a systematic way. This wealth of social scientific data can expand our informal schemas.

For example, a marketing manager's schema may be to check and see what her major competitor is doing in the market as a convenient way of assessing her options. However, a more formal model built by a researcher with a large database could be used to assess where innovation in the market comes from. Perhaps the data show that it comes from small innovators on the margin, not from central competitors. The findings from a more formal model might help this manager to update her schema. She may read about networks to understand her company's environment better and how ideas travel among researchers of this environment.

Of course, social scientists have their own favorite personal schemas for how to study the social world and how to construct a research project. Therefore, the insights and findings that we gain from social scientific research can be clustered into different types. The approaches in economics, psychology, anthropology, sociology, and political science are each distinctive.

This module focuses on three classic perspectives that weave together colorful strands from different social science disciplines. Each perspective embodies certain assumptions about human nature, about the meaning of organizing, about the relative power of different actors, and about how to collect and analyze data. Each perspective has developed from its own array of studies and models, like the simple example of a study of market innovation used as an example above. This research history makes the perspective a distinctive whole.

THREE CLASSIC LENSES ON ORGANIZATIONS

There are three readings that follow that describe these three classic perspectives. Think of each perspective as a different lens through which you can view the organization. These approaches reflect years of studies, interviews, observations, and participation in organizations. The readings highlight the important features of each lens, the history of the development of that lens, and the kinds of questions about organizational processes that each lens might guide you to ask in order to get a richer picture of an organization or to conduct an organizational analysis. The three lenses are:

- The Strategic Design Lens
- The Political Lens
- The Cultural Lens

The Strategic Design Lens

People who take this perspective look at how the flow of tasks and information is designed, how people are sorted into roles, how these roles are related, and how the organization can be rationally optimized to achieve its goals. What if you considered the problem mentioned in the opening paragraph of this introduction, about delays in manufacturing, from this perspective? Just one possibility is that you might decide that looking at the design/manufacturing interface is a good place to start to chart the flow of information and detect any disconnections between roles.

Ⓒ

7

ACADEMIC

The Political Lens

People who take this perspective look at how power and influence are distributed and wielded, how multiple stakeholders express their different preferences and get involved in (or excluded from) decisions, and how conflicts can be resolved. What if you considered delays in manufacturing from this perspective? Just one possibility is that you might decide that suppliers are critical stakeholders who must be considered, and you might explore whether they are influencing the delays to display their control over a crucial resource and gain influence in pricing.

The Cultural Lens

People who take this perspective look at how history has shaped the assumptions and meanings of different people, how certain practices take on special meaningfulness and even become rituals, and how stories and other artifacts shape the feel of an organization. What if you considered delays in manufacturing from this perspective? Just one possibility is that you might decide that overtime pay has a symbolic meaning to workers, that norms about who gets how much overtime have developed over the years, and that what look like delays might be attempts to spread out the overtime in ways that are valued as being more fair.

What Lens Do You Favor?

As you read about these lenses, try to surface your own implicit views of organizations. You might see whether you instinctively align with one of these three lenses. Compare and contrast what they say about organizational processes with what you have come to believe about organizational processes based on your own experiences.

THE THREE LENSES IN ACTION

Think about how you might use the three lenses differently to understand some of the changes that are taking place—or being thwarted—in organizations today. After the readings on the three lenses, there is a reading on using the three lenses to analyze the implementation of teamwork.

Analyzing Organizations

An organizational analysis often begins with an intuitive sense of where to look to understand an organization and describe its character to others. An organizational analysis is guided by an idea of how organizations work. Each of us has schemas that affect what we pay attention to and what we ignore. The three lenses provide a number of possible ways to expand your views of organizations and enrich your organizational analysis. Module 2A goes into even more detail about how to use the three lenses to do an organizational analysis.

Balancing Multiple Perspectives

You will have a chance to use all three lenses as you conduct the organizational analysis that is described in Part 5 of this module. At the same time, it is important to understand that sometimes these lenses suggest contradictory, not complementary, approaches or actions.

Throughout the term, you will have opportunities to work with other people who look at organizations differently or prefer a different perspective than you do, based on their different organizational experiences and standpoints.

We emphasize that there is not one clear, correct, optimal solution to a problem. That does not mean that any analysis is a good analysis. Some analyses are better than others—more thoughtful, more complete, more attentive to contingencies and tradeoffs, or more able to balance and integrate multiple perspectives. A failure to consider multiple perspectives represents an incomplete analysis.

ACADEMIC   8

REFERENCES

Fiske, Susan T., and Shelley E. Taylor. 1984. *Social Cognition.* New York: Random House.

Lord, Robert G., and Roseanne J. Foti. 1986. "Schema Theories, Information Processing, and Organizational Behavior." In H. P. Sims, Jr., and D. A. Gioia eds., *The Thinking Organization,* pp. 20–48. San Francisco: Jossey-Bass.

Ⓒ

9

ACADEMIC

PART 2: THE STRATEGIC DESIGN LENS

This part of Module 2 introduces you to the strategic design perspective on organizations. This is the first of the three perspectives introduced in this module, each of which provides invaluable insights for those who work and manage in organizations. The strategic design perspective is the dominant one in most management schools, and probably the one that managers find most congenial. It sees organizations as systems that have been deliberately constructed to achieve strategic goals, and takes as its fundamental assumption that organizations can be designed so as to maximize their efficiency and effectiveness in the environment in which they are operating. This module introduces you to the way this perspective "sees" organizations—the kind of lens it applies to them—and provides an overview of the basic elements of organization design.

Organization design is, in this perspective, a fundamental task of organizational life. It operates at all levels, from the design of the organization as a whole to the design of teams and work groups, right down to the design of individual tasks and jobs. You yourself are, or should be, engaged in designing an organization when you decide how to operate in teams in your classes. Understanding and working with the basic design principles introduced in this module can not only help you understand how complex organizations work; it can also have immediate application in your current activities.

This part of the module contains a class note on the strategic design perspective, which provides you with the fundamentals of how the world looks through this particular "lens" and introduces the basic principles of organization design. This is followed by a case study of an organization which is often held up as a model of good organization design: ABB (Asea Brown Boveri). ABB is an extremely complex firm: it operates in over 140 countries in several major businesses, with over 200,000 employees and over one billion dollars in sales. Yet its design allows it, as its former CEO, Percy Barnevik, has repeatedly stated, to be simultaneously big and small, centralized and decentralized, global and local. ABB is in many respects an exemplar of the networked, flat, flexible, and global organization that has so dominated the discussions of the organization of the future that have appeared in the business press over the last decade. And yet it is an organization that has its own roots in the nineteenth century, as does its core industry, heavy electrical equipment. ABB provides a complicated but fascinating example of the power of strategic organization design.

The purposes of this part of the module are, therefore, to:

- introduce the basic concepts and approaches of the strategic design perspective on organizations
- provide an overview of the fundamental principles of organization design at all levels of the organization
- exercise your understanding of those concepts and principles by asking you to apply them to an extremely complex but widely-admired company, ABB

Source: From *Competing By Design: The Power of Organizational Architecture* by David Nadler and Michael Tushman. Copyright © 1997 Oxford University Press. Used by permission of Oxford University Press, Inc.

ASSIGNMENTS

As you read the case, think about the following questions, which will frame the class discussion:

1. What are the strategic grouping structures? What are the principle linking mechanisms? What are the major alignment challenges, and how does ABB address them?
2. What do you see as the major strengths of ABB's organization design? Its major weaknesses? Would you like to work as an operating company manager in ABB?

ADDITIONAL SUGGESTED READINGS

Galbraith, Jay. 1977. *Organization Design.* Reading, Mass: Addison-Wesley. One of the classic texts of organization design.

Nadler, David A. and Michael L. Tushman. 1997. *Competing by Design: The Power of Organizational Architecture.* New York: Oxford University Press. A comprehensive and detailed guide to organization design, with many rich examples.

Miles, R. and C. Snow. 1994. *Fit, Failure, and the Hall of Fame.* New York: Free Press. A much-cited book that links strategy and strategic organizational design.

Taylor, William. 1991. "The Logic of Global Business: An Interview with ABB's Percy Barnevik." *Harvard Business Review* (March–April), pp. 90–104. A detailed interview with ABB's then-CEO, Percy Barnevik, who is widely credited with being the principal "architect" of ABB's organization.

11

ACADEMIC

THE ORGANIZATION AS STRATEGIC DESIGN

From Max Weber's discussion of "machine bureaucracy" at the turn of the century to business process re-engineering in the 1990s, the dominant perspective on organizations has viewed them as *strategic designs:* that is, as systems deliberately constructed to achieve certain strategic goals. This perspective asserts that by understanding basic principles of organization design, by aligning the organization's design with its strategy, and by making sure that both strategy and design fit the environment in which the organization is operating, managers can make their organizations successful. The strategic design perspective emphasizes the efficiency and effectiveness of the organization. *Efficiency* involves accomplishing strategic goals with the least possible expenditure of resources; *effectiveness* involves ensuring that goals are accomplished to the standard necessary for the organization to succeed.

More and more managers are coming to see organization design as a critically important source of competitive success, and to agree that "ultimately, there may be no long-term sustainable advantage except the ability to organize and manage" (Galbraith and Lawler, 1993). What does "the ability to organize and manage" involve? The strategic design perspective sees it as building on basic principles and processes involving:

- Setting the strategy or mandate of the organization (**strategic intent**)
- Establishing what activities the organization must carry out to achieve success in its strategies (for example, providing speedy and reliable servicing of products to customers, getting products from R&D to the market more quickly, etc.) and how the organization's capabilities might influence the strategies (for example, an organization with a widespread marketing organization might be better off using that organization to get fast and detailed information on customer needs than adopting a low-cost strategy that involves drastic cuts in marketing personnel). This is often referred to as **linking strategy and organization**.
- Deciding how the necessary activities are to be allocated into jobs, departments, divisions, and other units, and how people are assigned to each (**differentiation** or **strategic grouping**)
- Ensuring that people, jobs, departments, etc. are coordinated effectively with each other (**integration** or **strategic linking**)
- Making sure the different elements and processes in the organization work together to carry out the strategies (**alignment** of organization and strategy)
- Ensuring that the organization design meets the requirements of its external environment (**fit** between organization and environment)

The processes leading to the strategic design of an organization are summarized in Figure 2.1.

People working with this perspective often use metaphors of the organization as a mechanism or system, of "engineering" or "re-engineering," of organization-building and "organizational architecture," of the organization as a complex organism that can be "diagnosed" like a medical patient. Like engineering, architecture, or medicine, management is seen as a matter of understanding and applying basic principles and processes, and adapting them to the context in which one is operating.

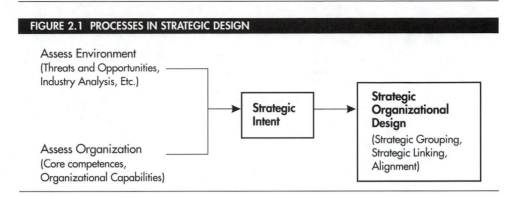

FIGURE 2.1 PROCESSES IN STRATEGIC DESIGN

KEY ELEMENTS OF ORGANIZATION DESIGN

One way to think about the strategic design perspective is that it involves simultaneously

- Drawing boundaries around clusters of tasks or activities (to define jobs, departments, and processes), **strategic grouping**
- Creating links across those boundaries, **strategic linking**
- **Aligning** other elements of the organization (such as rewards and incentives) with the chosen grouping and linking patterns with each other so that each part of the organization is oriented to accomplishing "what needs doing" in terms of its strategies

The basic assumption of the strategic design perspective, therefore, is that an organization is most effective when its strategy fits the conditions of its environment and when the organizational components are aligned with the strategy and with each other.

The basic element of organization design is often seen as the *task*: the smallest unit of the activities that need to be performed if the organization is to realize its strategic goals. Tasks vary in complexity, from the relatively simple, like inserting circuit boards into the CPU of a personal computer on an assembly line, to more complex, such as reprogramming an industrial robot on an assembly line, to the extremely complex, like setting up a new business division to develop, produce, and sell industrial robots. Tasks also vary in the level of routinization: that is, the extent to which the activity can be specified and programmed. Usually, simple tasks are more routinized, but even complex tasks can also be routinized. For example, the analysis of how software is designed and the breaking of what had been seen as a complex "art" or task into discrete programming steps has led to the creation of "software factories" with high levels of efficiency in producing certain kinds of software programs.

Tasks also vary in the nature of their interdependence. Some tasks are highly independent of other tasks, and can be performed quite separately from others. Most tasks that are incorporated into an organization, however, involve some level of interdependency. *Task interdependence* can be imagined as varying from low to high. It can also be seen in terms of the kind of interdependence. James Thompson (1967) developed a highly influential typology of task interdependence, identifying three different types: **sequential interdependence,** in which one task is completed and then handed off for the next stage; **pooled interdependence,** in which interdependent tasks are undertaken at the same time, and the results put together or pooled; and **reciprocal interdependence,** in which tasks are conducted in repeated interaction with each other (see Figure 2.2). In software engineering, sequential interdependence can be seen when the development of a software program is divided into distinct stages or phases, with "milestones" to mark the completion of one stage and the hand-off to the next. Pooled interdependence occurs when different groups work on modules of a program that are then put together to form the final program. And reciprocal interdependence characterizes complex

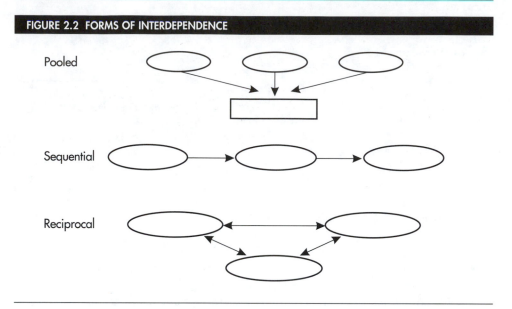

FIGURE 2.2 FORMS OF INTERDEPENDENCE

Pooled

Sequential

Reciprocal

programs where the different tasks involved in developing the program are carried on in dense interaction with each other, because the solutions to problems in one element of the program affect the solutions that can be implemented in others.

As these examples show, many complex tasks can be broken down into simpler activities. Nearly a century ago Frederick Taylor developed what came to be called "Scientific Management," using time and motion studies to analyze the most efficient set of movements needed to perform industrial tasks, such as shoveling coal in a steel mill. Then he re-aggregated the movements into a Standard Operating Procedure that defined the job. Nearly one hundred years later, this same approach of the disaggregation and careful analysis of tasks underpins Business Process Re-engineering, which analyzes the steps in delivering a product or service to the customer to eliminate unnecessary activities, and then re-combines tasks into more effective and efficient jobs and subunits.

Organizational design choices begin with strategic grouping: that is, the aggregation of activities, positions, and individuals into work units. Every set of grouping decisions must be accompanied by a complementary set of linkages, which provide the coordination mechanisms across the activities or groups separated by the grouping boundaries. Then the other elements of the organization must be aligned with the grouping and linking mechanisms, in order to implement the design.

Strategic grouping, linking, and alignment are relevant at every level of the organization, from the design of teams or departments to the overall design of the organization.

STRATEGIC GROUPING

Grouping decisions dictate the basic framework within which all other organizational design decisions are made. Grouping gathers together some tasks, functions, or disciplines, and separates them from others. It is (or ought to be) a direct outgrowth of the organizational unit's strategy. At its simplest level, it involves answering the question of how to cluster tasks and activities. Should people performing the same kinds of tasks in similar ways be clustered together, or should people performing complementary tasks be grouped together? How many subgroups should be created, and in how many layers? Grouping can be seen as "drawing the boxes" of the organization design. There are three basic forms or "ideal types" of grouping, each with a distinct set of strengths and weaknesses.

Grouping by Activity

Grouping by activity brings together individuals who share similar functions, disciplines, skills, or work processes. In other words, they perform similar tasks and engage in similar activities. At the level of the organization, grouping by activity gives rise to *functional organizations*, the oldest form of business enterprise and one which is still often the form first adopted in new organizations. In the functional organization, activities concerned with a particular function—product development/engineering, manufacturing, marketing, distribution, accounting, and so on—are grouped into separate divisions, as shown in Figure 2.3. Pharmaceutical companies are often organized functionally, with Research and Development, Manufacturing, and Marketing and Distribution forming separate departments or divisions of the company, and with the top management group consisting of the Vice-President of R&D, the Vice-President of Manufacturing, the Vice-President of Marketing, and so on. Grouping by activity is common in subunits of organizations. Even when pharmaceutical companies reorganize their organizations overall according to other criteria, they may continue to group their scientists in the research laboratory according to discipline (e.g., biology, chemistry, etc.).

Grouping by Output

Grouping by output organizes on the basis of the service or product provided. The people within the group perform a variety of different tasks and activities, but they are all contributors to the same final output (a product or set of closely related products or services). For example, firms with a range of product lines and markets usually find the functional organization too inflexible and instead adopt a *product line* or *multidivisional* structure. In this design, pioneered in the United States by DuPont and General Motors (Chandler, 1962) and in Japan by Matsushita, the functions are divided across the business or product line they support, as shown in Figure 2.4.

Grouping by User, Customer, or Geography

Grouping by user, customer, or geography gathers together people who perform different activities and tasks and produce different outputs but who serve the same customers or market segments. The most common dimension is geography. Large multinational companies operating around the world, for example, historically favored a geographic organization, grouping by geographic region and country (as shown in Figure 2.5).

Even domestic companies have often grouped by sales territories. But grouping by customer or user has also been common in some industries. Publishers, for example, are often organized on the basis of what customer group the division serves: textbooks (often subdivided by educational level—primary, secondary, college), business and professional books, mass market, etc.

There is no universally ideal grouping pattern. Each strategic grouping option comes with its own set of strengths and weaknesses. And every organization design must address all three elements of activity/function, business/product, and geography/customer. The critical grouping question is which dimension will be primary, and

FIGURE 2.3 FUNCTIONAL ORGANIZATION STRUCTURE

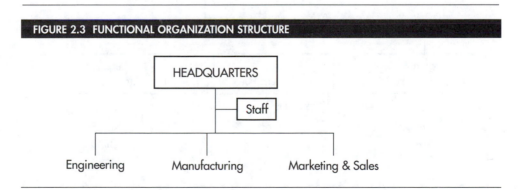

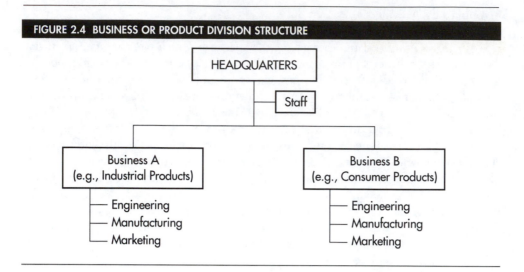

FIGURE 2.4 BUSINESS OR PRODUCT DIVISION STRUCTURE

how the others will be nested at the next levels: function within business within geography, for example.

In broad terms, grouping by activity, as in the functional organization, enables each major grouping in the organization to deepen its specialized knowledge and functional excellence. Activity-based organizations can achieve efficiencies through specialization and scale economies, and they can be extremely innovative in specific technologies or functions. The grouping by activity allows each group to create separate incentive and control systems suited to its needs and to reinforcement of these strengths. However, these advantages come at the cost of integration across activities. Functional organizations are often not very responsive to changes in markets or customers. As their level of specialization increases, individuals tend to develop narrower perspectives, and have difficulty in solving problems that require joint efforts with other groups. And it can be difficult in this kind of organization to assign accountability for the overall performance of the organization as a whole. A functional organization is frequently adopted by new organizations and maintained over time by organizations that have a single major business, or several businesses that share the same technologies and have very similar markets.

Output-based and customer-based organizations, in contrast, facilitate integration across activity clusters, but often at the cost of specialized knowledge and expertise.

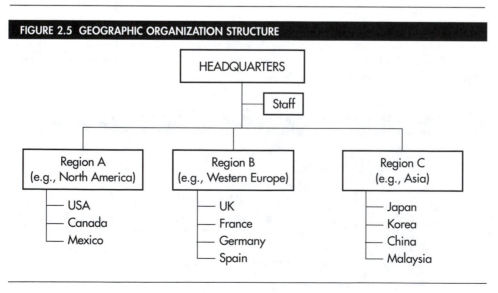

FIGURE 2.5 GEOGRAPHIC ORGANIZATION STRUCTURE

These types of organizations tend to be attentive to the markets and customers they serve, but less responsive to fundamental changes in underlying disciplines or functional areas. Grouping by output facilitates the integration of various functions and disciplines and is therefore more responsive to a rapidly changing market. Grouping by user allows the organization to become even more responsive to specific customer needs. But because functional specialists are separated into different groupings in the organization, they can lose their professional focus and become less attuned to breakthrough innovations in their fields (and this holds true across fields, from research fields to financial and accounting fields, to manufacturing operations). Moreover, units fail to share information and learning opportunities with each other, sacrificing the potential advantages of being parts of the same organization and acting instead like independent entities. And often companies find that they are duplicating resources across units: for example, a multi-divisional company will have several sales departments, each serving a particular segment. During the 1970s and 1980s, IBM and Xerox both employed vast sales forces—numbering in the tens of thousands—each selling their products to much the same array of customers.

Matrix Organizations

Fewer and fewer companies are finding that grouping on any single dimension—activity, output, customer or geography—is adequate. Corporate strategies frequently require attention to multiple priorities simultaneously, product and function, for example, or customers and technical expertise. Many organizations have turned to multifocused grouping structures in an attempt to break out of the constraints imposed by a single mode of strategic grouping, and to build a matrix structure.

The *multiple foci* or *matrix organization* places simultaneous emphasis on several strategic priorities, which are embedded in an organizational form that picks two strategic grouping dimensions and gives them equal weight in the organization structure, so that subunits have two "grouping" identities. In a business/functional matrix, for example, such as the one illustrated in Figure 2.6, the left side of the matrix contains the traditional functional departments: engineering, manufacturing, marketing, etc. The right side is composed of product groups, with a product manager coordinating the functional activities involved in developing and producing the product and getting it to the market. Thus, functional supervisors within the product line report to two bosses: the functional manager and the product line manager. The organization benefits from the information exchange and control provided by the grouping of people by function but also achieves integration across product-related activities. In a business/geography matrix, of the kind presented in Figure 2.7, the two dimensions of the matrix are product line and geography. This kind of structure is adopted by multi-business companies

© 17 ACADEMIC

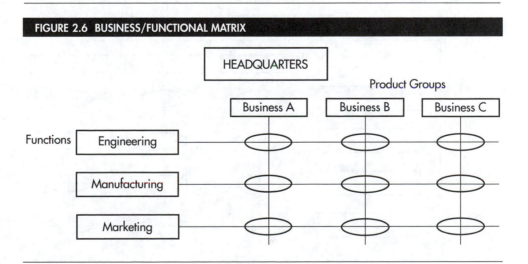

FIGURE 2.6 BUSINESS/FUNCTIONAL MATRIX

operating in many countries. Here, the manager of a business or product line in a region or country would report both to the top manager of the geographic grouping and to the top manager of that business.

Matrix organizations seemed to provide a way of balancing two equally important grouping dimensions. However, from every perspective they are more complicated than single-dimension organizations: they require dual systems, roles, controls, and rewards that reflect both dimensions of the matrix. Along with this complexity can come confusion, higher costs, delays in reaching decisions, and a heightened potential for conflict. Often, organizations that adopted a matrix structure found that despite the formal effort at balancing the two, one dimension tended to be more powerful than the other, negating the potential advantages of the matrix structure. Even when the balance was fairly even, many people found it extremely difficult to have two "bosses" (Steers and Black, 1994).

Grouping by Business Process

In the early 1990s, an additional mode of grouping emerged, one that identified as a key dimension of structure a specific *process*, rather than the conventional definitions of activity, output, or customer. *Grouping by business processes* involves putting together people engaged in a wide variety of tasks, each constituting a step in an overall process, such as order fulfillment, customer management, or product development. In its most radical form, as *Business Process Re-engineering*, it offered a way of fundamentally redesigning organizations by regrouping people into processes. It has proved difficult to redesign an organization on the basis of processes alone, although in some companies grouping by processes has become one dimension of a matrix form. Nadler and Tushman (1997), for example, provide the example of the redesign of the Health Plan and Hospitals operation of Kaiser Permanente's North California region, one of the country's largest not-for-profit Health Maintenance Organizations (HMOs). In the early 1990s, the operation implemented a major redesign in which one side of the matrix was based on grouping by Customer, and the other by seven "Core Processes," including Patient Care, Member Services, Information Technology, etc.

Matching the strategic grouping to the organization's strategy is crucially important, but this alone does not constitute an organizational design. The next crucial element of design is strategic linking.

FIGURE 2.7 PRODUCT/GEOGRAPHY MATRIX

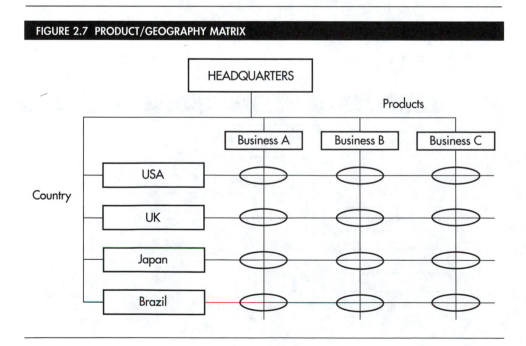

STRATEGIC LINKING

Linking involves designing formal and informal structures and processes to connect and coordinate organizational units and subunits whose tasks are interdependent but that have been separated by strategic grouping decisions. The level of interdependence across groups depends in part on the tasks they perform. We saw earlier that task interdependence can take three forms: pooled, sequential, and reciprocal. These tend to involve different needs for linking and integration. Each type of interdependence benefits from different types and intensity of linking mechanisms: to be effective, reciprocal interdependence demands more intense coordination than does sequential interdependence, which in turn demands greater coordination than pooled interdependence (Nadler and Tushman, 1997, p. 94). The key resource in interdependence is *information*.

Routinized task interdependence is not the only kind of interdependence, however. Professional scientists and engineers working in technical organizations need to maintain contact with their peers inside and outside the company in order to keep abreast of changes in a particular discipline. Different parts of the organization may draw on common resources: training facilities, for example, or corporate services. Temporary and abnormally high degrees of interdependence can also arise during emergencies, crises, or one-time efforts aimed at solving certain problems. In 1982 and 1986, for example, Johnson & Johnson rapidly mobilized people and resources from 160 different businesses, operating in over 50 countries, when several of its Tylenol painkillers were laced with cyanide by outsiders. The firm was widely praised for its rapid, unified response to the crises.

A growing challenge for organizations is the need to develop and maintain linking and coordination patterns that extend beyond the traditional external boundaries of the company, reflecting growing interdependence with customers, suppliers, and partners. The same basic linking patterns, however, are applicable to external as well as internal linking.

There are a range of linking mechanisms on which organizations can draw. As the need for coordination increases, organizations tend to resort to an array of these mechanisms to connect the different parts of their structures. These mechanisms include several components.

Formal Reporting Structures: Hierarchy

The most common form of structural linking is the formal assignment of responsibility for coordinating activities to specific positions in the hierarchy. In this regard, the organization chart is not simply a "map" of strategic grouping; it is also a map of who must keep whom informed and who has responsibility for linking which activities. For example, in a divisional grouping structure, functional managers report to their respective divisional general managers who, in turn, report to their respective divisional general managers who, in turn, report to the company president. Managers in different divisions at the same level coordinate their groups' activities via their common boss, who channels information, controls the type and quantity of information that moves among groups, and adjudicates conflicts. Often formal direct reporting structures include what is commonly called a "dotted line" hierarchical relationship, indicating that the lower-ranking person is formally responsible for supplying all relevant information to the higher-ranking person, but that the latter has no formal authority over the former beyond the information flow.

The formal hierarchy and reporting structures are the simplest and most pervasive of the formal linking mechanisms, but they are also quite limited. In particular, individual managers can quickly become overloaded as the number and complexity of coordination issues requiring their attention rises. As a result, key decisions may be delayed. There is also the risk of message distortion when orders and information pass up and down in a hierarchy. People at the top may be shielded from critical or negative information, while people at the bottom are sometimes excluded from information that could help them in their work. Formal reporting structures are therefore often inadequate when conditions change rapidly.

Liaison Roles

If coordination between two or more groups is important, a liaison is assigned responsibility for coordinating across the groups to specific individuals. Liaisons serve as conduits for information and expertise, and as contacts and advisors on the work involving their groups. Their roles are primarily information-focused; they rarely have the authority to impose decisions on others, especially those in other groups. One example might be the engineering liaison in a manufacturing plant, who is a member of the engineering organization but who is physically located in the plant to link the two units. The liaison role is often not a full-time responsibility, but is combined with other activities.

Permanent Cross-Unit Groups

These groups bring together representatives of different task or work groups, with a formal mandate to pool their expertise and coordinate the efforts of their respective groups vis-à-vis particular products, clients, markets, or problems. Examples include Technology Planning Boards, with representatives from engineering, manufacturing, various business units that share a base in certain core technologies, and even outside technical experts; Total Quality Management Councils, with the mandate to improve quality throughout an organization; and standing committees on various cross-unit issues such as environmental policy or diversity. Lucent Technologies, for example, relies on standing, cross-functional, cross-business committees called Process Improvement Teams (PMTs) to improve the quality of its software development processes on an ongoing basis. Membership on these groups is rarely a full-time assignment.

Temporary Cross-Unit Groups

These often resemble permanent cross-unit groups in their composition—they bring together representatives from various groupings in the organizations. These groups, however, are problem-focused, and exist only until the particular problem is solved or the assigned task is accomplished. Cross-functional project teams are a common example in today's organizations: they bring together a team of people from different functions to accomplish a task (such as developing a new product and getting it to market).

The task force is another increasingly common example of this form of cross-unit group: it represents a temporary patchwork on the formal structure, used to intensify communications links in times of high uncertainty or great pressure. For example, we see companies pull together task forces to analyze problems in customer satisfaction and to make recommendations for improvement, or even to analyze the organization's grouping and linking mechanisms and to make recommendations for changes in organizational design. Membership on these groups is more often a full-time assignment than is the case for the permanent cross-unit groups; members return to their original groups after the completion of the assigned task. However, many task forces are composed of people whose primary tasks lie elsewhere, just like the more permanent cross-unit groups.

Integrator Roles

Some situations may require a more general management perspective and swifter resolution of problems or issues involving several units than is offered by liaison roles or cross-unit groups. In such cases, organizations will sometimes assign to an individual the responsibility for acting as an integrator. Product, brand, geographic, program, and account managers are all examples of formal integrator roles. In each case, the task of the integrator is not to do the work but to coordinate the decision process. In effect, the integrator serves as a "little general manager" with responsibility for a particular decision process. Integrators usually report to senior management with a dotted line relationship to members of their teams. They must therefore rely on expertise, interpersonal skills, and team and conflict resolution skills in order to be effective. Research from the auto industry has found that in some of the most successful Japanese auto makers the "heavyweight product manager" is a key element of the remarkable speed of their new model development process. The heavyweight product manager coordinates the activities of a product development team on the one hand, and works with senior management to create an overarching product concept on the other.

Information Technology Systems

Computer and advanced telecommunications technologies have rapidly increased the linking and coordinating alternatives open to organizations, and they are profoundly changing the way companies organize and manage work. Computer networks, electronic mail, digital scanning and printing, desktop video conferencing, and collaborative software allow organizations to push back the constraints imposed by time and distance, disseminate information more broadly and quickly, and facilitate collaboration and teamwork. Salespeople in the field can communicate instantly with their offices, feeding in the latest information on their customers and their activities and drawing on shared databases on products and sales options. E-mail bulletin boards foster the cultivation of informal networks across departments. R&D organizations like Hewlett-Packard, Apple, and Microsoft and consulting firms like McKinsey maintain on-line databases, which codify knowledge and identify technical and customer "experts" within the firm. Decision-making and decision support systems also increasingly extend outside the company, creating links with customers and suppliers. Wal-Mart relies on an extensive information technology system for automatic order fulfillment by its suppliers. Increasingly, information and communications technology systems provide not only enhanced support for the linking and coordinating mechanisms chosen in an organization, they can be seen as linking mechanisms in their own right.

Planning Processes

At the peak of the era of strategic planning groups in the 1970s and early 1980s, hundreds of people were employed in Corporate Strategic Planning Offices, whose mandate was to generate a plan for each major grouping in the company. The focus was on the plan as roadmap for the organization. In the years since then, Strategic Planning Offices have fallen out of favor, but strategic planning remains important. Its importance for most organizations, however, lies less in the output—the plan—than in the planning process itself, as a linking mechanism for bringing people from different groups to work together to identify major challenges and develop jointly a set of goals for a certain time horizon.

Linking mechanisms connect people and units separated by strategic grouping and coordinate their activities as needed to achieve the organization's strategic goals. The flow of information is a critically important element of their role, and the challenge for managers is "to design the appropriate pattern of linkages that will create the clearest channels of information with the minimum commitment of people, time, money, and other organizational resources" (Nadler and Tushman, 1997). In other words, the challenge is to construct linking mechanisms that are both effective and efficient.

ALIGNMENT

The third strategic design process is *alignment*: that is, assessing the implications of strategic grouping and linking patterns for the rest of the organization's structures and processes, and making changes to ensure that the grouping and linking patterns can be implemented effectively. One of the reasons for the failure of so many organizational redesign efforts, according to this perspective, is misaligned systems and processes; organizational patterns that pull groups and individuals to behavior that undermines the strategic intent or that pulls different groups in opposing directions. Consider, for example, a company in which the manufacturing division is rewarded on the basis of gross margins while the sales division is rewarded for volume. No amount of linking mechanisms can prevent the two groups from working at cross purposes: sales will do everything possible to reduce the unit price in order to sell as much as possible, which hurts the manufacturing margin. Manufacturing may then respond by cutting corners in order to cut costs, thereby diminishing the product's quality or features and reducing its appeal to customers. What the organization design requires in this case is the alignment of incentives for the divisions. The following key features should be evaluated when aligning components of the organization.

Organizational Performance Measurement Systems

How will the organization's leaders know whether the strategic intent underlying the grouping and linking patterns is being realized? The system for measuring organizational performance should provide crucially important information that signals to an organization whether its design is effective. And that system should be aligned with the strategic intent. Some organizations have redesigned their organizations to improve responsiveness to customers, for example, but have continued to rely on older performance measures such as return on assets, sales growth, and market share, without adding measures of customer satisfaction. The growing popularity of the "Balanced Scorecard" as a system for measuring overall organizational performance reflects the need for organizations to align their measurement systems with their strategic intent.

Organizations also need to align the measurement systems used for different strategic groupings, so that they do not pull groups in incompatible directions that undercut linking mechanisms, as in the example of manufacturing and sales above.

Individual Rewards and Incentives

Most of us have experienced how powerful a tool for changing behavior a change in individual rewards and incentives can be. In most organizational change efforts, aligning individual rewards and incentives with the strategic grouping and linking patterns is regarded as one of the most important factors in the success or failure of the organization design. Bonuses, raises, and promotions have traditionally been the primary reward mechanisms in organizations. In flatter organizations, assignment to interesting projects, training opportunities, and greater choice in assignments often replace the more traditional incentives of promotions and large raises.

In their recent book on organization design, David Nadler and Michael Tushman set out the following general principles for reward and incentive systems:

- Incentives should clearly link performance to pay and should directly link performance to specific standards and objectives. If a team's objective is customer satisfaction, that should be the measure of performance, rather than volume or duration of service calls, which may bear little relation to whether the customer's needs were actually met.
- Rewards should relate directly to the nature of performance required at each level of the organization. At Corning, for example, in order to develop a true team perspective among top executives, the bonus plan for each member of the senior team is based largely on the entire company's success in meeting certain specific financial goals, such as stock price. But in other situations—fund managers in an investment firm, for example—it's more appropriate to base rewards on each person's individual performance.
- Rewards should be directly linked to objectives that are within the group's or individual's power to control.
- Incentive plans should match measurement periods for rewards to relevant performance periods; some goals can be assessed after three months, while it might not be practical to evaluate others in less than a year. Some incentive programs recognize that fact by containing both short- and long-term goals.
- Reward systems should be guided by the principle of equity, not equality (Nadler and Tushman, 1997, p. 107).

In the literature on individual rewards and incentives, we can observe two somewhat different sets of assumptions about the alignment of individual rewards. One view, sometimes called "Theory X," views individuals as oriented to material rewards and prone to "free ride" on the efforts of others, such that the behaviors that the organization wants must be very carefully measured and rewarded, while unproductive behavior brings down negative sanctions. The other, called "Theory Y," rests on the belief that most individuals basically want to do a good job, and that the main challenge in designing reward systems is to avoid misalignment that rewards behavior that does not meet the requirements of the organization's strategic intent and the demands of its grouping and linking systems (which economists call "perverse incentives"). A common example is reorganizing work into teams, but continuing to base evaluations and rewards solely on individual accomplishments.

Resource Allocation

Do the units created by the strategic grouping process have the resources they need to achieve their goals? Are the linking mechanisms accompanied by the allocation of adequate resources to be effective? Resources in this context includes people, money, physical assets (equipment, office space, etc.), and, most importantly, information and expertise. Assessing the adequacy of resources to carry out the assigned tasks can be the most demanding and difficult task in implementing an organizational design.

Human Resource Development

By strict logic, human resource development could be considered a subset of resource allocation. However, its importance is so great, and the distinction between *allocating* resources and *developing* or *creating* them so valuable, that it deserves separate consideration. Many organizational redesigns fail because they do not recognize the need to align human resources and skills and expertise with the new design. Often people need training in new ways of doing things; in team processes, for example. A change in design often needs a change in the way careers are designed: for example, moving from a functional to a business unit organization often works best if the organization fosters cross-functional mobility as part of the career structure of high-potential managers.

Informal Systems and Processes

The most elusive and challenging element of alignment involves the informal processes in the organization. No formal blueprint for organizational design can ever capture fully the processes and interactions that make the organization work. These emerge over time, as people adapt to the organization and to the demands of their jobs and their environments. Often an organizational redesign is less effective initially than its designers expect, or it initially seems to work but then runs into unexpected snags and glitches. Often this is because the redesign has wrenched apart the formal and the informal organization—and indeed it often has been deliberately designed to break established patterns and habits.

In the strategic design perspective, the informal systems constitute a somewhat difficult design element that can be structured through various alignment mechanisms, such as the creation of various arenas in which people can form new networks, discuss problems, and form new patterns. Sometimes this can be designed into training programs, or incorporated into linking mechanisms. Sometimes the worst problems of misalignment of the previous structure and the new design can be anticipated, and steps taken to counteract them: for example, by rotating personnel into different positions, or providing extra linking mechanisms early in the adjustment process. But overall, although this perspective recognizes that the realignment of formal and informal processes takes time, it assumes that such realignment is fundamentally a design challenge that can be solved.

© 23 ACADEMIC

THE STRATEGIC ORGANIZATIONAL DESIGN PROCESS

Design changes, once fairly rare events in an organization, are becoming a normal, on-going process in many enterprises. In fact, the ability to anticipate change and quickly implement new architectures may be among the most valuable organizational capabilities in today's competitive environment.

To some extent, managers are making design decisions all the time. Every time a specific job is designed, a procedure created, a process altered, or a task moved, the organization design is being changed. And yet we know that the very process of redesign, and especially the major redesigns of the organization that seem to be increasingly common in many companies, involve inherent and significant costs.

Disruption of the Normal Flow of Business

Redesign efforts obviously occupy the time and attention of managers and tie up organizational resources. People throughout the organization tend to focus on the implications of the redesign for themselves and their part of the organization, sometimes at the cost of their immediate tasks.

Risk to Long-Term Relationships with Key Customers and Suppliers

Established communications patterns are often severed, either temporarily or permanently, during redesign efforts, leaving customers and suppliers with no idea of whom to talk to in the company. Unfortunately, competitors will be more than ready to capitalize on the opportunity to satisfy those unmet needs.

Stress and Anxiety

Endless waves of restructuring can lead to enormous anxiety, a loss of continuity, the departure of key people, and may seriously damage the core competencies that made the company successful. People worry about losing their jobs, friends, status, or day-to-day routines. Anxiety often leads to a number of predictable reactions, ranging from panic or withdrawal to outright resistance.

A careful process of organization design is one way to develop the organizational capability for proactive change or for rapid reactive response, and can minimize the costs of change, although it can never expect to eliminate them entirely. Nadler and Tushman provide a model of ten steps in the organizational design process shown in Figure 2.8.

They also provide some general "ground rules" that underpin these steps:

> First, the best designs are those that emerge from consideration of the widest possible range of alternatives. Second, the best design processes involve people who fully understand the organization and its work; in large corporations, third- and fourth-level managers are positioned better than either the senior team or outside consultants to understand the way the organization works, both formally and informally. Third, the best designs are developed with implementation in mind. And design—like any organizational change—will have significantly better chance of success if the people responsible for making it work feel they were a part of shaping the change (Nadler and Tushman, 1997, p. 179).

No matter how successful a company may be at any point in time, there are powerful forces at work, both within an organization and in its external environment, that make redesign inevitable. Sometimes redesign is a response to the growth, evolution, and maturation of an organization and of its products. As organizations grow, for example, they become more complex, and simply multiplying existing units does not suffice to cope with the broader range of customers, employees, and products. Sometimes management succession provides the stimulus for change efforts, as a new CEO or division head seeks to put a personal stamp on the organization or to take advantage of the change in leadership to address some longstanding organizational problems. At other times, redesign is necessary because of internal problems, such as lack of coordination, excessive conflict, unclear roles, poor work flows, or a proliferation of ad hoc organizational units such as task forces, committees, and special project teams.

FIGURE 2.8 STRATEGIC ORGANIZATIONAL DESIGN PROCESS: SPECIFIC DECISION-MAKING STEPS

Steps	Objectives
1. Generate design criteria.	Create a series of statements that can serve as criteria for assessing different designs.
2. Generate grouping alternatives.	Create a large number of different grouping alternatives designed to meet the design criteria.
3. Evaluate grouping alternatives.	Assess grouping alternatives in terms of design criteria; eliminate, modify, and refine alternatives.
4. Identify coordination requirements.	For each grouping alternative, identify the information-processing needs, working from the design criteria.
5. Generate structural linking mechanisms.	For each grouping alternative, create a set of structural linking mechanisms that will be responsive to the coordination requirements and will enhance the extent to which the design meets the design criteria.
6. Evaluate structural linking mechanisms.	Assess each alternative in terms of the design criteria; eliminate, modify, and refine alternatives. Combine alternatives if necessary.
7. Conduct impact analysis.	Assess each surviving design alternative in terms of predicted impact on or fit with other organizational components.
8. Refine and eliminate designs.	Based on the impact analysis, eliminate designs, resulting in a first choice design recommendation, and refine designs as appropriate.
9. Identify issues for operational design and alignment.	Based on impact analysis, identify where operational design needs to be done and issues to be addressed by the design.
10. Identify issues for implementation.	Based on impact analysis, identify key issues to be considered in planning implementation of the design.

Source: Nadler and Tushman, *Competing by Design*, p. 189.

However, the most frequent stimulus to design changes is that the current design no longer fits the pressures from the external business environment. The organization is, in this perspective, seen as a "throughout-put" system that takes inputs from the environment, adds value to them through various internal processes, and then distributes them to users outside the organization; accordingly, the environment is primarily seen as a source of inputs and a market for outputs (the "input-set" and the "output-set"). Shifts in the firm's environment can make the established design inadequate: new competitors, technical innovations that affect either the nature of potential inputs or ways of distributing outputs (an example of the latter would be the rise of Internet marketing and sales), changes in markets and the customer base, changes in the supplier base or in the labor markets that supply personnel, regulatory changes that affect what inputs an organization can use ("green" restrictions on certain chemicals, for example, or labor legislation affecting the use of part-time labor). As the environment changes, the organization must adjust its design to "fit" the environmental pressures.

WHAT DO YOU LOOK FOR IN ANALYZING AN ORGANIZATION?

A key assumption of the strategic design approach is that organizations are fundamentally *rational*, in the sense that in a well-designed organization, each person and each part of the organization can and should be oriented to accomplishing its goals to the best available knowledge of its participants. In order to analyze an organization from this perspective, you need to know its *strategy* (what is it trying to accomplish?) and its *design*. Design questions include:

- How are activities grouped?
- How are the activity clusters linked and coordinated?

- Are its basic systems—control systems, resource allocation and decision-making systems, human resource management systems, evaluation and reward systems—aligned, so that they reinforce each other rather than pulling people in different directions?
- Does the organization design fit the demands of its environment? is it getting the kinds of inputs it needs? meeting the requirements of customers? effectively meeting the competition it faces?

Some of the most frequent sources of organizational ineffectiveness are summarized in Figure 2.9.

SUMMARY

A key premise of the strategic design approach is that in a well-designed organization, in which the strategic goals fit the demands of the environment, each person and each part of the organization can and should be oriented to accomplishing its goals. The major impediments to realizing this situation are that people do not adequately understand the goals or tasks (inadequate information), that they do not have the resources necessary to accomplish their assigned tasks, or that an inadequate organizational design is directing their efforts to subunit goals that get in the way of the overall goals. Strategic grouping, linking, and alignment are the key processes for ensuring that the organization does indeed provide the base for realizing its strategic goals.

REFERENCES

Chandler, Alfred D. Jr. 1962. *Strategy and Structure*. Cambridge, MA: MIT Press.

Galbraith, Jay R. and Edward E. Lawler. 1993. *Organizing for the Future: The New Logic for Managing Complex Organizations*. San Francisco: Jossey-Bass.

Nadler, David A. and Michael L. Tushman. 1997. *Competing by Design: The Power of Organizational Architecture*. New York: Oxford University Press.

Steers, R. M. and J. S. Black. *Organizational Behavior*. New York: Harper Collins Publishing.

Thompson, James D. 1967. *Organizations in Action*. New York: McGraw-Hill.

FIGURE 2.9   REASONS BEHIND ORGANIZATIONAL INEFFECTIVENESS

- **Lack of Clarity of Goals.** Strategic goals are not clear, or are not clearly communicated, or are not clearly linked to particular aspects of the organization's design.
- **Ineffective Grouping.** The strengths of the activity clusters do not generate the organizational capabilities the firm needs to perform effectively in its environment (for example, it uses a functional organization that provides deep functional competence but is slow to respond to shifting customer needs).
- **Ineffective Linking.** The activity clusters are not effectively integrated and coordinated with each other.
- **Lack of Internal Alignment.** The design of the organization is internally inconsistent, so that one element of the design gets in the way of another (for example, an organization introduces customer-focused teams in order to improve customer satisfaction, but continues to use an evaluation and reward system focused on measuring individual accomplishments and short-term financial performance).
- **Lack of External Fit.** The design does not fit the needs of its environment (for example, a company continues to use its non-technically-expert marketing people to sell its products, even after most of its customers have switched the responsibility for buying equipment from an umbrella purchasing department directly to its operating units, where purchasing decisions are made by engineers and production people).

ABB—THROUGH THE STRATEGIC DESIGN LENS[1]

"Asea Brown Boveri is seen by more and more global business leaders as the model of the way that organizations will have to operate to thrive in the 21st century—that is, streamlined in structure, rapid in transferring information, having employees who are highly empowered, committed to continuous learning, running world-class HRD [human resource development] programs, and teamworking and networking globally. ABB appears not only first in the alphabetical listing of companies, but also as one of the first among global learning organizations" Marquand, Michael, and Angus Reynolds. *The Global Learning Organization*. New York: Irwin Professional Publishing, 1996, p. 149.

"While ABB may not be a *model* that every other company can adopt, it is an example of what most companies can achieve." Ghoshal and Bartlett. *The Individualized Corporation*. London: Heinemann, 1997, p. 33.

"Percy Barnevik, president and CEO of ABB (Asea Brown Boveri), is a corporate pioneer. He is moving more aggressively than any CEO in Europe, perhaps in the world, to build the new model of competitive enterprise—an organization that combines global scale and world-class technology with deep roots in local markets." HBR introduction to an interview with Barnevik, 1991, p. 91.

Asea Brown Boveri (ABB) is an unlikely prototype for the 21st century organization. ABB was created by the merger in 1987–88 of two companies whose roots lie in the nineteenth century: Asea, founded in Sweden in 1890, and Brown Boveri, established in Switzerland in 1891. The two companies were among the surge of industrial enterprises established towards the end of the nineteenth century to provide equipment for the rapidly expanding electrical power industry, which involved generating, transmitting, and distributing power, and using it in industrial motors. The core business of ABB is still the electrical equipment industry, including power plants, transformers, industrial motors, instead of the industries that are supposed to be leading the way into the next century, like software, financial services, or Internet marketing. And yet ABB has become one of the most widely admired companies in the world today, not because of its products, or its innovative technology, but because of its organization. ABB prides itself on being an organization that its former CEO, Percy Barnevik, sees as being simultaneously global and local, big and small, centralized and decentralized.

Let us look more closely at the strategic context in which ABB's organization developed, before turning to the organization design itself.

STRATEGIC CONTEXT

ABB's largest business is producing and servicing the equipment for generating, transmitting, and distributing electrical power. The customers in this business are electric utilities around the world, many of which are state-owned or strongly state-regulated. Because national or local governments either directly own or indirectly control the utilities, they have a strong tendency to favor suppliers with a local manufacturing presence,

---

1 D. Eleanor Westney, "ABB—Through the Strategic Design Lens." Copyright © 1998 D. Eleanor Westney. Reprinted by permission of the author.

both because local companies are contributing to the local economy and because they can be relied upon for servicing and replacement parts for the complex power systems, any breakdown of which can have enormous costs for local business and for the reputation of the utility. And yet in the last two decades, utilities and their state regulators have also become increasingly worried about controlling their costs, and have pressed suppliers to lower their prices and increase the lifetime of equipment, cutting profit margins to the bone for suppliers that are unable to achieve greater efficiency in production.

ABB is also a world leader in rail transportation systems, such as locomotives, light rail vehicles, and signaling. Again, this is a business in which rail networks in much of the world are state-owned or state-regulated and which are subject to the same somewhat contradictory pressures to manufacture locally and to be locally responsive to customers, while achieving efficiency through scale economies and cost savings.

A third set of products in ABB is directed to a very different type of customer. Its building systems (a set of businesses that evolved naturally from its core expertise in electrical systems, and includes air handling equipment, refrigeration, and building service) and industrial production systems, from motors to robotics, are sold to industrial companies, whose concerns are much more focused on price than on whether their suppliers are providing jobs locally. However, even here, industrial customers want to be sure that their supplier has the capacity to provide speedy and effective local servicing for the systems it sells.

In other words, ABB's businesses require the company to be locally responsive and to maintain a credible local presence in each of its major markets, and simultaneously to be efficient and cost-competitive. Moreover, operating in 140 countries in a wide variety of product lines, many of which are closely related in the eyes of the customer, the company needs to have a high degree of intra-product and cross-product coordination if the company is to capture fully the benefits of its product diversity. However, it also needs to be able to respond quickly to customers and local problems, and to encourage its managers to take responsibility for their units. One of ABB's vice-presidents has asserted that "we are a collection of local businesses with intense global coordination" (Taylor, 1991, p. 96).

THE CREATION OF ABB AND ITS STRATEGIC DIRECTION

Asea in 1980 was "a slow-growing but respected Swedish electrical engineering company" (*Business Week,* July 30, 1990, p. 64). In that year, a new CEO, Percy Barnevik, was brought in by the company's leading shareholders, the Wallenbergs, to address the company's problems of lagging growth and low profitability. Barnevik directed a major redesign of the company that included dividing it into a number of separate profit centers and radically decentralizing decision-making. By 1986, Asea's sales had grown by 136 percent, far outstripping the growth rates of its competitors, and its profitability had increased from 1.3 percent return on sales in 1980 to 4.8 percent in 1986. It was less successful than Barnevik had hoped, however, in expanding its share of the major European markets outside the Nordic countries, and both its production and its research and development (R&D) activities were still heavily concentrated in its home country of Sweden, which had one of the highest labor cost structures in the world.

One of its major European competitors was the Swiss company Brown Boveri. BBC had almost twice the sales volume of Asea, and was renowned for its technology and its strength in R&D, which was distributed across several sites in Europe. However, it was on a very different trajectory. Its sales were falling, its return on sales was 0.4 percent (and had not risen above 1 percent throughout the 1980s), and it faced serious management problems. One of the most serious was that its strong national subsidiaries in Europe were still each producing to national market scale. The growing integration of the European market and competition from lower-cost producers, however, meant that this was increasingly inefficient, and that competitors with more concentrated production facilities could undercut BBC's prices. Yet its strong country subsidiaries resisted Headquarters' efforts to rationalize production and increase cross-border coordination: each could see the arguments for rationalization, but insisted that any reductions in capacity should come in some other location.

On August 17, 1987, after only six weeks of intense negotiations among the top managers and major shareholders, the boards of the two companies announced that they had decided to merge, creating ABB (Asea Brown Boveri), the largest European company in its industry. Percy Barnevik became the CEO of the new company, and Thomas Gasser, the former CEO of Brown Boveri, became his deputy. The announcement was a surprise to most analysts and people in the industry, and even to most employees of the two companies. The two companies announced that they would start functioning as a single entity in January, 1988, and that the headquarters of the newly formed ABB would be in Switzerland.

The business press at the time hailed the creation of a European champion in the industry, and saw it as symbolizing the cross-border mergers that were taking place in anticipation of the coming of the single European market in 1992. But Barnevik and his top managers had ambitions beyond Europe: they wanted to create not a European but a global company. After all, the company created by the merger had the largest sales in the world in the electrical engineering industry, nearly 50 percent larger than any of its major competitors (Siemens, Hitachi, and General Electric).[2] Many observers in August of 1987, however, pointed out that integrating the two formerly competing companies, with a total of 180,000 employees, selling in 140 countries but with all but 30,000 of its employees in Europe, might well prove to be a challenge that would keep the company occupied for several years.

In January, 1988, at a three-day meeting of nearly 300 managers selected from the ranks of the two companies, Barnevik presented his analysis of the business environment facing ABB. He also announced the strategic direction for the new company (a focus on the electrical power business, rapid changes to make the company simultaneously more efficient and more responsive to customers), introduced the specifics of the new organization design, and laid out the company's financial and growth targets. The strategic commitment to the power industry and to a global strategy was demonstrated in a rapid series of alliances and acquisitions. In October 1988 ABB acquired AEG's steam turbines business, and in February 1989 bought out Westinghouse's power distribution and transmission business (price tag $700 million), acquired the U.S. boiler and nuclear plant builder Combustion Engineering ($1.6 billion), and purchased a majority stake in the Polish manufacturer of turbines, Zamtech. These moves rapidly extended ABB's international reach into North America and Eastern Europe. The speed with which these acquisitions were integrated into ABB was widely admired, and was attributed to the flexibility of its new organization design (see, for example, *Business Week*. July 23, 1990, pp. 64–66).

BUILDING THE NEW ORGANIZATION DESIGN

One of the first steps taken after the merger was announced in August 1987 was the creation of a task force of five top managers from each of the two companies to generate an organizational architecture for ABB. The time frame was short: ABB had announced that it would begin operating as a merged company on January 1, 1988. Within two months, the task force had agreed on the principal features of the new organization. The structure was to be an international matrix of business and geography. This design had

29

CASE

---

2 GE, Siemens, and Hitachi had larger total company sales than ABB because they were more diversified. However, within the electrical engineering industry, the new ABB dominated.

been widely touted in the 1970s as the organization of the future, but companies as diverse as IBM and Citibank tried to make it work and abandoned it as too complicated. To make it work for ABB, the basic organizing principle was to create highly focused local companies reporting both to a worldwide business manager, who would be responsible for achieving efficiency in that product line and growing the business on a global scale, and to a country manager responsible for coordinating the various businesses within a particular country (this structure is described in greater detail later in this section).

While the task force was engaged in developing the details of the new structure, the task of identifying the upper-level managers for the new company engaged much of the time and attention of Barnevik and Gasser. Barnevik personally interviewed about 100 managers from BBC, while Gasser did the same for a similar group of Asea managers. Personnel directors from the two companies engaged in a similar exercise for several hundred more managers, with the Asea director interviewing BBC people and the BBC director talking with Asea managers. An article written in 1988 about the merger contains the following description of this process:

> In drawing up the shortlists, emphasis was placed on identifying flexible individuals who could cooperate in multi-cultural environments and for whom innovation, risk-taking and the ability to motivate others were almost second nature. "We sought people capable of becoming superstars," explains Barnevik, "tough-skinned individuals, who were fast on their feet, had good technical and commercial backgrounds and had demonstrated the ability to lead others." Singled out were managers willing to abandon old alliances and create new ones. In weeding out candidates, they looked for people with an added management dimension. "For the merger to work, it is essential that we have managers who are open and generous and capable of thinking in group terms," he says. (*International Management.* June 1988, p. 27).

Nearly 300 of the managers identified by this process were summoned to the meeting in January 1988, where Percy Barnevik outlined the key aspects of the new matrix organization. He stressed the importance of action. One of the many slides he presented contained the following principles:

1. To take action (and stick one's neck out) and do the right things is obviously the best.
2. To take action and do the wrong things is second best (within reason and a limited number of times).
3. Not to take action (and lose opportunities) is the only unacceptable behavior. (Uyterhoeven, 1992, p. 16).

And in keeping with the strategic intent of making ABB a faster-moving company that was simultaneously more responsive to its customers and more efficient, one of the goals of the new design was to push accountability, decision-making, and the responsibility for action far down the organizational hierarchy.

One of the first steps taken by the new top management was the radical reduction of the company headquarters. Barnevik announced this in terms of what he called the "30–30–30" principle: 30% of the HQ staff would have to find jobs in the business divisions, 30% would be spun off into service centers that would charge the businesses for their services, and 30% would leave the company. The remaining 10% would continue to work at the corporate headquarters. Within a few months, the headcount at corporate HQ in Zurich went from over 1,300 professional staff to just over 100.

Another crucial step in the process was the design of a company-wide information system, called ABACUS (for Asea Brown Boveri Accounting and Communication System), which was up and running by August 1988. ABACUS collected monthly performance data from each unit, put it into a standard currency (US dollars), and transmitted the information to its main data processing center in Sweden, which compiled the data and passed it to the top managers at the Swiss headquarters and to the designated managers at each level of the company. The database had two major capabilities: it provided standard monthly reports for management, and it also functioned as an inquiry database that allowed top managers to "dig down" into the performance numbers.

The Basic Building Blocks

The basic unit on which performance data are collected for ABACUS is the *profit center,* the smallest organizational unit in the new organization (see Figure 2.10). Most of the profit centers are focused on a single production site or service organization. Each month they report their performance data (orders received, revenues, gross margins, net earnings, etc.) to the next highest level of the organization, the *local operating company,* or the *business unit* (as it often came to be called by the early 1990s), which in turn put the data into the ABACUS system. The profit center manager is accountable for the performance of the center to the manager of the local operating company. Initially the design called for the establishment of 3,000–4,000 profit centers; by 1991, after the acquisitions, the number had risen to 4,500.

The *local operating company* or *Business Unit* (BU) has been seen from the beginning as the key unit of ABB's organization. It is composed of two or more profit centers (in rare cases the local operating company might itself be the only profit center), and is focused on single business and market. In most cases, the market is geographically defined. For example, the Norwegian ABB Robotics company produces robots in its factory in Norway and services local customers; the U.S. relays company produces relays and sells them to utilities throughout the United States. In a few cases, the local company itself has responsibility for a highly focused business on a global basis. The Gas Insulated Switchgear (GIS) business unit, for example, produces complete installations that are sold (often on a turnkey basis) to a small number of customers, and has responsibility for that business worldwide. In 1991, it had four profit centers in its organization; by 1994, it had six. When ABB makes an acquisition, such as the purchase of Westinghouse's power transmission and distribution business, the acquired operations are broken up into a number of local operating companies, or into profit centers allocated to an existing local operating company.

In 1988, ABB had 800 local operating companies; by 1991, this had expanded to 1,100. The average size of the local operating companies is about 200 employees, with about $50 million in annual revenues. ABB factories in many of its businesses tend to

31

CASE

FIGURE 2.10 ABB's ORGANIZATION DESIGN

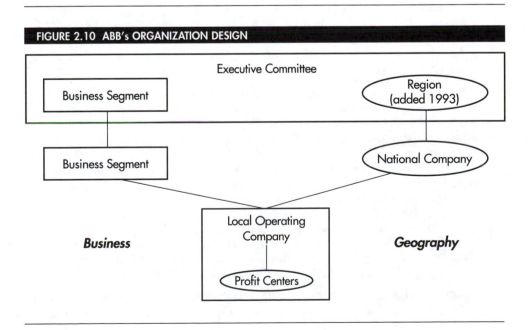

---

be smaller than those of its leading competitors. ABB's strategy is to concentrate on radically reducing costs in each site, reducing throughput times, maximizing design and production flexibility, and focusing on local customer needs. The transformers business, for example, has 25 local operating companies, each centered on a factory, with its own president and management team (production manager, marketing manager, design and engineering manager), and each providing 70 percent of their output to their local market (Taylor, 1991, p. 96).

The local operating company president has CEO responsibilities for his or her operations. Ghoshal and Bartlett have described the role of one such manager whose original employer (Westinghouse) sold the division for which he worked to ABB:

> From being an effective operational implementer working hard to be an effective part of a massive corporate machine, he was now cast in the role of an entrepreneurial initiator with full responsibility and accountability for the development of his own frontline company. As president of ABB Relays Inc., a separate legal entity created by ABB, he assumed full responsibility not only for his profit-and-loss statement but also for his balance sheet. This meant he had to focus on managing cash flows, paying dividends to the parent company, and making wise investments with his retained earnings, typically about 30 to 40 percent of total earnings. It also meant that he could borrow locally. . . . In short, he began seeing his job not simply as implementing the latest corporate program but as building a viable, enduring business (Ghoshal and Bartlett, 1998, p. 27).

The commitment of the local operating company manager to being competitive and meeting performance targets increases his or her commitment to rationalization and efficiency. However, in at least one important respect, the heads of the local operating companies differ from independent CEOs; they report to two bosses (see Figure 2.10). One is the Business Area manager; the other is the country manager for the country in which the operating company was located.

The Business Side of the Matrix: The Business Area

The Business Area (BA) manager is responsible for the worldwide strategy and performance of a business. In 1988, ABB set up 40 Business Areas; by the early 1990s, that had expanded to 65, which in 1993 were consolidated into 50. BA management tasks include coordinating technology development, deciding on transfer prices among local operating companies in the BA, transferring expertise within the BA (disseminating internal "best practice"), capturing economies of scale in purchasing, and, perhaps most important, allocation of markets and production to local operating companies. Depending on its efficiency, each local operating company can aspire to serve some export markets in certain product lines; the decision on what export markets it should serve is made at the level of the BA. Percy Barnevik has described the role of the BA manager as follows:

> The BA leader is a business strategist and global optimizer. He decides which factories are going to make what products, what export markets each factory will serve, and how factories should pool their expertise and research funds for the benefit of the business worldwide. He also tracks talent—the 60 or 70 real standouts around the world. Say we need a plant manager for a new company in Thailand. The BA head should know of three or four people—maybe there's one at our plant in Muncie, Indiana, maybe there's one in Finland—who could help in Thailand. . . . BA managers are crucial people. They need a strong hand in crafting strategy, evaluating performance around the world, and working with teams made up of different nationalities. . . . You see, BA managers don't own the people working in any business area around the world. They can't order the president of a local company to fire someone or to use a particular strategy in union negotiations. On the other hand, BA managers can't let their role degrade into a statistical coordination or scorekeeper. . . . So it's a difficult balancing act (Taylor, 1991, pp. 95–96).

Another top ABB manager, Goren Lindahl (Percy Barnevik's eventual successor as CEO), described the system in similar terms: "Although the BAs play a vital role in setting strategy, only the local companies can implement the plans and achieve the objectives" (Bartlett, 1993, p. 3).

The BA head is chosen from among the local operating company managers within the BA, and continues to manage that local company while simultaneously functioning as BA manager. The fact that the BA manager is also the head of a local operating company increases his or her motivation to push responsibility and decision-making down to the local operating companies, on the basis of time pressure, if not personal management philosophy. It also means that the "base" for the Business Area shifts when one manager succeeds another: Switzerland when the BA head is the manager of the Swiss local operating company, Germany when he or she is German, the United States when he or she is American. BA managers have a small full-time team of experienced managers from around the world to support them (4–5 people, including a controller and managers who provide worldwide expertise and coordination on key functions such as purchasing or technology development). In addition, they are supported by a BA Board, which meets 4–6 times a year and assists the BA manager in setting strategy, reviewing performance, and identifying and addressing key problem areas. The BA Manager selects the members of the Board, and membership varies considerably depending on the nature of the business. In most BAs, the members are a small number (5–8) of the heads of the largest and most efficient local operating companies from the key countries for that business. The BA Board is therefore an international group, and usually meets in a different location for each of its meetings over the course of a year.

In addition to the BA Board, the BA has a number of functional councils that bring together key managers in a function (such as R&D, purchasing, quality) for quarterly meetings to assess and exchange internal best practice and to identify and propose solutions for key problems in their area of expertise. For particular problems, the BA Board also forms task forces from among the high-potential younger managers in the BA. For example, a task force might be formed to develop a common product platform for a family of new products, or drawing on engineering talent from across the BA. Or a task force might be put together to assess the current strategy of the BA and propose a long-term plan for technology development or for geographic expansion. The Relays BA, for example, in the early 1990s picked nine high-potential managers from five major local operating companies to form the Relays Vision 2000 task force, which was given six months to develop a proposal for a long-term global strategy for the BA (Ghoshal and Bartlett, 1998, pp. 29, 203).

The BA manager receives monthly reports through ABACUS on the performance of each of the profit centers and operating companies in the BA. These performance data include orders received, revenues, gross margins, net earnings, costs, and headcount, and updated forecasts for the year. The BA manager decides how widely to disseminate this kind of information across the local operating companies. In the Power Transformers BA, for example, the BA manager decided to distributed detailed information on each of the 25 factories in the BA on critical parameters such as throughput times and inventories and receivables as a proportion of revenues, so as to generate internal benchmarks for the heads of the local units (Taylor, 1991, p. 97).

One of the most important roles of the BA is the dissemination of best practice. Sharing information about performance is one way to encourage this. Another is to expose managers to different ways of operating, through transfers and through travel. Sune Karlsson, BA manager for power transformers, has described the process as follows: "Show local managers what's been achieved elsewhere, let them drive the change process, make available ABB expertise from around the world, and demand quick results" (Taylor, 1991, p. 96). The combination of strict performance requirements with the resources for performance improvement is a powerful driver of change in ABB.

33

CASE

The Business Segment

The BA managers in turn report to Business Segment Managers. Business Segments are groupings of related BAs. ABB began in 1988 with four segments (Power Plants, Power Transmission, Power Distribution, and Industrial Equipment), and a cluster of BAs that did not fit under any of the segments and that were grouped into a fifth segment called "Various" or diversified businesses. By 1991, ABB had grouped some of these various businesses into an additional segment, Transportation. In 1993, however, it returned to four industrial segments, which differed from the original four: Power Plants, Power Transmission and Distribution, Industrial and Building Systems, and Transportation. The "Various" segment disappeared, with its BAs divided across the other four segments. A fifth segment, Finance, clustered within it both the internal finance function and the various financing services that ABB offered to its customers, including leasing and trade finance.

Each segment was headed by a member of the Executive Committee, the highest-level organizational unit in the company, which is described in greater detail below.

The Country Level

The local operating company managers also report to the country manager of the nation in which it is located. The country manager has profit-and-loss responsibilities for all ABB activities within that country. The country manager's task is to realize the potential synergies across the various ABB local operating companies, to present a "local face" for major projects within that country, to provide the legal and political infrastructure for operations, to coordinate certain personnel development programs, and to make sure that the local political and social environment is understood and considered appropriately in business decisions. Percy Barnevik has described the role of the national companies using Norway as an example:

> It is possible . . . to optimize every business area without regard for ABB's broad collection of activities in specific countries. But think about what we lose. We have a power transformer company in Norway that employs 400 people. It builds transformers for the Norwegian market and exports to markets allocated by the BA. But ABB Norway has more than 10,000 other employees in the country. There are tremendous benefits if power transformers coordinates its Norwegian operations with our operations in power generation, switchgear, and process automation: recruiting top people from the universities, building an efficient distribution and service network across product lines, circulating good people among the local companies, maintaining productive relations with top government officials. So we have a Norwegian company, ABB Norway, with a Norwegian CEO and a headquarters in Oslo, to make these connections. The CEO has the same responsibilities as the CEO of a local Norwegian company for labor negotiations, bank relationships, and high-level contacts with customers. This is no label or gimmick. We must be a Norwegian company to work effectively in many businesses. Norway's oil operations in the North Sea are a matter of great national importance and intense national pride. The government wouldn't—and shouldn't—trust some faraway foreign company as a key supplier to those operations (Taylor, 1991, p. 95).

The country manager receive monthly reports through ABACUS on the performance of each of the local operating companies in the country, and can use these data to identify common problems they face (such as exchange-rate-induced volatility) and individual difficulties (such as a failure by one of the local companies to meet its cost or quality targets).

Managing the Matrix: The Frontline

Reporting to two managers, each with a different mandate (global efficiency for the BA, local responsiveness for the country managers), is not an easy task. The heads of the local operating companies are supported in this balancing act by a Steering Committee, with representatives from the national company (the national company president in the case of the larger units), the BA, and other closely-related local operating companies in the same country. The president of ABB Relays Inc. in the United States, Don Jans, for example, had a seven-person steering committee, which met 3-4 times a year. As Ghoshal and Bartlett (1998, pp. 27-28) have described it,

> With membership drawn from ABB's global relays division (or worldwide business area in company terminology), the U.S. power transmission and distribution headquarters [the national company], and colleagues running related frontline companies within ABB, the steering committee became Jans's sounding board for new ideas (how to reorganize his unit, for example) and decision forum on key issues (such as approval for strategic plans and operating budgets).

They also note that Jans himself, as president of one of the largest local operating companies in his BA, was a member of the Relays BA Board, and sat on the steering committees of the Canadian and Puerto Rican relays companies.

Performance evaluations of the president of the local operating companies are conducted by both the BA head and the country manager. Each share the same basic performance metrics, but each has somewhat different expectations. Often the expectations and performance parameters collide, and then the local company president has to decide how to balance the potentially conflicting criteria. Ghoshal and Bartlett give the example of the President of ABB Relays in the United States, Don Jans, who believed that future growth in the business in the United States demanded the development of electronic relays. Jans wanted to budget development funds for the product, but although the BA manager favored it, the country manager resisted the proposal, because of shortfalls in U.S. performance overall, for which he was responsible. The local operating company's Steering Committee provided the arena in which the two positions were fought over, and eventually the conflict was resolved through a suggestion by the U.S. country head that, if the BA manager supported the program, he should find funding for the development out of his own budget. He did.

Managing the Matrix: The Top Management

At the bottom of the company, the two dimensions of the matrix meet at the level of the local operating company manager. At the top, they meet at the level of the Executive Committee, which is chaired by the CEO.

Initially, ABB's Executive Committee (or Executive Board—the two terms are used interchangeably in much of the writing about ABB and even within the company itself) consisted of Barnevik as CEO, Gasser as Deputy CEO, and ten Executive Vice-Presidents, five from each of the two merged companies. Barnevik chaired the Committee, and each of the ten Executive VPs had responsibility for one or more of the segments and countries. The extent of their individual responsibilities varied by the scope of the tasks. Goren Lindahl, for example, was assigned the responsibility for the Power Transmission segment, ABB's largest single segment. Sune Carlsson, who had the responsibility for the smaller Power Transmission segment, also had five of the diversified BAs reporting to him and three of the national companies (United Kingdom, Norway, and Ireland). Berthold Romacker had three of the diversified BAs and the corporate R&D function reporting to him. In other words, each BA manager and each country manager reported directly to a member of the Executive Committee. Even Percy Barnevik had one of the diversified BAs reporting to him, in addition to his duties as CEO and Chair of the Committee. The Executive Committee was supported by the very lean headquarters staff.

With ABB's acquisitions, the individual responsibilities assigned to Executive Committee members changed over time, especially in terms of geographies, and the membership grew to 13 by 1991. A major reorganization at the top in 1993 reduced the size of the Committee to eight (including Barnevik), and simplified the individual responsibilities. The major change was on geography: instead of having different members responsible for a portfolio of different national companies, geographic responsibilities

35

CASE

were clustered into three regions: Europe, the Americas, and Asia Pacific. Each member was assigned either one of the four industrial segments or one of three geographical regions. The position of Deputy CEO was abolished, and the CEO surrendered any direct BA reports. The goal was both to simplify the reporting responsibilities of the Committee members and to reduce the size of the Committee. The move to make the geography side of the matrix report to Committee members with regional rather than individual country responsibilities also reflected ABB's global strategy. Between 1990 and 1996, ABB cut 59,000 jobs in western Europe and North America and created 56,000 new jobs elsewhere, primarily in east Asia and eastern Europe (FT, Oct. 22, 1997). This required a strong balancing of regional priorities at the Executive Committee level.

Each Executive Committee member was involved in the annual planning process of each of the BAs and geographic units reporting to him. But as important were their collective responsibilities in charting the overall strategic direction for the company. Barnevik described the Executive Committee in 1991 as follows:

> Naturally these 13 executives are busy, stretched people. But think about what happens when we meet every three weeks, which we do for a full day. Sitting in one room are the senior managers collectively responsible for ABB's global strategy and performance. These same managers individually monitor business segments, countries, and staff functions. So when we make a decision—snap, it's covered. The members of the executive committee communicate to their direct reports, the BA managers and the country managers, and the implementation process is underway (Taylor, 1991, p. 99).

In the same interview, Barnevik described what he sees as a central role of the top management team: communication. He gave a very concrete example of a management development program he was about to attend:

> This afternoon, I'll fly up to Lake Constance in Germany, where we have collected 35 managers from around the world. They've been there for three days, and I'll spend three hours with them to end their session. Half the executive committee has already been up there. These are active, working sessions. We talk about how we work in the matrix, how we develop people, about our programs around the world to cut cycle times and raise quality. I'll give a talk at Lake Constance, but then we'll focus on problems. The manager running high-voltage switchgear in some country may be unhappy about the BA's research priorities. Someone may think we're paying too much attention to Poland. There are lots of tough questions, and my job is to answer on the spot. We'll have 14 such sessions during the course of the year—one every three weeks. That means 400 top managers from all over the world living in close quarters, really communicating about the business and their problems, and meeting with the CEO in an open, honest dialogue (Taylor, 1991, p. 101).

Such extensive communication in a company that operates in 140 countries requires a common language, which in ABB is English (or as Goren Lindahl has stated it, "The common language of ABB is broken English.") Since English is not the mother tongue of either of the two founding companies, its installation as the required ABB business language cannot be resented as headquarters imperialism.

Communication also takes place on a more individual level, between the Executive Committee and their direct reports, and even between the Executive Committee and the heads of the local operating companies. Ghoshal and Bartlett (1997, p. 190) have drawn on interviews with Goren Lindahl, then head of ABB's largest segment, to describe his role as follows:

> Lindahl saw his key role not as aligning, integrating, and blessing the plans of his various BA and regional managers in a ritualized annual review, but of questioning, probing, and challenging them in bimonthly meetings. He developed scenario exercises to force them to think about how they might change their strategic postures or priorities in response to various unplanned political, economic, or competitive developments."

Lindahl has also described the Executive Committee management style as "fingers in the pie" management. Executive Committee members have access to monthly performance data for all the operating companies, national companies, and business areas for which they are responsible. The ABACUS system provides rapid feedback on changes in the performance of any of these units, and the monthly data are routinely scrutinized carefully at the top of the company. Lindahl and other Committee members did not hesitate to call a local operating company manager whose monthly performance figures indicated a problem to ask, "What's the problem? What are you doing to fix it? How can we help you?" (Ghoshal and Bartlett, 1998, p. 189).

Alignment: Developing the Global Manager

One of the key challenges facing ABB has been developing managers who can work effectively in this demanding system. Obviously, local operating company managers need to be able to function effectively in the matrix, and this means developing a selection and training program to identify and prepare them. But most important is the development of the "global managers" who occupy the key positions in the Business Areas (both the BA managers and the small number of managers supporting them) and at the top of the company on the Executive Committee. In the 1991 interview published by *Harvard Business Review,* Barnevik responded to the question, "Is there such a thing as a global manager?" by saying: "Yes, but we don't have many. One of ABB's biggest priorities is to create more of them; it is a crucial bottleneck for us. On the other hand, a global company does not need thousands of global managers. We need maybe 500 or so out of 15,000 managers to make ABB work—not more. I have no interest in making managers more 'global' than they have to be" (Taylor, 1991, p. 94). Six years later, Barnevik reiterated this belief; although the number of managers in ABB had increased with ABB's geographic expansion, the number of global managers did not: "Building a mulitnational cadre of international managers is the key. It is one thing for a chief executive himself to be a global manager. It is quite another to persuade other executives to think and act globally. At ABB we have about 25,000 managers. But not all of them need to be global managers. We have about 500" (FT, Oct. 8, 1997, p. 10).

The global managers must be capable of balancing the often contradictory pulls of being locally responsive and globally efficient, pushing decision-making and responsibility for action down while enforcing accountability and control, and simultaneously encouraging local operating companies to be entrepreneurial while making sure that ABB does not lose the competitive advantage of being a multi-business global company. Such people are developed through the training programs, experience on cross-national teams, and rotation across locations. Barnevik has singled out the latter as particularly crucial: "There is no substitute for line experience in three or four countries to create a global perspective" (Taylor, 1991, p. 95). Those who aim for the top positions in ABB must expect that like the current members of the Executive Committee, they will spend some time in assignments on the geography side of the matrix as well as the business side.

One of the hallmarks of the cadre of global managers is that they spend a lot of their time travelling internationally. As CEO of ABB Barnevik himself spent most of his time travelling around ABB's international operations, estimating that he interacted personally with 5,500 ABB employees each year. In a 1992 article, Barnevik listed as the key qualities of the high-potential ABB manager as "patience, good language ability, stamina, work experience in at least two or three countries, and, most important, humility" (Rapo, 1992, p. 79). When asked whether this didn't eliminate women with young children or men with a strong family commitment from consideration, he replied that it did, but that "there are female executives who have chosen not to have a family, for example, or who have children, but their husbands have the kind of job, like teaching, that allows them to spend more time at home. . . . There are all kinds of people who are not tied down by family commitments. You have homosexuals, people who don't want to marry at all, people who want to be single, millions and millions of them. They are single not because their career forbids it but because they've chosen another lifestyle" (Ibid., p. 79).

A NEW ORGANIZATIONAL MODEL?

Ghoshal and Bartlett (1998) have argued that the key to understanding ABB is to think in terms of the way the strategic grouping and linking facilitate the differentiation of organizational roles. Specifically, they sum up ABB as follows:

- Frontline managers, heading small, disaggregated and interdependent units focused on specific opportunities, are the company's entrepreneurs. They are the builders of the company's businesses and competencies and take full responsibility for both the short-tern and the long-term performances of their units. Importantly, they face out to an external environment with which they build strong contracts and relationships, rather than upward into a hierarchy from which they expect direction and control.

- Like coaches who leverage the strengths of individual players to build a winning team, middle-level managers link these separate businesses and leverage the resources and capabilities developed in each of them. Overall, they play the role of capability developers—developing both the skills and competencies of the individual frontline managers through mentoring and guidance, and also the overall capabilities of the organization by integrating the diverse capabilities of the frontline units across businesses, functions, and countries.

- Top management provides the foundation for this activity by infusing the company with an energizing purpose—a sense of ambition, a set of values, an overall identity—so as to develop it as an institution that can outlive its existing operations, opportunities, and executives. Like social leaders, top management creates the challenge and commitment necessary to drive change and ensure that the company continuously renews itself. Rather than trying to control strategic content, top management focuses much more on shaping organizational context" (Ghoshal and Bartlett, 1998, pp. 205-206).

Perhaps the last comment should go to Nadler and Tushman, who see ABB as ". . . an organization that can act as a global powerhouse to amass resources, technological know-how, production innovations, and distribution networks to compete on a par with any major corporation even as it constantly emphasizes its deep connections to local markets and customers. The coordination of 210,000 employees, working in 300 companies and 5,000 profit centers in 140 countries, demonstrates the crucial role of linking mechanisms in turning a complex kaleidescope of grouping patterns into a smoothly functioning organization. ABB also illustrates how successful such designs can be; with net income of $1.3 billion, ABB saw its stock price double between 1992 and 1996" (1997, p. 90).

REFERENCES

Bartlett, Christopher A., 1993. "ABB's Relays Business: Building and Managing a Global Matrix." Harvard Business School Case #9-394-016, revised January 7, 1995.

Business International/Ideas in Action. 1988. "Asea Brown Boveri Becomes a European Powerhouse." May 9, pp. 14–20.

Business Week. 1990. "The Euro-Gospel According to Percy Barnevik." July 23, pp. 64–66.

The Economist. 1996. "The ABB of Management." January 6, p. 56.

Financial Times. 1997. "Own Words: Percy Barnevik, ABB and Investor: A Multinational Cadre of Managers is the Key." October 7, p. 10.

"ABB Axe Swings Back into Action." October 22, p. 20.

Ghoshal, Sumantra, and Christopher A. Bartlett. 1998. *The Individualized Corporation.* London: Heinemann.

International Management. 1988. "ABB: The New Energy Powerhouse." June, pp. 24–30.

Marquand, Michael, and Angus Reynolds. 1996. *The Global Learning Organization.* New York: Irwin Professional Publishing.

Nadler, David A., and Michael Tushman. 1997. *Competing by Design: The Power of Organizational Architecture.* New York: Oxford University Press.

Rapo, Carla. 1992. "A Tough Swede Invades the U.S." *Fortune.* June 29, pp. 76–79.

Taylor, William. 1991. "The Logic of Global Business: An Interview with ABB's Percy Barnevik." *Harvard Business Review* March-April, pp. 90–104.

Uyterhoeven, Hugo. 1992. "ABB Deutschland (A) (Extended)." Harvard Business School Case #9-392-065. Revised May 12, 1993.

Ⓒ

39

CASE

PART 3: THE POLITICAL LENS*

Power is shared in organizations; and it is shared out of necessity more than out of concern for principles of organizational development or participatory democracy. Power is shared because no one person controls all the desired activities in the organization (Salancik and Pfeffer, 1977, p. 7).

In the previous part, organizations are portrayed as monolithic, strategic, machine-like entities, capable of making and implementing rational decisions made by top executives in pursuit of the goal of the organization. However, this depiction of organizations does not jibe with our vicarious or real-life experiences of politics and power in governmental, religious, or business institutions. As the quote above expresses, sharing power is a necessity in organizations, but that necessity is itself a contested struggle for power and control among individuals and groups with quite different goals or interests. To manage in a real world organization, therefore, we need to augment the "strategic design" view of the organization with a political perspective.

A political perspective views an organization as composed of multiple "stakeholders," i.e., individuals and groups who contribute important resources to an organization and depend on its success but who also have different interests and goals and bring different amounts and sources of power to bear in organizational interactions (Freeman, 1984; Mitchell, et al., 1997; Kochan and Rubinstein, 1998). Moreover, organizational interactions are not (like selling your used car to a stranger) one-time events. In organizations, individuals and groups with different interests interact repeatedly over time and often carry into any specific interaction memories of how they fared in prior meetings or decision-making settings. So no specific organizational interaction is independent of the past or of expectations about the future.

The key analytical building blocks of a political perspective are quite simple. To use a political perspective you must:

1. Identify and map the relationships among the different *stakeholders* involved.
2. Uncover the most salient *interests and goals* the different stakeholders bring to the interaction and the extent to which the conflict or are congruent.
3. Assess the amount and sources of *power* of the different stakeholders.

With this analysis in mind, you can then design and implement group and organizational processes to produce joint gains or acceptable compromises among the stakeholders and their interests.

ANALYTICAL BUILDING BLOCKS

The *tools* managers can employ to act on a political analysis of a situation are equally straightforward. Putting a political analysis to work *requires acknowledging and legitimating differences in interests and goals,* exploring ways to better *align them* so solutions chosen produce joint gains, *building coalitions* to change the distribution of power, *negotiating* solutions or outcomes, and *resolving conflicts* where the situation does not lend itself to results that are joint gains for all the stakeholders. Over the

*This part of Module 2 developed by Paul Carlile.

longer run, a political perspective is useful in *designing and implementing organizational change* since any change will reconfigure and alter existing interests and power distributions and thereby encounter resistance from some and support from other stakeholders. Thus, the political perspective draws heavily on the negotiations and conflict management tools that are presented in greater detail in Module 13. In this Module we only introduce the analytical building blocks needed to put these tools to work. Specifically, we focus on the concepts of stakeholders, interests and goals, and power.

The Stakeholder Perspective

Viewing organizations as composed of multiple stakeholders is a relatively recent development, for management researchers and teachers as well as practicing executives. In fact, building a political perspective into organizational analysis and processes has itself been a political process of challenging what was a top-down view of organizations. This view implied that their formal positions gave top executives the most power in organizations. Those below them should therefore be expected to respond to their directives in support of some superordinate organizational goal, regardless of how doing so might affect the personal or group interests of those lower in the organization. (See the Appendix for this part for a brief intellectual historical of the treatment of politics in management and organizational theory.)

Gradually, however, reality overtook management theory and practice. Today it is more widely accepted that organizations consist of multiple stakeholders with varying interests. These interests arise from a variety of sources. Some reflect horizontal divisions of labor and organizational structures such as differences in functional responsibilities within the organizations (i.e., sales, R&D, production, etc.). Others reflect one's position in the vertical division of labor or hierarchy (e.g., differences between employees' interests in jobs and careers with high pay, employment security, and professional autonomy and their supervisors' interests in controlling costs and maximizing profits, maintaining flexibility, and coordinating or controlling his or her unit). And still others reflect the different concerns of numerous external constituencies the organization depends on (i.e., customers, suppliers, labor, investors, government regulators). Figure 2.11 maps some of the most frequently discussed stakeholder groups. All of these stakeholders, both internal and external to the organization, have different goals and interests that they are trying to maintain and expand. It is this part of organizational life—the natural struggle or conflict amongst interests or stakeholders—that a perspective on organizations as political systems helps to clarify and demystify.

Interests and Goals

Mapping the stakeholders involved in a given organizational interaction and their general interests provides only an initial portrait of the interests that may be represented in a given interaction. As such, it provides a first approximation of the specific goals the different participants will carry into a given organizational situation or interaction. Long ago, organizational theorists Herbert Simon and James March (1958) defined goals as the specific preferences individuals use to evaluate and rank the potential outcomes of a decision or interaction. Thus, the next step in using a political perspective is to uncover how the parties translate their broad interests into specific goals or preferences that will guide their behavior and the outcomes they will seek.

Accepting Goal Conflict   To do this effectively, a manager must first overcome what is often a psychological barrier. Identifying and working with the range of goals individuals and groups bring to an interaction requires manager to accept the *legitimacy and ongoing nature of* goal conflict among individuals, groups, and units in an organization. Although trying to create congruity among the numerous goals in an organizations is a large part of the managerial task and is what lies at the heart of many organizational change efforts—goal conflict will not go away. Indeed, goal conflict is consciously built into the design of most organizational interactions (for example

© 41 ACADEMIC

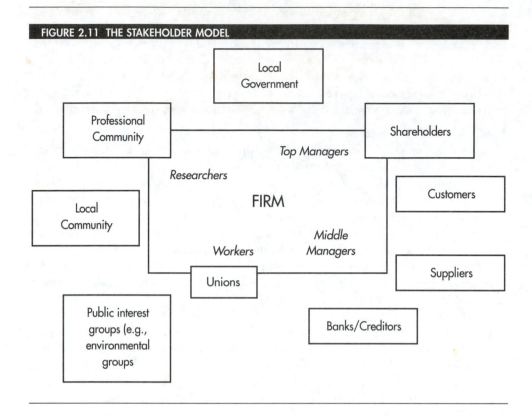

FIGURE 2.11 THE STAKEHOLDER MODEL

cross-functional teams are created to ensure that different requirements and knowledge bases are considered in a decision or product design process). As we will emphasize when we introduce negotiations and conflict resolution concepts and tools, acknowledging, legitimating, and surfacing the goals individuals bring to such processes are essential to effective group and team dynamics and performance.

Discovering and Surfacing Differences   The challenge is that individuals have multiple interests and stakeholder or group affiliations. So assuming goals or preferences based on group identity or stakeholder roles can be risky. And because individuals have multiple group or stakeholder affiliations and interests, often the goals they will favor are unclear at the outset of any given interaction and emerge and are shaped by the process itself. Thus, uncovering and surfacing interests and goals is an emergent and ongoing process of discovery. A critical part of a political analysis of a situation, therefore is to map the interests and goals most salient to the different participants in a given situation and to assess the degree to which the goals that emerge are congruent or conflicting.

Power and Politics

A political perspective defines power as the ability to get things done when goals conflict (Dahl, 1957, p. 203), or, in plain terms, the ability to get people to do something they would not do if acting alone in their own self interest. But power is not a fixed commodity or a "zero sum" game such that any power I gain is power that you must lose. There are two basic reasons why such a narrow conception is wrong. First, if we can find ways to realign stakeholder interests or achieve solutions that produce joint gains for the different stakeholders, all parties are not only better off but have increased their "ability to get things done" without giving up their power or sacrificing their self-interests. Module 13 will discuss models of negotiations specifically designed to search for these types of mutual gains' outcomes. Second, individuals and groups bring different sources or bases of power to bear in interactions that can be combined or utilized in complementary ways. This second point is worth exploring here since it offers considerable potential for utilizing power creatively and positively in organizational interactions, rather than simply viewing power as a "struggle" over who will come out on top.

Different Bases of Power   Figure 2.12 lists some of the different bases or sources of power commonly found in any organizational interaction involving multiple stakeholders. A sampling of these include formal authority or position power, contacts to or alliances with individuals or groups with higher power, the control of sanctions and rewards, specialized or technical knowledge, type of associations or referent groups, and access to critical information.

Henry Mintzberg (1983) summarized the numerous sources of power in three groups. The first group consists of resources, technical skills or specialized bodies of knowledge. These will be a basis of power if they have one or more of the following characteristics:

1. They are essential to the functioning of the organization.
2. They are concentrated, in short supply, or in the hands of a few individuals.
3. They are non-substitutable or irreplaceable.

The second group is formal power. This type of power lies in the ability to sanction behavior or impose choices—whether that is through formal position, legal rights or responsibilities, or ownership. The last group derives its power through access to individuals or groups who have power. This access may be through a personal network or lie in the collective power of an important constituency one represents.

Power Dynamics   So far power is portrayed as a relatively static phenomenon—a function of current position, control over information, resources, etc. But managers need to look at power as a dynamic, changing, and malleable phenomenon that is used by organizational members throughout the organization and in relations with external entities. Power (and interests) often evolve as relationships develop and mature. Two classical examples from prior organizational research illustrate the dynamic and evolving nature of power.

Michel Crozier's (1964) study of a cigarette factory in France furthered our understanding of the sources of power, conflict, and mutual control in organizations. One of the things that surprised him in his analysis is that the maintenance workers had a degree of authority and power that overstepped their formal position in the organization. Crozier found that while management was able to control the uncertainties of labor via piece-rate systems, and the uncertainties in supplies by stock piling material,

© 43 ACADEMIC

FIGURE 2.12 TYPICAL SOURCES OF POWER

- Formal authority—position power
- Control over scarce resources
- Rules, structure, regulations, standard operating procedures
- Control over decision process—access to decision making
- Information, knowledge, or specialized (scarce) skills
- Gatekeeping or control over the flow of information or access
- Ability to cope with uncertainty and ambiguity
- Alliances—ability to call on powerful resources
- Symbolic use of power—creating the perception of influence
- Countervailing power—ability to create new institutions
- Empowerment of weaker parties—use of third parties or legal rights
- Negotiating skills—shaping the process

Source: Adapted from Gareth Morgan, *Images of Organization.* San Francisco: Sage Publications, 1986, p. 365.

it lost control of operations when machinery critical to the production process broke down. Not surprisingly the lowly skilled maintenance workers who fixed this critical equipment had tremendous power and influence in the organization when breakdowns occurred. Management, on a number of occasions, tried to control the autonomy and curb the power of the maintenance workers, but by fixing the machines too slowly or in some cases performing outright sabotage the maintenance workers preserved the power that naturally belonged to their circumstances. Only when their "interest" in autonomy was recognized and respected by management did a negotiated relationship develop within which joint control over production was achieved.

Philip Selznick (1949) in his book studying how the Tennessee Valley Authority (TVA) cultivated "grassroots" power is a portrait of how power is exercised in relations between organizations interacting over time. He described this slow but effective political effort as a process of "co-optation" wherein "New Deal" values could infiltrate, co-opt, and control the conservative state and local water, farming, and electricity interest groups and policy making bodies in the mid-South. It is in this gradual process of co-optation that we see how alternative "interests" slowly legitimate themselves and in the end have the power to transform the interests (i.e., rural farmers, private utilities, state officials) that were opposing them. However, Selznick also observed that in some cases "New Deal" interests were likewise transformed or co-opted by various state and local groups. It is this story of co-optation on both sides that expresses both the negative (i.e., as a controlling force) and positive (productive) aspects of power and that result in many of the "unintended consequences" we observe in organizational life.

Both of these examples illustrate an important point: power is not a fixed commodity. At best it is ambiguous at any point in time, and often the relative power of different participants changes over time as events or decision-making processes unfold. Thus, one of the biggest tactical mistakes a person can make is to over-analyze the power relations prior to an event or interaction. If, for example, I believe that I enter into an interaction in a relatively low power position, I may behave in a way that makes my prediction a self-fulfilling prophecy! Or, if I believe my position or status should give me a power advantage and the right to control an interaction with others, I may be surprised and frustrated by my inability to "get things done!"

Managing "Resistance"   Neither individuals or groups tend to give up power voluntarily. Thus they can and should be expected to resist actions that are interpreted as putting their bases or sources of power at risk. Yet most organizational interactions, and particularly organizational change efforts, inherently change the distribution of power and enhance some sources of power while diminishing others. For example, restructuring from a functional to a product based organizational structure is almost always viewed by functional managers (e.g., manufacturing, marketing, finance, human resources, etc.) as reducing their power and enhancing the power of product or account managers. Similarly, delegating decision-making power to front line managers is almost always resisted by middle managers because it involves sharing some of the sources of their power.

These are realities that must be anticipated and taken into account in managing change. A political perspective, however, shifts the responsibility for addressing resistance to change from the resisters to the managerial change agents. That is, rather than view resistance as an illegitimate or irrational response, a political perspective not only views it as a natural response but anticipates it as a normal and legitimate part of organizational life. It becomes the *manager's* job to deal with this reality rather than ignoring it or leaving it to the individuals to cope with their diminished power.

Power Contests   Because power has value to individuals and groups, it is often sought after and contested inside an organization and in relations with external entities. Increasing one's power allows one to claim a greater portion of an organization's resources and rewards, individually or for one's stakeholder group. As power dynamics are played out interests and stakeholders get redefined—consider Selznick's co-optation example at the TVA or Crozier's example of how top management had to realize that lower level maintenance workers were stakeholders they needed to contend with.

Using Charles Perrow's (1986) discussion about power as initially a zero-sum game reinforces this point in terms of the contested nature of a political system and what it means to take action within one. First, as a zero-sum game power constrains organizational choices to the current entrenched interests, but by generating and then selling alternatives—*taking action*—to those entrenched interests that pie can be expanded. Going to a broader definition of power "as the ability to get things done," we can better visualize the character of power as a force that is both a constraining and producing force. And as a manager, who has to take action in a political system, being clear about the political terrain and the skills required to expand a constrained, zero-sum pie is paramount.

Given the changing and uncertain marketplace of an organization, both internally and externally, what is at stake for most of the stakeholders is always at risk (i.e., will the current bases of power remain essential, critical, or non-substitutable). To have power in the future in a given industry or a functional hierarchy is simultaneously a stake that one individual or group wants to preserve or a stake that one individual or group wants to transform. Transforming the stakes is about redistributing the critical resources, skills, and knowledge within an organization. For example, over time management in Crozier's cigarette factory took steps to try to redistribute more broadly the skills to fix critical machinery, thereby diluting the power base of the old-line maintenance workers. So, power dynamics are an ongoing and evolving organizational process and reality.

THE POLITICAL PERSPECTIVE AND TAKING ACTION IN THE NEW ORGANIZATION

Diversity

As workforce and organizational diversity increase, so too does the value of a political perspective and set of tools. The task of organizing and managing diversity in cultural background, language, occupations and professions, departmental affiliations, or representative responsibilities requires that all the parties to these processes be skilled in negotiating and problem solving. Interests of diverse parties need to be surfaced, not assumed. Moreover, as diversity increases and organization move decision-making authority around to gain value from the diverse resources and talents available, traditional interest group lines or stakeholder configurations get blurred. Indeed, this is necessary for a diverse organization to function effectively because if individuals carry narrow loyalties or interests into each organizational process in which they participate, the organization dissolves into multiple fiefdoms of negotiating barons. At this point, the organization itself loses its advantage to the competitive market or to other organizations that can better integrate and coordinate the interests involved on either a temporary (strategic alliance) or permanent basis.

Moreover, increasing numbers of organizational interest groups, sometimes known as caucuses, of blacks, women, or other demographic, professional, or occupational groups, seek a voice in issues affecting their key interests. Thus, as organizational diversity increases so do the demands for effective integration of multiple interests and resolution of differences in interest among often-shifting coalitions. The banding together of less-powerful groups is sometimes greeted with concern but can be a step toward surfacing, understanding, and even capitalizing on, and gaining value from differences.

Flattening Hierarchies

Flattening the organization means redistributing power to lower levels, power that was previously controlled by higher-level managers. And changing power relations is one of the most difficult political acts a manager will ever undertake, since power tends to be viewed from a zero-sum or win-lose perspective. Dispersing power among individuals and groups who have a mixture of common and conflicting goals also increases the potential for conflict, and, therefore, elevates the importance of being able to analyze situations from a political perspective and use the tools of effective negotiations and problem solving.

Globalization

A political perspective focuses attention on the recent recognition that firms in different societies design corporations in ways that give differential weight to different organizational *stakeholders* and on the increased need to understand the roles managers are called upon to play in alternative systems of organizational *governance*. A manager in a German firm, for example, finds employee representatives serving on the board of supervisors and elected councils of workers in each establishment with five or more employees. In Japanese firms, employee interests are typically ranked higher than those of shareholders, leading one Japanese scholar to describe the role of managers as mediators in an organizational coalition of owners and employees. Even in North America, models of human resource management and labor-management policymakers are searching for ways to promote mutual gains among the interests of shareholders, employees, and the broader society (Kochan and Osterman, 1994). Thus, globalization increases the importance of being flexible in adapting to different roles and relationships toward multiple internal and external stakeholders.

Flexibility

Finally, as boundaries of organizations blur in the flexible organization of the future, the complexity of interests to be accommodated further increases. In the early 1990s it has become common wisdom that firms must develop effective partnerships with their suppliers so as to increase quality, reliability and speed of delivery, and reduce the costs of product and process innovation. But in 1994 General Motors (GM) announced its highest quarterly profits in history following several years of disastrous losses. *Business Week* attributed the turnaround in large part to the hard-line, cost-cutting approach to suppliers taken by former GM executive José Ignacio Lopez. But, in the same article, *Business Week* went on to wonder whether this cost-cutting mentality was short sighted:

> To be sure, [GM's] suppliers have voiced similar anger before, and some of their most-dire predictions haven't come to pass. Still, they note that the auto industry's long lead times mean the full effects of Lopez' policies may not be seen until next year and later—when cars developed using parts sourced entirely under Lopez' watch rollout. Lopez may be gone, they say, but his ghost will haunt GM for years to come (*Business Week*. 1994, p. 26).

As cross-boundary relations become more important, so too will the need to decide when to take a traditional hard bargaining approach similar to what was described earlier as "end-game" behavior, as Lopez appeared to do for GM, and when to develop relations that better resemble the principles of effective ongoing negotiations and problem solving.

SUMMARY AND KEY QUESTIONS FOR A POLITICAL DIAGNOSIS

How can this political perspective be put to use in organizational diagnosis and action? To understand the political dimensions of a situation one must first attempt to map the interests at stake and the context in which the interaction will occur. Who are the key participants or stakeholders and what is most important to each of them? How fixed or malleable are these interests? How compatible are these interests? Can the situation or task be redefined to increase the potential for joint gains to the parties? Is the social setting or the history of the relations among the parties amenable to effective negotiations, conflict resolution, and problem solving, or should one first take steps to alter the climate or social norms that dominate?

Second, what source of power do the various parties bring to the situation? How evenly or unevenly is power distributed among the parties? Can this be changed in some way?

Third, how skilled are the various parties to the type of mixed-interest compromise of decision making that is likely to be needed to reach a successful result? Can these skills be enhanced or should skilled third parties (e.g., mediators, group facilitators, professional advocates, or God forbid, a lawyer or even two or more lawyers!) be brought in to assist?

Fourth, are the needed policies or systems in place to support effective negotiations, problem solving, and if necessary, conflict resolution? Are there adequate safeguards to protect the interests of the least powerful individual or groups involved? Are there interests excluded or not being heard in the process?

Fifth, will this process add value or is it dysfunctional or likely to leave one or all parties worse off than before? Not all conflicts need to be fought nor are all differences in interests resolvable. An effective decision-maker knows how to tell when this is the case and move on to more fruitful endeavors.

Finally, it is important to not overdo one's political analysis of situations. People do often look beyond their self-interests and act for the common good and welfare. Constantly looking for the self-interests motive or the "hidden agendas" that may lie behind individual or organizational action breeds an overly cynical society and one that fails to appreciate the innate need and willingness of most people do try to help others achieve what is important to them, regardless of its impact on themselves.

Concluding Comments

Given this discussion about multiple stakeholders, interests, and power we are left with a personal dilemma. As a person with management responsibilities, how do I decide upon the proper direction and means of expanding the pie of power in the organization? The purpose of shining the light on this dilemma is not to provide an answer or a way out, but to underscore that you will potentially face this problem, whether recognized or unrecognized, each time you try to take action and change the organization. What is required in the "proper management" of the resources of an organization, is to think about interests and power across the entire system, both internally and externally to the organization to help insure their effective utilization. This might include the overlooked concerns of a particular functional specialty, the unheard feedback from consumers, or the limited supply of a well-trained workforce. This complexity of organizational inputs, outputs, and interests should naturally encourage us to not just maximize our own immediate interests, but more systemically expand our view of "interests," the alternatives we propose, and the negotiation strategies that bridge these interests.

© 47 ACADEMIC

APPENDIX: A BRIEF INTELLECTUAL HISTORY OF THE POLITICAL PERSPECTIVE

Classical management theory and teaching, derived largely from models of military units, viewed the organization from the top down and developed principles designed to help executives control subordinate behavior in ways that overcame any human tendencies to deviate from loyalty to the firm's objective (Fayol, 1949). Conflict was to be avoided and viewed as a pathological breakdown of the command and control system of management.

Later, partly in response to outbreaks of worker unrest in the 1930s, organizational models and management began to emphasize human relations and the role of social interactions in the workplace. In these models, conflict was again viewed as a problem, this time arising because top management paid inadequate attention to the social needs of workers. As Chester Barnard (1938), one of the most widely read CEOs of his time, wrote in his classic book *The Functions of the Executive*, the key role of managers was to meet these social needs through policies that satisfied employees without losing control over decision making.

Meanwhile, as Barnard was writing, workers were taking control of auto plants through sitdown strikes, and industrial workers were joining unions in large numbers to use their new-found power to bargain collectively with management. This led to models of industrial relations that emphasized the inherent differences in economic interests between workers and managers. These models view organizations as divided into two fixed interest groups (labor and management) with clearly defined, enduring differences in goals (the size of a wage increase) but at the same time bound together by a set of common goals (e.g., firm survival and growth). This mixture of conflicting and common goals was described as a "mixed motive" relationship (Walton and McKersie, 1965).

By the 1960s some theorists began conceiving of organizations as coalitions of multiple interest groupings, some of which were quite fluid and emergent in nature, depending on the issues involved and the resources at stake (Cyert and March, 1963; Thompson, 1967). Rather than seeing organizations as having a limited number of fixed-interest groups defined by their positions in the vertical or horizontal division of labor, coalition models allow for interests to shift and vary depending on the issue or task at hand. More recent models stress the ambiguous nature of goals and interest and the fact goals often tend to emerge out of a problem as it is defined or "framed" by those involved (Bazerman and Neale, 1992). One seldom knows at the outset whose interests are at stake, what the goals are, or what processes can best deal with the task at hand.

More recently, the American model of the firm as solely a shareholder wealth-maximizing entity has been challenged by the view that organizations are composed of multiple stakeholders, each of which shares risks with owners and investors and therefore has legitimate claims over organizational resources and rewards (Freeman, 1984; Blair, 1994; Kochan and Rubinstein, 1998). How this debate plays out will have important implications for the future roles and responsibilities of managers.

REFERENCES

Barnard, Chester. 1938. *The Functions of the Executive.* Cambridge, MA: Harvard University Press.

Bazerman, Max. H. and Margaret A. Neale. 1992. *Negotiating Rationally.* New York: Free Press.

Blair, Margaret. 1994. *Ownership and Control.* Washington, D.C.: The Brookings Institute.

Business Week. 1994. "Hardball is Still GM's Game." August 8.

Crozier, Michel. 1964. *The Bureaucratic Phenomenon.* Chicago: University of Chicago Press.

Cyert, Richard M., and James G. March. 1963. *A Behavioral Theory of the Firm.* New York: MacGraw-Hill.

Dahl, Robert. 1957. "The Concept of Power." *Behavioral Science.* 20, pp. 201–215.

Fayol, Henri. 1949. *General and Industrial Management.* London: Pitman and Sons.

Freeman, E. Richard. 1984. *Strategic Management: A Stakeholder Approach.* Boston, MA: Pitman.

Kochan, Thomas. A., and Paul Osterman. 1994. *The Mutual Gains Enterprise.* Boston: Harvard Business School Press.

Kochan, Thomas. A. and Saul Rubenstein. 1998. "Dynamics of a Stakeholder Firm: The case of the Saturn Partnership." MIT Working Paper.

March, James G. and Herbert Simon. 1958. *Organizations.* New York: Wiley.

Mintzberg, Henry. 1983. *Power In and Around Organizations.* Englewood Cliffs, NJ: Prentice-Hall.

Mitchell, Ronald, Angle, Bradely, and Donna Wood. 1997. "Toward a Theory of Stakeholder Identification and Salience." *Academy of Management Review,* 22 (4), pp. 852–856.

Morgan, Gareth. 1986. *Images of Organization.* San Francisco: Sage Publications.

Perrow, Charles. 1986. *Complex Organizations: A Critical Essay.* (3rd Edition). New York: Random House.

Salancik, Gerald, and Jeffery Pfeffer. 1977. "Who Gets Power—And How They Hold on to It: A Strategic-Contingency Model of Power." *Organizational Dynamics.* (Winter).

Selznick, Philip. 1949. *TVA and the Grass Roots.* Berkeley: University of California Press.

Walton, Richard E., and Robert B. MaKersie. 1965. *A Behavioral Theory of Labor Negotiations.* New York: McGraw-Hill.

Ⓒ

49

ACADEMIC

POWER FAILURE IN MANAGEMENT CIRCUITS

The position, not the person, often determines whether a manager has power.

by Rosabeth Moss Kanter

When one thinks of "power," one often assumes that a person is the source of it and that some mystical charismatic element is at work. Of course, with some people this is undoubtedly so; they derive power from how other people perceive them. In organizations, however—says this author—power is not so much a question of people but of positions. Drawing a distinction between productive and oppressive power, the author maintains that the former is a function of having open channels to supplies, support, and information; the latter is a function of these channels being closed. She then describes three positions that are classically powerless: first-line supervisors, staff professionals, and, surprisingly, chief executive officers. These positions can be powerless because of difficulties in maintaining open lines of information and support. Seeing powerlessness in these positions as dangerous for organizations, she urges managers to restructure and redesign their organizations in order to eliminate pockets of powerlessness.

Ms. Kanter is professor of sociology and organization and management at Yale University, where she conducts research on organization design and change processes. She is the author of *Men and Women of the Corporation* (New York: Basic Books, 1977) and numerous other articles and books on life in today's organizations.

Power is America's last dirty word. It is easier to talk about money—and much easier to talk about sex—than it is to talk about power. People who have it deny it; people who want it do not want to appear to hunger for it; and people who engage in its machinations do so secretly.

Yet, because it turns out to be a critical element in effective managerial behavior, power should come out from undercover. Having searched for years for those styles or skills that would identify capable organization leaders, many analysts, like myself, are rejecting individual traits or situational appropriateness as key and finding the sources of a leader's real power.

Access to resources and information and the ability to act quickly make it possible to accomplish more and to pass on more resources and information to subordinates. For this reason, people tend to prefer bosses with "clout." When employees perceive their manager as influential upward and outward, their status is enhanced by association and they generally have high morale and feel less critical or resistant to their boss.[1] More powerful leaders are also more likely to delegate (they are too busy to do it all themselves), to reward talent, and to build a team that places subordinates in significant positions.

Powerlessness, in contrast, tends to breed bossiness rather than true leadership. In large organizations, at least, it is powerlessness that often creates ineffective, desultory management and petty, dictatorial, rules-minded managerial styles.

[1] Donald C. Pelz. 1952. "Influence: A Key to Effective Leadership in the First-Line Supervisor," *Personnel*, November, p. 209.

Accountability without power—responsibility for results without the resources to get them—creates frustration and failure. People who see themselves as weak and powerless and find their subordinates resisting or discounting them tend to use more punishing forms of influence. If organizational power can "ennoble," then, recent research shows, organizational powerlessness can (with apologies to Lord Acton) "corrupt."[2]

So, perhaps power, in the organization at least, does not deserve such a bad reputation. Rather than connoting only dominance, control, and oppression, *power* can mean efficacy and capacity—something managers and executives need to move the organization toward its goals. Power in organizations is analogous in simple terms to physical power: it is the ability to mobilize resources (human and material) to get things done. The true sign of power, then, is accomplishment—not fear, terror, or tyranny. Where the power is "on," the system can be productive; where the power is "off," the system bogs down.

But saying that people need power to be effective in organizations does not tell us where it comes from or why some people, in some jobs, systematically seem to have more of it than others. In this article I want to show that to discover the sources of productive power, we have to look not at the *person*—as conventional classifications of effective managers and employees do—but at the *position* the person occupies in the organization.

WHERE DOES POWER COME FROM?

The effectiveness that power brings evolves from two kinds of capacities: first, access to the resources, information, and support necessary to carry out a task; and, second, ability to get cooperation in doing what is necessary. (*Exhibit I* identifies some symbols of an individual manager's power.)

Both capacities derive not so much from a leader's style and skill as from his or her location in the formal and informal

EXHIBIT I SOME COMMON SYMBOLS OF A MANAGER'S ORGANIZATIONAL POWER (INFLUENCE UPWARD AND OUTWARD)

To what extent a manager can –

Intercede favorably on behalf of someone in trouble with the organization

Get a desirable placement for a talented subordinate

Get approval for expenditures beyond the budget

Get above-average salary increases for subordinates

Get items on the agenda at policy meetings

Get fast access to top decision makers

Get regular, frequent access to top decision makers

Get early information about decisions and policy shifts

---

systems of the organization—in both job definition and connection to other important people in the company. Even the ability to get cooperation from subordinates is strongly defined by the manager's clout outward. People are more responsive to bosses who look as if they can get more for them from the organization.

We can regard the uniquely organizational sources of power as consisting of three "lines":

1. *Lines of supply.* Influence outward, over the environment, means that managers have the capacity to bring in the things that their own organizational domain needs—materials, money, resources to distribute as rewards, and perhaps even prestige.

2. *Lines of information.* To be effective, managers need to be "in the know" in both the formal and the informal sense.

3. *Lines of support.* In a formal framework, a manager's job parameters need to allow for non-ordinary action, for a show of discretion or exercise of judgment. Thus managers need to know that they can assume innovative, risk-taking activities assume innovative

---

2 See my book. 1977. *Men and Women of the Corporation.* New York: Basic Books, pp. 164–205; and David Kipnis. 1976. *The Powerholders.* Chicago: University of Chicago Press.

without having to go through the stifling multi-layered approval process. And, informally, managers need the backing of other important figures in the organization whose tacit approval becomes another resource they bring to their own work unit as well as a sign of the manager's being "in."

Note that productive power has to do with *connections* with other parts of a system. Such systemic aspects of power derive from two sources–job activities and political alliances:

1. Power is most easily accumulated when one has a job that is designed and located to allow *discretion* (nonroutinized action permitting flexible, adaptive, and creative contributions), *recognition* (visibility and notice), and *relevance* (being central to pressing organizational problems).

2. Power also comes when one has relatively close contact with *sponsors* (higher-level people who confer approval, prestige, or backing), *peer networks* (circles of acquaintanceship that provide reputation and information, the grapevine often being faster than formal communication channels), and *subordinates* (who can be developed to relieve managers of some of their burdens and represent the manager's point of view).

When managers are in powerful situations, it is easier for them to accomplish more. Because the tools arc there they arc likely to be highly motivated and, in turn, to be able to motivate subordinates. Their activities are more likely to be on target and to net them successes. They can flexibly interpret or shape policy to meet the needs of particular areas, emergent situations, or sudden environmental shifts. They gain the respect and cooperation that attributed power brings. Subordinates' talents are resources rather than threats. And, because powerful managers have so many lines of connection and thus are oriented outward, they tend to let go

of control downward, developing more independently functioning lieutenants.

The powerless live in a different world. Lacking the supplies, information, or support to make things happen easily, they may turn instead to the ultimate weapon of those who lack productive power—oppressive power: holding others back and punishing with whatever threats they can muster.

Exhibit II summarizes some of the major ways in which variables in the organization and in job design contribute to either power or powerlessness.

POSITIONS OF POWERLESSNESS

Understanding what it takes to have power and recognizing the classic behavior of the powerless can immediately help managers make sense out of a number of familiar organizational problems that are usually attributed to inadequate people:

- The ineffectiveness of first-line supervisors
- The petty interest protection and conservatism of staff professionals
- The crises of leadership at the top

Instead of blaming the individuals involved in organizational problems, let us look at the positions, people occupy. Of course, power or powerlessness in a position may not be all of the problem. Sometimes incapable people *are* at fault and need to be retrained or replaced. (See the ruled insert on page 55 for a discussion of another special case, women.) But where patterns emerge, where the troubles associated with some units persist, organizational power failures could be the reason. Then, as Volvo President Pehr Gyllenhammar concludes, we should treat the powerless not as "villains" causing headaches for everyone else but as "victims."[3]

First-Line Supervisors

Because an employee's most important work relationship is with his or her supervisor, when many of them talk about "the company," they mean their immediate boss. Thus a supervisor's behavior is an

---

3 Pehr G. Gyllenhammar. 1977. *People at Work.* Reading, Mass.: Addison-Wesley, p. 133.

EXHIBIT II WAYS ORGANIZATIONAL FACTORS CONTRIBUTE TO POWER OR POWERLESSNESS

Factors	Generates power when factor is	Generates powerlessness when factor is
Rules inherent in the job	few	many
Predecessors in the job	few	many
Established routines	few	many
Task variety	high	low
Rewards for reliability/predictability	few	many
Rewards for unusual performance/innovation	many	few
Flexibility around use of people	high	low
Approvals needed for nonroutine decisions	few	many
Physical location	central	distant
Publicity about job activities	high	low
Relation of tasks to current problem areas	central	peripheral
Focus of tasks	outside work unit	inside work unit
Interpersonal contact in the job	high	low
Contact with senior officials	high	low
Participation in programs, conferences, meetings	high	low
Participation in problem-solving task forces	high	low
Advancement prospects of subordinates	high	low

important determinant of the average employee's relationship to work and is in itself a critical link in the production chain.

Yet I know of no U.S. corporate management entirely satisfied with the performance of its supervisors. Most see them as supervising too closely and not training their people. In one manufacturing company where direct laborers were asked on a survey how they learned their job, on a list of seven possibilities "from my supervisor" ranked next to last. (Only company training programs ranked worse.) Also, it is said that supervisors do not translate company policies, into practice—for instance, that they do not carry out the right of every employee to frequent performance reviews or to career counseling.

In court cases charging race or sex discrimination, first-line supervisors are frequently cited as the "discriminating official."[4] And, in studies of innovative work redesign and quality of work life projects, they often appear as the implied villains; they are the ones who are said to undermine the program or interfere with its effectiveness. In short, they are often seen as "not sufficiently managerial."

The problem affects white-collar as well as blue-collar supervisors. In one large government agency, supervisors in field offices were seen as the source of problems concerning morale and the flow of information to and from headquarters. "Their attitudes are negative," said a senior official. "They turn people against the agency; they put down senior management. They build themselves up by always complaining about headquarters, but prevent their staff from getting any information directly. We can't afford to have such. attitudes communicated to field staff."

Is the problem that supervisors need more management training programs or that incompetent people are invariably attracted to the job? Neither explanation suffices. A large part of the problem lies in the position itself—one that almost universally creates powerlessness.

4 William E. Fulmer. 1976. "Supervisory Selection: The Acid Test of Affirmative Action." *Personnel.* November–December, p. 40.

First-line supervisors are "people in the middle," and that has been seen as the source of many of their problems.[5] But by recognizing that first-line supervisors are caught between higher management and workers, we only begin to skim the surface of the, problem. There is practically no other organizational category as subject to powerlessness.

First, these supervisors may be at a virtual dead end in their careers. Even in companies where the job used to be a stepping stone to higher-level management jobs, it is now common practice to bring in MBAs from the outside for those positions. Thus moving from the ranks of direct labor into supervision may mean, essentially, getting "stuck" rather than moving upward. Because employees do not perceive supervisors as eventually joining the leadership circles of the organization, they may see them as lacking the high-level, contacts needed to have clout. Indeed, sometimes turnover among supervisors is so high that workers feel they can outwait—and outwit—any boss.

Second, although they lack clout, with little in the way of support from above, supervisors arc forced to administer programs or explain policies that they have no hand in shaping. In one company, as part of a new personnel program supervisors were required to conduct counseling interviews with employees. But supervisors were riot trained to do this and were given no incentives to get involved. Counseling was just another obligation. Then managers suddenly encouraged the workers to bypass their supervisors or to put pressure on them. The personnel staff brought them together and told them to demand such interviews as a basic right. If supervisors had not felt powerless before, they did after that squeeze from below, engineered from above.

The people they supervise can also make life hard for them in numerous ways. This often happens when a supervisor has himself or herself risen up from the ranks. Peers that have not made it are resentful or derisive of their former colleague, whom they now see as trying to lord it over them. Often it is easy for workers to break rules and let a lot of things slip.

Yet first-line supervisors are frequently judged according to rules and regulations while being limited by other regulations in what disciplinary actions they can take. They often lack the resources to influence or reward people; after all, workers are guaranteed their pay and benefits by someone other than their supervisors. Supervisors cannot easily control events; rather, they must react to them.

In one factory, for instance, supervisors complained that performance of their job was out of their control: they could fill production quotas only if they had the supplies, but they had no way to influence the people controlling supplies.

The lack of support for many first-line managers, particularly in large organizations, was made dramatically clear in another company. When asked if contact with executives higher in the organization who had the potential for offering support, information, and alliances diminished their own feelings of career vulnerability and the number of headaches they experienced on the job, supervisors in five out of seven work units responded positively. For them contact was indeed related to a greater feeling of acceptance at work and membership in the organization.

But in the two other work units where there was greater contact, people perceived more, not less, career vulnerability. Further investigation showed that supervisors in these business units got attention only when they were in trouble. Otherwise, no one bothered to talk to them. To these particular supervisors, hearing from a higher-level manager was a sign not of recognition or potential support but of danger.

It is not surprising, then, that supervisors frequently manifest symptoms of

---

5 See my chapter (coauthor, Barry A. Stein), "Life in the Middle: Getting In, Getting Up, and Getting Along," in *Life in Organizations*, eds. Rosabeth M. Kanter and Barry A. Stein. New York: Basic Books, 1979.

WOMEN MANAGERS EXPERIENCE SPECIAL POWER FAILURES

The traditional problems of women in management are illustrative of how formal and informal practices can combine to engender powerlessness. Historically, women in management have found their opportunities in more routine, low-profile jobs. In staff positions, where they serve in support capacities to line managers but have no line responsibilities of their own, or in supervisory jobs managing "stuck" subordinates, they are not in a position either to take the kinds of risks that build credibility or to develop their own team by pushing bright subordinates.

Such jobs, which have few favors to trade, tend to keep women out of the mainstream of the organization. This lack of clout, coupled with the greater difficulty anyone who is "different" has in getting into the information and support networks, has meant that merely by organizational situation women in management have been more likely than men to be rendered structurally powerless. This is one reason those women who have achieved power have often had family connections that put them in the mainstream of the organization's social circles.

A disproportionate number of women managers are found among first-line supervisors or staff professionals; and they, like men in those circumstances, are likely to be organizationally powerless. But the behavior of other managers can contribute to the powerlessness of women in management in a number of less obvious ways.

One way other managers can make a woman powerless is by patronizingly overprotecting her: putting her in "a safe job," not giving her enough to do to prove herself, and not suggesting her for high-risk, visible assignments. This protectiveness is sometimes born of "good" intentions to give her every chance to succeed (why stack the deck against her?). Out of managerial concerns, out of awareness that a woman may be up against situations that men simply do not have to face, some very well-meaning managers protect their female managers ("It's a jungle, so why send her into it?").

Overprotectiveness can also mask a manager's fear of association with a woman should she fail. One senior bank official at a level below vice president told me about his concerns with respect to a high-performing, financially experienced woman reporting to him, Despite *his* overwhelmingly positive work experiences with her, he was still afraid to recommend her for other assignments because he felt it was a personal risk. "What if other managers are not as accepting of women as I am?" he asked. "I know I'd be sticking my neck out; they would take her more because of my endorsement than her qualifications. And what if she doesn't make it? My judgment will be on the line."

Overprotection is relatively benign compared with rendering a person powerless by providing obvious signs of lack of managerial support. For example, allowing someone supposedly in authority to be bypassed easily means that no one else has to take him or her seriously. If a woman's immediate supervisor or other managers listen willingly to criticism of her and show they are concerned every time a negative comment comes up and that they assume she must be at fault, then they are helping to undercut her. If managers let other people know that they have concerns about this person or that they are testing her to see how she does, then they are inviting other people to look for signs of inadequacy or failure.

Furthermore, people assume they can afford to bypass women because they "must be uninformed" or "don't know the ropes." Even though women may be respected for their competence or expertise, they are not necessarily seen as being informed beyond the technical requirements of the job. There may be a grain of historical truth in this. Many women come to senior management positions as "outsiders" rather than up through the usual channels.

Also, because until very recently men have not felt comfortable seeing women as businesspeople (business clubs have traditionally excluded women), they have tended to seek each other out for informal socialization. Anyone, male or female, seen as organizationally naive and lacking sources of "inside dope" will find his or her own lines of information limited.

Finally, even when women are able to achieve some power on their own, they have not necessarily been able to translate such personal credibility into an organizational power base. To create a network of supporters out of individual clout requires that a person pass on and share power, that subordinates and peers be empowered by virtue of their connection with that person. Traditionally, neither men nor women have seen women as capable of sponsoring others, even though they may be capable of achieving and succeeding on their own. Women have been viewed as the *recipients* of sponsorship rather than as the sponsors themselves.

(As more women prove themselves in organizations and think more self-consciously about bringing along young people, this situation may change. However, I still hear many more questions from women managers about how they can benefit from mentors, sponsors, or peer networks than about how they themselves can start to pass on favors and make use of their own resources to benefit others.)

Viewing managers in terms of power and powerlessness helps explain two familiar stereotypes about women and leadership in organizations: that no one wants a woman boss (although studies show that anyone who has ever had a woman boss is likely to have had a positive experience), and that the reason no one wants a woman boss is that women are "too controlling, rules-minded, and petty."

The first stereotype simply makes clear that power is important to leadership. Underneath the preference for men is the assumption that, given the current distribution of people in organizational leadership positions, men are more likely than women to be in positions to achieve power and, therefore, to share their power with others. Similarly, the "bossy woman boss" stereotype is a perfect picture of powerlessness. All of those traits are just as characteristic of men who are powerless, but women are slightly more likely, because of circumstances I have mentioned, to find themselves powerless than are men. Women with power in the organization are just as effective—and preferred—as men.

Recent interviews conducted with about 600 bank managers show that, when a woman exhibits the petty traits of powerlessness, people assume that she does so "because she is a woman." A striking difference is that, when a man engages in the same behavior, people assume the behavior is a matter of his own individual style and characteristics and do not conclude it reflects on the suitability of men for management.

---

powerlessness: overly close supervision, rules-mindedness, and a tendency to do the job themselves rather than to train their people (since job skills may be one of the few remaining things they feel good about). Perhaps this is why they sometimes stand as roadblocks between their subordinates and the higher reaches of the company.

Staff Professionals

Also working under conditions that can lead to organizational powerlessness are the staff specialists. As advisers behind the scenes, staff people must sell their programs and bargain for resources, but unless they get themselves entrenched in organizational power networks, they have little in the way of favors to exchange. They are seen as useful adjuncts to the primary tasks of the organization but inessential in a day-to-day operating sense. This disenfranchisement occurs particularly when staff jobs consist of easily routinized administrative functions which are

out of the mainstream of the currently relevant areas and involve little innovative decision making.

Furthermore, in some organizations, unless they have had previous line experience, staff people tend to be limited in the number of jobs into which they can move. Specialists' ladders are often very short, and professionals are just as likely to get "stuck" in such jobs as people are in less prestigious clerical or factory positions.

Staff people, unlike those who are being groomed for important line positions, may be hired because of a special expertise or particular background. But management rarely pays any attention to developing them into more general organizational resources. Lacking growth prospects themselves and working alone or in very small teams, they are not in a position to develop others or pass on power to them. They miss out on an important way that power ran be accumulated.

Sometimes staff specialists, such as house counsel or organization development people, find their work being farmed out to consultants. Management considers them fine for the routine work, but the minute the activities involve risk or something problematic, they bring in outside experts. This treatment says something not only about their expertise but also about the status of their function. Since the company can always hire talent on a temporary basis, it is unclear that the management really needs to have or considers important its own staff for these functions.

And, because staff professionals are often seen as adjuncts to primary tasks, their effectiveness and therefore their contribution to the organization are often hard to measure. Thus visibility and recognition, as well as risk taking and relevance, may be denied to people in staff jobs.

Staff people tend to act out their powerlessness by becoming turf-minded. They create islands within the organization. They set themselves up as the only ones who can control professional standards and judge their own work. They create sometimes false distinctions between themselves as experts (no one else could possibly do what they do) and lay people, and this continues to keep them out of the mainstream.

One form such distinctions take is a combination of disdain when line managers attempt to act in areas the professionals think are their preserve and of subtle refusal to support the managers' efforts. Or staff groups battle with each other for control of new "problem areas," with the result that no one really handles the issue at all. To cope with their essential powerlessness, staff groups may try to elevate their own status and draw boundaries between themselves and others.

When staff jobs are treated as final resting places for people who have reached their level of competence in the organization—a good shelf on which to dump managers who are too old to go anywhere but too young to retire—then staff groups can also become pockets of conservatism, resistant to change. Their own exclusion from the risk-taking action may make

them resist *anyone's* innovative proposals. In the past, personnel departments, for example, have sometimes been the last in their organization to know about innovations in human resource development or to be interested in applying them.

Top Executives

Despite the great resources and responsibilities concentrated at the top of an organization, leaders can be powerless for reasons that are not very different from those that affect staff and supervisors: lack of supplies, information, and support.

We have faith in leaders because of their ability to make things happen in the larger world, to create possibilities for everyone else, and to attract resources to the organization. These are their supplies. But influence outward—the source of much credibility downward—can diminish as environments change, setting terms and conditions out of the control of the leaders. Regardless of top management's grand plans for the organization, the environment presses. At the very least, things going on outside the organization can deflect a leader's attention and drain energy. And, more detrimental, decisions made elsewhere can have severe consequences for the organization and affect top management's sense of power and thus its operating style inside.

In the go-go years of the mid-1960s, for example, nearly every corporation officer or university president could look—and therefore feel—successful. Visible success gave leaders a great deal of credibility inside the organization, which in turn gave them the power to put new things in motion.

In the past few years, the environment has been strikingly different and the capacity of many organization leaders to do anything about it has been severely limited. New "players" have flexed their power muscles: the Arab oil bloc, government regulators, and congressional investigating committees. And managing economic decline is quite different from managing growth. It is no accident that when top leaders personally feel out of control, the control function in corporations grows.

As powerlessness in lower levels of organizations can manifest itself in overly routinized jobs where performance measures are oriented to rules and absence of change, so it can an at upper levels as well. Routine work often drives out nonroutine work. Accomplishment becomes a question of nailing down details. Short-term results provide immediate gratifications and satisfy stockholders or other constituencies with limited interests.

It takes a powerful leader to be willing to risk short-term deprivations in order to bring about desired long-term outcomes. Much as first-line supervisors are tempted to focus on daily adherence to rules, leaders are tempted to focus on short-term fluctuations and lose sight of long-term objectives. The dynamics of such a situation are self-reinforcing The more the long-term goals go unattended, the more a leader feels powerless and the greater the scramble to prove that he or she is in control of daily events at least. The more he is involved in the organization as a short-term Mr. Fix-it, the more out of control of long-term objectives he is, and the more ultimately powerless he is likely to be.

Credibility for top executives often comes from doing the extraordinary: exercising discretion, creating, inventing, planning, and acting in nonroutine way. But since routine problems look easier and more manageable, require less change and consent on the part of anyone else, and lend themselves to instant solutions that can make any leader look good temporarily, leaders may avoid the risky by taking over what their subordinates should be doing. Ultimately, a leader may succeed in getting all the trivial problems dumped on his or her desk. This can establish expectations even for leaders attempting more challenging tasks. When Warren Bennis was president of the University of Cincinnati, a professor called him when the heat was down in a classroom. In writing about this incident, Bennis commented, "I suppose he expected me to grab a wrench and fix it." [6]

People at the top need to insulate themselves from the routine operations of the organization in order to develop and exercise power. But this very insulation can lead to another source of powerlessness—lack of information. In one multinational corporation, top executives who are sealed off in a large, distant office, flattered and virtually babied by aides, are frustrated by their distance from the real action.[7]

At the top, the concern for secrecy and privacy is mixed with real loneliness. In one bank, organization members were so accustomed to never seeing the top leaders that when a new senior vice president went to the branch offices to look around, they had suspicion, even fear, about his intentions.

Thus leaders who are cut out of an organization's information networks under- stand neither what is really going on at lower levels nor that their own isolation may be having negative effects. All too often top executives design "beneficial" new employee programs or declare a new humanitarian policy (e.g., "Participatory management is now our style") only to find the policy ignored or mistrusted because it is perceived as coming from uncaring bosses.

The information gap has more serious consequences when executives are so insulated from the rest of the organization or from other decision makers that, as Nixon so dramatically did, they fail to see their own impending downfall. Such insulation is partly a matter of organizational position and, in sonic cases, of executive style.

For example, leaders may create closed inner circles consisting of "doppelgängers," people just like themselves, who are their principal sources of or organizational information and tell them only what they want to know. The reasons for the distortions are varied: key aides want to relieve the leader of burdens, they think just like the leader, they want to protect their own positions of power, or the familiar "kill the messenger" syndrome makes

---

6 Warren Bennis. 1976. *The Unconscious Conspiracy: Why Leaders Can't Lead.* New. York: AMACOM.
7 See my chapter, "How the Top is Different," in *Life in Organizations.*

people close to top executives reluctant to be the bearers of bad news.

Finally, just as supervisors and lower-level managers need their supporters in order to be and feel powerful, so do top executives. But for them sponsorship may not be so much a matter of individual endorsement as an issue of support by larger sources of legitimacy in the society. For top executives the problem is not to fit in among peers; rather, the question is whether the public at large and other organization members perceive a common interest which they see the executives as promoting.

If, however, public sources of support are withdrawn and leaders are open to public attack or if inside constituencies fragment and employees see their interests better aligned with pressure groups than with organizational leadership, then powerlessness begins to set in.

When common purpose is lost, the system's own politics may reduce the capacity of those at the top to act. Just as managing decline seems to create a much more passive and reactive stance than managing growth, so does mediating among conflicting interests. When what is happening outside and inside their organizations is out of their control, many people at the top turn into decline managers and dispute mediators. Neither is a particularly empowering role.

Thus when top executives lose their own lines of supply, lines of information, and lines of support, they too suffer from a kind of powerlessness. The temptation for them then is to pull in every shred of power they can and to decrease the power available to other people to act. Innovation loses out in favor of control. Limits rather than targets are set. Financial goals are met by reducing "overhead" (people) rather than by giving people the tools and discretion to increase their own productive capacity. Dictatorial statements come down from the top, spreading the mentality of powerlessness farther until the whole organization becomes sluggish and people concentrate on protecting what they have rather than on producing what they can.

When everyone is playing "king of the mountain," guarding his or her turf jealously, then king of the mountain becomes the only game in town.

TO EXPAND POWER, SHARE IT

In no case am I saying that people in the three hierarchical levels described are always powerless, but they are susceptible to common conditions that can contribute to powerlessness. *Exhibit III* summarizes the most common symptoms of powerlessness for each level and some typical sources of that behavior.

I am also distinguishing the tremendous concentration of economic and political power in large corporations themselves from the powerlessness that can beset individuals even in the highest positions in such organizations. What grows with organizational position in hierarchical levels is not necessarily the power to accomplish—productive power—but the power to punish, to prevent, to sell off, to reduce, to fire, all without appropriate concern for consequences. It is that kind of power—oppressive power—that we often say corrupts.

The absence of ways to prevent individual and social harm causes the polity to feel it must surround people in power with constraints, regulations, and laws that limit the arbitrary use of their authority. But if oppressive power corrupts, then so does the absence of productive power. In large organizations, powerlessness can be a bigger problem than power.

David C. McClelland makes a similar distinction between oppressive and productive power:

"The negative . . . face of power is characterized by the dominance-submission mode: if I win, you lose. . . . It leads to simple and direct means of feeling powerful [such as being aggressive]. It does not often lead to effective social leadership for the reason that such a person tends to treat other people as pawns. People who feel they are pawns tend to be passive and useless to the leader who gets his satisfaction from dominating them. Slaves are the most inefficient form of labor ever devised by man. If a

EXHIBIT III COMMON SYMPTOMS AND SOURCES OF POWERLESSNESS FOR THREE KEY ORGANIZATIONAL POSITIONS

Position	Symptoms	Sources
First-line supervisors	Close, rules-minded supervision Tendency to do things oneself, blocking of subordinates' development and information Resistant, underproducing subordinates	Routine, rules-minded jobs with little control over lines of supply Limited lines of information Limited advancement or involvement prospects for oneself/subordinates
Staff professionals	Turf protection, information control Retreat into professionalism Conservative resistance to change	Routine tasks seen as peripheral to "real tasks" of line organization Blocked careers Easy replacement by outside experts
Top executives	Focus on internal cutting, short-term results, "punishing" Dictatorial top-down communications Retreat to comfort of like-minded lieutenants	Uncontrollable lines of supply because of environmental changes Limited or blocked lines of information about lower levels of organization Diminished lines of support because of challenges to legitimacy (e.g., from the public or special interest groups)

leader wants to have far-reaching influence, he must make his followers feel powerful and able to accomplish things on their own. . . . Even the most dictatorial leader does not succeed if he has not instilled in at least some of his followers a sense of power and the strength to pursue the goals he has set." [8]

Organizational power can grow, in part, by being shared. We do not yet know enough about new organizational forms to say whether productive power is infinitely expandable or where we reach the point of diminishing returns. But we do know that sharing power is different from giving or throwing it away. Delegation does not mean abdication.

Some basic lessons could be translated from the field of economics to the realm of organizations and management. Capital investment in plants and equipment is not the only key to productivity. The productive capacity of nations, like organizations, grows if the skill base is upgraded. People with the tools, information, and support

to make more informed decisions and act more quickly can often accomplish more. By empowering others, a leader does not decrease his power; instead he may increase it—especially if the whole organization performs better.

This analysis leads to some counterintuitive conclusions. In a certain tautological sense, the principal problem of the powerless is that they lack power. Powerless people are usually the last ones to whom anyone wants to entrust more power, for fear of its dissipation or abuse. But those people are precisely the ones who might benefit most from an injection of power and whose behavior is likely to change as new options open up to them.

Also, if the powerless bosses could be encouraged to share some of the power they do have, their power would grow. Yet, of course, only those leaders who feel secure about their own power outward—their lines of supply, information, and support—can see empowering subordinates as a gain rather than a loss. The two

8 David C. McClelland. 1975. *Power: The Inner Experience.* New York: Irvington Publishers, p. 263. Quoted by permission.

sides of power (getting it and giving it) are closely connected.

There are important lessons here for both subordinates and those who want to change organizations, whether executives or change agents. Instead of resisting or criticizing a powerless boss, which only increases the boss's feeling of powerlessness and need to control, subordinates instead might concentrate on helping the boss become more powerful. Managers might make pockets of ineffectiveness in the organization more productive not by training or replacing individuals but by structural solutions such as opening supply and support lines.

Similarly, organizational change agents who want a new program or policy to succeed should make sure that the change itself does not render any other level of the organization powerless. In making changes, it is wise to make sure that the key people in the level or two directly above and in neighboring functions are sufficiently involved, informed, and taken into account, so that the program can be used to build their own sense of power also. If such involvement is impossible, then it is better to move these people out of the territory altogether than to leave behind a group from whom some power has been removed and who might resist and undercut the program.

In, part, of course, spreading power means educating people to this new definition of it. But words alone will not make the difference; managers will need the real experience of a new way of managing.

Here is how the associate director of a large corporate professional department phrased the lessons that he learned in the transition to a team-oriented, participatory, power-sharing management process:

"Get in the habit of involving your own managers in decision making and approvals. But don't abdicate! Tell them what you want and where you're coming from. Don't go for a one-boss grass roots 'democracy.' Make the management hierarchy work for you in participation. . . ."

"Hang in there, baby, and don't give up. Try not to 'revert' just because everything seems to go sour on a particular day.

Open up—talk to people and tell them how you feel. They'll want to get you back on track and will do things to make that happen—because they don't really want to go back to the way it was. . . . Subordinates will push you to 'act more like a boss,' but their interest is usually more in seeing someone else brought to heel than getting bossed themselves."

Naturally, people need to have power before they can learn to share it. Exhorting managers to change their leadership styles is rarely useful by itself. In one large plant of a major electronics company, first-line production supervisors were the source of numerous complaints from managers who saw them as major roadblocks to overall plant productivity and as insufficiently skilled supervisors. So the plant personnel staff undertook two pilot programs to increase the supervisors' effectiveness. The first program was based on a traditional competency and training model aimed at teaching the specific skills of successful supervisors. The second program, in contrast, was designed to empower the supervisors by directly affecting their flexibility, access to resources, connections with higher-level officials, and control over working conditions.

After an initial gathering of data from supervisors and their subordinates, the personnel staff held meetings where all the supervisors were given tools for developing action plans for sharing the data with their people and collaborating on solutions to perceived problems. But then, in a departure from common practice in this organization, task forces of supervisors were formed to develop new systems for handling job and career issues common to them and their people. These task forces were given budgets, consultants, representation on a plantwide project steering committee alongside managers at much higher levels, and wide latitude in defining the nature and scope of the changes they wished to make. In short, lines of supply, information, and support were opened to them.

As the task forces progressed in their activities, it became clear to the plant management that the hoped-for changes

61
ACADEMIC

in supervisory effectiveness were taking place much more rapidly through these structural changes in power than through conventional management training; so the conventional training was dropped. Not only did the pilot groups design useful new procedures for the plant, astonishing senior management in several cases with their knowledge and capabilities, but also, significantly, they learned to manage their own people better.

Several groups decided to involve shop-floor workers in their task forces; they could now see from their own experience the benefits of involving subordinates in solving job-related problems. Other supervisors began to experiment with ways to implement "participatory management" by giving subordinates more control and influence without relinquishing their own authority.

Soon the "problem supervisors" in the "most troubled plant in the company" were getting the highest possible performance ratings and were considered models for direct production management. The sharing of organizational power from the top made possible the productive use of power below.

One might wonder why more organizations do not adopt such empowering strate-

gies. There are standard answers: that giving up control is threatening to people who have fought for every shred of it; that people do not want to share power with those they look down on; that managers fear losing their own place and special privileges in the system; that "predictability" often rates higher than "flexibility" as an organizational value; and so forth.

But I would also put skepticism about employee abilities high on the list. Many modern bureaucratic systems are designed to minimize dependence on individual intelligence by making routine as many decisions as possible. So it often comes as a genuine surprise to top executives that people doing the more routine jobs could, indeed, make sophisticated decisions or use resources entrusted to them in intelligent ways.

In the same electronics company just mentioned, at the end of a quarter the pilot supervisory task forces were asked to report results and plans to senior management in order to have their new budget requests approved. The task forces made sure they were well prepared, and the high-level executives were duly impressed. In fact, they were *so* impressed that they kept interrupting the presentations with compliments, remarking that the supervi-

---

THE REDISTRIBUTION OF POWER

The polarities that I have discussed are those of power and creativity. Workers who want to move in the direction of participative structures will need to confront the issues of power and control. The process of change needs to be mutually shared by all involved, or the outcome will not be a really participative model. The demand for a structural redistribution of power is not sufficient to address the problem of change toward a humanistic, as against a technological, workplace. If we are to change our institutional arrangements from hierarchy to participation, particularly in our workplaces, we will need to look to transformations in ourselves as well. As long as we are imbued with the legitimacy of hierarchical authority, with the sovereignty of the status quo, we will never be able to generate the new and original participative forms that we seek. This means if we are to be equal to the task of reorganizing our workplaces, we need to think about how we can reeducate ourselves and become aware of our own assumptions about the nature of our social life together. Unless the issue is approached in terms of these complexities, I fear that all the worker participation and quality-of-work-life efforts will fail.

Source: From Robert Schrank, *Ten Thousand Working Days*, Cambridge, MA. The MIT Press, copyright © 1978 by The Massachusetts Institute of Technology. Reprinted with permission of the author.

sors could easily be doing sophisticated personnel work.

At first the supervisors were flattered. Such praise from upper management could only be taken well. But when the first glow wore off, several of them became very angry. They saw the excessive praise as patronizing and insulting. "Didn't they think we could think? Didn't they imagine we were capable of doing this kind of work?" one asked. "They must have seen us as just a bunch of animals. No wonder they gave us such limited jobs."

As far as these supervisors were concerned, their abilities had always been there, in latent form perhaps, but still there. They as individuals had not changed—just their organizational power.

PART 4: THE CULTURAL LENS

The cultural perspective on organizations takes issue with a good deal of conventional managerial thought on how to run a business. It is a complex perspective that emphasizes the inherent limitations of managerial authority and influence and rejects claims that strictly structural, rational, or interest factors best explain human behavior. From the cultural perspective, people take action on the basis of their situations and, most critically, on the basis of what their situations mean to them. Assigning meaning is, of course, a mental and therefore cultural activity, since the terms, labels, concepts and languages we have available to us to make sense of the world come from the social and not physical or biological world. The cultural perspective on organizations focuses first and foremost on the meanings people assign to their respective work experiences. People are thus more than cogs in a machine or self-interested political actors. They are also meaning makers, symbol users, storytellers who are actively engaged in organizational life, and, through interaction with one another, they continually create, sustain, and modify organizational events, processes, and products.

THE CENTRALITY OF SYMBOLISM

The concern for meaning in organizations focuses attention on such matters as values, languages, beliefs, founding legends, social norms, myths, rituals, mental frameworks or maps, metaphors, superstitions, and ideologies shared by a few, many, or all organizational members. Meanings guide behavior. The key to the cultural lens is not meaning per se but the symbol—a more or less arbitrary but conventionalized sign that stands for something else. A symbol is a vehicle for meaning. A symbol such as a corporate logo, a marketing slogan or a time clock may stand for a particular company, a public claim of quality, or a managerial control device. A symbol may also invoke notions of personal identification and honor to some and alienation and distrust to others. The symbol is the unit on which the cultural perspective rests, and decoding what a given symbol or set of symbols means to a specific group of people is what cultural analysis is all about.

Symbols carry both denotative and connotative meanings. Denotative meanings refer to the direct, instrumental uses of a symbol, such as an annual report as standing for the performance of a given firm. Connotative meanings refer to the expressive, more general and broader uses of a symbol—the annual report as standing for a firm's meticulous record keeping and its concern for the financial well-being of its stockholders. To take a cultural perspective on organizations is to treat symbolism seriously and learn how meanings are created, communicated, contested and sometimes changed by individuals and groups interacting both inside and outside the organization.

There are at least four interconnected areas to be explored when the workings of a given symbol are at issue. First, symbols—both material (e.g., buildings, products, machines) and ideational (e.g., values, norms, ideologies)—are cultural objects or artifacts whose form, appearance, logic, and type can be categorized (although category systems differ and some differ spectacularly). Second, symbols are produced and used by specific people and groups within (and beyond) organizations for certain purposes and thus the intentions of the symbol creators and users must be understood. Third, symbols are always put forth within a particular historical period and social context, which severely shapes and limits the possible meanings a symbol may carry. Finally, symbols typically mean different things to different groups of people, so the receptive competencies and expectations of those who come into contact with given symbols must be examined. Since each domain plays off the others, the interpretation of symbols—even simple ones—can be complicated.

Take, for example, the Big Mac as a symbol of interest. Consider the audience first. To some McDonald's patrons, the Big Mac is the quintessential American meal, a popular and desirable hamburger served up in a timely and tasty fashion. To others, the Big Mac is food without nourishment, a travesty of a meal served up in a most sterile and unappetizing way. But social context is of considerable importance, too. A Big Mac in Paris is simply not the same cultural object as a Big Mac in Boston. Nor is the history of the Big Mac irrelevant to its current meaning, for this more or less edible symbol has been around for some time and comes packed with consumer myths, production rules, social standing, snappy advertising, and associated symbols all cross-referenced to an uncountable number of life's little pleasures—"you deserve a break today." Some of this is by design, some accidental, and some highly circumstantial and fleeting. A cultural perspective directs attention to how context helps shape meaning; how symbols are created, packaged, and, in a variety of ways, understood; how connotative meanings grow from denotative ones (and vice-versa); and, centrally, how various audiences receive and decode symbols and then act on the basis of the meaning the symbols hold for them.

The interpretation of symbols is at the heart of the cultural perspective on organizations, whether the organization of interest is a small and relatively autonomous work group within a corporation or a huge multinational firm operating in diverse social, linguistic, and political contexts around the world. Symbolism is also central to any concern for communication in organizations because communication itself rests on a coding framework that is shared by at least some, if not all, organizational members. Symbolism reaches into all aspects of organizational behavior because it is the process by which all organizational activities, ceremonies, objects, products, stories, services, roles, goals, strategies, and so on are made sensible and hence logical and perhaps desirable to given audiences both inside and outside recognized organizational boundaries. Leadership can therefore be seen as symbolic action, as can other organizational influence attempts such as selection, training, and reward practices. From a cultural perspective, symbolism is the elementary or fundamental process that makes organizational behavior both possible and meaningful.

A WORKING DEFINITION OF CULTURE

Culture is to social science as the concept of life is to biologists, or force is to physicists, or god is to theologians. It is without doubt one of the most complex and contentious concepts at play in everyday and scholarly life. In its broadest anthropological sense, culture refers to a way of life shared by members of a given society and includes knowledge, belief, art, morals, law, customs, and any other abilities and habits acquired by members of that society. Viewing culture generally as a "way of life" passed from one generation to the next avoids the ethnocentrism and elitism associated with definitions that flow from the arts and humanities (i.e., "culture as the best that has been thought, known, and produced"). But, alas, such a broad definition lacks precision and focus.

The current trend is toward trimming the culture concept down and making explicit distinctions about what exactly is to be the object of cultural analysis. Take the useful distinction between cultural *products* and cultural *processes* as an illustration.

© 65 ACADEMIC

Cultural products are tangible social constructions, symbolic goods, or commodities that are explicitly produced—business cards, TV sit-coms, or a raise and promotion handed out in a corporate setting. Cultural processes are more abstract, implicit features of social life itself that underlie and prefigure such products—the ways Japanese and Americans handle business cards, the ways gender roles are constructed and understood within a society, or the ways performance appraisals are conducted, interpreted, and used in different companies. The distinction between product and process helps not because one conception of culture is somehow deeper or more real than another, but because the distinction itself helps sort out the many ways to approach culture.

It is important also to distinguish culture from structure, although the two are intricately related. Structure represents those social and material conditions that characterize and more or less direct the communal, economic, and political life of a given society (organization or group). Culture represents the values, beliefs, assumptions, norms, and so forth that stand behind and legitimate—albeit, imperfectly—such patterns. The fit between structure and culture is, in theory, a close one. Harmony, not opposition, is ordinarily the rule, at least in settled times. Societies (organizations or groups) that persist are those in which structure and culture are more or less aligned and something of a balance is maintained over time through a process of mutual accommodation. As culture shifts, so too does structure. The reverse is often true as well, for structural change usually implies (however slow) cultural change. One without the other is incomplete and usually a recipe for trouble.

Does culture lead or follow structural shifts? This is a question on which a good deal of ink has been spent, but the best answer seems to be a timid one: "It all depends." In some cases, structural changes precede cultural ones, creating the proverbial cultural lag. Personal computers provide a convenient example. Rapid technological improvements and massive capital investments have made high power and, to varying degrees, user-friendly computers accessible to vast numbers of people in organizations. But the everyday use of such computers has typically lagged far behind the availability and presumed economic value of these computers because, for many workers and managers alike, they threaten to obliterate established and comfortable cultural meanings, routines, and relationships in the workplace.

On the other hand, examples of culture leading structure are not hard to find. Perhaps the most famous example is Max Weber's analysis of the role of the Protestant Ethic as the foundational "spirit" of capitalism. Consider too cultural innovations pushed by charismatic leaders (e.g., prophets, entrepreneurs, and artists) or groups of true believers (e.g., social movements such as psychoanalysis, business re-engineering, and abstract expressionism). These are cultural innovations that (arguably) emerge and prosper without any obvious structural push. Of course, the pull is not always apparent either. Take, for instance, the widespread belief in the United States that women deserve equal pay for equal work. Although the culture has seemingly shifted, the wage structure is slow to catch up, for women continue to earn far less than their male counterparts. The connection between structure and culture is not one to be reduced to formula.

Culture is indeed a multidimensional concept and is used in a number of ways. The term covers much ground and takes on many different shades of meaning. But, precisely because it is such an all-purpose label, any discussion of culture must be definitionally clear. As a working definition for the sections that follow, consider culture to refer to the symbolic or expressive side of human life—actions, objects, and ideas that stand for something else. Culture involves meaning, it is attached to both products and processes, and it both shapes and reflects social and material conditions. To take a cultural perspective is to consider the pattern of meanings that guide the thinking, feeling, and behavior of the members of some identified group.

ORGANIZATIONAL CULTURE

How does culture affect the way people deal with one another at work or the way organizations writ large manage to get things done in a world that is increasingly interconnected? People who work for profit-seeking firms ordinarily think of themselves as serious, practical types who are trying only to get the job done, beef up the bottom line, or, more often than not, fix this or that problem so the organization as they know it will function more smoothly. Yet, even as practical types, men and women of the corporation must inevitably deal with the symbolic and expressive side of organizational life. Making deals, establishing or meeting goals and standards, and getting products out the door are complicated everywhere and always by the fact that these activities must be accomplished collectively. Business organizations are social systems in which people must do things together, and therefore the management of meaning is as central to this collective task as is the management of money, production, and sales.

Organizations are positioned within and across cultures. But they also produce and house cultures of their own. Owners, workers, managers, customers, suppliers, legislators, and so on all participate in the creation and consumption of cultural products and processes that both help and hinder the workings of an organization. Moreover, culturally specific meanings are constructed within and across many levels of potential organizational analysis (e.g., individual and small work groups; larger clusters of employees such as departments, divisions, functional units, project teams, unions, and various other associational groups; or the organization as a whole as it is nested within sets of other organizations at home and abroad). Each conceptual level raises distinct questions of cultural relevance. Consider, first, the face-to-face or so-called micro levels of organizational culture.

Culture and Control

How does a boss get people to work hard, to coordinate what they do with others, to put themselves out for the good of the group, or, in general, to do things they might not otherwise do if left to themselves? These are quintessential top-down problems faced by any organization—from the mom-and-pop convenience store to the multinational corporation. Coercive theories hold that most people will respond accordingly only when management holds a (symbolic) whip over their backs. But the exercise of raw force is, of course, more than a little inefficient, not to mention inhumane and illegal. Running an organization as a forced labor camp or prison is simply not an option for most business organizations.

Exchange theories hold that most people work for tangible rewards such as money and the things that money will buy. Desire usually outstrips the means people possess, so they will work harder for more pay. But, however plausible these economic incentive or material reward theories appear on the surface (and there are many varieties), they do not seem to work very well. Numerous studies of work units have shown, for example, that groups develop their own standards for appropriate and reasonable behavior and, over time, manage to set and enforce their own internal rates of production—ones that are considered just and comfortable by most members of a work group. Regardless of what management might do to try to increase production, group members stick to their rates and ordinarily resist change. Those who overproduce are shunned as rate busters. Those who underproduce are usually aided by other members of the group to keep production rates at reasonable levels (from the perspective of the work group), even though it is often not in the self-interests of individual group members to do so.

From a cultural perspective, what is occurring in such situations is the creation of highly specific work norms and practices at odds with managerial ideals. Such cultural inventions may be highly unstable or relatively fixed. Members of a given work unit may share a good many norms and practices with others in the organization or very few. But subversion of managerial objectives by small groups of employees occurs virtually

ACADEMIC

everywhere in the world. If sheer economic incentives or the coercive imposition of rules and regulations cannot be used to predictably move people in managerially desired directions, what does work? Managers in organizations have tried a variety of methods and, at root, all involve attempts to forge a type of organizational culture (at various levels and segments of the organization) that values hard work and respect for managerially approved objectives.

One way to deal with motivational issues is to try to alter organizational structure in the hope that the culture will follow. Changing the organizational chart from one that is tall and thin to one that is short and fat is an illustration of trying to build a managerially approved work culture that conceivably might increase communications across the organization and reduce status differences among employees. Local rationalities might then give way to organizational rationality. It might also bring the average employee closer to the centers of control and decision making in the organization, thus, in the language of the day, "empowering" them. The greater influence employees have over what happens in the firm or, more critically, in their own segments of the firm, the more employees will presumably identify with and contribute to the goals of the organization.

Another way to tackle motivational problems is to try to create a preferred kind of organizational culture directly by recruitment, selection, training, placement, and career development. This tactic seems particularly favored by many Japanese companies noted—in Western eyes—for their intense, within-firm socialization practices. Such practices are not unknown elsewhere, of course. Disneyland is an example of an organization that relies heavily on selecting ride operators for the theme park who are by nature cheerful and extroverted and then training them to perform their "on-stage" work roles with as much enthusiasm as they can muster so that the explicit corporate goal of generating happy customers can be met. When service is the product that is, in fact, being sold, building a genuine concern among employees for the customer's comfort and pleasure is very likely to be at the core of an organization's culture.

A third way to motivate employees in managerially approved directions is to set up models of thought and action for employees to follow. Lobbies of corporate offices may be decorated with pictures of "employees of the month," or sales organizations may publicly honor those high performers who exceed their quotas for the year. If such ceremonial events and ritualized rewards are not overused, honored employees may become models of desirable behavior for other members of the organization to emulate. Other models for behavior come from the stories repeatedly told on formal occasions (e.g., orientation sessions or reward dinners) or conveyed, usually more effectively, by the informal exchanges that occur among employees in and out of the workplace about exemplary behavior—the telephone lineman who braved a flood to restore service to an isolated community or the computer technician who worked through the night to discover and rectify a bug in a system for an important client. Such tales, managers often assume, help create organizational loyalties and motivate employees in the proper direction.

It is the case, of course, that not all stories are exemplars in the eyes of management. Tales about insensitive bosses, managerial stupidities, and customers from hell are also common in organizations, and they too play a role in shaping organizational cultures. There are many stories circulating in organizations. Some filter up from the bottom, some ooze from the middle and some trickle down from the top. Censorship is virtually impossible in this domain and there is only so much the would-be culture shapers of the organization can do to encourage what from their (varied) perspective(s) are appropriate lines of behavior.

Perhaps most critical in terms of building organizational culture at the face-to-face level is what employees, particularly managers, pay attention to in their day-to-day dealings with others in the organization. Strict rules coupled with surveillance and harsh

discipline may create a culture of fear among employees. An obsessive focus on quarterly returns may produce a culture with little concern for long-run profitability. A sales- or marketing-driven company is distinguishable from one geared to manufacturing. What is consistently encouraged (or discouraged) as "the way we do things around here" can be expected to become the norm. Some actions may become so taken-for-granted as the "natural" way to go about one's work that members of the organization no longer consider alternative actions. It is in this sense that culture can become a blueprint for behavior.

All of the above means for motivating organizational members are usually in operation simultaneously. Many high-tech companies, for example, favor an organizational structure that is decentralized, project centered, rather vague, and continually in flux. Such a structure is more or less compatible with a faith in professional independence and self-management (i.e., the chain of command is not considered to be important), with norms encouraging information sharing and consensual decision making (i.e., positions and functions are not believed to be necessarily aligned with needed expertise), and with a strong emphasis on profit-oriented creativity and entrepreneurial advocacy (i.e., too much bureaucracy is thought to stifle innovation). Control in such contexts is primarily normative and put in place by selection, socialization, stories, rewards of many sorts, models of exemplary behavior, rituals of solidarity, and everyday routines. To a large degree, managers in such contexts tend to be quite aware of the norms they wish to foster in the organization and thus self-consciously promote an organizational culture to serve what they take to be the firm's best interest.

Subculture and Segmentation

Moving beyond managerially influenced work units and cultures, consider now the presence of subcultures within and across organizations. Subcultures are groups of people who share common identities based on characteristics that often transcend their organizationally prescribed roles and relationships. Subcultures emerge more or less autonomously in organizational settings and influence the behavior of organizational members in a variety of ways. As noted, groups of people who work together produce their own cultural understandings, but cultural production in organizations is not confined strictly to fixed work positions and units. The larger social context in which people live, beyond the organization, can be expected to play a role and that is where the idea of subculture is most relevant. For example, even though ethnicity is not supposed to count when performing a particular job, it certainly counts in the external world, and members of different groups bring different cultures with them to work. Employee subcultures may then form along ethnic lines because cultural similarities are strongly felt and people are drawn to others who share their meaning systems.

One of the most powerful divisions influencing subcultural development in organizations is between management and labor. Like soldiers and officers in the army, business firms usually draw clear lines between workers and managers. Symbolism reinforces the divide—the executive lounge, the worker's cafeteria; the manager's monthly salary, the worker's hourly wage; the suit and tie, the workshirt and hard hat; and so forth. The labor-management divide is also dependent on the larger social context within which a firm is located. In a relatively homogeneous society such as in Japan, company unions and worker-manager socializing may help bridge the gap. In Britain, class consciousness may sustain the gap that is bridged primarily by institutional means. In a heterogeneous society such as in the United States, where most working people—regardless of their positions—view themselves as middle class, ethnicity may help bridge the gap in some cases and amplify it in other cases.

Subcultural groupings may also emerge from professional interests and education backgrounds. Often these reflect functional boundaries in organizations—accountants working with other accountants, machinists with machinists, lawyers with lawyers, carpenters with carpenters, and so forth. Subcultural ties and interests are thus deepened. Some organizations may represent rather loose coalitions of occupational communities whose members share little sense of belonging to the same organizational culture but nonetheless display a fierce loyalty and commitment to their own vocational enclave. Managers too may develop their own sense of culture beyond that of their employing organization. Such a subculture is based on class interests, common work experiences, similar management training, and, importantly, opportunities for interaction and exchange across internal and external organizational boundaries.

In general, a focus on subcultures emphasizes a segmentalist or cleavage model of organizational culture. The classic fault line is between labor and management, but gender, religion, ethnicity, age, occupation, organizational function (e.g., engineering versus marketing), and so on can foster comparable subcultures of conflicting perspectives and actions. Subcultures, however, may be less stable and predictable these days than in times past. Fragmentation seems to be on the move. Many firms today are riddled with shifting and inconsistent goals and strategies. Work procedures and policies are often up for grabs. Many, if not most firms are in the midst of responding to rapid structural, technical, environmental, and even cultural changes taking place in the social and economic spheres that surround them. Internal shake-ups, downsizings, and reorganizations are common. Employees in many organizations move continually from one collaborative, perhaps cross-functional, work unit to another. Projects, not departments, define work identities. People come and go in organizations, making attachments to any given work unit uncertain at best. In such settings, there are no doubt numerous and competing versions of what constitutes appropriate lines of action.

Some observers of organizational life—particularly in the West—argue that the increased fragmentation at work and the understandably diminished loyalty employees offer to their respective organizations reflect a radical cultural shift in the meaning of the organization itself. The argument suggests that we have moved from viewing an organization as a bounded, corporate entity, a collective "body" akin to a small yet sacrosanct society, to viewing the organization as hollow fiction, having no natural or fixed boundaries and consisting of nothing more than a "bundle of contracts" among individuals, each subject to rapid revision or termination. Talk about an embracing or unifying organizational culture in this context becomes highly suspect.

Less speculatively, and perhaps more to the point, people within organizations—fragmented or not—are capable of taking multiple perspectives on what they do. A single employee is not so much an organization type (an IBM, Nat West, or Mitsubishi man or woman) or a member of a single identity group in the organization (a saleswoman, financial analyst, or salariman) as a repository for different cultural perspectives. Take, for instance, a married, politically liberal, African-American woman with three young children who is a practicing Catholic and is currently working in the Mergers and Acquisitions Division of a large, multinational bank. Different issues that arise in the workplace will tap different identities. A dispute over a particular acquisition may find her lined up with analysts in her work group arguing vigorously that the firm should move quickly on a specific matter, against higher-ups in the company who push for caution and further study. On a question of company-sponsored child care, she may line up with others who share her family interests and liberal leanings. Or, if the bank suddenly flounders in the marketplace, she may be willing to take a less desirable position in the firm or a salary freeze and try to ride out the economic downturn as a quiet and conforming company woman. The cultural perspective suggests that rather than try to find a single organizational culture (or most salient subculture) to explain individual or group behavior, the best approach may be to look for the kinds of issues that call up different meaning systems or cultures for the person or collectivity involved.

Organizations and Cultural Contexts

Thus far, we have considered culture as played out within membership boundaries of organizations. But what of the relationship between an organization as a whole and the cultural context in which it operates? Some organizational scholars and practitioners have suggested that large business firms in modern industrial states are inevitably converging toward a more or less singular and highly rationalized bureaucratic model that is based primarily on efficiency considerations. Yet, other scholars and practitioners are intrigued by the variations—modest to massive—in the bureaucratic model that occur in different societies. Coming to terms with such differences means examining closely the relationship between organizations and their surrounding cultures. And, at least at the moment, it appears that pronouncements about the inevitable convergence toward a singular organizational form—be it a bureaucratic "iron cage" or any other proposed form—are a trifle premature.

Indeed, since the early 1970s, interest in the cross-cultural context of organizational life has been intense. The increasing globalization of the economy is perhaps the central reason behind this interest. Numerous firms that had once operated within a restricted local or national context have now expanded internationally in terms of finance, production, and sales. For many organizations, rapid growth across country boundaries means that they must become knowledgeable about cultural differences from the slight to the spectacular if they are to be successful. Moreover, the global economy is itself being reshaped by the surprising—at least to many Westerners—success of Japan and (among others) the so-called Four Little Dragons of Taiwan, Singapore, South Korea, and Hong Kong. Little wonder that culture has become a hot topic.

Of considerable interest here are questions surrounding the applicability of certain organizational forms and work methods in different cultural contexts. For instance, do Japanese practices work in the United States as they do in Japan? The answer, it seems, is complicated: some do and some don't. Certain practices such as guarantees of job security, concentrated labor-management cooperation on quality issues, and a (relatively) high degree of worker participation in local decision making seem to increase worker commitment and satisfaction wherever they are applied. Japanese firms tend to engage in more of such practices, but the same relationships should, in principle, hold in virtually all organizations. Other practices, such as intense socialization to work, elaborate and frequent corporate rituals, and routine social contacts between workers and managers, do not appear to travel as well—at least not to the United States and Europe.

The key to research findings like these apparently reflects broad cultural differences across societies (although there are always numerous exceptions to the rule within societies). The Japanese, for example, seem to favor close relations with supervisors and working in groups, whereas Americans press for individual autonomy and independence. These differences influence work attitudes and behavior, yet they do not wash out the effects of other organizational matters such as participation in decision making. Other cross-cultural comparisons will no doubt produce different stories depending on the work practices and societies involved. In other words, one can expect particular cultural differences to influence employee behavior in a firm but such differences are subtle and specific, less sweeping and general than often portrayed by cultural chauvinists of various stripes.

A useful way to think of the links between cultural contexts and organizational forms or practices is to recognize the powerful role the former plays in legitimizing the latter. Enterprise groups in Taiwan and South Korea provide an example in this regard. Enterprise groups are sets of firms bound together by common ownership. They engage in mutual financial exchanges and, in general, are highly interdependent. Exact counterparts do not seem to exist in the United States. In South Korea, enterprise groups are quite centralized and vertically dominated by a founding company. In Taiwan, enterprise groups are typically smaller and less centralized, have more horizontal connections to noncompeting firms, and are backed by powerful single families. But what is most interesting is that in each country, enterprise groups take shape in a fashion that mirrors the way other institutions in that society—schools, families, government agencies, the legal system (itself a cultural product), and so on—are organized and managed. Thus, specific organizational forms and practices reflect unique cultural patterns—"patrimonialism" in South Korea and "familialism" in Taiwan.

In this regard, it is instructive to recall that the root word for organization is the Greek term *organon*, which means tool or instrument. English-speaking countries seem most comfortable with the highly utilitarian sense of the word—to serve collective purposes. But, as a cultural contrast, the two Chinese characters for organization mean "grouping" and "weaving." The Chinese notion of organization also implies collectivity and patterning, of course, but it lacks the direct sense of instrumentality that is present in the English term. It is not entirely fanciful, then, to wonder just what such a difference might mean to those who invent, manage, and work for organizations in such distinctive cultural contexts.

It is one thing, however, to recognize that cultural differences have an effect on how organizations are put together and operate in various parts of the world. It is another thing entirely to come to terms with such differences by having to actively coordinate business operations within a variety of cultures. This is as true for a company in Los Angeles attempting to manage a Mexican, Vietnamese, Arabic, and American workforce as it is for a multinational firm trying to manage its production flow in four different nations. In both cases, multiple cultural systems interact, and the pitfalls of dealing with such cultural differences are legendary. To take just one example, consider the comic but costly General Motors promotion of its economy-sized Chevy Nova in Mexico. Apparently, no one involved in the doomed project had recognized (or taken seriously) that *No va* translates to "it doesn't go" in Spanish.

The pitfalls of cultural differences go deeper, of course, than simply misunderstanding the relationship between words and referents. Since culture concerns shared meanings (however localized they may be), working with some success in different cultural contexts means understanding the assumptions and nuances on which different meaning systems rest. Knowing that *hai* is the Japanese equivalent of "yes" is a start, but it is of little value unless one is also familiar with the culturally-tuned uses to which *hai* can be put. To wit, it may mean that the speaker has heard what was said and is now thinking about a proper response, or it may mean simple agreement, or it may mean that the speaker has heard what was said but unfortunately cannot grant the request. Matters such as these are hardly to be taken lightly when doing business across cultural boundaries. General rules are difficult if not impossible to promote in this domain. There are obvious dangers in both underestimating and overestimating the degree of meaning overlap. Perhaps the best advice to be offered to both individuals and organizations when engaged in cross-cultural exchanges is to be alert at all times for colliding meaning constructions since incompatibilities at either the denotative or connotative level carry significant potential for disruption in both the short and the long run.

TOWARD A CULTURAL ANALYSIS OF ORGANIZATIONS

It seems that we now live in fast times. The world is increasingly interconnected, and new communication, production, and transportation technologies alter the way business is conducted at home and around the world. The international flows of people, information, goods, images, and entertainment suggest that all organizations must contend with cultural multiplicity and all the potential misunderstanding and hurt such multiplicity implies. Taking a cultural perspective on organizations helps predict areas of potential trouble and can help reduce such conflict, if possible, or at least

help manage it more effectively—and presumably more empathically—where and when it does arise. But, as this rather breathless class note suggests, the perspective is a broad one and covers much territory. Five features of the cultural lens on organizations stand out as particularly crucial, as summarized below.

1. Focusing on Symbols and Meaning

Taking a cultural perspective means trying to decipher what things mean to people in organizations. Strategies, goals, rewards, and so forth may well mean different things to different people, and discovering where and why such differences arise is a matter of considerable diagnostic and ultimately practical importance for the understanding and running of an organization.

2. Identifying Various Forms of Social Control

Organizations must develop the means to insure that employees act in ways that are more or less beneficial to the goals of the enterprise. Both individuals and groups may follow norms and standards that disrupt or otherwise interfere with managerially approved objectives. Identifying the ways in which satisfying and productive work cultures are created (or not created) in organizational settings is a crucial diagnostic task for managers and one that requires paying close attention to such matters as recruitment practices, socialization and training programs, reward policies (both formal and informal), corporate rituals, exemplary role models, and the stories that are frequently told in and around a company.

3. Recognizing Subcultures

Homogeneous organizational cultures are probably quite rare and, when present, are typically found in relatively small, closely held and highly focused firms. As organizations grow in size, subcultures emerge more or less naturally and on occasion challenge and resist managerial direction. Within a given organization, subcultures provide alternative identities for employees and allow meanings that flow from groups outside the firm's boundaries to find internal expression. Understanding subcultures is often a most practical matter, for it means being able to anticipate the different meanings that new policies or programs may take in various segments of the organization.

4. Diagnosing Organizational Culture

Despite considerable subcultural variation within large organizations, there is often a relatively small set of governing ideas or, in the words of organizational analyst Edgar Schein, "basic assumptions" that members draw on to guide thought and action within the firm. Such assumptions are built into the organization by way of mental maps or schemas members use as guides for "how we do things around here (and why we do them that way)." Such assumptions are essentially moral because violations are met with disapproval if not sanction from others. They are built up over lengthy periods of time, typically originate with the founder or founders of a firm, and establish the unique character and identity of the organization as experienced by the membership. Basic assumptions are not to be confused with organizational values or officially prescribed norms as put forth by senior managers. They may or may not reflect such publicly proclaimed virtues. Nor are assumptions to be confused with organizational artifacts—behavioral routines, structures, systems, symbols, rules, codes (official and unofficial) and so forth found within an organization. Values and artifacts are merely the "data" needed to identify the basic assumptions that make up a given organizational culture. Assumptions concern the way the many values and artifacts of an organization are patterned over time. Defining and diagnosing organizational culture is taken up in more detail in a subsequent reading in this module.

5. Looking Across Cultures

Strong cultural models claim that either national, local, or firm-specific culture (or some combination) fully explains organizational behavior. The counterpoint is taken up by either strong power or structural models that discount the potential lead culture takes in promoting or thwarting organizational change, or ignore the mediating and legitimating roles culture plays when stability is desired. The cultural perspective presented here rejects an either-or approach in favor of a more complicated mutual accommodation idea that stresses the cultural influences on power and structure and the need to always interpret both in light of a specific cultural lens. Such an approach is particularly helpful when an organization operates in more than one country and/or several cultural groups must work together in a single operational setting. Managers cannot control the cultural frameworks that make their operations (or products) meaningful in such settings, but they can appreciate their lack of control and inability to impose unitary meanings. Given such inherent limitations, managers can perhaps understand just when cultural incompatibilities will seriously challenge what they would like to do and thus act sensibly and respectfully in light of such understanding.

POSTSCRIPT: THE "NEW" ORGANIZATION

The "new" organization is essentially a structural description for the form business organizations seem to be moving toward at the moment in advanced capitalistic societies. Flattened hierarchies, greater workplace diversity, global scope, increased lateral communication and cooperation (within and across organizational boundaries), and increased flexibility are the definitional elements. Each element is not only complex but must be defined relative to historical trends and always local circumstances. As a result, each element is quite likely to take on a variety of meanings, each to a degree specific to a given cultural context. What diversity means in parts of Eastern Europe, where the terror of ethnic cleansing is an ugly fact of death, is most assuredly distinct from the meaning of diversity in the eastern United States.

Even within particular cultural contexts, the structural elements of an organization may be less critical than the relatively ignored cultural processes that must support the outcomes presumably fostered by "new" organizational forms. Flattened hierarchies are, for example, intended to encourage unbiased information flows up and down the chain of command. Yet unbiased information flows may have less to do with the number of people involved in a communication chain than with the degree to which people involved in such chains know and trust one another. Similarly, operating on a global scale for large consumer product firms that were founded in, say, small-market European nations may be far less troublesome than for similarly sized firms that originated in large home-market countries who, by contrast, have relatively little experience operating on foreign soil. In short, the different dimensions of the "new" organization are subject to numerous cultural qualifications.

Perhaps the most important and general qualification recalls our earlier discussion about cultural and structural lags. On the cultural side, it seems apparent that managers are becoming increasingly aware of the conserving nature of culture and the protective and defensive reactions of people when their customary and sometimes cherished ways are threatened. Culture probably buries more planned (and unplanned) changes than it ever advances. On the structural side, cautionary wisdom can be advanced as well. Redesigning an organization in the form of the "new" is perhaps not as great a challenge as that of bringing social practices in line with what the design is intended to accomplish. Culture may eventually follow design but it is unlikely to do so swiftly. The question a culturally sophisticated manager is likely to pose to advocates of the "new" organization is what guarantees are there that the structure the organization is currently pointed for is the one that will prove effective if and when the destination is reached. If all organizations assume the "new" organizational form, from where will competitive advantages derive? From this angle, we should keep in mind that organizations and the environments in which they sit are changing all the time. But what such changes mean are far from transparent. The "new" organization is therefore very likely to be a never-ending story.

RECOMMENDED FOR ADDITIONAL READING

Berger, Bennett M. 1995. *An Essay on Culture: Symbolic Structure and Socal Structure.* Berkeley: University of California Press. Cultural sociology at its best. A wide ranging treatment of the relations between social structure and culture with examples drawn from here, there, and everywhere.

Fantasia, Rick. 1988. *Cultures of Solidarity: Consciousness, Action and Contemporary American Workers.* Berkeley: University of California Press. A set of carefully written case studies concerning the emergence of strong worker movements in a variety of contemporary organizations.

Griswold, Wendy. 1992. *Cultures and Societies in a Changing World.* Thousand Oaks, CA: Pine Forge Press. A broad sociological treatment of culture in a rapidly changing world, including a number of illuminating examples of the interaction between structure and culture.

Hannerz, Ulf. 1992. *Cultural Complexity: Studies in the Social Organization of Meaning.* New York: Columbia University Press. A useful and quite accessible anthropological reworking of the culture concept in the context of a postmodern, information-intensive, and shrinking world.

Kunda, Gideon. 1992. *Engineering Culture: Control and Commitment in a High Tech Organization.* Philadelphia: Temple University Press. A lucid ethnography of an large computer company (circa 1987–88) focused on the skilled ways managers in the firm build and manipulate organizational culture.

Morrill, Calvin. 1995. *The Executive Way: Conflict Management in Corporations.* Chicago: University of Chicago Press. A candid and sophisticated look at the work lives of high level corporate executives focusing on the way corporate cultures shape informal social relations and networks in organizations.

Schein, Edgar H. 1992, 2nd ed. *Organizational Culture and Leadership.* San Francisco: Jossey-Bass. A careful, psychologically oriented look at the role founders and managers play in the creation, maintenance, and alteration of organizational culture.

Smith, Vicki. 1990. *Managing in the Corporate Interest: Control and Resistance in an American Bank.* Berkeley: University of California Press. A fascinating ethnographic study of a large but troubled California bank based on experiences of middle managers in the age of corporate restructuring.

Van Maanen, John. 1988. *Tales of the Field: On Writing Ethnography.* Chicago: University of Chicago Press. A general but quick glance at the ways culture has been diagnosed and captured in print by anthropologists and sociologists over the past 100 or so years.

ORGANIZATIONAL CULTURE

by Edgar H. Schein

Abstract: The concept of organizational culture has received increasing attention in recent years both from academics and practitioners. This article presents the author's view of how culture should be defined and analyzed if it is to be of use in the field of organizational psychology. Other concepts are reviewed, a brief history is provided, and case materials are presented to illustrate how to analyze culture and how to think about culture change.

To write a review article about the concept of organizational culture poses a dilemma because there is presently little agreement on what the concept does and should mean, how it should be observed and measured, how it relates to more traditional industrial and organizational psychology theories, and how it should be used in our efforts to help organizations. The popular use of the concept has further muddied the waters by hanging the label of "culture" on everything from common behavioral patterns to espoused new corporate values that senior management wishes to inculcate (e.g., Deal and Kennedy, 1982; Peters and Waterman, 1982).

Serious students of organizational culture point out that each culture researcher develops explicit or implicit paradigms that bias not only the definitions of key concepts but the whole approach to the study of the phenomenon (Barley, Meyer, and Gash, 1988; Martin and Meyerson, 1988; Ott, 1989; Smircich and Calas, 1987; Van Maanen, 1988). One probable reason for this diversity of approaches is that culture, like role, lies at the intersection of several social sciences and reflects some of the biases of each—specifically, those of anthropology, sociology, social psychology, and organizational behavior.

A complete review of the various paradigms and their implications is far beyond the scope of this article. Instead I will provide a brief historical overview leading to the major approaches currently in use and then describe in greater detail one paradigm, firmly anchored in social psychology and anthropology, that is somewhat integrative in that it allows one to position other paradigms in a common conceptual space.

This line of thinking will push us conceptually into territory left insufficiently explored by such concepts as "climate," "norm," and "attitude." Many of the research methods of industrial/organizational psychology have weaknesses when applied to the concept of culture. If we are to take culture seriously, we must first adopt a more clinical and ethnographic approach to identify clearly the kinds of dimensions and variables that can usefully lend themselves to more precise empirical measurement and hypothesis testing. Though there have been many efforts to be empirically precise about cultural phenomena, there is still insufficient linkage of theory with observed data. We are still operating in the context of discovery and are seeking hypotheses rather than testing specific theoretical formulations.

A HISTORICAL NOTE

Organizational culture as a concept has a fairly recent origin. Although the concepts of "group norms" and "climate" have been used by psychologists for a long time (e.g., Lewin, Lippitt, and White, 1939), the concept of "culture" has been explicitly used only in the last few decades. Katz and Kahn (1978), in their second edition of *The Social Psychology of Organizations,* referred to roles, norms, and values but presented neither climate nor culture as explicit concepts.

Organizational "climate," by virtue of being a more salient cultural phenomenon, lent itself to direct observation and measurement and thus has had a longer research tradition (Hellriegel and Slocum, 1974; A. P. Jones and James, 1979; Litwin and Stringer, 1968; Schneider, 1975; Schneider and Reichers, 1983; Tagiuri and Litwin, 1968). But climate is only a surface manifestation of culture, and thus research on climate has not enabled us to delve into the deeper causal aspects of how organizations function. We need explanations for variations in climate and norms, and it is this need that ultimately drives us to "deeper" concepts such as culture.

In the late 1940s social psychologists interested in Lewinian "action research" and leadership training freely used the concept of "cultural island" to indicate that the training setting was in some fundamental way different from the trainees' "back home" setting. We knew from the leadership training studies of the 1940s and 1950s that foremen who changed significantly during training would revert to their former attitudes once they were back at work in a different setting (Bradford, Gibb, and Benne, 1964; Fleishman, 1953, 1973; Lewin, 952; Schein and Bennis, 1965). But the concept of "group norms," heavily documented in the Hawthorne studies of the 1920s, seemed sufficient to explain this phenomenon (Homans, 1950; Roethlisberger and Dickson, 1939).

In the 1950s and 1960s, the field of organizational psychology began to differentiate itself from industrial psychology by focusing on units larger than individuals (Bass, 1965; Schein, 1965). With a growing emphasis on work groups and whole organizations came a greater need for concepts such as "system" that could describe

what could be thought of as a *pattern* of norms and attitudes that cut across a whole social unit. The researchers and clinicians at the Tavistock Institute developed the concept of "socio-technical systems" (Jaques, 1951; Rice, 1963; Trist, Higgin, Murray, and Pollock, 1963), and Likert (1961, 1967) developed his "Systems 1 through 4" to describe integrated sets of organizational norms and attitudes. Katz and Kahn (1966) built their entire analysis of organizations around systems theory and systems dynamics, thus laying the most important theoretical foundation for later culture studies.

The field of organizational psychology grew with the growth of business and management schools. As concerns with understanding organizations and interorganizational relationships grew, concepts from sociology and anthropology began to influence the field. Cross-cultural psychology had, of course, existed for a long time (Werner, 1940), but the application of the concept of culture to organizations *within* a given society came only recently as more investigators interested in organizational phenomena found themselves needing the concept to explain (a) variations in patterns of organizational behavior, and (b) levels of stability in group and organizational behavior that had not previously been highlighted (e.g., Ouchi, 1981).

What has really thrust the concept into the forefront is the recent emphasis on trying to explain why U.S. companies do not perform as well as some of their counterpart companies in other societies, notably Japan. In observing the differences, it has been noted that national culture is not a sufficient explanation (Ouchi, 1981; Pascale and Athos, 1981). One needs concepts that permit one to differentiate between organizations within a society, especially in relation to different levels of effectiveness, and the concept of organizational culture has served this purpose well (e.g., O'Toole, 1979; Pettigrew, 1979; Wilkins and Ouchi, 1983).

As more investigators and theoreticians have begun to examine organizational culture, the normative thrust has been balanced by more descriptive and clinical research (Barley, 1983; Frost, Moore, Louis, Lundberg, and Martin, 1985; Louis, 1981, 1983; Martin, 1982; Martin, Feldman, Hatch, and Sitkin, 1983; Martin and Powers, 1983; Martin and Siehl, 1983; Schein, 1985a; Van Maanen and Barley, 1984). We need to find out what is actually going on in organizations before we rush in to tell managers what to do about their culture.

I will summarize this quick historical overview by identifying several different research streams that today influence how we perceive the concept of organizational culture.

Survey Research

From this perspective, culture has been viewed as a property of groups that can be measured by questionnaires leading to Likert-type profiles (Hofstede, 1980; Hofstede and Bond, 1988; Kilmann, 1984; Likert, 1967). The problem with this approach is that it assumes knowledge of the relevant dimensions to be studied. Even if these are statistically derived from large samples of items, it is not clear whether the initial item set is broad enough or relevant enough to capture what may for any given organization be its critical cultural themes. Furthermore, it is not clear whether something as abstract as culture can be measured with survey instruments at all.

Analytical Descriptive

In this type of research, culture is viewed as a concept for which empirical measures must be developed, even if that means breaking down the concept into smaller units so that it can be analyzed and measured (e.g., Harris and Sutton, 1986; Martin and Siehl, 1983; Schall, 1983; Trice and Beyer, 1984; Wilkins, 1983). Thus, organizational stories, rituals and rites, symbolic manifestations, and other cultural elements come to be taken as valid surrogates for the cultural whole. The problem with this approach is that it fractionates a concept whose primary theoretical utility is in drawing attention to the holistic aspect of group and organizational phenomena.

Ethnographic

In this approach, concepts and methods developed in sociology and anthropology are applied to the study of organizations in order to illuminate descriptively, and thus provide a richer understanding of certain organizational phenomena that had previously not been documented fully enough (Barley, 1983; Van Maanen, 1988; Van Maanen and Barley, 1984). This approach helps to build better theory but is time consuming and expensive. A great many more cases are needed before generalizations can be made across various types of organizations.

Historical

Though historians have rarely applied the concept of culture in their work, it is clearly viewed as a legitimate aspect of an organization to be analyzed along with other factors (Chandler, 1977; Dyer, 1986; Pettigrew, 1979; Westney, 1987). The weaknesses of the historical method are similar to those pointed out for the ethnographic approach, but these are often offset by the insights that historical and longitudinal analyses can provide.

Clinical Descriptive

With the growth of organizational consulting has come the opportunity to observe in areas from which researchers have traditionally been barred, such as the higher levels of management where policies originate and where reward and control systems are formulated. When consultants observe organizational phenomena as a byproduct of their services for clients, we can think of this as "clinical" research even though the client is defining the domain of observation (Schein, 1987a). Such work is increasingly being done by consultants with groups and organizations, and it allows consultants to observe some of the systemic effects of interventions over time. This approach has been labeled "organization development" (Beckhard, 1969; Beckhard and Harris, 1977, 1987; Bennis, 1966, 1969; French and Bell, 1984; Schein, 1969) and has begun to be widely utilized in many kinds of organizations.

The essential characteristic of this method is that the data are gathered while the consultant is actively helping the client system work on problems defined by the client on the client's initiative. Whereas the researcher has to gain access, the consultant/clinician is provided access because it is in the client's best interest to open up categories of information that might ordinarily be concealed from the researcher (Schein, 1985a, 1987a).

The empirical knowledge gained from such observations provides a much needed balance to the data obtained by other methods because cultural origins and dynamics can sometimes be observed only in the power centers where elements of the culture are created and changed by founders, leaders, and powerful managers (Hirschhorn, 1987; Jaques, 1951; Kets de Vries and Miller, 1984, 1986; Schein, 1983). The problem with this method is that it does not provide the descriptive breadth of an ethnography nor the methodological rigor of quantitative hypothesis testing. However, at this stage of the evolution of the field, a combination of ethnographic and clinical research seems to be the most appropriate basis for trying to understand the concept of culture.

DEFINITION OF ORGANIZATIONAL CULTURE

The problem of defining organizational culture derives from the fact that the concept of organization is itself ambiguous. We cannot start with some "cultural phenomena" and then use their existence as evidence for the existence of a group. We must first specify that a given set of people has had enough stability and common history to have allowed a culture to form. This means that some organizations will have no overarching culture because they have no common history or have frequent turnover of members. Other organizations can be presumed to have "strong" cultures because of a long shared history or because they have shared important intense experiences (as in a combat unit). But the content and strength of a culture

have to be empirically determined. They cannot be presumed from observing surface cultural phenomena.

Culture is what a group learns over a period of time as that group solves its problems of survival in an external environment and its problems of internal integration. Such learning is simultaneously a behavioral, cognitive, and an emotional process. Extrapolating further from a functionalist anthropological view, the deepest level of culture will be the cognitive in that the perceptions, language, and thought processes that a group comes to share will be the ultimate causal determinant of feelings, attitudes, espoused values, and overt behavior.

From systems theory, Lewinian field theory, and cognitive theory comes one other theoretical premise—namely, that systems tend toward some kind of equilibrium, attempt to reduce dissonance, and thus bring basic categories or assumptions into alignment with each other (Durkin, 1981; Festinger, 1957; Hebb, 1954; Heider, 1958; Hirschhorn, 1987; Lewin, 1952). There is a conceptual problem, however, because systems contain subsystems, organizations contain groups and units within them, and it is not clear over what range the tendency toward equilibrium will exist in any given complex total system.

For our purposes it is enough to specify that any definable group with a shared history can have a culture and that within an organization there can therefore be many subcultures. If the organization as a whole has had shared experiences, there will also be a total organizational culture. Within any given unit, the tendency for integration and consistency will be assumed to be present, but it is perfectly possible for coexisting units of a larger system to have cultures that are independent and even in conflict with each other.

Culture can now be defined as (a) a pattern of basic assumptions, (b) invented, discovered, or developed by a given group, (c) as it learns to cope with its problems of external adaptation and internal integration, (d) that has worked well enough to be considered valid and, therefore (e) is to be

79

ACADEMIC

taught to new members as the (f) correct way to perceive, think, and feel in relation to those problems.

The strength and degree of internal consistency of a culture are, therefore, a function of the stability of the group, the length of time the group has existed, the intensity of the group's experiences of learning, the mechanisms by which the learning has taken place (i.e., positive reinforcement or avoidance conditioning), and the strength and clarity of the assumptions held by the founders and leaders of the group.

Once a group has learned to hold common assumptions, the resulting automatic patterns of perceiving, thinking, feeling, and behaving provide meaning, stability, and comfort; the anxiety that results from the inability to understand or predict events happening around the group is reduced by the shared learning. The strength and tenacity of culture derive, in part, from this anxiety-reduction function. One can think of some aspects of culture as being for the group what defense mechanisms are for the individual (Hirschhorn, 1987; Menzies, 1960; Schein, 1985b).

THE LEVELS OF CULTURE

In analyzing the culture of a particular group or organization it is desirable to distinguish three fundamental levels at which culture manifests itself: (a) observable artifacts, (b) values, and (c) basic underlying assumptions.

When one enters an organization one observes and feels its *artifacts*. This category includes everything from the physical layout, the dress code, the manner in which people address each other, the smell and feel of the place, its emotional intensity, and other phenomena, to the more permanent archival manifestations such as company records, products, statements of philosophy, and annual reports.

The problem with artifacts is that they are palpable but hard to decipher accurately. We know how we react to them, but that is not necessarily a reliable indicator of how members of the organization react. We can see and feel that one company is much more formal and bureaucratic than

another, but that does not tell us anything about why this is so or what meaning it has to the members.

For example, one of the flaws of studying organizational symbols, stories, myths, and other such artifacts is that we may make incorrect inferences from them if we do not know how they connect to underlying assumptions (Pondy, Boland, and Thomas, 1988; Pondy, Frost, Morgan, and Dandridge, 1983; Wilkins, 1983). Organizational stories are especially problematic in this regard because the "lesson" of the story is not clear if one does not understand the underlying assumptions behind it.

Through interviews, questionnaires, or survey instruments one can study a culture's espoused and documented *values*, norms, ideologies, chargers, and philosophies. This is comparable to the ethnographer's asking special "informants" why certain observed phenomena happen the way they do. Open-ended interviews can be very useful in getting at this level of how people feel and think, but questionnaires and survey instruments are generally less useful because they prejudge the dimensions to be studied. There is no way of knowing whether the dimensions one is asking about are relevant or salient in that culture until one has examined the deeper levels of the culture.

Through more intensive observation, through more focused questions, and through involving motivated members of the group in intensive self-analysis, one can seek out and decipher the taken-for-granted, underlying, and usually unconscious *assumptions* that determine perceptions, thought processes, feeling, and behavior. Once one understands some of these assumptions, it becomes much easier to decipher the meanings implicit in the various behavioral and artifactual phenomena one observes. Furthermore, once one understands the underlying taken-for-granted assumptions, one can better understand how cultures can seem to be ambiguous or even self-contradictory (Martin and Meyerson, 1988).

As two case examples I present later will show, it is quite possible for a group to hold conflicting values that manifest themselves in inconsistent behavior while having complete consensus on underlying assumptions. It is equally possible for a group to reach consensus on the level of values and behavior and yet develop serious conflict later because there was no consensus on critical underlying assumptions.

This latter phenomenon is frequently observed in mergers or acquisitions where initial synergy is gradually replaced by conflict, leading ultimately to divestitures. When one analyzes these examples historically one often finds that there was insufficient agreement on certain basic assumptions, or, in our terms, that the cultures were basically in conflict with each other.

Deeply held assumptions often start out historically as values but, as they stand the test of time, gradually come to be taken for granted and then take on the character of assumptions. They are no longer questioned and they become less and less open to discussion. Such avoidance behavior occurs particularly if the learning was based on traumatic experiences in the organization's history, which leads to the group counterpart of what would be repression in the individual. If one understands culture in this way, it becomes obvious why it is so difficult to change culture.

DECIPHERING THE "CONTENT" OF CULTURE

Culture is ubiquitous. It covers all areas of group life. A simplifying typology is always dangerous because one may not have the right variables in it, but if one distills from small group theory the dimensions that recur in group studies, one can identify a set of major external and internal tasks that all groups face and with which they must learn to cope (Ancona, 1988; Bales, 1950; Bales and Cohen, 1979; Benne and Sheats, 1948; Bennis and Shepard, 1956; Bion, 1959; Schein, 1988). The group's culture can then be seen as the learned response to each of these tasks (see Table 2.1).

Another approach to understanding the "content" of a culture is to draw on anthropological typologies of universal issues faced by all societies. Again there is a danger of overgeneralizing these dimensions (see Table 2.2), but the comparative studies of Kluckhohn and Strodtbeck (1961) are a reasonable start in this direction.

If one wants to decipher what is really going on in a particular organization, one has to start more inductively to find out which of these dimensions is the most pertinent on the basis of that organization's history. If one has access to the organization one will note its *artifacts* readily but

---

TABLE 2.1 THE EXTERNAL AND INTERNAL TASKS FACING ALL GROUPS

External Adaptation Tasks	Internal Integration Tasks
Developing consensus on:	Developing consensus on:
1. The core mission, functions, and primary tasks of the organization vis-à-vis its environments. 2. The specific goals to be pursued by the organization. 3. The basic means to be used in accomplishing the goals. 4. The criteria to be used for measuring results. 5. The remedial or repair strategies if goals are not achieved.	1. The common language and conceptual system to be used, including basic concepts of time and space. 2. The group boundaries and criteria for inclusion. 3. The criteria for the allocation of status, power, and authority. 4. The criteria for intimacy, friendship, and love in different work and family settings. 5. The criteria for the allocation of rewards and punishments. 6. Concepts for managing the unmanageable— ideology and religion.

Source: Tables adapted from Edgar H. Schein, *Organizational Culture and Leadership.* Copyright © 1985 by Jossey-Bass, Inc., Publishers. Used with permission.

TABLE 2.2 SOME UNDERLYING DIMENSIONS OF ORGANIZATIONAL CULTURE

Dimension	Questions to Be Answered
1. The organization's relationship to its environment	Does the organization perceive itself to be dominant, submissive, harmonizing, searching out a niche?
2. The nature of human activity	Is the "correct" way for humans to behave to be dominant/proactive, harmonizing, or passive/fatalistic?
3. The nature of reality and truth	How do we define what is true and what is not true; and how is truth ultimately determined both in the physical and social world? By pragmatic test, reliance on wisdom, or social consensus?
4. The nature of time	What is our basic orientation in terms of past, present, and future, and what kinds of time units are most relevant for the conduct of daily affairs?
5. The nature of human nature	Are humans basically good, neutral, or evil, and is human nature perfectible or fixed?
6. The nature of human relationships	What is the "correct" way for people to relate to each other, to distribute power and affection? Is life competitive or cooperative? Is the best way to organize society on the basis of individualism or groupism? Is the best authority system autocratic/paternalistic or collegial/participative?
7. Homogeneity vs. diversity	Is the group best off if it is highly diverse or if it is highly homogenous, and should individuals in a group be encouraged to innovate or conform?

Source: Tables adapted from Edgar H. Schein, *Organizational Culture and Leadership.* Copyright © 1985 by Jossey-Bass, Inc., Publishers. Used with permission.

will not really know what they mean. Of most value in this process will be noting *anomalies* and things that seem different, upsetting, or difficult to understand.

If one has access to members of the organization one can interview them about the issues in Table 2.1 and thereby get a good roadmap of what is going on. Such an interview will begin to reveal *espoused values,* and, as these surface, the investigator will begin to notice inconsistencies between what is claimed and what has been observed. These inconsistencies and the anomalies observed or felt now form the basis for the next layer of investigation.

Pushing past the layer of espoused values into underlying *assumptions* can be done by the ethnographer once trust has been established or by the clinician if the organizational client wishes to be helped. Working with motivated insiders is essential because only they can bring to the surface their own underlying assumptions and articulate how they basically perceive the world around them.

To summarize, if we combine insider knowledge with outsider questions, assumptions can be brought to the surface, but the process of inquiry has to be interactive, with the outsider continuing to probe until assumptions have really been teased out and have led to a feeling of greater understanding on the part of both the outsider and the insiders.

TWO CASE EXAMPLES

It is not possible to provide cultural descriptions in a short article, but some extracts from cases can be summarized to illustrate particularly the distinctions between artifacts, values, and assumptions. The "Action Company" is a rapidly growing high-technology manufacturing concern still managed by its founder roughly 30 years after its founding. Because of its low turnover and intense history, one would expect to find an overall organizational culture as well as functional and geographic subcultures.

A visitor to the company would note the open office landscape architecture; a high degree of informality; frenetic activity all around; a high degree of confrontation, conflict, and fighting in meetings; an obvious lack of status symbols such as parking spaces or executive dining rooms; and a sense of high energy and emotional involvement, of people staying late and expressing excitement about the importance of their work.

If one asks about these various behaviors, one is told that the company is in a rapidly growing high-technology field where hard work, innovation, and rapid solutions to things are important and where it is essential for everyone to contribute at their maximum capacity. New employees are carefully screened, and when an employee fails, he or she is simply assigned to another task, not fired or punished in any personal way.

If one discusses this further and pushes to the level of assumptions, one elicits a pattern or paradigm such as that shown in Figure 2.13. Because of the kind of technology the company manufactures, and because of the strongly held beliefs and values of its founder, the company operates on several critical and coordinated assumptions: (a) Individuals are assumed to be the source of all innovation and productivity. (b) It is assumed that truth can only be determined by pitting fully involved individuals against each other to debate ideas until only one idea survives, and it is further assumed

that ideas will not be implemented unless everyone involved in implementation has been convinced through the debate of the validity of the idea. (c) Paradoxically, it is also assumed that every individual must think for himself or herself and "do the right thing" even if that means disobeying one's boss or violating a policy. (d) What makes it possible for people to live in this high-conflict environment is the assumption that the company members are one big family who will take care of each other and protect each other even if some members make mistakes or have bad ideas.

Once one understands this paradigm, one can understand all of the different observed artifacts such as the ability of the organization to tolerate extremely high degrees of conflict without seeming to destroy or even demotivate its employees. The value of the cultural analysis is that it provides insight, understanding, and a roadmap for future action. For example, as the company grows, the decision process may prove to be too slow, the individual autonomy that members are expected to exercise may become destructive and have to be replaced by more disciplined behavior, and the notion of a family may break down because too many people no longer know each other personally. The cultural analysis thus permits one to focus on those areas in which the organization will experience stresses and strains as it continues to grow and in which cultural evolution and change will occur.

© 83
ACADEMIC

FIGURE 2.13 THE ACTION COMPANY PARADIGM

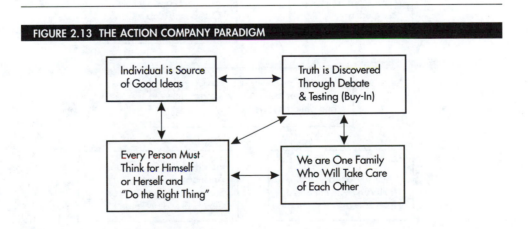

By way of contrast, in the "Multi Company," a 100-year-old multidivisional, multinational chemical firm, one finds at the artifact level a high degree of formality; an architecture that puts great emphasis on privacy; a proliferation of status symbols and deference rituals such as addressing people by their titles; a high degree of politeness in group meetings; an emphasis on carefully thinking things out and then implementing them firmly through the hierarchy; a formal code of dress; and an emphasis on working hours, punctuality, and so on. One also finds a total absence of cross-divisional or cross-functional meetings and an almost total lack of lateral communication. Memos left in one department by an outside consultant with instructions to be given to others are almost never delivered.

The paradigm that surfaces, if one works with insiders to try to decipher what is going on, can best be depicted by the assumptions shown in Figure 2.14. The company is science based and has always derived its success from its research and development activities. Whereas "truth" in the Action Company is derived through debate and conflict and employees down the line are expected to think for themselves, in the Multi Company truth is derived from senior, wiser heads and employees are expected to go along like good soldiers once a decision is reached.

The Multi Company also sees itself as a family, but its concept of a family is completely different. Whereas in the Action Company, the family is a kind of safety net and an assurance of membership, in the Multi Company, it is an authoritarian/paternalistic system of eliciting loyalty and compliance in exchange for economic security. The paradoxical absence of lateral communication is explained by the deeply held assumption that a job is a person's private turf and that the unsolicited providing of information to that person is an invasion of privacy and a potential threat to his or her

FIGURE 2.14 THE MULTI COMPANY PARADIGM

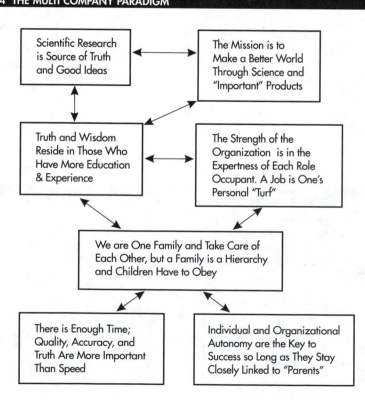

self-esteem. Multi Company managers are very much on top of their jobs and pride themselves on that fact. If they ask for information they get it, but it is rarely volunteered by peers.

This cultural analysis highlights what is for the Multi Company a potential problem. Its future success may depend much more on its ability to become effective in marketing and manufacturing, yet it still treats research and development as a sacred cow and assumes that new products will be the key to its future success. Increasingly the company finds itself in a world that requires rapid decision making, yet its systems and procedures are slow and cumbersome. To be more innovative in marketing it needs to share ideas more, yet it undermines lateral communication.

Both companies reflect the larger cultures within which they exist in that the Action Company is an American firm whereas the Multi Company is European, but each also is different from its competitors within the same country, thus highlighting the importance of understanding organizational culture.

CULTURAL DYNAMICS: HOW IS CULTURE CREATED?

Culture is learned; hence learning models should help us to understand culture creation. Unfortunately, there are not many good models of how groups learn—how norms, beliefs, and assumptions are created initially. Once these exist, we can see clearly how leaders and powerful members embed them in group activity, but the process of learning something that becomes shared is still only partially understood.

Norm Formation Around Critical Incidents

One line of analysis comes from the study of training groups (Bennis and Shepard, 1956; Bion, 1959; Schein, 1985a). One can see in such groups how norms and beliefs arise around the way members respond to critical incidents. Something emotionally charged or anxiety producing may happen, such as an attack by a member on the leader. Because everyone witnesses it and because tension is high when the attack occurs, the immediate next set of behaviors tend to create a norm.

Suppose, for example, that the leader counterattacks, that the group members "concur" with silence or approval, and that the offending member indicates with an apology that he or she accepts his or her "mistake." In those few moments a bit of culture has begun to be created—the norm that "we do not attack the leader in this group; authority is sacred." The norm may eventually become a belief and then an assumption if the same pattern recurs. If the leader and the group consistently respond differently to attacks, a different norm will arise. By reconstructing the history of critical incidents in the group and how members dealt with them, one can get a good indication of the important cultural elements in that group.

Identification with Leaders

A second mechanism of culture creation is the modeling by leader figures that permits group members to identify with them and internalize their values and assumptions. When groups or organizations first form, there are usually dominant figures or "founders" whose own beliefs, values, and assumptions provide a visible and articulated model for how the group should be structured and how it should function (Schein, 1983). As these beliefs are put into practice, some work out and some do not. The group then learns from its own experience what parts of the "founder's" belief system work for the group as a whole. The joint learning then gradually creates shared assumptions.

Founders and subsequent leaders continue to attempt to embed their own assumptions, but increasingly they find that other parts of the organization have their own experiences to draw on and, thus, cannot be changed. Increasingly the learning process is shared, and the resulting cultural assumptions reflect the total group's experience, not only the leader's initial assumptions. But leaders continue to try to embed their own views of how things should be, and, if they are powerful enough, they will continue to have a dominant effect on the emerging culture.

85

ACADEMIC

Primary embedding mechanisms are (a) what leaders pay attention to, measure, and control; (b) how leaders react to critical incidents and organization crises; (c) deliberate role modeling and coaching; (d) operational criteria for the allocation of rewards and status; and (e) operational criteria for recruitment, selection, promotion, retirement, and excommunication. *Secondary articulation and reinforcement mechanisms* are (a) the organization's design and structure; (b) organizational systems and procedures; (c) the design of physical space, facades, and buildings; (d) stories, legends, myths, and symbols; and (e) formal statements of organizational philosophy, creeds, and charters.

One can hypothesize that as cultures evolve and grow, two processes will occur simultaneously; a process of differentiation into various kinds of subcultures that will create diversity, and a process of integration, or a tendency for the various deeper elements of the culture to become congruent with each other because of the human need for consistency.

CULTURAL DYNAMICS: PRESERVATION THROUGH SOCIALIZATION

Culture perpetuates and reproduces itself through the socialization of new members entering the group. The socialization process really begins with recruitment and selection in that the organization is likely to look for new members who already have the "right" set of assumptions, beliefs, and values. If the organization can find such pre-socialized members, it needs to do less formal socialization. More typically, however, new members do not "know the ropes" well enough to be able to take and enact their organizational roles, and thus they need to be trained and "acculturated" (Feldman, 1988; Ritti and Funkhouser, 1987; Schein, 1968, 1978; Van Maanen, 1976, 1977).

The socialization process has been analyzed from a variety of perspectives and can best be conceptualized in terms of a set of dimensions that highlight variations in how different organizations approach the process (Van Maanen, 1978; Van

Maanen and Schein, 1979). Van Maanen identified seven dimensions along with socialization processes can vary:

1. *Group versus individual:* the degree to which the organization processes recruits in batches, as in boot camp, or individually, as in professional offices.
2. *Formal versus informal:* the degree to which the process is formalized, as in set training programs, or is handled informally through apprenticeships, individual coaching by the immediate superior, or the like.
3. *Self-destructive and reconstructing versus self-enhancing:* the degree to which the process destroys aspects of the self and replaces them as in boot camp, or enhances aspects of the self, as in professional development programs.
4. *Serial versus random:* the degree to which role models are provided, as in apprenticeship or mentoring programs, or are deliberately withheld, as in sink-or-swim kinds of initiations in which the recruit is expected to figure out his or her own solutions.
5. *Sequential versus disjunctive:* the degree to which the process consists of guiding the recruit through a series of discrete steps and roles versus being open-ended and never letting the recruit predict what organizational role will come next.
6. *Fixed versus variable:* the degree to which stages of the training process have fixed timetables for each stage, as in military academies, boot camps, or rotational training programs, or are open-ended, as in typical promotional systems where one is not advanced to the next stage until one is "ready."
7. *Tournament versus contest:* the degree to which each stage is an "elimination tournament" where one is out of the organization if one fails or a "contest" in which one builds up a track record and batting average.

Socialization Consequences

Though the goal of socialization is to perpetuate the culture, it is clear that the process does not have uniform effects. Individuals respond differently to the same treatment, and, even more important, different combinations of socialization tactics can be hypothesized to produce somewhat different outcomes for the organization (Van Maanen and Schein, 1979).

For example, from the point of view of the organization, one can specify three kinds of outcomes: (a) a *custodial orientation,* or total conformity to all norms and complete learning of all assumptions; (b) *creative individualism,* which implies that the trainee learns all of the central and pivotal assumptions of the culture but rejects all peripheral ones, thus permitting the individual to be creative both with respect to the organization's tasks and in how the organization performs them (role innovation); and (c) *rebellion,* or the total rejection of all assumptions. If the rebellious individual is constrained by external circumstances from leaving the organization, he or she will subvert, sabotage, and ultimately foment revolution.

We can hypothesize that the combination of socialization techniques most likely to produce a custodial orientation is (1) formal, (2) self-reconstructing, (3) serial, (4) sequential, (5) variable, and (6) tournament-like. Hence if one wants new members to be more creative in the use of their talents, one should use socialization techniques that are informal, self-enhancing, random, disjunctive, fixed in terms of timetables, and contest-like.

The individual versus group dimension can go in either direction in that group socialization methods can produce loyal custodially oriented cohorts or can produce disloyal rebels if countercultural norms are formed during the socialization process. Similarly, in the individual apprenticeship the direction of socialization will depend on the orientation of the mentor or coach.

Efforts to measure these socialization dimensions have been made, and some preliminary support for the above hypotheses has been forthcoming (Feldman, 1976, 1988; G. R. Jones, 1986). Insofar as cultural evolution is a function of innovative and creative efforts on the part of new members, this line of investigation is especially important.

CULTURAL DYNAMICS: NATURAL EVOLUTION

Every group and organization is an open system that exists in multiple environments. Changes in the environment will produce stresses and strains inside the group, forcing new learning and adaption. At the same time, new members coming into the group will bring in new beliefs and assumptions that will influence currently held assumptions. To some degree, then, there is constant pressure on any given culture to evolve and grow. But just as individuals do not easily give up the elements of their identity or their defense mechanisms, so groups do not easily give up some of their basic underlying assumptions merely because external events or new members disconfirm them.

An illustration of "forced" evolution can be seen in the case of the aerospace company that prided itself on its high level of trust in its employees, which was reflected in flexible working hours, systems of self-monitoring and self-control, and the absence of time clocks. When a number of other companies in the industry were discovered to have overcharged their government clients, the government legislated a system of controls for all of its contractors, forcing this company to install time clocks and other control mechanisms that undermined the climate of trust that had been built up over 30 years. It remains to be seen whether the company's basic assumption that people can be trusted will gradually change or whether the company will find a way to discount the effects of an artifact that is in fundamental conflict with one of its basic assumptions.

Differentiation

As organizations grow and evolve they divide the labor and form functional, geographical, and other kinds of units, each of which exists in its own specific environment. Thus organizations begin to build their own subcultures. A natural evolutionary mechanism, therefore, is the differentiation that inevitably occurs with age and size. Once a group has many subcultures, its total culture increasingly becomes a negotiated outcome of the inter-action of its subgroups. Organizations then evolve either by special efforts to impose their overall culture or by allowing dominant subcultures that may be better adapted to changing environmental cir-cumstances to become more influential.

CULTURAL DYNAMICS: GUIDED EVOLUTION AND MANAGED CHANGE

One of the major roles of the field of organization development has been to help organizations guide the direction of their evolution, that is, to enhance cul-tural elements that are viewed as critical to maintaining identity and to promote the "unlearning" of cultural elements that are viewed as increasingly dysfunctional (Argyris, Putnam, and Smith, 1985; Argyris and Schon, 1978; Beckhard and Harris, 1987; Hanna, 1988; Lippitt, 1982; Walton, 1987). This process in organiza-tions is analogous to the process of ther-apy in individuals, although the actual tactics are more complicated when multi-ple clients are involved and when some of the clients are groups and subsystems.

Leaders of organizations sometimes are able to overcome their own cultural biases and to perceive that elements of an orga-nization's culture are dysfunctional for survival and growth in a changing envi-ronment. They may feel either that they do not have the time to let evolution occur naturally or that evolution is heading the organization in the wrong direction. In such a situation one can observe leaders doing a number of different things, usu-ally in combination, to produce the desired cultural changes:

1. Leaders may unfreeze the present sys-tem by highlighting the threats to the organization if no change occurs, and, at the same time, encourage the organ-ization to believe that change is possi-ble and desirable.
2. They may articulate a new direction and a new set of assumptions, thus pro-viding a clear and new role model.
3. Key positions in the organization may be filled with new incumbents who hold the new assumptions because they

are either hybrids, mutants, or brought in from the outside.
4. Leaders systematically may reward the adoption of new directions and punish adherence to the old direction.
5. Organization members may be seduced or coerced into adopting new behaviors that are more consistent with new assumptions.
6. Visible scandals may be created to dis-credit sacred cows, to explode myths that preserve dysfunctional traditions, and destroy symbolically the artifacts associated with them.
7. Leaders may create new emotionally charged rituals and develop new sym-bols and artifacts around the new assumptions to be embraced, using the embedding mechanisms described earlier.

Such cultural change efforts are gener-ally more characteristic of "midlife" organ-izations that have become complacent and ill adapted to rapidly changing environ-mental conditions (Schein, 1985a). The fact that such organizations have strong subcultures aids the change process in that one can draw the new leaders from those subcultures that most represent the direction in which the organization needs to go.

In cases where organizations become extremely maladapted, one sees more severe change efforts. These may take the form of destroying the group that is the primary cultural carrier and reconstruct-ing it around new people, thereby allow-ing a new learning process to occur and a new culture to form. When organizations go bankrupt or are turned over to "turn-around managers," one often sees such extreme measures. What is important to note about such cases is that they invari-ably involve the replacement of large num-bers of people because the members who have grown up in the organization find it difficult to change their basic assumptions.

Mergers and Acquisitions

One of the most obvious forces toward culture change is the bringing together of two or more cultures. Unfortunately, in many mergers and acquisitions, the culture compatibility issue is not raised until after the deal has been consummated, which leads, in many cases, to cultural "indigestion" and the eventual divestiture of units that cannot become culturally integrated.

To avoid such problems, organizations must either engage in more premerger diagnosis to determine cultural compatibility or conduct training and integration workshops to help the meshing process. Such workshops have to take into account the deeper assumption layers of culture to avoid the trap of reaching consensus at the level of artifacts and values while remaining in conflict at the level of underlying assumptions.

THE ROLE OF THE ORGANIZATIONAL PSYCHOLOGIST

Culture will become an increasingly important concept for organizational psychology. Without such a concept we cannot really understand change or resistance to change. The more we get involved with helping organizations to design their fundamental strategies, particularly in the human resources area, the more important it will be to be able to help organizations decipher their own cultures.

All of the activities that revolve around recruitment, selection, training, socialization, the design of reward systems, the design and description of jobs, and broader issues of organization design require an understanding of how organizational culture influences present functioning. Many organizational change programs that failed probably did so because they ignored cultural forces in the organizations in which they were to be installed.

Inasmuch as culture is a dynamic process within organizations, it is probably studied best by action research methods, that is, methods that get "insiders" involved in the research and that work through attempts to "intervene" (Argyris et al., 1985; French and Bell, 1984; Lewin, 1952; Schein, 1987b). Until we have a better understanding of how culture works, it is probably best to work with qualitative research approaches that combine field work methods from ethnography with interview and observation methods from clinical and consulting work (Schein, 1987a).

I do not see a unique role for the traditional industrial/organizational psychologist, but I see great potential for the psychologist to work as a team member with colleagues who are more ethnographically oriented. The particular skill that will be needed on the part of the psychologist will be knowledge of organizations and of how to work with them, especially in a consulting relationship. Organizational culture is a complex phenomenon, and we should not rush to measure things until we understand better what we are measuring.

REFERENCES

Ancona, D. G. 1988. Groups in organizations; Extending laboratory models. In C. Hendrick ed., *Annual Review of Personality and Social Psychology: Group and Intergroup Processes*. Beverly Hills, CA: Sage.

Argyris, C., R. Putnam, and D. M. Smith. 1985. *Action Science*. San Francisco: Jossey-Bass.

Argyris, C., and D. A. Schon. 1978. *Organizational Learning: A Theory of Action Perspective*. Reading, MA: Addison-Wesley.

Bales, R. F. 1950. *Interaction Process Analysis*. Chicago: University of Chicago Press.

Bales, R. F., and S. P. Cohen. 1979. *SYMLOG: A System for the Multiple Level Observation of Groups*. New York: Free Press.

Barley, S. R. 1983. "Semiotics and the Study of Occupational and Organizational Cultures." *Administrative Science Quarterly*, 28, pp. 393–413.

Barley, S. R., C. W. Meyer, and D. C. Gash. 1988. "Culture of Cultures: Academics, Practitioners and the Pragmatics of Normative Control." *Administrative Science Quarterly*, 33, pp. 24–60.

Bass, B. M. 1965. *Organizational Psychology.* Boston: Allyn & Bacon.

Beckhard, R. 1969. *Organization Development: Strategies and Models.* Reading, MA: Addison-Wesley.

Beckhard, R., and R. T. Harris. 1977. *Organizational Transitions: Managing Complex Change.* Reading, MA: Addison-Wesley.

Beckhard, R., and R. T. Harris. 1987. *Organizational Transitions: Managing Complex Change.* 2nd ed. Reading, MA: Addison-Wesley.

Benne, K., and P. Sheats. 1948. "Functional Roles of Group Members." *Journal of Social Issues,* 2, pp. 42–47.

Bennis, W. G. 1966. *Changing Organizations.* New York: McGraw-Hill.

Bennis, W. G. 1969. *Organization Development: Its Nature, Origins, and Prospects.* Reading, MA: Addison-Wesley.

Bennis, W. G., and H. A. Shephard. 1956. "A Theory of Group Development." *Human Relations,* 9, pp. 415–437.

Bion, W. R. 1959. *Experiences in Groups.* London: Tavistock.

Bradford, L. P., J. R. Gibb, and K. D. Benne, eds. 1964. *T-Group Theory and Laboratory Method.* New York: Wiley.

Chandler, A. P. 1977. *The Visible Hand.* Cambridge, MA: Harvard University Press.

Deal, T. W., and A. A. Kennedy. 1982. *Corporate Cultures.* Reading, MA: Addison-Wesley.

Durkin, J. E., ed. 1981. *Living Groups: Group Psychotherapy and General Systems Theory.* New York: Brunner/Mazel.

Dyer, W. G., Jr. 1986. *Cultural Change in Family Firms.* San Francisco: Jossey-Bass.

Feldman, D. C. 1976. "A Contingency Theory of Socialization." *Administrative Science Quarterly,* 21, pp. 433–452.

Feldman, D. C. 1988. *Managing Careers in Organizations.* Glenview, IL: Scott, Foresman.

Festinger, L. 1957. *A Theory of Cognitive Dissonance.* New York: Harper and Row.

Fleishman, E. A. 1953. "Leadership Climate, Human Relations Training, and Supervisory Behavior." *Personnel Psychology,* 6, pp. 205–222.

Fleishman, E. A. 1973. "Twenty Years of Consideration and Structure." In E. A. Fleishman and J. G. Hunt, eds. *Current Developments in the Study of Leadership.* Carbondale: Southern Illinois University Press, pp. 1–39.

French, W. L., and C. H. Bell. 1984. *Organization Development.* 3rd ed. Englewood Cliffs, NJ: Prentice-Hall.

Frost, P. J., L. F. Moore, M. R. Louis, C. C. Lundberg, and J. Martin, eds. 1985. *Organizational Culture.* Beverly Hills, CA: Sage.

Hanna, D. P. 1988. *Designing Organizations for High Performance.* Reading, MA: Addison-Wesley.

Harris, S. G., and R. I. Sutton. 1986. "Functions of Parting Ceremonies in Dying Organizations." *Academy of Management Journal,* 29, pp. 5–30.

Hebb, D. 1954. "The Social Significance of Animal Studies." In G. Lindzey, ed. *Handbook of Social Psychology,* Vol. 2. Reading, MA: Addison-Wesley, pp. 532–561.

Heider, F. 1958. *The Psychology of Interpersonal Relations.* New York: Wiley.

Hellriegel, D., and J. W. Slocum, Jr. 1974. "Organizational Climate: Measures, Research, and Contingencies." *Academy of Management Journal,* 17, pp. 255–280.

Hirschhorn, L. 1987. *The Workplace Within.* Cambridge, MA: MIT Press.

Hofstede, G. 1980. *Culture's Consequences.* Beverly Hills, CA: Sage.

Hofstede, G., and M. H. Bond. 1988. "The Confucius Connection: From Cultural Roots to Economic Growth." *Organizational Dynamics,* 16(4), pp. 4–21.

Homans, G. 1950. *The Human Group.* New York: Harcourt, Brace, Jovanovich.

Jaques, E. 1951. *The Changing Culture of a Factory.* London: Tavistock.

Jones, A. P., and L. R. James. 1979. "Psychological Climate: Dimensions and Relationships of Individual and Aggregated Work Environment Perceptions." *Organizational Behavior and Human Performance,* 23, pp. 201–250.

Jones, G. R. 1986. "Socialization Tactics, Self-Efficacy, and Newcomers' Adjustments to Organizations." *Academy of Management Journal,* 29, pp. 262–279.

Katz, D., and R. L. Kahn. 1966. *The Social Psychology of Organizations.* New York: Wiley.

Katz, D., and R. L. Kahn. 1978. *The Social Psychology of Organizations.* 2nd ed. New York: Wiley.

Kets de Vries, M. F. R., and D. Miller. 1984. *The Neurotic Organization.* San Francisco: Jossey-Bass.

Kets de Vries, M. F. R., and D. Miller. 1986. "Personality, Culture, and Organization." *Academy of Management Review,* 11, pp. 266–279.

Kilmann, R. H. 1984. *Beyond the Quick Fix.* San Francisco: Jossey-Bass.

Kluckhohn, F. R., and F. L. Strodtbeck. 1961. *Variations in Value Orientations.* New York: Harper & Row.

Lewin, K. 1952. "Group Decision and Social Change." In G. E. Swanson, T. N. Newcomb, and E. L. Hartley, eds. *Readings in Social Psychology.* rev. ed. New York: Holt, Rinehard, and Winston, pp. 459–473.

Lewin, K., R. Lippitt, and R. K. White. 1939. "Patterns of Aggressive Behavior in Experimentally Created 'Social Climates.'" *Journal of Social Psychology,* 10, pp. 271–299.

Likert, R. 1961. *New Patterns of Management.* New York: McGraw-Hill.

Likert, R. 1967. *The Human Organization.* New York: McGraw-Hill.

Lippitt, G. 1982. *Organizational Renewal.* 2nd ed. Englewood Cliffs, NJ: Prentice-Hall.

Litwin, G. H., and R. A. Stringer. 1968. *Motivation and Organizational Climate.* Boston: Harvard Business School, Division of Research.

Louis, M. R. 1981. "A Cultural Perspective on Organizations." *Human Systems Management,* 2, pp. 246–258.

Louis, M. R. 1983. "Organizations as Culture Bearing Milieux." In L. R. Pondy, P. J. Frost, G. Morgan, and T. C. Dandridge, eds. *Organizational Symbolism.* Greenwich, CT: JAI Press, pp. 39–54.

Martin, J. 1982. "Stories and Scripts in Organizational Settings." In A. Hastorf and A. Isen, eds. *Cognitive Social Psychology.* New York: Elsevier.

Martin, J., M. S. Feldman, M. J. Hatch, and S. Sitkin. 1983. "The Uniqueness Paradox in Organizational Stories." *Administrative Science Quarterly,* 28, pp. 438–454.

Martin, J., and D. Meyerson. 1988. "Organizational Cultures and the Denial, Channeling, and Acknowledgement of Ambiguity." In L. R. Pondy, R. J. Boland, and H. Thomas, eds. *Managing Ambiguity and Change.* New York: Wiley.

Martin, J. and M. E. Powers. 1983. "Truth or Corporate Propaganda: The Value of a Good War Story." In L. R. Pondy, P. J. Frost, G. Morgan, and T. C. Dandridge, eds. *Organizational Symbolism.* Greenwich, CT: JAI Press, pp. 93–108.

Martin, J. and C. Siehl. 1983. "Organizational Culture and Counter-Culture: An Uneasy Symbiosis." *Organizational Dynamics,* 12, pp. 52–64.

Menzies, I. E. P. 1960. "A Case Study in the Functioning of Social Systems as a Defense Against Anxiety." *Human Relations,* 13, pp. 95–121.

O'Toole, J. J. 1979. "Corporate and Managerial Cultures." In C. L. Cooper, ed. *Behavioral Problems in Organizations.* Englewood Cliffs, NJ: Prentice-Hall.

Ott, J. S. 1989. *The Organizational Culture Perspective.* Chicago: Dorsey Press.

Ouchi, W. G. 1981. *Theory Z.* Reading, MA: Addison-Wesley.

Pascale, R. T., and A. G. Athos. 1981. *The Art of Japanese Management.* New York: Simon & Schuster.

Peters, T. J., and R. H. Waterman, Jr. 1982. *In Search of Excellence.* New York: Simon & Schuster.

Pettigrew, A. M. 1979. "On Studying Organizational Cultures." *Administrative Science Quarterly,* 24, pp. 570–581.

Pondy, L. R., R. J. Boland, and H. Thomas. 1988. *Managing Ambiguity and Change.* New York: Wiley.

Pondy, L. R., P. J. Frost, G. Morgan, and T. C. Dandridge, eds. 1983. *Organizational Symbolism.* Greenwich, CT: JAI Press.

Rice, A. K. 1963. *The Enterprise and Its Environment.* London: Tavistock.

Ritti, R. R., and G. R. Funkhouser. 1987. *The Ropes to Skip and the Ropes to Know.* 3rd. ed. New York: Wiley.

Roethlisberger, F. J., and W. J. Dickson. 1939. *Management and the Worker.* Cambridge, MA: Harvard University Press.

Schall, M. S. 1983. "A Communication-Rules Approach to Organizational Culture." *Administrative Science Quarterly,* 28, pp. 557–581.

Schein, E. H. 1965. *Organizational Psychology.* Englewood Cliffs, NJ: Prentice-Hall.

Schein, E. H. 1968. "Organizational Socialization and the Profession of Management." *Industrial Management Review* (MIT), 9 , pp. 1–15.

Schein, E. H. 1969. *Process Consultation.* Reading, MA: Addison-Wesley.

Schein, E. H. 1978. *Career Dynamics.* Reading, MA: Addison-Wesley.

Schein, E. H. 1983. The Role of the Founder in Creating Organizational Culture. *Organizational Dynamics,* 12, pp. 13–28.

Schein, E. H. 1985a. *Organizational Culture and Leadership.* San Francisco: Jossey-Bass.

Schein, E. H. 1985b. "Organizational Culture: Skill, Defense Mechanism or Addiction?" In F. R. Brush and J. B. Overmier, eds. *Affect, Conditioning, and Cognition.* Hillsdale, NJ: Erlbaum, pp. 315–323.

Schein, E. H. 1987a. *The Clinical Perspective in Fieldwork.* Beverly Hills, CA: Sage.

Schein, E. H. 1987b. *Process Consultation.* Vol. 2. Reading, MA: Addison-Wesley.

Schein, E. H. 1988. *Process Consultation.* rev. ed. Reading, MA: Addison-Wesley.

Schein, E. H., and W. G. Bennis. 1965. *Personal and Organizational Change Through Group Methods.* New York: Wiley.

Schneider, B. 1975. "Organizational Climate: An Essay." *Personnel Psychology,* 28, pp. 447–479.

Schneider, B., and A. E. Reichers. 1983. "On the Etiology of Climates." *Personnel Psychology,* 36, pp. 19–46.

Smircich, L., and M. B. Calas. 1987. "Organizational Culture: A Critical Assessment." In F. M. Jablin, L. L. Putnam, K. H. Roberts, and L. W. Porter, eds. *Handbook of Organizational Communication.* Beverly Hills, CA: Sage, pp. 228–263.

Tagiuri, R., and G. H. Litwin, eds. 1968. *Organizational Climate: Exploration of a Concept.* Boston: Harvard Business School, Division of Research.

Trice, H., and J. Beyer. 1984. "Studying Organizational Cultures Through Rites and Ceremonials." *Academy of Management Review,* 9, pp. 653–669.

Trist, E. L., G. W. Higgin, H. Murray, and A. B. Pollock. 1963. *Organizational Choice.* London: Tavistock.

Van Maanen, J. 1976. "Breaking In: Socialization to Work." In R. Dubin, ed. *Handbook of Work, Organization and Society.* Chicago: Randy McNally, pp. 67–130.

Van Maanen, J. 1977. "Experiencing Organizations." In J. Van Maanen, ed. *Organizational Careers: Some New Perspectives.* New York: Wiley, pp. 15–45.

Van Maanen, J. 1978. "People Processing: Strategies of Organizational Socialization." *Organizational Dynamics,* 7, pp. 18–36.

Van Maanen, J. 1988. *Tales of the Field.* Chicago: University of Chicago Press.

Van Maanen, J., and S. R. Barley. 1984. "Occupational Communities: Culture and Control in Organizations." In B. M. Staw and L. L. Cummings, eds. *Research in Organizational Behavior.* Vol. 6. Greenwich, CT: JAI Press.

Van Maanen, J., and E. H. Schein. 1979. "Toward a Theory of Organizational Socialization." In B. M. Staw and L. L. Cummings, eds. *Research in Organizational Behavior.* Vol 1. Greenwich, CT: JAI Press, pp. 204–264.

Walton, R. 1987. *Innovating to Compete.* San Francisco: Jossey-Bass.

Werner, H. 1940. *Comparative Psychology of Mental Development.* New York: Follett.

Westney, D. E. 1987. *Imitation and Innovation.* Cambridge, MA: Harvard University Press.

Wilkins, A. L. 1983. "Organizational Stories as Symbols Which Control the Organization." In L. R. Pondy, P. J. Frost, G. Morgan, and T. C. Dandridge, eds. *Organizational Symbolism.* Greenwich, CT: JAI Press, pp. 81–91.

Wilkins, A. L., and W. G. Ouchi. 1983. "Efficient Cultures: Exploring the Relationship Between Culture and Organizational Performance." *Administrative Science Quarterly,* 28, pp. 468–481.

PART 5: APPLYING THE THREE LENSES IN AN ORGANIZATIONAL SETTING

This part of the module asks you to apply all three lenses to the Dynacorp case on page 98. In order to do a thorough analysis and action plan, you should go back and review each of the three lenses: the strategic design, political, and cultural lenses. As you read through the case think about how each lens by itself and the three lenses together, help to analyze what is going on in the case and suggest actions for the major organizational members.

Before reading the case, read the example of applying the three lenses to the implementation of teamwork. This application should help you review the three lenses.

USING THE THREE LENSES: ANALYZING THE IMPLEMENTATION OF TEAMWORK

There is a "transformation" of work practices that has been widely heralded by researchers and practitioners. Transformed work practices include teamwork, job rotation, multiskilling, cross-training, and pay-for-skills, which together constitute a new way of dividing, monitoring, and rewarding labor. These practices are often considered fundamental to total quality management or re-engineering in organizations. They are also valued because they can enrich jobs, make work more interesting, and give employees more autonomy and decision-making authority. The gradual spread of transformed practices across organizations has been documented by researchers (e.g., Appelbaum and Batt, 1994; Bailey, 1992; Osterman, 1994).

Despite the enthusiasm for teamwork and some initial attempts at implementation, it has been slow to come to full fruition. There was optimism about teamwork in manufacturing settings, in particular because the logic of the work, the physical proximity of the workers, and the capacity to measure inputs and outputs seem to make teamwork more natural than in some other settings. The difficulties may be not just technical, but also social, involving the multiple meanings that actors have about the change process, from hopefulness to suspicion, from perceived gain to perceived loss (Donnellon, forthcoming; Scully and Preuss, 1994).

What are some questions that each of the three perspectives might pose to learn more about obstacles to the implementation of teamwork in a manufacturing setting? How do these analyses overlap? A few ideas are listed below. You should think of others.

THE STRATEGIC DESIGN LENS

- Focus on whether the right people are in the right roles. What are the formal procedures for selecting team members and team leaders? Is the matching process good? What skills are gained and lost with job rotation?
- Consider how the tasks are divided among the teams. Does each team follow a product from start to finish? Or does each team have a specialty that they apply across multiple products? Are the teams the right size and skill mix to accomplish their respective goals?
- Who is accountable for completion of tasks? Is the division of authority and accountability clear?

- What does the reward system look like? Have team-level rewards been created as incentives for team-level collaboration and the fulfillment of team-level goals (not just individual goals and rewards)?
- Does the choice of a team structure fit well with the conditions and demands of the organization's environment?

THE POLITICAL LENS

- Think about whether there are political squabbles between groups. Who stands to gain and who stands to lose in implementing team work? Will engineers feel that more highly skilled production workers are encroaching on their terrain? Do skilled production workers worry that they are being treated just like average team workers and losing some of the perks they worked for?
- Consider the history of labor and management relations. Has there been conflict or cooperation? Was labor consulted in the design of teamwork or presented with a finished blueprint?
- Are there processes in place for resolving disputes among team members? If team members are increasingly asked to monitor each other rather than be monitored by a supervisor, are they given training and resources to mediate disputes? What kinds of disputes arise most commonly? Can the system be revised to resolve some of these disputes more fundamentally?
- Who has the power to make critical decisions? Can team members stop the production line if they detect problems? Will they be allowed to defend their decisions?
- Is critical information shared with those who need it to make decisions? Or is information hoarded as a resource that confers power?
- If the teamwork system produces gains in productivity, who will share in those gains? Stockholders? Managers? The lowest level of employees?

THE CULTURAL LENS

- Focus on how change evolves within the social system, not how changes are decreed. Memos might tell employees about the benefits of teamwork, but what meaning does teamwork have to the members themselves? Do they share an identity as a team? They may be called the Blue Team, but is that a meaningful identity for members? Do they share any inside jokes, rituals, or understandings that ground their team identity?
- Consider how symbols that were meaningful before teamwork was adopted might linger. Were there old ways of operating (perhaps rituals like friendly competition for "employee of the week") that are inconsistent with the proposed new teamwork? Are there some roles that had significance, such as the "lead technician" or "foreman," that have been eliminated in the creation of self-managing teams but that are perceived as lost opportunities? What does the loss of formerly meaningful features of work mean for employees?
- Are there some unintended meanings? Does the elimination of individual recognition for team members unintentionally make people feel more depersonalized and powerless, instead of making the team feel more collaborative and less competitive, as intended?
- What are some new artifacts? Do the "measure and display" charts that adorn the walls have meaning to people? Do they look at them and use them? Or have they developed jokes about some of the new artifacts?

COMBINING LENSES

Clearly, any given practice might be interpreted from each of the perspectives. For example, the decision to elect team leaders (or not) is part of the strategic design, has political implications, and may be culturally symbolic. Sometimes the advice from the three perspectives may conflict. From a strategic design perspective, it might be important to appoint the best qualified person as team leader rather than a popular but inappropriate person who won the election. From a political perspective, it may be important to show that managerial decision-making power, particularly the power to appoint employees to roles, is being fully shared with teams. From a cultural perspective, what matters is understanding the meaning of the election to employees. Employees may care very much about this symbol of economic democracy; on the other hand, they may be frustrated if they think it represents a cavalier approach to setting up a team or represents management's opinion that one worker is pretty much like another worker. There can be ambiguity about employees' meanings.

To probe the implications of any of these perspectives, it helps to have data and observations from the organization. The next reading discusses conducting an organizational diagnosis.

REFERENCES

Appelbaum, Eileen, and Rose Batt. 1994. *Transforming Work Systems in the United States.* Ithaca, NY: ILR Press.

Bailey, Thomas. 1992. *Discretionary Effort and the Organization of Work: Employee Participation and Work Reform Since Hawthorne.* Unpublished manuscript.

Donnellon, Anne. Forthcoming. *The Paradox of Team Work.* Book manuscript.

Osterman, Paul. 1994. "How Common Is Workplace Transformation and How Can We Explain Who Adopts It?" *Industrial and Labor Relations Review.* 47, pp. 173–188.

Scully, Maureen, and Gil Preuss. 1994. "The Dual Character of Trust During Workplace Transformation." *Proceedings of the Forty-Sixth Annual Meeting of the Industrial Relations Research Association.* Madison, WI: Industrial Relations Research Association, pp. 12–22.

DYNACORP CASE

This activity is designed to generate data about how we look at and think about organizations. You are asked to take the role of a person conducting an analysis of a change initiative in a company.

BACKGROUND

The Dyna Corporation, known in the industry as Dynacorp, is a major global information systems and communications company. The company has been organized for the past two years into Product Focused Business Units. In addition, there are three major Customer Operations Groups that have responsibility for the "field" activities (including sales, customer support, and customer administration). The three Customer Operations Groups (one each for the United States, Europe, and Latin America–Asia/Pacific) are responsible for sales and support of the products of all Business Units (see organization chart on the following page).

Dynacorp's roots were in an office equipment company which was formed in the early 1960s. During the 1960s and early 1970s the company moved into high technology applications, which led to accelerated growth.

The 1980s was a very critical time for the company. It became known for its advanced and highly innovative, high-technology products. This came as a result of the very strong engineering and product development groups that were built in the corporation. Dynacorp developed a reputation for being first in the market with innovations and high-quality products. Customers would gladly wait months, and in the extreme, more than a year, to take delivery of products bearing the Dynacorp logo. The customers were typically sophisticated users who were willing to do some of their own applications work and figure out how to integrate Dynacorp's products with the rest of their operations. During this period, the company grew at a very fast rate and built a full set of national and international operations.

The last decade has been difficult for Dynacorp. Although the company has continued to grow, it has done so at a much slower rate and has experienced periods of decreased earnings. Outside observers have attributed this to a loss of technological "edge." Smaller companies and Japanese competitors have been developing systems with equally good technology. Perhaps more important, there seems to have been a shift in the market. Many customers are now demanding "complete solutions" to their business and information problems rather than simply wanting a good piece of hardware. Software, customer support, special applications, and high levels of professional services are all critical. More and more, they are looking for the vendor who can provide an integrated solution, rather than simply a set of good products. Sometimes this solution needs to be globally implemented, which involves different Customer Operations Groups. At the same time, quick delivery and high-quality installation are a requirement. Many were willing to forgo the latest or best technology in order to obtain these other benefits.

In recognition of these factors, Dynacorp's senior managers began to work on reorienting the company to accommodate the competitive realities of the present market.

Source: Dynacorp case study reprinted by permission of David Nadler, Chairman, Delta Consulting Group, Inc.

Two years ago, they reorganized the company-moving from a functional organization to a set of "end-to-end" Business Units, with responsibilities for development, manufacturing, and marketing. At the same time, senior management decided not to break up the field organizations to create multiple sales forces. Since products overlapped, the purchasers of different products were frequently the same people, and the cost inherent in replicating the field structure several times was prohibitive. (See Figures 2.15(a) and 2.15(b) for Dynacorp and Northeast Region organization charts.)

The U.S. Customer Operations Group has just reorganized into regions and a new sales team structure to improve customer responsiveness and better support the Business Units. The Northeast Region headquarters is located in the same building as the Corporate Center in New York City.

YOUR ROLE

You are a member of a student research team that is conducting an organizational analysis of a change initiative in a company of their choice for their class project in their organizational processes course. Carl Greystone, the current executive vice-president for U.S. Customer Operations in Dynacorp, is an alumnus of your school, and he has agreed to provide your team with access to his organization for your project. You have told him that you would like to talk with people at each level of his Customer Operations group, and he has agreed to select key informants for you to interview. Your team wants to develop an analysis of the current state of the change process in Dynacorp, to look at what is facilitating and what has been hindering the change, and to practice its analytical skills by identifying action steps that might make the change process work more effectively.

THE SITUATION

Greystone has suggested that your team focus on the recent change initiative in the U.S. Customer Operations Group that reorganized the sales force in each region into

FIGURE 2.15(a) DYNACORP ORGANIZATION CHART

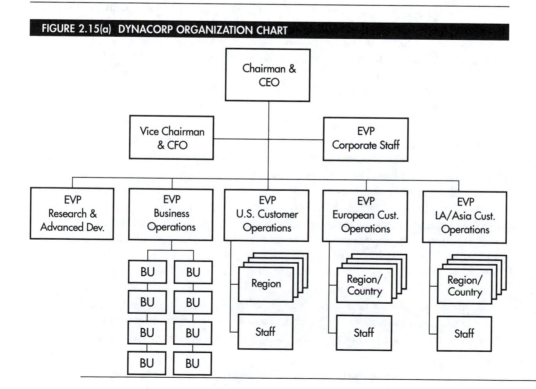

FIGURE 2.15(b) DYNACORP U.S. CUSTOMER OPERATIONS

Account Teams. Each Account Team focuses on customers in a particular market segment, defined by their industry (for example, financial services).

In your initial discussions, Greystone admitted that for the past year and a half, the U.S. Customer Operations Group has consistently been behind plan in both revenue and profit, and that the Business Unit presidents have expressed some frustration with the performance of his Group. But he is confident that the recent change initiative will turn the situation around. He tells you, "Recently, we've made a tremendous amount of progress. If you could have seen this place two years ago, when the company first created the Business Units, you would have been horrified. We've made the big changes—we've reorganized into Regions and Customer Teams, and we have our people thinking about the business in new terms. I think we're beginning to see the light at the end of the tunnel."

Greystone has agreed to talk with you himself, to provide an overview of the change initiative and its background, and then has arranged for you to meet with Ben Walker, the vice-president for the Northeast Region. Ben Walker in turn will give you his perspective on the change, and will then introduce you to one of his branch managers, to whom the Account Teams report. You also hope to sit in on an Account Team meeting, to get a clearer sense of how the teams are really working.

THE VISITS AND DISCUSSIONS

You spend the day at the Dynacorp building in New York, and are successful in getting time with people at each of the levels of the organization you wanted to talk with. (These visits are shown on the accompanying videotape. A transcript of the dialogue is included on the following pages.) It is now the following day, and your team is trying to make sense of what it has seen and heard.

DYNACORP VIDEO TRANSCRIPT NORTHEAST REGION

C. Greystone (EVP U.S. Customer Operations Group): . . . So the past few years have not been easy. As you know, both foreign and domestic competitors have been cutting into our market share, and our gross margins are way down. There was a time when our customers would pay high prices for our state-of-the-art technology. But now, they are looking for systems solutions, more customized software, and more value-added services. We've been forced to develop a strategy that more closely matches with the current marketplace. Customer Teams must now function as consultants by helping the customers identify their needs and providing high-quality products, integrated solutions, and customized services to fit those needs. To support the new plan, we've restructured the U.S. Customer Operations Group into regions and a new Customer Team Structure.

Now the way we go about that is to assign multifunction and multiproduct account teams to specific customers in specific industries instead of having them cover a mixed bag of clients in the sales territory. That way, our people are industry specialists, not just product knowledgeable. In addition, we are focusing the sales force on selling customized solutions based on integrating our products, rather than on selling fancy hardware. You see, we feel that by targeting our investments toward growth of sales in specific industries and developing solutions to fit their needs, we'll rebuild our market share and increase margins.

I'd like you to talk to Ben Walker, my most experienced general manager. I'll have my secretary call Ben and tell him that you'll be over to visit after we have lunch. Ben can fill you in on some of the details in his area.

B. Walker (VP Northeast Region): Carl outlined the new strategy. I think it's a move in the right direction. Finally we're able to compete with the foreign and domestic competitors that are grabbing the market with their emphasis on customized solutions. Our short-term problem is that we have a new structure, but the same people to fill the slots. There are too many people who know how to sell products but not solutions. Right now we have the customer teams functioning under new guidelines that force them to collect information on customer needs and develop solutions. But too many team members are still operating under the old attitude that the equipment sells itself and the customers will do the work of integrating our products into their operations. The notion of helping the customer from initial call through implementation and use of the system is still quite alien to many of our people. In fact, the skills and attitudes on many levels are mismatched with our current needs. Let me give you an example. Instead of focusing on the customer teams and making sure that they are being more responsive to customer needs, some branch managers seem to spend most of their time worrying about the new performance measurement system. You see, under our new structure, branch managers and product managers in the Business Units are compensated on performance against revenue and margin goals.

This causes considerable friction because no one in these jobs has the skills to be a team player. Honestly, I feel that with the help of early retirements, downsizing, and the addition of appropriately retrained staff, we'll be able to profit soon from our new approach. Unfortunately, we project that at least 25 percent of the current staff needs to be replaced.

Hopefully, that will show everyone that we are serious about change. It's not an easy answer, but I guess it's the price we pay for success in this new world. The market and the customers are very unforgiving.

One of the industry-focused branches is on the fourteenth floor. Let's go down and I'll introduce you to Martha Pauley, the branch manager. She's one of our best, and she'll show you the setup.

M. Pauley (Branch Manager): Excuse me for just one minute. I'll get back to you with that information later this afternoon.

Well, first let me tell you how we're set up. I work for Ben Walker and manage the six sales teams that handle financial institutions, insurance, and education in the Northeast Region. I share revenue goals for my teams with the product team's general managers in the Business Units. My teams are made up of account managers, product specialists, solution consultants, service technicians, customer administration specialists, and systems specialists. I haven't had a chance to develop a cohesive sales plan to show you. Everyone has been so busy trying to understand their new responsibilities while still keeping up with our customers that we have communicated only through e-mail messages. We haven't had time for the off site meeting that I had planned. Anyway, we're still getting modifications on the job guidelines from the staff group. You see, moving from a product salesperson to a provider of solutions is a big change. It involves knowledge of the industry and the company, the full line of products, our various software applications, and concepts of systems integration. Exactly who handles all the pieces of a sale like this is still unclear. In addition, different product team leaders in the Business Units are pushing different types of sales, depending on their particular product lines.

Another big issue is our ability to compete. Our prices are still higher than our competitors', and technical support services are way too slow. The new plant in Indonesia was supposed to help bring prices down, but they're having problems getting the factory up and running. Since I have no control over unit manufacturing costs or the availability of technical support resources, I can't help the team's effectiveness in these areas.

There is an account team meeting going on in the conference room down the hall. Under the current guidelines, they meet as a team once every two weeks. Let's take a quick look and then you can see some of how a team functions.

M. Pauley: Hi, how would you feel about having an overseas guest and me sit in on your meeting for a few minutes?

Sales Team Member 1 (Team Leader): It's fine with me. How do the rest of you feel? [Others nod and say fine.]

M. Pauley: Great, thanks a lot. What happened to the rest of your team? It looks like about half of you are missing.

Sales Team Member 1: It's true. Jim Davis, the head of the Large Systems Business Unit, is having a big meeting for the field to introduce his new product line. We thought we ought to send a few representatives.

M. Pauley: Oh yes, now I remember. Well, I guess we have to be responsive to them. I didn't mean to get you off track by my question.

Sales Team Member 1:   No problem, Martha. Listen, did the Boston bank make a decision yet on their system?

Sales Team Member 2:   Yes they did. We didn't get the contract. National Systems won the bid. They had lower prices and a much more comprehensive package. They were able to link their machines to the systems network. Plus, they have a partnership with a software applications company that is going to come in and customize their interface and provide training to all the employees. It's a pretty impressive package, even though their products are not as good as ours.

Sales Team Member 3:   This situation is getting very depressing. We have to figure out a new strategy pretty quickly or we are not going to make our quarterly targets.

Sales Team Member 1:   What about the Thompson account? Has that system been installed yet?

Sales Team Member 3:   We are still waiting on Technical Support. This is one of those custom systems that they just can't seem to gear up for. I'm meeting with our support person tomorrow and we are going to try to work out a schedule so that we don't miss the deadline.

102

CASE

Sales Team Member 2:   Well, anyway, Judy Brown called me yesterday. She's great. She's been a good customer of mine for years. I'm having lunch with her on Tuesday. She'll tell me exactly what she wants, and it looks like a whole set of standard off-the-shelf equipment for her bank. If only we had more customers like Judy.

M. Pauley: As I said earlier, there are some bugs to work out. But I think some training will do the trick once the guidelines are in place.

105

MASSACHUSETTS INSTITUTE OF TECHNOLOGY

ANCONA, KOCHAN, SCULLY,
VAN MAANEN, WESTNEY

Assisted by Amy Segal

MANAGING FOR THE FUTURE

Organizational Behavior & Processes

CONDUCTING TEAM
PROJECTS

module 2a

CONTENTS

MODULE 2A (M-2A)

CONDUCTING TEAM PROJECTS

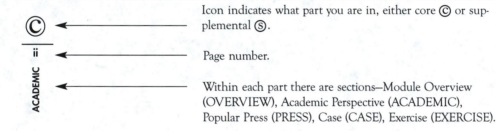

Icon indicates what part you are in, either core Ⓒ or supplemental Ⓢ.

Page number.

Within each part there are sections—Module Overview (OVERVIEW), Academic Perspective (ACADEMIC), Popular Press (PRESS), Case (CASE), Exercise (EXERCISE).

Dedicated to those who have inspired us to try to be better students and teachers. Special dedications to

Professor Jack Barbash
Professor Arthur H. Gladstein
Professor Marius B. Jansen
Professor Joanne Martin
Professor Edgar H. Schein

Acquisitions Editor: John R. Szilagyi
Developmental Editor: Jamie Gleich Bryant
Production Editor: Mardell Toomey
Production House: DPS Associates, Inc.
Cover Design: Michael H. Stratton
Marketing Manager: Rob Bloom

ISBN: 0-324-00725-6

1 2 3 4 5 6 7 D1 4 3 2 1 0 9 8

Printed in the United States of America

 South-Western College Publishing
an International Thomson Publishing company IⓉP®

Cincinnati • Albany • Boston • Detroit • Johannesburg • London • Madrid • Melbourne • Mexico City
New York • Pacific Grove • San Francisco • Scottsdale • Singapore • Tokyo • Toronto

CONDUCTING TEAM PROJECTS

This module provides a blueprint for a team project based on the course materials. The project or assignment that is detailed here is designed to provide you with an opportunity to apply the various theoretical frameworks covered in this course and utilize them in a "real life" organizational setting.

This assignment was developed with the belief that these analytical frameworks and tools are useful only if we employ them in examining real life organizations. They are of little use if they remain abstract concepts or models. You will see the real value of these frameworks and tools only if you practice using them. This assignment provides you with that practice. You will see firsthand how these analytic tools allow you to develop a more comprehensive view of organizations. With this more holistic view of organizations, you will be better equipped to take action and manage within an organization, especially during times of change.

This assignment was designed to develop your skills in analyzing organizations from a strategic, political and cultural perspective. Using these perspectives will better enable you to assess organizational situations and take informed actions based on those assessments. It will also cultivate your skills in looking at the organization of the future, one that is flatter, networked, diverse, flexible, and global.

Additionally, this assignment provides you with an opportunity to work in a team and enhance your team building skills. In working in a team, you will have to deal with such issues as setting team goals, dividing and coordinating the work among team members, managing the team's time, and collectively creating a deliverable product at the end of this course. Because this project is team based, you will have the chance to put the lessons about teamwork into practice. You will have to deal with such issues as conflict, influence, decision-making, and communication in the team. The synergies and multiple perspectives enabled by teamwork will enrich your analysis. However, serious problems that plague the team can hinder your efforts at completing a successful project. It is wise to be aware of the complexity of working in teams, so that you can try to avoid or deflect any potential problems. As you embark upon your project, you might wish to refer to the other modules on teamwork to assist you as you work together on this project. A well-functioning team will make the completion of this project that much easier.

The module consists of three parts:

- Project Instructions
- Organizational Analysis Guide
- Metaphor Readings

The **Project Instructions** are intended to provide you with a step-by-step procedure for conducting this organizational analysis. In the instructions, you will find a detailed discussion of the ethics involved in conducting this type of analysis. You will also find advice about how to manage the relationship with the organization in which you conduct your analysis, including suggestions on negotiating access with organizational members and then exiting the organization. The instructions contain detailed information about various methods for collecting data for your analysis, such as interviews, questionnaires, and archival data. These project instructions were meant to outline the various steps you will need to take in order to complete this assignment. You should read through all of the instructions so you can plan your time and develop intermediary goals.

The **Organizational Analysis Guide** will help focus and structure the content of your analysis. The Guide takes the frameworks and perspectives that you have studied and breaks them down into specific questions you should consider in conducting your analysis. These questions help examine the organizational initiative from the strategic, political and cultural perspectives. The Guide also provides questions that will assist you in looking at the organizational setting or context in which this initiative is taking place. These questions will focus your analysis around the features of the new organization. The questions in this Guide should assist in designing your data collection strategy and tools. The Guide also will help you focus the wealth of data you collect by posing questions to focus on likely outcomes of this initiative and develop concrete recommendations.

There is a supplemental reading on metaphors, **Using Metaphors to Understand Organizational Processes**. This reading introduces what metaphors are and the everyday ways in which they appear in organizational life. It discusses how managers use metaphors in ways that can either constrain or liberate their approach to organizational processes and change. For example, thinking about the organization as a machine suggests very different actions than thinking about the organization as an organism, or to use one of the metaphors of the new organizational form, a hologram. Testing and flexing our metaphors can be a helpful analytic tool, especially taking lessons from where metaphors break down. Some specific metaphors appear in the Appendices to this reading. You will see that one of the steps in the **Project Instructions** and one of the focal themes addressed in the **Organizational Analysis Guide** is selecting an overall metaphor to describe the organizational initiative you are studying. This reading on metaphors provides the background. A vivid metaphor can help you capture and convey your discoveries to your class.

Finally, there are two supplemental readings from the popular press that show you some metaphors used in the United States to describe how teams work and what the new organizational form will look like. Innovations like teamwork and virtual organizations come to life through metaphors, especially before new vocabulary emerges to catch up with these innovations.

In **"There's More Than One Kind of Team,"** from *The Wall Street Journal*, noted organizational advisor Peter Drucker illustrates three types of team coordination by analogy to differences among baseball, football, and tennis doubles teams. The article also shows the familiarity and popularity of sports metaphors in business writing.

In **"The Bureaucracy Busters,"** from *Fortune*, you will read about how team-based organizations were described in 1991 as they gained new popularity. The article colorfully evokes a range of new metaphors, from Busby Berkeley musicals to spiders to switchboard operators to the Möbius strip ("a geometric form that has no identifiable top or bottom, beginning or end"). These metaphors continue to be useful as organizations grapple with the real nature of teamwork, learning, and virtual organizing.

Notice how organizational processes and changes can be better communicated and understood when metaphors are used. These readings give you some ideas about how to convey the organizational processes that you are studying for your project.

M-2A

core

PROJECT INSTRUCTIONS

INTRODUCTION

These instructions outline the steps your team should undertake in conducting your organizational analysis. Before you embark on this project, read these instructions and think about the analytical process, so your team can plan accordingly. The Organizational Analysis Guide that follows will help you focus and structure the content of your analysis. You should use these sections in tandem to develop a timetable for your project and achieve your objectives in completing it.

PROJECT RESPONSIBILITIES

The steps for conducting your organizational analysis are outlined below:

1. Discuss and clarify your team's objectives.
2. Identify an organization in which you will conduct your analysis.
3. Negotiate entry and conditions.
4. Choose an initiative the organization is attempting to implement as the focus of your analysis.
5. Think about the central questions outlined in the Guide to help plan your data collection.
6. Collect a variety of appropriate data.
7. Analyze your data with respect to the questions outlined in the Guide.
8. Evaluate the initiative based on your analysis and make recommendations.
9. Select a metaphor to represent the organization's attempt to implement this initiative.
10. Deliver your presentation in class.
11. Prepare a final report, incorporating any feedback provided during the presentation in class.
12. Exit the organization and deliver whatever was agreed upon.

The team project map, shown in Figure 2A.1, outlines the steps you should take to complete the assignment. Each of these steps is described in greater detail later in this module.

This is a difficult, time-consuming, and exciting assignment. We hope you will find it as intriguing and worthwhile as many others have. Before we present the detailed instructions for the project, we want to emphasize some important ethical issues.

ETHICAL ISSUES

Confidentiality

You will be entering a real organization where many people have jobs, careers, products, and ideas at stake. You may be probing issues that are politically sensitive. It is essential that you honor any promises of **confidentiality** throughout your data collection and analysis. You may find that the most candid and provocative quotes are the ones that bring your final report alive. Remember that these are also comments that could

Team Project Map

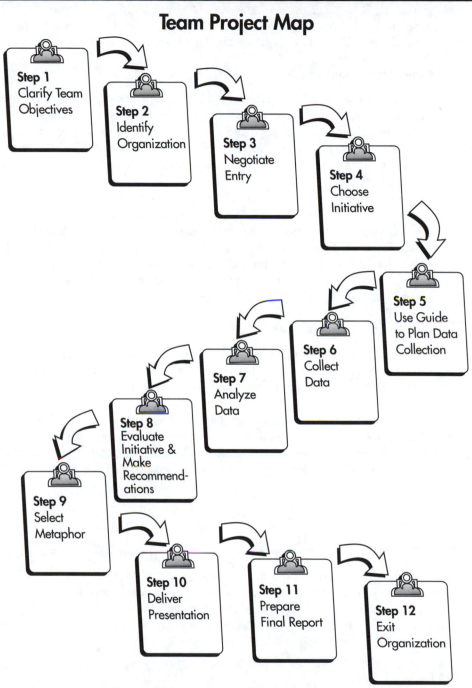

Step 1 Clarify Team Objectives

Step 2 Identify Organization

Step 3 Negotiate Entry

Step 4 Choose Initiative

Step 5 Use Guide to Plan Data Collection

Step 6 Collect Data

Step 7 Analyze Data

Step 8 Evaluate Initiative & Make Recommendations

Step 9 Select Metaphor

Step 10 Deliver Presentation

Step 11 Prepare Final Report

Step 12 Exit Organization

get people into trouble, affecting their relationships or reputations and potentially costing them promotions or even their jobs.

Anonymous Quotes

In most cases, you should expect that people with whom you talk will prefer that their names not be used. Even if people say something like, "Oh, it's okay. I'm not telling you anything I wouldn't say directly to my manager," be sensitive about how you quote them. You might still want to mask their names and identities in your report, in case their remarks to you were overly confident on their part. You might make up names for people you quote. Remember that other aspects of identity might give someone away. For example, if you say, "one of the young female engineers noted . . . ," you might get someone in trouble if there are only two young female engineers in the department.

Specific Information

In addition, quotations should be checked carefully to see whether they could violate confidentiality (for example, if someone says, "back when I was on the Megadeal project . . . ," the name "Megadeal" might give his or her identity away; you could change it to a fictitious name without losing the spirit of the quote). Often it is helpful to give aggregate data in order to protect identity ("many people interviewed cited their insecurities about layoffs").

At the end of the project, an enthusiastic manager who helped you get your organizational analysis off the ground may ask, "So, what did my marketing people say about the proposed initiative?" Even though you may be eager to provide feedback to this person, who has been so helpful, be careful not to let an offhand remark slip ("Well, the junior people hate it," or "Everyone but Mary seems to be on board"). You will have more time to be editorially thoughtful and discreet in your final report, so try to urge this manager to wait until you have worked out your final conclusions more thoroughly.

Confidential Corporate Data

In addition to data that are sensitive for particular individuals, you may be given some confidential data that are sensitive for the corporation. If the corporation shares information with you, but tells you not to duplicate or share it, please honor this agreement. The information can help form your overall impressions, if the company members agree to your making general statements ("Market share has been growing steadily"), without your having to disclose the specific numbers or details. If you have any uncertainty about which corporate data were meant to be confidential, check with your company contact person. (In public companies, certain data is already public; it is always advisable to double-check.)

Final Note

We trust that none of you will deliberately violate the standards of confidentiality. We would also like to caution you against doing so accidentally. All it takes is a notebook or tape cassette carelessly left behind in a meeting room (or left at the house of a friend who happens to work for the competitor) to get a lot of people into serious trouble. Please be very mindful of how you transport and store data (notes, quotes, etc.), as well as where you discuss the data you are collecting as a group. Remember, you never know who may be sitting next to you at a bar or restaurant.

TEAM PROJECT MAP

The instructions given below are designed to help you formulate a plan to approach and conduct all phases of the project.

Step #1: Discuss and Clarify Your Team's Objectives

Discuss team members' objectives. Some team members who have done this project in the past have been surprised to learn how varied their teammates' ideas about the project can be (e.g., "I want to write the best possible report"; "I want to learn about an organization in-depth to think about where I want to work"; "I just want to get a C in this class"; "I want to learn about diagnosing the politics and culture").

Think about how the steps in the project map onto a timetable. Discuss team members' strengths and preferences to decide on different roles and ways of sharing the workload.

Step #2: Identify an Organization

It is imperative that you identify an organization immediately. You might start by identifying several potential organizations, including one or more where team members have worked. The following are criteria you should consider in selecting the organization:

- The organization can be in the private, public, or nonprofit sector.
- It should be geographically accessible because you will need to visit it.
- It should be of moderate size (for example, not General Motors or even one plant of GM, but perhaps the shipping department for one product at one plant of GM).
- It should be of interest to team members.

Take the following steps in identifying an organization:

- Choose one individual who will serve as a liaison to each organization and ultimately to the final organization selected. This will facilitate communication with the organization and minimize confusion.
- Arrange initial and subsequent meetings with organizational members through the liaison.
- Emphasize what the organization has to gain by participating. You will be helping it examine a complex issue or an initiative at a time when organizations are changing rapidly.
- If you begin discussions with an organization and do not select it, be sure to let the company contact person know.

You should be aware that other teams in your section or other sections may be pursuing the same organizations. If there is interest, a space can be designated for teams to indicate which organizations they are contacting, (such as an easel in an accessible place). When you have successfully identified an organization, you should complete the form provided at the end of this module, indicating what organization your team has chosen to analyze and then submit it to your instructor.

Step #3: Negotiate Entry and Conditions

Once you have identified the participating organization, you should negotiate the conditions of your relationship with the organization. You should draft some form of informal contract—not a legal document, but a definition of what is expected of the team and of the organization. Some elements of the "contract" might include:

- The access the organization will provide to certain people, data, or events
- The team's assurance of confidentiality
- The final product the team will deliver to members of the organization

The team might agree to provide a brief written report, to share the final report written for the class, or to do an oral presentation for certain key people in the organization. Your team should think about whether you will want to share the final class report (some organizations may insist and others may not care). In previous years, some teams have been more critical in their final paper than they are comfortable sharing with the organization, so they write a more neutral account for the organization. On the other hand, some organizations welcome the opportunity for free evaluation and ideas from bright students and they ask the students to be critical.

It is important to reach agreement on the following expectations:

Sample Contract

Goals of the project . . .
- *To assess the work/family policies*
-
-

The team will provide . . .
- *Confidentiality*
- *Final presentation of findings to the human resources department*
-

The organization will provide . . .
- *Access to employees who have used the policies*
-
-

If this changes, we will renegotiate by . . .

- Student and organizational goals for the project
- Student and organizational resources and abilities applicable to the challenges the organization is facing in adopting this initiative
- A broad method of approach to the study
- Expected benefits to students and organization
- Issues of confidentiality. It is helpful to include the organization's real name in the final class report, but you should disguise the names and identities of organizational members with whom you speak.

In short, be clear about what you are going to do for the organization and what you will not do (e.g., you are not employees to work on a particular task nor consultants to solve a particular problem). Be careful not to encourage the organization to participate in your project by over-committing to play any of the roles familiar to consultants, such as expert, pair-of-hands, or collaborator, lest the organization develop mixed motives for participating.

 If the organization experiences significant change, such as new managers, downsizing, or a major strategy shift, you may need to renegotiate during the project.

Step #4: Choose an Initiative Around which to Focus the Analysis

 After communicating with your contact or contacts in the organization, you should jointly determine what organizational initiative you will study. Speaking with individuals within the organization will help you decide what initiative would be most useful to analyze within the organization. It may be an initiative that the organization has had difficulty implementing; it may be an initiative that is in the process of being developed and requires an assessment of its feasibility; or it may be an initiative that has been successfully implemented at one site or department and is being considered for replication in other sites or locations. Refer to the Guide for specific examples. You will be able to select an initiative only after talking to individuals within the organization and learning what major initiatives and changes are most significant within the company.

 Negotiate as a team around which initiative you wish to study. Everybody on the team should participate in order to come to an agreement.

Step # 5: Consider Focal Questions for the Project to Guide Data Collection

 When diagnosing an organizational initiative, you become an analyst examining the patterns of behavior within a particular organization. You want to be able to describe how the organizational initiative is being implemented and determine what works well and where there are problems. In conducting your analysis, use the concepts and refer to the readings from the course. Specifically, refer to the Organizational Analysis Guide for the questions you need to consider. With these in mind, you will be able to develop a data collection plan. New data may prompt new questions, themes, and approaches.

Also, teams frequently conduct their analyses in organizations where they have an "in": in some cases studying an organization where a team member formerly worked. If it is an organization about which a team member has a great deal of insider knowledge, ensure that your data collection plan allows for new views of the organization to emerge. You want to guard against collecting data that just confirms a previously held hypothesis. An individual who once worked or continues to work in an organization you are studying may have deeply held theories about what is or is not functional in the organization, particularly if the individual feels disgruntled. Be aware of existing biases your team might have before you begin your data collection.

 Consider at this stage how the team will collect data. Discuss who will be responsible for what.

When organization members tell you about issues, challenges, and problems, you need to remember that each person has a unique perspective and that multiple perspectives can be combined. You should also keep in mind that there can be interesting differences between the espoused values and practices of an organization and the actual values and practices. There is rarely one "true answer"; your goal is to consider how the multiplicity of views works together or creates tensions.

The well-known organizational consultant, Peter Block, discusses not only the importance of eliciting an organizational member's ("client's") perspectives, but also of adding new interpretations rather than taking them simply and literally:

> The client's initial attempt to describe to us the cause of difficulties is called the presenting problem. . . . I never accept the presenting problem as the real problem without doing my own data collection and analysis. The presenting problem and the real (or underlying) problem are usually different. . . . An important contribution is to redefine that initial problem statement for the client. (from *Flawless Consulting: A Guide to Getting Your Expertise Used.* Austin, TX: Learning Concepts, 1981.)

Often the value you can add is in helping the client better understand the underlying issues.

Step #6: Collect a Variety of Appropriate Data

 There should be a reasoned logic to your data collection plan and the research methods you employ. For instance, you probably do not want to start with a questionnaire as a form of exploratory data collection, given the fact that survey instruments are more useful for testing working hypotheses rather than developing them. Interviews and exploring archival data may be better suited for exploratory data inquiry. Consider which methods are useful for your exploratory phase of research. Then, as you develop a more refined understanding of what is occurring within the organization, you can tailor your data collection and use methods that allow you to test working hypotheses.

The methods of data collection can include the following, each of which is discussed in detail below:

- Interviews
- Questionnaires
- Direct Observation
- Archival Data
- Personal Experience

 Stretch yourself. Collect data in ways that you have not tried before to enhance the learning experience of this assignment.

Each of these methods of data collection has its pros and cons. Make sure you do not simply seek data that confirm your initial impressions or hypotheses about the organization. Instead, collect data that give you multiple views of the organization and leave open the possibility of interesting surprises from which you can learn. Some of the data may conflict. As this course emphasizes, you need not try to scour your data for one true portrait of the organization. You might discuss, as part of your findings in your final report, the contradictions that emerge, whether organizational members notice them, and how they cope with them.

Interviews   One-on-one interviews are a means of gathering information and developing a relationship with individual organizational members. You can get information from non-verbal as well as verbal cues and can press further on questions that have not been adequately answered. Interviews are an excellent format for building trust and becoming acquainted with a variety of perspectives.

In preparing for the interviews, project teams can generate a list of questions that address the issues outlined in the Guide and the concepts discussed in classroom discussion. This list of questions—also called an "interview protocol"—serves as a checklist during the interview process. Researchers often conduct what are called "semi-structured, open-ended" interviews. They are guided by and try to touch on all the areas in the list of questions, but there is no rigid order of recited questions. There is room for amplification or to pursue interesting tangents that might reveal unanticipated but crucial issues.

You should include different kinds of questions that each of the three perspectives would lead you to ask. Again, refer to the Guide to see the specific questions. You could include all three types of questions in an interview, or assign different team members to conduct separate interviews from a single perspective and then compare notes.

Prior to starting any interview, explain to each interviewee the purpose of the session and insure confidentiality. That is, the information collected will not be repeated to anyone inside the organization except in disguised or aggregate form. Emphasize that no one person's responses will be discernible.

The following are helpful rules of thumb for conducting an interview:

- Keep careful track of the conversation either by taking notes or by tape-recording the session if permission is granted by the interviewee (who may ask you to turn off the tape at points).
- Conduct the interview with a maximum of two team members.
- Start with simple, open-ended questions, then lead up to more personal and value-laden questions. End with a wrap-up question and thank the person for speaking with you.
- Ask interviewees at the end if there were other questions they expected to be asked or other issues they had hoped to raise that were not elicited by the questions.

- Inquire if it is acceptable for you to call back with follow-up questions. A follow-up phone call can be helpful to clarify a point or to ask a question that you discovered in later interviews was very provocative and useful, but that you had not asked this particular interviewee.

In general, in designing questions for both interviews and questionnaires, think about what kinds of variance you are trying to understand and explain. Ask questions that will generate an interesting variety of responses, rather than prompt everyone to give the same easy answer or platitude. (Of course, sometimes very different people give the same answer—understand what you are looking for and what constitutes an interesting and surprising finding.) If your questions seem to be eliciting only platitudes, then you can revise your questions for subsequent interviews.

Questionnaires   Questionnaires make it possible to get responses from a large number of people quickly and provide quantitative data that can be summarized in a table in your final report. Questionnaires can be "close-ended" (providing the respondent with a fixed list of choices), or "open-ended" (leaving the respondent room to write a short answer and explanation), or a mix of the two. It is not necessary to use a questionnaire to do a good organizational analysis.

Take the following steps in preparing questionnaires:

- Generate a list of questions that relate to the concepts from the readings, class-room discussions, and the Guide.
- Ensure that the responses will be confidential.
- Include a brief statement of purpose at the beginning.
- Seek feedback from the teaching assistant or instructor, who have sample surveys or standards that will help guide you.

If you choose to gather questionnaire data for statistical analysis, you should keep in mind what you have learned about sampling and statistical inference in any data, statistics, or econometrics courses you have taken. For example, you should not "select on the dependent variable." That is, if you are trying to learn what factors helped some product groups in the organization successfully become flat and flexible, do not sample only members of the product groups that had difficulties becoming flat and flexible (ones that remained hierarchical and rigid) to learn about the crucial, distinguishing factors. In selecting your sample for questionnaires and interviews, one rule-of-thumb is to have at least 30 respondents (which may require sending questionnaires to 60 people in the hope of a 50 percent response rate). You should also keep in mind that if you have categories of organizational members that you hope to represent (e.g., men and women, exempt and nonexempt, managers and independent contributors) than you should have about eight or more people in each category.

 These are a few limited pointers. Again, your team should consult a faculty member or teaching assistant for ideas or criteria in designing and creating a survey instrument.

Direct Observation   You can collect data about an organization simply by observing it. Observation allows you to evaluate behavior firsthand rather than through the lenses of its members. Once people get used to your presence, you can actually see how the people make decisions, treat their leader, communicate and so on. Observation is often time-consuming, but the rewards can be worth the commitment. Be creative. Some examples include:

- Hang out in the lobby or cafeteria and see what you observe (e.g., you might observe that your organization espouses the importance of balancing work and family, but that most employees do not leave until 8 p.m.).

- "Shadow" someone for a day or half day.
- Attend a social function for members of the organization.
- Attend an orientation day for new employees or a speech being given by the leader.
- Observe what kinds of cartoons people have on their doors or in their cubicles.

 It is probably a good idea to keep the number of observers in the organization at any one time to a minimum. There is nothing worse than having observation get in the way of normal group interaction. Observers should clarify why they are present at particular times and places.

Archival Data   Past records can be extremely helpful in understanding group behavior. Information about the organization and the initiative may be collected from library materials, the organization's documents, letters, e-mail, website, or similar means. Collecting this kind of data does not take as much time from organizational members, and if it is in the public domain (e.g., press announcements), then it is unobtrusive to the organization. However, some archival data from organizational records may be sensitive or confidential, and the organization may be reluctant to release such information. The following very diverse kinds of data may be helpful for your organizational analysis:

- Organizational charts
- Financial performance records
- 10K and annual reports
- Statistics on employee turnover or absenteeism rates
- Compensation trends for different occupational groups
- Memos
- E-mail
- Rules, policies, procedures
- Mission statements, mandates, charters, ethics codes
- Employee newsletters
- Handbook or videos about this new initiative
- Advertising brochures about the organization's products or services
- Newspaper articles about the organization or its key stakeholders

Personal Experience   Your personal reactions (and the organization's reaction to you) can provide important information on the climate of the organization. Does it feel tense, relaxed, cheerful, depressed, guarded, open, in crisis, optimistic? Do people in the organization return your phone calls? What might this tell you? Is it easy or difficult to get organizational members to participate in interviews or to fill out a questionnaire? Why do you think so?

 As a team you should compare your personal reactions. Are your team members' views consistent or conflicting? Discuss why.

Step #7: Analyze Data with Respect to the Focal Questions and New Issues that Emerged

The goal of your data collection is to better understand the initiative. The next step is to use all of the data your team has collected to piece together an analysis of the initiative. You should be relying extensively on the Organizational Analysis Guide to help structure your analysis. In conducting your analysis, look for themes across your data. Consider whether the data offer a consistent or inconsistent story. Often inconsistent data prove to be as informative as consistent data. For instance, if you are studying an organization's attempt to develop a more family-friendly environment, senior managers may tout the organization's new policies offering flexible work arrangements and leave, while employees who try to take advantage of these policies encounter resistance from middle managers. Consider whether you see different views across levels or types of roles in the organization when examining your data. Is the public view of the organization consistent with the private view held by employees? These types of inconsistencies should help point you to recommendations.

 In analyzing the data, remember to think back to your discussions of the team members' different kinds of expertise and roles. For example, some team members might be good at providing statistical summaries of questionnaire data, whereas others may be good at deriving categories and interpretations from a stack of interview notes. Some team members might be good at writing clear English prose, and others may be good at producing elegant graphics. Your team should think about a classic issue that arises for teams that are working under time pressure but who are also oriented toward continuous learning: Should team members do what they are already good at, or should they try something they want to learn? You should think about creative approaches (e.g., working in pairs where one person teaches and the other observes/learns).

Step #8: Evaluate the Initiative and Make Recommendations

 Given your analysis, evaluate the initiative and its degree of success. Again, refer to the Guide for the questions you should answer in your evaluation. You should also develop a set of *feasible* recommendations about how to increase the success of the initiative. Outline steps and actions the organization might take to enhance its success. Your recommendations should be as concrete as possible.

If we return to the previous example of the organization attempting to promote a more family-friendly workplace, it would be much more helpful to delineate a detailed set of recommendations to deal with the resistance reported among middle managers. The team could identify one or two isolated examples where managers had been successful in using these policies and then use those success stories as leverage to promote the policies further. The team could then outline a detailed marketing plan for the promotion of these successful cases, including showcasing them in the employee newsletter and planning brown bag lunches to highlight them. Additionally, the team could suggest a program that would partner those managers and employees who have effectively used these policies with managers who are resistant but considering their use in order to provide them with counsel.

Frequently we find that organizations are good at developing the content of a new initiative, but fail in the process of implementing it. Your insights and feedback may be extremely helpful if they incorporate suggestions on implementation. These are often areas where mutual observation and suggestions can provide real value for organizational learning. Rather than offer vague and generic recommendations, it is better to make them as specific as possible, even if the managers of the organization ultimately respond that they cannot adopt and enact your detailed recommendations.

 Solicit multiple viewpoints from the team about how team members would evaluate the initiative and what recommendations they would make based on their assessments. Don't shut down discussion too early, as a discussion reflecting different views may eventually lead to better and more fleshed out recommendations.

Step #9: Select a Metaphor

Your team should brainstorm a number of possible metaphors. Think about which metaphor best describes this initiative. Again, refer to the Guide and the readings in this Module that provide a detailed discussion of the use of metaphors.

Don't vote on the best metaphor and select one too soon. Hold a rich brainstorming session. Discussion can move you to a less obvious, more sophisticated metaphor to represent what you've observed.

© 13 EXERCISE

Step #10: Deliver Presentations in Class

It is expected that students will speak informally about the organization they are diagnosing at relevant times in class throughout the term (e.g., in discussions of the use of teams or the symbols of the organizational culture). Teams are also required to present their organizational analyses near the end of the term. For your presentation, start with the basics, as your team spent an entire semester analyzing this organization. Remember, your audience has a lot to learn, but don't inundate them with information. Keep it succinct and to the point.

Consider and plan as a team who should do what to prepare for this presentation. Think about visual aids that will help your audience better understand your organizational analysis. If you can present your analysis well, it probably means you understand it well.

Step #11: Prepare the Final Report, Incorporating Feedback from the Presentations

After presenting your final analysis, your team will receive verbal feedback from other classmates. You are expected to submit a final written report the week after you have presented your final analysis in class. You will have the opportunity in your final written report to incorporate feedback and consider unanswered questions.

Your final written report will be an executive summary (10 to 15 double-spaced pages) that briefly and succinctly outlines the major findings of your study. The content of the report should draw upon the issues and questions posed in the Guide. In addition, summarize what your team members learned about operating as a team by doing this assignment. While you will have collected a wide variety of data, you should certainly not be presenting it all. Undoubtedly, there will be data left on the cutting room floor. It is your job to sift through the data to decide which are relevant and support your evaluation and recommendations. Your final product will be much more incisive if you include only those salient data.

Don't wait until the end to summarize your learnings. Ask yourself at the end of each step/or specified time period what you are learning and take notes to aid in your final report preparation.

Step #12: Exit the Organization and Deliver Whatever Was Agreed Upon

Rather than abruptly leaving the organization at the end of the term, give some thought as to how to terminate your relationship. Have you given the organization what you promised? Have you been clear about the data and what can be done with it? Have you let organization members react to the analysis and answered their questions or concerns? Have you summarized what you accomplished for the company, as agreed upon? Have you written thank-you letters to the appropriate people?

As a team, you have accomplished a great deal in completing this project. Take time to recognize your achievement, even if the process of working together did not proceed as smoothly as you might have envisioned at the onset of this project.

ORGANIZATIONAL ANALYSIS GUIDE

INTRODUCTION

The major assignment for this class is to analyze an initiative that is in the process of being adopted in an organization. Organizations undertake initiatives in order to further their strategic or tactical business goals. Each team will have to identify an initiative, conduct a multi-perspective analysis, and relate it to what else is happening in the organization. In order to be effective, you will need to be able to analyze and tailor initiatives in ways that work. The purpose of this assignment is for your team to apply the frameworks introduced in class to a "real-life" organizational initiative or issue.

This Guide outlines the focal topics and questions you should consider before and while you conduct your analysis. The focal topics and questions provide structure for your data collection plan, your data analysis, and your final write-up. Your analysis will be complete if you answer these questions thoughtfully, considering the connections between them and supporting your answers with the data you collect.

This Guide covers the following topics:

1. Description of the initiative
2. Multiple perspectives (lenses) on the organizational initiative
   a. Strategic Design
   b. Political
   b. Cultural
3. Connection to what's going on in the organization
   a. Networked
   b. Flat
   c. Flexible
   d. Diverse
   e. Global/International
4. Evaluation of initiative and recommendations
5. Selection of a metaphor

FOCAL TOPIC #1: DESCRIPTION OF THE INITIATIVE

The project needs to focus on an initiative. There are many possibilities; you can choose to focus on a particular change that is occurring within the organization or an issue that has become salient within the organization. Some examples of initiatives that students

FIGURE 2A.3 FOCUSING ON AN INITIATIVE

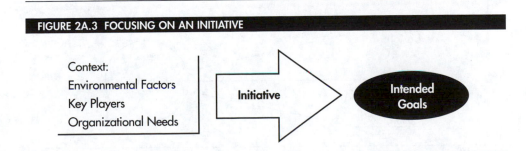

have considered include the following: introduction of new technology, the attempts of a middle manager to turn his belief in empowering employees into reality, or the merger of two departments in an organization. The initiative does not have to be top-down; it can be a change that is being driven from the bottom-up. For instance, it could be an attempt by parents in the company to develop a policy of billable hours for the purpose of providing flexible work hours.

As a first step in your analysis, describe the initiative, its history, and the organizational context.

Consider the following questions:

- What is the initiative?
- Why was the initiative developed?
- What environmental factors led to the adoption of this initiative?
- What organizational needs are being met?
- Who are the key parties involved?
- What are the steps that have been developed to implement this initiative?
- At what stage is the organization in adopting this initiative?
- What is/are the ultimate goal/goals of this initiative?

FOCAL TOPIC #2: LOOKING FROM MULTIPLE PERSPECTIVES

The next step in your analysis involves looking at the initiative from the three different lenses: strategic design, political, and cultural.

Strategic Design

Consider the following questions to understand how the formal structure and strategy of the organization influence this initiative:

- What is the strategy of this organization or work unit and how is it related to the initiative you are analyzing?
- Is this initiative consistent with the organization's strategy?
- Draw the formal structure or design of this organization or work unit. How does the formal design of the organization influence this initiative? Does the formal structure facilitate or hinder the adoption of the initiative?
- How does the way in which jobs are designed influence the initiative and how it is implemented?
- What coordinating and reward systems are in place that may affect the initiative and how it is successfully implemented?
- How does the initiative fit with the needs of the environment of the organization?

FIGURE 2A.4 THE THREE ORGANIZATIONAL LENSES

Political

Consider the following questions to understand the different interests and goals that guide individuals, groups, and departments both within and outside of the organization:

- Who are the parties involved and what are their interests?
- Who stands to gain and who stands to lose with this initiative? (Consider all of the various stakeholders who are involved and what each has to gain and lose. Include stakeholders who may be outside of the organization, such as customers and the community.)
- Map out the different stakeholders and indicate whether they are for or against the initiative.
- Are these interests compatible? If not, how malleable or fixed are those interests?
- What sources of power do the various parties bring to the situation? How evenly distributed is the power among these parties?
- Is the history of the relations among the different parties involved amenable to effective conflict resolution and problem-solving?
- Does this initiative alter power relationships within the organization?
- Have there been conflicts or disputes about this initiative? How have they been settled?
- Are there organizational structures in place to help resolve conflicts around this initiative?
- Are there any measures to allow the less powerful parties to voice their interests as they relate to this initiative?

Cultural

Consider the following questions to understand the meaning people attribute to this initiative and what it symbolizes within the organization:

- What symbolic meaning does this initiative have for the organization? Consider both the denotative and connotative meanings. Does it have different symbolic meaning for different people?
- How is this initiative related to the artifacts, values, and basic assumptions of the organization? Does it attempt to change them or reinforce them?
- Is this initiative designed to reinforce rituals and traditions or create new ones within the organization? How?
- What is formally being communicated about this initiative? How is it being packaged or framed?
- Are there ceremonies or other activities that are being used to introduce and implement this initiative?
- Does the initiative depend upon shared tacit knowledge within the organization or does it seek to unearth that knowledge and transform it?
- What stories are being told about this initiative? By whom? Are these stories shared? Are different stories being told by different parties?
- What type of language is used in discussing the initiative? Does it vary, depending upon who is speaking? How?
- Are there different subcultural responses? How are the people in these subcultures appropriating the initiative for their own use?
- How does this initiative relate to the larger cultural context within which the organization is situated?

Consider how looking at the initiative from the three perspectives influences the data you collect and how you interpret what is happening. Do the things you see through one lens change your view of the things you see through another lens? Consider how each perspective can inform the others. (i.e., How does your analysis from the strategic design perspective inform your analysis using a political lens and vice versa?)

Ⓒ

17

EXERCISE

FOCAL TOPIC #3: CONNECTION TO WHAT IS GOING ON IN THE ORGANIZATION

It is important to understand the organizational context in which this initiative is taking place, whether that is the total organization (if it is small) or the work unit. The following questions will help you to think about broader changes occurring within the organization. You then need to make the connections between these broader changes and the initiative you are analyzing.

Networked
Consider how the initiative is related to the levels of interdependence in the organization.

- How do different departments interact?
- Are teams used often? For what purposes? Are they cross-functional?
- How is information shared across the organization? Is it widely distributed and shared both vertically and horizontally?
- How do departments cooperate with one another? Are there set boundaries among the departments?
- Has the organization developed close relationships with suppliers, customers, and other key shareholders?
- Has the organization created cooperative networks with other organizations? For what purposes?

Flat
Consider how the degree of hierarchy within the organization influences the initiative.

- How many levels are there?
- To what extent are there clear lines of authority established for each position?
- Have lower-level employees been empowered to make decisions and solve problems? How?
- Have there been recent attempts to make the organization "leaner"?

Flexible
Consider how the initiative is related to the organization's ability to respond more quickly to the needs of employees, customers, and other stakeholders.

- To what extent is the organization governed by formal rules and operating procedures? How are those developed and changed?
- What has been done to adjust to and meet different customer demands?
- Has the organization kept pace with changing technologies?
- How is the labor force used to respond more flexibly to changing environmental conditions? What are those conditions?
- Are career paths upward and linear or lateral and flexible?

Diverse
Consider how the initiative is connected to how the organization accommodates a variety of perspectives, approaches, and needs.

- To what extent is there a single strong culture that demands conformity?
- How are organizational members attempting to develop a more demographically heterogeneous workforce?
- Are there different career trajectories that are being developed, particularly with regard to helping employees balance work and family?
- Is the organization open to people from a variety of backgrounds? How?

Global/International
Consider how the initiative is related to the organization's involvement in an increasingly global economy.

- Is the organization more locally or globally focused?
- Are there networks that have been developed that stretch beyond the organization's home market? For what purposes?
- What international links has the organization established? How and why?

Look at the interaction between the initiative and what is occurring in the organization. Describe how the successful implementation of the initiative may be facilitated or hindered by the movement toward this new model. Not all of these dimensions may influence the initiative in the same manner. For instance, if the initiative revolves around developing a more family-friendly work environment, the movement toward an increasingly global company may hinder that objective, because employees may be expected to travel frequently and be "on call" at all hours to service clients and other divisions who are located in different time zones. On the other hand, the flexible dimension may serve to facilitate as well as hinder this initiative. While it may provide alternative career paths and flexible hours to meet the needs of employees, the need to be flexible in response to customer demand may require employees to work longer hours and impede their ability to have a more balanced lifestyle.

As the readings have emphasized, all of the features of the new model are not always complementary. There are apparent contradictions and paradoxes in moving toward this new model. You may wish to consider how these contradictions may affect or be reinforced by this initiative.

FOCAL TOPIC # 4: EVALUATION INITIATIVE AND RECOMMENDATIONS

Given your analysis, how would you evaluate the initiative and its implementation? What do the three perspectives individually and collectively predict about the likely success of this initiative? Your analysis should lend insight into how the changes occurring in the rest of the organization will affect the likely success of this initiative. Consider the following questions:

- Are the intended goals of the initiative being realized within the organization?
- How are organizational members measuring whether this initiative is successful or not?
- Are these measures adequate? If not, what other measures could be considered?
- What factors will facilitate or hinder the success of this initiative?

Use your analysis to determine the likely outcomes from a broad set of organizational stakeholders. For example, will customers view the likely outcomes in the same way as employees? Will top managers view it from a similar perspective as middle managers and lower level employees? Also, identify the barriers that are currently working against the initiative.

Then, based upon your assessment of the initiative, develop recommendations for a manager who has an interest in making the initiative a success. Make sure that your recommendations are feasible given the current state and context of the organization. These recommendations should directly flow from your analysis. For example, if you have identified major political and cultural factors impeding this initiative, then your recommendations should revolve around ameliorating these political and cultural barriers. Don't, for instance, identify major cultural stumbling blocks and then propose recommendations that are more structural or strategic in nature.

In your recommendations, you should outline detailed steps or actions this manager should take. Remember, you should not only use the three lenses for your analysis, but should also base the actions this manager should take on all three perspectives.

Additionally, your recommendations must encompass implementation issues. For instance, when making recommendations, do not suggest creating and installing a new

© 19 EXERCISE

compensation system or organizational design without also delineating **how** to go about creating and installing it. You must consider which people need to be brought on board and how you will go about gaining their support, including any specific negotiations that need to be undertaken. When you are trying to encourage new models of behavior, you must think about whom should be picked to lead such an effort and how they will go about encouraging new behavior. Additionally, you must consider what types of cultural shifts need to take place to support the design and installation of a new system or structure. Recommendations should include the creation of new stories and symbols, as well as new reporting relationships. Your recommendations should then incorporate how to create those new stories and symbols.

FOCAL TOPIC #5: SELECTION OF A METAPHOR

There will be a lot of data, and you will need to present these data in a rich, yet concise way. A metaphor allows you to convey a picture of a complex set of features. Your team will want to brainstorm a number of possible metaphors. The metaphor might capture what the intended purpose of the initiative is, how well it has fared, or its relationship with the organization and the rest of the external environment.

For example, an attempt to adopt total quality management within an organization may not be receiving the type of continuous training and managerial support it needs to sustain it. Your team may decide that a fire engine without gas is a good metaphor to describe what is happening with this initiative. This metaphor may be apt, because the adoption of total quality management may be helping an emergency situation in the organization, but like a fire engine without gas, the solution will not be effective unless someone is supplying it with fuel.

As you think about the metaphor, you may be prompted to ask new questions about your organizational initiative. In the case with the fire engine metaphor, fuel can often be easily transported to the scene to rescue the stalled vehicle. Consider whether the support that is necessary to sustain the quality management program is just as easily available. By pursuing the metaphor playfully, creatively, and sometimes literally, you may push your thinking further.

Any metaphor highlights some features, even dramatically exaggerates them, at the expense of others. Consider how the metaphor you have selected is partial. What factors does it capture and what factors does it ignore? The following section on metaphors will help you think about their benefits and limits. Consider where your metaphor applies and where it breaks down. This question itself prompts deeper thinking about your organizational diagnosis. Consider the metaphor of the fire engine again; fire engines race to the scene even when it's a false alarm. Do the reasons behind the adoption of this initiative indicate a four-alarm fire or a false alarm?

This discussion suggests some ways to play with a metaphor to animate your analysis of this organizational initiative and make it easier to explain your findings to others.

ORGANIZATION IDENTIFICATION FORM

Organizational Processes
Term Project—Final Choice for Organizations

1. Team Members _____
   _____
   _____
   _____

2. Organization/Company Name _____
   _____
   _____

3. Industry/Primary Business _____
   _____
   _____

4. Initiative to be studied (If known now) _____
   _____
   _____
   _____
   _____

5. Any particular function or department targeted? ☐ yes ☐ no

5a. If yes, what is it? _____
    _____
    _____
    _____
    _____

6. Does someone in your group have a personal contact in the company? ☐ yes ☐ no

6a. If yes, explain how. _____
    _____
    _____
    _____
    _____

Please return to your instructor.

M-2A

supplemental

USING METAPHORS TO UNDERSTAND ORGANIZATIONAL PROCESSES

MANAGERIAL SKILLS

Some important skills for creative managers who want to lead a change effort are:

- Understanding which metaphors underlie the design and operation of organizations
- Knowing how to use metaphors to guide an analysis of an organizational issue
- Recognizing the metaphors that other people use, consciously or instinctively
- Seeing which implicit metaphors constrain or enable change

To take action in an organization, you have to be open and flexible in reading what is going on in the first place. Skill with metaphors can help.

> Effective managers and professionals in all walks of life, whether they be business executives, public administrators, organizational consultants, politicians, or trade unionists, have to become skilled in the art of "reading" the situations that they are attempting to organize or manage. . . . Skilled readers . . . have a capacity to remain open and flexible, suspending immediate judgments whenever possible, until a more comprehensive view of the situation emerges. They are aware of the fact that new insights often arise as one reads a situation from "new angles," and that a wide and varied reading can create a wide and varied range of action possibilities.
>
> Less effective managers and problem solvers, on the other hand, seem to interpret everything from a fixed standpoint. As a result, they frequently hit blocks that they can't get around; their actions and behaviors are often rigid and inflexible and a source of conflict. When problems and differences of opinion arise, they usually have no alternative but to hammer at issues in the same old way and to create consensus by convincing others to "buy into" their particular view of the situation. (Morgan, 1986, pp. 11–12)

To help you to become better managers who read situations well, the organizational diagnosis encourages you to select and use a metaphor for the organizational initiative you are studying.

Other members of your team may have different ideas about existing organizational metaphors or new ones that might suit your project. Observe how people talk using different metaphors. They may be unconscious of the metaphors that naturally creep into their speech. How does someone who describes organizational conflict as a "battle" talk to someone who describes it as a "negotiation?"

A CEO recently said the following at a strategic planning session: "What this outfit needs is fewer tight ends and more wide receivers." What vision of the organization does this metaphor convey?

From a strategic design perspective: What images of organizational design and role structure does this metaphor evoke? What possible designs does it exclude?

From a political perspective: Who might be left out or put at a disadvantage in this discussion? Who in organizations has the power to determine which metaphors are dominant?

From a cultural perspective: How do metaphors set the tone and give an organization its character? Which ones begin to crop up in everyday conversation and which ones are the source of jokes?

METAPHORS AND ORGANIZATIONAL PROCESSES

This reading discusses the helpfulness of metaphors for understanding organizational processes. It defines metaphors and how they can guide a more creative analysis, emphasizing the following points:

- Metaphors are already commonly in use for organizational processes—you should recognize them when you see them (for example, the organization as a machine or the organization as one big family).
- Metaphors can free up our thinking about organizations—but also constrain how we look for solutions (for example, if the organization is like a machine, we might just replace a broken part, but if the organization is like a family, we might take pains to help a struggling member).
- Metaphors can be extended to discover some unexpected aspects of an organizational issue—and are also informative at the point where the metaphor breaks down (for example, if you think of a contentious organizational issue as like a court case, extending this metaphor makes you think about how each side is carefully marshaling evidence, while looking at where the metaphor breaks down [there is no jury in an organization] reminds you to think about who, then, will decide between the sides).

WHAT'S AT STAKE?

Do metaphors matter? Having an outdated metaphor in mind, implicitly or explicitly, can hamper change. Some analysts see the loss of competitiveness of United States companies in the global marketplace as the result of clinging to an outdated machine metaphor for the organization. The strict adherence to following a flow diagram and a set of procedures made it difficult to improvise and to learn from feedback within the system. In contrast, other nations fostered more nimble and responsive companies, by viewing their organizations metaphorically as organisms, as small nation states, as families with trust and shared understandings, or as ongoing learning processes.

Thus, using metaphors is more than a fascinating parlor game. It can have an impact on how you do your work, for example, how productivity problems are investigated, how the talents of employees are cultivated, and ultimately how the organization performs and changes.

WHAT IS A METAPHOR?

Metaphor (definition): *a figure of speech containing an implied comparison, in which a word or phrase ordinarily and primarily used for one thing is applied to another (Ex: the curtain of night, 'all the world is a stage').*[1]

Metaphor is for most people a device of the poetic imagination and the rhetorical flourish—a matter of extraordinary rather than ordinary language. Moreover, metaphor is typically viewed as characteristic of language alone, a matter of words rather than thought or action. For this reason, most people think they can get along perfectly well without metaphor. We have found, on the contrary, that metaphor is pervasive in everyday life, not just in language but in thought and action. Our ordinary conceptual system, in terms of which we both think and act, is fundamentally metaphorical in nature (Lakoff and Johnson, 1980, p. 3).

Different metaphors constitute and capture the nature of organizational life in different ways, each generating powerful, distinctive, but essentially partial kinds of insight. . . . [N]ew metaphors may be used to create new ways of viewing organizations which overcome the weaknesses and blindspots of traditional metaphors (Morgan, 1980, p. 612).

---

1 Excerpted with permission of Macmillan General Reference, a Simon & Schuster Macmillan Company, from *Webster's New World* ™ *College Dictionary*, Third Edition (Updated). Copyright © 1997, 1996, 1994, 1991, 1988 by Simon & Schuster, Inc.

The world of business is full of metaphors. Scan the business press for everyday examples of the following:

- Sports metaphors
- Military metaphors
- Nautical metaphors

These metaphors make the speech of organizational leaders and business writers more colorful.

But more importantly, metaphors also have several features that are useful analytically: they are evocative, partial, elastic, and informative in their limits. Each of these attributes is discussed below.

Evocative

A metaphor is used when we want to describe a complex Thing A by likening it to a more familiar, vivid, or tangible Thing B. Thing A may be difficult to describe on its own terms without some colorful and evocative reference to Thing B. It is hard to describe the social world. When Shakespeare writes, "All the world's a stage" (the example of metaphor used in the dictionary), he gets us to think about all the world (a complex Thing A) by thinking about some specific traits of the stage (Thing B). Thus, the world is a place where people play roles, use certain well-rehearsed scripts, act self-consciously as if they know people are watching, try to set a mood, and experience the ups and downs of drama. All these features are conveyed in the shorthand metaphor of the stage. Spelling out the features of the metaphor helps us understand what we learn from the metaphor.

Partial

A metaphor captures only some of the features of what we are describing. For example, when we say "that person fights like a tiger," we refer to the strength and tenacity of the person (an example from Morgan, 1980). Our descriptive use of "tiger" evokes certain traits. We do not mean to say that the person has stripes and four legs. Nor do we mean to say we have captured everything about the person using the metaphor. Because the metaphor is partial, we leave out those non-tiger-like things about the person, who may also be a gentle storyteller. Because metaphors are partial, we sometimes need many metaphors to convey richly and more completely what we are describing.

To be most helpful a metaphor should be neither too far from nor too close to the thing being described. For example, if we say, "an organization is like a paper clip," this metaphor may be too abstract and distant to be helpful (although one could try!). However, if we pick something too close—an "organization is like an accounting department" or "an organization is like an assembly plant"—we are almost being tautological ("an organization is like an organization"). These metaphors are not "partial enough;" there are too many traits in common for them to spur creative thinking. The idea of partial overlap can be depicted graphically (drawing on Morgan, 1980, p. 612), as shown in Figure 2A.5.

Elastic

Playing with a metaphor makes it more useful. We might describe an organization as like an organism. What features of an organization does that make us think about that we might have overlooked? It has to adapt to its environment, finding the right "resource niche" in which to flourish. What else comes to mind when we play with the organism idea? Each organ or part has a specific function; when all the organs function together, the whole is healthy and productive. By further extending this metaphor of function and health, we can raise some provocative ideas about what the analogy of illness might mean. Illness might mean it is time to eliminate the problem area (like removing tonsils). Or illness can be an opportunity for diagnosis, feedback, and improvement (as when stress indicates that a person's regimen should be changed). The idea of "illness" or "failure" as an opportunity for learning in an organization is a provocative idea that has gotten a fair amount of attention in the academic and business press. Such ideas can be brought to life by taking a metaphor and playing with it.

FIGURE 2A.5 EFFECTIVE METAPHORS ARE PARTIALLY OVERLAPPING

(1) Abstruse

> A metaphor should not be too far from the entity it describes: "An organization is a paper clip."

(2) Creative

> * A metaphor should have partial overlap with the entity it describes: "An organization is a machine."

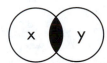

(3) Trivial

> A metaphor should not be too close to the entity it describes: "An organization is an accounting department."

Adapted from Morgan (1980, p. 612).

Knowing the details of the metaphor helps in this process; that is, knowing more about organisms reveals places to play with the metaphor. Philosophers use the term "analogic reasoning" to describe the process of understanding something by playing with a metaphor for it.

Informative in Its Limits

At some point, playing with a metaphor reveals where it breaks down, because metaphors are partial. Penicillin can cure an illness, but there may be no such wonder drug for organizational woes, precisely because organizations are not literally organisms. There are no reliable chemical interactions that occur in response to an intervention, because people in complex relationships inhabit organizations. They do not respond as predictably as chemical systems. However, even where a metaphor breaks down, there are lessons to learn. Precisely the fact that there is no organizational analogy to the wonder drug can make people think more critically about easy remedies that are offered for organizational problems.

Ⓢ

27

ACADEMIC

APPENDIX 1: "A SAMPLE METAPHOR: THE ORGANIZATION AS A MACHINE"[1]

The machine metaphor seems like a tired one today. But when it was used in earlier times, it captured the excitement that people felt in watching the smooth, intricate, well-coordinated workings of a machine. Machines were efficient. Their efficiency promised to make more things possible than people had imagined. Thus, the machine metaphor for an organization was evocative of the incredible efficiency that was thought possible if people worked together like the parts of a machine did. Every person had a role. The roles were coordinated by higher level systems (managers at higher levels). When it worked well, the machine was a thing of beauty. It was reliable and predictable. And when it broke, it could be diagnosed and fixed, applying rational principles of design.

While the machine metaphor of organizations may seem to apply best to organizations that use or make machines, its notion of fixed and repeated routines persists with the rise of the service industry. The machine metaphor and its ideal of efficiency and standardization describe many service industry jobs. For example, the details of taking a fast food order are very precise, down to the moment of inserting suggestive selling ("and would you like fries with that?") and the prescribed smile and "thank you."

As organizations try to become more flexible and adaptable, a number of problems have been traced to the machine-like conception of the organization:

- While every person has a role, job descriptions also let people decide what is not part of their role, resulting in a "pass the buck" mentality famous in bureaucracies but quite contrary to more current notions of shared ownership and commitment to getting a job done.
- When orders pass up and down a hierarchy, there is often distortion of the message, with people at the top being shielded from critical bad news and people at the bottom being excluded from data that might help them understand the business better.
- Machine-like organizations work better if everyone is willing to "fit in," but behaviors that are "irrational" from a machine mentality can "gum up the works," such as employees' building empires, hoarding resources, or "gaming the system" by rigging procedures to work in their favor. These are reasonable or likely behaviors from other perspectives.
- The organization designed like a machine is not flexible; it might have to shut down while a critical part is being repaired.
- A machine-like organization cannot adapt quickly to a changing environment; it would have to be redesigned almost constantly to accommodate new specifications in a world of rapid change.
- The designer of the machine is somehow invisible and outside the machine or organization, exerting a kind of unquestionable control that runs counter to ideas of employee involvement and the learning organization.

These are familiar critiques of the organizational problems that result when organizational managers and members conceive of their organization as a machine.

As a final note: Just as the organizational world is changing, so is the world of machine design. There are new kinds of machines that snap together, instead of being welded together. When a part is no longer needed, it can find a new life, in accord with principles of designing for environmental responsibility. Perhaps these new kinds of machines will inspire their own new metaphors for new organizational forms.

---

1 This brief summary draws upon Gareth Morgan. 1986. *Images of Organization.* Newbury Park, CA: Sage Publications.

APPENDIX 2: "A SAMPLE METAPHOR: THE ORGANIZATION AS A BRAIN"[2]

Can an organization be as flexible, resilient, and inventive as the functioning of the brain? The brain metaphor takes us beyond networks and matrices, which are just new ways of drawing lines and linking boxes, and are still essentially like a machine or engineering diagram. Nor does the brain metaphor suggest a central planning organ through which other functions are guided, as in the organism metaphor.

The idea of the organization as a brain requires understanding how all the functionality of the brain is distributed across its many parts. The brain used to be likened to a telephone switchboard or a library. A new point of reference now seems to capture best the functioning of the brain: The brain works like holography, storing the whole in all of its parts. The distinctiveness of the brain's functioning is captured in this passage:

> In a famous experiment, the American psychologist Karl Lashley removed increasing quantities of the brains of rats which had been taught to run in a maze. He found that, provided he did not remove the visual cortex and thus blind them, he could remove up to ninety percent of their cortex without significant deterioration in their power to thread their way through the maze. There is no man-made machine of which this is true. Try removing nine-tenths of your radio and see if it still brings in a signal! It would seem that each specific memory is distributed in some way over the brain as a whole.
>
> Similarly, you can remove considerable amounts of the motor cortex without paralyzing any one group of muscles. All that happens is a general deterioration of motor performance. The evolutionary advantages of such an arrangement are manifest: when pursued, it is better to run clumsily than not at all. But how this remarkable distribution of function is achieved we do not really understand. We see, at all events, that the brain relies on patterns of increasing refinement and not (as man-made machines do) on chains of cause and effect.[3]

A detailed description of the brain such as this one is helpful for extending the metaphor to the organization. What ideas does the above passage give us about how the new organizational form is like a brain? Here are a few examples; you will probably think of more. The distribution of decision-making power and information back down into local departments or teams mirrors the brain's function. Each cross-functional team can mirror the whole of the organization. If the top management team does not give orders, the subunit can still function toward the organization's aims, perhaps modifying the aims creatively along the way (like the way neural networks adapt). Whole parts of the organization can be removed, and the organization will continue to function. Certain parts of the organization might contain "core capabilities," analogous to the visual cortex. While certain specialized functions may be localized, an understanding of the whole is incorporated in each of the self-organizing parts. Redundancy becomes a positive source of creativity, rather than an inefficiency. Though independent, the parts are connected and respond to changes in one another's capacities. The brain is responsive to its environment, reorganizing its patterns of information and function in the process of learning new tasks, and moreover, of learning how to learn.

The above passages suggest some advantages and disadvantages of this structure that come to light in playing with the metaphor. An advantage is that it is good to be flexible and to remain able to function under adversity. It is helpful to distribute power and memory to local units. A disadvantage might be that the organization will "run clumsily" if too many portions are cut. To extend the metaphor further, just as parts of a person's personality might be lost if too much of the brain is cut out, the distinctiveness of an organization's culture may be lost if too many parts are cut out. How else can you extend the metaphor of the organization as a brain?

2 This brief summary draws upon Gareth Morgan. 1986. *Images of Organization*, Newbury Park, CA: Sage Publications.
3 From G. R. Taylor. 1979. *The Natural History of the Mind*. New York: Dutton. Quoted in Morgan, *op cit.*, p. 77.

APPENDIX 3: METAPHORS FROM RESEARCH ON ORGANIZATIONS

Metaphors can be used to describe an entire organization or one component of how an organization operates. Many metaphors for organizations have flourished in social science research on organizations. Here are some examples:[4]

1. *Cybernetic systems.* These metaphors were popular in the 1960s as the field of cybernetics flourished. This metaphor encourages us to view organizations as "patterns of information." Negative feedback in this pattern can be a source of learning about how to keep the overall system in homeostatic balance.

2. *Loosely coupled systems.* This metaphor emphasizes that the pieces fit together quite loosely (e.g., the organizational chart is only loosely related to how people really act). This metaphor is meant explicitly to counter the image of the machine metaphor that portrays organizations as tidy, efficient, well-coordinated, tightly coupled systems. Its central idea is that loose coupling is a good thing, not a problem to be fixed, and allows the organization some slack with which to be creative and adaptive. One piece can change without all the others having to be re-tooled.

3. *Population ecology.* This metaphor says that organizations should be studied, not one at a time, but in groups or populations. Populations of animals have weaker and stronger members. Populations of animals compete with populations of other animals for resources in order to survive. This metaphor has been used to explain the forces that affect the survival and growth of entire populations of organizations (for example, examining the birth and death of local newspapers in an entire region, instead of considering one newspaper alone). This metaphor emphasizes that changes in an organization's environment can cause it to be "selected against" (an evolutionary biology concept), even despite its attempts to "adapt."

4. *Theater.* This metaphor suggests that organizational life involves a series of performances. People learn how to put on different faces. Organizational actors may play multiple roles in different settings (in one setting the assertive team member, in another the attentive trainee, in another the dominant supervisor, in another the deferential subordinate). Researchers who have played with this metaphor emphasize that sometimes the conflict of roles can cause stress.

5. *Architecture.* The architecture metaphor emphasizes how an architect puts together the elements of a building—its purpose, the structural materials available, and any new innovations in style and aesthetics—so that they fit well together. As any of these elements change, so do the ways in which they can be fit together to create an architectural design. The architecture metaphor can be extended to raise some interesting issues. For example, new architectural possibilities, like the creation of high rise buildings, have necessitated new auxiliary systems, like the development of elevators and heating and air conditioning systems. These systems are called "collateral technologies." They are another element that must be fit into the whole to create a pleasing and coherent space. This metaphor urges us to think about similar instances where new organizational designs like the use of teamwork may necessitate new "collateral technologies." What might teamwork necessitate? Answers range from team meeting rooms to new procedures for evaluating team performance to new ways of rotating team roles when members go on leave. How will these new elements fit together into a coherent and well-balanced overall design?

6. *Lean and mean.* This metaphor for the changing shape of organizations is evocative of a fit, focused, athletic competitor. It is interesting that this metaphor has gained currency in the United States as the American passion for fitness is escalating. Old

4 The first four are summarized in Morgan (1980, p. 616), the fifth draws from Nadler and Gerstein (1992, p. 120-121), and the sixth appears throughout the business press.

organizational metaphors emphasized the importance of "buffers" or "slack" in organizations; for example, companies in the United States tended to have large inventories. "Fat city" was a good place to be. The positive view of slack has turned into a negative view of excess baggage. The lean idea follows from the implementation of some principles of "just in time" management, which discourages large buffers because they obscure where the underlying problems or bottlenecks may be. ("Just in time" management uses an interesting metaphor to convey this point: "You can see the rocks in the river only at the points where the river flow is most shallow.") The lean metaphor has been extended as an approach to human resource management as companies "shed" workers (a word evocative of "shedding" pounds to become lean).

Whether leanness with respect to labor is a good thing remains a subject of debate. Critics highlight the problems of using a "lean and mean" approach to human resource management, including the strain on employees who survive layoffs but feel overtaxed and put in marathon hours. While it is one thing to have a "lean and mean" game of tennis, it is quite another to approach staffing in a mean manner, and here the ways that the metaphor breaks down may be food for thought.

APPENDIX 4: METAPHORS AND DIVERSITY

Appreciating diversity reminds us that a metaphor makes sense from a particular vantage point. A full understanding of organizational forms and processes may require: (1) sharing and trying out many different metaphors, (2) making the meanings behind metaphors more explicit, and (3) understanding the metaphors that other people take-for-granted in planning their everyday approach to organizational issues.

Metaphors and Gender

The widespread use of sports metaphors in business has been given scrutiny as more women have entered the workforce, some of whom may not have been socialized to the language of sports. Women or men unfamiliar with a particular sport (such as U.S. football) may be unintentionally left out. (As more girls get the opportunity to play sports, their fluency in sports metaphors will change). One popular advice writer gives an example of what can happen when a taken for granted metaphor is not shared.[5]

> Sports metaphors abound in business talk, as might be expected. They are colorful, action-oriented, motivational words and usually have an incisive meaning. One neutral sports phrase can communicate a world of meaning (to receptive men) without forcing the speaker to long explanations or loaded words. If a male manager calmly and smilingly remarks to a male subordinate, "I like to think I'm the quarterback," he communicates volumes, depending on the context. He is saying any or all these things: "Watch out. You're stepping out of bounds. You're forgetting who's the boss. You've argued enough for your viewpoint, now drop it! I've heard you but I've made the decision. I know you might get hurt as a result of this action but do the best you can under the circumstances and you'll probably be okay."
>
> The male subordinate could laugh good-naturedly, say, "It was worth a try," and leave the office, their relationship unimpaired because none of the explosive words were ever said. They understood each other; they spoke each other's language. The same complacent comment made to a woman subordinate might be greeted with a blank stare or a flippant, "So?"

The consequences of a misunderstood metaphor can be high. One challenge of an increasingly diverse workforce will be to educate each other in the metaphors that we use and to expand the base of shared metaphors.

Metaphors in the Global Business World

The pitfalls of using metaphors in international business transactions are highlighted in a passage peppered with some favorite, taken-for-granted sports metaphors:

> Most of us [native speakers of American English] do not stop to realize how many of our metaphors come right off the playing field. . . . No matter how avid a golfer or baseball fan your foreign counterpart is, American sports terminology is still likely to leave him out in left field. Asking for a ballpark figure rarely gets you to first base. Aces, end runs, slam dunks, and playing for all the marbles are not worldwide business maneuvers. One U.S. firm lost a client simply by remarking, "This is a whole new ball game." The client did not consider the discussion a game.

Ⓢ

32

ACADEMIC

---

5 Harragan, Betty Lehan. 1977. *Games Mother Never Taught You.* New York: Warner Books, p. 103.

APPENDIX 5: METAPHORS FOR THE ORGANIZATION OF THE FUTURE

New metaphors may help liberate our thinking about organizations. Old metaphors can constrain it. Some metaphors become very familiar, to the point that we forget that they were metaphorical to start with. For example, we refer to "chain stores" quite naturally. When the term "chain" was first used, the image that was prompted was literally a chain, a "flexible series of joined links." This image captures well how a chain of department stores, like Sears, typically functioned. Chain stores used to be bound together (they may have relied upon the same advertising campaign) and depended upon their linkages to each other for success (the chain metaphor reminds us of the saying, "a chain is only as strong as its weakest link" and the importance of standardization across the chain for this reason).

Metaphors can limit what we see and how we think if we do not reexamine them periodically. In contrast to the chain metaphor, we may need new metaphors to describe new possibilities for how related organizations form links. There is much recent focus on flexible customization of products to serve the buying patterns of different local groups of customers (that is, stores in different cities stock different types and amounts of products). Some alternative metaphors for chain stores convey very different conceptions of organizations and provide a starting point for thinking creatively and critically about alternatives. What might these metaphors be? Perhaps metaphors like brains, neural networks, or satellites are helpful. A satellite metaphor suggests independent organizations orbiting in their own trajectory, although they retain a notion of a central entity around which the satellite moves (like a central headquarters). This metaphor may work for some groups of stores with strong central planning (perhaps like Walmart). A network metaphor may suggest that the nodes in the network are more equal and there is no center—an alternative depiction that might capture more loosely linked groups of stores (perhaps like independently owned franchises).

Ⓢ

33

ACADEMIC

REFERENCES

Harragan, Betty Lehan. 1977. *Games Mother Never Taught You.* New York: Warner Books.

Jackall, Robert. 1988. *Moral Mazes: The World of Corporate Managers.* New York: Oxford.

Lakoff, George, and Mark Johnson. 1980. *Metaphors We Live By.* Chicago: The University of Chicago.

Morgan, Gareth. 1980. "Paradigms, Metaphors, and Puzzle Solving in Organization Theory." *Administrative Science Quarterly.* 25, pp. 605–622.

Morgan, Gareth. 1986. *Images of Organization.* Newbury Park, CA: Sage.

Nadler, David A., and Marc S. Gerstein. 1992. "What is Organizational Architecture?" *Harvard Business Review,* September–October, pp. 120-121.

THERE'S MORE THAN ONE KIND OF TEAM

by Peter F. Drucker

"Team building" has become a buzz-word in American business. The results are not overly impressive.

Ford Motor Co. began more than ten years ago to build teams to design its new models. It now reports "serious problems," and the gap in development time between Ford and its Japanese competitors has hardly narrowed. General Motors' Saturn Division was going to replace the traditional assembly line with team work in its "factory of the future." But the plant has been steadily moving back toward the Detroit-style assembly line. Procter & Gamble launched a team-building campaign with great fanfare several years ago. Now P&G is moving back to individual accountability for developing and marketing new products.

One reason—perhaps the major one—for these near-failures is the all-but-universal belief among executives that there is just one kind of team. There actually are three—each different in its structure, in the behavior it demands from its members, in its strengths, its vulnerabilities, its limitations, its requirements, but above all, in what it can do and should be used for.

The first kind of team is the baseball team. The surgical team that performs an open-heart operation and Henry Ford's assembly line are both "baseball teams." So is the team Detroit traditionally sets up to design a new car.

FIXED POSITIONS

The players play *on* the team; they do not play *as* a team. They have fixed positions they never leave. The second baseman never runs to assist the pitcher; the anesthesiologist never comes to the aid of the surgical nurse. "Up at bat, you are totally alone," is an old baseball saying. In the traditional Detroit design team, marketing people rarely saw designers and were never consulted by them. Designers did their work and passed it on to the development engineers, who in turn did their work and passed it on to manufacturing, which in turn did its work and passed it on to marketing.

The second kind of team is the football team. The symphony orchestra and the hospital unit that rallies round a patient who goes into shock at 3 a.m. are "football teams," as are Japanese auto makers' design teams. The players on the football team or in the symphony orchestra, like those on the baseball team, have fixed positions. The oboe never comes to the aid of the violas, however badly they might flounder. But on these teams players play as a team. The Japanese auto makers' design teams, which Detroit and P&G rushed to imitate, are football-type teams. To use an engineering term, the designers, engineers, manufacturing people and marketing people work "in parallel." The traditional Detroit team worked "in series."

Third, there is the tennis doubles team—the kind Saturn management hoped would replace the traditional assembly line. It is also the sort of team that plays in a jazz combo, the team of senior executives who form the "president's office" in big companies, or the team that is most likely to produce a genuine innovation like the personal computer 15 years ago.

Source: Peter Drucker, "There's More Than One Kind of Team," first published in *The Wall Street Journal*, February 11, 1992. Copyright © 1992 Peter F. Drucker. Reprinted by permission of the author.

On the doubles team, players have a primary rather than a fixed position. They are supposed to "cover" their teammates, adjusting to their teammates' strengths and weaknesses and to the changing demands of the "game."

Business executives and the management literature have little good to say these days about the baseball-style team, whether in the office or on the factory floor. There is even a failure to recognize such teams as teams at all. But this kind of team has enormous strengths. Each member can be evaluated separately, can have clear and specific goals, can be held accountable, and can be measured—as witness the statistics a true aficionado reels off about every major-leaguer in baseball history. Each member can be trained and developed to the fullest extent of the individual's strengths. And because the members do not have to adjust to anybody else on the team, every position can be staffed with a "star," no matter how temperamental, jealous or limelight-hogging each of them might be.

But the baseball team is inflexible. It works well when the game has been played many times and when the sequence of its actions is thoroughly understood by everyone. That is what made this kind of team right for Detroit in the past.

As recently as 20 years ago, to be fast and flexible in automotive design was the last thing Detroit needed or wanted. Traditional mass production required long runs with minimum changes. And since the resale value of the "good used car"—one less than three years old—was a key factor for the new-car buyer, it was a serious mistake to bring out a new design (which would depreciate the old car) more than every five years. Sales and market share took a dip on several occasions when Chrysler prematurely introduced a new brilliant design.

The Japanese did not invent "flexible mass production"; IBM was probably the first to use it, around 1960. But when the Japanese auto industry adopted it, it made possible the introduction of a new car model in parallel with a successful old one. And then the baseball team did

indeed become the wrong team for Detroit, and for mass-production industry as a whole. The design process then had to be restructured as a football team.

The football team does have the flexibility Detroit now needs. But it has far more stringent requirements than the baseball team. It needs a "score"—whether it's the play the coach signals to the huddle on the field or the Mozart symphony everyone in the orchestra puts on his music stand. The specifications with which the Japanese begin their design of a new car model—or a new consumer-electronics product—are far more stringent and detailed than anything Detroit is used to in respect to style, technology, performance, weight, price and so on. And they are far more closely adhered to.

In the traditional "baseball" design team every position—engineering, manufacturing, marketing—does its job its own way. In the football team or the symphony orchestra, there is no such permissiveness. The word of the coach or the conductor is law. Players are beholden to this one boss alone for their orders, their rewards, their appraisals, their promotions.

The individual engineer on the Japanese design team is a member of his company's engineering department. But he is on the design team because the team's leader has asked for him—not because the chief engineer sent him there. He can consult engineering and get advice. But his orders come from the design-team chief, who also appraises his performance. If there are stars on these teams, they are featured only if the score calls for a solo. Otherwise they subordinate themselves to the team.

Even more stringent are the requirements of the doubles team—the kind that GM's Saturn Division hoped to develop in its "flexible-manufacturing" plant, and that any such plant does indeed need. This team must be quite small, with five to seven members at most. The members have to be trained together and must work together for quite some time before they fully function as a team. There must be one clear goal for the entire team and yet considerable flexibility with respect to the individual member's work and performance. And in this kind of team only the team "performs"; individual members "contribute."

All three of these kinds of teams are true teams. But they are so different—in the behavior they require, in what they do best, and in what they cannot do at all—that they cannot be hybrids. One kind of team can play only one way. And it is very difficult to change from one kind of team to another.

Gradual change cannot work. There has to be a total break with the past, however traumatic it may be. This means that people cannot report to both their old boss and to the new coach, conductor or team leader. And their rewards, their compensation, their appraisals and their promotions must be totally dependent on their performance in their new roles on their new teams. But this is so unpopular that the temptation to compromise is always great.

TEAMS ARE TOOLS

At Ford, for instance, the financial people have been left under the control of the financial staff and report to it rather than to the new design teams. GM's Saturn Division has tried to maintain the authority of the traditional bosses—the first-line supervisors and the shop stewards—rather than hand decision-making power over to the work teams. This, however, is like playing baseball and a tennis doubles match with the same people, on the same field, and at the same time. It can only result in frustration and non-performance. And a similar confusion seems to have prevailed at P&G.

Teams, in other words, are tools. As such, each team design has its own uses, its own characteristics, its own requirements, its own limitations. Team work is neither "good" nor "desirable"—it is a fact. Wherever people work together or play together they do so as a team. Which team to use for what purpose is a crucial, difficult, and risky decision that is even harder to unmake. Managements have yet to learn how to make it.

37

PRESS

THE BUREAUCRACY BUSTERS

by Brian Dumaine

If you were to ask a CEO in the year 2000 to take out his Montblanc and draw the organization chart of his company, what he'd sketch would bear little resemblance to even the trendiest flattened pyramid around today. Yes, the corporation of the future will still retain some vestiges of the old hierarchy and maybe a few traditional departments to take care of the boringly rote. But spinning around the straight lines will be a vertiginous pattern of constantly changing teams, task forces, partnerships, and other informal structures. Picture one of those overhead camera shots in a Busby Berkeley musical: Dozens of leggy dancers form a flower on stage, disband into chaos, and then regroup to form a flag or a flugelhorn. Like the dancers, in tomorrow's corporation teams variously composed of shop-floor workers, managers, technical experts, suppliers, and customers will join together to do a job and then disband, with everyone going off to the next assignment.

Call this new model the adaptive organization. It will bust through bureaucracy to serve customers better and make the company more competitive. Instead of looking to the boss for direction and oversight, tomorrow's employee will be trained to look closely at the work process and to devise ways to improve upon it, even if this means temporarily leaving his regular job to join an ad hoc team attacking a problem. Says Raymond Gilmartin, CEO of Becton Dickinson, a New Jersey maker of high-tech medical equipment: "Forget structures invented by the guys at the top. You've got to let the task form the organization."

So far, the adaptive organization exists more as an ideal than as a reality. But you can see aspects of it taking shape not only at Becton Dickinson but also at companies such as Apple Computer, Cypress Semiconductor, Levi Strauss, Xerox, and AES (formerly Applied Energy Services), a builder of co-generation plants. Last year, for instance, an informal Xerox team made up of people from accounting, sales, distribution, and administration saved the company $200 million in inventory costs. Cypress, a San Jose, California, maker of specialty computer chips, has developed a computer system that keeps track of all its 1,500 employees as they crisscross between different functions, teams, and projects. Apple is developing a computer network called Spider that, like a high-tech version of the dossiers Mr. Phelps used to choose his *Mission: Impossible* team, instantly tells a manager whether an employee is available to join his project, what the employee's skills are, and where he's located in the corporation.

If you look hard at your own organization, you'll probably see something quite similar already going on. In every outfit of more than a few people, there exists an informal organization—social scientists sometimes call it an emergent organization—that operates alongside the formal one. It consists of the alliances between people and the power relationships that actually get work done. It may be as simple as some workers banding together to go outside channels to do a job despite the obstacles set in their way by a pigheaded bureaucrat. This isn't new. What is new is that corporations are finally realizing the need to recognize the informal organization, free it up, and provide it the resources it needs.

The adaptive organization incorporates the informal organization and draws its power from the same fund of energy. It provides openings for the creativity and initiative too often found only in small, entrepreneurial companies. It does this by aligning what the corporation wants—innovation, improvement—with what turns people on, namely a chance to use their heads and expand their skills. Traditional hierarchies usually have the opposite effect. Says Paul Allaire, Xerox's new CEO (see article below): "When people know some order or memo is eventually going to come down from above and demand something different than what they want to do, it's easy to say, 'Hell, I've been burned enough times. I'm not going to do anything until I'm told to do it.' "

Some influential CEOs like Allaire now believe that unleashing this kind of energy is the best hope for U.S. competitiveness, better than any quality program. That's a thought to be taken seriously, coming as it does from the CEO of a company that won the Baldrige award in 1989. Explains Allaire: "We're never going to outdiscipline the Japanese on quality. To win, we need to

---

CAN HE MAKE XEROX ROCK?

If Paul Allaire gets his way, and CEOs often do, the rock & roll is going to start soon at Xerox's headquarters in Stamford, Connecticut. Says Allaire, 52: "We changed a lot in the 1980s, but in the next five years we'll have to change so much it will make the last ten look like a practice run."

Allaire, who succeeded David Kearns as CEO last year, plans to take a hammer to the bureaucratic walls that keep R&D, marketing, and manufacturing from capitalizing on each other's innovations. After all, why shouldn't Xerox exploit its own ideas as successfully as outsiders did? It was Xerox scientists who created the software that helped launch such startups as Apple, 3Com, and Sun Microsystems.

In Allaire's vision, Xerox, now officially dubbed the "Document Company," will concentrate on helping office workers create, use, and share reports, memos, and databases—not just push copiers. Says he, in a strong Massachusetts accent: "I have to change the company substantially to be more market driven. If we do what's right for the customer, our market share and our return on assets will take care of themselves."

The chief first learned about pleasing the customer when his father, who ran a quarry outside of Worcester, Massachusetts, taught him to hurl a few extra shovelfuls of gravel onto every order. After college and business school, he joined Xerox in 1966 as a financial analyst and in 1975 began an eight-year stint running Rank Xerox, the company's London-based overseas subsidiary. Allaire's successful restructuring of that operation—he cut staff 40% and reduced costs by $200 million—helped win him the CEO job.

Allaire doesn't give a hoot for most CEO perks. He drives himself to work and, when he takes a ski trip, flies coach. Nor is he a workaholic. While his day typically runs from 7 a.m. to 7 p.m., he makes it a rule to work only the occasional Sunday and never on Saturdays. In off hours, he likes to read books on politics—currently Tom Wicker's new study of Nixon, *One of Us*—or go riding with his wife, Kay, his two children, Brian and Christiana, and his horse, Patrick.

While he idolizes GE chief Jack Welch for his tough-mindedness, Allaire couldn't have a more different management style. Allaire is a listener who quietly sits in meetings, sizes things up, and then gets people quickly on to the next issue. But don't let the mild manner fool you. Says Leonard Vickers, a Xerox senior VP: "A mild rebuke from Paul is like a tongue-lashing from other people. You immediately get the point."

It will take years to find out whether Allaire can change Xerox. Wall Street, however, seems to be betting things will improve, especially since the new CEO has started to sell some of the money-losing financial service businesses the company picked up in the mid-eighties. Although Xerox's stock is selling below its 1987, pre-market-crash high of $85 a share, it nearly doubled over the past several months to a recent price of $56.

Ⓢ

39

PRESS

---

find ways to capture the creative and innovative spirit of the American worker. That's the real organizational challenge."

Many managers point out, and rightly so, that giving people this kind of freedom raises troublesome questions. If no one's watching over workers, how do you prevent them from heading in the wrong direction, or running off the rails? Who decides which person ends up on which team and for how long? How do you judge the performance of someone who is constantly rotating from team to team? What happens to careers where there's no clear ascent up the old hierarchical ladder? For some answers, read on.

In considering whether this model is for you, says professor Paul Lawrence, an organizational theorist at the Harvard business school, begin by imagining a spectrum with a traditional hierarchy at one end and the adaptive organization at the other. Generally speaking, companies in stable, slow-growth industries like oil, paper, and forest products should stay near the hierarchical end of the spectrum. Hierarchies were designed for stable situations, and if yours is one of those increasingly rare companies lucky enough to be in a relatively predictable market, it probably doesn't pay to change. By contrast, companies in fast-changing markets like computers, telecommunications, publishing, autos, and specialty steel probably need to move as far as possible toward the adaptive end of the line.

What will the adaptive organization look like? No one knows for sure, but that hasn't stopped an excited assortment of academics and consultants from trying to describe it. Raymond Miles, a management professor at Berkeley, likens it to a network where managers work much as switchboard operators do, coordinating the activities of employees, suppliers, customers, and joint-venture partners. Charles Sabel, a sociologist at MIT, dubs it the Möbius strip organization, after the geometric form that has no identifiable top or bottom, beginning or end. Sabel means to suggest a body that constantly turns in on itself, in an endless cycle of creation and destruction.

No matter what you call them, all these designs for an organization have one thing in common: fluidity. The adaptive organization will work much the same way that big construction firms such as Bechtel, Fluor, and Brown & Root do, gathering hand-picked groups of employees and outside contractors with the right skills for each new dam, refinery, or airport.

About four years ago, Becton Dickinson found itself worrying about the competition despite a history of fast growth and annual revenues of around $2 billion. To regain its edge, the maker of high-tech diagnostic systems such as blood analyzers started exploring ways to let its informal organization bust out. While the company still maintains traditional functions like marketing, sales and manufacturing, it now encourages its people to take the initiative and form teams to innovate and go after business in new ways. Explains CEO Raymond Gilmartin: "We're creating a hierarchy of ideas. You say, 'This is the right thing to do here,' not 'We're going to do this because I'm boss.'"

Instead of directing strategy from the top, Gilmartin lays out a very broad vision—develop proprietary ideas and beat the competition to market with them—and then lets his 15 divisions develop their own business strategies. Part of the point is to send a message to employees that there is no rigid master plan.

Left on their own, Gilmartin's division heads structure their businesses to meet their needs. Says Chuck Baer, head of the company's consumer products division: "We reorganized ourselves by the way we work. We organized cross-functional teams that include not only our own people but also vendors, suppliers and people from other divisions. We set the strategy and the team carries it out."

This is harder than it sounds, and less than completely democratic. In 1990, Becton Dickinson developed a new instrument called the Bactec 860, designed to process blood samples. A team leader was assigned and immediately put together a project team of engineers, marketers, manufacturers, and suppliers. While the group eventually launched the Bactec 860 some 25% faster than its previous best efforts, Gilmartin wasn't satisfied.

There was still too much time-wasting debate between marketing and engineering over product specifications, he found. Marketing argued that Bactec 860 needed more features to please the customer, while engineering countered that the features would take too long to design and be too costly. Further inquiry led management to the nub of the problem: Because the team leader reported to the head of engineering, he didn't have sufficient clout to resolve the conflict between the two sides. Today the company makes sure all its team leaders have access to a division head, which gives them the authority to settle disputes between different functions.

What's to keep an informal system from veering off in the wrong direction? Xerox's Allaire believes something as simple as that old rag "focus on the customer" is often enough to steer by. A few years ago, for instance, Xerox prided itself on its ability to ship a copier from its factory to a customer faster than the competition. Only one problem: That wasn't what Xerox's customers cared about. They wanted to know when the copier would arrive, to have it installed on schedule, in working order, and to be presented with an accurate bill. Unfortunately, Xerox didn't have much grasp of how to do that. When a customer asked when his copier would arrive, the salesperson would typically answer "two weeks" because he had no better information. Says Allaire: "It was a real embarrassment."

Allaire assigned a seasoned middle manager to tackle the problem. Taking the initiative, the manager pulled a group of people out of their regular jobs in such functions as distribution, accounting, and sales. The team developed a system that tracks each copier through the distribution process and makes sure that it and accompanying paperwork check out. Changing the process helped Xerox boost its customer satisfaction, as measured by a company survey, from 70% to 90%. Says Allaire: "You can't get people to focus on only the bottom line. You have to give

them an objective like 'satisfy the customer' that everyone can relate to. It's the only way to break down those barriers and get people from different functions working together."

It's not a one-shot deal either. Soon after Xerox revamped its distribution system, it tackled inventory by forming a so-called coordinating group that cuts across hierarchical lines. The team found that no one was coordinating the flow of copiers through the manufacturing process, into the warehouse, and out of the door. At every stage each department was ordering extra inventory, out of fear of being caught short. The coordinating team took a look at the whole chain, set in place procedures to make sure everyone along the line could always get as many copiers as they needed, and cut inventory costs by $200 million a year.

When people move from one team to another, they and their companies have to think about careers and pay in new ways. It's likely that tomorrow's workers and managers, instead of slowly climbing the ladder, will make more lateral moves, picking up expertise in different functions like marketing and manufacturing. For those who do well on teams, Becton Dickinson is trying out so-called lateral promotions, rotating, say, a financial person into a marketing or manufacturing job. In one division last year, the company rotated ten managers out of 50. These people got a raise and change of title, just as they would with a regular promotion, but they weren't necessarily put in charge of any more people.

Working in an environment where teams constantly band and disband requires new sets of skills. Stuart Winby, an organizational expert hired by Hewlett-Packard to ponder the future, argues that a team leader should be trained to spend the first two or three days designing the right way to get the job done. He would decide who would best fit the team, what reward system is appropriate, and what information technology is necessary.

Apple is working on a new computer system that should help leaders find the

41

right people for their teams. Now being developed in the company's Advanced Technology Lab in Cupertino, California, the Spider system combines a network of personal computers with a video-conferencing system and a database of employee records. A manager assembling a team can call up profiles of employees who work anywhere from Columbus to Cameroon. On the screen he'll see a color photo of the person, where he works, who reports to him, whom he reports to, and his skills. If the manager wants to interview a candidate in, say, Frankfurt, he can call him over the Spider network and talk with him in living color on the computer screen.

But how can a candidate's boss be persuaded to part with him, even for a temporary assignment? The experts don't have this one figured out completely, though they suspect that much barter will go on in the adaptive organization. One manager may be willing to run short-handed for a while, knowing that when he really needs the manpower he'll get it from elsewhere in the organization.

Another hallmark of the adaptive organization is its openness to outsiders. A greater appreciation of flexibility within seems to encourage a greater use of alliances, partnerships, joint ventures, and other relationships with parties from outside. While some companies that haven't embraced other aspects of the adaptive organization are also moving in this direction, they don't seem to do so with the same gusto.

One key to doing it right, says C. K. Prahalad, a professor at the University of Michigan and a consultant, is the company's ability to recognize its core competencies. A core competency, by his definition, is what a company does best. If its strength is engineering and design, for example, it might want to farm out manufacturing. Says Apple executive vice president Al Eisenstat: "If I can lop off one area of activity and say, 'Gee, I can join with such and such company,' then I can focus my resources on what I do best."

Companies such as Apple, Nike, and IBM (with respect to its PCs) have set themselves up as design, engineering, and marketing companies, farming out much of their manufacturing to those who can do it cheaper and better. Says Jay Galbraith, a management professor at the University of Southern California: "These companies control the flow of product from the factory to the retailer. They act like they own the place, but then don't."

To work smoothly with outsiders, companies must learn to stop thinking like xenophobes and open themselves to the larger world. As Jack Welch of GE puts it, tomorrow's organization will be boundaryless. It will work with outsiders as closely as if they were insiders. For instance, Apple has the Delta consulting firm of New York City hooked into the California company's computer network. Anyone at the New York firm can send a message to CEO John Sculley just as easily as an Apple employee could.

So here you are in the year 2000, and you've got a constantly changing, adaptive organization. How will you keep track of all this chaos? At Cypress Semiconductor, CEO T. J. Rodgers has a computer system that allows him to stay abreast of every employee and team in his fast-moving, decentralized, constantly changing organization. Each employee maintains a list of ten to 15 goals like "Meet with marketing for new product launch" or "Make sure to check with Customer X." Noted next to each goal is when it was agreed upon, when it's due to be finished, and whether it's finished yet or not.

This way it doesn't take layers of expensive bureaucracy to check who's doing what, whether someone has got a light enough workload to be put on a new team, and who's having trouble. Rodgers says he can review the goals of all 1,500 employees in about four hours, which he does each week. He looks only for those falling behind, and then calls not to scold but to ask if there's anything he can do to help them get the job done. On the surface the system may seem bureaucratic, but it takes only about a half-hour a week for employees to review and update their lists.

The toughest part of moving toward the adaptive organization may be selling it to managers. Says Michael Beer, a management professor at the Harvard business school: "It's a fundamental change in the way people think, work, and feel. It's gut wrenching." Xerox's Allaire concurs: "The hardest person to change is the line manager. After he's worked like a dog for five or ten years to get promoted, we have to say to him or her, 'All those reasons you wanted to be a manager? Wrong. You cannot do to your people what was done to you. You have to be a facilitator or a coach and, by the way, we're still going to hold you accountable for the bottom line.'"

In its efforts to become more adaptive, Becton Dickinson ran across much the same challenge. The company had dutifully created cross-functional teams and lectured everyone on the evils of bureaucracy. Even so, nothing seemed to change—the company still had too many middle managers who weren't willing to cede control to others. Says Jim Wessel, a vice president: "We had to get over the mind-set that said, 'I'm not in control, so it must be out of control.'"

A restructuring at Becton Dickinson serendipitously solved the problem by overloading the middle layers with responsibility. Managers found themselves working 14 hours a day just to keep up with the increased workload. According to Wessel: "After about a year of this, they said, 'I can't go on.' And then they started delegating."

Kenan Sahin, president of Kenan Systems Corp., a Cambridge, Massachusetts, software consulting firm, argues that in an adaptive organization, managers will have to change gears readily, following the lead of the person who knows most about the subject. Says he: "Before, when markets were slower, leaders had time to absorb information from experts. Now markets and technologies are becoming so complex, the experts will have to do the leading." In Sahin's vision, a skilled scientist or engineer or marketer who's a leader on one project may have to turn around and be a follower on the next.

AES, the builder and operator of co-generation plants, already takes this principle further than most companies. As part of encouraging everyone from the bottom ranks up to take more initiative, CEO Roger Sant invented something called work week. Once a year, every senior manager in the company must spend a week working in one of the company's generating plants. The employees get to pick what job the boss does. Two years ago, for example, Sant ended up driving a front-end loader, a piece of heavy equipment AES uses to scoop coal onto conveyor belts. Says the chief executive: "It was a mess; there was coal all over the yard."

Work week helped Sant descry some of the obstacles to a more open organization. At one point, workers in the plant told him they couldn't do something because "they" didn't want them to do it. "Who's 'they'?" asked Sant. "You know, 'they,'" replied the workers. Sant quickly realized there was no "they," just old, inefficient work habits and memories of being throttled by bureaucracy. In response, Sant started a "Theybusters" campaign, with appropriate buttons and posters. The result was some surprising employee initiatives: For example one AES worker figured out how to avoid costly plant shutdowns by using tennis balls to temporarily stop leaks in a pollution-control system.

Toward the same end—getting managers and employees to understand how much they have in common in pursuit of personal and corporate goals—Levi Strauss conducts what it terms leadership week. The company sends a top manager, a trainer, and 20 employees off site for up to a week. During that time, people perform a series of exercises designed to explore, among other things, why people work. All right, to make money. But the company believes there's more to it than that.

In one exercise, employees write their own obituaries, which tends to focus the attention wonderfully on what legacy a person would like to leave behind. Says Bill Eaton, a member of the Levi Strauss executive management committee who, like everyone else in the company, prefers to wear you-know-whats to the office: "People are driven not by little business achievements like how many jeans you got shipped through the door, but by things you've done to help other people grow."

Through leadership week, Lynne Southard, a Levi middle manager, realized that she was spending too much time as a slave to rules and regulations and not enough time helping along her employees. Says she: "I learned that leadership is like raising a kid. I clap for my child every time he takes a step." You have to be prepared, however, for the child to take an occasional tumble. Last year, for instance, one of Southard's people failed to buy enough fabric to meet a production run of jeans. It cost the company dearly. Says Southard: "We sat down and found out what went wrong and how to prevent it in the future in a nonthreatening way. Unlike in the old days, there was no blaming and finger pointing."

How nice, you may say, and how touchy-feely. But what does it do for the company? Well, reply the managers who have tried it, it just may give the organization the flexibility first to spot and then to respond to the challenges of the ever-quickening future. And along the way, they add, you can pick up a gratifying measure of personal satisfaction. As Levi Strauss's Eaton testifies, "On a day-to-day basis, my passion comes from backing people's efforts, getting them what they need to do the job, educating them, and working with them as a member of the team." If you like how that sounds, why not start ripping up your organization chart now?

MASSACHUSETTS INSTITUTE OF TECHNOLOGY

ANCONA, KOCHAN, SCULLY,
VAN MAANEN, WESTNEY

MANAGING FOR THE FUTURE

Organizational Behavior
& Processes

MAKING TEAMS WORK

module 3

CONTENTS

MODULE 3 (M-3)

MAKING TEAMS WORK

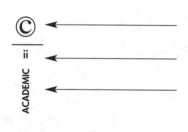

Icon indicates what part you are in, either core Ⓒ or supplemental Ⓢ.

Page number.

Within each part there are sections—Module Overview (OVERVIEW), Academic Perspective (ACADEMIC), Popular Press (PRESS), Case (CASE), Exercise (EXERCISE).

Dedicated to those who have inspired us to try to be better students and teachers.

Special dedications to:
Professor Jack Barbash
Professor Arthur H. Gladstein
Professor Marius B. Jansen
Professor Joanne Martin
Professor Edgar H. Schein

Acquisitions Editor: John R. Szilagyi
Developmental Editor: Jamie Gleich Bryant
Production Editor: Mardell Toomey
Production House: DPS Associates, Inc.
Cover Design: Michael H. Stratton
Marketing Manager: Rob Bloom

Copyright © 1999
by South-Western College Publishing
Cincinnati, Ohio

All Rights Reserved

The text of this publication, or any part thereof, may not be reproduced or transmitted in any form or by any means, electronic or mechanical, including photocopying, recording, storage in an information retrieval system, or otherwise, without the prior written permission of the publisher.

ISBN: 0-538-87690-5

1 2 3 4 5 6 7 D1 4 3 2 1 0 9 8

Printed in the United States of America

South-Western College Publishing
an International Thomson Publishing company ITP®

Cincinnati • Albany • Boston • Detroit • Johannesburg • London • Madrid • Melbourne • Mexico City
New York • Pacific Grove • San Francisco • Scottsdale • Singapore • Tokyo • Toronto

MAKING TEAMS WORK

Unlike other modules, this one does not correspond to a class. This module is designed to provide you with a shared vocabulary and model of teams, team performance, and teamwork, and to give you the tools to make your teams more effective. As you work through this module, you will not only learn about teams conceptually, but will also have the opportunity to practice creating, monitoring, and improving an ongoing team effort.

Our emphasis on learning skills in setting up teams, making them work, and improving their performance over time comes in response to an increased use of teams in today's organizations. This trend of giving more and more tasks to teams, as opposed to individuals, is predicted to continue well into the future as work becomes more complex, cross-functional, and subject to time constraints. In organizations that move to a more networked form, teams are a primary vehicle for coordinating people who have the various skills and expertise needed for a particular job. As managers shift organizational structures to be flatter and more flexible, teams are often configured and reconfigured as demands change. Managers will have to be able to quickly pull a set of individuals together to carry out a specific assignment. Increasingly, as organizations become more global and diverse, that set of individuals will be more heterogeneous in age, gender, race, functional background, priorities, and nationality. Thus, this module focuses primarily on the individual skills needed to promote effective teamwork in the organization of the future.

Unfortunately teams are complex entities that are often difficult to manage. Team members often complain of meetings that are a waste of time, of decisions that never get made, and of conflicts that never get resolved. This module provides pragmatic advice about how to make teams work in an effort to head off problems before they arise.

The module consists of three parts: a **Team Primer**, a **Team Handbook**, and a **Team Assessment Survey**. The **Team Primer** provides an introduction to the basic terminology of teams, the types of teams in organizations today, when to choose a team versus an individual structure, and a model of team effectiveness. The primer is meant to provide some basic level of knowledge about teams so that you begin work with a common vocabulary and some idea of what teams are all about. The model of team effectiveness is meant to show you the primary levers that can be used to improve effectiveness.

The **Team Handbook** is a workbook designed to help you jump-start your work as a team, to avoid common problems, and to continually improve over time. The handbook has concrete suggestions about what team members can do to make their time together more productive, and it contains tips and barriers to point out potential pitfalls and what to do about them. You can use the handbook as a resource when needed, or you can work your way through the entire handbook. It is probably a good idea to skim through the entire handbook before the team meets so that you can get a sense of those parts of the handbook that will be most useful to you.

The handbook is organized around five questions that your team will try to answer over the course of the term. They are:

1. Who are we? (i.e., understanding team composition)
2. What do we want to accomplish? (i.e., establishing team goals)
3. How can we organize ourselves to meet our goals? (i.e., setting a team structure)
4. How will we operate? (i.e., defining team operations)
5. How can we continuously learn and improve?

The **Team Assessment Survey** is a questionnaire designed to evaluate how well teams are doing in answering the five questions posed in the Team Handbook. You will complete the Team Assessment Survey midway through the term so that you can assess how well your team is operating and performing and so you can chart a course for improvement. Team members are not graded on the team assessment survey scores, but you might be graded on how well you use the information from the survey to take stock of the team and plan for the future.

Working on a team can be both a challenging and a rewarding experience. Good luck.

ADDITIONAL ACTIVITIES

The materials in this module represent a first step in making teams work. Other activities that would enhance learning in this area include the following:

1. Meet with your teammates to discuss prior team experiences. Each member can relate what worked and what did not work in these other experiences and what he or she has learned that can transfer to future team experiences. Then pool your learnings and make some decisions about how to integrate these learnings into the ongoing processes of your own team.

2. Call the human resource departments of some local companies to find out how they help teams to get started. Telephone interviews or actual visits might help you learn how team building is done in these companies and what resources are available when teams are first formed. This information can then be pooled and the team can decide if any of these organizational practices can be applied to your own team.

3. Try to obtain access to teams in local companies, in your university, or in volunteer agencies in your community. Through telephone or personal interviews, learn what particular early steps helped and hindered the work of these teams. Probe about what structures, activities, and decisions helped teams to move ahead and be productive, and which ones interfered with team progress. Again, this information can then be pooled and the team can decide if any of these organizational practices can be applied to your own team.

4. Take some time to think about your vision of the perfect team. Go into a fair amount of detail, including such things as how often the team would meet, the type of leadership that would exist, how members would handle conflict, how work would be allocated, etc. Then meet with your team to exchange visions. Discuss the similarities and differences across visions. Then negotiate among yourselves on what aspects of each vision you will try to incorporate into your own team.

5. Additional reading material might help you get more of a sense of how to build an effective team. Suggested readings include:

Hackman, J. 1990. *Groups That Work (and Those That Don't)*. San Francisco: Jossey-Bass.

Hanson, P. G. and B. Lubin. 1986. "Characteristics of an Effective Work Team." *Organization Development Journal*, Spring 1986. Hirschhorn, L. 1991. *Managing the New Team Environment. Reading*, MA: Addison-Wesley.

Reddy W. B. and K. Jamison, eds. 1988. *Team Building: Blueprints for Productivity and Satisfaction*. San Diego, CA: NTL Institute and University Associates.

Schein, E. 1969. *Process Consultation: Its Role in Organization Development*. Reading, MA: Addison-Wesley.

Smith K. K. and D. N. Berg. 1987. *Paradoxes of Group Life*. San Francisco: Jossey-Bass.

Tjosvold, D. 1986. *Working Together to Get Things Done: Managing for Organizational Productivity*. Lexington, MA: Lexington Books.

M-3

core

A TEAM PRIMER

Teams—it's a buzz word of the nineties. Everyone's talking about autonomous work teams and empowerment, about teamwork, and being a team player. Teams are a central element in the "new" organization and a mechanism to cope with downsizing and decentralized decision making. We discuss team processes and team structures. But what does it all mean?

Many of these words are so common that we all assume we know what each other is talking about. In reality, these terms mean different things in different organizations. Even team researchers do not agree on definitions. To make certain that we have a common understanding of the words and concepts all of us use in discussing teams, we offer this primer. We will start off by defining some key terms and types of teams, then discuss under what circumstances a team might be formed, and then provide an overall model of team performance, in which we define key terms and relationships.

KEY TERMS

One of the major distinctions that creates some order out of the chaos is that between a working group and a team.

A **working group** is defined as a small set of individuals (three to about twenty-five) who are aware of each other, interact with one another, and who have a sense of themselves together as a unit (Schein, 1992). A working group's performance is a function of what each member does as an individual because members do not work interdependently and do not share responsibility for each other's results. Successful working groups get together to share information, perspectives, and best practices; make decisions that help each member do his or her job better; and reinforce individual performance standards (Katzenbach and Smith, 1993). Many top management teams are really working groups in which members get together to help each functional or divisional manager do a better job. The firm's performance is the sum of each member's contribution, and each individual's performance has little to do with how the others are doing.

A **team** includes all of the characteristics of a working group but adds several others, including members working interdependently and being jointly accountable for performance goals. Thus, team members work both as individuals and jointly. While it is easy for a working group to point to what each member did and accomplished, teams meld member efforts and have a "collective work product" (Katzenbach and Smith, 1993). When you read a team report, it reflects members building on each other's contributions and communicating in a unified voice. Thus, all members are accountable for their joint products. Top management teams that really function as a team take joint responsibility and work together to create and meet the strategic and operational goals of the firm. Members of these teams are measured on how well the firm does and members' performance is a function of how well they work together.

The distinguishing characteristics of teams are intensity and interdependence. The team's effectiveness depends on how members work together. A team has more power and potential than a working group, but it requires more investment by members to realize that potential. A team is not better than a group; it is simply more effective when the task at hand requires interdependence and joint accountability. Teams may also be chosen over working groups when members want the greater intensity of the team experience, the opportunity to learn about how to work in a team, or the sense of belonging that comes from working so closely with others.

High-performing teams are those that excel in several categories of team effectiveness. Team effectiveness can be broken down into four components:

1. Performance (how well team members produce output, measured in terms of quality, quantity, timeliness, efficiency, and innovation)
2. Member satisfaction (how well team members create a positive experience through commitment, trust, and meeting individual needs)
3. Team learning (how well team members can acquire new skills, perspectives, and behaviors as needed by changing circumstances)
4. Outsider satisfaction (how well team members meet the needs of outside constituencies such as customers and suppliers)

High-performing teams somehow manage to do their jobs better than others thought possible by setting difficult and clear performance goals, structuring themselves to get the work done, taking into account member and outsider needs, and changing as circumstances warrant. These teams are often held up as exemplars throughout the organization.

Teamwork, a word often confused with teams, represents a set of values whereby members of some collective (a group, team, division, or organization) are encouraged to help one another, to listen and give feedback to others, and to provide support and recognition to others. Teamwork values can exist even if a team does not.

A **team player** is a member of some collective (a group, team, division, or organization) who embodies teamwork values. He or she is known for putting group or team needs above personal ambition and for being encouraging, being a good listener, and providing support and recognition to others. A team player works hard to make the collective meet its goals. In some organizations where teams and teamwork are widely used, employees are evaluated on how well they carry out the team player role.

TYPES OF TEAMS

As teams proliferate in organizations, they are taking many forms. Some of the more common types of teams include:

Quality Circles

Quality circles have become popular as a result of the total quality programs that have swept through Japan, the United States, and parts of Europe. Quality circles (QCs) are small groups of employees who get together to solve quality-related problems such as quality control, cost reduction, production planning, and even product design. Quality circle members get training in problem-solving techniques, meet together about once a week on company time, and report in to management on problems that are outside of their control (Nelson and Quick, 1994).

Quality circles first became popular in Japan after World War II as the Japanese imported and embraced the teachings of W. Edward Deming. Their use has also been widespread in Sweden, as companies like Volvo incorporated them and as workers demanded more involvement, and later in the United States as companies like Ford, Xerox, and Hewlett-Packard began to think of quality as part of a competitive strategy.

Cross-Functional Teams

Cross-functional teams consist of members that represent multiple functions within the firm, e.g., manufacturing, engineering, finance, marketing, and sales. These teams are formed to improve the coordination among functions in such areas as product development, process improvement, and allocation of resources. Cross-functional teams are thought to better link upstream and downstream organizational activity (so that, for example, manufacturing considerations can be designed into a product rather than being discovered after prototypes already exist), to push decision making down to those who have the real expertise, and to speed coordination. These teams bring the necessary expertise together but members often need time to learn how to bring their diverse views together.

Self-Managed Teams

Self-managed teams (also known as autonomous work groups) are ones that make decisions that were once restricted to management. These teams may be given the responsibility to hire members, allocate tasks and roles to members, determine work schedules and work flow, and handle disputes. As companies move to create self-managed teams, they are said to be empowering employees since power and decision making are moved downward in the organizational hierarchy. Members of these teams often receive training in problem solving and negotiation. Since these teams can be threatening to middle managers, a move to this type of structure needs to include appropriate change-management tools.

Office of the President

The office of the president is the term often given to the set of executives that run a corporation. While the dominant model of firm leadership still involves a COO (chief operating officer) reporting to a CEO (chief executive officer), with functional or divisional managers reporting to the COO, many organizations are moving to team leadership. Under this model the COO is eliminated and the functional or divisional managers report directly to the CEO. This set of executives is given the title of Office of the President and it collectively assumes the role of the COO in managing internal operations and helps the CEO formulate strategy and manage external relations. In order to carry out this task the executives need to shift their focus from their function or division to the corporation (Ancona and Nadler, 1989).

Transnational Teams

A transnational team is one composed of people from different nations. As organizations become more global in their operations, there has been a corresponding increase in the number of transnational teams, including joint-venture teams where the sponsoring companies are from different countries. Transnational teams pose a particular type of challenge as nationality has been shown to influence individuals' cognitive schema, values, nonverbal behavior, and language, all of which influence behavior in teams. As Linda Hill (1994) points out, there are cross-national differences on the individual-collective dimension (Erez and Earley, 1993). In individualistic cultures such as the United States and the Netherlands people tend to use personal achievements to define themselves, view relationships as more short-term, and value the individual more than the team. In collectivist cultures such as Japan and Brazil, however, there is high commitment to, and identification with, the team, and group harmony, unity, and loyalty are valued more than individual gain (Hill, 1994).

These observations are generalizations, however, and do not hold for all individuals. Furthermore, organizational culture can reinforce or reduce the impact of national culture on an individual. In addition, there is some evidence that the more people are exposed to multiple nationalities, the less likely they are to conform to the customs and beliefs of their own (Hambrick, et. al., 1994).

TEAMS VERSUS INDIVIDUALS

While teams have clearly become a fad of the nineties, it is equally clear that not all team initiatives have been successful. While teams create the promise of greater competitiveness, faster decision making, fewer levels of hierarchy, greater commitment and quality, and greater employee satisfaction, they can also be difficult to manage, evaluate, and support. Creating teams requires an investment in training and organizational design. It often means making changes in existing reward systems and in the corporate culture that surrounds the team. Therefore, one should not jump into team designs unless the potential advantages outweigh the costs.

When work is structured for individuals, there are a number of advantages for both the individuals and the company. Work often takes less time and individuals feel a greater sense of control over their work. Under this mode individual accountability is very high, and limiting the involvement of others can lessen their ability to interfere or obstruct work. It is easier to measure and reward good performance, and the costs involved in getting people to learn how to work together are not incurred.

Teams also offer advantages. A team design usually results in greater ownership of the final product and high levels of commitment to implementing the team's ideas. Teams are a vehicle to pool diverse views and perspectives as well as for refining raw ideas. Teams foster innovation and allow for coordination across individuals and departments. Finally, teams provide many social rewards to individuals who are seeking support, camaraderie, and assistance in their work.

So, how can one determine whether or not to use a team approach? The following conditions should be present:

- The work requires a range of different skills, views, or expertise.
- The different components of the work are highly interdependent.
- There is sufficient time to organize and structure team effort.
- The organizational reward structure and culture support a team approach.
- There is a need to build commitment to a course of action or set of decisions.
- The issues being worked on require refinement.
- There are high needs for innovation and coordination.
- Members can be trusted not to purposefully obstruct the team's efforts.
- Individuals desire a team experience.

(This list is based on those contained in *Developing Effective Work Teams*, published by the Delta Consulting Group).

A TEAM EFFECTIVENESS MODEL

Once a team is formed, what factors are likely to contribute to its success? Figure 3.1 presents a model of team effectiveness. The model shows the organizational culture, team design, and rewards leading to a set of team operations that contribute to team effectiveness. A feedback loop from effectiveness back to team operations shows that these two components interact over time.

As mentioned earlier **team effectiveness** is thought to have four components (see Sundstrom and McIntyre, 1994):

- *Performance*—how well team members produce output, measured in terms of quality, quantity, timeliness, efficiency, and innovation
- *Member satisfaction*—how well team members create a positive experience through commitment, trust, and meeting individual needs
- *Team learning*—how well team members acquire new skills, perspectives, and behaviors as needed by changing circumstances
- *Outsider satisfaction*—how well team members meet the needs of outside constituencies such as customers and suppliers

In turn, team effectiveness is a function of **team operations**, which have two components:

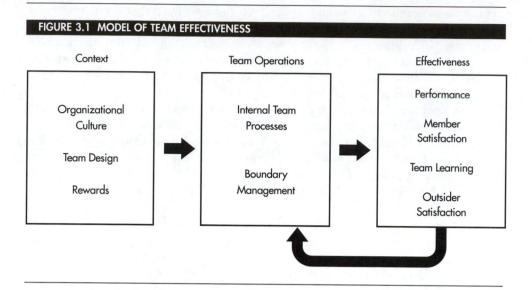

FIGURE 3.1 MODEL OF TEAM EFFECTIVENESS

- *Internal team processes*—the way in which team members interact with each other to accomplish the task and to keep themselves together as a team. Key processes include communication, influence, task and maintenance functions, decision making, conflict management, atmosphere, and emotional issues (see Module 5, Team Processes, for more detail about these processes).
- *Boundary management*—the way in which teams define their boundaries, identify key external constituencies, and interact with those outsiders. Key boundary management activities include buffering the team from political infighting, persuading top management to support the team's work, and coordinating and negotiating with other groups on work deadlines (see Module 6, Teams in Organizations, for more detail about these processes).

Team operations are the product of the **context** in which the team is created. Context includes the organizational culture in which the team resides, the way in which the team is designed, and the rewards given to the individuals that make up the team:

- *Organizational culture*—the values and underlying assumptions about teams and teamwork that are communicated through symbols, stories, and rituals. Attempts at creating teams have often failed because the underlying culture was very individualistic, despite the rhetoric of teams. Organizational cultures that emphasize cooperation, mutual responsibility, and the exchange of information are more supportive of teams than those that emphasize barriers and distinctions (Orlikowski, 1994). Other authors have stressed the importance of egalitarian cultures (Gittell, 1994) and those in which individualism and teamwork are both truly held up as the ideal.
- *Team design*—the way in which teams are put together, including their composition, the nature of their task, and their structure. Composition refers to the make-up of the team. The mix of skills, backgrounds, experience, and personalities found in team members profoundly affects the team's ability to work effectively on different tasks. In addition, the extent to which team members share values and perspectives affects members' ability to cohere and work together. The nature of the task refers to whether or not the team's task is designed to be interdependent. For example, two companies designed their computer repair units in very different ways. One firm gave each engineer a

given geographic territory and held him or her responsible for it. The other firm gave a team of engineers several geographic territories and let them jointly determine how best to service those areas. The first company provided individual-level feedback on customer satisfaction and average time to customer, while the second provided this data at the team level. Obviously some tasks lend themselves more easily to a team design, so the nature of the task needs to be considered when a team is formed. Structure includes the size of the team, the way in which members organize the work (e.g., when to work in subgroups, deadlines, what approaches to take for different tasks, and who will be responsible for what), the formal roles that members are given (e.g., facilitator or project manager), the goals of the team, and the norms—or expectations about how to behave—that team members bring to the team.

- *Rewards*—the rewards, both formal and informal, are a key determinant of how team members will interact with one another and those outside the team. Cross-functional teams whose members are evaluated by functional bosses often demonstrate higher levels of conflict than those whose members are evaluated by the team leader. Similarly, managers who promote employees based solely on individual achievement are sending a double message when they say that teams are important. Thus, the rewards need to support the type of teamwork that is desired in the organization.

While the model shown in Figure 3.1 identifies some key elements that affect team effectiveness, we have shied away from identifying universal characteristics of a good team. This is because there are a number of different ways to be effective and because teams in different environments need to be configured differently. Teams that exist in an environment with greater external demands, due to how threatening the environment is, its pace of change, its complexity, and its interconnectedness, must pay more attention to external boundary processes. Teams that have greater interdependence, more divergent membership, and a more complex task must work harder on their internal team processes, such as communication and conflict resolution. Similarly, different team designs may work for different types of teams and different organizational cultures.

Although there is no one best way, as organizations experiment in their quest to become the organizations of the future we learn more about how the key elements can be configured to produce effective teams. Consider, for example, Southwest Airlines, the fastest growing airline of the 1990s, with the best record for reliability, safety, and customer satisfaction. Southwest achieves these outcomes using fewer resources and has broken through the cost/quality boundary that was taken for granted in the airline industry, much as Toyota did with its lean production strategy in the auto industry (Gittell, 1995).

According to Gittell, Southwest's strategy relies on quick turnaround time. Airplanes arrive at the gate, are unloaded, serviced, reloaded, and depart in an average of 17 minutes, compared with the industry average of 43 minutes. Behind this strategy are cross-functional teams that coordinate up to 10 distinct functional groups, from pilots to cabin cleaners. Rather than add costly buffers between these different functional groups and have decisions made further up the hierarchy, Southwest has given frontline workers more decision-making responsibilities. These sets of cross-functional workers communicate often, work at improving their ability at working together rather than trying to blame one another for failures, and engage in rapid decision making as planes arrive at the gate. Team members keep each other informed of what is going on in other parts of the airport and about weather conditions. Thus, there is both internal and boundary management work going on. This interdependence is fostered by a project manager, shared accountability for outcomes across functional lines, an egalitarian organizational culture, shared monetary rewards, training and selection for teamwork skills, and flexible work rules. As Gittell notes, "Together this set of practices offers the means for employees to transfer information across functional lines, the incentive to do so, and a means to strengthen the underlying relationships" (1994, p. 4).

The Southwest example shows how specific contextual factors create teams that are able to engage in complex internal and boundary management processes. The key for using the model is creating the culture, design, and reward system that will best facilitate the processes that are needed for a given task. Under these conditions team effectiveness results. In turn, the effectiveness feeds back to enhance the motivation of the team and its ability to carry out the appropriate processes. Teams can then enter a positive cycle in which their processes and their effectiveness continue to improve. Unfortunately, many teams are not designed very well or exist in cultures that are not supportive. Under these conditions teams can enter into negative cycles in which team operations are not adequately carried out, resulting in low levels of effectiveness, which, in turn, create additional conflict and confusion in the team, further eroding effectiveness.

The team effectiveness model acts as a guide to team management. Once the team context is set, the model suggests a series of questions that act as a guide for effective team management. These questions include:

1. Who are we? (i.e., understanding team composition)
2. What do we want to accomplish? (i.e., establishing team goals)
3. How can we organize ourselves to meet our goals? (i.e., setting a team structure)
4. How will we operate? (i.e., defining team operations)
5. How can we continuously learn and improve?

In attempting to answer these questions we believe that teams will enhance their effectiveness. The Team Handbook that follows takes team members through some specific suggestions, tips, and barriers that will help them to jump-start their work together, avoid common problems, and continually improve over time.

The management of teams is fraught with difficulties. The terminology is often ambiguous, the decision to use teams involves many costs and benefits, and there are multiple roads to success and failure. This primer has attempted to clarify the terminology, outline the tradeoffs between individuals and teams, and present a model of team effectiveness. With this primer as background we hope that you can go on to make your own team experience a successful one.

REFERENCES

Ancona, D. G., and D. Nadler. 1989. "Top Hats and Executive Tales: Designing the Senior Team." *Sloan Management Review*, 19, pp. 19–28.

Delta Consulting Group, Inc. 1996. *Developing Effective Work Teams.*

Erez, M., and P. C. Earley. 1993. *Culture, Self-Identity, and Work.* New York: Oxford University Press.

Gladstein, D. 1984. "Groups in Context: A Model of Task Group Effectiveness." *Administrative Science Quarterly*, 29, pp. 499–517.

Gittell, J. H. 1994. *Crossfunctional Coordination and Human Resource Systems.* Submission to the Academy of Management, Organization and Management Theory Division.

Gittell, J. H. 1995. *Crossfunctional Coordination and Human Resource Systems: Evidence from the Airline Industry.* Dissertation, Massachusetts Institute of Technology, Sloan School of Management.

Hambrick, D. C., S. C. Davison, S. A. Snell, and C. C. Snow. 1994. *When Groups Consist of Multiple Nationalities: Toward a New Understanding of the Implications.* Lexington, MA: International Consortium for Executive Development.

Hill, L. 1994. *Managing Your Team.* Harvard Business School, N9-494-081.

Katzenbach, J. R., and D. K. Smith. 1993. "The Discipline of Teams." *Harvard Business Review*, March–April 1993, pp. 111–124.

Nelson, D. L., and J. C. Quick. 1994. *Organizational Behavior: Foundations, Realities, and Challenges.* St. Paul, MN: West Publishing Company.

Orlikowski, W. J. 1994. *Information Technologies as Integrative Mechanisms: Insights From Practice.* Submission to the Academy of Management, Organization and Management Theory Division.

Schein, E. 1992. *Organizational Culture and Leadership*, 2nd. ed. San Francisco, CA: Jossey-Bass Inc.

Sundstrom, E., and M. McIntyre. 1994. *Measuring Work-Group Effectiveness: Practices, Issues, and Prospects.* Working paper. Knoxville, TN: University of Tennessee, Department of Psychology.

Ⓒ

11

ACADEMIC

Team Handbook

CONTENTS

This handbook outlines a set of tools to enhance team effectiveness. It is designed to help team members (managers, students, consultants, etc.) to jump-start their work together, to avoid common problems, and to continually improve over time. The handbook can be used in its entirety to guide a team along its development, or it can be used in pieces to deal with specific issues as they arise.

The basic assumption of this handbook is that team effectiveness is enhanced when team members explicitly try to answer five important questions:

I. Who are we?
II. What do we want to accomplish?
III. How can we organize ourselves to meet our goals?
IV. How will we operate?
V. How can we continuously learn and improve?

For each question there is a brief *description* of what the team is meant to address. Then there are a series of *suggestions*, including *tips* and alerts to *barriers*, which ought to help the team as it works to answer the question. The suggestions included in the handbook are just that, suggestions, so feel free to be creative in designing your own method of answering the questions posed. Hopefully, this handbook will help your team experience to be both rewarding and fun.

15

HANDBOOK

A NOTE ABOUT GETTING STARTED

The start-up of any team is a unique time and opportunity to set core modes of operation. As Edgar Schein, Professor of Organization Studies at MIT, points out, it is also a time when four issues are raised for individuals: those related to identity (who am I in this team?); power/control (who will have it and what will that mean for me?); goals (which of mine will be met in this team?); and acceptance/intimacy (what will my emotional attachment be?). These questions play out over the life of the team, but are especially influential in the beginning stages. Stay aware of your own and others' expectations, and be aware that finding tentative answers to these questions is as important as getting other work done. Teams are dynamic, fascinating entities. As the old adage goes, look to make this team a whole that is greater than the sum of its parts.

I. WHO ARE WE?

DESCRIPTION

The team should begin by coming to terms with its composition (i.e., understanding the make-up of the team). Individuals approaching a team task each bring their own "baggage"—positive and negative—reflecting their backgrounds, experiences, personalities, and prejudices. Members represent different races, genders, and religions, as well as different hierarchical levels and functional backgrounds. Members bring different expectations, needs, and abilities to contribute to any particular task. Only through a process of mutual discovery can the team come to understand how to harness these differences toward the team's goals. By candidly exploring who is best suited to each task and each role, the team can configure itself to operate most effectively.

Before the team meets to start this process of mutual discovery, it is useful for each team member to think about what he or she brings in terms of expectations, needs, preferences, skills, experiences, biases, and commitment level. This information can then form the basis of initial discussions among members.

Plan to hold initial discussions in a setting where a comfortable atmosphere can be created. Members should try to listen carefully to one another, and try to put themselves in the shoes of the other person to understand what each team member needs and how those needs might be met. There should be some general discussion about how the team might best capitalize on the similarities and differences that exist. This discussion isn't a one-time event; it needs to be ongoing as member needs, preferences, and skills shift. Remember that the more individuals feel that their own needs are met, the more committed and productive they can be for the team as a whole.

HANDBOOK   16

SUGGESTIONS

To begin the process of getting to know each other:

1. Go around the team several times, having members convey the following:

- Birthplace, previous places lived

- College attended, major

- Hobbies and interests

- Work experiences

- Unique skills and areas of expertise

- Prior team experiences—the best and the worst

- What you most want to accomplish in this team

Alternative: Break up into pairs. Have each member of the pair interview the other using the questions in #1. Then have the pairs report each other's responses to the rest of the team.

2. Discuss your responses as a team.

3. Discuss how you can capitalize on the similarities and differences that exist.

TIPS

- Determine how much time you have for this activity and pace yourselves accordingly.

- Distribute addresses and phone numbers to aid communication.

- Hold the initial discussion in an informal setting, e.g., over dinner, at the beach, or at someone's apartment.

- Don't be too serious; humor help everyone to relax, and getting to know each other should be as much fun as it is work.

BARRIERS

- Some people have a harder time opening up than others.

- Be aware of cultural differences in participation.

(So be patient and respectful and consider using the suggested alternative.)

II. WHAT DO WE WANT TO ACCOMPLISH?

DESCRIPTION

Before a team can organize itself to work effectively members need to agree upon goals. Goals serve to focus team member activity on specific tasks and motivate members toward a similar endpoint. They also enable the team to set milestones and measure their progress. Clarity and specificity are important, because when goals are ambiguous they often create confusion and conflict. Team goals come in four categories:

- *Performance* refers to team output. Specific goals for the quality, quantity, time-liness, efficiency, and innovation levels that the team would like to produce will determine the work that members need to carry out. For example, new product development teams set goals related to budgets, schedules, technical specifications, and product innovation. Student teams need to determine the grades they want, the level of preparation for each class, the standards for assignments and the time they want to devote to the class.

- *Member satisfaction* involves providing team members with a positive experience. It is often related to the level of commitment and trust created within the team. Satisfaction is also related to meeting personal goals, such as having a good time, getting to know other team members, or establishing a supportive environment. Personal goals also include the time and commitment that members wish to offer.

- *Team learning* refers to the team's ability to survive, improve, and adapt to changing circumstances. Learning goals include finding innovative approaches to problems, becoming more efficient over time, acquiring new skills, and changing norms and procedures when external circumstances warrant change.

- *Outsider satisfaction* has to do with meeting the demands of, and pleasing, outside constituencies, such as customers, suppliers, clients, government agencies, or community groups. For example, if a product development team has a high-quality product but they cannot convince the marketing group and the customers of its appeal, then there is a problem. Similarly a student team may work many hours on a project, but unless the professor is satisfied, they may not reap the rewards of their labor.

18

HANDBOOK

SUGGESTIONS

To begin the process of establishing goals:

1. Have each person rate the importance of a list of goals that you generate as a team. Some examples might be:

- Getting an A on our team project

- Being well prepared for class and for team assignments

- Having a high level of camaraderie in the team

- Having a good time

- Having efficient meetings

- Learning a lot about organizational behavior and how to manage a team

- Satisfying the professor and other student teams

2. Tally up the results of your ratings. Then discuss the ratings, negotiate, and agree upon a preliminary set of team goals.

TIPS

- Identify some smaller goals that you can accomplish in the short term. Examples might be finding a firm for the course project within two weeks or finding a set time and place to meet every week.

- More challenging goals may give you more direction and a greater sense of purpose but require more commitment by all members.

- Continually test people's ongoing commitment to goals, and level of agreement. As deadlines approach and/or team norms settle, you may need to explicitly renegotiate.

BARRIERS

- Conflicting goals can be a major barrier to a team's progress.

- Teams struggle without a definition of goals.

(Don't assume that others will share goals. Getting an A and having fun may seem obvious to you, but to others they may not be worth the time or energy they demand. All goals need to be negotiable at the start.)

19

HANDBOOK

III. HOW CAN WE ORGANIZE OURSELVES TO MEET OUR GOALS?

DESCRIPTION

Once goals have been set, the team needs to organize itself to meet those goals. Teams will develop different levels of structure depending upon their tasks and make-ups. Very detailed and predictable work is better suited to high levels of structure than abstract and ambiguous work. Some people enjoy lots of structure and clarity while others like the free and easy approach. Your team can be creative in the way in which it structures its activities.

There are three major aspects to organizing a team:

- *Creating a work structure* requires that the team move from the goals to the work that needs to be done to achieve those goals. For example, if a new product team wants to be very innovative, it has to spend time brainstorming, looking at what the competition is doing, and experimenting with new materials. A student team that must analyze an organization needs to contact the organization, develop interview questions, analyze its data, and write up a report. Once the work has been identified, the team decides how it will organize itself to do the work. One key issue is determining when members will work alone and when they will work in subgroups or as a whole. Also important are when work must be done, what approaches will be taken, and who will be responsible.

- *Roles* are specific activities that are taken on by particular individuals. While there are many different role typologies that are available, here we focus on the roles of facilitator, project manager, and boundary manager. The **facilitator** focuses on task and maintenance functions during meetings. Task functions help the team to do its work, while maintenance functions hold the team together so that members can continue to get along with one another and even have some fun. The **project manager** organizes the work plan and sees that it is implemented. The **boundary manager** determines how the team will deal with key stakeholders such as clients, other teams, and upper management. As a team comes to understand its task and members better, additional roles will develop.

- *Norms* refer to expectations of acceptable behavior. They are unwritten rules enforced by team members. Norms can cover all aspects of team behavior. Norms that seem to cause the most disruption to team behavior if they are not discussed include meeting norms, working norms, communication norms, leadership norms, and consideration norms.

SUGGESTIONS—WORK STRUCTURE

Follow these steps to help you manage your work:

1. List the goals that need to be accomplished.

2. List the major pieces of work that need to get done to meet the goals.

3. Work backwards from final deadlines to define the due dates by which each piece of work must be completed. Set milestones to measure progress.

4. Decide whether each piece of work will be done by an individual, a subgroup, or the entire team and then assign people to responsibilities.

5. Clarify which members have primary responsibility for the task versus those who will contribute to the effort.

6. Prepare and build in time for contingencies, problems, and emerging issues.

TIPS

- Ensure that each member buys into his or her responsibilities at outlined.

- Use a responsibility chart as part of your plan. Include who is responsible for which pieces of work by when.

- Distribute the plan and use it to measure progress.

- Use the plan as a picture of current agreements among members, and change it as circumstances warrant.

- Celebrate when milestones are reached and people have met deadlines.

BARRIERS

- Initial enthusiasm may lead to commitments that are not kept.

- Inadequate preparation can lead to a poorly written plan.

- A plan that is too structured can harm creativity.

- Changes in the plan may result in members resenting those who have not followed through on their commitments.

SUGGESTIONS—THE FACILITATOR ROLE

A *facilitator* role is to:

1. Focus the team toward the task.

2. Engage participation from all members.

3. Protect individuals from personal attack.

4. Suggest alternative procedures when the team is stalled.

5. Summarize and clarify the team's decisions.

TIPS

- Be neutral, do not interject your views.

- Keep the team to its agreed time frame.

- Express out loud what you think is happening (e.g., "everybody seems to be very tense since John spoke").

- Don't be afraid to confront problems openly—that's your job.

- Listen carefully and test for understanding.

- Allow members to be silent if they do not wish to speak.

BARRIERS

- People often feel personal discomfort with conflict.

- People often fear that being an active facilitator will look like power grabbing.

(Just take a stab at the role; be prepared to discuss with others what you did well and what you did poorly.)

SUGGESTIONS—THE PROJECT MANAGER ROLE

The *project manager* role is to:

1. Develop the project plan.

2. Remind members of upcoming deadlines and commitments.

3. Bring up issues that may mean a plan revision is needed.

4. Confront the team when the plan is not followed.

TIPS

- Get everyone involved in developing and reevaluating the project plan. It should be a team, not an individual project.

- Do not delegate all work to individuals. If there is no joint work, you are just a collection of individuals, not a real team.

BARRIERS

- Some people will volunteer for too much work and others will not want to do anything.

- All the work that needs to be done will not be clear when the team is starting out.

(The project plan, like other aspects of the team's work, is an area for discussion and negotiation. Don't be afraid to confront problems and to push for clarification.)

SUGGESTIONS—THE BOUNDARY MANAGER ROLE

The *boundary manager* role is to:

1. Identify key stakeholders, people or groups who will influence, or be influenced by, the work you are doing.

2. Decide what to do with each stakeholder:

- Influence

- Inform

- Involve

- Get information

- Coordinate

- Get permission

3. Assign responsibility for each outsider to a specific team member.

TIPS

- Begin early and keep up the relationship with each stakeholder.

- Ensure that team members do not overlap or send mixed signals.

- Look in all directions, not just up.

BARRIERS

- It is not always easy to recognize who will affect the team.

- High levels of interaction with outsiders can make it harder to integrate across team members.

SUGGESTIONS—AGREEING UPON NORMS

Meet and discuss your team's norms. Include the following categories:

1. *Meeting norms.* Expectations include when, where, and how often to have meetings. What is expected of members with regard to attendance, timeliness, and preparation. Also, what is the balance between work and fun?

2. *Working norms.* Expectations involve standards, deadlines, how equally effort and work should be distributed, how work will be reviewed, and what to do if people do not follow through on commitments.

3. *Communication norms.* Expectations center on when communication should take place, who is responsible, how it should be done (phone, e-mail, etc.), and how to discuss feelings about the team or members.

4. *Leadership norms.* Expectations include whether a leader is needed, if leadership is rotated, responsibilities, and how to keep the leader from doing all the work.

5. *Consideration norms.* Expectations center on being considerate of members' comfort with things like smoking, swearing, etc., and their ability to change norms if they are uncomfortable with what is going on in the team.

TIPS

- Spend time discussing norms in order to agree upon a common approach.

- Keep norms simple and consistent (e.g., meeting every Friday at 1:00 p.m. is easier than picking a new time each week).

BARRIERS

- Subjects that are difficult to talk about often remain undiscussed.

- Members often shy away from responsibilities or team needs for leadership.

(The facilitator should push to see that all categories of team norms are discussed, especially when there are problems.)

IV. HOW WILL WE OPERATE?

DISCUSSION

One of the most interesting and exciting aspects of teams is the way their dynamics unfold. The interaction among team members is often unpredictable and different than anticipated when the team began. This interaction among team members is called team process. As team process unfolds it often reshapes the team's structure, which, in turn, creates a new process. Thus, structure and process remain interrelated throughout the life of the team.

Team process includes communication, influence, task and maintenance functions, decision making, atmosphere, and conflict resolution; that is, who talks to whom, how often, who is influencing decisions, how the team organizes itself, how conflict is handled, and what happens in and between meetings (see Module 5, Group Process Observation Guide, for more detail.) While the previous section outlined the plans for how the team will operate, team process focuses on the behaviors that actually take place among members. For example, while the plan may give responsibility for a certain activity to one member, influence on decisions may come entirely from another.

There are a number of tools that have been developed to help harness the potential of team process. Here we include agenda setting, brainstorming, multivoting, and tips on cross-cultural communication. Agenda setting helps to organize meetings and improve efficiency, brainstorming is a tool for generating a lot of creative ideas, and multivoting enhances the team's ability to reach consensus. Consensus means that there is a solution that is acceptable to all, not necessarily the top strategy or preference of any or all. It is achieved by negotiating key requirements among the parties so that everyone can "live with" the outcome. The suggestions for cross-cultural communication help communication among diverse team members.

SUGGESTIONS—PLANNING AN AGENDA

When planning an agenda:

1. Write down the major items that the team wishes to tackle.

2. Ensure that all team members have the opportunity to contribute.

3. Clarify what the team wants to accomplish for each item—discussion, brainstorming, making a decision, taking action, etc.

4. Prioritize items and allocate time to each.

5. Leave time at the end to discuss how the meeting went.

TIPS

- The first item on the agenda should be a "check-in," in which each person spends a minute or so telling other members what is currently on his or her mind. This activity legitimizes air time for everyone.

- Make the agenda available to members before the meeting.

- Assign a timekeeper to keep the team on track.

- Leave time to discuss the team process, not just the task.

BARRIERS

- An agenda that is too structured can stifle creativity and an open atmosphere.

- An agenda that is not followed can frustrate team members.

© 27 HANDBOOK

SUGGESTIONS—BRAINSTORMING

When brainstorming:

1. Clearly define the subject or problem to be discussed.

2. Give people time to think and write responses individually.

3. Invite everyone to call out their ideas (or go around the team).

4. Write down all ideas.

TIPS

- Don't evaluate. Something that sounds unrealistic or off the mark initially may spark a great new idea. (Beginning ideas aren't imperfect solutions, they are just beginning ideas.)

- Encourage creative and different thinking. (There are many creativity tools available.)

- Encourage people to hitchhike, i.e., build on others' ideas.

- Some people take longer than others to form their ideas. Allow some silence to get everyone's ideas out.

- Do not stop too soon. Eventually people will come up with more ideas.

BARRIERS

- People are sometimes afraid that their beginning ideas will be "wrong" or sound stupid. (This is why it's essential to avoid evaluating too early and to set up an uninhibited atmosphere.)

- Once you have generated a number of ideas, their quantity and lack of realism may be overwhelming. (This is why it is equally essential to set up a non-threatening way to select and build on those ideas with the most promise for a new but workable solution.)

SUGGESTIONS—MULTIVOTING

To multivote you should:

1. Brainstorm ideas.

2. Discuss what each idea means and how it will solve the problem at hand.

3. Have each person vote on the top four choices. You can split your votes any way you want to across the set.

4. Choose the three to five ideas that are the highest priorities.

5. Identify similarities and differences among ideas, then positive and negative aspects of each idea, then what is really important to each person.

6. Rework the top priorities as needed, and have each person vote on his or her top two priorities.

TIPS

- Sometimes ideas are similar and votes are split. Consolidate ideas so that strong support is not watered down.

- Try to be open to the ideas of others. You are trying to come to a team decision, not to win at all costs.

BARRIERS

- Some members will find this method too structured.

29

HANDBOOK

SUGGESTIONS—COMMUNICATING CROSS-CULTURALLY

Members of cross-cultural teams generated this list of suggestions based on their experiences over several months together:

1. Recognize the different cultures and languages represented in the team.

2. Meet in areas with minimal noise and distraction.

3. Have adequate time for meetings.

4. Start meetings with a check-in, in which each member spends a minute or so telling other members what is on his or her mind. This exercise forces everyone to contribute equally at the start of the meeting.

5. Record main points on a chalkboard or similar display. Distribute meeting notes.

6. Check frequently to make sure all members are in agreement with what the team has decided.

7. Get to know each other personally.

8. Assign pairs of buddies: one buddy from the host country and one from a foreign country.

9. Do not use slang or complex language.

10. Be aware that behavior is viewed differently in different countries. Check on what it means to interrupt, to resolve conflict, to discuss feelings, to disagree.

Be patient! Remember, the relationship you build in this team is not just for now, it can also bring great rewards in the future. Cross-cultural communication can demand a great deal of time and energy. Yet the relationships that are forged provide a network that bridges people, companies, and countries.

HANDBOOK 30

V. HOW CAN WE CONTINUOUSLY LEARN AND IMPROVE?

DESCRIPTION

In addition to goals, structure, and process, an essential component in a team's health is its ability to grow and learn from experience. This growth comes in the form of additional skills, enhanced ability to play the roles required of the task, and the team's willingness and ability to build a climate that encourages change and learning. A team's ability to be flexible in the face of obstacles and to learn about its own strengths and weaknesses is the core to keeping energy and motivation high and to achieving high performance results.

There are two critical tools for team learning. The first is assessment—both of oneself and the team. Self-assessment is an internal observation and reflection on what is working or not working about one's own behavior in pursuit of identified goals. Team assessment is the team's picture of the same issues, looking not only at individual behaviors, but at the team norms, processes, and climate, among other key areas.

The second key tool for team learning is feedback. Feedback is the non-judgmental observation that others offer. It is a picture of how effectively one's behavior or action is helping to move the person or team toward the desired outcome or goal.

Feedback and assessment should be ongoing activities in any team. Learning itself becomes an increasingly honed skill, and the team's evolution is dependent upon it.

31

HANDBOOK

SUGGESTIONS—GIVING FEEDBACK

In giving feedback to others, you should describe the problem and how it affects you and the team. State how you feel, and describe what you'd like instead. It is important that feedback:

1. Be specific, not general.

2. Describe behavior, not judge the person.

3. Start with the word I, not the word you (to avoid blaming).

4. Be timely.

TIPS

- When giving feedback, you can ask and expect people to change their behavior, not their feelings or attitudes.

- The more you give feedback, the easier it gets. It should not be focused only on one or a few people, but be a part of the whole team's norm of dealing with issues.

- Positive feedback about what is going well in the team is as important as negative feedback.

BARRIERS

- Initially, it is hard to give feedback. Take a deep breath and give it a try.

- Sometimes people do get angry or take negative feedback personally.

This shouldn't stop you from giving it, but makes it essential that you follow the guidelines on not being judgmental in tone.

32 HANDBOOK

SUGGESTIONS—ASSESSING YOURSELF AND THE TEAM

In assessing yourself or the team, ask the following questions:

1. *Goals*: Are my and our goals being met?

2. *Roles and structure*: What are our roles? How effectively are they being carried out? What works or doesn't work about our team structure?

3. *Process*: How effectively do we make decisions and resolve conflict? How do we communicate? What is the atmosphere in our meetings?

4. *Plans to change*: How can we improve any of these areas? What actions or ideas should we take?

TIPS

- To make team assessment a regular part of your routine, you might try a three minute "check-out" at the end of every meeting, to ensure that issues or problems are identified quickly.

- At key milestones (i.e., the midpoint, the delivery of the product, or concluding a major project phase) take the time to do a more structured team assessment covering all of the questions listed above.

BARRIERS

- Assessment can be time- and energy-consuming.

33

HANDBOOK

TEAM ASSESSMENT SURVEY

Please indicate the extent to which you, individually, think that your team exhibits the following characteristics and behaviors.

QUESTIONS

	To a very small extent		To some extent		To a very great extent
1. Team members understand the range of backgrounds, skills, preferences, and perspectives in the team.	1	2	3	4	5
2. Team member differences and similarities have been effectively harnessed toward achieving team goals.	1	2	3	4	5
3. The team cannot integrate diverse viewpoints.	1	2	3	4	5
4. Members view themselves as a team (e.g., they work interdependently, have joint accountability, and are committed to joint goals), not a collection of individuals who have their own particular jobs to do.	1	2	3	4	5
5. Team members have articulated a clear set of goals.	1	2	3	4	5
6. The team's goals are not motivating to members.	1	2	3	4	5
7. Team members agree on what goals and objectives are most important.	1	2	3	4	5
8. The team has an effective work structure (i.e., an understanding of what work needs to be done, when work needs to be completed, and who is responsible for each piece of work).	1	2	3	4	5
9. It is not clear what each person in the team is supposed to do.	1	2	3	4	5
10. Team members have devised effective time tables and deadlines.	1	2	3	4	5
11. Team members have a clear set of norms that cover most aspects of how to function.	1	2	3	4	5

	To a very small extent		To some extent		To a very great extent
12. Team members often disagree about ideas, procedures, and priorities.	1	2	3	4	5
13. Members take arguments personally and get angry with one another.	1	2	3	4	5
14. Every member does his or her fair share of the work.	1	2	3	4	5
15. A few members do most of the work.	1	2	3	4	5
16. A few people shirk responsibility or hold the team back.	1	2	3	4	5
17. Team members are imaginative in thinking about new or better ways to perform our tasks.	1	2	3	4	5
18. All team members participate in decision making.	1	2	3	4	5
19. Team members have the resources, information, and support they need from people outside team boundaries.	1	2	3	4	5
20. The team has a clear leader.	1	2	3	4	5
21. Team members take turns performing leadership roles.	1	2	3	4	5
22. Team meetings are well organized.	1	2	3	4	5
23. Team meetings are not productive.	1	2	3	4	5
24. Coordination among members is a problem: people seem not to know what to do and when to do it for smooth team functioning.	1	2	3	4	5
25. Members express their feelings freely in the team.	1	2	3	4	5
26. Team members support each other.	1	2	3	4	5
27. Team members are not effective at making decisions.	1	2	3	4	5
28. The quality of our work is superior.	1	2	3	4	5
29. The quantity of our work is superior.	1	2	3	4	5
30. All in all, I am satisfied with being a member of this team.	1	2	3	4	5
31. This team keeps getting more effective all the time.	1	2	3	4	5
32. A lot of learning goes on in this team.	1	2	3	4	5

	To a very small extent		To some extent		To a very great extent
33. Team members brainstorm creatively.	1	2	3	4	5
34. We have met the needs of our "clients."	1	2	3	4	5

This survey instrument was based on questions from the following sources:

Ancona, D., and D. Caldwell. 1992. "Bridging the Boundary: External Activity and Performance in Organizational Teams." *Administrative Science Quarterly*, 37, pp. 634–665.

Gladstein, D. L. 1984. "Groups in Context: A Model of Task Group Effectiveness." *Administrative Science Quarterly*, 29, pp. 499–517.

Hackman, J. R. 1983. *A Normative Model of Work Team Effectiveness*. Technical Report #2. New Haven, CT: Yale University, School of Organization and Management. Research Program on Group Effectiveness.

Ⓒ
37
ACADEMIC

INDEX

MASSACHUSETTS INSTITUTE OF TECHNOLOGY

ANCONA, KOCHAN, SCULLY,
VAN MAANEN, WESTNEY

MANAGING FOR THE FUTURE

Organizational Behavior
& Processes

DIVERSE COGNITIVE
STYLES IN TEAMS

module 4

CONTENTS

MODULE 4 (M-4)

DIVERSE COGNITIVE STYLES IN TEAMS

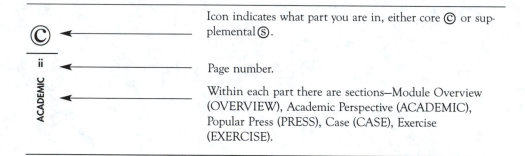

Icon indicates what part you are in, either core © or supplemental Ⓢ.

Page number.

Within each part there are sections—Module Overview (OVERVIEW), Academic Perspective (ACADEMIC), Popular Press (PRESS), Case (CASE), Exercise (EXERCISE).

Acquisitions Editor: John R. Szilagyi
Developmental Editor: Jamie Gleich Bryant
Production Editor: Mardell Toomey
Production House: DPS Associates, Inc.
Cover Design: Michael H. Stratton
Marketing Manager: Rob Bloom

ISBN: 0-538-87691-3

1 2 3 4 5 6 7 D1 4 3 2 1 0 9 8

Printed in the United States of America

South-Western College Publishing
an International Thomson Publishing company IⓉP®

Cincinnati • Albany • Boston • Detroit • Johannesburg • London • Madrid • Melbourne • Mexico City
New York • Pacific Grove • San Francisco • Scottsdale • Singapore • Tokyo • Toronto

DIVERSE COGNITIVE STYLES IN TEAMS

A QUICK OVERVIEW OF THE MODULE

This module on **Diverse Cognitive Styles** *in Teams* offers a close look at the different ways individuals selectively absorb and use information. The phrase cognitive style refers to the general way a person approaches and attempts to solve problems encountered in the world at large, including, of course, problems faced by teams in the workplace. Cognitive style represents a way of seeing and thinking—a perspective. The module is built around a consideration of cognitive style and makes use of the short self-assessment questionnaire that follows. You are to fill out this instrument, score it, and turn it in to your instructor prior to class. An in-class group exercise will follow (including a presentation by each group), and then the self-assessment instrument will be discussed. *There are readings assigned for this module but they should not be read until the group exercise and class presentations have been completed.* For class, then, all you need to do is complete the questionnaire and turn it in at the assigned time.

The instrument itself—called the **Cognitive Style Self-Assessment**—is based on the psychological-type theory developed by Carl Jung. This quick paper-and-pencil instrument is a loose variant of the much longer and more rigorously designed diagnostic inventory first developed by Isabel Myers and Katheryn Briggs in the 1940s and 1950s (and much refined since then by many researchers who follow the general Myers-Briggs approach to personality assessment). Our instrument is intended to give you a rough idea of your own cognitive style and just how your style might operate in team and organizational settings. A way to interpret your answers and summary scores on the various dimensions of the instrument (and based on the readings included in the module) will be provided in class.

ASSIGNMENT SUMMARY

1. Following the instructions on the instrument, complete the **Cognitive Style Self-Assessment** instrument. Page 15 is to be handed in sometime before class.
2. Come to class and take part in the group exercise for the session. Be sure to bring to class your Cognitive Style Self-Assessment answer sheet (pages 5 and 15).
3. Following the class session devoted to interpreting the instrument, read the two articles and class note included in the Module. *Again, do not read these articles and class note until you have gone over the self-assessment instrument in class.* This is important because the readings are likely to make a good deal more sense to you after the group exercise and in-class debriefing. The first reading listed below elaborates the concepts covered in the class discussion. The second reading addresses various ways organizations use (and sometimes abuse) personality-based testing. The third reading is a brief class note written to summarize some of the key learning points advanced in this module.

REFERENCES

Margerison, Charles, and Ralph Lewis. 1981. "Mapping Managerial Styles." *International Journal of Manpower* 2, 1:2–20, p. 24.

Golden, Daniel. "Give Me an E. Give Me an S." *The Boston Globe* (January 8, 1990).

Class Note, "Integrating Multiple Perspectives."

M-4

core

COGNITIVE STYLE SELF-ASSESSMENT

This is a set of questions designed to indicate your cognitive style. The answer you choose to any question is neither "right" nor "wrong." It simply helps to point out where your cognitive preferences lie.

Below you will find a number of paired statements and words. Please give every one a score so that each pair will add up to 5. For example:

"In describing my work, I would say it is:"
a. Challenging and exciting   4
b. Routine and dull   + 1
     = 5

Clearly, work can sometimes be challenging and sometimes dull. In the above example we have weighted four parts challenging and one part dull. The score could, in your case, be 3 + 2 or 5 + 0 or another combination.

Please choose your scores, one against another, from the following scale:

Minimum————————————————————Maximum
0   1   2   3   5

1. Are you influenced more by:

   a. Values   ____
   b. Logic   + ____
     = 5

2. When you have to meet strangers, do you find it:

   a. Something that takes a good deal of effort   ____
   b. Pleasant, or at least easy   + ____
     = 5

3. Does following a plan:

   a. Appeal to you   ____
   b. Constrain you   + ____
     = 5

4. Do you get along better with people who are:

   a. Creative and speculative   ____
   b. Realistic and "down to earth"   + ____
     = 5

5. Are you naturally:

   a. Somewhat quiet and reticent around others   ____
   b. Talkative and easy to approach   + ____
     = 5

© 5 MBTI

6. Is it harder for you to adjust to:

    a. Standard procedures   ____

    b. Frequent changes   + ____

                                        = 5

7. Is it better to be:

    a. A person of compassion   ____

    b. A person who is always fair + ____

                                        = 5

8. At a party, do you usually:

    a. Try to meet many new people   ____

    b. Stick with the people you know + ____

                                        = 5

9. When you learn something new, do you:

    a. Try to do it like everyone else does   ____

    b. Try to devise a way of your own + ____

                                        = 5

10. Are you at your best:

    a. When following a carefully worked out plan   ____

    b. When dealing with the unexpected + ____

                                        = 5

11. Do you get more annoyed at:

    a. Fancy theories   ____

    b. People who don't like theories + ____

                                        = 5

12. Is it better to be regarded by others as a person with a:

    a. Visionary outlook   ____

    b. Practical outlook   + ____

                                        = 5

13. Are you more often:

    a. Soft-hearted   ____

    b. Hard-headed   + ____

                                        = 5

14. When you buy a gift, are you:

    a. Spontaneous and impulsive   ____

    b. Deliberate and careful   + ____

                                        = 5

15. Do you find talking to people you don't know:

    a. Usually easy   ____

    b. Often taxing   + ____

                                      = 5

© 7 MBTI

Please allocate scores on the same basis to the following choice of words and phrases so as to indicate your preferences.

22. a. Personal   ____

     b. Objective   + ____

                              =   5

23. a. Timely   ____

     b. Casual   + ____

                              =   5

24. a. Reason   ____

     b. Feeling   + ____

                              =   5

25. a. Make   ____

     b. Design   + ____

                              =   5

26. a. Easy   ____

     b. Hard   + ____

                              =   5

27. a. Unjudgmental   ____

     b. Judgmental   + ____

                              =   5

28. a. Composed   ____

     b. Lively   + ____

                              =   5

29. a. Facts   ____

     b. Theories   + ____

                              =   5

30. a. Imaginative   ____

     b. Practical   + ____

                              =   5

SCORING SCHEME

Look back at the scores you allocated to each of the questions. Those scores should now be added up as shown below.

Dimension E

Question	Score Given
2b	____
5b	____
8a	____
15a	____
19a	____
21a	____
28b	____
Total:	____

Dimension I

Question	Score Given
2a	____
5a	____
8b	____
15b	____
19b	____
21b	____
28a	____
Total:	____

Dimension S

Question	Score Given
4b	____
9a	____
11a	____
12b	____
17b	____
25a	____
29a	____
30b	____
Total:	____

Dimension N

Question	Score Given
4a	____
9b	____
11b	____
12a	____
17a	____
25b	____
29b	____
30a	____
Total:	____

Dimension T

Question	Score Given
1b	____
7b	____
13b	____
16a	____
22b	____
24a	____
26b	____
27b	____
Total:	____

Dimension F

Question	Score Given
1a	____
7a	____
13a	____
16b	____
22a	____
24b	____
26a	____
27a	____
Total:	____

Dimension J

Question	Score Given
3a	____
6b	____
10a	____
14b	____
18a	____
20b	____
23a	____
Total:	____

Dimension P

Question	Score Given
3b	____
6a	____
10b	____
14a	____
18b	____
20a	____
23b	____
Total:	____

© 13 MBTI

Now transfer each of the Total Scores to the columns below. Thus, your total score under Dimension E should be placed next to the E, the total score under Dimension I should be placed next to the I, and so on.

	Total		Total
E	_____	I	_____
S	_____	N	_____
T	_____	F	_____
J	_____	P	_____

NAME: _____

15

MBTI

CLASS NOTE: DIVERSE COGNITIVE STYLES IN TEAMS

The articles in this module span a broad opinion spectrum. The writers of the first article, Charles Margerison and Ralph Lewis, are true believers in personality testing (not surprising because that is what they do for a living). Daniel Golden, the author of the second article, is at best skeptical (again, not surprising because he is a journalist trained to be suspicious of grand claims). We are somewhere in between these poles. The use and abuse of personality testing is too large a topic to take up here, but in this Class Note we quickly summarize our position on personality testing after first looking at why we think it is important to take seriously the role cognitive style plays in teams specifically and organizational life generally.

We are concerned in this module with individual differences and the role they so often play in the functioning of teams, groups, and organizations. There are many ways to classify and conceptualize individual differences, of course. Some of these are obvious and quite visible, such as gender, race, language, national origin, social background, and class. Other ways rest on less visible but nonetheless influential distinctions, such as cultural and educational differences. Here we are concerned with personality-based differences; in particular, differences in the manner individuals absorb and selectively use information available to them.

The phrase "cognitive style" refers to the way a person approaches and attempts to solve problems encountered in the world at large, including the problems faced at work. Viewed most broadly, cognitive style is a way of seeing and thinking—a perspective. Its origins are deep and diffuse—family origins, childhood socialization, schooling, higher education, work experience, and patterns of past success and failure all play a role. It can perhaps best be thought of as a fairly stable, though certainly not fixed, part of each individual's personality or character. Differences in cognitive style are often most apparent in organizations when individuals come together to jointly solve problems, negotiate agreements, or work together for extended periods of time in teams. Integrating multiple perspectives is then predominantly an interactive, not a structural, task. It requires a good deal of listening to others, empathy, and mutual give and take. It requires also an appreciation for what contrasting cognitive styles can offer a team, group, and organization.

To illustrate cognitive style and the role individual differences play in organizational life, we use the Cognitive Style Self-Assessment which is a short, altered, and rough variant of the much used (and approximated) Myers-Briggs Type Indicator (MBTI™) as discussed in the Margerison and Lewis reading. The instrument rests on Carl Jung's approach to personality.[1] Certainly other personality theories and measuring devices are available, but the Jungian approach we selected has several advantages.

1 The Myers-Briggs Type Indicator (MBTI™) is available from the Consulting Psychologists Press, Inc. at 577 College Avenue, Palo Alto, California, 94306. Sandra Krebs Hirsh and Jean M. Kummerow have a useful interpretive guide to the MBTI called *Introduction to Type in Organizations*, 2nd ed. (1990), available also from the Consulting Psychologists Press. Another useful guide is David Keirsey and Marilyn Bates's popular book called *Please Understand Me* (1984). The book is distributed by Prometheus Nemesis Book Company, Box 2748, Del Mar, California, 92014. This book contains a 70-item self-assessment instrument, called the Keirsey Temperament Sorter. In general, there are many instruments (and items,

First, the Jungian approach to personality is enormously popular at the moment. Many business, educational, and governmental organizations make use of the Myers-Briggs approach in their management training and executive development efforts. There is also a voluminous research literature devoted to both Jungian theory and its Myers-Briggs variant. Moreover, it is likely that a few students in any given class will already be familiar with the Myers-Briggs approach (or similar personality inventory) and can thus speak to the class about their past experiences—how accurate the assessment seemed at the time, how it was used, and how it compares with the Cognitive Style Self-Assessment. Part of the popularity of the Myers-Briggs approach and theory is perhaps that, unlike many other conceptual models of personality type, the Jungian model classifies individuals in positive terms, by what people like rather than what people lack.

Second, the emphasis of Jung's personality theory on the things people pay attention to and ways they make decisions matches up nicely with the key features of most managerial jobs. The Sensing/iNtuitive and Thinking/Feeling dimensions translate well to the interactionally dependent and informationally intensive world of managerial work. Jung's theory has a relevance not currently found in many other personality theories (although there is a good deal of overlap with other personality measures on several dimensions; notably, S-N and T-F). Crucially, Jung's work brings to the surface matters that can be seen and felt in familiar circumstances and thus gives order to the seemingly limitless variations of managerial thought and behavior.

Third, and perhaps most important, making use of individual differences in organizations is critical. Simply ignoring or merely tolerating such differences will not do. If the structural characteristics of organizations are shifting in accordance with a model of the "new" organization as outlined in Module 1—networked, flat, diverse, flexible, and global in orientation—differing cognitive styles are likely to be of vital importance. The challenges facing organizations are increasingly complex. The application of multiple perspectives is necessary if these challenges are to be addressed adequately. Relying on our own perspective or, more generally, a single and, within the team, group, or organization, dominant and (for most) comfortable perspective is quite limiting.

At the individual level, cognitive style is a way of ordering preferences for thought and action. As these preferences are incorporated into our personalities, they become taken for granted as natural, normal, even proper ways to think and behave. Others with different cognitive styles may then be regarded as odd, improper, perhaps out of sync with the way the world really works. To bridge these differing perspectives requires a common language and a genuine appreciation for those individuals whose cognitive styles differ from our own. Multiple perspectives cannot be integrated until they are understood.

This said, there remain important qualifications to be made. Personality typing is everywhere and always problematic. It is far from an exact science, and inordinate care, sensitivity, and restraint must be taken when characterizing individuals by the use of virtually any diagnostic device. One of the attractions of Jung's theorizing is his principled hesitation to classify individual personality in a static or timeless way. Personal growth and balance are inherent in Jungian approaches, and breaking from type is an important developmental task.

Nonetheless, there is always a danger of flattening and pigeonholing individuals and thus stereotyping them in unjustified and ignorant ways. Cognitive style is but a small part of personality. Its functioning and measurement are imperfectly understood. It is

theoretically and empirically made up of a complicated and shifting mix of analytically distinct preferences. And, most critically, it is difficult if not impossible to make strong behavioral predictions on the basis of cognitive style—simply too many influences are at work in the calculus of human behavior to isolate single causes.

Using personality typing, then, to select (or deselect) individuals for particular jobs or membership in a particular work team is, we think, inappropriate, both practically and ethically. Measures are at best primitive. And, even when there exist positive correlations among particular types and job performance, there is no guarantee that such correlations are stable. Job demands change, markets shift, new tasks replace old tasks. The modern work environment is simply too volatile to neatly locate the "right" person for the "right" job by means of personality testing.

Using personality typing loosely and discursively is, however, a different matter. It can provide a set of terms and concepts for talking about the role individual differences play in teams and the workplace. It can also provide a way of considering comparatively one's own perspective on the world. A good deal of personal insight, mutual understanding, and increased respect for one another can be fostered by collective discussion prompted by well-designed and thoughtful personality inventories. Differences in cognitive style may, for example, provide a relatively sound and nonjudgmental hypothesis to account for some—although certainly not all—of the personal misunderstandings and conflicts that characterize team and organizational activity.

Teams are about people doing things together. Common wisdom has it that the better individuals are able to get along with one another, the better will be the products of their interaction. Such practical wisdom is often played out in organizations as individuals with similar ways of thinking and acting cluster together—in groups, divisions, departments, and so forth. Homogeneity seems to increase as one moves up the hierarchy in most organizations. Bosses naturally favor subordinates who think along similar lines, and thus promote the interests and careers of like-minded subordinates. Homogeneity smoothes interaction, increases comfort levels, and, in general, eases the strains or tensions involved in doing things together. When the source of homogeneity is more or less invisible, as it is with cognitive style, the heightened similarity of thought and action among individuals may be unnoticed by them—although surely noticed by those not sharing the dominant mode.

But homogeneity has a price. In the classroom assignment of this module, for instance, groups are assigned the task of developing a new work arrangement for a few technical employees of an organization. These task groups were designed to be as homogeneous as possible, given the data that were collected on individual cognitive style. There was comfort in most of these groups but there was also a restricted range in terms of the possibilities considered for making the new arrangement work. The "best solution, it seemed, would be one that combined the insights of all the groups.

The point being made here is that cognitive diversity adds value to an organization and increases the likelihood that innovative solutions to work problems will arise. But making effective use of diverse cognitive styles does not come easy. The forces of homogeneity must be countered time and time again. Understanding diverse cognitive styles and recognizing the need for integration is only part of the answer. Ways of operating effectively in teams that are made up of diverse individuals must be developed and sustained. And, in many respects, this is a never-ending task. Not only are we growing, developing, and changing in a variety of ways that reflect the teams of which we are a part and the tasks to which we put our efforts, so too are the others who surround us in these teams and on our tasks.

MAPPING MANAGERIAL STYLES

by Charles Margerison and Ralph Lewis

MANAGERIAL MAPPING

We wish to produce a new way in which managers can look at how they manage themselves and their teams. We have called the approach Mapping Managerial Styles because it is possible for each person to assess his or her own approach to work and look at how it compares with other people's. This is particularly important for every manager.

The job of managing essentially involves motivating and leading other people. To do this a manager is required to have a good understanding of people's approach to work.

Indeed, it is common to hear managers complain that they need to know more about "what makes people tick" or what motivates people. People who are promoted to managerial positions have usually done well at the technical aspect of their jobs. They are usually intelligent. They are invariably people who are concerned about achieving things. They usually have quite a number of good ideas which they want to put into practice. The one issue which they commonly confront, which causes a lot of heart-searching, is how to get the energies of the people for whom they are accountable mobilized in such a way that they work together.

It is vital, therefore, that managers do have a theory which can govern their relationships with other people at work, particularly in the areas of selection, training, appraisal, work allocation and, probably above all, in building a successful team.

Up to now there have been very few theories which can help managers on an overall basis make the right kinds of decisions in these areas. The ones that have been put forward are in our view far too simple. They have concentrated on such things as having a high concern for production and a high concern for task, or being more democratic rather than autocratic. More recently we have moved towards what have been called contingency theories but these again have not provided a clear basis for managers to understand people's work preferences and motivations in depth.

And yet, this is the area that managers spend most of their time upon. There are numerous research studies which show that well over 70 percent and often 80 and 90 percent of managerial time is spent working with other people. Of all this time, perhaps the most important is the time spent in selection. Peter Drucker, reporting a conversation with Alfred Sloan, who was head of General Motors, had asked him why he spent as much as four hours of his personal time as committee chairman selecting a master mechanic in a small division of the company. Sloan replied, "Tell me what more important decision is there than that about the management of people who do the job. If that master mechanic is the wrong man our decision here on the 14th floor might as well be written on water." Sloan prided himself on the trouble he spent in making the right judgment when it came to people. As he said, "If we didn't spend four hours on placing a man right, we'd spend 400 hours cleaning up after our mistake."

Most managers would empathize with those words and recognize in their own decisions key points when they had not read the situation correctly. However, making the

Source: Charles Margerison and Ralph Lewis, "Mapping Managerial Style," *International Journal of Manpower, Special Issue*, Volume 2 (1), 1981, pp. 2–20. Reprinted by permission of MCB University Press.

right decision in itself is not the answer. Once people have been appointed the manager really needs to understand them as individuals and enable them to contribute to their best. This means understanding their strengths and enabling them to work in a way which maximizes their abilities. Moreover, it means developing a team of people who can work together.

In this we believe that it is vitally important that a manager understands his own style and motivational pattern and in doing so will more easily understand those of his team. To this end the current monograph outlines a very powerful explanatory theory of human behavior. It was originally developed by Carl Jung[1] in his book *Psychological Types*. Jung is better known as a psychiatrist and philosopher. However, he had a number of important insights and contributions to managerial thought which have long been ignored.

Our own work shows how the original theory can be applied to a number of areas of business life. In particular, we shall look at the relationships between the five key aspects of any work situation shown in Figure 4.1.

Each of these areas interacts with the other, within the constraints and opportunities of the market place. A key influence, however, in the internal working of the organizations are the motivational interests and styles that the individual members bring with them.

We have therefore adapted Jung's theory of personal (motivational) preferences and applied it to industrial and commercial organizations. This is based on a lot of research. In particular 849 managers contributed to the generation of information used in the mapping procedures.

The mapping process enables each person to identify the core values and ideas that he or she brings with them to the work situation. Now these core values relate to the way in which each person wishes to run his or her life. While the particular values may be religious, humanistic, political or utilitarian there is an overall pattern which can be identified and mapped. We are concerned with the underlying patterns which have also been well described recently by Myers.[2]

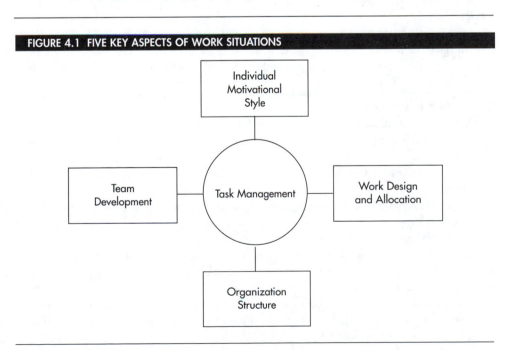

FIGURE 4.1 FIVE KEY ASPECTS OF WORK SITUATIONS

1 Jung, C. G. 1923. *Psychological Types*, London: Kegan Paul.

2 Myers, J. B. 1962. The Myers-Briggs *Type Indicator*, Princeton: Educational Testing Service.

The competitive nature of organizational life and the day to day pressures mean that we often find it difficult to live life in the way we prefer. Therefore, there is usually a fair degree of stress between one's own personal preferences and the job and the task to be done. Add to this the other pressures from other people who have different work patterns, the constraints about doing jobs on time and a host of other factors, then each person has to adapt his or her behavior accordingly. However, as we shall show, people rarely change their core values and basic motivational styles. Wherever possible they will revert to type and play the game in the way they know best. This will mean that people will try to reorganize their jobs and indeed the work of others to fit into their preferred pattern of working.

It is important that we understand these motivational style patterns which come from basic core values and preferences that people bring to work. The next section sets out how this can be done by using Jung's theory and method of application.

PERSONAL WORK STYLES

While work is a set of complicated activities there are four major things that everyone has to do each day. These four activities are:

1. Meeting with others
2. Generating information
3. Making decisions
4. Choosing priorities

Let us look briefly at each of these activities, all of which have two opposite dimensions.

Meeting with Others

In essence this is the way we prefer to relate and the sort of relationships we like to have. We shall therefore call this activity *managing relationships*.

According to Jung's theory there are two major ways in which this can be done. One approach he called *extroverted*. The other approach he called *introverted*. These terms have become widely acknowledged and used, even though they are not always fully understood.

As we shall illustrate, no one is totally introverted, nor is anyone totally extroverted. We all have the ability to behave either way at various times. However, we all have preferences on how we wish to relate with others and when, where and what we will relate about. It is these issues that require explanation.

Generating Information

Gathering information is crucial in all aspects of life, but particularly so at work. In order to make a contribution you have to find out a lot of information or explore a range of ideas.

There are two major aspects to this. One dimension is called *sensing* and the other *intuition*.

People who prefer sensing usually emphasize, among other things, getting the facts. They are good on detail and prefer information that is based on some form of measurement that can be done using one or more of the senses.

In contrast, other people prefer to generate information by intuition. This means developing data through the use of one's imagination and creative insight, as, for example, a novelist does.

Again the preferences are not totally independent of each other. Most of us gather facts and also express ideas. However, we all tend to prefer one of these more than the other when it comes to doing a job.

Making Decisions

Once the information has been gathered there is usually a requirement to do something with it. Here again there are two major options, one of which Jung called *thinking*, the other *feeling*.

Some people prefer to make decisions using a thinking or analytical approach. Others prefer to make decisions using a feeling, or decisions based upon personal convictions or beliefs, approach. As before, there is no right or wrong way; it is just a matter of motivational preferences. Most of us decide some things by thinking, and some things through feeling. However, we do usually have an overall preference for one or the other and will revert to this when free from other pressures.

Choosing Priorities

Finally, all of us have to make a choice in how we allocate our time. The priorities referred to here are those of either:

1. Getting more facts (sensing) or ideas (intuition)
2. Making decisions (thinking) or (feeling)

The more you are oriented towards generating data, the higher you will be on what the theory calls *perceiving*. The higher you are on making decisions, then the more likely you are to be *judgmental.* These are the two options associated with the priorities for time allocation. Again, neither is right or wrong, but choices usually have to be made. Moreover, most people tend to prefer one to the other.

The theory is not a hard and fast set of rules, but rather a set of guidelines within which people can assess their own preferences and those of others. The model below outlines the options from the factors mentioned above.

```
Extrovert  ————————  Establishing Relations  ———————  Introvert
Sensing  ——————————  Generating Information  ——————  Intuitive
Thinking  —————————  Making Decisions  ——————————  Feeling
Judgmental  ———————  Choosing Priorities  ——————————  Perceptive
```

WORK PREFERENCES

In this section we will look at the main dimensions in more detail, especially with respect to the way work is approached. Most emphasis will be placed on generating and using information with a briefer look at establishing relationships and priorities.

Establishing Relationships: Extrovert Approach

Extroverts require variety and stimulation. They can become easily bored. Their sociability may be just one facet of their desire to obtain stimulation. They often, therefore, try to keep a number of balls in the air at the same time and will take on a number of jobs which they try to do in parallel. Their interests are essentially those of going out and looking for new situations.

Because they talk a lot (in order to stimulate others) they are often seen to be influential although in reality this may not be so. Introverts can also be extremely influential, though they typically talk far less. Extroverts do, however, seem to be far less inhibited. They are more likely to put forward an idea before they have thought it through sufficiently and argue their way through to a conclusion. They will usually take the initiative in making new friends and establishing relationships. At business gatherings they will typically come up and introduce themselves rather than wait to be introduced. They will initiate the subject of conversation and feel quite at home in exchanging observations, views and ideas.

Extroverts, however are not easily organized. It is difficult for an extrovert to fit into a set of rules in a structured and a planned way of doing things. This is because typically they will be somewhat impulsive and do what they feel is required even if it does not conform to the plan.

An extrovert manager may well have an open door policy. That is, he might deliberately keep his door open so that he is in touch and stimulated by events going on in the office. He will probably actually enjoy people coming in and interrupting him from time to time so that he can get going on another problem. The telephone ringing is really not a major difficulty for the extrovert—it is stimulating!

The more extroverted a person is the more he will feel at ease in meeting with people he does not know, contributing to meetings, making an after-dinner speech, representing the company in negotiations and generally entering into situations that have high demands for interpersonal relationships. In this sense the caricature of the salesman who is the hail-fellow-well-met extrovert does in fact have some bearing in reality. However, it is unwise to take this too far. Everyone in business requires some degree of extroversion but, like most things, it can become a weakness rather than a strength if over-played. People get bored with too many funny stories and want to get away from the high pressure conversation.

If you have a boss who approaches work in an extroverted way then he will probably like a lot of meetings and try to get his information by going out into the world. If you have subordinates who are extroverts they will, no doubt, exert quite considerable pressure upon you as they will continually want to relate with you on a personal basis. They will have ideas, very often bubbling over with enthusiasm, and you will have to try and encourage them while at the same time making sure that they do not take up too much of your time.

Establishing Relationships: Introvert Approach

Introverts, on the other hand, like to take time to think things through clearly before they communicate. They may become over-stimulated by too much variety and consequently they spend their time trying to reduce the number and length of their contacts. One of the reasons they may not talk as much as extroverts is that this stimulates others to reply and perhaps gives the introvert too much information to work on in too short a space of time.

It must be remembered that the introvert is very open to information. He or she can pick up very subtle points of information or feeling and may well grasp ideas from very little information. Hence the need to switch off and to sit and think it through. This, of course, is a major strength. However, it can also be a weakness. Because of his sensitivity he may assume that others also understand the issues in the same way. The result is that the introvert may not communicate his understanding as he feels it is obvious. While it is obvious to himself, it is not always so for others. Therefore introverts are often accused of not being good at letting people know what they know or think. This is not entirely true. Introverts will communicate well with those they trust or when the situation demands it. Many an introvert makes a fine conference speech or presentation to a meeting but it is usually more of a strain than it is for the extrovert.

An interesting point is that although introverts and extroverts are equal in terms of intelligence, introverts predominate in the higher levels of the education system. This is because they can adjust to the routine and isolation of study more easily than extroverts. If organizations promote on qualifications rather than merit, they may end up with more introverts at the top. And introverts, as indicated earlier, may find it more difficult to communicate to the rest of the organization. Hence, the complaints of some employees about being kept in the dark!

Another point about introverts is that they will work at a problem in a concentrated way for quite a period of time. They will pursue an issue in depth. By doing so they feel that they can get in command and control of the situation so that when they do put forward an opinion or a proposition it is well founded.

Some introverts, however, get upset when their propositions in a meeting are met with rejection or doubt. Because they have thought them through so well, they find it hard to believe that anyone else cannot see the validity of their point of view.

If you have a boss who has an introverted approach, it may take a long time for you to get to know her. You may feel that she does not communicate as well as you would wish. However, she is likely to do so in her own way. For example, she is more likely to use memos rather than call informal meetings. To this extent you may well have to use the same form of communication if you are to get through to her.

If you have a subordinate who adopts an introverted approach, then likewise you may find him or her hard to understand at times. Introverts may seem to live in a world of their own. To a certain extent, this is true, in that they do put more credence upon their own ideas rather than going out and searching for other people's. However, to get communication at its best then one perhaps has to talk through quietly and on a confidential basis with these people on their own view. Perhaps it is best to ask them to write down their thoughts prior to a discussion. Certainly they appreciate the opportunity to think issues through before sounding off an opinion, and giving them forewarning of issues is very helpful. They are particularly good at looking at things in depth, providing you can organize sufficient time and freedom from successive interruptions.

The danger is that introverted people can often be overlooked. Indeed, they themselves can often be their own worst enemies and they do not go out and seek company. They will stick with the people they know even at coffee breaks and informal meetings. Their list of acquaintances, therefore, is often more limited than those of extroverts and, as a consequence, their opportunities for influence are likely to be less.

Summary

Extrovert Approach

- Will often think things out by talking them through
- Enjoys meeting other people and often seeks social gatherings
- Enjoys a variety of tasks and activities
- Stimulated by unanticipated interruptions
- When speaking publicly will often talk impromptu
- Likely to contribute a lot at meetings
- Can be impulsive

Introvert Approach

- Prefers to think things out before speaking
- Does not have a high need to meet regularly with others
- Likes to concentrate on few tasks at a time
- Dislikes unanticipated interruptions
- When speaking publicly will prepare in depth and speak to a plan
- May be more quiet at meetings
- More likely to consider things before acting

Generating Data: The Sensing Approach

People who use the sensing approach are usually very much matter of fact. They do not trust things unless they can touch them, weigh them, move them or in some way assess their worth through practical means. They like clear tasks with specific things to do. They enjoy developing and using their skills, and essentially are more interested in doing things where they can see that they have had an effect. These people are usually good at gathering information on mechanical methods, working on particular jobs which require manipulating physical materials, or assessing the practical implications of change, which involves the reorganization of physical things.

However, they tend to dislike problems unless there are standard ways of solving them. Problems must be approached logically or sequentially. Frustration occurs with ambiguous or complex situations which do not have tangible outcomes such as philosophical

25

ACADEMIC

16. Do you think it is a worse mistake to:

    a. Show too much emotion   ____
    b. Try to be too rational   + ____
                                   =   5

17. Do you prefer people who have:

    a. Vivid imaginations   ____
    b. Good common sense   + ____
                                   =   5

18. Do you usually:

    a. Organize and plan things in advance   ____
    b. Allow things to just happen and then adapt   + ____
                                   =   5

19. Do people get to know you:

    a. Quickly   ____
    b. Slowly   + ____
                                   =   5

20. At work, would you rather:

    a. Encounter an unscheduled problem that must
         be solved right away   ____
    b. Try to schedule your work so you won't be up
         against the clock   + ____
                                   =   5

21. When you are with people you don't know, do you usually:

    a. Start conversations on your own   ____
    b. Wait to be introduced by others   + ____
                                   =   5

© 9 MBTI

This is usually manifested in the fact that we choose certain jobs which play to our strengths. Therefore, if you find a person who likes practical detail, precision, and specific task working in a creative situation of ambiguity it is likely he or she will be dissatisfied. Equally, if you find a creative person working in a situation where he is tied down to specific work which has to be done in a specific time, he is also likely to get frustrated and leave the job. The task of the manager, therefore, is to identify the strengths of the people he has around him and be able to place them in jobs which best suit their work preferences.

The following summary gives the main elements of the sensing and the intuitive approaches.

Summary

Sensing Approach

- Prefers practical problems
- Prefers systems and methods
- Likes to work with tested ideas
- Likes to work with real things
- Patient with routine detail
- Will test establish facts
- Pays attention to facts and detail
- Wants to see detailed parts
- Likes schedule of working
- Searches for standard problem-solving approach

Intuitive Approach

- Enjoys ambiguous problems
- Gets bored with routine problems
- Regularly floats new ideas
- Sees possibilities and implications
- Frequently jumps beyond the facts
- May get facts wrong
- Has creative vision and insight
- Follows inspirations
- Searches for the new; innovation
- Likes complexity and searches for creative approaches

Making Decisions: The Thinking Approach

People who use the thinking approach subject information to a careful process of analysis before deciding. That is, they look, stand back and weigh the facts rather than give way to their feelings.

Such people will try to bring whatever analytical aids there are to help assess the situation. In the world of business they will like to use decision analysis, linear programming, cost benefit analysis, extrapolative forecasting, and other methods for cutting down the risk.

The emphasis on analytical reasoning sounds like a hard, cold, and logical process. However, for many people it is an exciting challenge. They like working with figures and assessing the conclusions of particular lines of action. They treat forecasting as a science. Their development of budgets and the preparation of plans are a fundamental part of the analytical approach. The use of statistical methods to work out probabilities is a key aspect. The aim is not to eliminate risk but to reduce it. Such methods can only work, however, where there are clear objectives. It is the objective-setting process which is perhaps the most difficult part of the thinking approach.

Those who favor the thinking approach often take a detached view of the decision-making process. They talk about markets rather than people. They talk about products rather than processes. They like to have clear criteria for assessing the decision to be taken.

If you have a boss who has a strong thinking approach, it is best to give him evidence. He will want to be convinced by data. Likewise, if you have subordinates who decide on a basis of analytical reasoning it is important that they see the factual basis upon which you come to a decision if they are to be motivated. Trying to get them to act on purely personal conviction will rarely be sufficient.

© 27 ACADEMIC

People who prefer a thinking and analytical approach to decision making may hurt other people's feelings without being aware of it. Because their concern is to do what "the situation" demands they may ignore people's concerns and emotions. Increasingly, managers are being made to comply with laws and codes which demand a cold analytical decision. For example, staff now have to be warned at least three times before they can be dismissed for inadequate work performance. No longer can the manager just make people redundant without giving thought to the social and legal aspects as well as the basic profit and loss aspects.

Making Decisions: The Feelings Approach

Most of us have strong beliefs, whether it be on how to bring up a family or the way in which society should be run or, indeed, the way in which business should be conducted. The question that we have to consider is how far these beliefs dominate our decision-making process.

People who have strong beliefs usually ask whether the decision that is to be taken will be congruent with their values. They will, therefore, look at things very much in terms of their own personal standpoints rather than sit back and decide things on the basis of cold analysis. People with strong religious, political or humanitarian views will therefore look very much at the extent to which the decision is related to their own perspectives on life.

People who have strong feelings can be enormously helpful to those who they feel could be converted to support their own views. They are often very friendly people who like to see that there is a great deal of commonality in the way people see the world.

However, if other people do not see the world in their terms equally they can be fierce opponents. They will polarize the issues as being for or against.

This can be seen in various facets of the business. At one level the shop steward is often a person with very strong convictions. He judges the decisions of management as to whether or not they accord with his views on the way in which a business should be run. Likewise the businessman can be equally strong in his convictions. He may well ignore the logic of the situation to press for what he believes is right. Indeed, Henry Ford did this producing the original Model T car. However, when other competitors developed their cars, Ford was still insisting on the standard Model T. It nearly ruined his business. Eventually he had to face the cold hard facts and make his decisions upon an analytical basis. However, by that time he had lost millions and it took a long time to get the organization profitable again.

Beliefs are therefore critical. It is very important that people do have standards and ideals against which they can measure their facts. It is not a question of just deciding everything according to conviction or, alternatively, deciding everything according to the facts. There must be a mixture of both.

Summary

Thinking Approach

- Tries to establish objective decision criteria
- Measure decisions against payoffs
- Can be seen as detached and cold
- Believes in deciding according to situation
- Is likely to be flexible depending on situation

Feelings Approach

- Has personal subjective decision criteria
- Measure decisions against beliefs
- Can be seen as over-committed to a point of view
- Believes in deciding on personal considerations
- Is likely to be nostalgic, holding to traditional ways

— Negotiates on the evidence	— Negotiates on rights and wrongs of the issues
— Has concern for fairness based on the rules	— Believes fairness relates to values and beliefs
— Likes analysis and clarity	— Likes harmony based on common values
— Sets objectives and beliefs follow	— Objectives emerge from beliefs
— Task orientated	— Principles orientated

Establishing Priorities: The Judging Approach

We all have an inclination to get into action or wait until we have information. These priorities considerably influence our overall preferences.

People who are high on judging like to have issues clarified and resolved. They will often come across as detached, impersonal decision makers. They will, however, be more open to change, providing people can convince them with hard evidence that has been subject to careful review. They do essentially respect the logic of problem solving, but do not like to spend too much time before getting into action.

Judging is clearly a vital aspect of any manager's role. The higher the manager gets in the organization, the more he has to balance the considerable information required for decision making with the need for clarity and order. Those concerned with judging will put more weight on the decision process of either thinking or feeling as described above. In short, the judgmental process leads towards decision making. The opposite is true for the perceptive approach.

Establishing Priorities: The Perceptive Approach

People who prefer the perceptive approach will put a priority on getting as much information as possible. Therefore, perceptive people put more weight on either the sensing or intuitive factors. The perceptive sensing person will focus heavily on in-depth investigations to dig up the facts associated with the problem. They will put pressure on others for "hard" data and they will not be easily put off with generalizations, hearsay, or other circumstantial evidence. They may even demand information way beyond what you feel is necessary in order to make the decision. That is not seen as important by perceptive persons. It is their concern to know and understand that dominates. They can frustrate their colleagues, subordinates and boss by not taking decisions. Of course, this can also upset others who do not wish to be bothered by more inquiries.

If the person is high on perceiving and also on intuition, then it may be more difficult to observe the process that goes on. The reason for this is that the intuitive process is based on insight, imagination and developing new ideas. So, rather than going outside of herself to generate data, the perceptive intuitive person may sit around doodling, scribbling and waiting for the inspiration. In short, such people are waiting for the great idea to strike them, or trying to link a set of ideas into a coherent whole. The perceptive person, therefore, does not mind letting things hang loose. Although maybe frustrated that he does not have enough information, he is usually prepared to hang on till he does.

It is also noticeable that some perceptive people tend to take on a number of projects simultaneously and never do justice to any. However, it satisfies their concern to be involved in a lot of activities, and to be aware and knowledgeable. Therefore, in summary, the perceptive person has a lot to contribute but needs to be focused towards time schedules, output quotas, and commitments if he is to make the best use of his abilities.

29

ACADEMIC

Summary

Judging Approach	Perceptive Approach
— Like clarity and order	— Enjoy searching and finding
— Concerned with resolving matters	— May procrastinate in search of even better information
— Dislike ambiguity and loose	— Can tolerate ambiguity
— Very orderly	— Concerned to know, not organized
— May rush to quick decisions	— Take in lots of data—maybe too much
— Can be somewhat inflexible once judgement is made	— Open minded and curious
— Concerned to work to a plan	— Work according to the requirements of the data
— Emphasize decision making over information getting	— Emphasis on diagnosing over concluding and resolving
— Concern with implementation	— Concern with knowledge
— Like to get things resolved and operating	— Like to find out as much as possible before action

Overall Profiles

In summary, each person has a personal way of working and living which is influenced considerably by a number of important factors. These, of course, are not by any means the only factors. However, they are very influential in the way a person organizes his or her work.

We can summarize these preferences in the following way:

E Extrovert Preference	or	**I Introvert Preference**
Prefers to live in contact with others and things		Prefers to be more self-contained and work things out personally
S Sensing Preference	or	**N Intuition Preference**
Puts emphasis on fact, details, and concrete knowledge		Puts emphasis on possibilities, imagination, creativity and seeing things as a whole
T Thinking Preference	or	**F Feeling Preference**
Puts emphasis on analysis using logic and rationality		Puts emphasis on human values, establishing personal friendships; decisions mainly on beliefs and dislikes
J Judging Preference	or	**P Perceiving Preference**
Puts emphasis on order through reaching decisions and resolving issues		Puts emphasis on gathering information and obtaining as much data as possible

The initial letter of each preference provides a shorthand reference to the factor for understanding and discussion. Each one carries the initial letter of the factor except for intuition which is coded N, so that it does not conflict with I for introvert.

We shall use these letters to describe the factors and make up the maps to describe managerial styles and teamwork. This will be based upon the research we have conducted and this we shall not describe.

A BASIS FOR SELF-UNDERSTANDING

The individual descriptions, while valuable, are insufficient. It is the combination of the various preferences that gives us a better indication of how a person will manage.

There are 16 combinations from the alternatives outlined. These can be seen from the following model, which builds upon the shorthand letters that have been adopted for each factor. Therefore:

E = Extrovert ——————— I = Introvert
S = Sensing ——————— N = Intuitive
T = Thinking ——————— F = Feeling
J = Judgement ——————— P = Perceiving

The range of options that emerges is shown in Figure 4.2:

Each combination has detailed explanations of its views and values in the Myers-Briggs Handbook. The resulting descriptions make fascinating reading. For example, the "INTP" type is often considered to be the most "academic" of all the types, whilst the "ESFP" is seen as the most sociable. Clearly, however, it is impossible for us to go into depth here. Our concern will be the relation of the types to managerial roles.

Our research, based on 849 managers attending business school short courses, showed the following breakdown.

	Extrovert	Percentages Total	Introvert	
ESTJ	20.7	44.5	23.8	ISTJ
ESFJ	5.9	12.4	6.5	ISFJ
ENTJ	8.8	15.3	6.5	INTJ
ENFJ	1.6	4.0	2.4	INFJ
ESTP	3.9	8.2	4.4	ISTP
ESFP	1.2	2.4	1.2	ISFP
ENTP	4.2	7.1	2.9	INTP
ENFP	2.9	6.0	3.1	INFP

It can be seen that the "STJ's" form by far the largest chunk of the senior and middle managerial ranks. This suggests that not only are there certain types of people who are attracted to managerial roles, but also that they are selected more often than not. Also of interest, is the low proportion of "SFP's"—the most "sociable" of the types. Does this mean that managers are not "sociable" or at least that they find it difficult to maintain relationships with others? This is one of the issues to be explored later. For the moment we shall use the four basic conceptual types that were outlined earlier.

FIGURE 4.2 COMBINATIONS OF PREFERENCE ALTERNATIVES

The percentage breakdown for these in our sample are as shown:

	Total	ST	SF	NF	NT
Managers	849	52.8%	14.8%	10%	22.4%

The implications of these figures will be discussed in the next section on applications.

The preceding sections have discussed the basic model of work preferences and have shown that different preferences lead to different ways of working. However, of more interest is that application to managerial and organizational issues. The ones we shall comment on are:

1. Managerial style and decision making
2. Organization structure
3. Approaches to change
4. Creativity and innovation
5. Career development, appraisal, and training

Managerial Style and Decision Making

A number of authors have discussed the need for different types of conceptual skill and style within the managerial context. For example, Mintzberg[3] in his article "Planning on the Left Side, and Managing on the Right" describes the implications of research on the human brain. It has been suggested that the human brain is specialized with logical, linear functions occurring in the left hemisphere and holistic, rational functions occurring in the right. Managers with the left hemisphere more developed would, Mintzberg suggests, be much better at planning and analytical work, which managers with the right hemisphere developed would be better at imaginative overall control. This appears to reflect the sensing/intuitive dimension postulated by Jung.

Leavitt[4] also contrasts the analytical approach to management as exemplified in America by the MBA student with that of a more imaginative integrated approach based upon "consciousness raising." He comes to the conclusion that "we need to integrate wisdom and feeling with analysis." Again one can see some parallels with the typology through the need to integrate the thinking and feeling functions. McKenney and Keen[5] have also developed research on cognitive styles concerned with the differences between management scientists and general managers. They said management scientists were more logical and analytical than general managers who operate by the seat of their pants.

By far the majority of the work in this context has been done by Kilmann and Mitroff[6] using the four conceptual types outlined earlier. Their work has a tremendous number of applications. One of these is the preference of the different types for certain stages in decision making. Essentially:

1. The NF type prefers ambiguity, creating, feeling, problems/opportunities.
2. The NT type prefers defining problems/opportunities, identifying basic objectives and policies, establishing criteria for success.

---

3 Mintzberg, H. 1976. "Planning on the Left Side and Managing on the Right," *Harvard Business Review,* July–August, pp. 49–58.

4a Leavitt, H. J. 1975. "Beyond the Analytic Manager," *California Management Review,* Vol. XVII No. 3, pp. 5–12.

4b Leavitt, H. J. 1975. "Beyond the Analytic Manager: Part II," *California Management Review,* Vol. XVII No. 4, pp. 11–21.

5 McKenney, J. L. and P. G. W. Keen. 1974. "How Managers' Minds Work," *Harvard Business Review,* pp. 79–80.

6 Mitroff, I. I. and R. H. Kilmann. 1975. "Stories Managers Tell: A New Tool for Organizational Problem Solving," *Management Review,* pp. 18–28.

3. The ST prefers defining solutions and planning their implementation.
4. The SF type prefers to be practical but work on the basis of what he feels to be the right way to go.

This suggests that cognitive styles will be different between staff and line managers, as each has to concentrate on different parts of the decision-making process. Kilmann and Mitroff go slightly further; not only do they postulate the existence of these different types of managers but they make three further propositions.

1. All types are necessary for an effective balanced solution that is implemented.
2. The views of each type, being so essentially different, will lead to difficulties in communication between them.
3. Not only their way of working will be different, but also their long-term goals.

What therefore are the implications for managers based on our sample?

If we consider the sample of managers, we can see that managers are predominantly the "ST" type. They will be concerned first and foremost with practical and logical problems. They will also prefer problems that are concrete and specific rather than ambiguous and abstract, hence, their impatience and distrust of issues that to them seem nebulous and not based on tangible factors. This is not to say that some managers do not prefer problem exploration and definition. As can be seen from the table, all the basic types are represented. However, it is also of interest to note that the types most concerned with people problems are outnumbered 3:1 by those most concerned with technical problems. Perhaps this explains the need for "interpersonal" skills courses for managers. The "SF's" are a low proportion—these are the types which act as "lubricant" to the social mechanism of management and again perhaps their low proportion explains some of the industrial relations problems that occur in organizations.

Organization Structures

One of the constant themes of our work has been that people see and organize their world, including the world of work, in very different ways. This is why we are concerned with the mapping of personal spaces. Following the preferences given earlier it might be expected that the types of organizational structures set up will reflect these preferences. Again Kilmann and Mitroff have investigated this aspect. Table 4.1 gives a summary of some of their findings.

TABLE 4.1 ORGANIZATIONAL PREFERENCES OF DIFFERENT TYPES

Areas	Types			
	Practical (ST)	Social (SF)	Idealistic (NF)	Theoretical (NT)
Structure	Practical bureaucratic, well-defined hierarchy, central leader	Friendly, hierarchical but open	Completely decentralized, no clear lines of authority, no central leader	Complex organization, flexibility, changing authority, task forces
Emphasis in interactions	Task orientation, complete control, specificity, fixed	Human qualities of people doing	Humanitarian, general concern for	Goals, clients, effect of environment
Organizational goals	Productivity work flow	Good interpersonal relations	Personal and humanitarian	Macroeconomic theoretical

It can be seen that NF's prefer an organizational structure which is decentralized, which has no clear line of authority and no central leader. On the other hand, ST's prefer an authoritarian and bureaucratic organization with a well defined hierarchy and central leadership. The reasons for this stem from the nature of the work preference types. The NF person requires a high degree of autonomy and freedom in order to exercise his preferences and feeling. He prefers making contact with people regardless of their level and organization before he can work effectively. The ST type, on the other hand, prefers a well defined structure because this enables him to get on with what he enjoys doing–practical, everyday matters at hand. Discussions with people about feelings and intuition are often seen by ST people to be a waste of time and barriers to getting the task done.

Richek[7] found that sensing types had more positive attitudes to authority than intuitives. He also found that reality was perceived in different ways ranging from tangible material reality to intangible imaginative reality. One of the findings of the Aston studies was that the organizational structure of the company studied and the data collected were very much dependent on the attitudes of managers in each function. For example, the accountants often saw the organization very differently from the marketing people and also had different wishes for the type of structure they wanted. Handy[8] also examines this link between structure and individual most amusingly and instructively in *Gods of Management*.

Most managers are ST's and NT's with the thinking-judgmental style predominating. Organizations in which they worked, therefore, would be expected to follow a hierarchical principle, and this appears to be true of most industrial organizations. On the other hand, there exist organizations such as the theatre, or to a certain extent, academic institutions, in which there is relatively little hierarchy. Our own work[9] examined the preferences of academics in a business school and shows that their dominating preference was intuition, which accords with a loose form of organization.

What is being said, therefore, is that as people perceive organizations in different ways they will tend to try and reinforce this perception by creating organizational structures that will leave them free to work in the way they most prefer. *This is one of the main motivating forces behind the action of individuals in organizations. It has major implications for top manager selection and development–when people select others in their own image.*

Approaches to Change

One of the major issues of importance in behavior is the individual's responsiveness to change. This is reflected in his or her attitude towards time.

It had been suggested by Mann et al.[10] that the different Jungian types react to time and change very differently; that is:

Sensation types	—	present orientation
Intuitive types	—	future orientation
Feeling types	—	past orientation
Thinking types	—	time as a linear continuum

---

7 Richek, H. G. and O. H. Brown. 1968. "Phenomenological Correlates of Jung's Typology," *Journal of Analytical Psychology*, Vol. 13, pp. 57–65.

8 Handy, C. 1978. *Gods of Management*, Souvenir Press.

9 Margerison, C. J. and R. Lewis. 1979. "Management Educators and Their Clients" in Beck, J. and C. Cox, eds. *Advances in Management Education*, John Wiley.

10 Mann, H., M. Siegler. and H. Osmond. 1965. "The Many Worlds of Time," *Journal of Analytical Psychology*, Vol. 13, pp. 33–56.

These approaches appear to have been borne out by some of the work that Kilmann and Mitroff[11] did in getting some groups within the American Bureau of Census to plan ahead to the year 2000. They concluded that:

> To summarize, ST's can be characterized as real-time, operational-technical, problem-solvers; NT's are future-time, strategic-technical problem generators; and SF's are real-time operational-people problem solvers related to intuitives; the planning horizon of sensing people is extreme; however the extreme sensing people are not interested in planning at all. They do not believe that one can talk sensibly about the future because one cannot sense it directly.

Again, if we look at the distribution of managers we can see that the majority (the sensing-thinking types) will be concerned with the present here-and-now. They will not be interested in long-term theoretical issues but those of immediate value. Hence, from a study of the types, it would be expected that for management educators to try to get managers to concentrate on theoretical ideas of general interest will not work. There is a reluctance to examine issues that are not directly pertinent to the current job.

Creativity and Innovation

It might be expected from the preceding section that innovators would essentially be the intuitive types. However, this must depend on how creativity and innovation are viewed. Certainly, intuitive types predominate in creativity that involves redefinition of the problem with new and different ideas. The work of McKinnon[12] has shown a preponderance of intuitives in "creative" professions such as architecture and novel writing. However, creativity can and does also involve coming up with many different solutions and alternatives rather than redefining the problem area. Kirton[13] defines these two different types of creativity as adaptor-innovator. The adaptor can find many different ways of solving a problem but within the context of the rules and system—the innovator goes outside the accepted system and comes up with one or two radical proposals. Thus all types may be said to be creative but in different ways.

It is also in order to look at the prime areas in which the various types usually operate well and show their strengths.

Sensing—Thinking	ST	Practicality
Sensing—Feeling	SF	Social Relations
Intuitive—Feeling	NF	Idealism
Intuitive—Thinking	NT	Theory

Creativity to an ST, for example, may well be in redesigning or building machinery, a brick wall, or sewing a dress, etc. Creativity for the SF could be selling, or making people happy. For the NT, it could be developing a new model or concept and for the NF in creative writing, or communication. This is fine as long as each type recognizes the creativity implicit in each other's chosen personal space.

From our sample we can see that the majority of managers would find it easiest operating within a system and working to rules and regulations. They will not want to continually question the basic framework within which they would be operating. Hence, again with some exceptions, because of the different types, managers would be uncomfortable with radical and drastic changes coming about through innovation. They would prefer "adaption," and gradual change.

11 Mitroff, I. I., V .P. Barabba and R. H. Kilmann. 1977. "The Application of Behavioral and Philosophical Technologies to Strategic Planning: a Case Study of a Large Federal Agency," *Management Science*, Vol. 24 No. 1, September.

12 McKinnon, D. W. 1962. "The Nature and Nurture of Creative Talent," *American Psychologist*, Vol. 17, pp. 484–95.

13 Kirton, M. J. 1977. *Kirton Adaptation-Innovation Inventory*, National Foundation for Educational Research.

Career Development, Appraisal and Training

The model of work preferences that we have been discussing is based on the original theories and ideas of Jung. In essence, he was interested in a developmental guide to the path or career that an individual follows throughout his life. This aspect has recently been examined by Sheehy,[14] for example. In this context the ideas of Jung are well worth following up as they do appear to facilitate the understanding of problems of career change and development. They are extremely complex ideas if considered only in theory, but when related to individual life patterns develop clarity and simplicity.

One such idea is that of the shadow. This is the "opposite" of the preferred type of orientation and as such is an area in which the individual prefers not to work. He or she also would find it very difficult to understand others of the shadow type. For example, logical thinking types would have as their shadows feeling types. How often have "thinkers" dismissed with scorn the "softness" of feeling types—and in return the feeling types characterized thinkers as cold and heartless.

The dilemma is, however, that whilst there may be misunderstanding or even hostility towards "shadow" in other people, it also exists within our personalities. In order to end up a balanced, mature individual Jung believed we must develop this "shadow" self. If we do not, he argued, it will develop itself—either in the form of a breakdown or over-compensation. Careers can be seen in this light.

What we are suggesting, and in fact have used, is that this concept of "shadow" is of great use in appraisal and training. The majority of managers would have their shadow in the area of "theory" if our sample is a guide. There would also seem to be from our sample a considerable need for interpersonal skills development to help understand and improve relations with others. The dilemma is that this type of training, whilst absolutely necessary for balance, may be rejected because it is in the shadow—the hidden and feared part! This may well be the cause of the unease that some managers feel with regard to participation. A knowledge of type can therefore be of immense use to the trainer.

OTHER READINGS BY THE AUTHORS

Lewis, R. and C. Hibbett. 1980. "Career Development: Meeting Individual and Organizational Needs," *Journal of European Industrial Training*, Vol. 4 No. 4.

Margerison, C. J., R. Lewis, and C. Hibbett. 1978. "Training Implications of Work Preferences," *Journal of European Industrial Training*, Vol. 2 No. 3, pp. 2–4.

Margerison, C. J. 1950. "Leadership Paths and Profiles", *Leadership and Organization Development Journal*, Vol. 1, No. 1.

The Centre for Applications of Psychological Types acts as a reference centre for Myers-Briggs Type Indicator. Their address is 1221 Norwest 6th Street, Suite B 400, Gainesville, Florida 32609, USA.

14 Sheehy, G. 1978. *Passages: Predictable Crisis of Adult Life*, Corgi.

M-4

supplemental

GIVE ME AN E. GIVE ME AN S.
Or how about an I or a P? Or a left-brained type?
Sound like gibberish?
It's the language of personality testing,
corporate America's hot new tool.

by Daniel Golden

Author's apology to detail-oriented, random, quantitative readers: The personality tests I have taken over the past few months indicate that I am intuitive, sequential, and abstract—in other words, just the opposite of you.

Although I've tried to flex my less dominant sides in this article, I'm afraid it will bore you. Please try to learn my language, and remember that differences enhance team-building. As Rocky Balboa once said about his girlfriend, Adrian: "I've got gaps. Together we fill gaps." If a left-brained extrovert like the Italian Stallion and a right-brained introvert like Adrian can hit it off, so can we.

After a mutual friend introduced them this past August, it wasn't long before psychologist Otto Kroeger was offering to pump up morale and improve communication at Ralph Jacobson's troubled company.

Jacobson, the chief executive officer of Draper Laboratory in Cambridge, was intrigued. Draper had long specialized in guidance systems for underwater missiles, but much of that research had been torpedoed by glasnost, and the company had undertaken a variety of smaller projects. This shift required a reorganization. In August 1988, employees who had worked together for years were divided into specialized teams. Not surprisingly, some were unhappy with the change, and tensions ensued between teams responsible for scheduling deadlines and those in charge of engineering. This past July, the firm laid off 60 employees.

So Jacobson listened to the ebullient Kroeger and then read his book, *Type Talk*, an introduction to the Myers-Briggs Type Inventory, one of the world's most frequently used personality tests. At his office in Fairfax, Virginia, Kroeger trains more than 500 people a year to administer the MBTI. He also does "interventions" at U.S. and foreign companies.

In September the psychologist flew to Cambridge and gave the MBTI to Jacobson and six of his top aides. The seven executives answered 126 questions, including, "In your way of living, do you prefer to be original or conventional?" and "Do you prefer to arrange dates, parties, etc., well in advance or be free to do whatever looks like fun when the time comes?"

On the basis of their responses, the test-takers were categorized as Introverts (I) or Extroverts (E), Sensors (S) or Intuitives (N), Thinkers (T) or Feelers (F), and Judgers (J) or Perceivers (P). Then they discussed their types. Although Kroeger and Jacobson are reluctant to talk about the test results, Kroeger does say, "Sixty percent of the managers of any company are TJs." Top executives tend to be Is; Es are too indiscreet to advance that far.

Jacobson found the discussion so helpful that he brought Kroeger back in November to give the test to 40 more managers. "The experience and outcome of the day produced better understanding," says Joseph O'Connor, Draper's vice president for human resources and administration, who took the test in September. "The instrument was an amazingly accu-

Source: Daniel Golden, "Give Me an E. Give Me a S." *Boston Globe Magazine*, January 8, 1990. Reprinted courtesy of *The Boston Globe*.

rate predictor of my own personality, and the others felt the same way."

Reflecting the values of the baby boom generation and the influence of the Japanese model of corporation-as-family, more and more American businesses are recognizing that their success may depend not on technological innovation but on human factors such as teamwork, communication, and leadership—elusive goals that in the end boil down to the interaction of personalities. And, for an inexpensive but supposedly accurate reading on the personalities of job applicants and employees, U.S. firms increasingly rely on personality testing.

Long used by career counselors and government agencies but disdained by most companies out of skepticism or fear of bad publicity, personality testing is becoming a mainstay of the corporate world. Advocates believe that testing can help companies ease the pain of layoffs, build support for affirmative-action policies, and make the transition from entrepreneurial start-up to established institution. Wayne Camara, director of scientific affairs for the American Psychological Association, estimates that in the past five years the number of tests available to industry has tripled. Major corporations such as Digital Equipment Corp. have behavioral psychologists on staff who develop tests for in-house use.

In many offices, guessing your personality type is the hottest fad since the team decision-making technique known as quality circles. Members of this cult of personality have Myers-Briggs four-letter type designations inscribed on their license plates or nameplates. Or they pin schematic diagrams of their brains on their bulletin boards to identify themselves as predominantly right- or left-brained.

Ideally, personality tests match employees to tasks, teams, and environments that suit their temperaments, thereby raising productivity. One nationwide trucking firm recently hired University of Tulsa psychology professor Robert Hogan, developer of the Hogan Personality Inventory, to analyze the personalities of its drivers. The local delivery men were alienating customers, while long-distance truckers complained of boredom. The test showed that most of the local drivers were introverts uncomfortable with personal contact, while the long-distance ones were extroverts who needed stimulation. The company switched their assignments, and the complaints decreased.

Test-testing carries risks as well. The field is largely unregulated by the government. It is perfectly legal to sell or administer a bogus test as long as it does not discriminate against protected groups such as minorities and women. Most tests do not have to be administered by psychologists, which reduces their price but makes it harder for organizations such as the APA to monitor them. "We have no good gauge on test misuse in employment," Camara says.

Although the association and its division of industrial psychologists publish professional guidelines, many test developers refuse to show their questions and scoring systems to the APA or *Buros'* *Mental Measurements Yearbook*, the leading review publication. Test developers say are worried about plagiarism. "Psychologists steal from each other all the time," says Arnold Daniels, chairman of Praendex Inc. in Wellesley, which markets the Predictive Index. Daniels' company has never submitted the index to the yearbook, although it did commission two Harvard Medical School staffers to analyze the test's reliability.

Some academic psychologists contend that test developers are simply afraid of scrutiny and test business customers aren't interested in spending the time or money necessary to learn about what they're buying. Seymour Epstein, a University of Massachusetts at Amherst psychology professor who developed the Constructive Thinking Inventory several years ago, says several companies contacted him about using it. But when he responded that he would not let them use the test until research showed how it applied to their companies, they lost interest. Even when he told some companies that he would compare his test—for free—with the ones they were already using, there were no takers. "It's become not a scientific thing, it's a business thing," Epstein says. "There's a lot of black magic and mumbo jumbo."

According to Camara, companies often find themselves deluged with test offers, without the sophistication to choose the best one for their needs. "Organizations that have no expertise are trying to make a decision from 10 different salesmen all pushing their own test," he says. "They're exposed to a lot of hype, and they're at an extreme disadvantage."

There is also the risk of oversimplification. People enjoy knowing about their personality type as much as they like reading their horoscope—it's a conversation piece, a way to connect. Yet personalities may be too varied to be easily categorized, and many people don't fall into any one type. If they are shoehorned by co-workers or bosses into a type that doesn't fit them, or if they're regarded as misfits because they won't play the game, personality typing can turn into a dangerous kind of stereotyping.

"A lot of management tests put you in categories that aren't justified statistically," says Boston psychologist Kenneth Kraft, who favors administering several different tests to avoid pigeonholing employees. "They want you to walk away with a label, `I'm a this or I'm a that.'"

Personality typing, of course, is nothing new. Medieval philosophers divided humanity into four humors, or temperaments—phlegm, melancholy, blood, and cholera. Victorian phrenologists analyzed personality by feeling bumps on the skull. The advent per modern psychiatry spurred more scientific testing starting with the Rorschach, or ink-blot, test, a staple of clinical treatment for half a century.

The grandfather of modern personality indicators is the Minnesota Multi-Phasic Inventory. Designed as a clinical measurement of neurosis, it is also used by many government agencies and private employers to weed out unstable applicants. Because it includes such true-false questions as "I am very strongly attracted by members of my own sex" and "I believe in

the second coming of Christ," the MMPI remains controversial. Most recently, a California department store that administers the MMPI was sued on invasion of privacy grounds by an applicant for a security guard job. The case is pending.

Today, the MMPI is just one of hundreds of tests. They are not proliferating because psychologists are discovering new aspects of personality. Quite the contrary. An increasingly accepted theory among academic psychologists synthesizes personality traits into five spectrums, nicknamed the "Big Five": abstract to concrete, self-confident to depressed, prudent to impulsive, outgoing to shy, and empathic to hostile.

What's happening, instead, is that consultants design tests just original enough to call their own. Most of the tests on the market try to assess one or more of the Big Five dimensions on and many of them ask similar questions. Only the interpretive jargon changes. What the Myers-Briggs calls intuitive, for example, overlaps considerable with what other tests label as abstract, conceptual, or right-brained.

Once consultants develop a test, they try it out on executives in the industries they want as customers until they can show that patterns of answers correlate with behavior on the job. Then they translate these patterns into management personas: inspirer, perfectionist, assimilator, accommodate, implementer, experimenter.

Even the most ardent proponents of personality testing concede there is a lack of statistics or studies showing that it improves productivity or lowers attention. Yet tests steadily gain ground in the workplace. Because their results are couched in terms of style and preference rather than aptitude and intelligence, they seem unthreatening to most employees. And for employers who are trying to hire, they come at a time when other sources of information are drying up.

For example, intelligence and aptitude tests are more likely than personality tests to discriminate on the basis of race—which makes them more vulnerable to legal challenge. Another traditional tool, checking an applicant's references, has lost its usefulness because many past employers won't speak frankly for fear of being sued. Since Congress outlawed the lie detector test for private employment in 1988, many companies have turned to pen-and-pencil honesty tests.

Changes in the corporate world trigger demand for testing. Many firms, including *The Boston Globe*, use tests to ease tensions associated with affirmative action and drive home the lesson that personality types know no race or gender. If a white male and a black female discover at a workshop that they are both introverted judgers, perhaps that bond will erase any mutual suspicion.

With deregulation of financial services, many banks want customer-service workers to change from being passive order-takers to aggressive salespeople. Testing may show which workers can adapt most easily. Other companies have shifted from a hierarchical organization to a structure based on equal and interdependent teams. That structure delegates more responsibility to midlevel employees and makes chemistry more crucial. In choosing team members, again, personality testing often plays a role.

A few companies, though, are disillusioned. The Knight-Ridder newspaper chain, long a proponent of personality tests, still gives them to managerial candidates and uses them for [hiring decisions but they no longer use] them for prospective reporters because it could not demonstrate any link between personality traits such as high levels of energy and the ability to write on deadline. "Tests are not to be used as an excuse to throw brains out the window," says Ivan Jones, assistant vice president of personnel research and development for Knight-Ridder. "That's the trouble with tests. They're quick, they're easy, their value is easy to overemphasize, so hiring managers rely on them."

Just for fun, let's divide companies that use personality tests into two types: communicators and evaluators. Communicators test employees at workshops in which participation is usually voluntary. Employees often score their own tests and do not have to share the results with their bosses. The tests, then, are used not to assess performance or potential but to spark conversation about morale or team-building. While this approach reduces concerns about privacy and stereotyping, its benefits are often limited because of a lack of follow-up.

Says one therapist who used to give the Myers-Briggs at businesses: "It's hard to change patterns that have been going on for a long time unless a structure is set up, such as a process time to discuss communication before each meeting. When things get stressed out, when your profits go down, that's when you most need this stuff, and it's not there."

Unlike communicators, evaluators have enough faith in testing to rely on it for hiring and promotion. And while communicators boast about their trendy workshops, evaluators sound defensive. They decline comment or describe their questionnaire as a tool, an instrument, an indicator—anything but a test. They realize that many people agree with the Boston woman who withdrew her application for a management job in the Sheraton hotel chain after being asked to take a battery of personality [tests].

"When you accept a job, it should be based on your skills," she says. "If a psychologist is making the decision, you don't need to work there. My interpretation of dots, or whatever they use, is nobody's business."

Tobias Fleishman Shapiro and Co., a Cambridge accounting firm, is one of the few companies willing to discuss its personality testing for prospective employees. For the past five years, TFS has required most applicants to take the Predictive Index, which has been available since 1955. Praendex chairman Arnold Daniels based the index on his work in World War II with a psychologist who studied Air Force bomber crews. The corporations using the test range from banks to fast-food chains, and their number has more than doubled in a decade, from 800 in 1979 to 1,700. The index lists two identical sets of adjectives—"eloquent," "conscientious," "life of the party," etc.—on either side of a sheet of paper. On one side, applicants check the adjectives that describe their behavior; on the other, they mark the ones that describe how others expect them to act. According to Daniels, the self-description indicates personality traits, and comparing it with the perceived expectations suggests the individual's pattern of adjustment.

The total number of adjectives checked is supposed to reflect the individual's energy level. But that seemed dubious in one case. A highly respected Globe writer who took the PI anonymously for the purposes of this article was surprised to be told that, according to Daniels' analysis of his responses, he held a subordinate position and was frustrated by the routine nature of his job. When Daniels was asked how he had reached his conclusion, he said it was because the writer checked only a few adjectives.

In a world where recruitment agencies charge $10,000 to find an entry-level accountant, TFS executives regard the Predictive Index as insurance against making an expensive hiring mistake. The additional cost of personality testing for TFS is minuscule: $1,400 to train recruiting director Laura Share to administer the index, plus a $400 annual licensing fee.

Share says that the ideal entry-level accountant is a detail-oriented extrovert, equally at ease with numbers and clients. If the results signal introversion or inattention to detail, TFS executives probe those areas in interviewing the applicant and calling references. "If we see someone who's opposite to everyone here, we want to make sure they'd be happy here," Share says. "Otherwise, chances are they won't stay long."

TFS executives recognize that using the Predictive Index could drive away potentially valuable employees. Occasionally, they waive the test for especially desirable applicants. After praising the index for the better part of an hour, Tracy Gallagher, director of administration, concedes that he decided not to give it to Lawrence Kaye, for fear of alienating him. Kaye is now manager of training and education.

On the other hand, since an important part of happiness at the office is getting along with the boss, TFS often tests not only the job applicant but also the supervisor for that position, to see if their personalities would be compatible. Share says, "If the supervisors say they want someone who is independent, and they're dominant themselves, you ask, 'Are you sure? Do you really want someone like yourself?'"

It doesn't take long to realize that Manny Elkind is artistic, visionary, turned off by sequences and numbers—in a word, right-brained. When a reporter interrupts Elkind's fluid exposition of the left-brained personality ("You like to think it through, then you say, 'Okay, let's get it done'") to ask permission to accompany him to a workshop, Elkind agrees. Checking his calendar, he says he will lead a session on brain dominance technology at an insurance company the following Monday. Elkind calls the company and informs an answering machine of the reporter's wish: "I've got a good feeling about this guy," he tells the machine. Only after hanging up the phone does he realize that he has the date wrong. He conducted the workshop the previous week.

Like a cat in a dog pound, Elkind worked for years as an operations manager in the left-brained milieu of Polaroid. There, he says, he saw promising innovations, such as a plan for cameras to be put together by small teams rather than on assembly lines, thwarted by supervisors reluctant to give up control. Realizing that managers need to understand themselves to work effectively with others, he began attending workshops on self-awareness—including est, the controversial California-based movement that flourished in the late 1970s. In 1979, Elkind became Polaroid's senior manager of experimental projects, with an opportunity to implement what he had learned.

Ned Herrmann, developer of the Hermann Brain Dominance Instrument, visited Polaroid in 1983 and gave a seminar on left- and right-brained personalities. According to Herrmann, everyone questions. Their concern is to deal with practical issues and generate information which can have a bearing upon the specific outcome. Such people enjoy the present and deal with the practicalities of life, rather than theorizing or developing grand ideas of how life should be.

If you are the manager of people who have a strong practical base, then it is important to give them work which does have some tangible aspect to it. It is no good bringing such a group together to develop radical new ways of working. They will not necessarily be very successful in generating new ideas or brainstorming. However, they will be extremely valuable in applying their minds to a specific problem and utilizing their experience. Such people can be very effective when asked to develop a more effective way of organizing the work process or mending or rectifying situations which are getting out of control. They can be as clever as anyone else, but they like to use their abilities to deal with practical problems, particularly in the here-and-now situation.

Generating Data: The Intuitive Approach

People who use the intuitive approach tend to stress more the imaginative side of their personalities. They are like the novelist who perhaps sees two people fighting in the street and then goes home and writes a novel about urban violence and the breakdown of law and order. The novel emerges out of a specific incident which the writer then develops according to his insight. They often do not know themselves what is happening and why. Nevertheless they do come up with ideas and possibilities, some of which may be worthwhile, some not!

The characteristics of the intuitive person would include the following points. First of all, she concentrates on the whole field, rather than specifics. This means that she can be poor in attending to detail. Such people do not like routine. They get impatient, frustrated and show anxiety when they have to engage in such work. The effect of this is that they may sometimes take short-cuts and play hunches. Such people are often difficult to talk with. Their minds are racing ahead, looking for the consequences and the implications.

It is of no use putting people who have the high capacity for intuition into jobs which demand repetitive behavior over a period of time. Such people enjoy tackling new jobs and are extremely good on project work. They love learning a new skill. Indeed, having learned a new skill they may not then want to use it but instead go quickly to the next interesting assignment.

Often such people work in quick and energetic spells. They may seem to be lazy at times and not be applying themselves. However, as Andrew Carnegie, the great industrialist, used to say, "I've got the flash," and would then rush off to tackle a new project.

Such people can be exciting individuals to have alongside you. However, they are not easy to understand. It is necessary, though, if we are to develop an effective team or organization, to harness the talents of such people. Typically this is difficult to do because of their dislike of routine, and their enjoyment of complexity.

Examples of such teams are the research and development laboratories of major organizations. Many of these are separated away from the operational side of work, such as manufacturing or refining. Many of the researchers will often come in late in the morning and work till all hours of the evening if they are pursuing something that they feel has value. In one sense the creative process cannot be tied down to time and the nine-to-five day has little meaning for someone who is extremely creative.

We have distinguished here between two ends of a continuum. We have referred to people as having either more of a sensing or more of an *intuitive* approach to gathering information. In reality all of us have some degree of both. Therefore, what we are talking about is the emphasis that we place on one in contrast to the other. This is a matter of preferences. Clearly we develop over a period of time and gather strength in one or both of the dimensions. Therefore we will move towards using our strengths and often reinforce them.

prefers one or more of four styles: cerebral left (analytical, mathematical); cerebral right (creative, holistic); limbic left (controlled, conservative); and limbic right (interpersonal, emotional). "This technology was the best combination of most valuable and least threatening," Elkind says. "It's a whole-brain concept. It appeals to everyone. I had an immediate vision of what I could do with it."

The following year, Elkind began using Herrmann's test for workshops he conducted at Polaroid. They were so popular that he invited other corporations to send their employees. The number of people enrolled in his seminars increased from 300 in 1984 to 4,000 in 1988. Then Elkind became concerned about Polaroid's future after a takeover attempt, and he grew frustrated because, as he puts it, the company would not support "the more intensive training people need to move into." He left to start Mind-Tech Inc. in Stoughton. His workshop remains popular with Massachusetts companies: It is required for loan officers at Bank of Boston and for senior managers at John Hancock Mutual Life Insurance Co.

Among his other activities, Elkind gives a daylong workshop every month at Bentley College in Waltham, open to anyone. This past November about 30 people paid either $215 apiece, the corporate rate, or $125, the rate for employees of nonprofit enterprises, to attend the session. The group, which had twice as many women as men, included a dozen employees from Bank of Boston's customer relations division, a Bank of New England employee who was evaluating the workshop for use in the bank's training program, and four employees of a Texas Air subsidiary that has suffered from high turnover and low morale.

Elkind's genial manner makes the group feel at home. He encourages its members to change seats every 45 minutes: By the afternoon, everyone has met everybody else. The activities are a fast-paced melange of lecture, films, discussion, and exercises. Asked to draw a flower, left-brainers depict no-frills stems and petals of mathematical exactness,

while right-brainers, emptying their crayon boxes, scrawl impressionistic blossoms.

"The thinking preferences affect you at every level of your life," Elkind says. "The way you choose cars, the way you choose clothes, the way you choose careers."

At one point, Elkind tells the group that Herrmann's theory does not depict the brain's actual division of labor. It is just a schematic, a metaphor, with no more claim to a physiological basis than other models of personality. He urges his audience to explore other typologies, such as the distinction between matchers and mismatchers. Matchers, he says notice similarities, while mismatchers see differences.

"I'm a matcher, and my wife is a mismatcher," Elkind says. "I'd suggest going out to dinner, and she'd say, 'I can't do it either Tuesday or Thursday.' I'd get angry, thinking she was negative. I'd tell her, 'Don't tell me when you can't do it. Tell me when you can do it.' I finally realized that her mind worked by process of elimination. She was telling me that she could do it Monday, Wednesday, and Friday."

Before his first workshop in 1984, Elkind gave Herrmann's questionnaire to the Polaroid executives who had volunteered to participate. When he graded the tests, he was distressed to find that everyone in the group was left-brained. Since the workshop needed a mix of personalities, he asked the executives to invite the most creative, free-wheeling people they knew to take the test. Any right-brainers, he said, could come for free.

Miriam Kronish, an elementary school principal in Needham, heard about Elkind's offer from a school media specialist who was married to a Polaroid manager. Kronish had wondered for years if she was unsuited to her job because she was bored by budgets and schedules. Intrigued by the concept of personality types, she took the test, which showed that she was very right-brained. Then she went to the workshop. It was an "epiphany," she says. "It changed my way of looking at myself professionally."

Since then, Kronish has matched wits with the *New York Times* crossword puzzle

Ⓢ

43

PRESS

every day to develop her left brain. Along with other Needham teachers and administrators who had been impressed by Elkind, she attended workshops that applied personality types to the classroom. Today, the Needham elementary school curriculum is not only divided into right- and left-brained activities but is tailored to four learning styles: innovative, analytic, common sense, and dynamic.

At the John Eliot School, where Kronish is principal, a recent unit on the physically impaired appealed to all four styles. A concert by a band of physically impaired people at a school assembly, which culminated in teachers and students dancing in the aisles, gave innovative learners the emotional reason they need to study a topic. Analytic learners, who used to be called bookworms, absorbed facts galore. Common sense learners, seeking sensory experience, tried on crutches and braces. And dynamic learners designed a better wheelchair.

Unlike many corporations, which have neglected to transfer the lessons of the workshop to the office, school systems such as Needham's have woven personality theory into everyday interaction. Since teachers rather than students take the tests, there is less danger of stereotyping children.

Every teacher in Newburyport is required to take a workshop about Anthony Gregorc's theory, which divides learners into four "mindstyles"; abstract-random, abstract-sequential, concrete-sequential, and concrete-random. (They correspond roughly to Needham's innovative, analytic, common sense, and dynamic learners.) The school system also paid for several teachers to receive advanced training. They act in their spare time as peer coaches, helping their colleagues to implement the theory.

One peer coach is Nancy Duclos, a geometry teacher at Newburyport High School. Giving a lesson on congruent triangles to her class of sophomores and juniors one recent afternoon, Duclos, like an expert fisherman, floated a lure for each type of learner. She reviewed the textbook for sequential learners and enticed randoms with a freewheeling discussion. Then she divided students into groups to draw their own triangles, pleasing concretes as well as abstract-randoms, who enjoy collaborating.

"When I learned this, I didn't want to put a label on kids," Duclos says afterward, still holding her yardstick and chalk-tipped compass. "All I know is that when I'm at the front of the room, it's possible that I have at least one kid of every learning style in my classroom. It's my job to do something that each of those kids would like."

"I could have gotten up there and given it to them from the book. Two days later, I'd have to give it to them again, because they'd forget it. This way, they've discussed it, they've experienced it, and they'll remember it."

After a 1988 federal law banned the use of lie detector tests for job applicants in private industry, Wackenhut Corp. had to find a substitute. The international security firm based in Coral Gables, Florida, chose the Phase 2 Profile Integrity Status Inventory, a questionnaire that claims to measure, among other things, "Basic Dishonest Attitudes," "Ability to Measure Dishonesty," and "How Often a Person Thinks or Plans About Doing Something Dishonest."

Today, Wackenhut officials say that the Phase 2 is more accurate than the polygraph. They boast that only 10 percent of employees who passed the test turn out to be dishonest, although a skeptic might wonder whether other Phase 2-approved workers, might be stealing undetected. The firm uses it in every state except Massachusetts, where honesty testing has been prohibited since 1986. Without the test, Boston-area manager James Healey complains, he has to conduct in-depth background checks, which are both more expensive and less reliable.

Honesty tests are the fastest-growing type of personality test in the United States, and the most controversial. Desperate to arrest employee theft, which costs American business an estimated $40 billion per year, 10,000 companies now administer the tests to 3 million people annually. Test marketers do not guarantee that an applicant with a passing score is honest or that one with a failing score is crooked, but they do claim that failing applicants represent a higher risk to the employer.

Critics of the tests contend that they are meaningless and that even if they are valid in the aggregate, it is fair to reject an individual because he or she has a 30 percent or 40 percent probability of stealing on the job. Both the APA and the US Office of Technology Assessment are now studying the issue.

"The use of so-called honesty tests to make hiring or promotion decisions is on the same shaky ground as are the polygraphs . . . and is the equivalent of a random procedure," wrote University of Illinois psychology professor Benjamin Kleinmuntz in a review of the Phase 2 in *Buros' Mental Measurements Yearbook.* "They are themselves dishonest devices. They are dishonest toward employers because they reject many potentially productive workers, hence causing greater costs than savings. And they are dishonest toward prospective employees because they constitute an unfair method of screening."

Kleinmuntz and other critics point out that such testing rests on a paradox: It relies on dishonest people to make honest admissions of dishonest acts. Yet marketers say that no matter how strange it seems, many applicants confess to crimes. Of 10,000 applicants in 1988 who took a test developed by Reid Psychological Systems of Chicago, 7 percent admitted stealing money or merchandise from an employer, and 5.6 percent admitted using marijuana, amphetamines, or cocaine at work.

The reason for these admissions, according to test marketers, is that dishonest people rationalize their behavior by convincing themselves that the rest of mankind is more corrupt than they are. If they don't acknowledge a few bad acts, they think, they will look like liars. That is why, besides directly asking about criminal behavior, most tests probe the applicant's view of human morality. Anyone who answers "No" to "Do you think

police officers are usually honest?" is off to a bad start.

The flaw in this approach is that workers in certain world-weary professions tend to believe, regardless of their own conduct, that other people are crooks. Reporters usually fail honesty tests—unless they take the Phase 2, which has a built-in cynicism factor, according to its designer, Gregory Lousig-Nont.

Another assumption underlying the tests is that honest people want harsher penalties for crime than dishonest people do. There are exceptions to this rule as well, the best known being a nun who sought a job in a Minneapolis bookstore and was given an honesty test. As a believer in Christian mercy, she favored leniency for thieving employees. She flunked.

Your wife will die of cancer tomorrow unless she takes a new miracle drug. It costs $2,000, but you only have $1,000. Should you steal it from the drugstore?

In a cozy Prudential Center apartment, its window shades half-drawn to keep out the light, 10 managers from *The Boston Globe* ponder this hypothetical question. Some say they would do anything to save their spouses' lives. Others object, asking what would happen if everyone broke the law when it suited their needs.

There is no right answer, organizational consultant Emily Souvaine tells the group. The differing responses reflect personality types. Fs—feelers—make decisions subjectively. Ts—thinkers—make them objectively. In the business world there is pressure to be a T. "This day is a way of honoring the F side of decision-making, as well as the T side," Souvaine says.

Like their cohorts at Draper Laboratory, all managers at the Globe have attended these workshops to learn about themselves and their co-workers. Based on the work of Carl Jung, the Myers-Briggs Type Indicator theorizes that there are 16 different personalities, derived from four pairs of contrasting types. ISTJs (or introverted, sensing, thinking judgers), for example, are serious and quiet and succeed by concentration and thoroughness. Among their most popular careers is

45

PRESS

pollution control, and their least favorite is dental hygiene.

Developed from 1945 to 1962 by a mother-and-daughter team, the MBTI was available only for research until 1975. During the next decade it was mainly used in religious organizations, government, and higher education. In 1980 the University of Maine at Orono began giving the test to all incoming freshmen. As often as possible, it matched roommates who shared two of their four types so that they would support each other while leaving room for understanding differences. The university found that roommates selected with the MBTI had higher grade point averages and lower dropout rates.

The indicator proved equally helpful in explaining a rash of vandalism in one dormitory. By studying the types of residents, university officials found that the dorm contained more than its share of EPs—extroverted perceivers, who need lots of stimulation and physical activity. The university started a health club and aerobics classes in the dorm, and vandalism returned to normal levels.

Now corporations are supplanting universities as leading users of the MBTI. Of the nearly 2 million MBTI answer sheets sold each year in the United States, 30 percent go to private industry. (Until 1985, the Japanese were the world's largest users of the MBTI, and they still rank second.) *The Type Reporter*, a promotional newsletter, has devoted several recent issues to the MBTI's role in the workplace, using headlines such as, "How to Keep Ss from Getting Stuck on Specifics," "How to Keep Ps from Procrastinating," and "How to Keep Js from Jumping to Conclusions."

A study by Jean Kummerow, co-author of *Introduction to Type in Organizational Settings*, found that 62 percent of workers who took the MBTI in one study felt that it assessed their types correctly. Of the 10 people in the *Globe's* workshop, five agreed with their MBTI results, and four said that it had identified three of their four types. One person said that only two types were correct.

For those who disagree with their type, a frequent comment is that the MBTI has no middle ground: You must be either E or I, S or N, and so on. Yet some people lack a strong preference in at least one dimension. This analysis applies to most personality tests. They tend to be more vindicating for people with strongly defined personalities, such as Manny Elkind or Miriam Kronish. Those in the middle of the spectrum—call them well-balanced or, in MBTI jargon, "undifferentiated"—may find their results more perplexing than revealing. "People come to me and say, `Shall I answer this the way I am at home or at work?' " says Caroline Weaver, a consultant who uses the MBTI for corporate team building.

The MBTI is not recommended for hiring, mainly because it is rather transparent, and takers could skew answers to fit the job description. Computer Sciences Corp., a high-tech company with 21,000 employees, uses the indicator to improve its hiring indirectly: Its instructors take the MBTI before training managers to interview job applicants. At the San Jose Mercury News, a group of editors used to interview each job applicant together. After being exposed to the MBTI, they realized that this process felt threatening to introverts, and they considered switching to one-on-one interviews.

The workshops at the *Globe* indicate that 70 percent of its managers are introverted—a surprising finding, since 70 percent of Americans are extroverted. Dolly King, *The Charlotte Observer's* director of organizational development, says most editors in the Knight-Ridder newspaper chain are ENTJs—"hearty, frank, decisive leaders."

Back at the Prudential Center, Souvaine poses another stumper: You are vacationing in Paris, and this morning you plan to visit the Louvre. On your way, you pass a lively street fair. Do you stick to your schedule or postpone the museum to enjoy the fair?

If you head straight for the "Mona Lisa," you must be a judger, Souvaine says. If you veer off to eat a croissant or watch a juggler, you are a perceiver.

"Are you still a J if you plan to be a P?" one member of the group asks.

"That's a totally J question," Souvaine answers. "How can you plan to be spontaneous?"

To tell you the truth, I'm still a bit confused about my personality. On the Myers-Briggs, I come out as an INTJ—skeptical, critical, independent, stubborn, most likely to become an architect and least likely to become a food-counter worker. The Predictive Index concurs: I am analytical, quick-thinking, tense, and driven, although I'm trying to conform to demands made by an organization or leader and be more patient than I really am. "When we're out selling our program people like you are among our toughest prospects," says Arnold Daniels who developed the PI.

But the Herrmann Brain Dominance Instrument sees me differently. Like "the clear majority of women, I'm creative holistic, interpersonal and feeling—right-brained to the max." I'm suited to be a teacher, social worker, or nurse.

So what's the true me?

Guess I'd better take some more tests.

INDEX

MASSACHUSETTS INSTITUTE OF TECHNOLOGY

ANCONA, KOCHAN, SCULLY,
VAN MAANEN, WESTNEY

MANAGING FOR THE FUTURE

Organizational Behavior & Processes

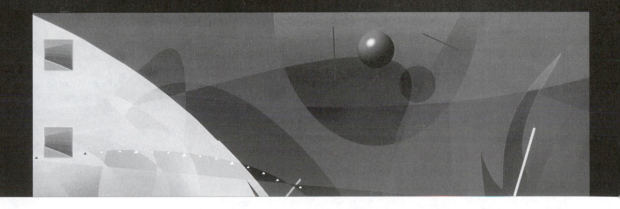

TEAM PROCESSES

module 5

CONTENTS

MODULE 5 (M-5)

TEAM PROCESSES

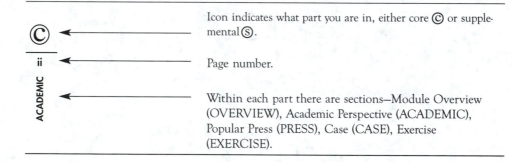

Icon indicates what part you are in, either core © or supplemental Ⓢ.

Page number.

Within each part there are sections—Module Overview (OVERVIEW), Academic Perspective (ACADEMIC), Popular Press (PRESS), Case (CASE), Exercise (EXERCISE).

Dedicated to those who have inspired us to try to be better students and teachers.

Special dedications to:
Professor Jack Barbash
Professor Arthur H. Gladstein
Professor Marius B. Jansen
Professor Joanne Martin
Professor Edgar H. Schein

Acquisitions Editor: John R. Szilagyi
Developmental Editor: Jamie Gleich Bryant
Production Editor: Mardell Toomey
Production House: DPS Associates, Inc.
Cover Design: Michael H. Stratton
Marketing Manager: Rob Bloom

ISBN: 0-538-87692-1

1 2 3 4 5 6 7 D1 4 3 2 1 0 9 8

Printed in the United States of America

South-Western College Publishing
an International Thomson Publishing company IⓉP®

Cincinnati • Albany • Boston • Detroit • Johannesburg • London • Madrid • Melbourne • Mexico City
New York • Pacific Grove • San Francisco • Scottsdale • Singapore • Tokyo • Toronto

TEAM PROCESSES

This module is designed to help you learn about and practice observing ongoing internal team processes. It is also geared to help you think about how to manage and change existing processes. Internal team processes refer to the ways in which team members interact with one another. The major categories of team processes are task and maintenance functions, decision making, communication, influence, conflict, atmosphere, and emotional issues. All groups and teams exhibit team processes that shift over time in response to changes in membership, task, external influences, or the growth that members exhibit as they work together. In this module you will have the opportunity to analyze your own team processes or those of a decision-making group.

Internal team processes, although only one determinant of team effectiveness (see Figure 5.1, Model of Team Effectiveness—a model covered more fully in Module 3, **Making Teams Work**) constitute the aspect of teams over which members have the most control and which has the most influence on team member satisfaction. The amount of learning that takes place in teams is also very much influenced by team processes. Once you learn more about what team processes are and how to observe them, you should be better able to manage them to achieve better team effectiveness.

It is predicted that the understanding and management of team processes will be important skills in the organization of the future. As the work of teams becomes more complex, crossfunctional, and varied, there are more demands put on the members of those teams. As organizations become more diverse and global, team membership becomes more heterogeneous, and the possibilities for conflict and poor communication increase. All of this occurs in a competitive setting in which the demands for high performance are ever increasing. Managers will have to be able to create smooth team processes in the face of these challenges if they are to succeed.

FIGURE 5.1 MODEL OF TEAM EFFECTIVENESS

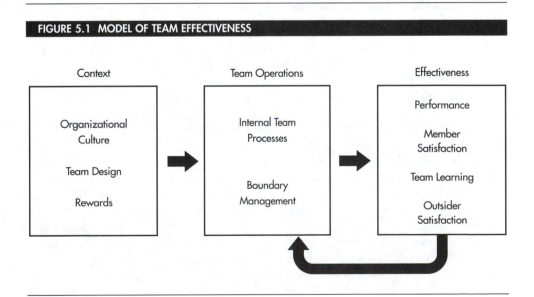

This module consists of three readings and an exercise. The core reading, **Team Process Observation Guide**, provides some detail about each of the major categories of internal team processes, why each category is important, and hints about how to carefully observe the category in an ongoing team. This reading points out that although most of us have participated in many different teams, we seldom take the time to systematically observe and analyze them. Observation and analysis are, however, precursors to understanding and managing teams. As you read through the Observation Guide you should try to think about how you can use the concepts to better understand your own team or a team that you might observe. What aspects of the team will you monitor? Why? How will you go about monitoring how the team members are interacting with one another? What conclusions will you be able to draw from your observations?

The first supplemental reading, **Team Decision Making**, focuses on one important category of internal team processes. Decision making is singled out for greater emphasis because the work of many teams is essentially decision making. Decision making is becoming more difficult as decisions need to be made more quickly than ever before, using greater amounts of more complex information. This reading focuses on the key steps in team decision making, what can go wrong as team members try to follow those steps, and ways to improve decision making.

Unlike the other two readings, the second supplemental is from the popular business press, *Fortune* magazine. This article, **"The Trouble with Teams,"** investigates the myth that everybody loves teams. Instead, it focuses on the difficulties that people and companies encounter as they try to implement team designs. The article emphasizes creating the right types of teams and sets the stage for understanding the context in which team processes will evolve.

Conceptual understanding of internal team processes is very important, but this module also emphasizes the application of those concepts. Therefore, you will be asked to participate in an exercise in which you have to observe and analyze team processes and think about how to improve them. You might be asked to observe a film of a decision-making group or to work with other team members to create a new product. In either case, you will be called upon to use the readings to interpret what goes on in a team meeting and to suggest how the dynamics among members might be reshaped. Team processes are very complex and exciting; they should be more comprehensible after you complete this module.

ADDITIONAL ACTIVITIES

You can expand your learning about internal team processes in several ways. One is to start to keep a journal documenting what is occurring on a team you are a part of. This could include a student team, an athletic team, or even your family. As you write your entries, try to cover all the categories of team processes that are discussed in the readings. What insights occur as you systematically observe what is going on? How are communication, influence, decision making, and conflict handled? Who takes care of task and maintenance activities? What does your analysis suggest about what you wish to do on this team?

Another way to learn more about team processes is to get permission to observe a team in a local company or in your school. You might want to create an observation form that helps you to organize the data you collect while you are observing. When you enter the team, your presence may seem to interfere with its regular work, but over time your presence will become quite natural. After you have finished your observations you might want to offer to share your reactions with the team members, or you may be more comfortable simply thanking them for their participation.

Finally, you can think back over the team experiences that you have had in the past. Try to figure out which aspects of team processes were most satisfactory to you and which ones were most distressing. How did these processes come about? What could you have done to make your bad experiences better? What can you do in the future to create the types of processes that work best for you?

For those who wish to learn more about internal team processes the following references are suggested.

REFERENCES

Donnellon, A. 1996. *Team Talk: The Power of Language in Team Dynamics.* Boston, MA: Harvard Business School Press.

Eisenhardt, K. M. 1990. "Speed and Strategic Choice: How Managers Accelerate Decision Making." *California Management Review,* 32(3), pp. 1–16.

Gabarro, J. J., and A. Harlan. 1983. "Process Observation." In L. Schlesinger, R. Eccles, and J. J. Gabarro, eds. *Managing Behavior in Organizations.* New York: McGraw Hill, pp. 57–66.

Gersick, C. J., and J. R. Hackman. 1990. "Habitual Routines in Task-Performing Teams." *Organizational Behavior and Human Decision Processes,* pp. 47, 65–97.

Janis, I. 1972. *Victims of Groupthink.* Boston: Houghton-Mifflin.

Katzenbach, J. R., and D. K. Smith. 1993. *The Wisdom of Teams: Creating the High-Performance Organization.* Boston, MA: Harvard Business School Press.

Nadler, D. A., and J. L. Spencer, Delta Consulting Group. 1998. *Executive Teams.* San Francisco, CA: Jossey-Bass Publishers.

Patton, R., K. Giffin, and E. Patton. 1989. *Decision-Making Team Interaction.* New York: Harper & Row.

Schein, E. 1982. "What to Observe in a Team." In *NTL Reading Book for Human Relations Training.* Bethel, ME: NTL Institute, pp. 72–74.

Schein, E. 1988. *Process Consultation: Its Role in Organization Development,* second edition. Reading, MA: Addison-Wesley.

Yukl, G. 1994. *Leadership in Organizations,* third edition. Englewood Cliffs, NJ: Prentice Hall.

M-5

core

TEAM PROCESS OBSERVATION GUIDE

Although most of us have been in various kinds of teams throughout our lives, we seldom take time to systematically observe and analyze how they function.[1] Yet observation and analysis are the first steps in understanding teams, shaping their dynamics, and, ultimately, improving their performance. Every team, be it a family, sports team, task force, or platoon, can be characterized as a set of individuals who depend on each other to reach certain goals. Team process observation focuses on these individuals and the ways in which they interact with one another.

MEMBERSHIP

Before observing a team it is useful to understand something about the individuals who comprise it. Differences in personality, style, race, and gender often play a role in team dynamics. Within organizations, differences in hierarchical level, functional background, and commitment to team goals also contribute to the level of cohesion or conflict within a team. In addition, length of association among members affects team functions. Teams in which members are familiar or strongly tied to each other are better at sharing unique information, while groups of strangers outperform familiar teams when members possess redundant knowledge (Gruenfeld, Mannix, Williams, and Neale, 1996). Key questions concerning membership include:

- Do team members have the required expertise and authority to carry out the task? Are all individuals who have a stake in the team's decisions included in the team?
- What are the personalities and styles of team members? How does this combination affect the team?
- What is the racial and gender mix within the team? How does this combination affect the team?
- How committed are individual members to the team? In what ways are conflicts over different levels of commitment resolved?
- Which hierarchical levels and functional teams are represented? How does this affect the team?
- Is the team made up of strangers, or members that know each other well? With what effect?

ORGANIZATIONAL CONTEXT

The larger organization in which a team operates also contributes to its success or failure. Groups need appropriate institutional direction, information, and resources. Problems occur when the organizational mission is unclear, tasks are poorly defined, teams are not allowed sufficient autonomy, or rewards are granted to individuals rather than to teams. Key questions regarding a team's organizational context include the following:

1 This reading builds heavily on the chapter "Process Observation," pp. 57–68 in Gabarro and Harlan (1983), and on Schein, (1988).

- Have the goals and tasks of the team been clearly identified?
- Are team members rewarded for individual rather than team performance?
- Has management granted the team enough autonomy to accomplish its task?
- Does the team have access to the information and resources needed to perform its task?

TEAM PROCESSES

Process observation focuses on the process, not the content, of team discussion. That is, it is less concerned with what the team is doing or discussing than in how the team is going about its task. For example, it does not focus on the specific details of the new car that a product development team is designing, but on who is talking to whom, who is influencing decisions, how the team organizes itself, how conflict is handled, and what happens in and between meetings. The major categories of team process are task and maintenance functions, decision making, communication, influence, conflict, atmosphere, and emotional issues.

TASK AND MAINTENANCE FUNCTIONS

In order for teams to operate effectively, they must engage in task and maintenance functions. Task functions help the team members to organize themselves to get the work done. They include activities such as setting team agendas, keeping the team on target, prioritizing tasks, structuring the way the team makes decisions, and proposing alternative ways to solve problems. Maintenance functions hold the team together so that members can continue to get along with one another and even have some fun. Table 5.1 outlines the task and maintenance functions identified by Benne and Sheats (reported in Schein, 1988). Questions associated with task and maintenance functions follow.

Task Functions

- Do team members make suggestions as to the best way to proceed? How frequently?
- Do members give or ask for information, opinions, feelings, and feedback, or indicate that they are searching for alternatives?
- How is the team kept on target?
- Are all ideas presented given adequate discussion before evaluation begins?
- Does the team summarize what has been covered? Does the team review who is responsible for doing what, when team member inputs are due, or when the team will meet again? How?

Maintenance Functions

- Are all team members encouraged to enter into the discussion?
- Are there attempts by any team members to help others clarify their ideas?
- Are team members careful to reject ideas, and not people? In what way?
- Are conflicts among members ignored or addressed in some way?
- Are all team members treated respectfully?

DECISION MAKING

Groups make decisions all the time, both consciously and subconsciously. Those decisions may concern the task at hand, team procedures, norms or standards of behavior, or how much work the team will take on. Many key decisions that subsequently shape the team are made early—sometimes at the first meeting—and are notoriously difficult to reverse. Therefore, understanding how decisions are made is key to team functioning.

TABLE 5.1 FUNCTIONS REQUIRED FOR EFFECTIVE GROUP FUNCTIONING

	Function	Description	Example
Functions that build task accomplishment	Initiating	Stating the goal or problem, making proposals about how to work on it, setting time limits.	"Let's set up an agenda for discussing each of the problems we have to consider."
	Seeking Information and Opinions	Asking group members for specific factual information related to the task or problem or for their opinions about it.	"What do you think would be the best approach to this, Jack?"
	Providing Information and Opinions	Sharing information or opinions related to the task or problem.	"I worked on a similar problem last year and found . . ."
	Clarifying	Helping one another understand ideas and suggestions that come up in the group.	"What you mean, Sue, is that we could . . .?"
	Elaborating	Building on one another's ideas and suggestions.	"Building on Don's idea, I think we could . . ."
	Summarizing	Reviewing the points covered by the group and the different ideas states so that decisions can be based on full information.	Appointing a recorder to to take notes on a blackboard.
	Consensus Testing	Periodic testing about whether the group is nearing a decision or needs to continue discussion.	"Is the group ready to decide about this?"
Functions that build and maintain a group	Harmonizing	Mediating conflict between other members, reconciling disagreements, relieving tensions.	"Don, I don't think you and Sue really see the question that differently."
	Compromising	Admitting error at times of group conflict.	"Well, I'd be willing to change if you provided some help on . . ."
	Gatekeeping	Making sure all members have a chance to express their ideas and feelings and preventing members from being interrupted.	"Sue, we haven't heard from you on this issue."
	Encouraging	Helping a group member make his or her point. Establishing a climate of acceptance in the group.	"I think what you started to say is important, Jack. Please continue."

The four key steps in decision making are (1) identifying the problem or opportunity, (2) analyzing the problem, (3) proposing and evaluating solutions, and (4) implementing the decision. Teams often need to cycle through these steps several times as new information and changing circumstances shift decision premises. Decision making seldom evolves smoothly; poor organization, interpersonal conflicts, bias, and even subconscious processes can work to distract the process. Too often the multiple steps of decision making are ignored as team members rush toward a quick decision and implementation. This "solution mindedness" relieves the anxiety of not having a solution to a problem, but often results in decisions needing to be revisited later (for more information on decision making, see Team Decision Making in this module).

Within teams, members often feel pressure to conform to the majority opinion. Subtle and not so subtle pressures from the majority often push those with differing opinions to remain silent. The chances of a minority being able to shift the majority rise dramatically when more than one person presents the minority opinion. Even when a minority opinion is not able to shift the decision, however, it serves a very useful function. It forces the team to think about alternative views, to justify the majority opinion, or to find creative ways to alter the decision to meet a broader set of criteria. Thus, even if there is no minority dissent in a team, it is often useful to create a "devil's advocate" who forces the team to consider other options and look at the possible negative consequences of their chosen option.

Consensus decision making allows all team members to feel that they are a part of the decision-making process and increases their commitment to a chosen course of action. However, consensus decision making can be very time consuming. Many corporate decision teams, in particular, are finding that consensus decision making takes too long. In a study of top management teams in the fast-paced mini-computer market, Eisenhardt (1990) found that although teams strive for consensus, they also have fall-back plans (e.g., they let the leader decide or they vote) if consensus is not easily forthcoming.

Questions concerning decision making include the following.

- Does the team follow the four steps of decision making? With what consequences?
- Does one person make the decisions for everyone? With what consequences?
- Does the team vote on decisions and let the majority rule? With what consequences?
- Does the team strive for consensus? With what consequences?
- Does the team encourage minority opinion?

COMMUNICATION

Communication patterns offer clues as to who is influencing the team, which subgroups and coalitions exist, how well the team is progressing, and how members are feeling. Those who participate most frequently are often, but not always, the most influential individuals. Influence often falls to aggressive and highly articulate team members who are able to sway the team discussion in their favor. In addition, ideas that are repeated over and over are usually adopted more readily than those that are mentioned only once.

Where coalitions exist, members will "trigger" each other to support a particular alternative (e.g., "John's idea to have customers pay for this service is a great one!") or oppose another (e.g., "I think we're better off with Debbie's suggestion of trying to cut costs."). Quiet members may be content just to listen, or may be angry or disconnected from the team.

Team communication patterns can easily be measured by use of a sociogram (see Figure 5.2 on page 10). In a sociogram each team member is represented by his or her initials. Directional arrows run between the sets of initials, indicating a verbal exchange between individuals, and from the initials to the center of the diagram, indicating a communication to the team as a whole. Each time a member of the team talks to another individual or to the team as a whole, the observer puts a mark on the appropriate arrow. Each time a team member interrupts another, the observer places an "i" above his or her initials; each time a member encourages another, the observer places

FIGURE 5.2 SOCIOGRAM OF GROUP COMMUNICATION

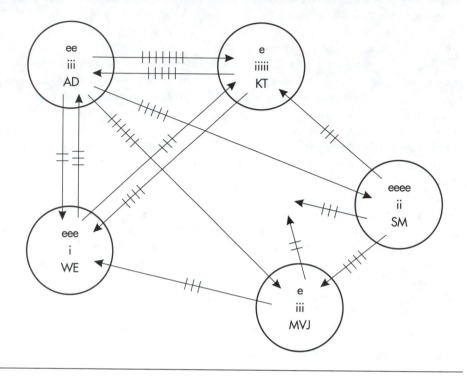

an "e." For example, the sociogram shows that AD has the highest number of communications with other team members (two to WE, six to MVJ, five to SM, and five to KT). MVJ has the fewest communications (two to the whole team and three to WE). KT interrupted others five times, and WE interrupted only once. SM was the most encouraging.

Sociograms can help provide clues to the following questions.

- Who are the most frequent participators? Why? What is the effect of their participation?
- Who are the least frequent participators? Why? What is the effect of their lack of participation?
- Are there shifts in participation? What causes these?
- Who talks to whom? Who responds to whom? Who triggers whom?
- How are "silent" and "noisy" members handled?
- Are team members with the requisite information contributing?

INFLUENCE

Although the formal leader often has the most power and influence in the team, it is common for influence to shift throughout a team's history. Influence, like communication, is often related to a member's status within the organizational hierarchy, level of experience, and personality. It is also a function of an individual's ability to argue articulately and persuasively for his or her position. The most effective arguments are those that are vivid, offer new information, and reflect team rather than individual goals.

Team members can also influence one another through the use of "influence tactics" (see Table 5.2 for a listing of these tactics). Team leaders typically exert the most influence by using a combination of these tactics. The choice of tactics, for leaders and members alike, depends on the situation at hand and the individual's preferences.

TABLE 5.2 INFLUENCE TACTICS

Rational Persuasion: The agent uses logical arguments and factual evidence to persuade the target that a proposal or request is viable and likely to result in the attainments of task objectives.

Inspirational Appeals: The agent makes a request or proposal that arouses target enthusiasm by appealing to target values, ideals, and aspirations, or by increasing target self-confidence.

Consultation: The agent seeks target participation in planning a strategy, activity, or change for which target support and assistance are desired, or is willing to modify a proposal to deal with target concerns and suggestions.

Ingratiation: The agent uses praise, flattery, friendly behavior, or helpful behavior to get the target in a good mood or to think favorably of him or her before asking for something.

Personal Appeals: The agent appeals to target feelings of loyalty and friendship toward himself or herself when asking for something.

Exchange: The agent offers an exchange of favors, indicates willingness to reciprocate at a later time, or promises a share of the benefits if the target helps to accomplish a task.

Coalition Tactics: The agent seeks the aid of others to persuade the target to do something, or uses the support of others as a reason for the target to agree also.

Legitimating Tactics: The agent seeks to establish the legitimacy of a request by claiming the authority or right to make it, or by verifying that it is consistent with organizational policies, rules, practices, or traditions.

Pressure: The agent uses demands, threats, frequent checking, or persistent reminders to influence the target to do what he or she wants.

Source: This material was taken from Yukl. 1994. p. 225.

Early on, power struggles may occur in any team. As individuals vie with one another for leadership, they may impede team progress if they push for their suggestions and ideas regardless of appropriateness. Early power struggles are normal, but if they persist and become a normal part of team operations, team effectiveness can suffer.

Helpful questions in observing influence patterns include the following.

- Who has the most impact on the team's actions and decisions?
- Whose ideas are ignored? What is the result?
- What tactics do members use to influence one another?
- Is there rivalry in the team? What effect does it have?
- How does the formal leader exert his/her influence?

CONFLICT

Opinions about conflict in teams range from "it encourages innovation and creativity" to "it hampers a team's ability to implement decisions." Recent research on conflict (see Jehn, 1991; Pelled, 1994) suggests that conflict can be advantageous or problematic, depending on what type of conflict it is. The "good" kind of conflict is called *substantive* conflict, which consists of differences of opinion about the team task and how it should be carried out. The "bad" kind of conflict is called *affective* conflict, which consists of interpersonal clashes due to personality or perceived differences in style, background, or values.

Substantive conflict may help a team by pushing members to exchange more task-related information, explore alternative positions, and examine issues in more depth. This type of conflict may also energize team members to get more involved in team activities. Affective conflict is problematic in that relations among members become characterized by frustration and hostility. These emotions disrupt work, lower team performance, and cause members to withdraw from team activity.

A frequent problem in cohesive teams is a phenomenon called "groupthink" (Janis, 1972). Here, team members avoid all types of conflict and shy away from deviating from what appears to be the team consensus. Despite doubts, fears, and personal disagreement, team members remain silent, feeling compelled to avoid creating dissension. Under these conditions, team members need to find ways to create the opportunity for substantive conflict. The key for teams is to find ways to encourage substantive conflict while taking time out to improve relations among members when affective conflict is apparent. Team-building activities, stressing team goals over individual interests, and discussion of similarities as well as differences among members can help to alleviate affective conflict. Key questions regarding team conflict include the following:

- How often do members disagree about the work to be done?
- To what extent are there arguments about which procedure should be used to do the work?
- To what extent do people take the arguments in the team personally?
- How often do members get angry with one another while working?
- Do team members feel free to disagree?

ATMOSPHERE

Group members bring with them many assumptions about how teams should function. These expectations may not be shared by all team members. One member may feel that team meetings are "strictly business," whereas another may want to include many social activities; one member may prefer that the team have a single leader, whereas another may want to share leadership; or one member way have high standards for the team, whereas another is satisfied if the team just finishes the job. The way in which these expectations and assumptions are expressed and resolved often determines what the climate or atmosphere in the team will be. If members have been able to air their differences and find common ground, the team will operate very differently than if they have been unable to do so.

Groups can evolve into trusting, supportive units or tense, conflict-ridden environments. Table 5.3 lists characteristics of both.

TABLE 5.3 SUPPORTIVE AND DEFENSIVE ENVIRONMENTS

Characteristics of a supportive environment

Provisionalism: Members encourage flexibility, experimentation, and creativity.

Empathy: Members attempt to listen and to understand each other's views and values.

Equality: Members respect the positions of others and no one is made to feel inferior.

Spontaneity: Members express ideas freely and honestly without hidden motives.

Problem Orientation: Members openly discuss mutual problems without rushing to give solutions or insist on agreement.

Clear Description: Communications are clear and describe situations fairly. Members share perceptions without necessarily implying a need for change.

Characteristics for a defensive environment

Evaluation: Members' manner of speech, tone of voice, or verbal content is perceived as critical or judgmental of others in the team.

Control: Communication is perceived as an attempt to manipulate or dominate the recipient.

Stratagems: Members are seen as operating from hidden motives, playing games, feigning emotion, withholding information, or having private access to sources of data.

Superiority: Members convey an attitude of condescension toward others.

Dogmatism: Members insist that their own points are best and try to foist them on the team.

Source: Patton, Giffin, and Patton (1989).

Questions that help to characterize the atmosphere in a team include the following:

- Are people friendly and open or very formal with one another?
- Are people involved and interested? Is there an atmosphere of work? Play? Competition?
- Are people in constant conflict or disagreement?
- Is there any attempt to avoid unpleasantness by ignoring tough issues?

EMOTIONAL ISSUES

In certain cases, individual members may become very disruptive as they deal with some of the basic problems and emotional issues associated with teams. Groups tend to ignore such behavior, to the detriment of the unit and the member who is having difficulty.

The main issues that individuals may face in teams concern the following:

Identity: Who am I in this team? Where do I fit in? What role should I play?
Goals and Needs: What do I want from this team? What do I have to offer? Can the team's goals be made consistent with mine?
Power and Control: Who will control what we do? How much power and influence do I have?
Intimacy: How close will we get to each other? How much trust exists among us?

Group members may react to these issues in different ways and at different times. The disruptive behaviors they may exhibit in response to these problems include the following:

Fighting and Controlling: Asserting personal dominance. Attempting to get their own way regardless of others.
Withdrawing: Trying to reduce discomfort by psychologically leaving the team.
Dependency and Counterdependency: Waiting passively for a leader to emerge who will solve the problem or, contrarily, opposing or resisting anyone in the team who represents authority.

TAKING ACTION

These seven categories of team process combined with membership and context provide the building blocks for analyzing team dynamics, and also the cues for managing and changing that process. If a team is not producing as required, is mired in conflict, or is not meeting member needs, then these categories suggest a range of interventions. The key is to do a careful analysis of the problem so that the appropriate intervention is found.

A team might require a structural intervention, such as assigning task and maintenance functions, appointing a devil's advocate, imposing an agenda and allocating time for each phase of decision making, or setting norms with negative consequences for noncompliance. Team issues can also be addressed through shifting the power and influence in the team. Team members and leaders can empower other members, form new coalitions and break up existing ones, negotiate new norms, and work to resolve affective conflicts. Simply finding a new way to bring silent members into team discussion can alter existing patterns of dominance.

Finally, team issues can be addressed by interventions aimed at shifting a team's underlying culture. Members can point out aspects of the team that create a defensive environment and try to model the empathy, spontaneity, and equality of a supportive environment. Members can observe other teams and note how their values and assumptions differ, and how they might want to change. Often all three types of interventions, structural, political, and cultural, are needed to create significant changes within a team.

REFERENCES

Eisenhardt, K. M. 1990. "Speed and Strategic Choice: How Managers Accelerate Decision Making." *California Management Review,* 32(3), pp. 1–16.

Gabarro, J. J., and A. Harlan. 1983. "Process Observation." In L. Schlesinger, R. Eccles, and J. J. Gabarro. eds. *Managing Behavior in Organizations.* New York: McGraw Hill, pp. 57–66.

Gruenfeld, D. H., E. A. Mannix, K. Y. Williams, and M. A. Neale. 1996. "Group Composition and Decision Making: How Member Familiarity and Information Distribution affect Process and Performance." *Organizational Behavior and Human Decision Processes,* 67, pp. 1–15.

Janis, I. 1972. *Victims of Groupthink.* Boston: Houghton-Mifflin.

Jehn, K. A. 1991. *Benefits and Detriments of Group Conflict,* Working Paper, Northwestern University.

Patton, R., K. Giffin, and E. Patton. 1989. *Decision-making Team Interaction.* New York: Harper & Row.

Pelled, L. H. 1994. "Team Diversity and Conflict: A Multivariate Analysis." *Academy of Management Best Paper Proceedings.* Madison, WI: Omni Press.

Schein, E. 1982. "What to Observe in a Team." In *NTL Reading Book for Human Relations Training.* Bethel, ME: NTL Institute, pp. 72–74.

Schein, E. 1988. *Process Consultation: Its Role in Organization Development,* second edition. Reading, MA: Addison-Wesley.

Yukl, G. 1994. *Leadership in Organizations,* third edition. Englewood Cliffs, NJ: Prentice-Hall, Inc.

M-5

supplemental

TEAM DECISION MAKING

Organizations today face a competitive world in which decision making has to be accomplished more quickly and with ever larger amounts of complex information. Authority and responsibility are being pushed downward in the organization and work is spreading across functional boundaries. Under these conditions, individuals do not have the expertise and ability to make decisions on their own. Thus, the need for team decision making is on the rise.

Decisions made by teams have many advantages over those made by individuals. An individual may be limited by his or her professional training, technical expertise, status within the organization, or the amount of information he or she can process, but in a team a broader information base can be incorporated into the decision-making process. Teams provide a forum where members can exchange valuable information about their own particular areas within the organization, which not only helps teams make decisions but also enhances coordination among the various parts of the organization. The informal communication network found in teams is likely to facilitate problem solving in the future by allowing formal hierarchical information channels to be bypassed with a simple telephone call or e-mail message.

Team decision making is also a useful device for linking upstream and downstream organizational activities, such as those that are designing new products with those that are manufacturing them. By including representatives from different functions, hierarchical levels, and/or areas of expertise, the team signals the importance of each of the various organizational constituencies. Doing so also creates a valuable flow of information, allowing those who must complete the work of others to become sufficiently involved. Feedback from team members with different views and expertise helps to locate problems early so they can be corrected before they become too costly. Finally, making decisions as a team facilitates their implementation across the organization much more comprehensively than any individual decision could.

As organizations become more diverse with more fluid boundaries, representatives of different constituencies within and outside the organization, such as women, minorities, and customers, increasingly demand roles in organizations. Thus, team decision making is also a vehicle that allows for their greater participation. What is meant by decision making? How do team decisions differ from individual decisions? Can we learn to maximize the effectiveness of team decision making? These are the questions addressed in this reading.

STEPS IN TEAM DECISION MAKING

Step 1. Identifying the Problem or Opportunity

The first step for a team solving a problem or taking advantage of an opportunity is to gain a clear understanding of it. In organizations problems are often ambiguous or hidden behind symptoms. When a drop in profits occurs, for example, there are usually several possible explanations. Before corrective action can be taken, the team must correctly identify the cause of the problem. A task force on quality improvement for instance, would not solve the underlying problem if price or delivery times were the real issue.

Step 2. Analyzing the Problem

Once the team has identified the problem or opportunity, it must then determine its scope. How big is it? How complex is it? Who is involved? What areas are affected? Next, the team must explore why the situation exists. What are the forces that keep the situation from changing?

The team must analyze both how crucial and critical the issue is. "Crucial" refers to its degree of importance, whereas "critical" refers to its timeliness. A crucial problem or opportunity is one that is central to the team or organization and therefore must be addressed. A critical problem is one which must be taken care of immediately. For example, it might not be crucial to replace a boiler in a particular plant, but it would be critical if the repairman said it could blow up at any time. Teams often can agree easily on the nature of the problem or opportunity at hand but disagree profoundly on the importance and urgency of the necessary action.

Next, the team must be thorough in gathering all relevant information about the issue. Team members must look carefully at all sides of the situation they are studying, search for the data beyond what is given to them, and constantly check their underlying assumptions and approach to the problem against new information.

Step 3. Proposing and Evaluating Solutions

Once the problem has been analyzed, the team needs to move to generating a large list of alternative solutions and choosing among them. Complete information about alternative solutions and their consequences is not always available. As decision making proceeds, new information and circumstances that may change the parameters of a decision must be taken into account. Trying to determine the probabilities of outcomes and their consequences is often a guessing game at best. Typically, decision makers will generate a limited set of alternatives and select the first that seems to best meet some set of criteria that the team has set. Choosing among alternatives is often a grueling process as differing values among team members come into play.

Several techniques for improving alternative generation and selection have been developed. First, alternative solutions are best generated in an open atmosphere that is free from criticism and social pressure. Second, individuals generate more ideas when they work independently and then pool their ideas in a roundrobin fashion than when they work together from the start. Third, teams work best when they compare alternatives simultaneously, rather than sequentially, and when they enlist the support of outside advisors. Fourth, selection is facilitated when members can agree on selection criteria and when members shy away from quickly choosing the first alternative that satisfies those criteria. Finally, in today's fast-paced organizations, meeting often and intensively helps teams cope with evolving decision-making demands.

Step 4. Implementing the Decision

After a team has reached agreement on the best solution, they must consider how to put that solution into operation. Patton, Giffin, and Patton (1989) have outlined a five-step plan to facilitate the process.

1. Members should identify everything that needs to be done.
2. The team must determine the equipment, materials, information, and other resources needed for each step of the process.
3. The team should delegate individual tasks, taking into account both individual wishes and abilities; all members should be familiar with the overall plan and should keep abreast of other members' progress and needs for assistance.
4. The team must devise contingency plans in case of emergencies because plans seldom happen without a hitch.
5. The team should evaluate the plan after it has been implemented so that members can learn from their ongoing experiences.

While the above five steps are the ideal trajectory for team decision making, the process often unfolds in unpredictable ways that are dictated by the dynamics among team members. Problems may arise when the primary goals of the team and the scope of its mandate are not articulated, for example. Members may analyze issues superficially, generate few alternatives, or pay little attention to implementing a good solution. The following section addresses such issues.

PROBLEMS IN TEAM DECISION MAKING

Lack of Organization

Problems can arise at the very beginning of team formation if members start to work without structuring and planning their activities, without properly identifying the problem to be addressed, or without discussing what the individual priorities of team members are.

The push to find answers without taking the time necessary to address these issues is a phenomenon called "solution mindedness." It can arise when external pressures, such as time constraints, force the team to find answers quickly. It can be fostered by internal pressures as well. Members are often uncomfortable with problems that have no obvious answer, and seek to relieve their anxiety by finding a quick solution. Unfortunately, decisions that are arrived at without adequate consideration often have to be revisited later, causing even more discomfort.

Lack of organization may also occur when there is a leadership vacuum, when no one takes on the task of keeping the team on track. There is clearly a problem when no one prepares an agenda, keeps records of what the team has decided, or reminds the team of what they are trying to accomplish.

This does not mean that teams must be regimented or formal. In fact, even the most effective teams rarely move neatly from problem identification to analysis to solution. Team process involves many iterations, as new information shows old assumptions to be inaccurate or solutions to be impossible. It also requires time out for fun. But teams need at least some level of structure so that activities can be coordinated.

Interpersonal Issues

Team norms and political agendas can also have a negative impact on team decision making. Team norms refer to expectations regarding others' behavior that are generally held by most members. These expectations, for example, might concern whether it is necessary to arrive at meetings on time, whether it is acceptable to smoke and wear particular types of clothing, or even whether members can lie. Members conform to norms because they desire the friendship, help, and recognition of others. Although conformity helps the team to become unified and maintain standards, it can also lead to the suppression of conflict and ideas. Team members may consciously or subconsciously avoid expressing contrary feelings in discussion because they see them as antithetical to the nature of the team. This ultimately denies the team access to important information. Unexpressed doubts generally linger, making it likely that team members will feel uncommitted to the adopted solution. If resistance to a decision can be brought into the open, however, doubts can be resolved or can become part of a dialogue that leads to an even better solution.

Problems can also arise when extroverted, dominant, socially aggressive individuals with superior social and verbal skills have a disproportionate influence on decisions or when team members defer to those with higher status, regardless of the quality of their contributions. This can result in the loss of valuable input from other, quieter members, who may have greater expertise.

Difficulties also ensue when differences in age, gender, ethnicity, and experience lead to unproductive conflict. In some cases, tension over differences lead members not to want to work with one another; to become frustrated, jealous, and angry; and to take arguments personally. This type of conflict can undermine the decision-making process.

Finally, team members may actually subvert the team process for their own political ends. Where personal agendas are covert, conflict and the inability to reach consensus are more likely. For a team to succeed, differences must be aired, agreements among sub-teams must be negotiated, and a commitment to common goals must be built.

Systematic Bias in Information

Teams often make poor decisions when they are based on biased information. Bias can occur when information provided by one member is not checked by others and proves to be incorrect or slanted according to the individual's perspective. It can also occur when team members are swayed by a majority opinion that is shifted toward one pole of an issue. This "team polarization" often leads to more risky decisions. Lastly, bias may be reflected in a team's tendency to take credit for success that should be attributed elsewhere or to blame failure on outside circumstances or bad luck. This is common in teams.

In addition, "heuristics," the simplifying strategies decision makers use to guide their problem solving, may also cause bias. One such heuristic—the "availability" heuristic—is the tendency to overestimate the likelihood of an event if an instance of it can easily be recalled. Thus, if a manager can easily remember an instance of product delay, he or she might be likely to assume that delays will be frequent in the future. Individuals tend to overestimate the likelihood of disasters and underestimate the probability of more common events. Such bias is magnified in the team context. Furthermore, individuals are also more risk averse when seeking gains than when avoiding losses, even if the probability of each is identical. Thus, a different bias can occur, depending on how a given problem is framed. (For more information about heuristics and their effects, see Tversky and Kahnemann, 1981 or Bazerman, 1990.)

Unconscious Mechanisms

Wilfred Bion (1975) believes that there are two forces operating in every team—one conscious and one subconscious. The first is the healthy drive of the "work team" that leads to task accomplishment, agenda setting, decision making, and so forth. This is the logical and conscious aspect of teams. The second force comes from the subconscious "basic assumptions" that a team might hold. These assumptions may include beliefs that the team is totally dependent on the leader and can act only with a good deal of direction from that leader, or that the team must constantly fight off enemies. These kinds of basic assumptions interfere with work and lead to contradictory behaviors, especially during stressful situations.

Unproductive Roles

Individual team members may fall into unproductive roles as well. Edgar Schein (1988) has identified several roles: blocker, recognition seeker, dominator, and avoider. A blocker stubbornly resists all attempts by the team to move ahead, is constantly negative, and frequently returns to rejected issues and ideas. A recognition seeker calls attention to himself or herself by boasting and acting as if he or she were superior. A dominator manipulates the team to pursue his or her agenda, interrupts others, and frequently tries to gain attention. An avoider remains apart from others and passively resists the team. Members will not necessarily take on these roles all of the time, but may do so during stressful periods in particular. Also they can take on these roles while simultaneously taking on positive task and maintenance roles in the team.

Noncooperation with Outsiders

Teams often pay too little attention to key external constituencies, such as providers of information, resources, support, and feedback, preferring to work on their own issues in relative isolation and at their own speed. Teams fail when they do not negotiate and communicate with upper management about the scope of their decision making, the resources and support they need, the time they need to complete the task, or what they will deliver when the work is done. Teams also have problems when they do not communicate horizontally throughout the organization. They need to get feedback on ideas, push other teams to come through on their commitments, or get updated on new developments within the corporation and with competitors and customers.

Groupthink

The phenomenon of "groupthink" occurs when members fail to disagree, to bring up doubts and fears, or to bring up information that contradicts the team's decision. Suddenly, they are going in a direction that makes no one happy simply because no one wants to cause conflict. Irving Janis (1972) cites many examples of groupthink in major policy decisions in business and government, such as the Cuban Bay of Pigs fiasco. At the time, President Kennedy's top advisory team agreed that the best action was to invade, but in retrospect, Kennedy asked, "How could we have been so stupid?" The decision, according to Janis, was a result of the nondeliberate suppression of critical thoughts on the part of a foreign policy advisory team whose members had become so loyal to one another that they felt compelled to avoid creating dissension.

Janis (1972) has identified a number of symptoms of groupthink, which result in an *illusion of unanimity* around a majority view, summarized below.

1. An *illusion of invulnerability* that arises among team members, which leads them to become overly optimistic and willing to take extraordinary risks.
2. *Rationalizations* that members collectively construct to discount warnings and other negative feedback.
3. An unquestioning belief by members in the team's inherent *morality* and *stereotyped* negative views of the "enemy" around them.
4. *Direct pressure* on any individual who expresses doubts about the team's shared illusions or who questions the validity of the majority view.
5. *Reluctance to deviate* from what appears to be team consensus despite misgivings, and a tendency to minimize personal doubts. (Arthur Schlesinger, for example, blamed his silence, despite real disagreement, on the "circumstances of the situation.")

Members may even appoint themselves as "mind guards" to keep anyone with differing views and information away from other members.

WAYS TO IMPROVE TEAM DECISION MAKING

Certainly all of the problems raised in the previous section show that the team decision-making steps of problem identification, analysis, alternative generation and choice, and implementation are more complex at the team level than one might have imagined. Unfortunately, no current theory or technique can prevent teams from experiencing the imprecise, and at times chaotic process of decision making. Nonetheless, years of experience and research have highlighted several ways to improve team decision making, which are described in this section.

Getting Started

As stated earlier, the first priority of any team is to define the problem it is to address. However, it is important that team members also have some time to get acquainted, in order to ease the initial stress of team formation. Members need an opportunity to openly express their expectations about the team's purpose and scope of activity as well as to negotiate shared goals. Helping team members to get to know one another is often best accomplished in an informal setting, even before the team begins its formal task. Setting up a few easy tasks early on that will give members "small wins" can also get the team started on a successful course.

Once the team has actually started working on problem definition and analysis, it is important to leave enough time for adequate examination of the issues. Team members

Ⓢ

20

ACADEMIC

need to consciously put the breaks on any "solution mindedness," encouraging members who want to prematurely close on a simple or inaccurate definition of the problem to explore further.

When the team gets started it is also useful to establish a precedent of discussing how to carry out a particular task before that task is actually carried out. For example, a simple, "What's the best way to organize ourselves to gather all of this information?" can save the team a lot of time. Another useful device for helping the team to continuously improve the way it goes about its work is to take a few minutes at the end of each meeting to analyze and evaluate how effectively the team organized itself. If there are problems, the team may want to change the way the next meeting is run, or may want to seek help from a process consultant.

Mapping the Key Outsiders

In the new, networked organization it is critically important to build and maintain critical links with external contacts, such as top management, other teams within the firm, and key customers, suppliers, or competitors outside the firm. Failure to elicit support from others, particularly those that may have other interests, may limit a team even more than poor internal organization. Furthermore, when a team has external support and resources, members tend to feel more like they can succeed and are more likely to get along with other team members.

It is important to build the critical links with these external constituencies early in a team's life. Teams can begin to do this by putting together a "map" of key outsiders. Members should first list those individuals and teams who have information or resources that the team needs. They may also want to determine who supports and who opposes the work of the team. The team can then organize itself to collect needed information, lobby for resources, build on existing support, and devise strategies to limit any damage that could be done by the "opposition."

Before teams begin to work on problem definition, members may even want to interview critical outsiders to understand their perspectives and views of the problem. Early interviews can also focus on what these individuals hope to see the team accomplish. Questions such as, "So if we came up with a list of the key reasons that their product is outselling ours by April 19, would you be happy?" help to align expectations. Bringing high level executives to early team meetings helps team members gather this type of information and build top-level support. It also signals to members that their work is important.

Maintaining and sustaining external contacts throughout the team's life is also essential. Outsiders will need to be informed of major breakthroughs and problems and will need to be consulted for feedback at key milestones. This will help teams keep their work connected to ongoing strategic and operational initiatives.

Structuring Decision Making

Once the team's problem has been formulated and analyzed, the team needs to organize itself to generate and evaluate alternatives. Several techniques have been devised to help structure these steps: brainstorming, consensus mapping, and the nominal group technique.

Brainstorming helps a team to generate many creative alternatives. It is a process whereby the team generates many ideas within a short period of time, usually on a single issue. Members are encouraged to spontaneously introduce as many ideas as possible, no matter how wild, and to suspend criticism and evaluation, opening new avenues of thought. Some consultants stress the informal nature of brainstorming and advocate that it be done "off-line"—in the woods or at a camp, just not in the office—and have created many techniques to help executives break down inhibitions and think creatively. These include using math or visual symbols rather than words to express ideas, creating analogies, and looking at situations in reverse (e.g., thinking about an uncomfortable chair in order to understand how to design a comfortable one).

Consensus mapping can help a team that is having difficulty agreeing on the problem they are to address or the scope of their work. Borrowed from the techniques involved in quality improvement, consensus mapping begins with each member of the team writing down key dimensions of the problem as he or she sees it on individual notes. Members then cluster and recluster the notes on a wall according to theme until there is some agreement as to how to represent the problem at hand in all of its complexity. Members may revise these classifications as new information and team discussion warrant.

The *nominal group technique* is a process designed to structure several phases of decision making. It is meant to allow for creativity in generating ideas, to provide a mechanism for resolving differences in ranking those ideas, and to balance participation among members. The steps involved are as follows:

1. Silently generating ideas in writing
2. Round-robin recording of ideas in terse phrases on a flip chart
3. Adding ideas and building on the ideas of others
4. Discussing each idea for clarification and pros and cons
5. Preliminary voting
6. Discussing the vote and revising alternatives
7. Final ranking

Recent advances in this technique include keeping sources of ideas anonymous and employing private, not public, voting. Anonymity is facilitated using computers, thereby minimizing social pressure and reducing the advantage held by verbal, aggressive individuals.

Overcoming Conformity

Given a team's tendency to use biased information, to create uniformity of opinion, and to shut down opposing ideas, members need to fight back. One tool to do this is to appoint a "devil's advocate." This role includes disagreeing with the majority, finding flaws in team logic, and championing unpopular ideas. By championing minority or different views, the devil's advocate helps to stimulate divergent thinking and the production of novel solutions. As Charlan Nemeth (1986) has pointed out, whereas majorities induce concentration of their chosen alternative, minority opinion stimulates thinking about more aspects of the situation and more creative solutions. Thus, attention and thought are spent on new interpretations and solutions to the problem, not simply supporting the chosen solution.

Making Decisions Fast and Well

Given the time pressures inherent in the modern era, it may be difficult for many teams to gather sufficient information or examine options thoroughly. Mixed scanning, hedging bets, and scenario construction are three techniques a team may use to improve its effectiveness.

Mixed scanning, an approach recommended by Amitai Etzioni (1989), involves focused trial and error. This approach borrows from the medical model used by doctors whereby they get a sense of the general health of the patient by focusing on the patient's troubled area, initiate a tentative treatment, and try something else if it fails. The team "focuses" first on whatever trouble spots are suggested by the initial information gathered. It then uses "trial and error" to check outcomes periodically and modify interventions. This allows for solutions to be constantly modified as new data become available. Like a good physician, who may prescribe a medication for two weeks but amend that treatment if the patient exhibits terrible side effects and no change in condition, a team should initially view any course of action as tentative.

Ⓢ

22

ACADEMIC

Hedging bets is another adaptive strategy. Although betting strongly on one option lets a team prioritize resources, it is often handy to have some other possibilities ready to go in case that option proves problematic. Again, Etzioni argues that effective decision making in a world of time pressure and change requires caution and a capacity to adapt. He advocates "humble" rather than "rational" decision making, which takes into account our own limits.

Scenario construction is a third technique for decision making in a fast-paced environment. This involves testing the team's solution by discussing a variety of scenarios that could occur. For example, the team might ask questions such as, "How will this product sell if company P comes out with its product in July? What if the economy gets worse instead of better? What if our team loses two members?" By thinking through a number of different situations, the team can prepare contingency plans, alternative solutions, and adaptive procedures. All of these help the team to shift work with changing circumstances.

SUMMARY

As changing markets and technologies require ever-greater organizational flexibility, teams are becoming less a tool for getting work done and more a part of the basic structure of the firm itself. The role teams play in decision making will become increasingly important in years to come. Although there are many problems inherent in team decision making, there are also many ways that teams can overcome them. Learning and testing the actions that leaders and members alike can take to improve the decision-making process will greatly enhance the toolset of managers in organizations of the future.

REFERENCES

Ancona, D. G., and D. Caldwell. 1992. "Demography and Design: Predictors of New Product Team Performance." *Organization Science,* 3(3), pp. 321–341.

Bazerman, M. 1990. Judgment in Managerial Decision Making, second edition. New York: Wiley.

Bettenhausen, K., and J. K. Murnighan. 1985. "The Emergence of Norms in Competitive Decision-Making Teams." *Administrative Science Quarterly,* 30, pp. 350–372.

Bion, W. S. 1975. "Selections from Experiences in Groups." In A. D. Colman & W. H. Bexton, eds., *Group Relations Reader.* Sausalito, CA: Grex, pp. 11–20.

Dougherty, D. 1992. "Interpretive Barriers to Successful Product Innovation in Large Forums." *Organization Science,* 3(2), pp. 179–202.

Eisenhardt, K. M. 1990. "Speed and Strategic Choice: How Managers Accelerate Decision Making." *California Management Review,* 32(3), pp. 1–16.

Etzioni, A. 1989. "Humble Decision Making." *Harvard Business Review* (July–August), pp. 122–126.

Gersick, C. J., and J. R. Hackman. 1990. "Habitual Routines in Task-Performing Teams." *Organizational Behavior and Human Decision Processes,* pp. 47, 65–97.

Gabarro, J. J., and A. Harlan. 1983. "Process Observation." In L. Schlesinger, R. Eccles, and J. J. Gabarro, eds. *Managing Behavior in Organizations.* New York: McGraw Hill, pp. 57–66.

Gordon, J. 1993. A Diagnostic Approach to Organizational Behavior. Boston: Allyn and Bacon.

Hatvany, N., and D. Gladstein. 1982. "A Perspective on Group Decision Making." In D. Nadler, M. Tushman, and N. Hatvany, eds. *Managing Organizations Readings and Cases.* Boston: Little, Brown, pp. 213–226.

Janis, I. 1972. *Victims of Groupthink.* Boston: Houghton-Mifflin.

Nemeth, C. J. 1986. "Differential Contributions of Majority and Minority Influence." *Psychological Review,* 93, pp. 23–32.

Patton, R., K. Giffin, and E. Patton. 1989. *Decision-Making Team Interaction.* New York: Harper & Row.

Schein, E. 1982. "What to Observe in a Team." In *NTL Reading Book for Human Relations Training.* Bethel, ME: NTL Institute, pp. 72–74.

Schein, E. 1988. *Process Consultation: Its Role in Organization Development,* second edition. Reading, MA: Addison-Wesley.

Sinclair, A. 1992. "The Tyranny of a Team Ideology." *Organization Studies,* 13(4), pp. 611–626.

Tversky, A., and D. Kahnemann. 1981. "The Framing of Decisions and the Psychology of Choice." *Science 211,* pp. 453–458.

THE TROUBLE WITH TEAMS

by Brian Dumaine

Corporate America is having a hot love affair with teams. And why not? When teams work, there's nothing like them for turbocharging productivity. Beguiling examples abound: Scores of service companies like Federal Express and IDS have boosted productivity up to 40% by adopting self-managed work teams; Nynex is using teams to make the difficult transition from a bureaucratic Baby Bell to a high-speed cruiser on the I-way; Boeing used teams to cut the number of engineering hang-ups on its new 777 passenger jet by more than half. Says Boeing President Philip Condit: "Your competitiveness is your ability to use the skills and knowledge of people most effectively, and teams are the best way to do that."

But wait a minute. Forget all the swooning over teams for a moment. Listen carefully and you'll sense a growing unease, a worry that these things are more hassle than their fans let on—that they might even turn around and bite you. Says Eileen Appelbaum, author of *The New American Workplace:* "It's not that teams don't work. It's that there are lots of obstacles."

That may explain why the use of high-performance teams like the ones that got the results mentioned above hasn't spread as fast as you might have expected. The Center for Effective Organizations at the University of Southern California recently conducted a survey of FORTUNE 1,000 companies showing that 68% use self-managed or high-performance teams. Sounds like a lot—but the study also shows that only 10% of workers are in such teams, hardly a number betokening a managerial revolution. "People are very naive about how easy it is to create a team," says USC's Edward Lawler, the management professor who oversaw the study. "Teams are the Ferraris of work design. they're high performance, but high maintenance and expensive."

The most common trouble with teams: Many companies rush out and form the wrong kind for the job. Quality circles, primitive types in which people take a few hours off each week to discuss problems, didn't die in the 1980s, though they declined. While they may provide incremental gains in productivity, they'll never give you high-octane boosts. Those come from self-managed or high-performance teams, whose members are truly empowered to organize their work and make decisions. What often happens is that a company afraid to let go of control will create a humdrum quality circle where what's really needed is a dynamic self-managed team, and then wonder why its teams don't work.

To compound the problem, teams often get launched in a vacuum, with little or no training or support, no changes in the design of their work, and no new systems like E-mail to help communication between teams. Frustrations mount, and people wind up in endless meetings trying to figure out why they're in a team and what they're expected to do. Says Paul Osterman, a professor of management at MIT's Sloan School: "When teams are introduced in combination with other organization changes, they work. When they're introduced as an isolated practice, they fail. My gut feeling is most are introduced in isolation."

Boeing's Condit identifies another problem: "Teams are overused." Remarkably, many companies will create teams where they're not really needed. What they don't realize is that workers who are lone wolves or creative types aren't necessarily better off in a team. Making them sit in a team meeting waiting to reach a consensus can even stifle creativity. The key is to analyze the work before you form a team. Does the task really require that people interact with each other? Can the work be done faster by a single person? After all, teams take a lot of time and energy to set up. Says Henry Sims, a management professor at the Maryland business school and author of *Business Without Bosses:* "You don't use teams with insurance salesmen and long-haul truckers."

When it comes to paying teams, most managers still throw up their hand-held computers in despair. Pay the team as a group? Then won't your star performers feel slighted? Pay for individual performance? What does that do to encourage teamwork? Companies that use teams best generally still pay members individually, but with a significant difference: They make teamwork—a sharing attitude, the ability to deal well with others—a key issue in an individual's annual performance review.

The reengineering craze is also taking its toll on teams. Executed ruthlessly, reengineering can corrode the esprit de corps vital to teamwork. Listen to US West's Jerry Miller, whose team of billing clerks in Duluth, Minnesota, got downsized out of existence last month: "When we first formed our teams, the company came in talking teamwork and empowerment and promised we wouldn't lose any jobs. It turns out all this was a big cover. The company had us all set up for reengineering. We showed them how to streamline the work, and now 9,000 people are gone. It was cut-your-own-throat. It makes you feel used." US West, which argues that in the long run reengineering will enhance teamwork, admits that for now, "People's stress levels will be high, and some people will be sad and angry."

For all the trickiness entailed in getting them right, corporate America obviously shouldn't give up on teams. Used cor-

rectly, they still increase productivity, raise morale, and in some cases spur innovation. Smart companies like Textron, Nynex, Boeing, and Allina navigated the bumps and potholes of team building. Their stories offer compelling examples of how to overcome the troubles with teams. Here's what they've learned.

USE THE RIGHT TEAM FOR THE RIGHT JOB

A common mistake among managers is to think a team is a team is a team. To the contrary, a more accurate taxonomy reads like Homer's catalogue of ships in the *Illiad:* problem-solving teams, product-development teams, self-managed teams, and virtual teams, to name just a few. Too often a CEO will get excited about the idea of teams and order them up as if only one type existed. That kind of unthinking, one-tool-for-all-jobs application is bound to send tremors through the ranks. The CEO of a Western manufacturing company suddenly announced that from now on everybody was going to be in a team. The next day absenteeism soared.

Understanding the history of teams helps in choosing the right kind. Widespread use of teams in America started in the 1980s when industries like autos and steel, trying to combat growing Japanese competition, began forming quality circles, in which workers meet weekly or monthly to discuss ways to improve quality. These teams helped companies cut defects and reduce rework, but enthusiasm for them has ebbed. The USC study of FORTUNE 1,000 companies found that 65% of companies used such groups last year, down slightly from 1987. Professor Ed Lawler says that quality circles are losing appeal because they operate parallel to work processes rather than within them. In other words, they're good for solving minor quality problems, but because they don't accompany changes in the way work is done, they can't spark quantum leaps in productivity.

The teams most popular today are of two broad types: work teams, which include high-performance or self-managed teams, and special-purpose problem-solving teams. Problem-solving teams, in particular, differ from quality circles in important ways. Where quality circles are permanent committees designed to handle whatever workplace problems may pop up, problem-solving teams have specific missions, which can be broad (find out why our customers hate us) or narrow (figure out why the No. 3 pump keeps overheating). Once the job is done, such teams usually disband. The USC survey found that 91% of American companies use problem-solving teams, about a third more than seven years ago. And on average, about 20% of a company's employees are beavering away at any given time on such teams.

While problem-solving teams are temporary, work teams, used by about two-thirds of U.S. companies, tend to be permanent. Rather than attack specific problems, a work team does day-to-day work. A team of Boeing engineers helping to build a jet would be a work team. If a work team has the authority to make decisions about how the daily work gets done, it's properly described as a self-managed or high-performance team. Common tests for a self-managed team are: Can it change the order of tasks? Does it have budgets?

CREATE A HIERARCHY OF TEAMS

Time and again teams fall short of their promise because companies don't know how to make them work together with other teams. If you don't get your teams into the right constellations, the whole organization can stall. The problems at DEC, America's second-largest computer maker, stand as a striking illustration. The Maynard, Massachusetts, company announced in July it was abandoning its matrix team structure. Under the old system, workers in functional areas—engineering, marketing—also served on teams organized around product lines like minicomputers or integrated chips. The teams spent endless hours in meetings trying to build a consensus between the two factions in the matrix: the functional bosses and the team bosses. Its sheer organizational weight left DEC a laggard in the fast-moving technology sector.

Boeing has an organizational structure similar to DEC's but with a critical difference. Its structure encourages teams to work together and seize initiative. Says Henry Shomber, a Boeing chief engineer: "We have the no-messenger rule. Team members must make decisions on the spot. They can't run back to their functions for permission." This kind of freedom allowed Boeing to use teams to build its new 777 passenger jet, which flew its first successful test flight this summer with fewer than half the number of design glitches of earlier programs.

When the Seattle aerospace giant set out to design the 777, a massive project eventually involving 10,000 employees and more than 500 suppliers, it knew it wanted an entirely team-based organization but wasn't sure how to make it all work. In the end the company created a hierarchy of teams, a structure meant to get all Boeing's work teams pulling in the same direction. "Our goal," says Boeing's Condit, "is a barrier-free enterprise where all are working to satisfy the customer."

Boeing's 777 project looks like a traditional organizational pyramid, but instead of layers of management, it has three layers of teams. In all there are over 200 cross-functional teams, each made up of people from departments like engineering, manufacturing, and finance. At the top of the pyramid is a management team of the five or six top managers from each discipline who, as a group, have responsibility for the plane's being built correctly and on time. Underneath this management group is a large group of the 50 or so leaders—half each from engineering and operations, set up in 25 to 30 two-person teams—who oversee the 200-plus work teams that have responsibility for specific parts of the plane. These work teams are typically cross-functional groups of five to 15 workers. Examples: a wing team, a flap team, a tail team, and so on.

The top management team holds a weekly meeting. The members of the second tier communicate with the top team through their leaders in engineering and operations, and also hold meetings in which they handle major issues like schedule delays or quality problems with suppliers. The group of 50 then returns to the work teams with solutions to big problems. While this team structure worked well to move information quickly up the organization, Boeing realized near the end of the 777 project that information wasn't moving well horizontally. In other words, the wing teams weren't necessarily communicating as well with the cockpit team as Boeing would have liked, causing design glitches. To solve the problem, the company added a fourth layer of what it calls airplane integration teams—five groups, each with 12 to 15 people drawn from the work teams.

These teams act like the corpus callosum, the part of the brain that transfers information back and forth between the left and right hemispheres. Top management makes sure the integration teams have access to everyone in the organization. Says Scott Forster, an integration team leader: "We can go and get any information now. I can go to the chief engineer. Before, it was unusual just to see the chief engineer."

A few months ago, two Boeing work teams discovered a conflict: one had designed the passengers' oxygen system in the same spot that the other had put the system for the gasper, the little nozzle that shoots fresh air toward the passenger. One of the teams, noticing the conflict, called in an integration team, which got everyone thinking about what was best for the airplane. Within hours the three teams, working together, came up with an ingenious solution: a special clamp that holds both systems. At the old Boeing a problem like that probably wouldn't have been caught until the plane was being manufactured or, as at DEC, would have been pushed up the traditional hierarchy and taken weeks to resolve.

YOU CAN'T HAVE TEAMS WITHOUT TRUST

Reengineering presents a devilish paradox for teams. As a company reengineers, it cuts out layers of middle management, pushing work down. Employees, forced to find new ways to do more work, naturally gravitate toward teams. but the very thing that often gives rise to teams—reengineering—can have a devastating effect on team spirit.

Nynex, the Baby Bell for New York and New England, must restructure itself to prosper in the Information Age. That means shedding 17,000 workers, 30% of its work force, most of whom work in local telephone operations, the company's traditional business. To keep team morale high, Nynex in April signed a landmark labor agreement. Instead of wholesale layoffs, Nynex and the Communications Workers of America, a tough union that conducted a bitter four-month strike against the company in 1989, have a new contract that virtually guarantees no involuntary layoffs. For workers near retirement it adds six years to the person's age, plus six years of service, and supplements Social Security payments. (It didn't hurt that Nynex's pension fund was overfunded.) For those who either can't or don't want to retire, the contract guarantees training for a new job inside Nynex or one with another company. The training provision is particularly generous: A worker can take two years off and receive $10,000 a year for tuition or can work four days a week and go to school for the fifth, again for two years. Says CEO Ferguson: "It costs in the short term, but I believe we'll build shareholder value in the future by doing this."

TACKLE THE PEOPLE ISSUES HEAD-ON

So you've created the right types of teams, built an atmosphere of trust, and changed your organizational structure—and your teams still seem to be misfiring. What's the rub? Most likely it's clashing personalities. Asks Robert Baugh, a workplace specialist at the A.F.L.-C.I.O.: "How do you get people who have been at each other's throats for years to start to cooperate?"

Companies must train managers and workers to deal openly and frankly with other team members. While this sounds elementary, most companies don't do an adequate job. There's no secret or magic formula. While a motivational consultant or two may help loosen people up, most team members pick up new behavior by watching closely how management acts.

A company that set a good example for teamwork is Allina, which runs 17 non-profit hospitals in Minnesota. The company tried to form teams through the 1980s but always failed. It had the kind of hostile relations with labor unions that could make a World Cup match look genteel. A nurses' strike in 1984 basically shut a hospital for six weeks. Some Allina managers who had been working there for as long as 20 years had never even met a union official. The unions weren't blameless either. A worker remembers being taught by union officials that all you need to know is that boss spelled backward is double SOB. Says Jack Dobier, Allina's labor-management coordinator: "You'll fail with teams if you don't change people's attitude."

Allina did this by forming a team of management and union officials and giving it the power to make a difference. For instance, it found a way to close one of Allina's hospitals without leaving employees stranded. The team set up an employment center that placed 95% of the closing hospital's employees elsewhere in Allina or in other companies.

Not only did this gesture raise morale generally and save the company $8 million in severance costs, but more important, it also showed that management was serious about working with labor. Allina has since created worker-management teams in 11 of its 17 hospitals, with stunning results. One of these problem-solving teams saved the company $200,000 a year by suggesting that maintenance on some hospital equipment, such as emergency electrical

generators and operating room lights, be done by the company's own staff.

Ellen Lord, a team leader at Davidson Interiors, a division of Textron in Dover, New Hampshire, found that to keep teams happy, managers must have the patience and presence of mind to act like a parent, teacher, and referee all at once. Lord's product-development team in 1992 created a new product called Flexible Bright—a high-tech coating that makes plastic for cars look exactly like chrome but won't rust, scratch, or crack. The grille of Ford's new Lincoln Mark VIII contains this new material, and the auto maker plans to use it in other lines.

But that success followed an emphatically unpromising start. Team members in the early days sometimes got into fights. A neatnik sitting next to a slob lost his cool. People were becoming emotional about what kind of coffee was brewing in the pot. The manufacturing types thought the engineering members were focused on trivia and bluntly let them know this.

Lord argues that no matter how bad it gets, you must keep people together and talking until they feel comfortable, a process that can take months. Says she: "We threw all the people in one room and forced them to work together. If people from different functions don't get to know each other, they can't ask favors, and teamwork stalls." Lord believes the infighting would have been much worse if she hadn't carefully screened team members before inviting them to join: "As long as all of them were doers who had a depth of knowledge they could apply, I knew the personalities would work themselves out."

Yes, teams have troubles. They consume gallons of sweat and discouragement before yielding a penny of benefit. Companies make the investment only because they've realized that in a fast-moving, brutally competitive economy, the one thing sure to be harder than operating with teams is operating without them.

INDEX

MASSACHUSETTS INSTITUTE OF TECHNOLOGY

ANCONA, KOCHAN, SCULLY, VAN MAANEN, WESTNEY

MANAGING FOR THE FUTURE

Organizational Behavior & Processes

TEAMS IN ORGANIZATIONS

module 6

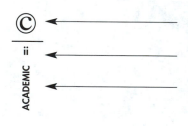

Ⓒ ← Icon indicates what part you are in, either core Ⓒ or supplemental Ⓢ.

ii ← Page number.

ACADEMIC ← Within each part there are sections—Module Overview (OVERVIEW), Academic Perspective (ACADEMIC), Popular Press (PRESS), Case (CASE), Exercise (EXERCISE).

Dedicated to those who have inspired us to try to be better students and teachers. Special dedications to

Professor Jack Barbash
Professor Arthur H. Gladstein
Professor Marius B. Jansen
Professor Joanne Martin
Professor Edgar H. Schein

Acquisitions Editor: John R. Szilagyi
Developmental Editor: Jamie Gleich Bryant
Production Editor: Mardell Toomey
Production House: DPS Associates, Inc.
Cover Design: Michael H. Stratton
Marketing Manager: Rob Bloom

ISBN: 0-538-87693-X

1 2 3 4 5 6 7 D1 4 3 2 1 0 9 8

Printed in the United States of America

South-Western College Publishing
an International Thomson Publishing company I(T)P®

Cincinnati • Albany • Boston • Detroit • Johannesburg • London • Madrid • Melbourne • Mexico City
New York • Pacific Grove • San Francisco • Scottsdale • Singapore • Tokyo • Toronto

TEAMS IN ORGANIZATIONS

This module is designed for you to apply some of the key concepts of team processes and boundary management to real teams in organizations. Through a case analysis you will examine how one team leader and those assigned to work with him set up a temporary team, got the team started, worked with others in the organization, presented the team's recommendations, and ended the team. By analyzing this team in depth you will have a chance to understand how concepts such as participation, goal setting, conflict management, and boundary management can be used to understand why some teams work and others do not. You should also come away with a greater understanding of the dynamics of task forces with diverse membership.

As organizations become more networked, both literally through the use of information technology, and structurally through the implementation of networked forms of organization, the use of temporary teams is on the rise. These teams are created for a short time to deal with an immediate problem or issue that cannot be solved through the standard practices of the organization. Temporary teams often have very diverse membership and must deal with many people and groups outside of the team. Due to their short-term nature and diverse composition, these teams provide flexibility to the organization and an ability to learn new things. Unfortunately, the diversity, short-term nature, and challenge to the status quo also pose unique management challenges. Finding ways to meet these challenges is critical, however, as management theorists predict that the organization of the future will be built around such temporary teams.

There are two core readings, one supplemental reading, and a case in this module. The first reading, **Outward Bound: Linking Teams to Their Organizations**, introduces the concept of boundary management. Boundary management refers to the way in which a team handles interactions with those outside its boundary. It is one of the major categories of team operations and plays a key role in creating and maintaining team effectiveness (see Figure 6.1—Model of Team Effectiveness—which is introduced in Module 3—**Making Teams Work**). Although most managers and researchers focus their attention on internal team processes, boundary management is actually more predictive of team performance. In today's business environment, teams can no longer work in isolation—members must learn to effectively interact with top management, other functions and units within the organization, as well as suppliers, customers, and distributors outside the firm. This boundary management function is critical to achieving cross-functional coordination, the speedy delivery of new products, and integration across nations and firms. The first reading provides concrete suggestions as to how to effectively carry out boundary management.

The second core reading, **A Summary of "The Tyranny of a Team Ideology,"** warns us to be careful of this very popular concept of teams. Although the business press generally extols the virtues of teams, Amanda Sinclair reminds us that teams are an arena in which coercion and conflict are the norm, and emotions—both positive and negative—run high. At a time when managers are rushing to join the bandwagon of those using teams everywhere for every task, Sinclair reminds us that teams are not suited for all types of work and can be costly in terms of time and energy.

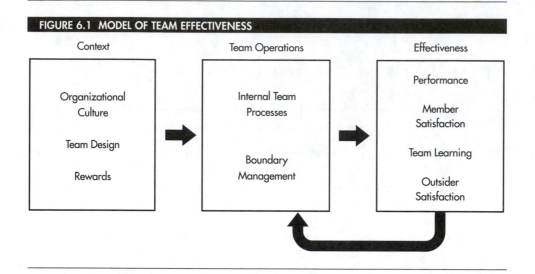

FIGURE 6.1 MODEL OF TEAM EFFECTIVENESS

The supplemental reading, **The Discipline of Teams**, reports on a study of teams in organizations carried out by Jon Katzenbach and Douglas Smith of McKinsey & Company. The reading expands upon the differences between groups and teams, and how to make them work effectively. Building on a number of case studies across different firms, the consultants provide some key guidelines that have helped all types of teams accomplish their goals.

In the case in this module, **Aston-Blair, Inc.**, you will follow the struggles of one team leader who tries to handle the many challenges of running a temporary team. Through his example you will be able to monitor the complexities inherent in blending the management of internal team processes and external boundary management. You will see how quickly a team culture forms and how politics often plays a major role in cross-functional teams. By putting yourself in the team leader's place, you can think through how you would meet the challenges he faces. What would your first steps be? How would you plan the first team meeting? How would you monitor progress? How would you handle boundary management? How would you prepare for your major presentation? Through trying to answer these questions, applying the concepts in the readings, comparing your responses to those of your classmates, and engaging in class discussion, you should be better prepared to be an effective team leader and member.

Also included in this module are copies of transparencies and work materials that should be taken with you to class. These will help you to follow the professor's introduction to boundary management, to follow the case discussion, and to keep track of what you have learned from this module.

ADDITIONAL EXERCISES

You can expand your learning about boundary management in several ways. First, you can analyze the boundary issues for a team in which you are currently a member, or one in which you were a member, or one that you have read about. What are the key interdependencies for this team? That is, who, besides the team members, has resources or information that can impact the team? Who can aid or sabotage the work of the team? What would be the best way to deal with outsiders? Who must be influenced? Who must be provided with information? With whom must negotiations take place?

Second, you can interview someone who has recently been part of a task force. Ask that person what boundary management issues arose and how they were handled. Find out how the organizational context helped and hindered the work of the team. Find out how the team member would handle boundary management activity in the future. By carrying out a few interviews like this you can learn more about how boundary management is handled in real task forces.

Finally, you can read up on boundary management and related concepts. The following references serve as a guide for further reading.

REFERENCES

Allen, T. J. 1984. *Managing the Flow of Technology: Technology Transfer and the Dissemination of Technological Information Within the R & D Organization.* Cambridge, MA: MIT Press.

Ancona, D. G. 1990. "Outward Bound: Strategies for Team Survival in the Organization." *Academy of Management Journal*, 33, pp. 334–365.

Ancona, D. G., and D. Caldwell. 1992. "Bridging the Boundary: External Activity and Performance in Organizational Teams." *Administrative Science Quarterly*, 37, pp. 634–665.

Ancona, D. G., and D. Caldwell. 1997. "Making Teamwork Work: Boundary Management in Product Development Teams." In M. L. Tushman and P. Anderson, eds., *Managing Strategic Innovation and Change: A Collection of Readings*, New York, NY: Oxford University Press. pp. 433–442.

Dougherty, D. and C. Hardy. 1996. "Sustained Product Innovation in Large, Mature Organizations: Overcoming Innovation-to-Organization Problems." *Academy of Management Journal*, 39, pp. 1120–1153.

Gresov, C. 1989. "Exploring Fit and Misfit with Multiple Contingencies." *Administrative Science Quarterly*, 34, pp. 431–453.

Lipnack, J. and J. Stamps. 1993. *The Team Net Factor: Bringing The Power of Boundary Crossing Into the Heart of Your Business.* Essex Junction, VT: Oliver Wight Publications, Inc.

Pfeffer, J. 1981. *Power in Organizations.* Marshfield, MA: Pitman.

Tushman, M. 1979. "Work Characteristics and Subunit Communication Structure: A Contingency Analysis." *Administrative Science Quarterly*, 24, pp. 82–98.

M-6

core

OUTWARD BOUND: LINKING TEAMS TO THEIR ORGANIZATION

The new computer project was a grand success. The cross-functional team was stellar, turning out an amazing new system that worked faster than anyone had thought possible. Then management killed the project. No team is an island.

It is not enough anymore to work well around a conference table or in the laboratory; it is not enough to know how to build internal consensus and effective team decision making; it is not even enough to work well as a cross-functional team on concurrent engineering or horizontal processes. Unless you know how to manage within and across the new organization, you lose. The only way to survive is to manage the external environment: "boundary management."

Teams need to manage their boundaries, to protect their territory and also to build bridges. The new product is now part of a "family" of products. The new service must interface with the computer and accounting systems. And all innovation must fit into a strategic direction that is changing at a faster rate than ever before. All of this is in a context in which the competition is trying to do the exact same thing. The need for new information, feedback, and coordination with outsiders means that teams must have dense linkages within and outside the firm. Here we focus on those within the firm.

Most researchers have tended to concentrate their efforts on understanding internal group dynamics. Others have been looking at how teams function in the larger environment of corporate realities and how their external strategies and styles affect performance. In studies of project teams, product development teams, R & D groups, sales teams, consulting teams, and management teams, clear patterns have emerged. Here we concentrate on the work of Ancona and Caldwell (1992) in their exploration of team boundary management.

The external strategies of teams are a complex matter. The team leader or project manager may play a key role in managing outside relations, or the work may be distributed across several team members. Teams need to manage various interfaces and interconnections with numerous parts of the organization. These interactions can be thought of across several dimensions: influence, task coordination, and information.

The *influence* dimension is vertical. The important external connections in this dimension are upward. Few teams become high performers without learning to "manage up." They need ambassador activities, whereby individuals who are skilled in diplomacy and know how to play organizational politics work the power structure, effectively marketing the project and the team as well as building and maintaining a good reputation through their representation of the team and its interests. Whether for good or bad, public relations can have a lot to do with team success. A team's reputation can become a self-fulfilling prophecy: "good" teams get the pick of projects and people and priority access to shared resources, whereas no one returns phone calls to those thought to be failing. Upward communication can also help a team to align its goals with that of top management.

Key to ambassadorial activity is the need to identify secure effective sponsorship within upper management, so that the team is protected from the shifting winds of

Source: This reading is based on Constantine (1993).

influence and interests as divisions are sold, companies are acquired, middle managers move, or projects are canceled. It is also key to identify potential threats to the team so that damage can be limited.

Task coordination is essentially a horizontal matter, involving lateral connections across functions and managing a team's work interdependence with other units. Teams that excel at this activity bargain with other groups, trade services or essential resources, and get feedback from others as to how their work meets expectations. These teams coordinate with other groups, pushing them to meet deadlines and to come through on commitments made to the team. They keep the work flowing in and out of the team, joining together upstream and downstream activity so that work moves quickly through the firm, not back and forth between warring functions or divisions.

The *information*, or scouting, activity is also largely lateral. Liaison here involves investigating markets, technologies, and competition, gathering information on what is going on in other parts of the organization, and bringing lots of data to the team.

Just as teams develop distinct styles of working internally, specializing in different aspects, they also seem to develop characteristic ways of managing their boundaries and interacting with the rest of the organization. Four different styles of teams have been observed: ambassadorial, researcher, isolationist, and comprehensive.

Ambassadorial teams specialize in "working vertically" or concentrating their efforts on good relations with top management. Researcher teams are specialists in scouting out and gathering information, whereas isolationist teams keep themselves apart, protecting and patrolling their tightly closed boundaries. They have relatively few external contacts and are not very well connected in terms of power, work flow, or information. Comprehensive teams are extremely active in dealing with many other groups. They are well integrated with other teams and functions through the work-flow network, and are connected up the hierarchy in the power structure. Thus, these teams combine large levels of ambassador and task coordinator activity.

TEAM EFFECTIVENESS

How did these various styles fare in the real world? Team performance can be looked at from the inside or from the outside, as team members see it or as the larger organization and management see it. Early on, members of the ambassadorial and isolationist teams thought that they were doing a great job, whereas researcher and comprehensive teams were less sure. The latter two sets of teams were having a more difficult time coming together and agreeing on goals and priorities. At this time management had a different view. They tended to rate the ambassadorial and comprehensive teams as top performers, both of these types being better tapped into the power structure.

A different picture emerges over the long haul. When teams were evaluated a year and a half to two years later, when their work was completed, the ambassadorial teams had fallen from grace, earning some of the lowest performance ratings. Apparently, these were teams that excelled at public relations but could not produce. These were the teams that most disappointed management, who had built up very high expectations for them.

Researcher teams, who sometimes never got beyond information gathering, often ended up disbanded by management. These teams kept searching for more and more information, and they had trouble moving away from problem definition and generation of alternatives toward choosing a solution and implementing it.

Isolationist teams turned out to be a mixed bag. Most of these self-contained teams failed miserably, but a few were outstanding successes. These teams often produced the most innovative products, but they had a very difficult time convincing the rest of the organization to adopt their ideas. With no support or coordination built up at the start, outsiders were reluctant to listen to these teams later in the process. Members of these teams were the most frustrated, tending to blame the organization for all of their problems.

The comprehensive teams, with their well-orchestrated and diversified strategies, came out the corporate winners. Such teams balanced internal performance with external demands. They got the information they needed but did not get stuck in perpetual research. They worked the system in terms of the power structure and work flow to meet their goals. Although the early history of these teams can be a bit rough, as they attempt to tackle internal and external issues, over time these become the high-performing teams. As external groups show their support, internal operations become smoother and a positive cycle is produced. In short, the winning strategy is moving outward bound.

MOVING OUTWARD BOUND

The notion of managing beyond one's borders is counterintuitive to many team managers. We have all been taught that team building begins with setting goals and priorities and having team members get to know one another. Nothing is said about checking those goals against management objectives or getting feedback from other parts of the organization. Thus, the first move to successfully carrying out boundary activity is to educate team members about its importance.

Next, team members need to organize themselves to carry out a comprehensive strategy. The team might begin by listing those individuals and groups within the organization that have information, expertise, control, or resources that the team might need. Members might also list those whose support will help the work of the team, and those who may be antagonistic to the team or its work. Then the team must decide how to allocate the work of managing all of this liaison work. The team leader might manage more of the vertical communication, whereas lateral communication is more distributed within the group.

Team members might begin by interviewing key outsiders about what they expect from the team, what they would really like the team to produce, and how the team's product affects them and their group. This information can help to shape the way the team defines its task and its output. Outsiders need to be informed all along of the history of the team. Those who may do damage need to be courted or controlled; those who have expertise and a stake in the team's output need to be brought into team decision making at the appropriate times. The team may also need to limit its exposure to those who would influence it in negative ways. Thus, there is a delicate balance between too much and too little interaction with those beyond the team's border. Team members often need to spend a lot of time explaining and "talking up" what they are doing, as well as pushing others to come through on earlier commitments.

Organizations have changed; the new flat, flexible, networked, diverse, global organization is very often team-based. These teams cannot work the way they have in the past. Success depends on linking up with other organizational members to get the job done. The teams that can best pull together the expertise of the firm and move their ideas and products quickly through the organization are those that will succeed.

USING THE THREE LENSES TO ANALYZE AND MANAGE THE EXTERNAL ENVIRONMENT

Another way to think about external boundary spanning is through three analytic lenses (see Module 2); strategic design, political, and cultural. From a strategic design perspective team members need to analyze those providing inputs and accepting outputs from the team in order to improve efficiency and effectiveness. From this view of the world ambassadorial activity is important in getting key resources from top management, task coordinator activity is key to insuring a smooth work flow to and from the team, and scouting assures the input of accurate and up-to-date information. Improving the flow of resources, work, and information is the major goal here.

From a political perspective team members need to identify the key "stakeholders" external to the team. Stakeholders play a role in the survival and success of the team and are affected by its activities—they have a stake in its operations. Here the focus is on assessing the environment's influence and potential influence on the team and the team's bargaining power vis-à-vis that environment.

In the stakeholder model the focus is on stakeholders' interests (what do they want?), their power and influence (how much do they have and what form does it take?), the negotiations that take place between them and team members, and the coalition building used by team members with outsiders to spread their agendas.

From this perspective ambassadorial activity is aimed at influencing top management, a major stakeholder. Here the goal is to align firm and team interests and to garner support for team interests from this powerful group. Task coordination activity is aimed at negotiating with the groups and divisions that members represent, as well as those that are not represented in the team. Special interest groups, professional groups, customers, suppliers, and employee groups might also have a stake in team outcomes and require ambassadorial and task coordinator activity. Scouting activity involves identifying the interests of other professional groups and divisions, customers, and suppliers.

The cultural perspective focuses on the artifacts, norms, values, and assumptions of the organization in which the team resides, as well as the overall societal view of teams in general. Here we look at the pressures on team members to design their teams in particular ways and to act according to standard scripts. Empowered teams, quality circles, and high-performance teams are all models of appropriate behavior that are currently being imposed on many teams. We also look at the team members' attempts to change the cultural expectations that limit and constrain behavior.

Ambassadorial, task coordinator, and scouting behavior can be used to learn more about the expectations facing the team, the "rules of the game," and what happens when those rules are broken. For example, one member of a product development team who often took on ambassadorial activity, fought long and hard to gain acceptance for allowing his team members to talk directly to customers. The "rules" in the organization made customer interaction solely a marketing activity.

Thus, external boundary activity is essential to team performance. Ambassadorial, task coordinator, and scouting activity allow the team to improve the efficiency of receiving inputs and exporting outputs, to negotiate and build coalitions with key external stakeholders, and to understand and possibly change cultural expectations.

REFERENCES

Ancona, D. G. 1990. "Outward Bound: Strategies for Team Survival in the Organization." *Academy of Management Journal*, 33, pp. 334–365.

Ancona, D. G., and D. Caldwell. 1992. "Bridging the Boundary: External Activity and Performance in Organizational Teams." *Administrative Science Quarterly*, 37, pp. 634–665.

Constantine, Larry. 1993. "People-Ware, Team Politics." *Software Development* (August), pp. 96–97.

ACADEMIC 9 ©

A SUMMARY OF "THE TYRANNY OF A TEAM IDEOLOGY"

by Amanda Sinclair

INTRODUCTION

Teams have become commonplace within organizations and are often viewed by both management theorists and consultants as the panacea for many organizational problems. Teams are seen as simultaneously satisfying needs at every level of the organization, including individual needs for productivity and effectiveness, and societal needs, for alleviating the alienation of the modern industrial age. This view is based on a dominant ideology of teamwork which is simplistic and masks many real and pervasive problems and issues within teams, including the role of power, emotions, conformity, coercion, and conflict. This ideology therefore creates inappropriate expectations around teams which ultimately hampers their use.

There are four elements or assumptions that underpin this dominant ideology:

1. *Definitions of Teams and Group Work*
   Narrowly conceived definitions of work groups and group work are based on the assumption that mature teams are almost exclusively task-oriented and have successfully minimized any impulses which interfere with the task. Yet even established teams still experience anti-task behavior. Additionally, some of what is labeled anti-task behavior, such as fantasy, may actually help and strengthen the group's creative process.

   Researchers have attempted to measure the output of work by teams. However, none of these measures provides a simple means of diagnosing when and what work occurs in groups or what group work looks like when it does occur. Additionally, groups are assigned ill-defined tasks and often have considerable scope to define their own tasks. These factors make it hard to measure the work of the team. Often researchers end up looking at decision making as the predominant group work indicator. Yet this is a poor indicator of work because the focus should be on the process by which the decision is reached rather than simply the decision itself. For example, meetings which rate high on decisions are often characterized by low participation rates, a dictatorial leadership style, and a dejected group mood. The work of any group is a unique and changing mix of decision making, exchange of information, conflict, and fantasy. A more complex and context-specific definition of group work is required, which reflects the diversity of tasks, environment, and composition of each team.

2. *The confluence of individual, group, and organizational interests*
   A unitary view of the organization is adopted which assumes confluence, not conflict, between the individual, group, and organizational goals. Many managerial theorists contend that work in groups generates heightened job satisfaction. However, individuals frequently experience substantial and continuing internal tensions as group members. Group participation is

Source: From Amanda Sinclair, "The Tyranny of a Team Ideology," *Organizational Studies*, 13(4), 1992, pp. 611–626. Adapted with permission of the author.

stressful for individuals due to more ambiguous performance standards, often based on the judgment of their peers. Group membership is typically unsatisfying for individuals, particularly those workers who are better suited to solitary work environments. Yet even when there is greater satisfaction derived from working in a group, there is little evidence that actual task performance improves, leading to greater organizational effectiveness.

Moreover, there is the assumption that individual goals are aligned with organizational goals. Conflict is thereby treated as an abnormality rather than as a constant within organizations. Alternative perspectives suggest that behavior is fundamentally political and that group activity is a consuming and irresolvable struggle for power. Consequently, the worker is not a natural group member who subordinates his or her own needs for the ultimate tasks of the group or of the organization. The over-reliance on teams may therefore mean that organizations are not getting the best performance from many of its members.

3. *Requirements of group leaders*
Rather simplistic views of the superiority of participative leaders are held. "One of the virtues of work groups lauded by organizational theorists is their capacity for self-management." With the advent of the flat organization, decision making is pushed down to groups, and workers are able to take on greater responsibility and participate in decision making, thereby increasing their level of commitment to group decisions. With the emphasis on creating a participative style, many work groups have suffered because they have ignored issues of leadership. Group process theorists are unanimous in their view that all groups will experience phases of identifying with, rejecting, and working through issues of authority. Other research confirms that the most critical ingredient of team success is its leadership. The refusal to recognize the importance of leadership can

lead to a group obsessed with authority relations, which can then paralyze the group. Additionally, teams are not a substitute for strong visionary leadership within an organization. Leadership needs to be considered as an essential element of any team.

4. *Power, conflict and emotions as subversive forces in work groups*
Power, emotions, and conflict are all viewed as regrettable forces which divert groups from their work. Power is seen by fervent team proponents as a tendency exercised by individuals who fail to identify with the collective task of the group. This view has minimized the impact of power within the group and diverted attention away from the ways power works in groups towards both constructive and destructive ends. Rather than viewing power as a threat to teams, "group behavior could be analyzed as a conflict between individuals seeking to exercise power in different ways." For instance, a team's reputation for decision making and effectiveness may be a result of decisions made unilaterally and may not reflect a quality exchange of ideas among group members.

Groups often generate pressure to conform and impede rather than encourage the healthy exchange of different opinions. The insistence upon a consensual view of teams conceals any conflicts, coercion, and power discrepancies occurring within groups. Conflicts are an inevitable part of any group and it will only facilitate our understanding of them if we acknowledge their existence.

Likewise, emotions have been seen as a disruptive force in groups, and their expression has been discouraged. Yet emotions are a mobilizing force of all groups and individuals. Groups naturally create a conflict for individuals between the need for belonging and the desire to maintain their individuality. This is an ongoing struggle for every team member. The expression of emotion may be an essential ingredient for dealing with these issues openly.

ASTON-BLAIR, INC.

Bringing Aston-Blair's June 12 executive committee meeting to a close Wynn Aston, III, chief executive officer and chairman of the board, asked Peter Casey, vice-president of marketing, and Chris Trott, vice-president of corporate planning, to seriously reexamine the company's procedures for forecasting sales. Aston hoped that improved product demand projections would lead to better inventory control, financial planning, and production scheduling. Aston-Blair had suffered significant losses in the first quarter of 1991 and expected even greater losses in the second quarter (the first losses the company had experienced since 1975). Aston felt that poor forecasting was one of several underlying factors contributing to the firm's poor performance.

Casey and Trott subsequently met with Richard Pack, president and chief operating officer, to briefly discuss his ideas on the subject. The two men then decided to form a task force to investigate the forecasting problem. Casey and Trott agreed to put Michael Bacon, a recent graduate of Stanford's Graduate School of Business, in charge of the task force. Bacon had been with Aston-Blair for two years and was currently a special assistant to Chris Trott. Prior to his present assignment, Bacon had worked as a financial analyst in Trott's financial planning group, and he was now assigned to Trott's market planning group. The assignment to market planning was an intentional move on Trott's part to broaden Bacon's exposure to different aspects of Aston-Blair's business. Bacon was regarded by both Trott and Casey as an especially promising and capable individual.

COMPANY BACKGROUND

Aston-Blair was the third largest U.S. producer of precious metal alloys and other specialized alloys for commercial and industrial use. The medium-sized company was headquartered in Chicago and had four major sales offices and five plants throughout the United States. Its products included alloys of silver, gold, platinum, and other precious or rare metals. The company sold its alloys in the form of ingots, bars, coil, strip, and wire. Most of its raw material was purchased from abroad. Aston-Blair sold its products to a wide range of customers including dealers in precious metals, jewelry manufacturers, scientific firms, and electronic and other industrial companies which used precious metals or other alloys in the manufacture of instruments and other devices.

The company's present difficulties were precipitated by two sets of related events. The first was the economic slowdown in the early 1990s which had affected the company's sales to both industrial customers and jewelry manufacturers. The second factor was the declining price of gold beginning in 1991. On the day President Bush announced the air strike against Iraq, the price of gold fell $27 an ounce, and the price continued to decline throughout 1991. The combination of the declining price of gold

Note: "Aston-Blair, Inc." Copyright © 1993 by the President and Fellows of Harvard College. Harvard Business School Case 9-494-015. This case was prepared by Professor John J. Gabarro with the assistance of Professor Deborah Ancona as the basis for class discussion rather than to illustrate either effective or ineffective handling of an administrative situation. Reprinted by permission of the Harvard Business School.

and Aston-Blair's overly optimistic sales forecasts for the first two quarters of 1991 had resulted in excessive inventories of overvalued gold, silver, and platinum, and sizable losses.

Aston-Blair's current problems stood in dramatic contrast with the company's recent record of outstanding growth and profitability. The company had been founded by Aston's great-grandfather in 1881, and it had always enjoyed a reputation for being a premiere supplier of precious metals. During Aston's 10-year stewardship as chief executive officer, the firm had quadrupled in size and had become the most profitable firm in the industry. Aston attributed this recent success to the company's aggressive marketing efforts and to its ability to identify potential users of precious metal alloys and to work with them in developing products tailored to their requirements. Under Aston and Pack's direction, the company was the first firm in the precious metals industry to develop a marketing organization where market managers and product managers were responsible for focusing on specific market segments and applications areas. (Pack had been vice-president of marketing prior to his promotion to president in 1989.)

Despite his family's obvious influence in the company, Aston had come up through the ranks and had a solid grounding in the business. Himself an MBA, Aston had made a concerted effort to hire business school-trained managers since becoming chief executive officer and had hired a number of MBA's from Columbia, Dartmouth, Harvard, MIT, Stanford, and Wharton. It was generally acknowledged that many of these MBAs were received with some resistance from industry old-timers, although several of them had gained considerable influence and success within the company, including Casey (a Harvard MBA) and Trott (an Amos Tuck MBA), both of whom were now vice presidents.

CASE 14

FORMATION OF THE TASK FORCE

After some discussion, Trott and Casey concluded that the major area for the task force to study should be the Marketing Division, because it was the four market managers who made the final forecasts for product demand. The market managers based their forecasts on information they received from their product managers, the vice-president of sales, the vice-president of manufacturing, and the macro-economic forecasts made by the vice-president of economic analysis and forecasting (see Exhibit 1 for company organization chart).

Having decided on the task force's mandate, Casey and Trott met with Bacon and described the problem as they saw it. Casey said that he would appoint three product managers to the task force to represent the Marketing Division. He suggested that it would not be necessary to involve the market managers (to whom the product managers reported), since they were very busy and had been resistant to similar changes in procedures in the past. Trott, in turn, said that he would ask Jed Burns, vice-president of Sales, to appoint a representative from Sales to the task force. He also suggested that two others, in addition to Bacon, be assigned from Corporate Planning. The first was Vicki Reiss, a young Harvard MBA, whom Trott felt would add analytic strength to the group; and the second was Robert Holt, a man in his middle 50s, whom Trott thought would add balance because he was an old-timer and would be able to relate well to the product managers. Trott also added that he would ask Dr. Russell Cornelius, vice-president of economic analysis, to appoint a representative from his group.

The three then agreed that the task force would report back to Trott, Casey, and the market managers on August 4. After the August 4 presentation, Trott would arrange for a subsequent presentation to the president and chairman of the board later in the month.

Aston-Blair, Inc.

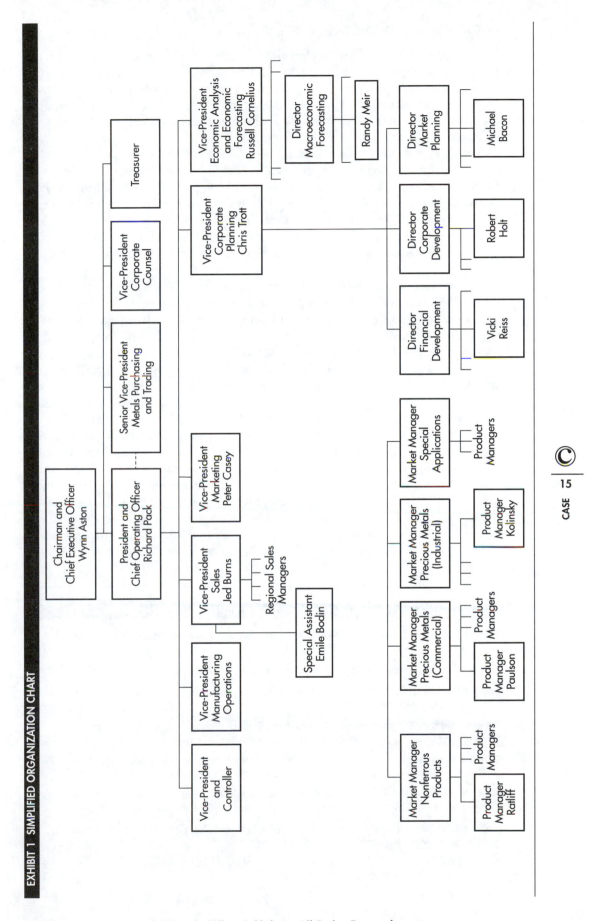

EXHIBIT 1 SIMPLIFIED ORGANIZATION CHART

CASE Ⓒ **15**

INITIAL MEETING OF THE TASK FORCE

A week after his discussion with Trott and Casey, Bacon had his first meeting with the newly appointed task force. In addition to himself, Vicki Reiss, and Robert Holt, it included the three product managers from the Marketing Division, Randy Meir, an economic analyst from Dr. Cornelius' group, and Emile Bodin, a special assistant to the vice-president of Sales. (See Exhibit 2 for the names and positions of the task force members.)

The three product managers were all men in their middle to late 40s; all were obviously uneasy at the beginning of the meeting. Bacon had had few prior contacts with them and did not know them well. By contrast, he knew Vicki Reiss and Robert Holt fairly well because they also worked for Trott in Corporate Planning. Bacon had previously worked with Reiss and had come to admire her analytic ability, quickness, and perceptiveness. Although he had never worked directly with Holt, he knew that Holt was widely respected within the company for his competence, knowledge, and thoughtfulness.

Randy Meir, the representative from the Economic Analysis and Forecasting group, was a Wharton MBA and a contemporary of Bacon and Reiss. Bacon had once worked with Meir on a project before Meir had been transferred from Corporate Planning to Cornelius' group. Bacon had found this experience to be less than satisfying, and he and Meir disagreed over several issues while working together.

Emile Bodin, the representative from the Sales Division, was in his late 50s and had spent almost all his career in sales. His last five years had been as a troubleshooter, and special assistant to the vice-president of sales. Bodin, like Holt, was well-liked and widely respected within the company.

The meeting had a slow and awkward beginning, with Emile Bodin, Vicki Reiss, and the three product managers saying almost nothing. In contrast, Randy Meir was quite vocal and emphatic about the need to develop a model for the internal forecasting process. Meir argued that it was essential for the task force to identify the basic assumptions on which the present product demand forecasts were based, and then to make a model of the entire process. Reiss finally interrupted Meir to say that although she agreed a forecasting model might be useful in the future, she thought the creation of such a model should not be the task force's purpose. Rather, it might be one of the

---

EXHIBIT 2   MEMBERS OF THE FORECASTING TASK FORCE

Michael Bacon, 28, chairman: Market planning analyst and assistant to the vice-president of Corporate Planning; (Stanford MBA).

Vicki Reiss, 27: Financial planning analyst; representative of Corporate Planning; (Harvard MBA).

Robert Holt, 54: Corporate development specialist; representative of Corporate Planning; (B.S., Missouri School of Mines, Rolla).

Peter Ratliff, 47: Product manager (Nonferrous Products Market Group); representative of Marketing Division; (B.S., Wayne State).

Charles Paulson, 43: Product manager (Precious Metals, Commercial Applications Market Group); representative of Marketing Division; (B.S., Illinois Institute of Technology).

David Kolinsky, 48: Product manager (Precious Metals, Industrial Applications Market Group); representative of Marketing Division; (M.S., City University of New York).

Emile Bodin, 58: Special assistant to the vice-president of Sales; representative of the Sales Division; (B.M.S., Massachusetts Maritime Academy).

Randy Meir, 29: Economic analyst; representative of the Economic Analysis and Economic Forecasting Group; (Wharton MBA).

---

recommendations that the task force might make based on what they found. She also added that it was much more difficult to develop a single-firm forecasting model than it was to develop the macroeconomic models that Dr. Cornelius and his group worked with.

After a long pause, Robert Holt suggested that the task force divide up its work so that he and the three product managers could concentrate on the Marketing Division and Meir could concentrate on gathering whatever hard data he felt were necessary for a model. Bacon thought that this was a good idea. He then asked Vicki Reiss and Emile Bodin if they would be willing to concentrate on the Sales Division's inputs into the forecast. Reiss and Bodin exchanged ideas briefly and then agreed to take responsibility for this part of the project. Shortly thereafter the meeting adjourned, the consensus being that individual subgroups would stay in contact with Bacon.

PREPARATION OF THE TASK FORCE REPORT

In the following five weeks, Bacon spent much of his time working with Holt and the three product managers on the Marketing Division's part of the study and with Reiss and Emile Bodin on the Sales Division's part. Holt and the product managers worked well together and Bacon found his meetings with them to be enjoyable and at times exciting. He also found that he, Reiss, and Bodin enjoyed working together and that the three of them were making considerable progress in identifying how the regional sales managers prepared the sales estimates for the vice-president of Sales (which in turn constituted the Sales Division's inputs to the market managers).

Meir, on the other hand, spent most of his time traveling to the various sales offices gathering data on historic sales trends, as well as interviewing all of the product managers in the company headquarters. Bacon's exchanges with Meir were brief and infrequent and occasionally strained. Bacon suspected that Meir resented Bacon's more rapid progress within the company. He had also heard through the grapevine that Meir's boss, Dr. Cornelius, was disturbed that he had not been asked by Aston to look at the forecasting problem, or by Trott and Casey to head the task force. Several of Meir's comments reinforced Bacon's suspicions, since Meir made it clear that the internal product demand forecasting should be done by Cornelius' group instead of the market managers.

By July 23, Bacon felt that the group had made enough progress to report back to Trott, Casey, and the market managers. The next day, he called the members of the task force together to share their findings and to discuss a strategy for presenting their recommendations to Casey and Trott on August 4. All of the task force members attended, except Meir who was in New York City gathering sales data and could not make the meeting. Holt and the three product managers were quite enthusiastic about several recommendations that they were sure would improve the quality of the product-demand forecasts. Bodin and Reiss also reported that they had found what they described as some systematic biases in the Sales Division's inputs into the forecast. They felt that they needed more time, however, before they could make any specific recommendations. They did think that they could make some recommendations of a general nature at the August 4 presentation.

After the meeting ended, Emile Bodin took Bacon aside and explained that the information he had on how the regional managers made their sales estimates was quite sensitive, and that he needed to discuss it with Jed Burns, the vice-president of Sales, before proceeding further. Bodin said that he would first prepare a report of his findings for only Bacon and Reiss to look at; then, after the three had discussed it, he would take the report to Burns. He said that he did not yet have all the information necessary and that the report would probably not be ready before the August 4 presentation. He also added that it would take several discussions with Burns before his findings could be presented to the rest of the task force since he thought his report would place the Sales

Division in an embarrassing situation. He expected, however, that once Burns understood the report and its implications, some significant changes could be made to improve the Sales Division's inputs into the market manager's forecasts. He also felt that Burns would support these recommendations. Reiss joined Bodin and Bacon partway through their conversation, and she concurred that all of this work could not possibly be completed by August 4. She suggested that their general recommendations be followed up at a later date with more specific recommendations after Bodin had discussed his report with Burns.

During the following week Robert Holt and the product managers spent most of their time preparing for the presentation, while Emile Bodin worked as rapidly as he could on his report for Burns. Vicki Reiss, in addition to consulting with Bodin on the report, concentrated on preparing some general recommendations about the Sales Division's input into the forecast.

Bacon had spoken with Meir as soon as he returned from New York and briefed him on the results of the earlier meeting. Meir agreed to outline a proposal for the development of an internal planning model as his part of the August 4 presentation. Meir added that gathering his data had been a frustrating experience, and that he suspected that the regional sales managers were hiding information from him.

THE AUGUST 4 REPORT OF THE TASK FORCE

Prior to the task force's oral presentation on August 4, Bacon, Holt, and the three product managers agreed that Holt should be the one to report his subgroup's findings and recommendations. The three product managers felt that if they made the presentation, it would put them in an awkward position with their bosses, the market managers, because several of their conclusions were critical in nature. Bacon agreed with this strategy; he also decided (with the approval of the other members of the task force) on a tentative agenda. The plan was for Bacon to begin the oral report with a 15-minute summary of the group's purpose, what they saw as the general problems, and their major recommendations. He was to be followed by Meir, who would recommend that an internal forecasting model be developed to assist the market managers in making their individual product-demand forecasts. Meir would also report on the historic sales data and on what he thought were the critical, underlying assumptions that needed to be clarified in developing an internal forecasting model. Then, Holt would report his subgroup's findings on how the Marketing Division should restructure its procedures for making future product-demand forecasts. After Holt's report was completed, Reiss would present her general recommendations concerning the Sales Division's inputs into the product-demand forecasts.

The presentation was scheduled to last from 10:00 a.m. to 1:00 p.m. in Peter Casey's office. Bacon arrived at his own office at 8:00 a.m. to go over his notes and slides. Shortly after 9:00 a.m., Emile Bodin came into Bacon's office with a copy of the report he had been working on all week. Bodin had stayed up most of the night typing it himself so that Bacon could see it before going into the meeting. Bacon skimmed the six summary statements on the first page and was indeed surprised by what they said. It was clear that the regional sales managers were consistently overstating their sales estimates in order to insure adequate inventory and rapid delivery. He called Reiss on the telephone and the three decided to discuss Bodin's report the next day, but not to report any of its findings at the presentation.

The presentation began promptly at 10:00 a.m. Everyone seemed very much at ease, except for the three product managers. The meeting went smoothly until Meir finished his portion of the presentation. Meir asked if there were any questions, and one of the market managers said he hoped that what the others had to say would be more relevant than Meir's recommendations. He added, "You guys in Cornelius' group can't even forecast what the economy is going to do; how the hell are your models going to tell me what our customers are going to do?" The other market managers laughed at this remark, and to save Meir further embarrassment, Bacon said that Meir's recommendations would make more sense after the market managers heard the other reports.

Holt then presented the report on the Marketing Division's procedures for forecasting product demand and the task force's recommendations on how they should be changed. During Holt's presentation, the product managers asked him several questions of a clarifying nature, which Bacon felt were useful in getting certain points across to the market managers. At the conclusion of Holt's presentation, Paulson, one of the product managers, said that all three of them felt that the conclusions and recommendations were sound, and that they were prepared as individuals to stand solidly behind them and take personal responsibility for their consequences.

Following this remark, Casey, the vice-president of Marketing, asked his market managers what they thought of Holt's presentation. One of them said he thought the recommendations might improve the forecasts, while the other three said that the recommendations could not possibly work. Their comments included such arguments as the recommendations would not allow enough room for necessary subjective factors, and that the new procedures would involve too much red tape. The discussion became quite heated, with most of the questions being addressed to Holt. Several times the product managers were cut off by their bosses, in their attempts to answer the questions or clarify certain points. Finally, one of the marketing managers said to Holt, "Robert, frankly, I'm amazed that this kind of nonsense could come from you. I would expect it from a tenderfoot like Bacon or Reiss or Meir, but from you? You've been around here long enough to know our business better than to come up with this nonsense." A second market manager added, "Look, I'm just getting things under control again so we won't lose money next quarter. The last thing I need is this garbage." He then turned to Casey and said, "In no way am I going to swallow this stuff." Casey began to respond, when Trott interrupted to say that he thought tempers were hot and that the recommendations were not as controversial as they might first appear to be. He suggested that the meeting be adjourned until 3:00 p.m. to give everyone a chance to cool off and think things over. Casey agreed that the suggestion was a good one and the meeting ended at 11:30 a.m.

Trott asked Bacon to remain after everyone else had left. Trott then closed the door and said to Bacon, "We've got one hell of a mess here, and you better figure out what you're going to do at 3:00. In the meantime, Casey and I will put our heads together and see what we can come up with." Bacon picked up his notes and left.

When Bacon returned to his own office, he found Meir sitting at his desk thumbing through the report that Emile Bodin had left for him earlier in the morning. Bacon explained that the report had been loaned confidentially to Bacon for study purposes only, and that Bodin had to discuss the report with his boss before presenting it to the full task force. Bacon added that none of the report data would be presented in the afternoon meeting, except in the most general terms. He said that it was important to respect Bodin's wishes and that the report would be shared with the task force when the time was right. Meir responded by saying that Bodin's data would certainly have made his own task much easier; he suspected all along that the regional sales managers had been withholding information from him. Meir added that he was angry that he had not received more support from Bacon and Reiss when the market mangers had attacked him during the morning meeting. Bacon explained his rationale for wanting to move the discussion on to another topic—one of his reasons for doing so was to get Meir out of the tough spot that he was in. He said he was sorry that Meir had interpreted it as a lack of support. Meir accepted his apology and left.

A few moments later, Reiss came in to ask Bacon to join her for lunch. The two spent most of their lunch discussing what Bacon should do when the meeting reconvened at

19

CASE

3:00 p.m. After lunch, Reiss accompanied Bacon back to his office where they found Dr. Cornelius waiting at Bacon's door. Cornelius said that he wanted some information on two of the points that Bodin had made on the first page of his report. Bacon noticed that Cornelius was holding a piece of yellow lined paper with Bodin's six major points written on it. Cornelius stated that he needed this information for a meeting that he had scheduled for 4:00 p.m. with Jed Burns, the sales vice-president (and Bodin's boss), to get "some real progress going on the forecasting problem." Bacon replied that it was impossible to give him that data, and that the report was considered confidential. Cornelius smiled and asked how company information could be thought of as confidential when it was a corporate vice-president who was asking for it. Cornelius left by saying that he would get the information he needed from Burns himself when they met at 4:00 p.m.

Reiss who had overheard Bacon's exchange with Cornelius, seemed incredulous at what had transpired. Bacon explained that Meir had seen the report before lunch and that he had explained its confidentiality to him. Meir had presumably understood the situation, although he had not actually said that he would keep it confidential. Reiss was by now quite angry, and said that if Emile Bodin was in any way hurt or compromised by this turn of events, it would be Bacon's responsibility. She said that Bodin had taken a personal risk in sharing the information with them and that if Bodin ended up in trouble because of it, Bacon's word would not be "worth a plugged nickel" in the future. Bacon attempted to again explain what had happened, but Reiss cut him off by saying, "You've got a problem, man, which you'd better fix in a hurry."

20

CASE

CASE WORK MATERIAL

WORK MATERIAL 6.1 MAJOR PLAYERS IN THE CASE

Wynn Aston III—CEO and Chairman of the Board

Peter Casey—VP Marketing

Chris Trott—VP Corporate Planning

Richard Pack—President and COO

Jed Burns—VP Sales

Russell Cornelius—VP Economic Analysis

Michael Bacon, Task Force Leader—Corporate Planning

Vicki Reiss, Harvard MBA—Corporate Planning

Robert Holt, old-timer—Corporate Planning

Randy Meir, Wharton MBA—Economic Analyst

Emile Bodin, old-timer—Special Assistant to the VP Sales

Peter Ratliff, Charles Paulson, David Kolinsky—Product Managers

---

WORK MATERIAL 6.2 TIPS ON MANAGING TASK FORCES

I. GETTING STARTED

  A. Think strategically about whether a task force is needed to carry out the assignment.

  B. Clarify the task, the objectives, and the output of the task force. Is the task force to conduct a preliminary investigation, engage in problem solving, or implement an agreed-upon change?

  C. Meet with management to go over goals, purpose, and final products. To follow up, write a memo summarizing project objectives and ask the managers to react to it.

  D. Meet with management to determine task force resources and operating guidelines.

  - How many members? Full- or part-time?
  - When should the task be completed?
  - How often will the team leader meet with management?
  - What information will be available to the team?
  - How much decision-making power has been delegated to the team?
  - What will the team's budget be?

  E. Select task force members carefully. Members should have:

  - Task knowledge
  - Problem-solving and decision-making skills
  - Interpersonal and team skills
  - Organizational influence and credibility
  - Ability to represent all areas that will be affected by the team's work
  - Time to devote to the team and an interest in the problem

© 21 CASE

F. Manage boundary processes.

- Clarify who will evaluate and receive the team's proposals.
- Do a political environmental scan—whose interests are at stake and how much power does each interest have to block or support proposals?
- Meet with the major interests to get their expectations and suggestions for the task force.
- Scan for needed resources and begin to negotiate for them.

G. Prepare for the first meeting.

- Ask the commissioning managers to attend.
- Review all that you know about the problem, resources, members, and outside interests.
- If possible meet with team members to determine initial reactions.
- Take a first pass at defining the often ill-structured problem.

II. CONDUCTING THE FIRST MEETING

A. Start with commissioning managers to discuss the importance of the task force and its work.

B. Get members to introduce themselves.

C. Reach a common understanding of the team's task and goals.

- Encourage everyone to participate.
- Achieve general agreement on the nature of the problem.
- Prevent a premature consensus on a solution.
- Test the team's view of the problem with key outsiders.
- Develop a sense of joint responsibility and appropriate next steps.

D. Define working procedures and relationships.

- The frequency and nature of full task force meetings
- The need for subgroups and, if needed, their structure
- Ground rules for communication and decision making between meetings
- Decision-making and conflict-resolution norms
- Schedules and deadlines
- Ground rules for dealing with sensitive issues
- Procedures for monitoring and reporting progress
- A process to critique and modify processes and procedures
- A procedure for boundary management

III. RUNNING THE TASK FORCE

A. Manage internal team dynamics.

- Hold full task force meetings often enough to keep all members informed and up-to-date on team progress.
- Meet with all subgroups and encourage appropriate team process principles.
- Do not align yourself with any one position or subgroup too early.
- Set interim project deadlines.
- Be sensitive to conflicting loyalties created by task force membership.
- Bring in new information and challenge team assumptions.
- Spend part of every meeting assessing how well the team is carrying out its task.

B. Manage external dynamics.

- Keep externals informed; use them to deal with other key outside constituencies to clarify or negotiate conflicts.
- Appraise key external interests beforehand of what will be presented in public meetings; get their reactions and help them to understand who might be

Aston-Blair, Inc.

opposed, and see if they are willing to go to bat for your recommendations in
the face of expected opposition.
- Offer to help team members with their boundary or constituency problems—a letter of support, joint visits, take the blame, "side payments."

IV. BRINGING THE PROJECT TO COMPLETION

- Prepare a tentative outline of the report and circulate it among team members.
- Try to reach team consensus before presenting any recommendations.
- Carefully plan and organize the final presentation.
- Rehearse the presentation to obtain feedback and fine-tune key points.
- Brief key managers and other constituencies before the final presentation to prevent
defensive reactions and rejection of the proposal. If necessary, negotiate changes to
make the proposal more acceptable.
- Plan two meetings: one to summarize findings and recommendations and one to
decide upon action.
- Remember to praise and reward team members and outsiders who have put a lot of
time and energy into the report.

23

CASE

Source: This material has been adapted from James Ware, "Managing a Task Force." In L. A. Schlesinger, R. G. Eccles,
& J. J. Gabarro, eds., *Managing Behavior in Organizations: Texts, Cases, and Readings,* pp. 16–126. New York,
McGraw-Hill, 1983.

M-6

supplemental

THE DISCIPLINE OF TEAMS

by Jon R. Katzenbach and Douglas K. Smith

Early in the 1980s, Bill Greenwood and a small band of rebel railroaders took on most of the top management of Burlington Northern and created a multibillion-dollar business in "piggybacking" rail services despite widespread resistance, even resentment, within the company. The Medical Products Group at Hewlett-Packard owes most of its leading performance to the remarkable efforts of Dean Morton, Lew Platt, Ben Holmes, Dick Alberting, and a handful of their colleagues who revitalized a health care business that most others had written off. At Knight-Ridder, Jim Batten's "customer obsession" vision took root at the *Tallahassee Democrat* when 14 frontline enthusiasts turned a charter to eliminate errors into a mission of major change and took the entire paper along with them.

Such are the stories and the work of teams-real teams that perform, not amorphous groups that we call teams because we think that the label is motivating and energizing. The difference between teams that perform and other groups that don't is a subject to which most of us pay far too little attention. Part of the problem is that *team* is a word and concept so familiar to everyone.

Or at least that's what we thought when we set out to do research for our book *The Wisdom of Teams*. We wanted to discover what differentiates various levels of team performance, where and how teams work best, and what top management can do to enhance their effectiveness. We talked with hundreds of people on more than 50 different teams in 30 companies and beyond from Motorola and Hewlett-Packard to Operation Desert Storm and the Girl Scouts.

We found that there is a basic discipline that makes teams work. We also found that teams and good performance are inseparable; you cannot have one without the other. But people use the word *team* so loosely that it gets in the way of learning and applying the discipline that leads to good performance. For managers to make better decisions about whether, when, or how to encourage and use teams, it is important to be more precise about what a team is and what it isn't.

Most executives advocate teamwork. And they should. Teamwork represents a set of values that encourages listening and responding constructively to views expressed by others, giving others the benefit of the doubt, providing support, and recognizing the interests and achievements of others. Such values help teams perform, and they also promote individual performance as well as the performance of an entire organization. But teamwork values by themselves are not exclusive to teams, nor are they enough to ensure team performance.

Nor is a team just any group working together. Committees, councils, and task forces are not necessarily teams. Groups do not become teams simply because that is what someone calls them. The entire work force of any large and complex organization is never a team, but think about how often that platitude is offered up.

Source: Reprinted by permission of *Harvard Business Review*. "The Discipline of Teams" by Jon R. Katzenbach and Douglas K. Smith, *Harvard Business Review*, March/April 1993. Copyright © 1989 by the President and Fellows of Harvard College; all rights reserved.

To understand how teams deliver extra performance, we must distinguish between teams and other forms of working groups. That distinction turns on performance results. A working group's performance is a function of what its members do as individuals. A team's performance includes both individual results and what we call "collective work-products." A collective work-product is what two or more members must work on together, such as interviews, surveys, or experiments. Whatever it is, a collective work-product reflects the joint, real contribution of team members.

Working groups are both prevalent and effective in large organizations where individual accountability is most important. The best working groups come together to share information, perspectives, and insights; to make decisions that help each person do his or her job better; and to reinforce individual performance standards. But the focus is always on individual goals and accountabilities. Working-group members don't take responsibility for results other than their own. Nor do they try to develop incremental performance contributions requiring the combined work of two or more members.

Teams differ fundamentally from working groups because they require both individual and mutual accountability. Teams rely on more than group discussion, debate, and decision; on more than sharing information and best practice performance standards. Teams produce discrete work-products through the joint contributions of their members. This is what makes possible performance levels greater than the sum of all the individual bests of team members. Simply stated, a team is more than the sum of its parts.

The first step in developing a disciplined approach to team management is to think about teams as discrete units of performance and not just as positive sets of values. Having observed and worked with scores of teams in action, both successes and failures, we offer the following. Think of it as a working definition or, better still, an essential discipline that real teams share.

> A team is a small number of people with complementary skills who are committed to a common purpose, set of performance goals, and approach for which they hold themselves mutually accountable.

The essence of a team is common commitment. Without it, groups perform as individuals; with it, they become a powerful unit of collective performance. This kind of commitment requires a purpose in which team members can believe. Whether the purpose is to "transform the contributions of suppliers into the satisfaction of customers," to "make our company one we can be proud of again," or to "prove that all children can learn," credible team purposes have an element related to winning, being first, revolutionizing, or being on the cutting edge.

Teams develop direction, momentum, and commitment by working to shape a meaningful purpose. Building ownership and commitment to team purpose, however, is not incompatible with taking initial direction from outside the team. The often-asserted assumption that a team cannot "own" its purpose unless management leaves it alone actually confuses more potential teams than it helps. In fact, it is the exceptional case-for example, entrepreneurial situations-when a team creates a purpose entirely on its own.

Most successful teams shape their purposes in response to a demand or opportunity put in their path, usually by higher management. This helps teams get started by broadly framing the company's performance expectation. Management is responsible for clarifying the charter, rationale, and performance challenge for the team, but management must also leave enough flexibility for the team to develop commitment around its own spin on that purpose, set of specific goals, timing, and approach.

The best teams invest a tremendous amount of time and effort exploring, shaping, and agreeing on a purpose that belongs to them both collectively and individually. This "purposing" activity continues throughout the life of the team. In contrast, failed teams

FIGURE 6.2 NOT ALL GROUPS ARE TEAMS: HOW TO TELL THE DIFFERENCE

Working Group	Team
• Strong, clearly focused leader	• Shared leadership roles
• Individual accountability	• Individual and mutual accountability
• The group's purpose is the same as the broader organizational mission	• Specific team purposes that the team itself delivers
• Individual work-products	• Collective work-products
• Runs efficient meetings	• Encourages open-ended discussion and active problem-solving meetings
• Measures its effectiveness indirectly by its influence on others (e.g., financial performance of the business)	• Measures performance directly by assessing collective work-products
• Discusses, decides, and delegates	• Discusses, decides, and does real work together

rarely develop a common purpose. For whatever reason—an insufficient focus on performance, lack of effort, poor leadership—they do not coalesce around a challenging aspiration.

The best teams also translate their common purpose into specific performance goals, such as reducing the reject rate from suppliers by 50% or increasing the math scores of graduates from 40% to 95%. Indeed, if a team fails to establish specific performance goals or if those goals do not relate directly to the team's overall purpose, team members become confused, pull apart, and revert to mediocre performance. By contrast, when purposes and goals build on one another and are combined with team commitment, they become a powerful engine of performance.

Transforming broad directives into specific and measurable performance goals is the surest first step for a team trying to shape a purpose meaningful to its members. Specific goals, such as getting a new product to market in less than half the normal time, responding to all customers within 24 hours, or achieving a zero-defect rate while simultaneously cutting costs by 40%, all provide firm footholds for teams. There are several reasons:

- Specific team performance goals help to define a set of work-products that are different both from an organization-wide mission and from individual job objectives. As a result, such work-products require the collective effort of team members to make something specific happen that, in and of itself, adds real value to results. By contrast, simply gathering from time to time to make decisions will not sustain team performance.

- The specificity of performance objectives facilitates clear communication and constructive conflict within the team. When a plant-level team, for example, sets a goal of reducing average machine changeover time to two hours, the clarity of the goal forces the team to concentrate on what it would take either to achieve or to reconsider the goal. When such goals are clear, discussions can focus on how to pursue them or whether to change them; when goals are ambiguous or nonexistent, such discussions are much less productive.

- The attainability of specific goals helps teams maintain their focus on getting results. A product-development team at Eli Lilly's Peripheral Systems Division set definite yardsticks for the market introduction of an ultrasonic probe to help

CONCLUSION

The ideology of teamwork that prevails among management consultants and experts does not reflect the deep and complex understanding we have of teamwork from the vast amount of research that has been conducted on this topic. The mutually beneficial characteristics of teams have been widely overstated, with little acknowledgment given to the inequities, costs, and risks that accompany teams.

The effectiveness of teams is dependent upon understanding them in their complexity and carefully appraising whether they can offer satisfying and productive contexts in which to work. The dominant ideology tyrannizes because it encourages teams "to be used for inappropriate tasks and to fulfill unrealistic objectives." By developing a more critical appreciation of the costs and limitations of teams, they will be put to better use.

12

PRESS

- *Technical or Functional Expertise*
  It would make little sense for a group of doctors to litigate an employment discrimination case in a court of law. Yet teams of doctors and lawyers often try medical malpractice or personal injury cases. Similarly, product-development groups that include only marketers or engineers are less likely to succeed than those with the complementary skills of both.

- *Problem-Solving and Decision-Making Skills*
  Teams must be able to identify the problems and opportunities they face, evaluate the options they have for moving forward, and then make necessary trade-offs and decisions about how to proceed. Most teams need some members with these skills to begin with, although many will develop them best on the job.

- *Interpersonal Skills*
  Common understanding and purpose cannot arise without effective communication and constructive conflict, which in turn depend on interpersonal skills. These include risk taking, helpful criticism, objectivity, active listening, giving the benefit of the doubt, and recognizing the interests and achievements of others.

Obviously, a team cannot get started without some minimum complement of skills, especially technical and functional ones. Still, think about how often you've been part of a team whose members were chosen primarily on the basis of personal compatibility or formal position in the organization, and in which the skill mix of its members wasn't given much thought.

It is equally common to overemphasize skills in team selection. Yet in all the successful teams we've encountered, not one had all the needed skills at the outset. The Burlington Northern team, for example, initially had no members who were skilled marketers despite the fact that their performance challenge was a marketing one. In fact, we discovered that teams are powerful vehicles for developing the skills needed to meet the team's performance challenge. Accordingly, team member selection ought to ride as much on skill potential as on skills already proven.

Effective teams develop strong commitment to a common approach, that is, to how they will work together to accomplish their purpose. Team members must agree on who will do particular jobs, how schedules will be set and adhered to, what skills need to be developed, how continuing membership in the team is to be earned, and how the group will make and modify decisions. This element of commitment is as important to team performance as is the team's commitment to its purpose and goals.

Agreeing on the specifics of work and how they fit together to integrate individual skills and advance team performance lies at the heart of shaping a common approach. It is perhaps self-evident that an approach that delegates all the real work to a few members (or staff outsiders), and thus relies on reviews and meetings for its only "work together" aspects, cannot sustain a real team. Every member of a successful team does equivalent amounts of real work; all members, including the team leader, contribute in concrete ways to the team's work-product. This is a very important element of the emotional logic that drives team performance.

When individuals approach a team situation, especially in a business setting, each has preexisting job assignments as well as strengths and weaknesses reflecting a variety of backgrounds, talents, personalities, and prejudices. Only through the mutual discovery and understanding of how to apply all its human resources to a common purpose can a team develop and agree on the best approach to achieve its goals. At the heart of such long and, at times, difficult interactions lies a commitment-building process in which the team candidly explores who is best suited to each task as well as how individual roles will come together. In effect, the team establishes a social contract among members that relates to their purpose and guides and obligates how they must work together.

S
30
ACADEMIC

No group ever becomes a team until it can hold itself accountable as a team. Like common purpose and approach, mutual accountability is a stiff test. Think, for example, about the subtle but critical difference between "the boss holds me accountable" and "we hold ourselves accountable." The first case can lead to the second; but without the second, there can be no team.

Companies like Hewlett-Packard and Motorola have an ingrained performance ethic that enables teams to form "organically" whenever there is a clear performance challenge requiring collective rather than individual effort. In these companies, the factor of mutual accountability is commonplace. "Being in the boat together" is how their performance game is played.

At its core, team accountability is about the sincere promises we make to ourselves and others, promises that underpin two critical aspects of effective teams: commitment and trust. Most of us enter a potential team situation cautiously because ingrained individualism and experience discourage us from putting our fates in the hands of others or accepting responsibility for others. Teams do not succeed by ignoring or wishing away such behavior.

Mutual accountability cannot be coerced any more than people can be made to trust one another. But when a team shares a common purpose, goals, and approach, mutual accountability grows as a natural counterpart. Accountability arises from and reinforces the time, energy, and action invested in figuring out what the team is trying to accomplish and how best to get it done.

When people work together toward a common objective, trust and commitment follow. Consequently, teams enjoying a strong common purpose and approach inevitably hold themselves responsible, both as individuals and as a team, for the team's performance. This sense of mutual accountability also produces the rich rewards of mutual achievement in which all members share. What we heard over and over from members of effective teams is that they found the experience energizing and motivating in ways that their "normal" jobs never could match.

On the other hand, groups established primarily for the sake of becoming a team or for job enhancement, communication, organizational effectiveness, or excellence rarely become effective teams, as demonstrated by the bad feelings left in many companies after experimenting with quality circles that never translated "quality" into specific goals. Only when appropriate performance goals are set does the process of discussing the goals and the approaches to them give team members a clearer and clearer choice: they can disagree with a goal and the path that the team selects and, in effect, opt out, or they can pitch in and become accountable with and to their teammates.

The discipline of teams we've outlined is critical to the success of all teams. Yet it is also useful to go one step further. Most teams can be classified in one of three ways: teams that recommend things, teams that make or do things, and teams that run things. In our experience, each type faces a characteristic set of challenges.

TEAMS THAT RECOMMEND THINGS

These teams include task forces, project groups, and audit, quality, or safety groups asked to study and solve particular problems. Teams that recommend things almost always have predetermined completion dates. Two critical issues are unique to such teams: getting off to a fast and constructive start and dealing with the ultimate handoff required to get recommendations implemented.

The key to the first issue lies in the clarity of the team's charter and the composition of its membership. In addition to wanting to know why and how their efforts are important, task forces need a clear definition of whom management expects to participate and the time commitment required. Management can help by ensuring that the team includes people with the skills and influence necessary for crafting practical

31

ACADEMIC

recommendations that will carry weight throughout the organization. Moreover, management can help the team get the necessary cooperation by opening doors and dealing with political obstacles.

Missing the handoff is almost always the problem that stymies teams that recommend things. To avoid this, the transfer of responsibility for recommendations to those who must implement them demands top management's time and attention. The more top managers assume that recommendations will "just happen," the less likely it is that they will. The more involvement task force members have in implementing their recommendations, the more likely they are to get implemented.

To the extent that people outside the task force will have to carry the ball, it is critical to involve them in the process early and often, certainly well before recommendations are finalized. Such involvement may take many forms, including participating in interviews, helping with analyses, contributing and critiquing ideas, and conducting experiments and trials. At a minimum, anyone responsible for implementation should receive a briefing on the task force's purpose, approach, and objectives at the beginning of the effort as well as regular reviews of progress.

TEAMS THAT MAKE OR DO THINGS

These teams include people at or near the front lines who are responsible for doing the basic manufacturing, development, operations, marketing, sales, service, and other value-adding activities of a business. With some exceptions, like new-product development or process design teams, teams that make or do things tend to have no set completion dates because their activities are ongoing.

In deciding where team performance might have the greatest impact, top management should concentrate on what we call the company's "critical delivery points," that is, places in the organization where the cost and value of the company's products and services are most directly determined. Such critical delivery points might include where accounts get managed, customer service performed, products designed, and productivity determined. If performance at critical delivery points depends on combining multiple skills, perspectives, and judgments in real time, then the team option is the smartest one.

When an organization does require a significant number of teams at these points, the sheer challenge of maximizing the performance of so many groups will demand a carefully constructed and performance-focused set of management processes. The issue here for top management is how to build the necessary systems and process supports without falling into the trap of appearing to promote teams for their own sake.

The imperative here, returning to our earlier discussion of the basic discipline of teams, is a relentless focus on performance. If management fails to pay persistent attention to the link between teams and performance, the organization becomes convinced that "this year we are doing 'teams.'" Top management can help by instituting processes like pay schemes and training for teams responsive to their real time needs, but more than anything else, top management must make clear and compelling demands on the teams themselves and then pay constant attention to their progress with respect to both team basics and performance results. This means focusing on specific teams and specific performance challenges. Otherwise "performance," like "team," will become a cliché.

TEAMS THAT RUN THINGS

Despite the fact that many leaders refer to the group reporting to them as a team, few groups really are. And groups that become real teams seldom think of themselves as a team because they are so focused on performance results. Yet the opportunity for such teams includes groups from the top of the enterprise down through the divisional or functional level. Whether it is in charge of thousands of people or a handful, as long as the group oversees some business, ongoing program, or significant functional activity, it is a team that runs things.

The main issue these teams face is determining whether a real team approach is the right one. Many groups that run things can be more effective as working groups than as teams. The key judgment is whether the sum of individual bests will suffice for the performance challenge at hand or whether the group must deliver substantial incremental performance requiring real, joint work-products. Although the team option promises greater performance, it also brings more risk, and managers must be brutally honest in assessing the trade-offs.

Members may have to overcome a natural reluctance to trust their fate to others. The price of faking the team approach is high: at best, members get diverted from their individual goals, costs outweighs benefits, and people resent the imposition on their time and priorities; at worst, serious animosities develop that undercut even the potential personal bests of the working-group approach.

Working groups present fewer risks. Effective working groups need little time to shape their purpose since the leader usually establishes it. Meetings are run against well-prioritized agendas. And decisions are implemented through specific individual assignments and accountabilities. Most of the time, therefore, if performance aspirations can be met through individuals doing their respective jobs well, the working-group approach is more comfortable, less risky, and less disruptive than trying for more elusive team performance levels. Indeed, if there is no performance need for the team approach, efforts spent to improve the effectiveness of the working group make much more sense than floundering around trying to become a team.

Having said that, we believe the extra level of performance teams can achieve is becoming critical for a growing number of companies, especially as they move through major changes during which company performance depends on broad-based behavioral change. When top management uses teams to run things, it should make sure the team succeeds in identifying specific purposes and goals.

This is a second major issue for teams that run things. Too often, such teams confuse the broad mission of the total organization with the specific purpose of their small group at the top. The discipline of teams tells us that for a real team to form there must be a *team* purpose that is distinctive and specific to the small group and that requires its members to roll up their sleeves and accomplish something beyond individual end-products. If a group of managers looks only at the economic performance of the part of the organization it runs to assess overall effectiveness, the group will not have any team performance goals of its own.

While the basic discipline of teams does not differ for them, teams at the top are certainly the most difficult. The complexities of long-term challenges, heavy demands on executive time, and the deep-seated individualism of senior people conspire against teams at the top. At the same time, teams at the top are the most powerful. At first we thought such teams were nearly impossible. That is because we were looking at the teams as defined by the formal organizational structure; that is, the leader and all of his or her direct reports equals the team. Then we discovered that real teams at the top were often smaller and less formalized—Whitehead and Weinberg at Goldman, Sachs; Hewlett and Packard at HP; Krasnoff, Pall, and Hardy at Pall Corp; Kendall, Pearson, and Calloway at Pepsi; Haas and Haas at Levi Strauss; Batten and Ridder at Knight-Ridder. They were mostly twos and threes, with an occasional fourth.

Nonetheless, real teams at the top of large, complex organizations are still few and far between. Far too many groups at the top of large corporations needlessly constrain themselves from achieving real team levels of performance because they assume that all direct reports must be on the team; that team goals must be identical to corporate goals; that the team members' positions rather than skills determine their respective roles; that a team must be a team all the time; and that the team leader is above doing real work.

BUILDING TEAM PERFORMANCE

Although there is no guaranteed how-to-recipe for building team performance, we observed, a number of approaches shared by many successful teams.

Establish urgency, demanding performance standards, and direction. All team members need to believe the team has urgent and worthwhile purposes and they want to know what the expectations are. Indeed, the more urgent a and meaningful the rationale, the more likely it is that the team will live up to its performance potential, as was the case for a customer service team that was told that further growth for the entire company would be impossible without major improvements in that area. Teams work best in a compelling context. That is why companies with strong performance ethics usually form teams readily.

Select members for skill and skill potential, not personality. No team succeeds without all the skills needed to meet its purpose and performance goals. Yet most team s figure out the skills they will need after they are formed The wise manager will choose people both for their existing skills and their potential to improve existing skills and learn new ones.

Pay particular attention to first meetings and actions. Initial impressions always mean a great. When potential teams first gather, everyone monitors the signals given by others to confirm, suspend, or dispel assumptions and concerns. They pay particular attention to those in authority: the team leader and any executives who set up, oversee, or otherwise influence the team. And, as always, what such leaders do is more important than what they say. If a senior executive leaves the team kickoff to take a phone call ten minutes after the session has begun and he never returns, people get the message.

Set some clear rules of behavior. All effective teams develop rules of conduct at the outset to help them achieve their purpose and performance goals. The most critical initial rules pertain to attendance (for example, "no interruptions to take phone calls"), discussion ("no sacred cows"), confidentiality ("the only things to leave this room are what we agree on"), analytic approach ("facts are friendly"), end-product orientation ("everyone gets assignments and does them"), constructive confrontation ("no finger pointing"), and, often the most important, contributions ("everyone does real work").

Set and seize upon a few immediate performance-oriented tasks and goals. Most effective teams trace their advancement to key performance-oriented events. Such events can be set in motion by immediately establishing a few challenging goals that can be reached early on. There is no such thing as a real team without performance results, so the sooner such results occur, the sooner the team congeals.

Challenge the group regularly with fresh facts and information. New information causes at team to redefine and enrich its understanding of the performance challenge, thereby helping the team shape a common approach. A plant quality-improvement team knew the cost of poor quality was high, but it wasn't until they researched the different types of defects and put a price tag on each one that they knew where to go next. Conversely, teams err when they assume that all the information needed exists in the collective experience and knowledge of their members.

Spend lots of time together. Common sense tells us that team members must spend a lot of time together, scheduled and unscheduled, especially in the beginning. Indeed, creative insights as well as personal bonding require impromptu and casual interactions just as much as analyzing spreadsheets and interviewing customers. Busy executives and managers too often intentionally minimize the time they spend together. The successful teams we've observed all gave themselves the time to learn to be a team. This time need not always be spent together physically; electronic, fax, and phone time can also count as time spent together.

Exploit the power of positive feedback, recognition, and reward. Positive reinforcement works as well in a team context as elsewhere. "Giving out gold stars" helps to shape new behaviors critical to team performance. If people in the group, for example, are alert to a shy person's initial efforts to speak up and contribute, they can give the honest positive reinforcement that encourages continued contributions. There are many ways to recognize and reward team performance beyond direct compensation, from having a senior executive speak directly to the team about the urgency of its mission to using awards to recognize contributions. Ultimately, however, the satisfaction shared by a team in its own performance becomes the most cherished reward.

As understandable as these assumptions may be, most of them are unwarranted. They do not apply to the teams at the top we have observed, and when replaced with more realistic and flexible assumptions that permit the team discipline to be applied, real team performance at the top can and does occur. Moreover, as more and more companies are confronted with the need to manage major change across their organizations, we will see more real teams at the top.

We believe that teams will become the primary unit of performance in high-performance organizations. But that does not mean that teams will crowd out individual opportunity or formal hierarchy and process. Rather, teams will enhance existing structures without replacing them. A team opportunity exists anywhere hierarchy or organizational boundaries inhibit the skills and perspectives needed for optimal results. Thus, new-product innovation requires preserving functional excellence through structure while eradicating functional bias through teams. And frontline productivity requires preserving direction and guidance through hierarchy while drawing on energy and flexibility through self-managing teams.

We are convinced that every company faces specific performance challenges for which teams are the most practical and powerful vehicle at top management's disposal. The critical role for senior managers, therefore, is to worry about company performance and the kinds of teams that can deliver it. This means that top management must recognize a team's unique potential to deliver results, deploy teams strategically when they are the best tool for the job, and foster the basic discipline of teams that will make them effective. By doing so, top management creates the kind of environment that enables team as well as individual and organizational performance.

INDEX

MASSACHUSETTS INSTITUTE OF TECHNOLOGY

ANCONA, KOCHAN, SCULLY,
VAN MAANEN, WESTNEY

MANAGING FOR THE FUTURE

Organizational Behavior & Processes

WORKFORCE MANAGEMENT:
EMPLOYMENT RELATIONSHIPS
IN CHANGING ORGANIZATIONS

module 7

**WORKFORCE MANAGEMENT: EMPLOYMENT
RELATIONSHIPS IN CHANGING ORGANIZATIONS**

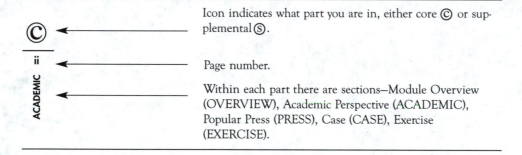

Icon indicates what part you are in, either core Ⓒ or supplemental Ⓢ.

Page number.

Within each part there are sections—Module Overview (OVERVIEW), Academic Perspective (ACADEMIC), Popular Press (PRESS), Case (CASE), Exercise (EXERCISE).

Dedicated to those who have inspired us to try to be better students and teachers. Special dedications to

Professor Jack Barbash
Professor Arthur H. Gladstein
Professor Marius B. Jansen
Professor Joanne Martin
Professor Edgar H. Schein

Acquisitions Editor: John R. Szilagyi
Developmental Editor: Jamie Gleich Bryant
Production Editor: Mardell Toomey
Production House: DPS Associates, Inc.
Cover Design: Michael H. Stratton
Marketing Manager: Rob Bloom

ISBN: 0-538-87694-8

1 2 3 4 5 6 7 D1 4 3 2 1 0 9 8

Printed in the United States of America

South-Western College Publishing
an International Thomson Publishing company IⓉP®

Cincinnati • Albany • Boston • Detroit • Johannesburg • London • Madrid • Melbourne • Mexico City
New York • Pacific Grove • San Francisco • Scottsdale • Singapore • Tokyo • Toronto

CONTENTS

WORKFORCE MANAGEMENT: EMPLOYMENT RELATIONSHIPS IN CHANGING ORGANIZATIONS

Workforce management is a significant part of a manager's job. You can understand its many dimensions by using the three lenses that guide our analysis of organizations. From the strategic design perspective, managers determine where and how employees work, deploy them onto one or more teams, and provide incentives. The workforce is viewed as both a major cost and an increasingly important asset to an organization. The manager must therefore find the right balance between investing in this asset for competitive advantage and controlling labor costs.

But employees are more than commodities—as everyone from Karl Marx to Peter Drucker has stressed. Workers have their own interests. They generally want the firm to succeed and also want a share of that success. Many want a life that balances work with interests outside of work. In deciding how to work, they take into account their labor market alternatives and bring to bear their personal values, experience, and ideas. From a political perspective, then, the manager's job is to find ways of integrating employees' personal interests and aspirations with the needs of the organization to produce "mutual gains." Managers must negotiate equitable compromises when interests or expectations conflict.

As people work together, the organizational culture evolves, gets passed along, and is sometimes changed. From a cultural perspective, therefore, the art of managing the workforce lies in understanding how a given request, decision, or proposal for change will affect the cherished cultural norms that the workforce has created or the particular norms of a subgroup. All these factors determine how loyal, secure, empowered, and motivated employees will feel—and, ultimately, whether a manager can mobilize his or her group to get the work done.

We approach workforce management through the study of the "employment relationship." The employment relationship is the set of practices that govern the exchange between employees and employers. In its simplest form, employees provide effort toward the achievement of employers' goals and receive compensation in return. In more developed forms of the employment relationship, employees may provide loyalty and extra commitment in exchange for lifelong employment and a sense of belonging. Employees may develop special, firm-specific skills and receive a wage premium for remaining with their employer to use and further develop these skills.

Instead of the usual approach, which looks at loyalty and motivation as individual personality traits that a manager works around, this module considers the broader system in which workforce management occurs. Employees' loyalty, commitment, and sense of fairness arise from the structures and incentives that are part of their work world. From a more systemic perspective, we can see how managers have to regard the pieces of workforce management as parts of a larger whole.

This module present historical and international comparative examples. Knowing more about history helps the smart manager to think ahead and see how trends are cyclical. Today's solutions sometimes breed tomorrow's problems. Consider the many corporations that are now scrambling to re-hire and rebuild loyalty in the wake of layoffs that were justified not so long ago as necessary, and final, readjustments in staffing levels. Knowing more about other countries' arrangements helps the smart manager understand that there is no single right policy as determined by technology and markets. Many varieties are on the menu. Managers can try other options more in line with their analyses of the situations, their understanding of the broader implications and possible future ramifications, and their values about which stakeholders must be respected.

The larger context for workforce management is characterized by an ongoing but incomplete transformation from old to new organizational forms. During this transformation, managers face special challenges. They have to create a committed group of employees in the midst of the insecurity caused by layoffs. They have to encourage people to share information and build trust as team members, even as team membership keeps changing in the face of rapidly shifting assignments and downsizing. They have to encourage people with rewards, even as the promise of upward advancement is diminishing, and new lateral moves and broad job titles are still vague and not as highly valued as promotions.

How can you, as a manager, take action in this context? The first step toward wisely guided action is to understand the system in which you work and how its many components go together (or sometimes, contradict one another). You may not be able to change your company's policies, but you can be aware of how they are affecting your employees and your performance. Managers can waste a lot of time on carefully worded memos and work plans, but if they do not understand and address employees' concerns, they will be left puzzled as to why their neat plans are not working. Participation and open discussion go a long way toward helping employees address their concerns. Signaling your awareness of the complexity—rather than papering over the issues with simplistic assurances—is a good start toward building an effective work group. Finally, taking action may sometimes involve pushing back on corporate policies with which you do not agree. You can pick your battles. If you have a broader understanding of the system, you will have better grounds for registering your concerns about negative repercussions and unintended consequences.

If you have read Module 1—or if you read the business press and keep up with the coverage of real, and sometimes exaggerated, trends—you are aware that a new model of employment appears to be emerging to replace the old. While the old was bounded, hierarchical, fixed, homogenous, and local, the new promises to be networked, flat, flexible, diverse, and global. These promises, whether hype or real, affect the way that corporations plan and justify their policies. They shape the context for workforce management.

The following are a few examples of how each of these changing dimensions pose some exciting opportunities that may motivate and empower employees (+), some problems and uncertainties that will make workforce management very difficult (–), and some questions that remain unsolved but that today's manager must understand in order to take well-considered action:

- As organizations move from **bounded to networked**:

  + There will be interesting opportunities for collaboration with new colleagues across boundaries, making work stimulating.
  – But careers will involve a patchwork of jobs in different organizations, with some measure of uncertainty and stress.
  ? How can managers maintain loyalty between employees and companies and between employees and teams as memberships are in flux?

- As organizations move from **hierarchical to flat**:

  + More employees at all levels will have access to decision-critical information and may be involved in projects that were formerly restricted to higher levels.
  – But there will be fewer vertical promotion paths and some confusion about what "career success" means.

? How can managers motivate employees without the traditional promise of promotions (will the promise of more stimulating work become a meaningful reward)?

- As organizations move from **fixed to flexible**:

  + Employees will have a range of ways to organize the time and space in which they work.
  - But it may be difficult to coordinate the efforts of employees working under different arrangements.
  ? How can managers balance flexibility and coordination?

- As organizations move from **homogeneous to diverse**:

  + A range of new approaches to work will be stimulated as new groups are increasingly included.
  - But differences may breed contests between groups over what is fair and who should get what considerations (such as who gets special hours to balance work and family, who gets invited to be in the mentoring program, etc.).
  ? How can managers be responsive to diverse constituencies in ways that respect differences but are also fair and consistent?

- As organizations move from **local to global**:

  + New ways to include multiple stakeholders will be added to the menu (for example, different national approaches to temporary workers or to employer-provided training or to labor/management relations).
  - But the range of choices will make it more challenging to present any one choice as legitimate (for example, it may be hard to argue that temporary workers should not get benefits if they are known to in other countries).
  ? How can managers learn from different global examples?

READINGS AND ASSIGNMENTS

Core Readings

There are three main readings. The first reading, **Managing a Changing Workforce in Turbulent Times**, provides a foundation. It tracks some of the important changes in the employment relationship.

The second reading, **The Changing Social Contract for White-Collar Workers**, addresses what happens as more employees try to redefine themselves as "free agents." The social contract is the moral underpinning of the employment relationship; it is a deep set of assumptions about what is right, reasonable, and fair in the exchange between employees and employers. Lifelong employment was once regarded as "best practice." The dismantling of lifelong employment options is a breach of the social contract. A new social contract has not yet emerged.

The third reading, **A Brave New Darwinian Workplace**, is from *Fortune* magazine. It captures the uncertainty and stress that people are talking about as the lifelong career appears to be in decline. Like many new popular business press articles, it encourages employees to "manage their own careers." Although this article appeared in 1994, it remains relevant today for understanding the long shadow cast by the age of rapid downsizing. Employees will still eye employers—and each other—warily, as they worry about their personal livelihoods. Even as corporations attempt to rehire and a new spate of articles about loyalty is reappearing, it is important to remember the fairly recent history that was part of many employees' experience.

Supplementary Readings

In addition to the readings discussed, there is a supplementary case and some supplementary readings that your instructor might ask you to prepare. The supplementary case is called **The Case of the Part-Time Partner**. The case grapples with some of the issues managers will face with employees' new, flexible arrangements, which create a variety of responses from employees who are affected differently. To prepare this case, consider this scenario:

> Imagine that you are a partner at this firm and you have to vote "yes" or "no" in each partnership decision. Analyze the arguments about the partnership decisions in the case and come to class prepared to defend your votes. A "yes" or "no" vote will be taken at the start of class:
>
> **1.** Would you vote to make Julie partner? Why or why not?
> **2.** Would you vote to make Tim partner? Why or why not?

The first supplementary reading shares a vision of remaining workforce challenges as viewed by Robert B. Reich as he finished his term as United States Secretary of Labor.

The second supplementary reading, "Patterned Chaos in Human Resource Management," suggests that this period of uncertainty and change can also have positive implications if some creative new approaches to work are invented, particularly ones that accommodate work and family balance.

The third supplementary reading, on "The Contingency Work Force," describes trends in using temporary workers. The final supplementary reading, on "Burned-Out Bosses," addresses the stress felt, not only by those who are laid off, but by those who have to deliver the bad news.

ADDITIONAL SUGGESTED READINGS

See the references at the end of the readings, particularly "Managing a Changing Workforce in Turbulent Times." Also consider these readings:

- On background data on the changing workforce, from a widely quoted report commissioned by the United States Department of Labor, which has influenced managers' and policy makers' perceptions and approaches:

  Workforce 2000: Work and Workers for the 21st Century. Indianapolis: Hudson Institute, 1987.

- On analyzing changes in employment, grounded in the empirical evidence about changes in work and the employment relationship:

  Capelli, Peter (with Laurie Bassi, Harry Katz, David Knoke, Paul Osterman, Michael Useem). 1997. *Change at Work*. New York: Oxford University Press.
  Osterman, Paul, ed. 1996. *Broken Ladders*. New York: Oxford University Press.
  Pfeffer, Jeffrey. 1998. *The Human Equation*. Cambridge, MA: Harvard Business School Press.

- On the changing nature of jobs, employment relationships, and work, from two books receiving popular attention:

  Bridges, William. 1994. *Job Shift: How to Prosper in a Workplace Without Jobs*. Wesley, MA: Addison-Wesley.
  Rifkin, Jeremy. 1995. *The End of Work: The Decline of the Global Labor Force and the Dawn of the Post-Market Era*. New York: G.P. Putnam's Sons.

- On several aspects of managing workers, teams, projects, empowerment, fast cycle times, and shifting loyalties in the new organizational form, by two sets of leading academics:

Donnellon, Anne, and Charles Heckscher, eds. 1994. *The Post-Bureaucratic Organization: New Perspectives on Organizational Change.* Newbury Park, CA: Sage.

Galbraith, Jay R. and Edward E. Lawler, eds. 1993. *Organizing for the Future: The New Logic for Managing Complex Organizations.* San Francisco: Jossey-Bass.

- On how one innovative Brazilian company is approaching jobs and subcontracting differently:

Semler, Ricardo. 1993. *Maverick: The Success Story Behind the World's Most Unusual Workplace.* New York: Warner Books.

- On how labor and management can play different kinds of roles in negotiating employment relationships, in different national policy contexts (in the future in the United States, and looking comparatively at Germany):

Kochan, Thomas, and Paul Osterman. 1994. *The Mutual Gains Enterprise: Human Resource Strategies and National Policy.* Cambridge MA: Harvard Business Review Press.

Osterman, Paul. *Making America Work.* New York: Oxford University Press, forthcoming.

Wever, Kirstin S. 1995. *Negotiating Competitiveness: Employment Relations and Organizational Innovation in Germany and the United States.* Boston: Harvard Business School Press.

doctors locate deep veins and arteries. The probe had to have an audible signal through a specified depth of tissue, be capable of being manufactured at a rate of 100 per day, and have a unit cost less than a pre-established amount. Because the team could measure its progress against each of these specific objectives, the team knew throughout the development process where it stood. Either it had achieved its goals or not.

- As Outward Bound and other team-building programs illustrate, specific objectives have a leveling effect conducive to team behavior. When a small group of people challenge themselves to get over a wall or to reduce cycle time by 50%, their respective titles, perks, and other stripes fade into the background. The teams that succeed evaluate what and how each individual can best contribute to the team's goal, and, more important, do so in terms of the performance objective itself rather than a person's status or personality.

- Specific goals allow a team to achieve small wins as it pursues its broader purpose. These small wins are invaluable to building commitment and overcoming the inevitable obstacles that get in the way of a long-term purpose. For example, the Knight-Ridder team mentioned at the outset turned a narrow goal to eliminate errors into a compelling customer-service purpose.

- Performance goals are compelling. They are symbols of accomplishment that motivate and energize. They challenge the people on a team to commit themselves, as a team, to make a difference. Drama, urgency, and a healthy fear of failure combine to drive teams who have their collective eye on an attainable, but challenging, goal. Nobody but the team can make it happen. It is their challenge.

The combination of purpose and specific goals is essential to performance. Each depends on the other to remain relevant and vital. Clear performance goals help a team keep track of progress and hold itself accountable; the broader, even nobler, aspirations in a team's purpose supply both meaning and emotional energy.

Virtually all effective teams we have met, read or heard about, or been members of have ranged between 2 and 25 people. For example, the Burlington Northern "piggybacking" team had 7 members, the Knight-Ridder newspaper team, 14. The majority of them have numbered fewer than 10. Small size is admittedly more of a pragmatic guide than an absolute necessity for success. A large number of people, say 50 or more, can theoretically become a team. But groups of such size are more likely to break into subteams rather than function as a single unit.

Why? Large numbers of people have trouble interacting constructively as a group, much less doing real work together. Ten people are far more likely than fifty are to work through their individual, functional, and hierarchical differences toward a common plan and to hold themselves jointly accountable for the results.

Large groups also face logistical issues, such as finding enough physical space and time to meet. And they confront more complex constraints, like crowd or herd behaviors, which prevent the intense sharing of viewpoints needed to build a team. As a result, when they try to develop a common purpose, they usually produce only superficial "missions" and well-meaning intentions that cannot be translated into concrete objectives. They tend fairly quickly to reach a point when meetings become a chore, a clear sign that most of the people in the group are uncertain why they have gathered, beyond some notion of getting along better. Anyone who has been through one of these exercises knows how frustrating it can be. This kind of failure tends to foster cynicism, which gets in the way of future team efforts.

In addition to finding the right size, teams must develop the right mix of skills, that is, each of the complementary skills necessary to do the team's job. As obvious as it sounds, it is a common failing in potential teams. Skill requirements fall into three fairly self-evident categories:

M-7

core

MANAGING A CHANGING WORKFORCE IN TURBULENT TIMES

Mobility. Empowerment. Teams. Cross-training. Virtual offices. Telecommuting. Reengineering. Restructuring. Delayering. Outsourcing. Contingency. If the buzzwords don't sound familiar, they should: They are changing your life. The last decade, perhaps more than any other time since the advent of mass production, has witnessed a profound redefinition of the way we work (*Business Week*, 1994, p. 86).

OVERVIEW: THE CHANGING EMPLOYMENT RELATIONSHIP

You may have read the buzzwords above. But how do you make sense of them? For employees, are they good news, with their promises of increased flexibility? Or are they bad news, with the lurking threats of downsizing, longer hours, and greater stress? For organizations, are they a carefully considered pathway to effectiveness? Or are they short-sighted fads that could generate as many unintended problems as solutions?

This reading will give you a context for assessing how the employment relationship is changing. The employment relationship is the set of arrangements and work practices that describe and govern the relationship between employee and employer. This relationship runs deeper than an economic arrangement. There is a "social contract" (or "psychological contract") between employees and employers—a shared cultural understanding of what is right, good, and fair about the ongoing exchange. The social contract that had evolved up until the past few years specified a longer term, substantive relationship between employee and employer for their mutual benefit. Employees not only contributed their skills but were often encouraged to bring their whole selves to work, contributing their loyalty, commitment, ingenuity, and extra effort. Employers not only paid a wage, but provided job security, offered additional benefits ranging from health care to on-site child care to substance abuse counseling, and even promoted the image of the company as a big family.

This employment relationship and the social contract that bolstered it are changing. Two very different stories—the good news and the bad news from the employee's perspective—accompany these changes. First, the good news story sings the praises of flexible arrangements that allow employees to balance work and family time better. Images abound of telecommuters sitting on beaches with laptops. Instead of job insecurity, employees are encouraged to look at the bright side and all the new avenues they can pursue when they become free agents managing their own careers. Second, the bad news story points to the harsh realities of downsizing, job insecurity, and the constant hustle for the next assignment or contract. Temporary jobs can be associated with difficult conditions, low pay, and no benefits. Companies once praised for their "best practices" in forging long-term employment relationships have made headlines over the past few years for their "restructuring" and elimination of positions. In some more recent cases, companies that may have gone too far in wielding the axe are trying to hire employees back and cajole loyalty from them again. Books on loyalty are once again popular, reminding us that these trends go in cycles.

Source: From Jack Patterson, "Welcome to the Company That Isn't There," *Business Week*, October 17, 1994. Reprinted by permission of Business Week.

This reading assesses these trends and their implications in four sections:

- **The "Old" Versus "New" Employment Relationship**—looks at four features of work and how they are shifting and considers the challenges accompanying the changes.
- **Flexibility: What Kind, What is Changing, and For Whom?**—considers the different types of flexibility and their positive and negative implications for employers and employees.
- **Putting More Options on the Menu for the New Employment Relationship**—considers alternative approaches to the emerging need for flexibility, including debates about traditional and alternative forms of worker voice and their effects on organizational performance.
- **Attending to Perceived Inconsistencies and Unintended Consequences**—discusses the implications for management during a time of turbulence and change, emphasizing the need to think about the coherence of employment practices and their perceived legitimacy to different constituencies.

THE "OLD" VERSUS "NEW" EMPLOYMENT RELATIONSHIP

As you examine this material, you might ask yourself some questions that have arisen in numerous articles and debates about the changes in employment relations:

- Has the implicit social or psychological contract in employment relationships broken down or changed for the better?
- Have the terms of the exchange between employees and employers shifted to create a new set of "winners" and "losers?"

There is a common historical picture that leads up to the present day debates. From the end of World War II through the 1970s, workers and firms enjoyed a sustained period of shared prosperity, with real wages and personal income rising in tandem with increases in productivity in the American economy. Employee loyalty (especially for white collar, managerial, and professional employees) and long tenure generally were rewarded by increased employment security and a rising level of income. Many employees worked in "internal labor markets" that were characterized by a constellation of features: long-term employment with an employer, internal advancement up a company job ladder, well-defined jobs linked in a progression that defined a career, and individual compensation based on merit, seniority, or some combination thereof. This system was called an "internal labor market," because in general, neither employees nor managers went back to the "open" market to apply or hire for openings above entry level, but instead counted on the promotion of trained, talented people from within. These features worked together as a system, because collectively they made sense and reinforced one another. They were the consistent pieces of a firm's overall human resource strategy (Osterman, 1992).

Since the mid 1970s, however, productivity growth has slowed down, real wages have stagnated for all employees except those at the very top of the occupational and income distribution (senior executives and the highly educated and mobile professionals), and inequality in the income distribution has greatly increased. Restructuring produced a significant number of white collar and managerial layoffs. New jobs were created, but fewer of these new jobs, largely created in the lower half of the income distribution, had wages or benefits equivalent to the higher level jobs that were lost. The phenomenon of "the working poor"—people employed in full-time jobs that do not pay a living wage—jarred with the image of prosperous American employment from preceding decades (Bane and Elliott, 1993). More jobs are now filled by turning to the external market rather than promoting from within, especially in firms facing changing technologies and rapidly changing product markets. Peter Cappelli (1998) describes the new employment relationship as "market mediated" rather than an internal labor market process.

Keep this broad characterization of recent changes in mind as you examine the material in this module. Ask yourself: What do employees and managers need to do to adjust to these changes? How might we redefine the social contract in ways that are responsive to the current environment? Can we define a legitimate, new social contract that is successful in doing what a social contract is expected to do: to meet "the broad expectations and obligations that employees, employers, and society have for work and employment relationships?"

In the following paragraphs, you will read about four features of the employment relationship that are changing to greater and lesser degrees. Many of the "old" features of work were once taken for granted.

Because the old set of features functioned as a system, it is difficult to change particular features in a piecemeal fashion. However, piecemeal change typically occurs in a time of transition. As some features change more rapidly and others more slowly, contradictions and inconsistencies may appear that make managing more difficult, as discussed in the final section.

Employment Security: Long Term Versus Short Term

From the 1950s to the 1970s, many employees and employers in the United States expected the employment relationship to be long term. They enjoyed employment security, while the company gained the benefits of the "firm-specific skills" their employees acquired. Of course, there were always jobs in the "periphery" of the economy, jobs that were disproportionately held by women and racial minorities and that offered low wages and no security nor advancement opportunities. Despite these counterexamples, the dominant model that infused the management press was that of the long-term employment relationship. "The images that best characterize the American corporation as an employer in the 1950s are ones of stability and uniformity, shared gains among multiple stakeholders, and world model" (Kochan, 1994).

The 1980s brought a change in this "implicit contract" between employees and employers. Large companies long known for lifelong careers and promises of employment security began to lay off employees. For example, IBM, once 406,000 employees strong, cut some 170,000 employees from 1986 to 1994. In recent years, companies with household names such as Xerox, AT&T, Boeing, Chase Manhattan/Chemical Bank, and others all announced large-scale layoffs as part of restructuring processes despite the fact that each of these firms was earning profits at the time. Each firm was also hiring new employees at the same time it was displacing others. In fact, during this same time, the U.S. economy was viewed world-wide for its ability to create new jobs at a high rate—outstripping the job losses experienced in these organizational downswings and restructuring.

There were a number of forces and rationales that drove these changes in the United States, including:

- International competition prompted companies to look for areas of "excess."
- Changing technologies were producing demand for employees with new skills.
- Companies found it easier to hire workers on the external labor market with the skills needed for the current technologies and markets than to retrain employees whose skills had become outmoded.
- The wage bill often appeared to be the obvious choice to slash first.
- It was time to get rid of "dead wood"—whether because some employees were regarded as complacent in the face of lifelong employment or because longer-term employees, with more skills and more deferred compensation due to them, were more expensive.
- Competition over quality and faster cycle time prompted companies to find ways to "do more with fewer people."
- The power of unions declined, making it difficult for employees to exercise a collective voice and bargain for employment security.

- Companies began to find it more economically appealing and socially legitimate to use subcontractors and temporary workers, whether by hiring cheaper labor through temporary agencies domestically or sourcing work abroad to areas where labor was cheaper.

The increase in anxiety over job security is happening around the globe. European workers have experienced a decade of unemployment averaging ten percent or more. New markets have opened in some countries, like Mexico and India, which produce new jobs in new industries but are accompanied by precariousness and restructuring from instability in currencies and elimination of jobs in industries previously protected by import restrictions or state subsidies. In Japan, long considered the paragon of lifetime employment, this institution is being reconsidered in the wake of prolonged economic stagnation. In early 1998, for the first time since Japan recovered from the effects of World War II, unemployment rose to above 3 percent—a number that was important symbolically as well as substantively in Japanese society. The deep financial crises that hit South Korea, Indonesia, Thailand, and other developing Asian countries in 1998 forced a number of multinational firms to close facilities or scale back investment plans, and forced many local firms to likewise abandon long-standing employment security practices.

The "old" employment relationship was sometimes criticized as too paternalistic. Perhaps the new employment relationship corrects this tendency to an extreme. Employees have been empowered and are now expected to shoulder the responsibility for their own employment. The phrase "lifetime employment" (provided by the employer) has been replaced by the phrase "lifetime employability" (traits that are supposed to be polished continuously by the employee). One of the questions that remains is whether employers will provide training to help employees stay current, continue to learn new skills, and remain employable. New arrangements that form the overall system that bolsters the new employment relationship are still evolving.

Advancement: Climbing the Ladder Versus Moving in Circles

Traditionally, employees spent a career advancing within a company, a classic feature of the bureaucracy. Many large companies were "tall," with 10 to 30 levels in the bureaucracy. These levels were designed to correspond to the way a task must be broken down into a "means-ends chain" in order for complex work to get done. For example, people at level 8 passed their information and results up to people at level 9, who collected it and passed it with additional information up to people at level 10. The people at level 10 made decisions and passed commands back down the chain. This bureaucratic method of working was taken for granted.

The "flattening" of job ladders has removed the numerous levels of approval that are now seen as slowing down decision-making in an era where faster turnaround is needed. At the same time, flattening of the hierarchy has resulted in fewer—or a very different type of—advancement opportunities for those employees who remain with an employer. Lateral advancement or advancement up the levels of a skill set relevant to one's own job (often called pay-for-skills plans) are common substitutes. The expectation of a promotion every few years has changed radically. This promise of promotions may have been part of the "psychological contract" between employers and employees in the "old" employment relationship. Thus, flattening of the organization may be greeted with ambivalence. On the one hand, employees may enjoy greater decision-making authority. On the other hand, there are fewer opportunities for promotion, ironically just at a time when employees are shouldering more of the responsibilities that used to signal readiness for promotion.

Job Titles: Fixed and Bounded Versus Changing and Multi-Dimensional

The prototypical organizational chart contained boxes with distinct job titles and showed the reporting links among jobs. The new division of labor in organizations may defy a two-dimensional chart. Tasks and relationships connect in every which way to form a complex web. A number of features of the new employment relationship are breaking the boundaries of the old job.

First, individual jobs are increasingly defined as "multi-skilled." Employees are encouraged to "cross train" and learn a variety of tasks, in order to "job rotate." Job rotation provides flexibility in that the same group of people, if they are multi-skilled, can be employed in a number of different configurations to accomplish a number of different tasks. While some employees express enthusiasm at the prospect of making their jobs more interesting by learning new tasks, others express ambivalence, fearing that job rotation can also be a path to layoffs, lost overtime, or greater stress (Scully and Preuss, 1994). Ideally, multi-skilling makes a workforce more productive, and increased productivity allows the creation of jobs with more reasonable hours, as a result of working smarter. The scenario that many fear is that, instead, many people will be laid off and those who remain must work harder, faster, and longer at a more complex chain of tasks.

Second, the once distinct job is changing as more companies use teamwork. Individuals may be pulled onto multiple teams, bringing a variety of skills to each. Reporting relationships become blurry, because employees may be accountable to a team leader and to their home function at once. Rather than progressing up a ladder of linked jobs, employees may rotate laterally into different jobs and teams. Lateral promotions and multi-skilling may be elements that go together in a new system of employment.

Third, the very notion of a job itself, as a discrete bundle of tasks, is being questioned:

> The job is a social artifact, though it is so deeply embedded in our consciousness that most of us have forgotten its artificiality or the fact that most societies since the beginning of time have done just fine without jobs. The job is an idea that emerged early in the 19th century to package the work that needed doing in the growing factories and bureaucracies of the industrializing nations. Before people had jobs, they worked just as hard but on shifting clusters of tasks, in a variety of locations, on a schedule set by the sun and the weather and the needs of the day. The modern job was a startling new idea—and to many, an unpleasant and perhaps socially dangerous one. Critics claimed it was an unnatural and even inhuman way to work. They believed that most people wouldn't be able to live with its demands. It is ironic that what started as a controversial concept ended up becoming the ultimate orthodoxy—and that we're hooked on jobs (Bridges, 1994).

The changes posed today include reconceptualizing work as a set of tasks that can be clustered and bundled in many different ways, accomplished across many different combinations of people, in many different space and time locations. These changes perhaps seem just as radical and risky today as did the introduction of the job. Like most changes, they hold both promises and threats—work could become more interesting but livelihoods could become more precarious. Changes like these do not happen in a vacuum and must be supported by other related changes in employment and social systems. For example, unemployment insurance might be provided, not just for people who are not working at all, but for people who are working fewer hours while they are in between assignments or seeking their place within another web of tasks. Changes in compensation and the distribution of wealth may be the most difficult of the many pieces of the employment relationship to change, but nonetheless one of the most crucial for bringing about the transition from old to new.

Compensation: Individualistic Versus Team-Oriented

The "old" employment system was shaped from the 1920s to the 1950s by the New Deal legislation, which created minimum employment standards, including minimum wages, and by the democratic exercise of voice by unions representing employees in collective bargaining. These factors essentially "took wages out of competition." Employers did not try to compete by cutting wages. Pay was administered inside the

internal labor market. Pay levels were matched to grades in the hierarchy and/or to levels of seniority.

In this system, a fair amount of attention was focused on getting promoted, which was an important part of the reward system. Individual performance evaluations were typically conducted annually for employees in stable internal labor markets. These were used to determine annual pay raises and to assess promotion candidates. The performance evaluation system was designed to provide rationality and legitimacy to the reward system. Numerous studies have been conducted to determine whether performance evaluation practices were, in fact, accurate and whether employees believed they were fair (summarized by the National Research Council [1991]). The evidence taken together suggests that individualistic performance measures have had only mixed success. Moreover, they may generate employee skepticism about their fairness and legitimacy (Scully, 1993), a tendency to fix the wrong parts of the system (Deming, 1986), and an inclination to grub for rewards rather than love the work intrinsically (Kohn, 1993).

The merits of this type of reward system may be debated by researchers, managers, and employees, but participants had some idea of what the intention of the design was. This approach to rewards fit with the system of other characteristics described above: long-term employment, promotion ladders, and individual job titles. As these other features change, the reward system should change with them. However, the dismantling of the old system may leave a vacuum of legitimacy, as employees who based their careers and aspirations around the old system are left skeptical about whether to trust a new system.

Furthermore, alternative systems have proved very difficult to conceptualize and implement. Many managers now can see that individualistic rewards are not well-matched with the values emphasized by teamwork. But individualistic competition for advancement is a deeply rooted value in the United States. From a cultural perspective, it is easy to find language and symbols that celebrate individual status attainment: the Horatio Alger stories of "rags to riches," testimonials from influential executives that "I started on the shop floor," and the general belief that "you can get what you want if you work hard."

Some of the new pay systems that are getting attention in the 1990s are, in many ways, a continuation of an individualistic approach to rewards. Some approaches try to "bring wages back into competition" by tying individual pay more closely to the market and to the contribution to the bottom line. Examples of this approach include "pay for contribution" and employee stock option programs. In both cases, there is a desire to make a link between individual effort and corporate performance, but such a link is difficult to measure and demonstrate. Another new approach is "pay for skills" or "pay for knowledge," where employees receive pay increases for increasing their skills, for example, through a series of courses taken on or off the job. This approach fits with other features of the new employment relationship in that it de-emphasizes advancement up a job ladder and substitutes advancement within a broadly classified job with multiple layers of skills. However, it retains a focus on individual pay.

Other alternatives shift the locus of reward from the individual to the team. Companies are experimenting with several kinds of team-based reward systems. A nod to teamwork is made when individual evaluations include an indication of whether the person is a good team player and has contributed to teams. This system is still essentially individualistic. Peer evaluations are sometimes used within teams, although these can do more to damage than heighten team-spiritedness. Sometimes teams are encouraged to compete against each other for a team level reward. This practice may simply raise the competitive spirit from the individual to the team level, hampering cooperation and coordination across teams. The tough problem of how to divide a team reward among team members remains, with potential disputes over whether to divide the reward into equal shares or try to find an algorithm for dividing it proportionally to contribution. The problem of how to measure contribution reappears—is it the time spent on the team project? the effort exerted? the quality of ideas contributed? the technical value of the skills? the process and facilitation skills that kept the team together?

It is easy to critique the various team reward schemes that have been devised so far. The problem with many of them is that they are only a small increment removed from individualistic rewards and may keep an organization locked in the old bureaucratic mode of working (Donnellon and Scully, 1994). While it may be important to retain some elements of individualistic motivation and reward within a team context, it is also important to find types of rewards that fit better into the new employment relationship. The new reward system may have to take into account not just how rewards are divided within and between teams, but also how work and livelihood are coupled, how the surplus generated by increased productivity should be shared by the many potential contributors to it, and how the gap between the most and least well off is affected. This level of thinking about compensation requires a deeper understanding of what we mean by flexibility and an ability to consider more approaches on the menu of choices, issues taken up in the following sections.

Assessing the Performance Effects of the New System

The old set of features described above made sense as a system. The new features, when taken together and functioning cohesively, are sometimes referred to as the "high performance work system." Firms struggling to achieve a high performance work system and its benefits seek to get all the pieces in place in a way that produces mutually beneficial results for employers and employees.

The increased uncertainty in white collar work and rise of flexible employment coincided with equally important shifts in the employment practices governing many hourly workers. The same competitive pressures and need for flexibility drove companies in industries as diverse as apparel, autos, steel, office products, semiconductors, and telecommunications to change their internal labor market systems from ones focused on individual job descriptions, wage rates, limited discretion, tight supervision, and complex work rules to systems that emphasize flexible job assignments, pay-for-skills, team forms of work organization, and employee involvement in problem solving and performance improvement efforts. Because these are aimed at improving firm performance, and because they work best when implemented as a package, they are often referred to as "high performance work systems." The evidence is quite strong that when implemented together in a systemic way, these workplace changes outperform more traditional work systems, producing significantly higher quality, productivity, and profitability (Ichniowski, et al., 1996). Not surprisingly, these practices spread steadily in the 1990s, especially in those industries and firms facing increased competitive pressures to upgrade the quality of their products and services.

FLEXIBILITY: WHAT KIND, WHAT IS CHANGING, AND FOR WHOM?

The demand for flexibility in work arrangements is often traced to the entrance of women into the paid workforce in increasing numbers (the contribution of women's unpaid work at home to national productivity is a separate issue). In 1950, 32 percent of women were in the labor force compared to 58 percent in 1993 (Kochan, 1994). The latest data show significant changes in the sex and race composition of the U.S. workforce.

The table that follows shows some data from the *Workforce 2000* report commissioned by the United States Department of Labor. These data are widely quoted (and sometimes technically misinterpreted). What they show, as discussed clearly by DiTomaso (1993), is the composition of the "net additions" to the labor force (note that "net additions" are distinct from the overall composition). The net additions are markedly more diverse and contribute to a labor force that will look different in the year 2000 and beyond. These data have received a lot of attention by corporations, particu-

TABLE 7.1 CHANGES IN THE DISTRIBUTION OF THE U.S. LABOR FORCE BY SUBGROUP, 1994 TO 2005 (NUMBER IN THOUSANDS, PERCENT IN PARENTHESES)

Labor Force Subgroup	1994	New Entrants	Leavers	2005	Net Additions	Change in %
Non-Hispanic White Men	54,306 (41.4)	12,937 (32.9)	10,814 (46.4)	56,429 (38.4)	2,123 (13.2)	–3.0
Non-Hispanic White Women	46,157 (35.2)	13,122 (33.4)	7,363 (31.6)	51,916 (35.3)	5,759 (35.9)	0.1
Non-Hispanic African American Men	6,981 (5.3)	2,314 (5.9)	1,512 (6.5)	7,783 (5.3)	802 (5.0)	0.0
Non-Hispanic African American Women	7,323 (5.6)	2,557 (6.5)	1,271 (5.5)	8,609 (5.9)	1,286 (8.0)	0.3
Hispanic Men	7,210 (5.5)	3,321 (8.4)	1,039 (4.5)	9,492 (6.5)	2,282 (14.2)	1.0
Hispanic Women	4,764 (3.6)	2,765 (7.0)	690 (3.0)	6,838 (4.6)	2,074 (12.9)	1.0
Asian and Other Men	2,317 (1.8)	1,148 (2.9)	326 (1.4)	3,139 (2.1)	822 (5.1)	0.3
Asian and Other Women	1,994 (1.5)	1,180 (3.0)	274 (1.2)	2,900 (2.0)	906 (5.6)	0.5
Totals	**131,051 (99.9)**	**39,343 (100)**	**23,289 (100.1)**	**147,106 (100.1)**	**16,054 (99.9)**	**0.0 ***

* Does not add up to zero due to rounding error.

Source: From Judith Friedman and Nancy DiTomaso, "Myths About Diversity; What Managers Need to Know About Changes in the U.S. Labor Force." Copyright © 1996, by The Regents of the University of California. Reprinted from the *California Management Review*, Vol. 38, No. 4. By permission of the Regents.

larly those that are creating diversity programs so that they will be able to hire and retain employees from a more diverse group and not face a crisis or shortage of labor. The *Workforce 2000* report is often referenced in the opening passages of a corporate diversity strategy to strengthen the case for implementing such a strategy.

Much attention has been given to the increasing numbers of women entering the workforce. At the same time, it is important to remember that women have been in the workforce for a long time (32% in 1950, as cited above) and have long faced issues of balancing work and family. Women of color in particular have had a long history of workforce participation, in disproportionately greater numbers than white women. There is much to be learned from their experiences of balancing work and family before there was a broader societal dialogue and some corporate support for the issue.

It is interesting, though not surprising, that it is the rise of white, middle class women into higher positions in organizations that has prompted new dialogues about ways to balance work and family. These women may have had somewhat more capacity to bargain for new conditions of work, even though it is risky to raise the issue or deviate from career norms. The dialogue has gradually expanded from "just a women's issue" to include fathers' taking leave, "parental leave time" more generally, leave time for adopting children, and flexible time arrangements for caring for elderly parents or ill family members.

And the dialogue continues to expand to include all employees, whether parents or not, who want to be able to pursue meaningful leisure time activities and not be tied to their work lives for long hours. For example, community involvement, hobbies, volunteer work, and political work are all at the heart of a well-functioning democratic community, but require time.

Though this need for flexibility is increasingly well articulated, the capacity of employees to lobby for changes is low, because so many people are worried about simply keeping the jobs they have, under whatever conditions. This section examines the different types of flexibility that are gaining attention and considers what types of changes in what aspects of work are actually involved. This section also considers the positive and negative sides of flexibility in terms of quality of work life and asks about the differential benefits of flexibility for more and less powerful stakeholders.

The Positive Side of Flexibility: Choices, Balance, Varied Work

It is important to understand what features of employment are being made flexible in each of the various trends that appear under the umbrella of "flexibility." Analyzing the different types of flexible arrangements in this way is helpful for understanding just what and how much is changing. Some kinds of flexibility will pose greater challenges to workplaces and managers than to others. Very often the types of flexibility are considered as one batch, as the quote at the beginning of this reading suggests. The types of flexibility that are included here as the "positive" side of flexibility for employees are sorted into several types: flexible space, flexible time and allocation of tasks, and flexible career paths.

Flexible Space. Telecommuting allows employees to work at home, at distant sites, or on the road. Usually these employees are linked electronically to the main site by computer modem and fax machine and are often expected to be available at certain regular hours or to report to work in person at specified times. They may do the same job, and even work longer hours, just in a different place. Systems for ensuring their accountability are evolving. They range from those based on strict monitoring to those based on high trust.

One corporate approach to reducing costs is to weaken employees' link to one physical space and establish a "virtual office." The number of square feet maintained per employee is an indicator receiving greater attention and may be decreasing. A virtual office is like a hotel, where employees check in at fixed times when a certain cubicle is theirs and a "concierge" helps put the right files into cubicles for that day's occupant. Flexible space will have to fit with other elements of the new employment system; for example, employees will need to work effectively as teams over electronic links, and learn when face-to-face contact needs to be scheduled.

Flexible Time and Allocation of Tasks. In its simplest form, flexibility in the hours of work came in the form of "flex time," where employees had some choice in their start and end times. The basic nature of the job was unchanged. Part-time work and job sharing involve different partitioning of work. Part-time work may involve a schedule that is reduced on a weekly basis (e.g., five half days or three full days) or an annual basis (seasonal employment). Job sharing involves two employees sharing the responsibilities that were typically associated with one job description, devising ways to communicate across their roles.

As the preceding section suggests, the very notion of what set of tasks constitutes "the job" is being reconsidered. Discussions of flexible time and tasks have evolved from "flex time" to much more fundamental questions about work. Thinking about the flexibility of time and tasks now involves more than thinking about how to carve up traditional 40 hour jobs into different start and end times or into two 20 hour jobs. The promise of technology used to be that it would reduce the working week to about 30 hours and generate more time for leisure pursuits. Instead, the number of hours of work is increasing, not just for individuals, but also for family units that have more than one person employed for pay. As long as jobs are conceptualized as 40—or more—hours per week, there may continue to be an imbalance between people who are overworked and stressed out, on the one hand, and people who are underemployed and unable to

generate a sufficient salary from 30 hours or fewer of work, on the other hand. Again, from a holistic perspective, reducing the number of hours of work will require thinking concomitantly about a variety of changes, such as changes in pay systems to provide sufficient wages and benefits for employees who work fewer or more highly variable hours.

Flexible Career Paths. Career paths in the "old" employment relationship were more linear—employees climbed a job ladder with a company. Of course, a political perspective on organizations reveals that, in fact, successful employees often skipped levels, jumped between ladders, and engaged in political maneuvers to enhance their career prospects. The logic and the cultural language of "ladders" prevailed.

New approaches to career paths are being discussed with the entrance of more women into organizations. The old career path does not coincide well with up-and-down demands of balancing work and family over a lifetime. Often the period of "proving oneself" occurs in an employee's thirties, particularly in up-or-out promotion systems such as law firms, public accounting firms, and universities. Women with advanced degrees often begin families in their thirties, making this a bad time to be subjected to demands and evaluations at work that will have ramifications for years to follow. Increasingly, men are also seeking ways to get the parenting and workplace clocks in better synchrony. There are few models for achieving this, but new language to describe roller coaster, rather than linear, career paths is emerging (Bailyn, 1993). Employees might alternate periods of more intense workplace commitment while family demands are lower with periods of less intense workplace commitment while family demands are higher. The issue for employers is to figure out how to retain employees through cycles when they have other demands and then get them back on track to contribute their skills (rather than derail them permanently onto a separate "mommy track") and how to do this in ongoing cycles across a career. Employees who work on teams may need to learn to cover each other during leaves, capacities that will be enhanced as "multi-skilling" and "job rotation" develop. As careers begin to span multiple companies, rather than involving a long term relationship with a single employer, the shaping of these new career paths will be increasingly challenging.

The Negative Side of Flexibility: Uncertainty, Anxiety, Lowered Morale
As noted above, it is important to understand what features of the employment relationship are being made flexible, how much of a change this flexibility actually represents, and what the implications are for different parties.

Flexible Workforce Size and Firm Boundaries. The so-called "virtual" corporation is one where multiple activities are spun off to subcontractors, an arrangement that might at once allow flexible adaptability to changing market conditions and create tenuous employment relationships. These relationships cause anxiety and are prompting people to ask normative questions about the severing of the bond between employer and employee, as in the passage below from *Business Week*:

> In computerese, a virtual disk exists only in the computer's memory; when the computer is turned off, the virtual disk is obliterated. By analogy, I suppose, people who work for the new virtual corporations can be called virtual employees. What happens to these people when the power is turned off and their virtual employer disappears? Do they vanish along with the electrons? Are they put together again somewhere when some chief executive loads another virtual corporation into memory? (Patterson, 1994, p. 86)

The 1990s brought greater attention to the use of temporary workers as a way to keep firm size elastic. Manpower, Inc., which not only provides temporary workers to large firms but also carefully screens and sometimes trains them, became one of the largest employers in the United States, with some 600,000 workers on its rolls in the mid-1990s. Combined with downsizing, the use of temporary workers changed the size and boundaries of many firms. As Jeffrey Pfeffer notes in his book *The Human Equation*

(1998) on the consequences of downsizing: "The two decisions considered here—where to draw the organization's boundaries or how much temporary help and contract employment to use and what kind of implicit or explicit agreement about the continuity of employment to offer to the firm's people—are two of the most basic, important, and fundamental choices organizations make."

The espoused appeal of temporary employees for companies is that they can expand and contract the size of their workforce as changes in demand and technologies dictate. There have been some cases that received a lot of publicity where large employers laid off their permanent employees, claiming that changing markets and competitive measures reduced their need for a large workforce, only to rehire almost the same number of employees through temporary agencies. Some so-called "temporary" workers remain with an employer for years. These cases highlight the fact that a principal motive of employers for flexing the number of permanent employees may be the savings in wages and benefits.

The hidden costs of downsizing include loss of employee loyalty and commitment, which are increasingly important if teamwork and shared decision-making are to be implemented effectively, the loss of "firm specific skills" that permanent employees develop over a longer term relationship, and the stresses and damaged working relationships experienced by managers who have to announce layoffs and select who will be laid off.

As Pfeffer (1998) notes:

> The question is not just what people cost, but what they do and what value they create for the organization. The question for managers is whether they will be swept up in the fads and rhetoric of the moment or will recognize some basic principles of management and the data consistent with them. As Peter Hartz, the senior personnel executive at Volkswagen reminds us, the competitive environment defines the requirements, but each company can define the solutions. In fact, that is precisely the job of leadership—to craft creative responses to competitive conditions that build competence, capability, and commitment in people, not to do things that destroy organizational memory, wisdom, and loyalty.

Who Benefits from Flexibility?

Clearly, there are different types of flexibility that have different costs and benefits. It is important to think about which stakeholders will gain or lose. If a proposed kind of flexibility appears threatening to a constituency, a whole array of proposed changes may be met with unexpected resistance.

Some kinds of flexibility are supposed to benefit the customer. Flexibility may increase turnaround time and get resolutions to problems more quickly. On the other hand, flexible task assignments and job rotation may make it difficult for customers to know whom to call for assistance.

Some kinds of flexibility may benefit highly educated employees but not others. For example, some telecommuting, part-time, or family leave arrangements are available to employees who have skills that are perceived to be more crucial to the organization. Employers may be willing to give these employees special arrangements in order to retain them. Increased flexibility may become a new type of reward.

However, employees not eligible for these special arrangements may be resentful. The emerging employment relationship could create a situation where work arrangements are wonderful for a few and tenuous, insecure, and essentially inflexible for many. The occupations that grew the most rapidly from 1975 to 1990 were at both ends of the wage continuum: highly paid executive, managerial, and technical positions on one end and low wage service jobs at the other. Temporary work for these two groups may have very different faces: autonomous consulting from the Rocky Mountains versus precarious positions at the edge of the poverty line in urban areas.

Putting More Options on the Menu for the New Employment Relationship

The weakening of the employee/employer bond was only one solution to the competitive, technological, and social pressures facing companies in the United States. It is

important to bear in mind that this response was but one choice from a menu of possible responses. Sometimes, both the research literature and the business press convey a sense that the current changes in the employment relationship, such as downsizing and the increasing use of temporary employees, are an inevitable and unfortunate new development, rather than a choice. These developments are portrayed as the necessary outcome of market and technological changes, such as faster cycle time and an increasing demand for high quality standards. However, one could imagine, for example, that the increased demand for quality could result in the hiring of more workers and an increased reliance upon employee loyalty to a single firm.

Downsizing is sometimes bemoaned as the unfortunate but inevitable outcome of market and technological changes. However, it has not proven to be a panacea for companies. In a 1993 Conference Board survey of human resource executives, many reported lowered morale among layoff "survivors" and greater need for training as costly and sometimes unanticipated consequences of downsizing. "An American Management Association (AMA) survey of companies that had made 'major staff cuts' between 1987 and 1992 found that, despite the reduced labor costs, less than half improved their operating earnings—while one in four saw earnings drop. More ominously, said the AMA's report, 'these figures were even worse for companies that undertook a second or third round of downsizing.' Many companies that fail to get their expected results with the first round of cuts simply repeat the process" (Bridges, 1994, p. 64).[1]

It is difficult to discern the causal relationship between downsizing and poor performance, but this cycle of crises and cuts may be an example of the kind of negative feedback loop that systems dynamics theorists warn companies about. Given the complexity of restructuring, it makes sense to look for other solutions, rather than simply to make cuts. Ideas for other solutions may come not just from abroad but from a deeper analysis and understanding of what exactly is changing, what is at stake and for whom, and how a new system of arrangements will hold together in a fashion that makes sense. Some new arrangements for companies include reduced hours as a way to share productivity gains, redistribution of pay ranges across types of jobs, more ongoing training and creation of trainer positions, or assistance to employees in spinning off new ventures and becoming suppliers. Other new arrangements will be crafted at the policy level, to provide new incentives and supports for many companies to innovate.

Human Assets and Organizational Forms

Since labor costs are normally the largest variable cost in most firms, employees are traditionally viewed as a cost that needs to be tightly controlled. This is one reason why staff cuts or "headcount" reduction is often used as a short term tactic for cost reduction. But human resources are also an important asset in many firms, particularly those in which employee knowledge is a critical competitive resource. In consulting, law, and other professional service firms, for example, employees who leave take significant portions of the firm's assets (their knowledge and sometimes their clients) with them. The organizational forms adopted in these situations often reflect this risk by creating partnerships in which crucial employees share in the ownership, profits, and governance processes of the firm. We might wonder, therefore, if other organizations will begin to take on more of these features as knowledge becomes a more important strategic asset (Blair, 1993). The organization of the future may therefore need to find new ways to bind these critical knowledge workers to the firm or risk losing significant capital.

Global Comparisons

One of the best ways to understand what other choices exist is to think globally and look at the responses of a variety of industrialized nations. Faced with the same international

---

[1]From William Bridges, "The End of the Job." Reprinted from the September 19, 1994 issue of *Fortune* by special permission; copyright 1994, Time Inc.p

and technological pressures, for example, Japan and Germany have made different choices. These countries have different institutional arrangements, which embed different historical choices and shape different approaches to similar challenges. Both countries have emphasized and maintained longer term employment relationships. When this relationship is threatened, their alternative approaches include maintaining a greater number of employees and having them work shorter hours (an example of one kind of flexibility discussed above), and at a societal level, providing unemployment insurance (one approach to the sweeping sense of anxiety over unstable employment).

For example, one of the questions raised above was whether employers will provide ongoing training for employees, particularly if they will not have a long-term relationship with these employees. Ideas for alternative approaches to training may come from countries such as Germany, which has an elaborate apprentice system that provides the highly skilled technicians that will be in increasing demand with new technologies. As another example, the language of business in the United States has tended to emphasize maximizing shareholder value. In contrast, in Japan, the company is conceived as a coalition of multiple "stakeholders"—shareholders and employees—with managers acting as mediating agents to maximize the return for all. A new view of the "mutual gains enterprise" that involves both labor and management has been proposed for the United States (Kochan and Osterman, 1994). These different conceptions of the corporation and its mission prompt decision-makers to put different types of alternatives on the menu.

Past and Future Models of Employee Representation

Consider one final challenge for managing the workforce of the future. One of the biggest labor market developments of recent years has been the decline in union representation. In the United States unions declined from their peak of representing about 35 percent of the private sector labor force in the mid 1950s to representing about 10 percent of private sector workers (14.5 percent of all private and public sector workers) in 1998. This trend, while less dramatic in magnitude, is visible in most other highly industrialized countries around the world. Britain, Japan, Australia, and even some of the European countries with strong labor-social democratic traditions such as Sweden experienced significant declines in union membership in the 1980s and 1990s (International Labor Organization, 1997).

Are we witnessing the end of unionism? Will unions rebound in response to the anxieties many workers are experiencing today? Or, will new organizations emphasizing new strategies arise to provide workers with a voice on their jobs and the assistance needed to move across firms as job opportunities come and go? These questions are difficult to answer. However, history teaches us that no democratic country has existed for long periods of time without some significant independent force advocating and representing employee interests. Perhaps the next century will witness the creation of new organizational forms for representing employees that are better matched to the nature of the new economy, the new organization, and the contemporary workforce. If so, one important question will be how will—and how should—managers react to these organizations? Should they resist and undermine them? Share power with them? Attempt to work with them and shape them in ways that fit the needs of employees and the organization? These will be questions managers of the future are likely to encounter. For this reason we include as the next reading an essay by Charles Heckscher speculating about these issues.

ATTENDING TO PERCEIVED INCONSISTENCIES AND UNINTENDED CONSEQUENCES

Managers need to keep in mind how the policies they are implementing hold together. If employees perceive inconsistencies, they may well become cynical or accuse management of hypocrisy. For example, a group of employees may take a training course on teamwork that emphasizes the importance of group loyalty and trust. Later that week, they may receive a memo about impending layoffs. Both of these trends—the encouragement of teamwork and the justification of layoffs—are occurring simultaneously. Often, they are considered separately, but taken together, they reveal how inconsistencies cause tensions.

Managers also need to keep in mind unintended consequences. The threat of layoffs may make employees quite half-hearted about their team membership. Perhaps teamwork was supposed to help the company revive its flagging quality. If team members are skeptical about getting involved when their futures are insecure, they may not produce the hoped-for results, which may result in a corporate decision to resort to more layoffs. The result is a dysfunctional dynamic.

Indeed, as labor markets tighten (as they have in the late 1990s in the face of unemployment rates that fell below 5 percent for the first time in over twenty years) for professionals and technical workers with scarce skills, many employers have experienced difficulty in attracting and retaining employees and rebuilding employee loyalty and commitment. One member of a group of engineers described this process in a classroom discussion as follows:

> Companies are now paying for their past sins. They showed no loyalty to us and so now we have to take care of ourselves and move to where we get the best offers. Today the most talented people in our companies can do this without even uprooting their families and so they ask themselves: Why would I stay here?

It is in this context that the management of today's workforce takes place—a context in which the loyalty and commitment of both firms and employees to each other has been weakened by the memory of past and recurring downsizings and restructurings.

Clearly, managing transitions requires some new habits of mind. What are some steps to taking this new approach? Several ways to broaden the range of factors that are brought into consideration include:

- Bringing multiple stakeholders with different perspectives into the change process (such as including people who are *and* are not likely to take parental leave so that issues of fairness are considered before they threaten a program)
- Not delegating one person to make only one dimension of change without broader consultation (it is too easy to become narrowly focused and believe one has optimized one's own small piece of the pie)
- Recalling examples of failed and successful change efforts from the organization's past (organizations tend to have short memories but can sometimes learn from the past)
- Drawing upon examples from other companies (designating someone to "scout" outside the organization)

SUMMARY

This reading has focused on the issues that arise in managing employees during a time of transition and increasing flexibility and uncertainty. It has highlighted some of the potential advantages and disadvantages of flexibility from the perspectives of varied constituencies of employees. The impact on employees should be of concern to you as a manager, because successful performance is affected by employee recruitment, retention, motivation, and, in particular, the willing contribution of effort and skill where self-managing and shared decision-making are increasingly important.

There is enthusiasm in the business press for flexible and virtual organizations because they can enhance the focus on "core competencies" and allow the organization to adapt quickly to a changing environment. At the same time, there is reservation about these practices, because they seem to create a world of chaos and insecurity, at least in the short run, during the transition to new organizational forms. In the longer run, new practices may be devised that take into account employees' concerns for balancing work in their lives, that provide institutional supports at both the organizational and societal levels for flexible working arrangements, and that help to resolve some of the unexpected consequences and perceived contradictions that arise during the transition.

This introductory reading was designed to make you aware of the tensions that can arise so that you are not taken by surprise, to urge you to think analytically about what it is that is changing when "change" is so broadly discussed, and to inspire you to think more broadly and creatively about some of the options and changes that can be devised.

In conclusion, here are some things to keep in mind:

- The overall coherence of the multiple pieces of your approach—the old system was indeed a system and new pieces need to make sense together and to be bolstered by a new social contract.
- The possible negative consequences of a "mismatch" of practices—for example, teamwork and downsizing do not go together well, nor do teamwork and individualistic, competitive rewards.
- The occasional positive consequences of a "mismatch" of practices—for example, the realization that teamwork requires a new reward system is pushing companies to innovate.
- The perceived legitimacy of practices to multiple stakeholders—for example, some people will feel pleased and motivated and some will feel cheated if companies begin to change the shape of career paths, and it is difficult to assess the net impact on motivation, withheld effort, and ultimately, productivity.
- The need to think of creative alternative ways to get work done—for example, how staffing needs can be met flexibly in a way that creates jobs that people want to have and that recognizes the role that business plays in shaping the quality of life in societies.

REFERENCES

Bailyn, Lotte. 1993. "Patterned Chaos in Human Resource Management." *Sloan Management Review*, Vol. 34, #2 (Winter 1993), pp. 77–83.

Bane, Mary Jo, and David Elliott. 1993. "Is American Business Working for the Poor?" *Harvard Business Review*.

Blair, Margaret. 1993. *Ownership and Control*.

Bridges, William. 1994. "The End of the Job." *Fortune* (September 19, 1994), p. 64.

Business Week, "The New World of Work." (October 17, 1994), p. 76.

Deming, W. E. 1986. *Out of the Crisis*. Cambridge, MA: Massachusetts Institute of Technology Center for Advanced Engineering Technology.

Donnellon, Anne, and Maureen Scully. 1994. "Teams, Merit, and Rewards: Will the Post-Bureaucratic Organization Be a Post-Meritocratic Organization?" In Anne Donnellon and Charles Heckscher, eds., *The Post-Bureaucratic Organization: New Perspectives on Organizational Change*. Thousand Oaks, CA: Sage Publications.

Kochan, Thomas. 1994. "The American Corporation as an Employer: Past, Present, and Future Possibilities." Unpublished paper. Sloan School of Management, Massachusetts Institute of Technology, p. 4.

Kochan, Thomas, and Paul Osterman. 1994. *The Mutual Gains Enterprise: Human Resource Strategies and National Policy*. Boston: Harvard Business School Press.

THE CHANGING SOCIAL CONTRACT FOR WHITE-COLLAR WORKERS

by Charles Heckscher

The unprecedented attack on middle management during the past decade creates a new theoretical and moral challenge to our employment relations system. The impact goes far beyond numerical body counts from corporate layoffs; what has been shaken is not just individual lives, but an implied social contract that has long governed employment relations at the management level. The disruption of expectations has profoundly affected much of the workforce, undermining the sense that one can predict and understand the future and resulting in a dangerous sense of drift and confusion.

THE THEORETICAL CHALLENGE

The theoretical challenge for our field stems from the fact that much of the industrial relations system is based on a model of stable hierarchical companies. At the white-collar level, managers have long been treated as part of a corporate "family" protected from market fluctuations; this is part of the reason why they have been exempted from the Wagner Act protections and located instead within a legal framework positing a need for loyalty. At the blue-collar level, too, periodic contracts have sought to "lock in" a system that can provide reliable benefits to employees; and a sense of loyalty, of life-long relation to a large employer, has been a crucial part of the "good life" built by unionized workers. If employees, after the current wave of restructurings, are less tied to a single employer, and if middle managers are in the same boat as blue-collar employees, then the current system of representation falls to the ground: neither contracts nor paternalistic family-feeling provide protection.

The moral issue is still more profound: the layoffs undermine the contract that has helped managers make sense of the world. As I have talked to middle managers and professional employees in large corporations, I have been struck by the sense of moral violation they have experienced. Their life as employees has been governed by a relatively simple rule of loyalty: as one expressed it,

> My basic mind set was, there's an implicit contract. I expect that the company will provide me a career, development opportunities, and reasonable pay and benefits; and they, in turn, should expect from me that I'm willing to work very hard for them. When either one of us is unhappy with that situation, the contract is broken. And up until the past two years, as a corporation I had faith that that would occur.[1]

But when downsizings reached these ranks, the whole world-view began to come apart:

> Loyalty comes with trust and believing, and this has been cast out across the whole company as being not the way to run things. And then when you look around you see takeovers and the crumbling of everything in the whole economy.

Source: Charles Heckscher, "The Changing Social Contract for White-Collar Workers," *Perspectives on Work*, Vol. 1, No. 1, 1997, pp. 18–21. Reprinted by permission of the Industrial Relations Research Association.

1 This and other quotes are drawn from my book *White-Collar Blues: Management Loyalties in an Age of Corporate Restructuring*. NY: Basic Books, 1995.

With "the crumbling of everything" people begin to cast about to make sense of the world. Many of them simply put their heads down and try to block out the reality of the change, hoping that they can make it through to retirement; others brush up their resumes and in a more-or-less meandering way test out their prospects in the outside world. No one gains much by these moves: not the companies, who find their employees acting more timid and bureaucratic and less entrepreneurial than before; and certainly not the employees themselves.

A RETURN TO THE PAST? THE LIMITS OF LOYALTY

One major response has, not surprisingly, been to lament the passing of the old ethic and to wish for its return: hardly a day passes without a newspaper article decrying the unfeeling heartlessness of corporate downsizings. From there it is only a short and common step to proposing that managers be *forced* to maintain the familiar system through bargaining or government regulation. It seems like a highly reasonable idea: it would bring us back to an order that we know how to deal with, that makes sense, and that has provided to a reasonable degree for many people the main things we look for from society: happiness, wealth, order.

The last forty years of political history, however, should make us wary of trying to engineer the social order. Loyalty in its heyday was not forced or engineered—few regulations *before* the '80s tried to guarantee employment security. Security for the core labor force arose naturally, as it were, out of the economic system, as a way of promoting needed cooperation within large oligopolistic bureaucracies. Chester Barnard, a former president of New Jersey Bell, said without equivocation in the '30s, "The most important single contribution required of the executive . . . is loyalty."

Today Barnard's counterparts say no such thing. As they chop at the previously accepted obligations of loyalty, many have tried to stop them. Plant-closing legislation and security clauses as a center of collective bargaining are recent phenomena, countering a shift already in motion. But unless we understand *why* business leaders have shifted their grounds—what are the underlying forces that have eroded an order that previously seemed "natural"—we should be cautious about attempts to hold that order in place.

Put that way, it should be obvious what has happened. Building a long-term culture of trust within an organization was eminently sensible in Barnard's era: it was a period in which the economy hit a stride, with a dominant group of large companies producing a relatively stable group of products. But today we are in the midst of instabilities of quite a different magnitude. The list of transformative pressures is familiar but worth repeating in order to take stock of how deeply the new employment relation is bound to overwhelming social change: information technology, scrambling entire industries and changing methods of work in almost every corner of the economy; the opening of international competition, forcing a reconfiguration of production patterns; the maturing of the consumer economy, creating new demands for innovation and customization; and the rising educational level of the workforce, generating a reserve of intelligence never used by traditional bureaucracies.

With all that, the long-term and hierarchical pattern of loyalty just doesn't fit. The problem is not that today's corporate leaders are somehow more callous than their predecessors. It is that the conditions of the existing moral contract no longer hold.

If we wanted to go back to a stable system of loyalty, we would also have to recreate some elements that are perhaps more controversial: a lower level of technology; a less capable and independent workforce; less demanding consumers; and closed borders. This is not only impractical, it is on the whole undesirable from a *moral* point of view. For in our nostalgia for employment stability and the ethic of loyalty, we often forget the less pleasant side.

The condition of security in the contract of loyalty, as Barnard understood, was a kind of paternalistic domination.

Consider, for instance, the conclusion of his dictum just cited: "The most important single contribution required of the executive . . . is loyalty,"—and here the part I omitted—"*domination by the organization personality.*"[2] The traditional corporation was a closed world and managers were expected to keep within it. They might be taken care of, but they were not to question the care. Women and minorities, as Rosabeth Kanter notably documented,[3] were not welcomed into this tight informal world; on the contrary, as wives they were expected to support their husbands, following wherever corporate needs took them. Executives were expected to follow a dress code, join the right clubs, and speak an internally coded language.

So if we want to go back to loyalty, we would also have to give up what I would consider significant moral advances of recent years. In an increasingly international world, executives have to be more mobile than ever—how could this be possible without submissive wives to follow along? Loyalty demands a high level of conformity—how could it incorporate the demands of an increasingly diverse workforce? The demands of paternalistic corporations extend deep into the private lives of their employees, and we have only begun to make progress in separating private choices in things like political or sexual orientation from the demands of work. Loyalty demands subordination, acceptance of what one is told. We are just beginning to move to greater "empowerment," participation, and sharing of information in corporations. Let us not be too quick with our condemnation of change.

MOVING ON: FREE AGENCY AND PROFESSIONALISM

If loyalty is gone, many assume that there is only one alternative: a cold logic (as one manager expressed it to me) of "give and get, give and get," watching out only for oneself—a vision of free agency, conjuring up images of spoiled, high-paid baseball players and investment bankers, entailing no moral obligations.

This attitude—I can't call it an ethic, because it is really nothing other than the absence of a moral contract—is almost universally unpopular: none of the managers I have interviewed, nor (as far as I can remember) any of my business students, embraces such an approach. Sometimes those who have been made cynical by the violation of prior obligations *say* they are going to go over to an attitude of pure self-interest; but if you push them at all they immediately express their distaste for the whole idea.

The absence of a moral alternative is one powerful factor that makes so many hold on to traditional loyalty. The fact is—and this would not have surprised Adam Smith, though it might surprise Milton Friedman—that few people arc willing to leap into an abyss of amoral self-interest. But the traditional ethic of loyalty, with its flaws, is not the only alternative to this doom. Many managers are developing a new ethic, or a new vision of a social contract, that accommodates a more flexible and less paternalistic relationship. I have called it "professional," though it is rather different from the professionalism of closed societies like doctors and lawyers. It entails centrally an *open negotiation of obligations between employee and employer.*

Where loyalty is diffuse and eternal, the professional ethic is relatively specific and time-limited. Its core assumption is that the employment relation is a meshing of interests between parties who are independent and changing. That assumption both reflects the real world and allows far more moral autonomy to the employee than the traditional relationship. It does not, however, lead to an atomized concept of self-interested individuals: the employment relation does create *obligations* that cannot legitimately be ignored.

The first obligation is honesty:

What's the psychological contract? The main thing is to keep things open. We have agreed to have open agendas,

2 Barnard, Chester I. 1938. *The Functions of the Executive.* Cambridge, MA: Harvard University Press, Italics added.

3 *Men and Women of the Corporation.* NY: Basic Books, 1977.

nothing bidden, no hidden agendas, to be open and honest with each other.

Thus, as these managers view it, they have both a right and an obligation to make known their personal agendas—what they hope to accomplish, what limits they set on their willingness to obey, and whether they are looking for other opportunities. The company, for its part, has an obligation to be open about its business prospects, what it expects for the employee, and what challenges it can provide in the future.

Both sides of this obligation, it should be stressed, are unfamiliar in a relationship of loyalty. The loyal employee is not expected to set limits—to say, for instance, that family obligations prevent a major move is seen as a violation of loyalty and therefore a "career killer." And the company is not expected to reveal its plan—business information flows less freely, and evaluations of career prospects are largely hidden for fear of "demotivating" people.

The second key obligation is for each party to work for the health of the other. If a company's business plans change—a financial crisis, a change in strategy, a takeover—"professional" managers do not expect to be taken care of permanently, but they do expect the company to do all it can to put them in a position of strength for the future. This means, among other things, that the company should constantly encourage and help employees to develop generalized skills that can be transferred to the world outside.

Again, those of a loyalist perspective see this as madness, and it drives many HR leaders crazy—they reason that if you want people to remain loyal you certainly don't want to encourage them to leave. The professional logic, by contrast, is that if you want people to contribute with their full intelligence you want them to stay only as long as *they* want to.

On the other side of this obligation, "professional" employees do not feel justified in leaving at a moment's notice or merely for money. If some circumstance causes them to leave—and a major new career challenge counts as a legitimate reason—they feel obligated to finish the proj-ects they are working on and to assist the company in replacing their skills and knowledge.

In the best of circumstances, this relationship escapes paternalism by establishing a kind of equality between the organization and the individuals—an exchange of abilities for challenge, in place of the loyalty bargain of effort for security. It accepts the reality of downsizing and restructuring, as well as of career change and growth, without tossing everything into the pit of naked self-interest. This is, I would emphasize, not merely a theorist's ideal-type, but a real construction of certain managers faced with the "crumbling of everything" from the familiar world of loyalty.

THE CONDITIONS FOR PROFESSIONALISM

There is just one flaw in this picture: though the professional ethic exists in some people's minds, it does not exist in the society at large. A new ethic must develop not just an abstract concept of obligations, but an employment relations *system* that provides the conditions for fair negotiation and enforcement of obligations.

The existing system supports instead the old pattern of long-term loyalty. The legal order, for instance, takes it as a given that the manager's obligation of loyalty supersedes almost everything else, including (in many cases) the duty to obey the law. The educational system is set up to set people on the path of occupational life, and then withdraw to allow companies to take over training and career formation throughout adulthood. Prestige is heavily tied to one's employer. There are few kinds of certification that enable someone to carry a reputation from one firm to another. And, of course—most concretely—health care and retirement benefits are still generally tied to tenure with a single company.

Thus those who take the ethic of professionalism seriously—who take seriously the widespread rhetoric about "shaping your own career" and "maintaining employability"—find themselves naked and alone. There are still very few employers that encourage the development of generalized skills; few educational mechanisms for gaining certification for new careers in adulthood; only the beginnings of portable health insurance; and very poor mechanisms of information about available jobs.

There is still a need for institutions of employment relations, but redesigned to encourage the new contract rather than the old. Collective bargaining will surely not disappear, but is becoming a special case of the broader process of negotiation.

Many levels of innovation are needed, but I would stress two. The first is collective action, or association. Though negotiation around the professional ethic is more individualized than the centralized contracts of industrial relations, group support is still essential. The burden of negotiating the professional relation is far too much for anyone to handle alone. Managers find a constant need to establish networks and get information and advice from others in similar situations.

Thus support groups and associations are acquiring increasing significance in helping people navigate unpredictable career shoals. And many are beginning, in a tentative way, to act also as pressure groups, using publicity and mobilization of internal networks to hold management to its own rhetoric of empowerment and openness. This is the logic behind the formation of *Working Today*—an organization that aims to represent employees under the new social contract.

Nor is this need restricted to managers and true professionals: more and more blue-collar and service workers see themselves as similarly "on their own" in the work world, unable to depend on a company. Unions have been slowly but increasingly looking for ways to support them through services of "associate membership" and representation outside a collective bargaining contract.

The second major innovation involves the role of government. Though associations can do a great deal, they need a

foundation of obligations embodied in law. The existing governmental role, of regulating organizing and bargaining processes under the Wagner Act, seems ineffectual and beside the point for many employees today—but that doesn't mean there is no needed government role. A century's worth of law, affirming (in the words of one key decision) that "there is no more elemental cause for discharge of an employee than disloyalty to his employer," needs to be recast on a different foundation. A labor relations system conceived around a balance of power between stable bureaucracies must give way to one that facilitates individual mobility within a collective vision of fairness—the obligations of the new social contract have to find their way into enforceable law. There is also a critical role for government in developing portability of benefits and various kinds of "disaster insurance" in an increasingly risky world—either by directly providing these benefits or by backing up private insurance mechanisms.

A social contract is both far simpler and far deeper than contracts bargained on the open market or through shows of force: it shapes daily lives and expectations through a huge range of different roles in a society. The wave of downsizings, driven by forces that are only partly understood, has left a void that is easily filled with individualistic cynicism or backwards-looking reaction.

Our field has, I believe, a major role to play in revitalizing the employment relation, as it led the way once before in the creation of the industrial relations system. But it has to start from a clear acceptance of (as the old prayer has it) "what cannot be changed" in the current developments—that business organizations are becoming more flexible and responsive to rapid environmental change and therefore less stable and protective. Our problem is to conceptualize fairness, and a way to enforce it, within that context.

Charles Heckscher is a Professor at Rutgers University and chair of the Labor Studies and Employment Relations Department. His research explores alternatives to bureaucratic systems of management. He has worked for many years as a consultant on organizational transformation, especially in joint union-management settings.

A BRAVE NEW DARWINIAN WORKPLACE

by Stratford Sherman

The greatest social convulsions of the years ahead may occur in the workplace, as companies struggling with fast-paced change and brutal competition reshape themselves—and redefine what it means to hold a job. Apple Computer CEO John Sculley made the point recently to Bill Clinton: The continuing "reorganization of work itself" is part of a social transformation as massive and wrenching as the industrial revolution.

Deep thinkers as diverse as futurist Alvin Toffler, author Tom Peters (*Liberation Management*), and Allied-Signal CEO Lawrence Bossidy agree: The demise of the old authoritarian hierarchies, from the U.S.S.R. to General Motors, is a global, historical phenomenon that none can evade. Like it or not, everyone who works for a living is helping create a new relationship between individual and corporation, and a new sense of self for employer and employee alike. Bit by bit, the forces of technology and economics are destroying the artificial constructs—such as rigidly hierarchical schemes for organizing work—that since the 19th century have limited the ability of people, organizations, and markets to behave in natural ways. The next few years of transition will be brutal for all concerned, but the result promises to be worth some suffering. The workplace will be healthier, saner, more creative, and yet more chaotic—like nature itself.

By the time the most radical of the restructuring is done, workers and companies will be more accustomed to negotiating voluntary relationships that benefit both parties, this instead of the rigid and ultimately alienating liaisons and dependencies of the machine age. Businesses will benefit from an abler, more flexible, and vastly more responsible work force. Job holders will get more respect, and their work may become more engaging, as employers seek employees' ideas.

Anyone who wants to be around for the fun part needs to start adapting now. Those who can't, sadly, will number in the millions. Major political shifts, notably pension and health care guarantees and large-scale training programs, may be the price of peace on the streets.

Abraham Zaleznik, a psychoanalyst and professor emeritus at the Harvard business school, believes the theme of the dawning era is greater accountability on the part of both individuals and corporations. Says he: "We're all up against a relentless, impersonal reality called the marketplace, which will reward those who do good jobs and punish those who don't."

If the ax falls on you, try hard not to take it personally: Odds are the causes have nothing to do with you, but rather with structural changes in organizations and industries. Ameritech, the Chicago-based regional Bell company, has eliminated almost 2,000 white-collar jobs since 1984. Now—despite record profitability—the Baby Bell is cutting 2,500 more such jobs, 12% of its managers. The harsh truth is that Ameritech, remaking itself to meet the challenges of the 21st century, simply doesn't need so many people. If big corporations honestly examined themselves—and just about every one will, sooner or later—most would reach the same conclusion. William Morin, chairman of the Drake Beam Morin outplacement firm, estimates that roughly a quarter of the U.S. workforce

29

PRESS

Source: Stratford Sherman, "A Brave New Darwinian Workplace." *Fortune* (January 25, 1993), 50–53.

is still imperiled by downsizing. "It's rough out there," says Harvey Mackay, author of the upcoming self-protection guide, *Sharkproof*. He adds, with a touch of hyperbole, "The worried people are the ones who've *got* the jobs."

That goes double for managers. Bluntly put, the United States has too many for the number of conventional managerial jobs around, and the gap will only grow. Says Nicole Morgan, a professor of public administration at Queen's University in Kingston, Ontario, and author of *Nowhere to Go*, a book about how people plateau in their careers: "What we have is a lot of ambitious people with huge career expectations competing for a diminishing number of positions."

Widespread denial makes the transition all the tougher. C. K. Prahalad, a business professor at the University of Michigan, explains why the changes are hard to accept: "You are telling top management that their accumulated intellectual capital is devalued, that their 30 years of personal experience is less valuable as we move forward. This is so traumatic that senior managers find it hard to change unless there's a crisis."

James Clawson, a professor at the University of Virginia's Darden School and a consultant to Comsat and GE, estimates that over 80% of employees haven't yet faced up to the consequences of abolishing the old hierarchical ways. "That's a great improvement!" he says. "Regardless of the hardness of the facts and the clearness of the data, there will always be those in denial. It's going to take a generation for the old dogs to die."

For anyone with the courage to face reality, the implications of the workplace revolution are becoming clearer. The most important:

EACH PERSON MUST TAKE FULL RESPONSIBILITY FOR HIS OR HER CAREER

James Taylor, CEO of the research firm Yankelovich Partners, says one of the most important trends in American society is a new determination of people to control their destinies. Only 12% of survey respondents trust public statements made by corporations, but an unprecedented seven out of ten agree with the statement "I'm the one in charge of my life." According to Taylor, "That's a real change in the psychology of being an employee. It's the price corporations are paying for breaking the loyalty bond."

Ralph Waldo Emerson's classic 152-year-old essay "Self-Reliance" offers perhaps the best advice for coping with the brave new world of employment: "Trust thyself. . . . Accept the place the divine providence has found for you, the society of your contemporaries, the connection of events. Great men have always done so, and confided themselves childlike to the genius of their age, betraying their perceptions that the absolutely trustworthy was seated at their heart, working through their hands, predominating in all their being."

Achieving such serenity doesn't mean you just sit there and hope for the best. Those who would take charge of their careers should commit themselves to a lifetime of learning—including exploring new job possibilities. Richard Nelson Bolles, the Episcopalian minister who wrote the job hunter's bible, *What Color Is Your Parachute?*, argues that a great lesson of the 1990s recession is that victims of layoffs rarely get much warning. Along with other experts on careers, he advises everyone to inventory his or her skills, add to them every single year, and always have a ready answer to the questions: What would you do if you lost your job tomorrow?

THE OLD CAREER PATH NO LONGER EXISTS

Fewer middle-management jobs means less vertical mobility, which the wise will translate into giving less importance to making the next rung. A decade or so ago at GE, many ambitious executives scored functional posts in such areas as manufacturing or finance in favor of the general-manager jobs that came with control of a profit-and-loss statement. But as CEO Jack

Welch has streamlined the GE organization, the number of general-manager jobs has declined by two-thirds: Only one such job per 5,500 employees remains. That is forcing the company and its employees to search together for ways to enrich functional jobs.

WORKERS WILL BE REWARDED FOR KNOWLEDGE AND ADAPTABILITY

Specialization is out, a new-style generalism is in. The most employable people will be flexible folk who can move easily from one function to another, integrating diverse disciplines and perspectives. Similarly, people who can operate comfortably in a variety of environments will fare better than those stuck in the mindset of a particular corporate or even national culture. Michigan's Prahalad argues that people will need the ability not only to learn fundamentally new skills but also to unlearn outdated ways.

TEAMWORK WILL REPLACE HIERARCHY AS THE DOMINANT FORM OF ORGANIZATION

Tom Peters suggests a movie production company as the new model: It brings together a group of highly skilled people to complete a focused project and then disbands. Anyone who has observed a film being made may scoff at the notion of emulating such inefficiency. But look at the larger picture—America's unchallenged domination of the multibillion-dollar world market for movies—and the genius of this apparently chaotic system becomes apparent. Peters also observes that more people are working for a company for a year or two, then going off to labor on behalf of somebody else, then returning to their original employer when they're needed again.

While most organizations may never become quite so flexible, managers are sharing more power with people they once regarded as subordinates, and employees of nominally lower rank are experiencing the joys and burdens of increased responsibility. With so many middle managers gone, there's no practical alternative to empowering workers.

This makes people skills supremely important, and as Prahalad points out, even leaders will have to learn how to follow. "A team is not like a pack of sledge dogs, with one dog the leader," he explains. "It's more like the flight of wild geese: The leader always changes, but they fly in a flock." The paired forces of globalization and information technology imply an increased likelihood that teams of people will be working together across great distances, requiring yet another type of relationship skill.

WORKERS WHO CAN FLOURISH IN THE NEW ENVIRONMENT WILL BE SO PRIZED BY EMPLOYERS THAT COMPANIES WILL GO OUT OF THEIR WAY TO BUILD A NEW CORPORATE LOYALTY

So argues Martin Strasmore, president of the Silvermine Consulting Group in Darien, Connecticut, a consultant to Chase Manhattan Bank and Siemens. "Every time you hire a person, you have to make a significant investment to get him up to speed and in tune with your vision and culture," he argues. "You'll continue to invest in your employees, training them in new skills and giving them the tools to manage change. That implies, if not a lifelong pact, at least a long-term pact with your people."

Companies that haven't made such pacts may suffer. "As soon as the economy turns around, many people are going to bolt from the company they are working for," says Mitchell Marks, a principal at the William M. Mercer consulting firm. "All this downsizing is going to come back to haunt companies. Executives are going to have to spend a lot of energy to recover esprit de corps."

Employers may bind valued workers with contracts, larger gobbets of freedom, or a bigger share of profits. For models, look at any business that depends on highly skilled—and therefore highly mobile—professionals; for instance, advertising agencies on Wall Street investment banks.

31

PRESS

Offering some form of security makes sense. People terrified of being laid off—and Yankelovich Partners' survey data suggest most workers still are—tend to become risk-averse. That renders them unlikely to produce the new, creative ideas that companies will need to prevail in competitive markets.

IT PAYS TO OFFER LEARNING OPPORTUNITIES TO EMPLOYEES

Besides improving the skills of your workforce, an investment in training can help you attract and retain desirable employees. Writes professor Karl Weick of the University of Michigan: "Training and management development . . . can increase [employee] commitment if it is used to teach knowledge that is *less* firm-specific and more generalizable. Ironically, in-house management development may produce more committed workers and higher performance if it focuses on skills that are needed by *other* firms than if it focuses on skills needed within its own firm." This may prove the core of the "new psychological contract" that companies such as Apple are offering workers: increased employability in return for hard work and commitment.

CORPORATE VALUES WILL BECOME CENTRAL TO LEADERSHIP

It goes without saying—or should—that as relations between employers and employees begin to rely more on voluntary behavior, the niceties of relationship become more important. A key role of leadership is to give people permission to change. That means allowing a reasonable measure of dissent and, as Prahalad says, careful differentiation between simple business failure and experimentation that results in learning. The perception of fairness, rationality, and reward based on merit is essential—and actions speak louder than words. "It's very analogous to a marriage," says psychologist Dee Soder, president of Endymion, an executive assessment and counseling firm. "If you're shallow and just out for one-night stands,

you could lose. You get from it what you put in. You have to work at these relationships."

AGE IS AN INCREASINGLY IMPORTANT FACTOR IN DEFINING THE OPPORTUNITIES AND CHALLENGES WORKERS WILL FACE

In general, says Harvard business school professor John Kotter, " . . . the older you are, the less prepared you are for this." On the other hand, older people tend to be much better off financially—and not only because they've been working longer. Here's how the outlook breaks down by generation:

Baby-boomers, having won the White House, will soon move into other centers of power. Financially, boomers have barely kept their heads above water by maintaining two-income families, but now their generation is poised to inherit enormous wealth from parents. On the job, boomers are fast transforming their unconventional career choices—working more at home, for example—into a new status quo.

Generation 13, as historian and author Neil Howe dubs the 80 million people born between 1961 and 1981, will continue to scramble for the boomers' meager leavings. Street smart but cynical, members of the 13th generation born since the American Revolution may feel they have been cruelly slighted. Raised to an unprecedented extent by absentee parents, under-35-year-olds are earning 20% to 30% less in real terms than people their age did in the 1970s.

People ages 50 to 60, though still energetic, are being passed over, pushed out, or shot with the so-called silver bullet of early retirement in extraordinary numbers. In general they can afford to cope with their reduced career prospects. Most will hang on to their jobs as long as they can; some will switch to new careers. Like everyone else, they should identify their most valuable aptitudes—basics like salesmanship or problem solving or three-dimensional thinking—and find ways to enhance them.

The new workplace will be ferociously Darwinian for corporations and individuals alike. Without the financial strength that comes with well-managed operations, companies won't be able to afford to focus on what used to be called the softer management issues that are becoming all-important. Without inner strength, individuals may hesitate to accept responsibility for their lives.

As Harvard's Kotter warns: "Just because people watch out for No. 1 doesn't mean they manage their careers intelligently. A lot of people manage their careers just as badly as some corporations have managed themselves."

For the transformation of the workplace to establish a new equilibrium, employers and employees must somehow find ways for workers to lead balanced lives. Empowerment and shared responsibility are undeniably good—but paradoxically, they increase the burdens on people who are already overstressed. Workers who lack the time and emotional energy to lead balanced lives risk burnout, and the companies that depend on them will lose. Find the solution to that one—somebody has to—and you'll be the biggest hero of the new world of work.

M-7

supplemental

THE UNFINISHED AGENDA

by Robert B. Reich

> I will leave office in a few days and can't resist a last word.

There *is* much to celebrate. As we all know, nearly 11 million jobs have been added to the economy over the past four years and most of them have paid above the median wage. The rate of unemployment remains relatively low (5.3 percent in December, 1996), and there is still no sign of accelerating inflation. This administration has overseen an increase in the minimum wage to nearly 10 million working Americans, an expansion of the Earned Income Tax Credit, the passage of the Family and Medical Leave Act, and improvements in the protection and provision of worker pensions and health care.

THE INEQUALITY GAP

Today, I want to focus on the work that remains to be done. The unfinished agenda is to address widening inequality. Over 15 years ago, inequality of income, wealth, and opportunity began to widen, and the gap today is greater than at any time in living memory. All the rungs on the economic ladder are now farther apart than they were a generation ago, and the space between them continues to spread. We worked to reverse this in the first Clinton administration, with some real success. Incomes have become less unequal, partly because more people are employed and they're working more hours, and because elderly retirees are doing better. But earnings inequality among full-time adult wage earners has

continued to widen—right up to the third quarter of 1996, the most recent data we have. This is not a statistical fluke. It has nothing to do with how we measure changes in productivity or prices.

How should we respond? There is one short-run imperative: First, and least, do no harm. As we reclaim mastery of our economic destiny by imposing control over the federal budget, the ultimate test is not simply whether the deficit reaches zero, but whether it does so in a way that, at a minimum, does not worsen inequality in America. The ultimate test for reform of Social Security and Medicare is not merely whether the trust funds are replenished, but whether they are replenished in a way that doesn't encourage the healthiest and wealthiest among us to opt out of these insurance pools. Nor should these reforms disproportionately increase payroll taxes or premiums for lower-income workers.

But beyond the immediate issues of the day, how should America deal with this long-term trend that threatens to blight an otherwise promising future? There are three unhelpful reactions: denial, resignation, and silence.

Some deny that inequality is increasing. Simply said, they are wrong. But rather than try to refute their arguments here, I will let the data speak for itself. Figures 7.1 through 7.5 summarize some of the key dimensions of increasing inequality: declining real wages, income shares of families in the bottom 40 percent and the top 5 percent of the distribution, the growth in the difference in earnings of high school and college grad-

Source: Robert B. Reich, "The Unfinished Agenda," *Perspectives on Work*, Vol. 1, No. 1, 1997. Reprinted by permission of the Industrial Relations Research Association.

FIGURE 7.1 CUMULATIVE CHANGE IN REAL WAGES SINCE 1980

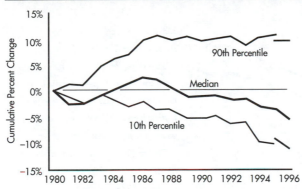

Between 1980 and 1995, the inflation-adjusted earnings of an adult at the top tenth of full-time workers rose by 10.7 percent. Over the same period, the median adult worker's wages fell by 3.6 percent, and the wages of a worker at the bottom tenth of the distribution fell by 9.6 percent. Although family income inequality has decreased since 1993, the disparity in the earnings of the highest and lowest earners has not declined markedly between 1993 and 1995 and quarterly figures indicate no improvement in 1996.

Source: Bureau of Labor Statistics, usual full-time earnings weekly earnings of wage and salary workers 25 years and older. The CPI-U is used for deflation. Lines from 1979 to 1995 represent annual averages; lines from 1995 to 1996 are based on third quarter figures.

uates, declining health coverage of employees, and job displacement rates.

Some are resigned to it. They view widening inequality as the byproduct of structural changes in our economy—most notably technological advances and global economic integration, both of which tend to reward the well-trained and penalize those with the poorest education and skills. The same phenomenon is occurring the world over, they say. Nothing can be done about it. We must adapt to this inevitability.

They are wrong for a different reason than are those who deny, but the consequence of resignation is the same.

They're wrong because the evidence of other countries and, even more important, of our own country's history shows that inequality rises and falls with the choices we make, that we are not powerless to decide what kind of future we will have. And they are wrong because we are not merely an economy, but also a culture. It has never been economics alone that defines America. If we choose, as a culture, to push against the economic forces that would otherwise divide us, it is within our ability to do so. And the consequence of choosing otherwise—by pretending that the choice is not ours to make—is to cease being a society.

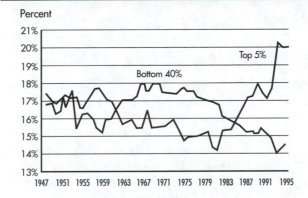

A greater share of our nation's income goes to the richest 5 percent of families than to the bottom 40 percent. In 1995, the richest 5 percent of families received 20.0 percent of aggregate income and the bottom 40 percent of families received 14.6 percent.

Source: Census Bureau, Current Population Survey. Data for 1993–1995 are not directly comparable with earlier data beacause of a redesign in the Current Population Survey that included new top codes for income.

FIGURE 7.3 COLLEGE-HIGH SCHOOL WAGE DIFFERENTIAL FOR MEN AND WOMEN, 1979–1996

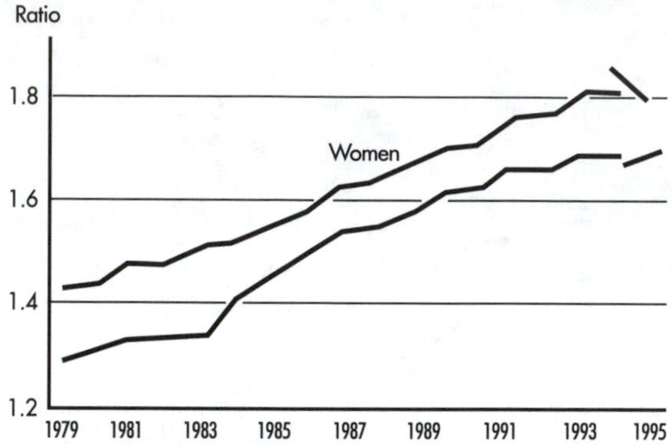

The returns of a college education increased throughout the 1980s. In 1995, the median full-time female college graduate earned 81 percent more than the typical woman working full time who finished high school only, up from an earnings differential of 43 percent in 1979. For men, the equivalent numbers are 67 percent in 1995, up from 29 percent in 1979.

Source: *Bureau of Labor Statistics, usual weekly earnings of full-time and salary workers 25 years and older. Lines from 1979 to 1995 represent annual data; those beginning in 1995 represent data for the third quarter.*

Silence is perhaps the most insidious response of all, because it erases the issue from the national mind. Inequality is widening slowly enough that absent a sudden or dramatic event that automatically galvanizes public concern, we are able to avert our eyes and talk about other things.

Here is where I drop my mask and stand revealed as a conservative. My concern with inequality is driven, I'll confess, by a conservative conviction that the future must keep faith with the direction of America's recent past, my own past. In the America of my youth, we were growing together. We still had a long way to go to overcome racism and sexism—and still do—but the remarkable thing about the first three decades after World War II is that prosperity was widely shared. Most people in the top fifth of the income ladder saw their real incomes double and so did most people in the bottom fifth. Broadly shared prosperity—the assumption that we were all in this together—highlighted and fortified something about the character of America that was the envy of the rest of the world.

THE IMPLICIT SOCIAL COMPACT

As we cross to the next century, the conservative in me insists we carry some precious baggage from the past. We need to carry with us the implicit social compact that, for nearly half a century, gave force to the simple proposition that American prosperity could include almost everyone.

This implicit social compact had three major provisions.

The first pertained to the private sector. As companies did better, their workers should as well. Wages should rise, as should employer-provided health and pension benefits, and jobs should be reasonably secure. This provision was reinforced by labor unions, to which, by the mid-1950s, about 35 percent of the private-sector workforce belonged. But it was enforced in the first instance by public expectations. We were all in it together, and as a result grew together. It would be unseemly for a company whose profits were increasing to fail to share its prosperity with its employees.

The second provision of the social compact was social insurance through which Americans pooled their resources against the risk that any one of us—through illness or bad luck—might become impoverished. Hence, unemployment insurance, Social Security for the elderly and disabled, Aid to Families with Dependent Children, and Medicare and Medicaid.

The third provision was the promise of a good education. In the 1950s our collective conscience, embodied in the Supreme Court, finally led us to resolve

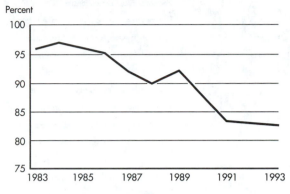

FIGURE 7.4 DECLINE IN EMPLOYEE HEALTH COVERAGE

Percent of full-time employees participating in Employer-Sponsored Health Plans, Medium and Large Private Establishments.

Benefits

Employer-provided benefits are also distributed unequally and their inclusion in total compensation does little to alter the long-term trends in inequality.

The percent of full-time employees in medium and large establishments participating in employer-sponsored health plans has fallen from over 95 percent in 1983 to 82 percent in 1993.

Source: *Based on Data from the Bureau of Labor Statistics, Employee Benefits Survey.*

that all children, regardless of race, must have the same—not separate—educational opportunities. For an ever-larger portion of our population, we also offered schooling beyond 12th grade. The GI Bill made college a reality for millions of returning veterans. Others gained access to advanced education through a vast expansion of state-subsidized public universities and community colleges.

It is important to understand what this social compact was and what it was not. It defined our sense of fair play, but it was not about redistributing wealth. There would still be the rich and the poor. It merely proclaimed that at some fundamental level we were all in it together, that as a society we depended on one another. The economy could nor prosper unless vast numbers of employees had more money in their pockets; none of us could be economically secure unless we pooled risks; a better-educated workforce was in all our interests.

THE BREAKDOWN IN THE SOCIAL COMPACT

In recent years, however, all three provisions of the social compact have been breaking down. Profitable companies now routinely downsize. As the Bureau of Labor Statistics has shown, layoffs in the current expansion are occurring at a higher rate even than in the expansion of

the 1980s. The corollary to "downsizing" and "down-waging" might be called "down-benefitting." Employer-provided health benefits are declining, as co-payments, deductibles, and premiums rise. Defined-benefit pension plans are giving way to 401(k)s without employer contributions, or to no pensions at all.

The widening wage gap is reflected in a widening benefits gap Top executives and their families receive ever more generous health benefits and their pension benefits are soaring in the form of compensation deferred until retirement. Although they have no greater job security than others, when they lose their jobs it is not uncommon for today's top executives to receive "golden parachutes" studded with diamonds.

The second provision—that of social insurance—is also breaking down. We see evidence of this in who is being asked to bear the largest burden in balancing the budget—disproportionately the poor and near poor, whose programs have borne the largest cuts. President Clinton is intent on rectifying this, particularly those aspects of the new welfare legislation that reduce food stamps for the working poor and eliminate benefits for legal immigrants.

Unemployment insurance now covers a smaller proportion of workers than it did twenty years ago—only about 35 percent of the unemployed. This is partly because states have competed to reduce

39

PRESS

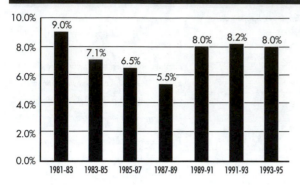

FIGURE 7.5 PERMANENT JOB LOSS: OVERALL DISPLACEMENT RATES, 1981–1995

Source: *Bureau of Labor Statistics, Displaced Worker Survey, unpublished data. Data before the survey covering 1991–93 are not adjusted for nonresponse and are therefore not strictly comparable with data covering 1991–93 and 1993–95.*

Displacement

Permanent job loss continues as a problem for American workers, despite robust job growth during the recent expansion. Between January 1993 and December 1995, 8.0 percent of workers were displaced from their jobs due to plant closure, insufficient work, or elimination of their position. This displacement rate has fallen from 8.2 percent in 1991–1993, but is still much higher than the rate at a similar point in the business cycle in the 1980s.

the premiums they charge businesses, and thus been forced to draw eligibility rules ever more tightly.

In fact, the entire idea of a common risk pool is now under assault. Proposals are being floated for the wealthier and healthier among us to opt out. Whether in the form of private "medical savings accounts" to replace Medicare, or private "personal security accounts" to replace Social Security, the ultimate effect would be much the same: the wealthier and healthier would no longer share the risk with those who have a much higher probability of being sicker or poorer.

The third part of the social compact, access to a good education, is also under severe strain. This administration has expanded opportunities at the federal level—more Pell grants and low-interest direct loans for college, school-to-work apprenticeships, and proposed tax breaks for education and training. But there are powerful undertows in the opposite direction. As Americans increasingly segregate by level of income into different townships, local tax bases in poorer areas simply cannot support the quality of schooling available to the wealthier. De facto racial segregation has become the norm in large metropolitan areas. And across America, state-subsidized higher education is waning under severe budget constraints and its cost has risen three

times faster than median family income. Young people from families with incomes in the top 25 percent are three times more likely to go to college than are young people from the bottom 25 percent.

America is prospering, but the prosperity is not being widely shared, certainly not as widely shared as it once was. During the last four years we have made progress in growing the economy. But growing together again must be our central goal in the future.

Why is the social compact coming undone? Is it because we no longer face the common perils of Depression, hot war, or cold war, and no longer feel the same degree of interdependence? Or is it that in the new global economy we no longer are as dependent on one another? Or is it because the wealthier among us are no longer under a "veil of ignorance" about their likely futures, to use the philosopher John Rawls' phrase, and know in advance that a social compact is likely to require they subsidize others rather than to improve their own well-being?

THE BRIDGE TO THE FUTURE

Perhaps some of each. But there should be no doubt that, unchecked, the disintegration of the social compact threatens the stability and the moral authority of this

Kohn, Alfie. 1993. *Punished by Rewards: The Trouble with Gold Stars, Incentive Plans, A's, Praise, and Other Bribes.* Boston: Houghton Mifflin.

National Research Council. 1991. *Pay for Performance: Evaluating Performance Appraisal and Merit Pay.* Washington, D.C.: National Academy Press.

Osterman, Paul. 1988. *Employment Futures: Reorganization, Dislocation, and Public Policy.* New York: Oxford University Press.

Osterman, Paul. 1992. "Internal Labor Markets in a Changing Environment: Models and Evidence." In David Lewin, O. S. Mitchell and P. D. Sherer, eds., *Research Frontiers in Industrial Relations and Human Resources.* Madison, WI: Industrial Relations Research Association, pp. 273–308.

Patterson, Jack. 1994. "Welcome to the Company that Isn't There." *Business Week,* October 17, p.86.

Pfeffer, Jeffrey. 1998. *The Human Equation.* Cambridge, MA: Harvard Business School Press.

Scully, Maureen. 1993. "The Imperfect Legitimation of Inequality in Internal Labor Markets." Working Paper #3520-93, Cambridge, MA: Sloan School of Management, Massachusetts Institute of Technology.

Scully, Maureen, and Gil Preuss. 1994. "The Dual Character of Trust During Workplace Transformation." *Proceedings of the Industrial Relations Research Association.* Madison, WI: Industrial Relations Research Association.

Workforce 2000: Work and Workers for the 21st Century. Indianapolis: Hudson Institute, 1987.

Ⓒ

23

ACADEMIC

nation. It threatens to strip away much of what we love about America and render our country little more than an arid economic unit. And needlessly so. Because it is within our power to restore the culture of broadly shared prosperity. But the bridge to America's future must first traverse the chasm of inequality.

I'm leaving the administration because I have two young teenage boys who are growing up all too fast. I don't want to miss it as they cross into adulthood. But neither do I want them to live their adult lives in a nation divided between rich and poor. And I don't believe most parents want to bequeath to their children that kind of country. What I want is the opposite of class warfare—it is a reaffirmation of our heritage that Americans must not be walled off from each other by class divisions.

As we congratulate ourselves, justifiably, for renewed growth and a diminished deficit, we must recognize that our circumstances allow us to take up the unfinished agenda. Our circumstances allow it, and our consciences compel it.

There is much to celebrate about America. The future is filled with possibility. But there is no escaping the underlying moral question, which is also a political one. Are we, or are we not, still in this together?

41

PRESS

Robert B. Reich is Professor and the Maurice B. Hexter Professor of Social and Economic Policy at Brandeis and its Heller Graduate School. Before joining Brandeis, he served as the nation's 22nd Secretary of Labor during President Bill Clinton's first term. Before heading the Labor Department, Secretary Reich was on the faculty of Harvard University's John F. Kennedy School of Government. He served as an assistant to the Solicitor General in the Ford Administration where he represented the United States before the Supreme Court, and he headed the policy planning staff of the Federal Trade Commission in the Carter Administration. He has written five books and numerous articles on the global economy and the U.S. workforce.

PATTERNED CHAOS IN HUMAN RESOURCE MANAGEMENT

by Lotte Bailyn

Human resource professionals are often caught between organization demands and employee concerns. To handle these competing pressures, they tend to develop elaborately structured and tightly controlled systems for managing people. Bailyn suggests a new approach: patterned chaos. As people and their needs differ, so should their work be organized in different ways. This article is based on a keynote address given to the Boston chapter of the Association of Part-time Professionals on 2 May 1992 in Needham, Massachusetts.

Lotte Bailyn is T. Wilson Professor of Management, MIT Sloan School of Management.

Three professionals—an architect, an accountant, and a human resource professional—were contemplating a profound existential question. What, besides the obvious, was the oldest profession?

The architect spoke first: "God created the world in six days, and that took a master design. So, obviously, architecture is the oldest profession."

"Not at all," replied the accountant. "You misunderstand what God really did. What He did in those six days was to create order out of chaos. And that is what accountants do, so accountancy is obviously the oldest profession."

But the human resource professional had the last word: "And who do you think created the chaos?"

I would like to suggest that organizations need more chaos, at least the kind of patterned chaos that is described by the new science of that name. And further, most human resource professionals do not create enough of it.

I am not a mathematician, and I do not understand much about the underpinnings of the science of chaos. It is hard for me to imagine how scientists deal with such complex phenomena. But what has been written for the layman and portrayed on TV is quite compelling. Take, for example, the description given by the physicist Joseph Ford of the Georgia Institute of Technology, who was an early proponent and contributor to chaos theory. He talked about "dynamics freed at last from the shackles of order and predictability," of "liberated systems" with "exciting variety, richness of choice, a cornucopia of opportunity."[1] This description comes close to my vision of the new organizational world.

One aspect of chaos theory that has particular resonance in current organizational concerns is popularly called the butterfly effect. This effect, more correctly known as sensitivity to initial conditions, refers to the phenomenon that a butterfly flapping its wings over Tokyo can affect New York weather some time hence. Similarly, small organizational decisions, often about highly circumscribed concerns, can have profound effects on larger problems that emerge considerably later—problems whose relevance to the initial decision is buried in the organization's ordinary practices.

For example, engineering companies often hire many engineers at the beginning of a project, but when the project ends they

1 Ford, Joseph. Quoted in J. Gleick, 1987. *Chaos: Making a New Science.* New York: Viking, p. 306.

Source: Lotte Bailyn, "SMR Forum: Patterned Chaos in Human Resource Management," *Sloan Management Review, 34,2* (Winter 1993), pp. 77–83.

are left with underutilized and demoralized employees. A possible solution is to hire more technicians. They can do some of the "engineering" work, and, when demand declines, their skills are more easily transferred to the ensuing maintenance jobs. One company, when confronted with this "obvious" solution, resisted its implementation. It took a while to establish that the resistance stemmed from a compensation decision made long before. At that time, trying to determine the proper incentive system for its engineering managers, the company decided to base their compensation, in part, on the number of engineers—not technicians—that reported to them!

A second example comes from a company that set its professional salaries by benchmarking against other companies in the same geographical area. Salaries are often set this way, and, of course, consulting firms make good money providing the benchmarking data. But the company also wanted to attract the best people it could by being the employer of choice. So it decided to provide overtime pay for its exempt employees up to a certain level. This financial incentive complemented the company's cultural dynamic that time spent at work was an indicator of commitment and high performance. But then the economy changed, and the company had to introduce cost-cutting measures, one of which was to reduce the amount of overtime. Still, certain tasks occasionally required extra work. What could the company do? It might have allowed employees to adapt their hours to fit the needs of the work, putting in more or less time when necessary, so that their hours would balance out in the end. But the company had another policy, evolved for very different reasons, that prohibited "comp time," that is, conversion of overtime into time off. This early decision had significant repercussions in a changed environment.

These examples show how embedded practice can constrain innovation in an organization's relationship to its employees. But let's step back and ask why such innovation is so necessary today in most organizations. Why do we need a new organizational vision? Why do we hear so much talk of organizational transformation, even organizational revolution?

Most of this concern stems from economic fear, from worry about U.S. productivity and foreign competition. But equally important are other new forces. More diverse family patterns are emerging in this country, and the younger generations have new and more varied values. What is problematic is that these two forces—the international economic situation and domestic demographic and life-style changes—lead to mutually contradictory responses. Companies try to increase productivity through cost-cutting and downsizing, which polarize the workforce: some people are under- or unemployed and others are completely overworked.[2] Recent demographic and life-style changes, however, call for a middle ground in which more people work but on reduced schedules. This solution seems peculiarly difficult for U.S. companies to accept. They find it culturally easier to provide day care, even sick child care, than to provide time and space for professionals to combine their commitment to work with their commitment to their private concerns.

Why should this be so? For one thing, U.S. companies have certain responsibilities—for social security and health insurance—that make part-time workers expensive. If a $100,000 job is held by one professional, the company pays social security tax on only half this salary. But if the same job is shared by two people, the company must pay this tax on the whole salary. Likewise, the company gets a greater return on health insurance costs if each covered employee does a greater proportion of the required work. In the short run, part-time work is economical for the organization only if it implies low wages and restricted benefits—not exactly the picture that most of us have in mind when we consider alternative ways of working.

S
43
PRESS

---

2 This effect has been well documented by Juliet Schor in her book. See J. Schor. 1991. *The Overworked American: The Unexpected Decline of Leisure*. New York: Basic Books.

But there are deeper, more complex reasons than these "simple" economic ones that account for the reluctance of U.S. companies to deviate from traditional employee practices. One reason is the myth of management control and the corresponding assumption that responsibility can't be shared. Managers are in the peculiar position of being held responsible for work they do not do. Their response, traditionally, has been to keep a tight control over the people who *do* do the work. Managers want their subordinates to be in sight, to be available at all times, and to be loyal and committed above all else to work. These are understandable responses, given the manager's position, but we all know that they actually defeat the goals they are intended to meet. People who feel controlled and mistrusted do not do their best work. That's why we hear so much talk about the multi-skilled workforce, the use of teams, and the elimination of management layers. These changes are attempts to increase productivity by empowering the people who actually do the work and by shifting managerial attitudes from control to trust.

The effects of such changes are often dramatic. I compared a group of home-based systems developers, many of them working part time, with an equivalent full-time group that was office based. The home-based employees were more involved with their work, more experienced, and more eager and willing to learn new skills. They were also more loyal to their organization, less involved in careerism, and less likely to expect to leave in order to start their own enterprises.[3]

Yet such alternatives as reducing schedules for organizational professionals or shifting the location of work between office and home are highly resisted by most managers and, indeed, by many employees. They fly in the face of entrenched career procedures, which evolved when the professional workforce consisted primarily of people who had full-time family support at home and therefore could—indeed were expected to—give complete priority to their work and their careers. We all know what these procedures entail. They put heavy emphasis on the early years of the career—you either prove yourself early or you won't get ahead. To prove yourself during this time you have to be visible; you have to be perceived as putting all your effort into your work; and you have to indicate your desire and willingness to accede to company demands.

These procedures are based on the assumptions that work is everyone's prime priority and that everyone plans on long-term career continuity. And it is these assumptions that have made life so difficult for the increasing number of women who have moved into the professional workforce as well as for the many men whose lives no longer fit into the traditional mold.

To accommodate the different ways of living with work, organizations should take a more chaotic approach to their employees. I realize that this suggestion flies in the face of a number of forces that support a more structured, controlled, and orderly system. Among these forces, ironically, are the very human resource systems that have been put into place to ensure lack of discrimination. Because of the threat of litigation, the fear of setting a precedent, and the erroneous belief that the only way to be fair is to assume that everyone is exactly alike and therefore has to be treated exactly equally, human resource professionals have actually created less chaos than might be optimal.

A good example of someone who got caught up in these assumptions is Doris. Her story came out of a series of networked interviews with MBA graduates, their spouses, their bosses, and their work colleagues.[4] After receiving her MBA, Doris joined a progressive high-technology firm that followed the tenets of the new high-commitment organization. It prided itself on its flexibility in dealing with

3 Bailyn, L. 1989. "Toward the Perfect Workplace?" *Communications of the ACM 32*, pp. 460–471.

4 Andrews, A. 1991. "Flexible Working Schedules in High-Commitment Organizations: A Challenge to the Emotional Norms?" Cambridge, Massachusetts: MIT Sloan School of Management, Working Paper No. 3329-91-BPS, August.

employees. Doris was immediately successful and received a number of commendations. Her work attracted the attention of an up-and-coming manager, and he enticed her to join his unit. However, as is customary in such an organization, he was shortly shifted to another part of the company, and he left her in charge of one of the other managers. Not long after, this manager took maternity leave and arranged with her boss to work one day a week at home after her return. All of this was good news to Doris, who also wanted to have a child.

Doris soon became pregnant and arranged for her own maternity leave. She wanted to return to her unit, and her managers wanted her back. Her husband supported her plans to continue her career. It seemed an ideal situation in which to negotiate a flexible schedule. As her maternity leave drew to an end, Doris began to negotiate for some kind of project that would require twenty-four hours a week. Such a project was identified; in fact it was the continuation of a project she had already successfully handled. All agreed it could be done in twenty-four hours a week—but there was a catch. Her managers wanted to make sure that the work was her primary commitment. For example, they wanted to know if she could come in for a meeting if one was called. She asked them to schedule meetings for times when she was already planning on being in the office. She needed to set limits on her time in the office in order to better manage both her work and her baby. But her managers needed to be assured that Doris would continue to give work her top priority over all else. Eventually they drew up a letter that said that Doris would have to come to all meetings that were called and that the part-time arrangement could be canceled at any time if it seemed to be interfering in any way. This was an unheard of formality in this loose organization. Doris's manager had had no such formal agreement with *her* boss when negotiating a more flexible schedule. But

she was willing to assure her boss that work would come first, despite the arrival of her baby. Flexibility was possible only if this show of primary commitment was made. But this was not what flexibility and accommodation to employee concerns meant to Doris, and so she quit.

What this story reveals is that in Doris's company, and indeed in most U.S. companies, work quality is not in itself a sufficient condition for high performance. Something else is required: proof that no matter what, the needs of the work always come first. Many companies require employees to prove their commitment by working long hours. But when long hours are not possible—as when an individual needs a different, more flexible schedule—the requirement nonetheless remains. In such a case, the willingness to shift one's private schedule whenever the organization demands, even when those demands seem capricious, provides the necessary "proof" of the required attitude.

Thus, in order to meet the needs of the changing workforce without sacrificing the competitive needs of U.S. industry, we must reevaluate the meanings of time and commitment in the workplace. This is the first principle in my vision of a chaotic organizational system (see Table 7.2). The output of complex, professional work is hard to specify, and it is hard to identify it with the efforts of one particular person. So we fall back on proxy indicators. If we can't know precisely the quality of a person's work—or we can't know it soon enough—we can at least know the level of his or her commitment. And we can measure people's commitment levels by the amount of time they are willing to give to their jobs and by the priority of work in their lives. Indeed, in a number of "how to" books on managing commitment, this is exactly the definition that is given. One states that a key "characteristic that we associate with committed employees is their willingness to make personal sacrifices to reach their team's organization's goals."[5]

45

PRESS

5 Kinlaw, D. C. 1989. *Coaching for Commitment: Managerial Strategies for Obtaining Superior Performance.* San Diego, California: University Associates, p. 5.

TABLE 7.2 PRINCIPLES OF CHAOS

1. Reevaluate Meanings
   - Time
   - Commitment
2. Test the Assumptions
   - Continuity vs. discontinuity
   - Uniformity vs. variety
   - Prespecification vs. self-design
3. Change the Boundaries
   - Looser link between organization and employee
   - Closer link between public and private life

Time, in its new meaning, should be less closely tied to cultural expectations and more closely linked to task. What we want is for our people to work smart, not long hours. That may mean that long hours become a sign of inefficiency rather than of committed performance. Jack Welch, the CEO of General Electric, is reported to have said that anyone who cannot do the job in forty hours is inefficient. We have to make a similar reevaluation of the meaning of commitment, defining it not in terms of time or loyalty but as taking responsibility for tasks in relation to organizational goals. Doris was willing to take such responsibility and was sure she could do it along with meeting the demands of her newly expanded family. But this was not enough in a culture where commitment went beyond task and constituted also a substitute form of control by the organization over its employees.

The second principle of this envisioned world requires testing and rethinking the assumptions on which the current career system is based. Three such revisions seem to me to be particularly critical. The first concerns the assumption of career continuity (which is in jeopardy anyway because of the recent spate of downsizings and layoffs). As I have already suggested, employers expect employees, particularly in the early career years, to put work above all else. But doing so may have serious repercussions down the road. Symptoms of the dangers of this assumption include burnout, plateaued careers, accumulation of "dead wood," and mid-life crises. Although these maladies are often seen as residing in individuals, it is actually the traditional career structure that contributes to these outcomes.

A new assumption of discontinuity, in contrast, would seem to be more effective in the long run. Organizations and employees would negotiate to divide careers into independent segments, each segment with its own distribution of commitments between work and other aspects of life. Low-commitment work segments would be judged differently from high-commitment segments, and they would involve different portfolios of tasks with different reward levels. Significantly, a period of some withdrawal from work would not be considered evidence of failure or of an inability to be productive; it would not be a blemish that would stay with the employee for the rest of his or her career. Nor should periods of low commitment reduce the effectiveness of organizations, because there are many organizational tasks that could be accomplished by employees in such a period. There is always work that is less visible, more circumscribed, perhaps less complex, that could be allocated to these workers. What is critical is that evaluation not be the same for these tasks as for those requiring greater employee investment of time and energy; evaluation must be relevant to the actual requirements of the tasks being performed.

The second assumption in need of reconsideration is the myth of uniformity; that is, the belief that employees can be handled identically. Employees, even in the same positions, bring with them very different needs and orientations. Further, as decades of research have shown, differences also vary over any given person's life span. Therefore, we need a system that responds to variety. Organizations must provide multiple career paths that are responsive to this ever-increasing diversity. Naturally, they must take care that such individualized paths are truly individual and do not turn into assignments based on stereotyped expectations about people's abilities or circumstances. In other words, we need a more chaotic situation than we currently have, in which the needs of tasks intersect with the needs of the people who perform them.

The third assumption, then, involves this intersection. The present system is based on matching people to carefully defined jobs and to all the presumed work requirements that have become attached to these jobs. I suggest that we need to allow people more flexibility to define for themselves how to do the necessary work. Some of this is happening already as companies try to become more innovative and adaptable. However, many of these modifications in work process don't allow employees discretion over the timing and location of work. Companies need to provide more opportunities for employees to design their own jobs, guided by both their individual needs and the needs of the tasks.

A final principle of this new world, which is congruent with the first two principles, relates to the boundaries between an employee and an organization and between a person's public and private life. As I've said, our current processes assume that the employee is closely tied to the employing organization's demands; that is, work must come first, organizational demands must be met. Hence there is assumed to be a clear separation between the person as worker and the person at home. I suggest that we need to *loosen* the link between organization and employee and thus to allow a closer linking of public and private life.

An example occurs in the management of fast food stores. An interesting study compared those stores that were franchised and managed by individual owners with those that were wholly owned by the central company and managed by one of its employees.[6] The latter case represents the typical link between employer and organization, whereas the franchise represents a looser link. The study found that central companies had a harder time controlling their franchisees, as one might expect. For example, when Pizza Hut decided to include evening delivery in its services, one franchisee refused because he did not want to spend his evenings working. He had that option as a franchisee, whereas an employee manager did not. The company, naturally, found such individuality problematic. But the study found another difference between the two employment relationships, this one in the area of innovation. The central control imposed on the employee manager did not provide a favorable atmosphere for new ideas. Most innovations came not from the wholly owned outlets but from the franchises. The Egg McMuffin, for example, was a franchise idea. This indicates that loosening the links between the organization and the employee may help both sides.

These then are the principles of a more chaotic, but nonetheless patterned way of thinking about personnel issues in organizations. They represent a different vision of the organizational world, which I believe would help both companies and employees. And they seem to fit better the conditions we currently face. They represent work organized by task rather than by time, based on trust more than on hierarchical control, and permitting a different—more integrated, less segmented—relationship between an employee's work life and private life.

So far I have considered organizational employees, who are subject to regulations they do not control. But what about entrepreneurs? Certainly people who start their own businesses should exhibit a greater variety of ways to organize their work lives. Indeed, in the data from our study of business school graduates, we have found two styles of entrepreneurship.[7] The differences between them are exemplified by the choices of Karen and Bill.

6 Bradach, J. L. 1992. "The Organization and Management of Chains: Owning, Franchising, and the Plural Form," Boston: Harvard Business School, Doctoral Diss.

7 Andrews, A. and L. Bailyn. Forthcoming. "Segmentation and Synergy: Two Models of Linking Work and Family," in *Work, Family, and Masculinities*, ed. J. C. Hood, Newbury Park, California: Sage.

Karen and Bill received their MBAs from the same school in 1979. For several years after graduation, their paths were almost identical. Both of them began in a prestigious, high-profile corporation position and moved on to a venture capital start-up a few years later. In both cases, the venture capital concerns failed to take root. At that point, Karen launched a consulting company combining her experience and expertise in biotech and computers; Bill opened the doors of his own investment company. Along the way, each of them married and began having children.

At this point, their lives became significantly different. Karen's decision to strike out on her own came as a result of a reevaluation of her aspirations and priorities: "Five years ago, I wanted to be a power player and run something. Now, I don't care about the fast track. I just want an interesting way to make money and stay flexible with my time." Bill, in contrast, gave the following three reasons for becoming an entrepreneur: "(1) dissatisfaction with corporate life and management; (2) identification of a significant business opportunity; and (3) need to get wealthy."

Karen feels that her work is well respected and that she could generate more income if she so desired. However, she is not willing to invest all of her time in the work. Bill, driven by the desire to build a successful business from scratch, works long hours and travels extensively.

Karen sees her work as a complement to the rest of her life. She has traveled extensively for pleasure in the past five years, and, at the time of our survey, she was taking six months off to stay with her new baby. Karen feels that her relationship with her husband, a software developer and consultant, has facilitated her progress in her career. She feels that their respective careers have allowed them the money and time to pursue their personal interests together. Karen names her husband as her primary source of emotional support and says that she has no problems with stress whatsoever.

For Bill, in contrast, it seems that other claims on his emotional or temporal energy create stress. They limit his ability to invest all in the new venture. He characterizes his relationship with his wife as a "constraint" on his progress at work; he also includes "presence of a two-year-old son" in the list of constraints. He says his wife, a business student, "has deferred to [his] career goals and resents it." Asked who provides support when problems arise, he responds "no real support."

Although Karen and Bill began their careers on parallel tracks, ten years after their graduation from business school they are living very different lives. They have both chosen to strike out on their own, to design and create their own professional opportunities. What is different is the degree to which they have decided to design their work around their personal and family lives. Bill's goals are rooted outside his home, in the marketplace and its monetary rewards. Karen's goals are centered within her home, in her own interests and the interests she shares with her husband. Their work lives appear to reflect these very different aspirations.

For both men and women, entrepreneurship is a way out of the dilemmas created by large bureaucratic organizations. But they seem to do it differently. Men often create situations that increase the personal pressures on them—even as they gain a sense of autonomy—whereas women use this route to integrate their lives. Two-thirds of the female entrepreneurs in our study structured their enterprises around their personal lives and said that their organizations fit their personality. Only 15 percent of the male entrepreneurs gave this response, and fully three-fifths said they have had to modify their behavior either some or a lot to fit into their *own* organizations.

I am not suggesting that this distinction reflects an essential difference between the sexes. Rather, it reflects a construction of the world of work based on the assumption that professional employees can give their all to work because someone else is taking care of nonwork concerns. This construction evolved at a time when caretaking responsibilities were the domain of people—women—who were not also involved in paid employment. As demographics and lifestyles have changed, so must this view of the world of work change. Under current conditions, such a worldview forces women to meld employment with caretaking and denies men the possibility of doing the same.

We tend to think that the excessive time demands of organizations reflect only the requirements of work, whereas in actuality, it seems likely that these demands also serve the purpose of measuring individual worth when performance criteria are difficult or impossible to specify. Traditionally, high performance is gauged by a commitment to work that is demonstrated by time and visibility. But the world is changing, and organizations will have to learn to respond more flexibly to their employees. Such individual flexibility may appear chaotic. One hopes, however, that it will be as constrained, as orderly, and as beautiful as the "chaotic" patterns portrayed by the new science of chaos. And if it provides the "exciting variety, richness of choice, and cornucopia of opportunity" that is associated with that science, we will all be the beneficiaries.

49

THE CONTINGENCY WORK FORCE

by Jaclyn Fierman

Like the tolling of an iron bell, a gloomy statistic has begun to resonate with many Americans: By some calculations, one out of four of us is now a member of the contingency work force, people hired by companies to cope with unexpected or temporary challenges—part-timers, freelancers, subcontractors, and independent professionals. As the name suggests, such workers typically lead far riskier and more uncertain lives than permanent employees; they're also usually paid less and almost never receive benefits. In large U.S. companies, their numbers have been growing lately in the scramble to get leaner and more efficient by shedding full-time workers for contingent ones. Indeed, a few analysts of trends predict that by the year 2000 fully half of all working Americans—some 60 million people—will have joined the ranks of these freelance providers of skills and services. Does this bell toll for you?

Absolutely, says Charles Handy, the British consultant who eloquently and accurately outlined the trend in his 1991 best-seller, *The Age of Unreason*. Handy's latest book, *The Age of Paradox*, due out in March, carries to an even scarier plane the concept of corporations that operate with a small core of permanent workers and a swirling mass of contingent ones. "Instead of being a castle, a home for life for its defenders, an organization will be more like an apartment block," he predicts, "an association of temporary residents gathered together for mutual convenience." Corporations will still conduct business, Handy says, "but to do so they will no longer need to employ."

If this prospect makes you feel like hurling yourself off the nearest bridge, stop—and take a closer look at the phenomenon. Start with that much cited one-out-of-four figure, which, on examination, may be less frightening than it seems. The way most analysts estimate the size of the contingency work force is by lumping together government statistics on part-timers and the self-employed. The latter account for about 8.5% of American workers—just as they did in 1980—and include many well-paid doctors, dentists, lawyers, and other professionals. These are not exactly the folks who spring to mind when articles bemoan the rise of "disposable" or "throwaway" workers.

Here's a second surprise: The size of the contingency work force, broadly defined, actually hasn't gone up. Add together part-timers and the self-employed for 1983, and you find that 27% of employed Americans were contingent workers a decade ago: a percentage point *higher* than today. Says Thomas Nardone, keeper of the employment figures at the Bureau of Labor Statistics (BLS): "We hear a lot of anecdotal data about the growth of the contingent work force, but we can't pinpoint the numbers." At a minimum, the available statistics suggest those infamous projections showing contingent workers accounting for 50% of the U.S. labor force by the year 2000 are sheer nonsense, while prophecies like Charles Handy's of full-time jobs soon becoming extinct are, to put it politely, far-fetched.

For all the doomster excess, other data confirm, though, that a profound, wrenching, and permanent change in the

Source: Jaclyn Fierman, "The Contingency Workforce," *Fortune* (January 24, 1994), pp. 30–36.

nature of employment is taking hold in the American workplace. The evidence:

- For as long as BLS has kept score, there have never been so many Americans working part-time who say they would rather have full-time jobs—roughly 6.4 million in 1993, out of 21 million part-timers. These include people like Chanel Lewis, 30, who teaches courses on self-esteem and social skills to girls in a jail in Chester, Virginia. She earns no benefits and is furloughed every seven months or so while the state reviews the funding for her job.

- The number of people working for temporary-employment agencies—national powerhouses like Manpower and Kelly Services as well as boutiques with names like Viva Temps and Contemporary—has jumped 240% in the past ten years, from 470,000 to 1.6 million. Temporary or part-time jobs accounted for roughly 20% of the 18 million jobs created since 1983, up slightly from earlier postwar decades. Result: Manpower, the biggest of the 7,000 U.S. temp agencies, is now also the nation's biggest private employer, with roughly 600,000 people on its payroll. That's some 200,000 more employees than General Motors and 345,000 more than IBM.

Temps once mainly filled in for a secretary who called in sick. What's fueling their proliferation is that companies now rely on outsiders to fill slots at every level of the organization. Some even sit in at the top. Cover subject Matthew Harrison, 49, works for Imcor, a Stamford, Connecticut, firm that provides companies with temporary senior executives. He has held high-level posts at four different businesses in seven years. "There can be real value in having a throwaway executive, who can come in and do unpleasant, nasty things like kill off a few sacred cows," says Harrison.

- Spurred by global competition and rapid technological change, large corporations continue to squeeze out inefficiencies. Wherever possible, many are reducing fixed labor costs by farming out work that contractors can do more cheaply or that telecommuters are happy to perform from home. Big companies, in particular, continue to downsize. Since 1979 the FORTUNE 500 industrials have eliminated 4.4 million jobs, one out of every four they once provided.

A new FORTUNE CEO Poll confirms that this trimming isn't about to end. Of 203 chief executives among the FORTUNE 500 queried in late November by the opinion research firm Clark Martire & Bartolomeo, 44% said they rely more on contingent workers now than they did five years ago. Only 13% used fewer, while the rest employed about the same level. An equally large percentage—44%—indicated that they expect to employ still more here-today, gone-tomorrow workers five years from now. Warns John Bryan, CEO of Sara Lee: "Any worker still expecting to hold one job from cradle to grave will need to adjust his thinking."

51

PRESS

TABLE 7.3 CEO POLL		
	Compared with 1988, my company's use of contingent workers has:	Five years from now, my company's use of them will have:
Increased	44%	44%
Decreased	13%	9%
Remained the same	43%	44%
Not sure	—	3%

All of which raises a very large question: Will this apparently inexorable trend, on balance, be good for the U.S.? Yes, say 48% of the FORTUNE 500 chief executives we polled, vs. just 25% who see it as clearly bad news. Supporters argue that greater use of contingent workers, by increasing companies' flexibility, lowering costs, and listing competitiveness, will enable them to provide greater job security—and fatter paychecks—for the far larger number of permanent workers who remain. In addition, notes Melvin Goodes, CEO of Warner Lambert: "Contingent work can provide the flexible job opportunities many people are looking for."

All true, but what troubles a vocal minority of business leaders is the devastating effect the temping of the work force can have on incomes, mental health, even the social fabric. Says Boeing CEO Frank Shrontz: "When it comes to medical help or retirement, contingent workers, who don't usually have benefits, are left hanging. That's not good for society." Some also insist that excessive reliance on temporary outsiders can drag productivity down, not up. "Having lots of part-time workers doesn't create the loyalty and ownership of results that being a regular part of the team does," says Martin D. Walker, CEO of M.A. Hanna, the Cleveland rubber company. "They should be used only on an emergency basis."

Worst off are the growing numbers of people being forced unwillingly into part-time-ism and self-employment. Again, the data are sketchy and anecdotal—tales of ex-steelworkers, say, who made $33 an hour before and are now freelancing down at the local body shop for $20 and hour. But one clear sign these people are facing relatively harder times is a sharp decline in their overall incomes. According to the Census Bureau, since 1989 the real median income of Americans who work for themselves fell 12.6% to $18,544 in 1992. During the same period, median wages and salaries for all employed Americans fell only 1.1% to $19,819.

If President Clinton's health plan survives Congress, the biggest fear of most full-time job holders—that a layoff could cost them their health coverage or force them to pay an exorbitant premium on their own—would be alleviated. But don't give the prospect of universal coverage more than two cheers. Because the President wants to finance his generous plan by making employers pick up most of the bill, mandatory health insurance may also swell the size of the contingency work force by persuading yet more companies that they can no longer afford to keep as many full-time employees on the payroll.

What's the view from the firing line? Like America's CEOs, many contingent workers are ambivalent. Karen Mendenhall, who had made a career of temping, captures the feeling in a new book, *Making the Most of the Temporary Employment Market:* "It is wonderful, exhilarating, rewarding, and challenging. And it is also horrible, demeaning, thankless, and boring."

For young people, such low-commitment work has traditionally been a useful way to explore career options. It still is. Since graduating from Williams College in 1992, Jillian Perlberger, 23, has toured the secretarial pools at New York City law firms and ad agencies. Temping at $16 an hour pays the bills while she contemplates what to do next. Law school is one possibility; cooking school another. "The only thing I've ruled out," she says, "is medical school."

What Perlberger dislikes most about temping is how quick people are to assume that temps are know-nothings. "One lawyer told me if he has to use a temp, he considers it a lost day," she says.

TABLE 7.4 CEO POLL	
	The trend toward using more contingent workers is:
Good for the U.S.	48%
Bad for the U.S.	25%
Neither	20%
Not sure	7%

In fact, 82% of temporary workers have finished high school, and 35% have completed at least two years of college. Says Frank Liguori, CEO of Olsten, one of the largest providers of temporaries: "We're not in the business of teaching people how to read and write."

Many older job hunters, especially those with children, find the contingent life considerably more stressful. Last June, Leo Zerrudo, 47, a chemical engineer, was laid off by aerojet propulsion division of GenCorp in Sacramento, which has cut 1,600 jobs in the past two years. For two months Zerrudo sent out close to 100 resumes. "Most companies didn't even bother to answer," he says. "My finances were going down. I was eating up my savings."

Finally LabForce, which places scientists in temporary jobs across the U.S., found a spot for Zerrudo analyzing potable water and hazardous waste on the evening shift at Enseco, Corning's environmental-lab subsidiary in West Sacramento. The original assignment was for one month. But Zerrudo has already been there four months. Though the job offers no benefits, he has matched his previous salary of $35,000 a year by working six to eight hours overtime a week.

Like most unwilling contingent workers, Zerrudo hopes eventually to land a permanent job. Temp work is often the way to do that. "We get a lot of our full-timers that way," says William Cooper, CEO of TCF Financial Corp., a bank holding company in Minneapolis. The National Association of Temporary Services, the industry's trade group, estimates that temp assignments lead to permanent work roughly a third of the time. While he waits, Zerrudo pounds the pavement every morning before reporting to work at Enseco—just in case.

For many others, the last-resort world of contingent work is becoming a first choice. Among this group are working mothers who want greater flexibility and are trying to tip the balance in their lives more toward home. Laura Masurovsky, 36, a 1983 graduate of Harvard Law School, cut back to part-time hours, so called, at Washington, D.C.'s prestigious Williams & Connolly after her second son was born. "But part-time was still nine to six," she says. "Full-timers live there."

Masurovsky opted out altogether last January after her third son was born. She launched her own part-time practice and helps pay overhead with occasional assignments from Attorneys Per Diem, and agency that finds just-in-time employees for law firms in the Baltimore area. Masurovsky values her new freedom: "I don't have to look over my shoulder when I have three pediatrician appointments in a row. And I don't have to answer to anyone if I have only three billable hours one day." She can also see more of her husband, Marc, 37, who is completing a doctorate at American University.

Masurovsky feels temping is less of a stigma than being mommy-tracked as a second-string player in a large law firm. "It's very professional. I find people are grateful for my help. I come in, do battle, and come up with a brilliant option for the counsel. Then I leave it on his desk and go home."

Corporate demand for interim professionals and executives has created a whole new industry over the past few years. David Lord, editor of *Executive Recruiter News*, estimates that firms dedicated to this endeavor mushroomed from 40 in 1990 to 110 today. Says John Thompson, head of Imcor, a leader in this end of the temp business: "What's core today can be considered contingent tomorrow."

While many executives use the Imcors of the world to cover expenses until the next full-time job comes along, at least a third, Thompson figures, opt for impermanence as a permanent way of life. Among them is Matthew Harrison, whose last assignment was turning around a frozen-food processor. Today he heads a troubled, family-controlled manufacturing company in Queens, New York, whose name he'd rather not divulge, lest its anxious creditors become even more so.

A former lieutenant colonel in the U.S. Army, Harrison earned his leadership stripes over two decades that included

FIGURE 7.6 THE GROWING ARMY OF TEMPS

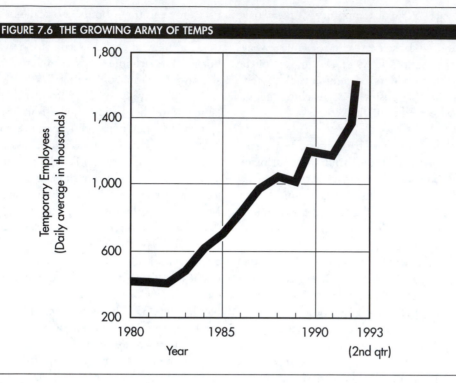

two years in Vietnam as a company commander. Says he: "I was in charge of 140 riflemen, most of whom were draftees and didn't have a lot of interest in getting killed. So keeping these guys focused on what we were supposed to be doing was a big challenge."

Harrison's first civilian job was vice president of administration at Wedtech Corp., the New York defense contractor that collapsed in a sea of scandal just weeks after he signed on in 1986. "That was actually a lucky break because, since I was about the only honest executive there, the creditors asked me to stay on and run the place," he says. Harrison subsequently wrote a well-received book, *Feeding Frenzy*, on the experience.

Much as he thrives on crisis and change, Harrison says he sometimes tires of constantly having to wield a turn-around ax. "It's not easy and never will be," he says. "Yesterday I had to get rid of a senior executive who worked here 35 years." The insecurity of his rootless life also gnaws at him. He never knows where his next job will take him, or when it will materialize. Says he; "I worry all the time."

For people who choose to work like gypsies, drifting from one job to the next, such feelings go with the territory. Some learn to live with it. Says Jerry Warshaw, 64, who has freelanced in the Chicago area for three decades as an illustrator: "I don't live on credit cards, so I never spend the money until the check comes in. When it does, I try to put 25% in the bank to cover taxes." To keep the work coming, Warshaw sends postcards of his illustrations every month to about 600 art directors and potential employers. "If you stop hustling," he says, "everything stops."

For companies that employ large numbers of contingent workers, managing them well poses "a tear-your-hair-out challenge," as Dee Daley of GE Medical Systems in Atlanta summarizes it. Start with the financial side of the equation. At the typical U.S. corporation, benefits—Social Security and other mandatory employment taxes, health and life insurance, vacations and sick leave, pensions and bonuses—add about 30% to total labor costs. So hiring temps and part-timers translates into big savings. Right?

Not necessarily. Depending on their skill level, independents sometimes command higher hourly wages than permanent workers. Nor do the people provided by good temp agencies, which have to recruit, screen, and pay employment taxes for their workers, come cheap. The bill to corporate clients can run as much as 50% above a regular worker's hourly wage, though smart managers can whittle that premium to as low as 20% by striking deals with just a few suppliers. Executives who try to save money simply by replacing workers with full-time temps or rehiring ex-employees as permanent consultants risk bringing down the wrath of an increasingly vigilant Internal Revenue Service—and could incur huge corporate and even *personal* tax liabilities (see above).

In addition, companies are discovering that, like permanent employees, contingent workers need to be trained and managed. If they're not, excessive turnover and low productivity are the costly consequences.

Consider Kolmar Laboratories, a cosmetics maker in Port Jervis, New York. Desperate to curb labor costs, the company a few years back began filling openings and covering work surges with temps. By the summer of 1992, roughly half its 600 assembly-line workers were temps, says Bill Brooks, Kolmar's general manager until last fall. These temps, who earned $5.60 an hour with no benefits, worked in teams with permanent employees who received, for the same work up to $9 an hour plus benefits, depending on their output. Fights broke out regularly between the groups. Says Brooks, who now runs one of American Home Products' largest plants: "All day long people shouted, 'go faster; you're holding us up.' But the temps had no incentive to work faster." Turnover was enormous.

HIRING TEMPS FULL-TIME MAY GET THE IRS ON YOUR TAIL

After more than a decade as an executive publishing computer magazines, Jay Whitehead, now 34, in October 1985 suddenly found his world falling apart. That's when the state of California launched the first of six employment audits of the magazines he worked for. Alerted by California, the IRS soon joined the chase. Between them the state and the feds have slapped the publications, among them *PC Magazine* and *Computer Register News*, with fines and penalties totaling $2.85 million—so far. As a principal of three of the hunted firms, Whitehead personally faced liabilities of over $300,000. "It was a life-shattering experience," he says.

Could this happen to you? You bet. Like many in his industry, Whitehead and his colleagues relied on a regular stable of temporary writers, art directors, and photographers. Their sin wasn't trying to hide the income they paid out to these people. They reported every dime. Their mistake was using the wrong form, the 1099s sent out to independent contractors rather than the W-2s mailed to regular employees. To the taxmen, who collect withholding and other employment taxes from W-2s but not from 1099s hiring part-timers to do jobs also filled by permanent workers—but accounting for them differently—is a tax error that costs the federal government alone $2 billion a year in lost revenues.

Aware of the growing market for temporary and freelance work and eager to get its due, the IRS since the mid-1980s has been cracking down hard on companies that misclassify contingent workers. The tally so far: $678 million collected in fines and back taxes, and some 439,000 independent contractors recategorized as full-time employees. Any business, large or small, can be at risk. But the IRS is especially interested in temp-intensive industries such as publishing, entertainment, telecommunications, advertising, software, and construction.

How can you avoid getting hit? The law can be pretty vague, but here's one handy rule to remember: Send 1099s only to people who truly work out of the office. Provide a phone and a desk for more than a few days to someone who does tasks similar to those your regular staff perform, and you'd better withhold taxes and send that person a W-2. Another red flag: hiring back former employees or retirees on a contract basis. Again, consider those folks employees, not freelancers.

Still uncertain about a worker's true tax status? Here's another solution: Hire part-time or self-employed staff only through an outside agency. That hoists the risk onto someone else's shoulders—and lets him deal with the hassle of distributing paychecks and paying income and employment taxes.

Convinced by his own unfortunate experience that such a service could prove a booming business, Jay Whitehead in early 1993 reinvented himself as head of a new division at Uniforce, a California temp agency. Known as Payroll Options: The 1099 Compliance System, Whitehead's operation promises to make any company IRS-audit-proof—at least when it comes to misclassifying workers. His toll-free number is—what else?—1-800-291-1099.

—Ani Hadjian

What did Kolmar gain at the end of the day? "It was a wash," says Broods. "What we saved on hourly rates we paid for in rework, recruiting costs, and training." Kolmar greatly improved team spirit at the plant when it stopped paying permanent employees on the basis of output and compensated them instead for the number of skills they acquired and put to use. And as openings occurred, temps were offered full-time work. Today, says Kolmar senior vice president Dale Cook, virtually none of the company's 400 assemblers are temps.

Still, many companies find that temps can pay off when they're managed right. At GE Medical Systems, the customer service call-in center offers extensive training to ensure that its 27 contingent employees work the phones as effectively as its 33 permanent employees. Manpower recruits the workers and puts them through a four week customer service course designed and largely paid for by GE. While temps don't earn what regulars do, the training does seem to lift their morale. "This can go on their resume," points out Dee Daley, who runs the operation. "It can be a building block for their careers."

Fierce competition among temp agencies may encourage this trend toward giving part-timers more skills. In Memphis, home of Federal Express and a distribution center for many national manufacturers, there is great demand for workers who can process orders and pack them accurately. Norrell Services responded by adding a 4,000-square-foot training center to its regional office, complete with warehouse equipment similar to that used by Snap-On-Tools, Nike and other clients. Permanent employees at Nike, for instance, pack some 210 pairs of sneakers an hour; Norrell has trained the temps it sends Nike to pack 267 pairs.

For Georgia-Pacific, the quest for top quality temps ultimately led to a new business. When the company moved its headquarters to Atlanta in 1982, it encountered a terrible turnover problem among clerical workers—close to 40% in the first year. "We were working with 20 temp agencies at the time to fill the gaps," says CEO Pete Correll. In response, the company started an in-house agency, Georgia Temp, that proved so successful—turnover quickly dropped to 9% at headquarters—that it soon began marketing its recruits to outsiders. Georgia Temp now supplies about 250 people a day to its parent and roughly the same number of people to other firms around Atlanta.

Despite that success, Correll, for his part, expresses no interest in hiring contingent workers for anything more than shuffling paper at headquarters. "Temps have their limits," he says. "Our manufacturing facilities need operators who are well trained and who understand the quality requirements of the job. You can't just drop someone into that. We want workers who will buy into our dream, which is to be the highest-quality, most competitive forest products company in the world."

As that comment suggests, at some point corporate America's drive for flexibility and cost cutting runs head-on into another key imperative: the growing belief that competitive advantage hinges

BURNED-OUT BOSSES

by Lee Smith

Because we believe in you, we are raising your sales quota 20%. But your relationship with customers is already strong, so we're trimming your travel budget. Also, would you mind sharing your secretary with several other managers? Finally, over the next few months we want you to reduce your staff by a third. Oh, one more thing . . .

As corporations restructure, they are forcing managers through one of the most harrowing stress tests in business history. It is more than just the searing pace of change that makes bosses feel pressed—it's what's happening where their business touches their lives every day. The sales and production quotas they have to meet go up relentlessly, but everything else about their careers seems headed down: operating budgets, travel allowances, expense accounts, salary increases, and opportunities for promotion.

Most painful of all, managers who were trained to build are now being paid to tear down. They don't hire; they fire. They don't like the new mandate, but most have come to understand that it's not going to change. That realization makes the daily routine different: Work no longer energizes; it drains.

If this is something you see in others—or feel yourself—you're not alone. A growing number of line managers, senior staff, and other executives suffer some stage of burn-out. Though not a precisely defined medical condition, burnout has recognizable symptoms and is a result of prolonged stress, says Dr. Donald E. Rosen, a psychiatrist who directs the Professionals in Crisis program at the Menninger Clinic, the celebrated psychiatric hospital in Topeka. "Victims are lethargic, feel empty, no longer able to take satisfaction in what they once enjoyed," says Rosen. "They have a deep questioning of the value of the tasks they perform." In everyday parlance, they hate to go to work, not just on an occasional morning but on most mornings.

Companies devote vast resources to dealing with trauma of downsizing, but most of that goes to the most obvious victims—those let go. Outplacement firms that help the displaced find new jobs collected $700 million in fees last year. But over time, many *survivors* may suffer more psychological damage than the departed. The dismissed sales manager who goes to work for a small but growing fish may settle for less income and fewer benefits at the new company but be more content than the colleague who remains behind with a whale struggling to turn itself into a shark.

Observes Daniel Yankelovich, the public opinion scholar whose organization recently completed a survey of top executives on the tactics of reorganization: "Most managements don't have as firm a hand on the human aspects of restructuring as they do on finance and technology." That shortcoming can wind up costing employers greatly in lost talent and lower sales.

David Noer, and expert in organizational behavior at the Center for Creative Leadership in Greensboro, North Carolina, calls the misery of those left clinging to the big fish "survivor sickness." No one knows for sure how many

Source: Lee Smith, "Burned-Out Bosses," *Fortune* (July 25, 1994), pp. 44–52.

executives suffer from it. Companies that are aware of the problem in their midst are not eager to talk about it. But a striking increase in the number of disability claims for mental and nervous illness may be an indicator. UNUM Life Insurance, which writes more private disability policies than any other U.S. insurer, says the number of such claims it processed rose from 7.8% of its total in 1989 to 10.2% in 1993.

Survivors, says Noer, go through a process of psychic numbing that is similar in many ways—although certainly far less shattering—to that of those who have lived through plane crashes or similar disasters where other people perished. Even though there may be a rationale to the reorganization, survivors often feel guilty because from their perspective it is arbitrary; they are no worthier than those who were fired, only luckier.

Under the circumstances it seems almost immoral to take much joy in work. So they become morose and cautious, worrying that they will be washed away in the next wave of discharges. Meanwhile, they work harder and longer to make up for the toil of those who have left. Fatigue and resentment begin to build.

A director of marketing reflects with contempt and exhaustion on the reorganization that the television station she works for has gone through. When she joined the company in 1985, she respected her employer and enjoyed managing her staff of eight. Two years ago a handful of senior executives unexpectedly revealed plans for a top-to-bottom restructuring.

"We down in the trenches had no voice," she says. The effect on her department was paralyzing: She lost half her staff to layoffs. "Things that once happened as automatically as breathing ceased to work," she says. "I walked in one day last summer and discovered I had three full-time jobs. With a load that size, I hate them all. As a result, my employer is getting 10% of my former creativity and maybe 50% of my energy. I'm the classic employee who quit but still shows up to pick up her paycheck."

But nothing—not overwork, not confusion, not lost perks, not apprehension—is as deadening to a manager's morale as firing subordinates. To do it once is traumatic enough, but subsequent dismissals wear down one's resilience. The American Management Association's most recent survey of employment practices at 870 companies found that almost half had reduced their work forces from mid-1992 to mid-1993. For two-thirds of those companies, this was at least their second year of downsizing in a row.

Unlike most other duties executives undertake, cutting staff is not something they get better at; they often get worse. More precisely, it gets worse for them. David Sokol sprinted into his fast-track career at the age of 27, ten years ago. He built a garbage-to-electricity co-generation business from scratch to 1,100 employees and $350 million a year in revenues. Three years ago Sokol and a partner made a major investment in California Energy, which sells power to utilities, and gained management control. The previous managers had so burdened the company with unneeded staff that earnings on revenues of $90 million were only $5 million, a profit margin far below the industry average. The new management decided to let 150 people go. Sokol fired 15 personally. "It made me angry because it wasn't the employees' fault," he says. His stomach twisted into a knot before each dismissal.

One year later Sokol left California Energy to become president of a much larger company and discovered to his dismay that it had even more serious financial problems. There he had to fire half a dozen senior people and supervise the dismissals of several hundred other employees. "You get through firing people the first time around, accepting it as part of business," says Sokol. "The second time I began wondering, 'How many miscarriages is this causing? How many divorces, how many suicides?' I worked harder so that I wouldn't have to think about it."

Adam Zak, an executive recruiter in Chicago, in the course of a search visited a prospect he had known before as an assertive, powerful executive. Since their last encounter, Mr. Take Charge had gone through several rounds of firing subordinates. Zak describes him: "He was smoking, had lost weight, had trouble looking me in the eye, was extremely nervous. It seemed to me that a few months of telling people they were out the door had gone a long way in destroying his personality."

In another case, a rapidly rising executive in a major communications company had been required to eliminate several thousand jobs a couple of years age. It bothered him, but he soldiered on, putting in more hours at work. Last year he was promoted, and a month later he was asked to oversee the elimination of several thousand more positions. Within weeks of that new assignment he began losing his appetite and had trouble sleeping. Although he had never had difficulty making decisions before, he started to second-guess himself. Was he cutting the wrong jobs? Occasionally he began to cry spontaneously. One day he couldn't get out of bed.

With the help of medication and psychotherapy, this executive is back on the job. But the incident helped illuminate for his employer the depth of the crisis among the senior staff. Hundreds of managers have had to tell waves of subordinates they were finished. And they see no end to it. "People there don't know when the rain is going to stop," says one of the company's retired executives. The toll on managers rises: The human resources department reports an increase in absenteeism and alcoholism among managers. The medical department has called in consulting psychologists.

In the course of continuing restructurings, IBM has eliminated more than 100,000 jobs over the past four years. Listen to a former marketing vice president who spent 20 years with the now struggling computer maker. "Through most of the years, I loved that company so much I would get excited on Sunday night about going to work on Monday," she says. But beginning in 1986 and every year since, IBM has been shrinking. "Every year we'd call it something

different—early retirement, reorganization, reengineering," she recalls. "It was slow water torture."

At first she could tell subordinates that they could have jobs if they were willing to be mobile. Moving from Armonk to Oklahoma was unrealistic for most IBMers, tied down by spouses with other jobs, houses, schools, and commitments. Still, she wasn't actually firing anyone. As those faraway opportunities began to vanish, the executive spent days on the telephone trying to find "catchers," colleagues who might be able to scoop up the talented people she had to let go. "I came home every night worried how this one or that one was going to support himself. I snapped at my husband. I had trouble sleeping." At Christmastime in 1992, she promised herself that the next time a decent retirement package was offered, she would take it. So in the middle of the following year she left IBM. "Reorganization had been five years out of my life," she says, "and when I quit, I felt the biggest load in the world had been lifted from my shoulders." As she circulated her resume elsewhere, one prospective employer was attracted by her experience in downsizing. He had the same thing in mind for his company. She fled the prospect.

Some managers are able to cope easily with successive dismissals—employees call them the "hatchets." But many more executives loathe it. For 15 years Nolan Brohaugh, a senior associate at the Menninger Clinic, has helped conduct weeklong seminars in which managers take a break from their routine and reflect on their work. "I've never met one of those caricature executives with blood dripping from his teeth," says Brohaugh. "In my experience, they have a lot of trouble even firing people who deserve to get canned."

Dismissal is clearly an attack on the ego of the person being fired, but in ways that are less obvious it also assaults the ego of the person wielding the ax. Dr. Gerald Kraines, a Harvard psychiatrist and CEO of the Levinson Institute, which advises companies on organizational strategies, explains how. "We all carry around internal aspirations, generally ideals from our childhood," he says, "Anything that increases the gap between what we think we ought to be and what we are actually doing drives down our self-esteem."

Overwork doesn't do that. Toiling 70 hours a week may be exhausting, but it's consistent with the American ethic. Taking the redeye overnight flight from Los Angeles to New York so as not to miss a day's work is as much an occasion for boast as complaint. Firing is something else. Its underlying principles are un-American—authoritarian and classist. Like nothing else in a manager's repertoire, it accentuates I'm-the-boss-and-your-not. Also, from kindergarten through business school, Americans are taught to expand and build to the horizon. Firing has the smell of defeat and retreat.

As the manager's self-esteem is threatened, he is inclined to work harder—beyond what is required by the reduction in staff—to feel good about himself again. The reason for that response, says Kraines, has to do with a physiological defense mechanism: "When there's a threat—whether it's to our bodies or to our self-esteem—the mind ratchets up a few notches." For short spurts, that can help prepare an effective response to the threat. But if the brain stays in racing gear for too long, mental and physical reserves run down, and burnout begins to set in.

One of the first things to go as the flame flickers is creative spirit. Managers undergoing prolonged threats react in one of several ways, says Kraines. They become hostile toward those around them or toward themselves—depression—or they try to impose strict control on everything within their jurisdiction. "All of those postures discourage the easy flow of ideas, which is the basis of creative output," Kraines observes. Once this syndrome takes hold in an organization, the result can be a cadre of uptight managers with little energy or imagination.

What makes the waves of dismissals in recent years especially damaging is that so often workers have been fired not for cause but because their skills were no longer needed. They were accountants, perhaps, when the times cried out for salespeople. Consider the torment of a 49-year-old controller of a Midwestern utility. He is active in his church and not long ago led a major fund-raising drive on behalf of a paralyzed girl. He has generally found business compatible with his faith and generous nature. Even when he occasionally had to dismiss a misfit, someone not cut out to be an accountant, he felt okay about it. "One young man started a string of quality photo shops, and we became customers," he recalls.

But late last year the controller had to fire 18 accountants because the utility had sold off some of its properties and no longer needed so large a staff. "That was very different," he says. "I no longer had the crutch of being able to say this was the best thing that could happen to them. It wasn't. One woman had been with the company for 15 years. She told me her father had just died, and her mother was sick. I felt as if *I* was the one being fired."

CEOs don't enjoy handing out pink slips any more than lower executives do, but at least the CEO gets some balancing psychological benefits out of a downsizing. The company's outside directors and security analysts, to whom the layoffs spell higher profits, applaud his courage for doing what has to be done—excellent salve for the self-esteem. Subordinate managers don't receive that applause. Muses Levinson's Kraines: "Misery flows downhill."

Another reason for managerial angst is that midlevel bosses face two incompatible assignments: Be a cold-blooded cost cutter, and be liked. Notes the Menninger Clinic's Dr. Rosen: "He has been told that the new management style of the Nineties is to think of himself and his people as teammates." But in front of his subordinates the manager has to play contradictory roles: He is their friend; he may also be their executioner. The strain of reconciling these personas fans the flames of stress and resentment.

61

In firing longtime employees, managers feel that they have violated a trust. "You joined AT&T knowing you would never own the biggest house in the neighborhood," says Chuck Taylor, 56, a former division controller there. "But in exchange for lower income, you got an implicit guarantee of lifetime employment." Or did until the mid-Eighties, when Taylor and hundreds of other managers began to dismiss what eventually amounted to 140,000 workers. Typically, those whom Taylor fired were men between 45 and 55 with a child or two in college and a wife who stayed home. One of the men broke down and shouted abuse at him. Security came and escorted the distressed employee out of the building.

Taylor's morale sank. "When I was in high school trying out for football, there was a guy who put a slip of paper in your locker if you were cut from the team," he says. "We called him the Turk. Nobody wanted to get near him. We looked the other way when he came by. At AT&T, I began to feel like the Turk." So in 1989, after participating in three rounds of downsizings, Taylor accepted a generous retirement package and left.

What can companies do to help thousands of other valuable, experienced managers before they burn out and leave? The Levinson Institute's Kraines insists that the first thing top management must do is walk managers below them through all the steps that led to the decision to restructure the company. What was happening in the marketplace that made it necessary? Why did they have to reorganize in this way and not in some other? Were there mistakes made at the top? This kind of information can lessen the guilt and enhance the performance of the managers who stay behind.

AT&T may be getting the message. When James Smith, 47, a division manager in Indianapolis, had to fire 20 of his 80 subordinates in 1988, he fretted that if he had led his troops better he might have prevented the downsizing. His guilt grew into a sense of personal failure. "I would characterize my reaction as depression," he says, "waking up at 2 A.M., crying at times, feeling out of control of things." Unlike Taylor, Smith stayed on. He is still cutting staff, but AT&T has made the anguish of his assignment more bearable. The company has taken great pains to explain how changes in the global marketplace and not managerial failures forces the restructuring. The financial benefits for those who are leaving have improved as well.

Top executives also need to spell out which of the company's traditional values will be preserved, says Kraines. Lifetime loyalty to employees is gone. What else is out the window? Will prestigious products be junked if their profit margins erode a bit? "People join companies for more than paychecks," Kraines points out. "You don't want people signing a new psychological contract they can't live with."

Sound advice, no doubt, but it doesn't do much to relieve the anguish of layoffs. Top management ought to acknowledge the pain. "A restructuring is always presented in nothing but a positive way, as an opportunity to get lean and mean or whatever," observes one psychologist who counsels senior executives on relations with colleagues. "That may be true, but it creates a taboo against talking about the other side of the restructuring. It doesn't give people permission to say, 'This is hell.'"

Constant restructuring has become a fact of business life in this era of change. Well and good, but companies that don't acknowledge the stress that survivors undergo and support those who are in danger of burning out may find that their glistening, reengineered enterprises end up being run by charred wrecks.

THE CASE OF THE PART-TIME PARTNER

by Gary W. Loveman

> HBR's cases are derived from the experiences of real companies and real people. As written, they are hypothetical, and the names used are fictitious.
>
> Gary W. Loveman is an assistant professor at the Harvard Business School, where he teaches organizational behavior and human resource management.

Meeker, Needham & Ames, a long-established metropolitan law firm, employs 100 associates and 20 partners and is preeminent in corporate litigation. Each year, the promotions committee nominates associates for promotion. This year, the partner nominations carried particular weight; MN&A's overall billings and partner incomes were stagnating, showing the effects of intensified competition and in-house corporate counsel. The three associates under consideration had all worked for the firm seven years, meeting the minimum requirement for partner.

Chairing the meeting was George Hartwig, 53, for three years the managing partner. Also on the committee were Maury Davidson, 62, a senior partner and managing partner for seven years before Hartwig; Pamela Fisher, 44, a tax law specialist and the only female partner; and Jim Welch, 47, director of litigation.

The day after the meeting, Hartwig circulated the minutes. Memos from Fisher and Davidson appeared on Hartwig's desk the same day.

MEEKER, NEEDHAM & AMES
Minutes of the Promotions Committee Meeting September 1, 1990

Present: George Hartwig, chair, Maury Davidson, Pamela Fisher, Jim Welch; Absent: None

Mr. Hartwig called the meeting to order at noon. He began by reminding the committee that although there was no fixed number of slots available for partners, the committee must consider carefully who it decided to recommend for promotion. Given the severe competition facing the firm, he said, the decision carried with it both risk to the incomes of existing partners and opportunities for new and increased billings. He also stated that the committee should nominate all worthy candidates but should carefully evaluate merit in terms of client service and the ability to generate revenues. He then asked Mr. Davidson to begin the consideration of Rick Stewart.

Mr. Davidson said that he believed that Mr. Stewart should not be promoted to partner. "While Rick has done well in this firm," said Mr. Davidson, "he hasn't really distinguished himself. Nor has he developed a practice that will generate new clients."

Mr. Welch supported Mr. Davidson's position. "Rick's work as a litigator has been solid, as his file indicates. But I don't think he'll become the kind of attorney who can capture the confidence of the high-level executives we want to represent."

Mr. Hartwig asked if anyone wished to support Mr. Stewart. Hearing no one, he declared Mr. Stewart's candidacy dropped and asked Mr. Welch to speak to Tim Brower's candidacy.

Source: Reprinted by permission of Harvard Business Review, "The Case of the Part-Time Partner," by Gary W. Loveman (September–October 1990). Copyright © 1990 by the President and Fellows of Harvard College; all rights reserved.

Mr. Welch stated that, in his opinion, Mr. Brower could serve as a model for the young, hard-working, committed attorneys the firm would need to attract in the future. "Tim has distinguished himself in virtually every way possible," said Mr. Welch. "He has consistently handled difficult cases with exceptional results and has earned praise from clients. He volunteers for more work and can be found at the office nights and weekends. And he has more than once proposed new legal avenues for us to pursue, based on his expertise in some of the more technical areas of our practice."

Mr. Hartwig asked if there were any reservations to Mr. Brower's candidacy.

Mr. Davidson responded that his only concern was that Mr. Brower seemed more interested in legal technicalities than in pursuing new clients.

Ms. Fisher remarked that his file clearly indicated a lack of new-client development.

Mr. Welch responded that Mr. Brower's networking and client-development abilities were definitely weak but that the rest of his performance was so outstanding that he was certain Mr. Brower could improve in these areas.

Mr. Hartwig asked for the sense of the committee. It unanimously supported Mr. Brower's candidacy for partner.

Mr. Hartwig said that he would introduce the candidacy of Julie Ross. He reminded the committee members that they all had firsthand knowledge of Ms. Ross's capabilities since she had worked for each of them at various times. Her file indicated that they had found her performance exemplary. Her work had ranked among the best in the firm, displaying both keen insight into legal issues and top-notch courtroom litigation. Moreover, Mr. Hartwig stated, in the past two years Ms. Ross had shown a growing capability for attracting new business. In most cases, she had received additional work from existing clients, but in two instances, satisfied clients had given her name to other companies that had then engaged MN&A as their main counsel.

Mr. Hartwig said that the main issue the committee needed to address was Ms. Ross's part-time status. "When Julie had her baby three years ago," he said, "she requested and was given a reduction in her client load. We should consider her promotion in light of how it will affect firm perceptions and policy on part-time status in general."

Mr. Welch asked Mr. Hartwig to review the agreement made with Ms. Ross as well as the firm's other part-time arrangements.

Mr. Hartwig responded that Ms. Ross had negotiated a flexible schedule that permitted her to work "as necessary" to meet the needs of her clients. She and the firm understood that this would require approximately 50% of the billable hours of her colleagues, with salary and benefits reduced accordingly. Mr. Hartwig recalled that there had been much debate about the agreement and that many senior partners had been adamantly opposed to part-time work. Nevertheless, Mr. Hartwig had agreed to the proposal, making MN&A the first firm of its size in the city to implement part-time schedules for its attorneys.

Mr. Hartwig said that after negotiating the agreement with Ms. Ross, he had issued a memorandum stating that the firm would entertain similar requests from other attorneys, would have no general policy on part-time professional work, and would work out decisions and details case by case. Since that time, two other female junior associates had been granted part-time status. Both had negotiated fixed schedules of three days per week.

Ms. Fisher stated that although Ms. Ross exhibited outstanding skills, she was not qualified for promotion. "We all had these skills when we were up for partner. But what distinguished us from the others was our dedication to the firm and to our clients through years of exceptionally hard work and long hours." Ms. Fisher said that as an associate, she had worked a minimum of 70 hours per week, as had most associates who made partner. These long hours were not only evidence of commitment but had also been invaluable in giving her a feel for the firm's distinctive culture and an understanding of its needs. "We have all just agreed that Mr. Brower should be made partner, in part because of his demonstrated commitment to the firm. Skills alone are not enough," she concluded.

Mr. Welch stated that he agreed with Ms. Fisher that Ms. Ross should not be nominated. "Julie's performance may have been excellent, but it has been based on a less-than-equal standard," Mr. Welch said. He noted that partners had refrained from assigning Ms. Ross the most complex and demanding work because of her limited schedule and her inability to go on lengthy trips. He concluded that he could not support her candidacy unless she returned to work full-time on the same kinds of cases and under the same conditions as her peers.

Ms. Fisher pointed out that the committee needed to address the issue of establishing precedent. "If we promote Julie without demanding an equal commitment to the firm," she stated, "we will be telling all of our associates that we no longer value motivation and dedication."

Mr. Hartwig agreed with Ms. Fisher that Ms. Ross's case would affect the firm's future direction, but he disagreed with her conclusion. He said that the proportion of female law school graduates was increasing each year and with it the number of female associates joining the firm. He pointed out that 40% of new hires in the past five years had been female, yet the firm still had only one female partner. "Our best female associates aren't staying around long enough even to be considered for partner," he stated. "Unless we establish a more flexible environment, we'll continue losing them. Julie is the only promising female candidate we'll have for the next two years. Promoting her will help us attract and retain the best people." Mr. Hartwig concluded that it was in the firm's best interest to balance the costs of nontraditional work schedules against the benefit of keeping people like Ms. Ross.

Mr. Davidson stated that establishing a flexible environment was important to men as well as women. Although no men had yet shifted to part-time schedules, he noted, the firm had recently lost several outstanding male associates who had left to pursue careers that gave them more time with their families. "This is not purely an issue of gender," Mr. Davidson said. "It is an issue of how we structure our work and the demands we place on all of our people. When I came up through the ranks, I expected to work and to do little else. All of us in the partnership paid a very high price in our home and family life, including separation and divorce. Today many of our best associates are unwilling to live as we did, and I can't say I blame them." Mr. Davidson concluded that the firm would have to make some changes in order to keep the best attorneys, and that included promoting Ms. Ross.

Mr. Welch reminded Mr. Hartwig of the debate that had ensued when Ms. Ross was given part-time status as an associate. He predicted that making Ms. Ross a part-time partner would produce an even greater crisis. Mr. Welch said, "I am not convinced that the threat of losing Julie and people like her is worth putting this firm through the convulsions that would follow her promotion. We can always attract enough people like Pam Fisher, Tim Brower, and ourselves among the many associates we hire each year to keep this firm growing and prosperous."

Mr. Hartwig stated that the committee was clearly divided on Ms. Ross's candidacy. Mr. Hartwig said that he would recommend Tim Brower for promotion and would draft a report describing each committee member's arguments regarding Ms. Ross's candidacy. He would circulate the report among the partners and schedule a meeting of the partnership for an open discussion.

Mr. Hartwig adjourned the meeting of the promotions committee at 3:30.

SEPTEMBER 2, 1990

To: **George Hartwig**
From: **Pam Fisher**

I've just looked over the minutes of the promotions committee meeting, and there are two things I'd like to add.

First, I have to point out, George, that the entire discussion wouldn't have been necessary if, at the time you made the part-time agreement with Julie, you had been explicit about how it would affect her chances of making partner. I don't understand why the issue wasn't clarified from the beginning.

Second, I see an important distinction between part-time associates and part-time partners. I respect Julie's decision to spend time at home with her young child. As an associate, I probably would have made the same decision if I'd had children. But I would not have expected to make partner. Associates can cover for other associates, but nobody can cover for a partner; we are the critical link to the client. I need not remind you that this firm is in trouble. I don't think we should consider making someone a partner who would not be working full-time to help us out of this situation.

9/2/90

George—

Nice job handling the discussion at the meeting. You've got a tough assignment ahead of you outlining for the partners the committee's divergent positions on Julie.

I don't mean to complicate the matter, but to me the issue isn't simply about making Julie a partner. Her case will effectively establish the firm's policy on part-time work. The relevant issues here include flexible work schedules, motivation of both male and female associates, the reaction of the firm's clients, and the concerns of the existing partners.

But even more important, our decision will reflect our beliefs as an organization about how the quality of one's personal life affects one's work at the firm.

I think you know my position on this. I intend to spend more time with my family—I don't want to wait until retirement to begin enjoying my grandkids. Furthermore, I'm convinced that doing this will make the time I spend at the firm more productive.

Maury

SHOULD MEEKER, NEEDHAM & AMES MAKE JULIE ROSS A PARTNER?

Ⓢ

66

CASE

Five experts from both inside and outside the law profession consider this question.

Sally C. Landauer *is a partner at Ball, Janik & Novack, a Portland, Oregon law firm, where she has worked a four-day week for the past eight years. At a previous firm, she was one of the first part-time partners on the West Coast.*

Meeker, Needham & Ames is a law firm in trouble. It is an associate mill, grinding out young lawyers so rapidly that by the seventh year, only 3 of its 100 associates are left to be considered for partnership.

This should be an economic disaster for the firm. It means that each year it must hire some two to three dozen new associates. Even its second-year associate load must be very heavy. John P. Weil, an Orinda, California law firm consultant, warns that the first-year cost of hiring an associate fresh from law school is $100,000. That includes capital costs, but it also takes into consideration revenue generated. If MN&A hires 30 new associates, it will spend $3,000,000. MN&A cannot afford to lose Julie Ross—despite her part-time status—because she is, by admission of the partnership committee, a client getter.

The committee, however, focused on how Ross's partnership would affect firm perceptions and policies on part-time work in general. The two partners arguing against Ross focused only on her lack of "dedication" to the firm. Pam Fisher, in particular, confuses Ross's part-time schedule with a lack of motivation and dedication. As a mother of three who tried for four years to be a full-time lawyer and an adequate mother, I can assure Fisher that motivation and dedication are not the problem. Despite my present four-day-a-week schedule, I have developed sufficient expertise and enough clients to be asked to join three firms as a partner.

What are the firm's options? Having made the initial mistake of not establishing Julie Ross's position on or off the partnership track at the time she requested part-time status, there are still a number of ways the firm can make Ross a partner. It can:

1. Delay her partnership by an amount of time equivalent to her reduced number of hours. A delay of a year and a half (50% of the three years of part-time work) would enable Ross to reassess whether to stay on a part-time basis at the end of that time or return to full-time work.

2. Establish an income partnership. This option is becoming more common in law firms around the country as competition squeezes profits and as more lawyers reject the 70-hour-a-week work schedule that has traditionally aided partnership entry. With this kind of partnership, Ross would be entitled to partnership status, a guaranteed income rather than points and profit sharing, and the right to vote on all matters except points (compensation) for partners and mergers. She would have no equity investment. She would not share in upside potential, but she would not be exposed to risk, either.

3. Establish a nonequity partnership in which part-time partners participate in profit and loss but make no capital investment and share in none of the firm's assets.

4. Make Ross an equity partner, but establish her level of compensation and investment at 50% of the lowest level of the average compensation of the partners who entered the class ahead of her, her class, and the class behind her. Her points would be determined in the same manner. She would always be compensated less than others similarly situated, but this is the price she must pay for the privilege of part-time status.

5. Make her a nonequity partner for five years, with a move up to equity after that time.

One final note. A litigation-only firm will have more difficulty with part-time associates and part-time partners than a business or transactional firm; court appearances, depositions, and trials frequently cannot be arranged around a part-time schedule. A transactional attorney, on the other hand, can often arrange his or her practice around the part-time schedule.

To be competitive in today's recruiting marketplace, MN&A must change its policies. It is throwing years of investment down the hole if it rejects Julie Ross as a partner. She will have no choice but to seek employment elsewhere, taking her considerable skills and her obviously growing practice with her. MN&A cannot afford to lose Julie Ross or to set a precedent that part-time is a career dead end.

Marsha E. Simms *is a partner at Weil, Gotshal & Manges, a New York City law firm.*

"Julie Ross wants a job—not a career."

My gut reaction as a woman was that of course Julie Ross should become a partner at MN&A. But when I considered the issue in light of the realities of today's law firms and businesses, I concluded that she should not. A partner in any professional firm has to have made a conscious decision to have a career. Julie Ross has decided she wants a job—not a career.

Part-time partnership raises important issues for clients, peers (male and female), and other women in the firm.

67

CASE

THE FIRM'S CLIENTS

While there will be some clients who can work within a part-time partner's time constraints, most clients expect a partner to be available whenever needed. A partner also has to be willing to work to expand the client base and to work with any client of the firm who needs that person's expertise. Julie Ross wants to limit her practice to meeting the needs of only *her* clients (so long as those needs are not full-time), not the firm's.

THE PART-TIME PARTNER'S PEERS

Without a doubt, making someone a partner who has not "suffered" as much as his or her peers creates resentment in the partnership. While most lawyers have reached a point where they accept "stopping out" for a limited period of whatever reason (maternity leave or a sabbatical, for instance), they expect their partners to be the people who have made and are willing to continue to make the same commitment as they have to the firm over an extended period. If someone is not willing to make that commitment, then peers will question whether that person should be given a status that symbolizes the commitment.

OTHER WOMEN IN THE FIRM

Most women who have attained a level of professional success have done so by consciously sacrificing other aspects of their lives—whether it be marriage, children, or community involvement. They have discovered that they *can't* have it all and have had to choose what they want most. Creating a new set of partnership criteria for part-time associates, most of whom will be women, risks alienating women who have earned their status in the traditional way and have made the sacrifices Julie Ross was unwilling to make. Such a policy might also imply that women should be judged by a different, less demanding set of criteria, which brings into question the competency and commitment of all professional women.

I am not suggesting, however, that MN&A reject for all time the possibility of making Julie Ross a partner. If she ever returns to work full-time, then she should be considered for partnership. If at that time she is still performing at the same level that she is now, she should be made a partner.

MN&A could have avoided its dilemma by discussing with Julie Ross (and then making it a part of its announced policy) at what point, if any, an associate who works part-time would be considered for partnership. Unfortunately, most firms have no policy on part-time employment or other nontraditional work roles and instead treat each case on an ad hoc basis. This approach makes it difficult for those who are contemplating a part-time arrangement to evaluate how it might affect their futures. Also, the resulting disparate treatment of different part-time requests creates its own set of problems.

The most workable policy in a law firm, therefore, is one in which associates are permitted to take leaves of absence or work part-time schedules with the understanding that they will have to return to work full-time before they can be considered for partnership. For those who do not want to be considered for partnership, the firm should try to work out a mutually satisfactory schedule. As one MN&A partner mentioned, the firm cannot afford to lose intelligent lawyers because of its unwillingness to be flexible.

Walter R. Trosin *is vice president of strategy and development for Merck & Co., Inc., where he oversees personnel and human resources planning, strategy, policy, and development activities worldwide.*

"The issue goes beyond partnership to the whole question of work and families."

This case raises an important question: Given that most employees who are parents have a spouse who also works, how can companies address the needs of employees who have dual obligations?

In Julie Ross's case, MN&A could not begin to answer this question because it did not think through the implications of her part-time arrangement at the time it was made. George Hartwig should have, for instance, asked Ross what kinds of expectations she had from the firm and whether she would be willing to make child-care arrangements when emergencies arose at work. And he should have let her know the extent of the firm's commitment to her and what chance she had for partnership.

At this point, the firm can at least revisit the terms of the agreement it made with Ross. For instance, did a part-time schedule mean she would be working 25 hours a week or 40? This will also force the firm to examine its requirements for partner. Given the reality of pressures from an increasingly stressful world outside the office, including but not limited to family obligations, is MN&A (and other businesses) really benefiting from a tradition of working its employees 70 hours a week?

Within MN&A's present culture of "hit the ground running and keep your nose to the grindstone," I would be very reluctant to make Ross a full-time partner. In such a firm, it would send a signal that hard work is not necessary to move forward. Still, MN&A should discuss with Ross the possibility of granting her a limited partnership status or allowing her to share her partnership with another person who has a similar arrangement.

At Merck, we base promotion decisions on how well individuals perform and on our judgment of their ability to perform at a higher level. We expect people to work hard and to be dedicated—but we do not expect them to give up their families. In fact, I believe (as Maury Davidson implies in his memo) that workers are most effective when they do *not* work constantly.

As in the case with a growing number of companies, Merck has part-time work policies—and we have found that they have unexpected payoffs: for example, part-time employees frequently focus more on task completion and getting jobs done rather than simply on attendance. And doing the job, after all, is what we pay employees for.

Nevertheless, it is only nonmanagers that work part-time at Merck; we don't have managerial part-time work. It would be very difficult for a senior manager to work part-time because, let's face it, supervising is a full-time job. The only possible way managers could work part-time is on a job-sharing basis. The rules here are still emerging; Merck, for instance, has not yet dealt with this. Given the increasing need in our diverse work force for more flexible approaches, however, we may have to address this sooner rather than later.

Barbara Mendel Mayden *practices law in New York City and is a member of the American Bar Association Commission on Women in the Profession.*

"Never mind hours worked; what about talent, efficiency, and values?"

Let me get this straight. Julie Ross has displayed exemplary performance as a lawyer, and unlike her colleague Tim Brower who is being nominated for promotion, she has demonstrated revenue-generation skills. She passes the tests articulated by the firm.

Why should the number of hours Ross works, an arrangement approved by the firm, determine whether she should be made a partner? Is it some sort of initiation rite? While a firm may decide that the attributes it is looking for in a partner may take longer to attain working part-time, when those criteria are met, what does a threshold number of hours add to the equation?

Experience, expertise, and other effects of tenure that Ross gained while working an alternative schedule should not fall into a black hole. She is a lawyer who has attained skills, has garnered firm and client respect, and has presumably done her *pro rata* share of *pro bono*, community service, and firm administration. She should accordingly be promoted.

Yet Pam Fisher argues that because she and her colleagues worked 70-hour weeks, so should anyone who comes up behind them. Fisher's memory may be a little clouded by fatigue; legal management firms tell us that the billable-hour spiral is much higher than this. In the late 1970s, average annual billables for associates hovered around 1,700 hours, which today would be considered "part-time" compared with the more than 2,000 billable hours associates now average.

So should Ross, who bills, say, 1,500 hours a year working part-time, take home the same amount of money as Brower, who bills 3,000 hours? Of course not. (After all, the

3,000-hour-a-year lawyer will likely have alimony and child support to pay.) Hours worked may be relevant to the size of Ross's piece of the pie but not to her ability to sit down at the table.

Jim Welch believes that the firm needs a young, hard-working, committed attorney for a model. But maybe the focus of that model ought instead to be talent, efficiency, and values. Reporter Marilyn Goldstein, in an article appearing last year in *New York Newsday*, wrote:

"The question should not be what's wrong with a woman who doesn't want to work 12-hour days but what's wrong with a man who does—and a culture that . . . applauds, glorifies, promotes people who put their jobs before their families. . . . This penchant for promotions via . . . overtime reflects an assumption that those willing to work long hours are the best and brightest [but] maybe the ones willing to work long hours are just the ones willing to work long hours. . . . What if we discover the answer to moving American commerce and industry ahead is finding those smart enough *not* to work 12-hour days and turning the reins of business over to them? Who knows, we might come up with a mother lode of talent."

Implicit in the discussion about whether to make Ross a partner is that it is uneconomic to do so. Some of the most successful law firms in the country, however, have shown that, alternative work schedules that don't "mommy track" women into pink-collar, no-room-for-advancement ghettos can be profitable. Those firms report that their reduced-schedule lawyers—both partners and associates—demonstrate increased productivity with a higher ratio of billable hours to hours worked. Fixed costs relating to such lawyers can be reduced. Fears about part-time partners being unable to supervise or to deal with client concerns have not been borne out; more often than not, the partner on an alternative work schedule is more accessible than the 2,500-hour-a-year workaholic juggling too many matters.

Firms that don't provide a work environment where family and professional responsibilities can be reconciled will lose their most valuable resources—many of their best people—to firms that are more "family friendly." Retention of valued, experienced professionals produces distinct value. Firm costs escalate with lawyer turnover. When firms don't offer options, they lose lawyers just when they have become profitable. (It has been noted that a woman professional's most productive years are also her reproductive years.) Clients become frustrated finding their matters constantly being shifted to new lawyers unfamiliar with their circumstances.

How firms deal with balancing family and work responsibilities is not just a women's issue, as Maury Davidson points out in the case. Perhaps women were the first to notice these issues, but what is becoming increasingly evident is that men are now leaving firms in greater numbers. No longer is the prototypical new lawyer a man who was put through school by a working wife who remains at home after her husband becomes a lawyer and devotes herself to providing her husband and children with a well-organized home life. Today both women and men are dealing with more responsibilities at home, in addition to those at the office. Men are increasingly opting out of those firms that cultivate an obvious "bottom-line only" environment. The managing partner of a major New York law firm recently noted that even men who don't intend to work part-time or take parental leave look for these kinds of policies in firms because they reveal how much importance a firm places on family issues.

Jim Welch is naive to think that without flexible policies, MN&A will continue to attract young lawyers of the quality of Fisher and Brower. While the lure of the big money was once all-powerful, law students are not becoming aware of the downside of a law firm environment where a 2,500-hour-billable-year expectation is not uncommon. In evaluating law firms, they are looking beyond the highest bidder and at the importance of lifestyle and family issues.

Pam Fisher is concerned about the message the firm will send by making Julie Ross a partner. With proper guidance from the top (and a written policy clearly articulating the firm's reasoning and the parameters of the policy), the other associates and potential recruits will see that Ross is a hard-working lawyer who has excelled in her field and who has traded the extra hours demanded of others for a significant cut in pay and benefits. And they will see MN&A as an organization that has responded to the demographics of the 1990s and that understands the importance of maintaining human values in a busy, successful legal practice.

D. Timothy Hall *is a professor of organizational behavior and associate dean for faculty development in the school of management at Boston University. He is the author of several books on career management.*

"The rules must change because the game has changed."

It is crucial at this point in MN&A's history that it take innovative action: it should promote Julie Ross.

First, let's look at the state of affairs for law firms and businesses alike. The emergence of global marketing and technological innovations means that our world has never been more competitive. And the most competitive assets for any business, as the saying goes, leave the building each night (however late the departure might be!). The only way to grow a business in these uncertain times is through a clear strategy of recruiting and grooming the finest talent available.

MN&A's three central criteria in evaluating partner candidates are: (1) legal performance, (2) commitment to the firm's work, and (3) client service and ability to generate new business. There is no doubt that Ross's performance is outstanding on the first and third criteria. But she has also been outstanding in the second area—when measured against the expected commitment level the firm negotiated with her. Furthermore, based on what George Hartwig says, Ross is the kind of lawyer who is committed to do whatever it takes to serve a given client, regardless of the number of hours a week she has agreed to work.

MN&A has to redefine the word "commitment" to mean whatever it takes to meet client needs—not a particular number of hours spent at the office each week. It must then let everyone at the firm know that this new commitment to *service* (rather than *hours*) will be its major strategic advantage. In effect, this will create a new psychological contract between the firm and its staff: if an employee performs well, shows commitment and flexibility, and opens up new areas of business, the firm will provide financial rewards, professional growth opportunities, a long-term relationship, and flexible work options.

For MN&A's current partners, this means new rules. MN&A acknowledged that the rules had changed when it implemented flexible work for associates. The rules have had to change because the game has changed: employees in all business realms are needing and insisting on more flexibility.

The most important thing is to make changes discussable. MN&A employees need information about what to expect under the new contract. For example, employees working part-time may need to modify their career goals and expect to be promoted more slowly than their full-time counterparts.

As part of this communication process, MN&A will also need to give suitable recognition to its current partners who made family trade-offs so they could serve the firm full-time. George Hartwig needs to let people like Pam Fisher and Tim Brower know how much he values their contributions and that he realizes that they had fewer options. As MN&A communicates its new career contract more widely, inside and outside the firm, not only will it retain and develop key assets like Julie Ross but it will also be better able to attract other women and men of her caliber who want a work-family balance that other firms aren't yet offering.

This kind of new contract is an opportunity for a business to create a strategic human-resource-development plan. This would entail examining future needs for skills and experience, the extent to which those needs are already being met, what gaps exist, and a plan for addressing those gaps by recruiting, selecting, developing, retaining, and rewarding future staff.

A staff task force could be appointed to work on this plan. It could survey clients to assess their future needs, and it could survey staff at all levels to assess career and personal needs. The task force could then develop an overall plan with policy recommendations addressing issues like flexible work arrangements, career timetables, compensation and benefit policies, career coaching and mentoring, and dependent care. The plan could be communicated and discussed with all staff in a variety of settings—regular staff meetings, a company newsletter, partner meetings, or "brown bag" lunch seminars.

Included in such a plan could be a lengthened timetable for part-timers. If a major objection to Ross's candidacy is that she has not yet done the same volume of work as her full-time peers, MN&A might require her to work additional years until she has.

Similarly, it might establish different levels of partnership to deal with the compensation issue and the concern that part-time partners might bring in less new business. One level would be fully participating partners who would share in the profits of the firm. A second level would be salaried partners who would not share in firm profits. Salaried partners would be either part-timers or technical specialists who would not generate business; in addition to lower financial return, they would have the advantage of lower risk since they would not sign firm loans or otherwise participate in the firm's investments. A few Boston law firms have already adopted this structure, and public accounting firms have implemented comparable structures.

Another option might be to allow employees to move from one level to another as their circumstances change. In addition to keeping the full-partner role open for part-timers, this could also be a way for older, fully participating partners to phase gradually into retirement or to continue working longer than they otherwise would—without the pressures of full-profit participation and contribution.

Regardless of what the new plan includes, the key is to make it discussable. This should be easy in a firm the size of MN&A. George Hartwig should act quickly to meet the needs of both the staff and the firm and use this opportunity to gain a strategic advantage over competitors.

Ⓢ

72

CASE

MASSACHUSETTS INSTITUTE OF TECHNOLOGY

ANCONA, KOCHAN, SCULLY,
VAN MAANEN, WESTNEY

MANAGING FOR THE FUTURE

Organizational Behavior & Processes

MANAGING CHANGE
IN ORGANIZATIONS

module 8

MODULE 8 (M-8)

MANAGING CHANGE IN ORGANIZATIONS

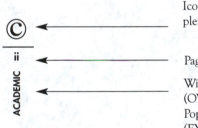

Icon indicates what part you are in, either core Ⓒ or supplemental Ⓢ.

Page number.

Within each part there are sections—Module Overview (OVERVIEW), Academic Perspective (ACADEMIC), Popular Press (PRESS), Case (CASE), Exercise (EXERCISE).

Dedicated to those who have inspired us to try to be better students and teachers. Special dedications to:

Professor Jack Barbash
Professor Arthur H. Gladstein
Professor Marius B. Jansen
Professor Joanne Martin
Professor Edgar H. Schein

Acquisitions Editor: John R. Szilagyi
Developmental Editor: Jamie Gleich Bryant
Production Editor: Mardell Toomey
Production House: DPS Associates, Inc.
Cover Design: Michael H. Stratton
Marketing Manager: Rob Bloom

Copyright © 1999
by South-Western College Publishing
Cincinnati, Ohio

ISBN 0-538-87695-6

1 2 3 4 5 6 7 D1 4 3 2 1 0 9 8

Printed in the United States of America

South-Western College Publishing
an International Thomson Publishing company IⓉP®

Cincinnati • Albany • Boston • Detroit • Johannesburg • London • Madrid • Melbourne • Mexico City
New York • Pacific Grove • San Francisco • Scottsdale • Singapore • Tokyo • Toronto

CONTENTS

ORGANIZATIONAL CHANGE AND TRANSFORMATION

At the beginning of each term we ask our students which of the following three statements best describes the last organization for which they worked.

1. The "new" model of organization
2. The "old" model of organization
3. An organization in transition—trying to move from the old to the new

Invariably, about 10–15 percent indicate they came from an "old," bureaucratic-type organization. Many of these are from government agencies or from staff units within large well-established firms operating in monopoly market settings. Another handful, usually less than 10 percent, classify their work settings as fitting most of the features of the "new" organization. These tend to come from small, relatively young, private sector service (most often consulting) firms operating in competitive and rapidly changing markets and often owned or managed by relatively young executives. This leaves the vast majority, usually between 70 and 80 percent, in transition situations—settings in which efforts are underway to change practices, but the organizations face considerable uncertainty over where they are going and how they will get there.

In many respects these responses reflect the essence of management today. Organizations are likely to be in a state of constant transition, with some forces tending to pressure for change and others reinforcing the status quo. Even those organizations that believe they have arrived at the "organization of the future" are likely to quickly find that the solutions implemented to solve past problems have now created a new set of unanticipated consequences—more problems to solve and more changes and transitions to implement. For example, the massive downsizing of companies and the outsourcing of work that occurred in the late 1980s and 1990s created leaner organizations that now ask fewer workers to do more with less. Although this did produce many positive changes and opened the door to other features of the new organization, it also added considerable stress to workers' lives, increased the hours they must spend at work, spilled over to increase work–family tensions, and reduced the economic security and standard of living of large numbers of middle-aged or older employees. Undoubtedly, these consequences will produce a backlash reaction that will influence organizational interactions in the future.

The art of management is therefore in large part the art of managing change. This means that skills in managing change are critical to all participants in the organization of the future. The materials in this module explore the multiple models used to understand and guide change and the multiple perspectives with which organizational participants experience and interpret change processes. The introductory class note explores a number of different models of organizational change and transformation and the managerial tools associated with these models. Then we draw on a paper written by three experienced change consultants, Rosabeth Kanter, Barry Stein, and Todd Jick, to illustrate the challenges involved in implementing change in organizations. We study the Xerox Corporation to bring these issues alive by exploring how

M-8

1

OVERVIEW

the transformations experienced in that company in the 1980s and early 1990s were perceived from two different vantage points—from the top and the bottom of the organization. We then stay with the Xerox case to look ahead at the issues that will challenge organizations to change in the future. We use the issue of the "overstressed" workforce to illustrate how the solutions of one decade (transformations to improve productivity, quality, and competitiveness) can often produce the problems for the next decade. In this way we emphasize a key point: Change is one of the few constants in organizational life!

M-8

core

CLASS NOTE: AN INTRODUCTION TO MODELS OF ORGANIZATIONAL CHANGE

It is impossible to review all the models of organizational change developed by scholars, consultants, and managers over the years. Instead, we will focus on those used most prominently in recent years, given our view that the change processes and results of one period create unanticipated consequences and reactions at some future point. The central question of interest here is what model(s) of change will work best in the years ahead as organizational participants struggle with the ongoing task of managing change and transformation? Yet we also believe that every generation must learn from and build on the lessons of its predecessors. Therefore, we also are interested in the question what did we learn from the change models that dominated in recent years that should inform future efforts?

FROM ORGANIZATIONAL DEVELOPMENT TO ORGANIZATIONAL TRANSFORMATION

The dominant feature distinguishing change efforts in the past decade from earlier models is an effort to move from incremental, gradual, planned changes to more decisive, rapid, fundamental transformations of organizational practices and design. In the 1960s, models of organizational development (OD) (Beckhard, 1969; Schein, 1969) gained popularity. These planned change efforts grew out of a behavioral science literature that had documented the inherent tendencies of individuals and organizations to resist change (Coch and French, 1948). That work was based on the theoretical foundations of Kurt Lewin's (1952) notion that change efforts go through three distinct phases: (1) unfreezing from existing patterns, (2) experimentation and implementation, and (3) refreezing or institutionalizing either new practices or retreating back to prior patterns. A force-field analysis was recommended as the major analytic and change agent tool in which the forces pressuring for and fostering change were compared to the forces leading organizations to resist change and move back to reintroduce past patterns.

The OD models of the 1960s attempted to move beyond the analysis of fostering and restraining forces to develop more action-oriented guides to consultants and participants who saw themselves as change agents. These change models were largely based on theories of interpersonal influence, conflict, leadership, and social-psychological theories of motivation and group behavior. OD models stressed the intervention of consultants as change agents or facilitators who used interviews, surveys, and observation to collect and feed back data on group processes and interpersonal interactions. These data and the feedback sessions in turn served as an impetus for changing behavior and improving decision making.

From these models evolved work stressing the need to understand and manage organizational culture (Schein, 1985) discussed in a previous module. These models are still widely used, and used effectively, in settings where change *within the cultural norms* of the organization is the task at hand. But these models were criticized eventually for being too focused on top organizational leaders or executives, and for assuming there were strong, widely shared cultural norms throughout the organization. OD models also were recognized as being limited in value in settings where change involved multiple interests or major shifts in structure or power of the parties since the underlying issues could not be resolved through increases in trust or interpersonal understanding and empathy. Stronger tools were needed that reflected the diversity of organizational participants and their interests, differences in power, and the ability to strategically restructure operations.

THE EUROPEAN ALTERNATIVE: SOCIO-TECHNICAL THEORIES

In Europe, another approach to planned change evolved from the work of the Tavistock Institute in Britain and Scandinavia known as socio-technical theory. Building on experiments in the 1950s with teams of coal miners, socio-technical change agents argued, as their name implies, for effective blending of the social and technical aspects of the work process. The key argument for this model is that technical and social dimensions of a work process must be changed together; changing one aspect without the other will not work. Socio-technical theorists advocated use of autonomous work groups to achieve the effective integration of social considerations with technical requirements. This approach in some ways served as a forerunner of the workplace reforms that would gain considerable popularity in the 1980s.

Like their OD counterparts in the United States, European socio-technical theorists stressed the importance of planned change, although they differed in an important respect. Whereas OD change agents tended to work with executives and focused on building interpersonal trust among those at or near the top of organizations, socio-technical change agents worked from the bottom up and stressed the importance of involving rank and file workers in the design of their jobs and the use of workplace technologies. But their major tool—the autonomous work group—did not fit all work settings, and, therefore, this model remained limited in its application.

UNPLANNED CHANGE: MUDDLING THROUGH

Not surprisingly, in keeping with the dialectic pattern of change processes, models of planned change were followed by the development of the view of organizational life that was appropriately labeled the "garbage-can" theory (Cohen, March, and Olsen, 1972). The essential view here was that most organizational actions are in fact unplanned reactions to events. Actions are taken in response to some change in the environment, and these actions are then considered to be solutions to problems that have yet to be defined. Only then do organizations tend to define problems to fit the solutions. For example, we buy lots of computers and then decide everyone ought to be networked!

TOP DOWN: THE TRANSFORMATIONAL LEADER

Gradually the popular press and some academic work replaced both OD models of planned change and the more agnostic or muddling through approach of the garbage-can models with visions of transformational organizational leaders or executives. This view was best epitomized by the title of a book extolling the leadership and change skills of Jack Welch, CEO of General Electric Corporation, *Control Your Own Destiny or Somebody Else Will* (Tichy and Sherman, 1993). This book presented a strong top-down model of change that mixed charismatic and tough analytic leadership by a CEO who was willing to make hard decisions even if these meant imposing personal costs on considerable numbers of current employees for the sake of maximizing the value of the firm to shareholders. It also recognized that the "market for change" was getting impatient with the pace of change achieved in more incremental or softer approaches.

© 5 ACADEMIC

The tools of the transformational leader varied considerably, incorporating some of the language, rhetoric, and team-building methods of the OD and cultural change models with the restructuring and strategic planning tools consistent with the strategic design perspective on organizations. This approach places great reliance on selecting (and replacing) top managerial personnel to build a team that shares the same vision and strategy for the organization.

BOTTOM UP: LABOR–MANAGEMENT PARTNERSHIPS

But top-down change was not the only approach to come along in reaction to the incrementalism of the 1950s and 1960s. In workplaces across the world a bottom-up approach was emerging: workers, their representatives, and grass roots managers were engaged in fundamental rethinking of the ways employee relations and work systems should be structured. Again, much of this change was market driven, and the impetus to get started often came from the top executives who felt the market pressure the most and the earliest. But the action was at the workplace, involving small groups of frontline workers, supervisors, and in some cases unions or workers' councils. Labor–management partnerships were formed in which workers, and, if present, unions, joined with managers in problem-solving processes to empower workers, increase teamwork, and gain the flexibility needed to improve quality, productivity, and customer satisfaction. An additional motivation behind these efforts was to overcome the adversarial relations between workers and managers and/or between union and management representatives.

This bottom-up model employed many of the buzzwords of the 1980s—labor–management cooperation, quality of working life, quality circles, total quality management, and so forth. This model also challenged the prior more incremental bargaining and adjustment of personnel policies that proved to be too slow and too much imprisoned by the work structures and traditions of the past. A more fundamental transformation of employee relations and workplace relations was needed, and indeed it began.

REENGINEERING

Left out of most of these change models were the opportunities afforded by the advances in information technologies (IT). Indeed, throughout much of the 1980s and early 1990s, researchers and organizational practitioners (particularly accounting and finance executives) noted a paradox: "Given all the money we spent on new information technologies we still don't see the payoff." As Noble Prize-winning economist Robert Solow put it, "Technology shows up everywhere but in the productivity numbers!" Why was this the case? The answer to this paradox is complex but most agree that it lies somewhere in the learning process—most organizations have not learned how to make full use of new technologies; when they do, quantum leaps in productivity and performance are possible. Alas, a new model of organizational change, "process reengineering," arrived on the scene in the early 1990s to solve this paradox and show organizations how to achieve the full potential of IT by totally "reengineering" their operations and organizations (Hammer and Champy, 1993).

Whether reengineering will produce the quantum leap forward it promises remains to be seen, but if history is a guide, it probably will fall short of the high expectations it has created for itself. One reason is that reengineering downplays many of the human costs that are imposed by the restructuring it recommends. This approach embodies a particularly narrow U.S. engineering conception of technology as "hardware." Japanese engineers and workplace experts have demonstrated that the real quantum leap gains promised by new technologies come when the hardware (and software) features of new technologies are combined with a sensitivity to what some call "humanware" (Shimada

and MacDuffie, 1987). That is, the most significant productivity and quality gains from new technology are achieved when technologies are conceived, designed, and implemented in ways that make full use of the ingenuity, skills, and motivations of the people who will be working with the machinery (Thomas, 1994; MacDuffie, 1995). This approach stresses continuous improvements throughout the life of the technology as opposed to the one-time quantum leap envisioned by reengineering models. One Japanese scholar describes this approach as "giving wisdom to the machines" (Monden, 1982).

EXTERNALLY INDUCED CHANGES

All of these change models focus on internal organizational operations and practices and leave intact the basic conceptions and roles of the corporation in society. But a longer historical and comparative perspective on organizational practices would recognize that many of the most important and fundamental changes in organizations come not from planned changes or even fundamental restructuring initiated by top management in response to market pressures or opportunities. The biggest changes are more likely to be externally induced by the economic environment—opening of new markets, entry of new competitors, and so on, or the actions of government or other external political and social forces seeking to change the role or behavior of corporations in society.

These externally induced changes can either be incremental—the invisible hand of the market or the more subtle hand of the government taxing authorities that change incentive structures and investment payoffs—or more transformational, such as the nationalization of private firms as was common in Latin American countries in the 1960s, or the reverse—the move to deregulate and privatize state-owned enterprises following the collapse of communism in Eastern European countries. In between these cataclysmic and marginal adjustments lie debates over whether the large networked *keiretsu* in Japan or the *chaebol* in Korea are too slow and closed to the outside influence of shareholders to be efficient and flexible in today's world markets or whether the U.S. shareholder-maximizing principle of corporate governance still fits a world with diverse stakeholders.

Organization theories have little to say about how to handle or manage these changes. One school of thought, labeled "population ecology" (Carroll, 1988), takes a Darwinian perspective—new organizations that fit the features of the changed environment are somehow born and prosper while older organizations fitted to a prior world shrink and die off. Moreover, there is a certain risk, or "liability to newness," experienced by start-ups. Those that read the environmental cues wrong or that get the cues right but the timing wrong (i.e., a good idea before its time) will also fail but will provide information for others to correct their errors.

This evolutionary perspective provides little guidance to organizational participants other than to choose their place of employment carefully or to time their start-up carefully!

Another school of thought, known as "institutional theory" (Zucker, 1988) suggests looking for safety in numbers—basically managers need to scan their environment to see who is doing well and to see what they are doing. That is, managers should identify new, emerging "best practices" and then copy or mimic these quickly and effectively.

One problem with this theory is that it tells managers little if anything about which practices to mimic and it says nothing about where these new ideas or practices come from in the first place. It says only copy what is already out there! While this sounds rather mundane, it may in fact be the dominant model of change used by most managers today. It reduces risk by allowing others to be what game theory economists call "first movers." First movers tend to experience high payoffs if they choose a winning strategy, but they also risk a high failure rate. Followers can select among the winning strategies and thereby reduce their risk, and if they are really good learners, followers can then adapt and improve upon what works for others to fit their particular situation. This cautious "adaptive learning" approach to change has been described as a key source of Japanese management strategy, both historically and currently (Westney, 1987).

More recently, organization theorists have been exploring ways to develop and sustain trust among networks of organizations, in part in response to the recognition of the importance of "cross-boundary networks" (Piore and Sabel, 1984). Yet sustained cooperation has proved to be more elusive in some cultures and institutional settings than others, and much remains to be done to develop effective change models that involve cross-boundary relations among organizations with partly shared and partly competing interests. Models of these types of interactions rely heavily on modern negotiations theory, as discussed in the political perspective on organizations introduced in Module 2.

IMPLICATIONS FOR THE FUTURE

Can we now build on the lessons of these change models and anticipate the types of models that will best address the problems of the future? We draw on two key lessons from approaches to change developed in the literature and tried in organizations in past years.

First, no *single* model or strategy fits all problems or organizational situations. The manager of the future will need to be adept at diagnosing change situations and skilled at choosing among different models and using the tools best suited to the moment. Indeed, we believe that the change strategies reviewed here correspond well to the strategic design, political, and cultural perspectives on organizational diagnosis developed in earlier modules. The strategic design perspective, for example, leads one to consider top-down restructuring of operations and organization design to better fit the organization to its environment. This is the essence of reengineering models, with a strong emphasis on the use of information technologies. Addressing the cultural dimensions of organizations and producing change consistent with prevailing cultures can best be done by applying the OD techniques of probing and collecting data on the underlying values, assumptions, interpersonal dynamics, and world views of managers and executives. A political perspective helps alert organizational members to the interests that need to be addressed in changes that challenge the existing culture, redistribute power, or produce more fundamental transformations in internal or external relationships.

Second, if history is a guide and our dialectic view of change is accurate, clues to the problems of the future are likely to be found in the solutions of the present. We will explore this point in more detail in the readings and exercises to follow.

CHANGE STRATEGIES IN THE ORGANIZATION OF THE FUTURE

How do these change models relate to the picture of the organization of the future? In understanding this, we must consider the following:

1. A flatter organization will bring into closer contact any bottom-up or top-down initiatives. Top executives will need to be skilled in managing worker-management or labor-management partnerships and work redesign efforts, whereas rank and file workers will be more exposed to and require the interpersonal skills and techniques of organizational development. The circle of contacts of top executives will be broader—more exposure to frontline employees at the workplace and vice versa. This increases the need for all organizational participants to understand and have the skills to manage change. Change will be too important to leave to managers or designated "change agents!"

2. Flexible boundaries and networked organizations mean that organizational participants will more frequently be exposed to externally induced changes and influences. Dual loyalties (both intergroup and interorganizational) will become an increasing part of the dynamics of change in the future. Skills in balancing the need to represent one's group or organizational interests with the need to build trust and cooperative alliances with external groups or organizations will be critical to managing change through cross-boundary networks.

3. Diversity increases the importance of the skills offered by the OD models. But it also suggests that the notion that change can be "planned" by a small cadre of top executives or change agents is outmoded. Diversity means that multiple cultural norms and styles of decision making will be present in organizations and that change will be initiated from many different people and organizational units. Managing change effectively will therefore require a greater openness to changes suggested by others rather than those planned or conceived by an organizational elite. Facilitating change initiated by others, therefore, will be an important managerial skill in the organization of the future.

4. Globalization of economic activity now implies that efforts to scan the environment for "best practices" will require a global lens and perspective. But choosing among "best practices" found in other cultural and institutional environments will require even greater skills in adaptive learning. Adaptive learning requires developing a deep understanding and appreciation for what makes practices used in another setting effective, along with an equally deep understanding of how to adapt them to fit into one's own setting. Experimentation with others' "best practices," therefore, will become an increasingly common and critical task in the organization of the future. But improved communications technologies will mean that organizations will have less time to exploit "second-mover" advantages implied in the institutional model of change.

What we have tried to do here, therefore, is to demonstrate that in some ways all of the concepts and tools discussed earlier are the building blocks for managing change. Now let us see if we can put these concepts and tools to use in actual case situations.

REFERENCES

Beckhard, Richard. 1969. *Organizational Development: Strategies and Models.* Reading, MA: Addison Wesley.

Carroll, Glenn R. 1988. *Ecological Models of Organizations.* Cambridge, MA: Ballinger.

Coch, L., and J. R. P. French. 1948. "Overcoming Resistance to Change," *Human Relations*, 1, pp. 512–532.

Cohen, M. D., J. G. March, and J. P. Olsen. 1972. "Garbage-Can Model of Organizational Choice," *Administrative Science Quarterly*, 17, pp. 178–184.

Hammer, Michael, and James Champy. 1993. *Reengineering the Corporation.* New York: Harper Business Books.

Lewin, Kurt. 1952. "Group Decision and Social Change," in G.E. Swanson, T. N. Newcomb, and E. L. Hartley, eds. *Readings in Social Psychology.* New York: Holt, Rinehart and Winston.

MacDuffie, John Paul. 1995. "Human Resource Bundles and Manufacturing Performance: Organizational Logic and Flexible Production Systems in the World Auto Industry," *Industrial and Labor Relations Review*, p. 48.

Mondon, Y. 1983. *The Toyota Production System.* Norcross, GA: Institute of Industrial Engineering.

Piore, Michael, and Charles Sabel. 1984. *The Second Industrial Divide.* New York: Basic Books.

Schein, Edgar. 1969. *Process Consultation.* Reading, MA: Addison-Wesley.

Schein, Edgar. 1985. *Organizational Culture and Leadership.* San Francisco: Jossey-Bass.

Shimada, Haruo, and John Paul MacDuffie. 1987. "Industrial Relations and Humanware," MIT Sloan School of Management Working Paper.

Thomas, Robert. 1994. *What Machines Can't Do.* Berkeley: University of California Press.

Tichy, Noel, and Stratford Sherman. 1993. *Control Your Own Destiny or Someone Else Will: How Jack Welch is Making General Electric the World's Most Competitive Company.* New York: Doubleday.

Westney, D. Eleanor. 1987. *Imitation and Innovation.* Cambridge, MA: Harvard University Press.

Zucker, Lynn G. 1988. *Institutional Patterns and Organizations.* Cambridge, MA: Ballinger.

THE CHALLENGES OF EXECUTION: ROLES AND TASKS IN THE CHANGE PROCESS

by Rosabeth Moss Kanter, Barry A. Stein, and Todd D. Jick

> Our company is in need of a profound transformation. We've read all the books. We know all the concepts and theories: transition management, frame-breaking, paradigms, empowerment, culture change, and so on. But we don't know how to implement the transformation. We don't even know how to make the theories operational.
>
> —Manager in a leading Fortune 100 company

Implementing change. The phrase sounds reasonable enough, and yet "managing" change is probably one of the most troubling and challenging tasks facing organizations today. Implementing a major and lasting change requires managers to develop skills akin to a juggler's. Instead of balls, however, managers must juggle tasks, striking a delicate balance between individual and collective actions, paying attention to the content as well as the process of change, and pursuing both short-term and long-term goals.

Considering the complexity of the task, it is no wonder that many managers feel overwhelmed—unable to keep all the balls of change in the air at the same time. The vice-president is too busy to add "change" related tasks to her already crowded schedule of "normal" activities; the production manager nods his head during the meeting on managing change, but forgets the message as soon as he's back on the factory floor; or the company launches a change effort with great fanfare and enthusiasm, but then loses momentum one year into the program and calls it quits. Consider the results of a 1990 *Wall Street Journal* survey of 164 chief executive officers. Although the CEOs recognized that personal communication helps create more employee commitment to change, 86 percent said other demands prevented them from devoting more time to communicating.

Another study examined the large gap between declared participatory management styles and what is actually practiced. A survey of 485 upper-level managers from 59 firms found unequivocal support for the concept of participatory management and a willingness and desire to support such a change. Nevertheless, managers generally did not install such systems, blaming an absence of opportunities to discuss the implementation process and lack of leadership (Collins, Ross, and Ross, 1989).

To help address such problems, change experts have devised tactics over the years to help managers do a better job on everything from crafting a vision to rewarding employees for productive behavior. Most managers at medium-to-large-size U.S. companies have been exposed to these tenets. Yet the track record overall is disappointing. As many of the portraits in this book illustrate there continues to be a great deal of disquiet in the workplace over the effectiveness of change efforts. Despite volumes of literature on planned change, legions of consultants, and the best efforts of corporate leaders, organizational change still appears to be a chaotic process. It is frequently mismanaged, beset by unexpected developments, and often largely unfulfilled.

Source: Reprinted with the permission of The Free Press, a Division of Simon & Schuster from *The Challenge of Organizational Change: How Companies Experience It and Leaders Guide It* by Rosabeth Moss Kanter, Barry A. Stein, and Todd D. Jick. Copyright © 1992 by Rosabeth Moss Kanter, Barry A. Stein, and Todd D. Jick.

This chapter examines why seemingly sensible advice on implementing change is solicited, accepted, and then often ignored. It then also offers suggestions on key steps that can improve the implementation process. We present two broad themes: (1) Change is extraordinarily difficult, and the fact that it occurs successfully at all is something of a miracle. (2) Change is furthered, however, if and when an organization can strike a delicate balance among the key players in the process. No one person or group can make change "happen" alone—not the top of the organization mandating change, not the middle implementing what the top has ordained, and not the bottom "receiving" the efforts.

We stress the difficulty of change efforts to dispel well-intentioned attempts to portray "change" as a discrete process, which when followed "correctly" leads more or less inevitably to the new desired state. Implicit in this notion is the idea that the benefits of change, while perhaps not immediately perceived, will eventually be realized, and the whole organization will go forward thriving on the chaos that the process drags in its wake. Anyone who has been even marginally connected with a change effort knows this isn't so.

Our second theme—that no one makes change happen alone—sounds a more positive note. Successful change builds on constructive interactions among multiple groups within an organization. Three basic groups must be coordinated if change is to be effectively implemented: change strategists, change "implementors," and change recipients. As we shall show, each group carries its own assumptions, agendas, and reactions. Unless these are considered both at the outset and during the unfolding of the change process, the most well-meaning efforts will be thwarted.

A brief illustration makes this point. A consultant describes an experience he had teaching managers in a large company about engineering change:

> When I went to this company, it seemed all their efforts to change were stricken with paralysis. I started off by talking to the middle managers The group seemed very receptive, but afterwards, someone came up to me and said, "That was a very well-done workshop with interesting ideas, but you had the wrong group here. It's not middle managers who make change happen. It's our bosses."
>
> So I offered the same workshop to the senior managers. Again, the crowd responded eagerly, but a manager broke in near the end and declared, "That was a fascinating workshop, and we know there are many changes we have to manage. But you really ought to be talking to the vice presidents and the president. They are the ones who can make change happen."
>
> Finally, assuming that the company's leaders would readily accept responsibility for implementing change, I presented my ideas one more time to the top of the organization. "That's all very well," responded the president. "But there's a limit to how much we can do. Most of the time, it's the middle managers who actually determine whether change gets implemented or not."

While each level acknowledged its dependence on the others, there was clearly no process for working through change issues together. As a result, change in this company seemed destined to fail. In more successful change efforts, the key players have developed a process that enables them to work together.

THE MESSY TERRAIN OF CHANGE

> How are you supposed to change the tires on a car when it's going 60 miles per hour?
> —Epitaph of a change agent

Real-life stories of corporate change rarely measure up to the tidy experiences related in books. The echo of the consultant's enthusiasm fades as the hard work of change begins. No matter how much effort companies invest in preparation and workshops—not to mention pep rallies, banners, and pins—organizations are invariably insufficiently prepared for the difficulties of implementing change. The responsibility for this situation lies in several areas.

Both the popular press and the academic literature tend to consider organizational change as a step-by-step process leading to success. Recent writings have grown more sophisticated—taking into account the often divergent methods called for in different change scenarios (Dunphy and Stace, 1989; Nadler and Tushman, 1989; Allaire and Firsirotu, 1985; Goodman *et. al.,* 1982); acknowledging that corporate transformation should be a continuous, ongoing process rather than a short-term fix (Kilmann and Covin, 1988); and recognizing change as a reciprocal learning process between the top of the organization and the bottom (Beer, 1988). But all too often many treatises on organizational change fail to concede that difficulties lie along the way.

This unrealistic portrayal of the change process can be dangerous. Already organizations are inclined to push faster, spend less, and stop earlier than the process requires. Such inclinations are further strengthened by an illusion of control that in fact does not exist. Managers are sometimes misled by consultants or authors who make change seem like a bounded, defined, discrete process with guidelines for success. They feel deceived; instead of a controllable process, they discover chaos.

In the real world, organizations cannot plot one change to be rationally and tenaciously pursued. Most corporations must stake out multiple changes at once, and the change goals themselves must be continually reexamined, altered, added to, or even abandoned. Instead of one vision to guide an organization's overall direction, many companies find they must pursue separate and sometimes even competing visions, such as a quality vision, a customer vision, and a human resources vision. Instead of one powerful, centralized, and charismatic change leader, many companies now rely on teams of collaborating individuals who hammer out the emerging details of the change process through bargaining, compromise, and negotiation.

The larger and more complex the change, the more likely it is that this kind of overlap and complexity will occur. The organizational analysts David Nadler and Michael Tushman (1989) have identified one set of characteristics that can bedevil the change process. Any large-scale change, they claim, entails at least some of the following four traits:

- *Multiple transitions.* Rather than being confined to one transition, complex changes often involve many different transitions. Some may be explicitly related; others are not.
- *Incomplete transitions.* Many of the transitions that are initiated do not get completed. Events overtake them, or subsequent changes subsume them.
- *Uncertain future states.* It is difficult to predict or define exactly what a future state will be; there are many unknowns that limit the ability to describe it. Even when a future state can be described, there is a high probability that events will change the nature of that state before it is achieved.
- *Transitions over long periods of time.* Many large-scale organizational changes take a long time to implement—in some cases, as much as three to seven years. The dynamics of managing change over this period are different from those of managing a quick change with a discrete beginning and end.

What is the experience of implementing change really like? Here is how the chief executive officer of a major U.S. airline describes managing multiple changes during the tempestuous period of the late 1980s:

It beat any Indiana Jones movie! It started out with a real nice beginning. Then suddenly we got one disaster after another. The boulder just missed us, and we got the snake in the cockpit of the airplane—that's what it's all about! You've got to be down in the mud and the blood and the beer.

This vivid description captures a sense of the drama involved in wrestling with complex, real-time issues day after day in a changing environment. Today's companies are composed of and affected by so many different individuals and constituencies—each with their own hopes, dreams, and fears. For these companies, operating in a global environment—with all the regulations, competition, and complexity that implies—managing organizational change does indeed require a juggler's skills.

Unfortunately, the unsettling nature of this process is often neglected in change "success" stories, leading those who "make" change to judge their own performance too harshly. Instead of the crisp, logical, and forward-moving process they have seen described, their own best efforts may feel like just "muddling along"—poking their fingers in the dike as a flood of demands and forced modifications threatens to pour down over them. One manager implementing multiple changes at a large Midwestern manufacturing company described her sensations this way: "I feel like I need to be smarter. There's just no way I can do it. Then I realize it's not related to my inexperience at all, it's just the situation."

This kind of frustration is part of the terrain of change. In fact, while the literature often portrays an organization's quest for change like a brisk march along a well-marked path, those in the middle of change are more likely to describe their journey as a laborious crawl toward an elusive, flickering goal, with many wrong turns and missed opportunities along the way. Only rarely does a company know exactly where it's going, or how it should get there. Indeed, "Everything looks like a failure in the middle. In nearly every change project, doubt is cast on the original vision because problems are mounting and the end is nowhere in sight" (Kanter, 1991).

Change is often messy, chaotic, and painful, no matter what leaders do to smooth the process. Take the case of the manager of a venerable control systems company trying to face up to the reality of shrinking orders and dwindling market share. After a careful analysis of market needs and corporate capabilities, the manager decides to shift the company's focus from producing a large range of systems to manufacturing a smaller stable of more advanced, value-added products. To accomplish this, she must lay off almost one-fourth of the company's most senior employees. Although she does her best to make the layoffs humane—offering generous retirement packages, as well as counseling services—both the employees who leave and those who remain respond with anger, bitterness, and distrust. Did the manager bungle this change effort?

Probably not. In fact, there is no way to make laying off employees pleasant, and yet it can be an important and necessary step in restructuring an organization and returning it to competitive form. Change agents generally make unpopular decisions. An organization is made up of many different constituencies, and each group is likely to be affected by—and to react to—any given change differently.

A manager need not do anything as drastic as laying off workers to trigger intense reactions within an organization. Realigning a company's chain of command, shifting resources from one part of an organization to another, or even introducing new computer systems can result in temporary chaos. The well-known change expert Chris Argyris (1985) argued that almost any action that disturbs the organizational status quo or represents a threat to an individual's habitual way of doing things is likely to provoke defensive, and often counterproductive, behaviors—behaviors learned early in life. "Defensive routines are probably the most important cause of failure in the implementation of sound strategy . . . ," Argyris wrote. "[W]e are dealing with how we are taught from a very early age to cope with threat."

Those who make change must also grapple with unexpected forces both inside and outside the organization, as discussed in the earlier chapters in this book. No matter how carefully the leaders prepare for change, and no matter how realistic and committed they are, there will always be factors outside of their control that may have a profound impact on the success of the change process. Those external, uncontrollable, and powerful forces are not to be underestimated, and they are one reason why some researchers have questioned the manageability of change at all.

Take the case of Northwest Airlines. In 1985 the carrier launched a carefully plotted cultural overhaul aimed at improving communication and increasing worker participation. As the program was beginning to take hold in 1986, Northwest acquired its Minneapolis rival Republic Airlines—the largest airline merger by that point. The aftermath was far more turbulent than the successful merger of Western and Delta.

Within hours of the acquisition's completion, the effort to merge the systems of the two Minneapolis-based carriers exploded. Union leaders, enraged by what they insisted was inept handling of the merger, encouraged workers to protest—leading to strikes and eventually sabotage. One year later, in the midst of continuing turmoil, Northwest Flight 255 crashed after takeoff from Detroit, killing 156 people in the nation's second worst aviation accident to date. Finally, in 1989, Northwest became the unwilling object of a hostile takeover attempt. A few months after a friendly buyer stepped in, most of Northwest's management team resigned. So much for planned changes.

While this may be an extreme example of the forces that buffet a change process, any number of events outside a company's control can render the best change plan obsolete. Shifts in government regulations, union activism, competitive assaults, product delays, mergers and acquisitions, and political and international crises are all realities of corporate life today, and leaders cannot expect to implement their plans free of such interruptions. All forms of motion are in play simultaneously. The world does not stand still while leaders manage a change.

This, then, is at least part of the terrain of change and the resultant challenge of implementation. Change is usually more complex than expected. Change agents may feel overwhelmed with frustration, or "lost" in the middle of the process. In order to realize their goals, managers may have to make decisions that are unpopular with at least part—if not all—of the organization. And throughout the process, the rest of the world continues to grow, change, and make demands. As experts note, "Change management is not a neat, sequential process" (Beckhard and Harris, 1987). Unfortunately, it is a process that defeats many who strive for substantive change.

Given that change is far more complex than the literature—and consultants—often suggests, is there anything useful to be drawn from such advice? Should managers simply fold up their tents and forgo any attempt to implement change systematically? Of course not. Moreover, there are many examples of successful change that have been built on reasonable advice. Our point is that rational suggestions for implementing change are most useful when they are addressed to the entire range of people involved in the change process. In the next section we shall meet the players whom we believe to be the real implementors of change and explore their differing roles in the process. Subsequently we shall look at the typical advice given to these "changemakers" and see how that squares with our cast.

THE CHANGEMAKERS: STRATEGISTS, IMPLEMENTORS, RECIPIENTS

Organizational change is typically modeled as a three-part process that takes the flawed organization, moves it through an arduous transition stage, and deposits it at the end in the enriched, desired state (see Figure 8.1). Whether the three phases are called Unfreezing, Changing, and Refreezing (Lewin, 1947), a Three-Act Drama (Tichy and Devanna, 1986), or a transition from current state to future state (Beckhard and Harris, 1987), the same major themes emerge:

- The company must be awakened to a new reality and must disengage from the past, recognizing that the old way of doing things is no longer acceptable.
- Next, the organization creates and embraces a new vision of the future, uniting behind the steps necessary to achieve that vision.

FIGURE 8.1 MODELS FOR THE CHANGE PROCESS

Model	Process		
Lewin (1947)	Unfreezing	Changing	Refreezing
Beckhard and Harris (1977)	Present State	Transition State	Future State
Beer (1980)	Dissatisfaction X	Process X	Model
Kanter (1983)	Departures from Tradition and Crises	Strategic Decisions and Prime Movers	Action Vehicles and Institutionalization
Tichy and Devanna (1986)	Act I Awakening	Act II Mobilizing	Act III (Epilogue) Reinforcing
Nadler and Tushman (1989)	Energizing	Envisioning	Enabling

- Finally, as new attitudes, practices, and policies arc put in place to change the corporation, these must be "refrozen" (as Lewin put it) or solidified.

This model is a prescription for creating a *temporary stability* so that things will work (i.e., can change) for some period of time. Further, a specific category of people—namely, change "agents"—are meant to fulfill this prescription. Indeed, some argue that the planned change literature is largely aimed at the "experts" in the change process, namely external consultants! (Covin and Kilmann, 1989).

But recall, however, how many forces "conspire" to frustrate change and to destabilize the process. Moreover, change is effected by a combination of actors, a much more varied group than the literature often suggests. Because there are multiple parties (and stakeholders) involved in making change happen, and because their assumptions, perspectives, and even agendas may not always converge, there is in fact a natural *instability* built into the change process. Thus, both external and internal dynamics are at work to rock the change boat. But whereas many of the external forces we mentioned are truly uncontrollable, or at a minimum unpredictable, organizations can control the way the various actors in the change drama interact. And if these actors share an understanding of what change is needed, of how that can be effected, and of the "price" to be paid, then the change process has a far better chance of succeeding.

Who, then, is really involved in implementing change? We would argue that change is successful only when the entire organization participates in the effort. But the organization isn't a monolith; it can be divided into three broad change categories: change strategists, change implementors, and change recipients.

Strategists lay the foundation for change and craft the "vision." They oversee the links between the organization and its environment—its marketplace, its stakeholders—that give the organization its identity; they specialize in managing the first of our three kinds of motion.

Implementors develop and enact the steps necessary to enact the vision; they manage the coordination among parts and the relationships among people that give the organization its internal shape and culture, specializing in our second kind of motion, the internal development of the organization.

Recipients, finally, adopt—or fail to adopt—the change plan. Their response to the promised distribution of tasks and rewards determines whether interest groups mobilize to support or oppose the change effort, either "refreezing" the organization in new habits or resulting in political turmoil—corresponding to our third kind of motion. Recipients, in fact, give the desired change its ultimate shape and sustainability.

Strategists and implementors who fail to take that fact into account do so at their peril.

Breaking all the players in a company into three distinct groups is, of course, an oversimplification. The roles often overlap, and any given person in an organization is likely to assume each of these roles at some point during the different phases of the change process. Nevertheless, these dramatis personae roughly correlate to the phases of the ideal change process; each group also more or less embodies the tasks that accompany the effort. And there are concrete numbers involved: for a given change, the strategists are few; the implementors constitute a larger group, and the recipients are the most broadly represented. Let us examine these roles—and their assumptions—more closely, and see how they interact.

Change Strategists

Change strategists are responsible for identifying the need for change, creating a vision of the desired outcome, deciding what change is feasible, and choosing who should sponsor and defend it. They tune into the external and internal environment, assessing the forces for change. CEOs, top management, and consultants typically, but not exclusively, are change strategists. They involve themselves in broad design issues related to the resources their change ideas will absorb; they do the big-picture work, reading the external signs and the perceived pressures for change. With their overview of the organization, they attempt to master the possibilities.

As initiators and conceptualizers, strategists inherently experience more *control*: since they originate the need, the "plan," and the impetus for change, the idea is lodged within them. Positively, this means they feel compelled to influence others to pay attention to their issues and to develop or modify the change agenda. Negatively, their "vision" can congeal. Having fixed on the solution to the problem they have delimited, they can "lead" their organizations into ill-fated efforts.

A growing literature is devoted to providing guidelines for what is often called the "leadership" role (e.g., Allaire and Firsirotu, 1985; Tichy and Devanna, 1986; Nadler and Tushman, 1989, 1990; Hambrick and Cannella, 1989; Beer and Walton, 1990). Theoretically, while the role may be performed by a group, it tends to be described in terms of a single person. David Nadler and Michael Tushman (1989) see this individual as having a special "feel" or "magic," and thus use the term "magic leader": someone who helps articulate the change and capture and mobilize the hearts and minds of the organization.

Embedded in this leadership role are several tasks: determining the ultimate extent of the change needed and its degree of urgency; assessing whether the change is short- or long-term; deciding if the change is cultural, structural, etc. These interwoven tasks, in turn, become represented in distinctive behaviors—envisioning, energizing, and enabling (Nadler and Tushman, 1989). The leaders are typically portrayed as the critical ingredient in instituting change; if they are missing, the change is not likely to occur (Collins, Ross, and Ross, 1989).

Implicit in these leader-centered descriptions, however, are indications that while the role is necessary it is hardly sufficient. Implementation must be part of a change's earliest formulation—one reason why we prefer change strategist to change leader to describe this role. And strategists must pay attention to all the constituencies that must be "sold" on change, not just to what should be changed (Hambrick and Cannella, 1989). The need thus goes beyond envisioning, energizing, and enabling to encompass crafting the implementors' task. It includes recognizing that a change strategy is as much a matter of selling as it is of substance. That is, many constituencies will have to live with the change, and their support is critical to its diffusion, as well as its success.

In sum, while change strategists can fairly easily impact organizational structures and resource allocation, it is more difficult for them to influence cultures and individuals

(Allaire and Firsirotu, 1985). These are more directly shaped by change implementors and change recipients.

Change Implementors

Change implementors "make it happen," managing the day-to-day process of change. They are concerned with the motion inside the organization, with coordination and habits. They are often assigned their role and given a mandate to institute the change on behalf of the change strategists. Depending on the extent of the "vision" they are given, they can either develop the implementation plan or shepherd through programs handed down to them. Simultaneously, they must respond to demands from above while attempting to win the cooperation of those below.

Thus, implementors are "sold" on the change in some fashion, whether personally believing in its merits or doing it because the boss said so. In addition, they are monitored and rewarded (or punished) according to the perceived effectiveness of the change's implementation.

Most organizational development literature has been directed at these change implementors, although more recently the perceived audience has been broadened to include managers at large (see Beer and Walton, 1987, for example). This voluminous literature tends to address step-by-step practical advice (e.g., Lippitt, Langseth, and Mossop, 1985; Kirkpatrick, 1986; Beckhard and Harris, 1987; Woodward and Buchholz, 1987). And it has an overwhelmingly positive premise. Change is beneficial. There tends to be little advice on how to arrest change or how to resist becoming an "adopter" (Fitzgerald, 1988).

Thus, the focus is on the major issues facing implementors: intervention tactics for overcoming resistance; communication tools; how to develop transition structures; training and development; reward systems; and the like. Advice may be directed at technical, cultural, or political dimensions (Tichy, 1983), and may focus on individuals, groups, or the entire organization.

The more complex and large-scale the change, the more important it becomes that interventions be well thought out and consistent with each other (Mohrman, Mohrman, and Ledford, 1989). A series of choices among tactical options is thereby needed (Lawler, 1989). This includes whether to use a pilot test or to go pan-organization; whether to be as participative throughout the process as the goals might warrant; whether to change certain systems sequentially or simultaneously; whether to reject the old or accentuate the new; whether to use a "programmatic approach" or to have each unit develop its own interpretation; and whether to drive change bottom-up or top-down.

Change strategists may often—but not always—play a secondary role in making these choices. For their part, change recipients are more focused on the outcomes and consequences of the choices. Partly as a result of this, implementors often gripe about being caught in the middle. As the list of decisions they must make demonstrates, implementors face a daunting task. They often feel that they have insufficient authority to make change happen entirely on their own, and that they fail to receive the support from above to move forward. And the more the "recipients" balk at the decisions implementors make, the more frustrating the task becomes.

Change Recipients

Change recipients represent the largest group of people that must adopt, and adapt to, change. Thus, their response and reaction to change can fundamentally reshape that change. These are the institutionalizers: their behavior determines whether a change will stick. The concept of "organizational readiness to change" that is frequently assessed in the early phases of a change effort is an indication of how important the "users" actually are. Another indication of change recipients' influence on the course and nature of a change process is the high failure rate of change. One study, for example, found that

dissatisfied leaders who attempted to impose change on organizational members who were not "ready" usually failed (Spector, 1989). Therefore, it is important for leaders to spread *dissatisfaction* if lasting change is to occur.

Recipients appear in the organization change literature primarily as sources of resistance. However, what is vital to a successful change effort is understanding how recipients perceive the change and how they experience it. This point of view is all too often underplayed by leaders, managers, and experts alike. Indeed, if the majority of the organization that "uses" a change is considered only in terms of potential resistance, a self-fulfilling prophecy can result—treated as likely resistors, they fight the change.

Consider an example that tracks recipients' response to a change over time. One case study of a "highly effective" turnaround of an ailing assembly plant described the "euphoria" expressed almost universally by the management team. By all indications, workers (i.e., recipients) shared this enthusiasm: absenteeism, turnover, and grievances were all down. Despite these positive signs, however, line workers interviewed following the three-year turnaround were largely unimpressed with the improvements and claimed that their jobs remained fundamentally the same (Guest, Hersey, and Blanchard, 1977). Perhaps the recipients were less a part of the "turnaround" than others assumed.

Recipients are often too distant from the source of the change. One observer put it this way: "Visionary light, like any other, diminishes in proportion to the square of the distance, so it may not shine very brightly out on the shipping dock or in the union hall down the street" (Fitzgerald, 1988).

Resistance to change is not an inevitable by-product of change efforts, nor is it purely emotional. Recipients resist change for reasonable and predictable reasons; for example (Kanter, 1985):

- *Loss of control.* Too much is done *to* people, and too little done *by* them.
- *Too much uncertainty.* Information about the next steps and likely future actions is not available.
- *Surprise, surprise!* Decisions are sprung full-blown without preparation or background.
- *The costs of confusion.* There are too many things changing simultaneously, interrupting routines and making it hard to know the proper way to get things done.
- *Loss of face.* The declaration of a need for change makes people feel they look stupid for their past actions, especially in front of peers.
- *Concerns about competence.* People wonder about their ability to be effective after the change; will they be able to do what is required?
- *More work.* Change requires more energy, more time, more meetings, and more learning.
- *Ripple effects.* One change disrupts other, unrelated plans.
- *Past resentments.* A legacy of distrust based on unkept promises or unaddressed grievances makes it hard to be positive about the change effort.
- *Real threats.* The change brings genuine pain or loss.

Unless carefully conceived, therefore, even change programs aimed specifically at eliciting more employee participation can backfire. For example, workers will not participate in decision-making when an organization's real decisions are made outside those forums; when their jobs do not benefit from participative decision-making; when seniority continues to "count" more than competence; or when other such mixed messages exist (Neumann, 1989). Sometimes "participation [can be] something the top orders the middle to do for the bottom" (Kanter, 1983). In fact, being ordered to participate does not feel much different from being ordered to do anything else. And when the rhetoric of participation does not match the actual ways people are included, cynicism follows.

© 19 ACADEMIC

SHIPS PASSING IN THE DAY: HOW VIEWS OF CHANGE DIFFER

As this brief tour of changemaker roles demonstrates, the understanding and impact of a change effort can vary considerably from one group to another (see Figure 8.2). Implementors, for example, are fighting the near daily fires, interruptions, and impediments attendant to working through the change effort, while often doing their "real" jobs at the same time. Meanwhile, the strategists anxiously await and test for positive results, striving to harmonize the effort and seeking to emphasize collective dedication and agreement. Recipients, for their part, are being confronted by often conflicting signals about what is important. They tend, as a result, to be far more testy about both the need for change and its ability to be implemented than either of the other two groups. That these three groups—strategists, implementors, and recipients—usually represent hierarchical realities confounds the problem further. Thus, the varying experiences, tasks, priorities—and ongoing work—of these three change groups lead to very different assumptions about a change effort.

The following description is at once extreme and typical, but it demonstrates our point. Imagine an effort at a quality transformation, originated and motivated by senior management strategists. After a couple of years, the strategists are more likely to judge the change a success than either the implementors or the recipients. They want to declare victory and go forward. Implementors, having lived with frustration and disappointment that the change has not moved fast enough or deep enough, are more critical of the results. The Indiana Jones scenario mentioned earlier is all too apparent to them. Finally, recipients, the "beneficiaries" of conflicting signals emanating from the other two groups, often think "this too shall pass."

In addition to the different frame of reference each group brings is the fact that each enters the change process at a different point. As often happens, the change strategist is impatient for action and exhorts the implementor to minimize time-consuming involvement steps. Even when participation is seemingly attempted, recipients will often report that they were insufficiently heard, involved, or informed. And when

FIGURE 8.2 THREE KEY CHANGEMAKERS

	Role and Mind Set	Orientation to Change (Kind of Motion)	Action Focus	Typical Organizational Level	Dominant Stage of Involvement
Change Strategist	Visionary	External environment	Ends	Top	Unfreezing
	Instigator		Corporate values and business results		
	Corporate view				
Change Implementor	"Project image"	Internal coordination	Means	Middle	Changing
	Translator		Overcoming resistance		
	Division or department		"Project image"		
Change Recipient	User and adapter	Distribution of power and proceeds	Means-ends congruence	Bottom	Refreezing
	Institutionalizer		Personal benefits		
	Personal view				
	Operational				

things break down, the implementor regretfully reflects, "I thought they understood and supported the change!"

Strategists are notorious for initiating major organization alterations by issuing a decree to the recipients, directly bypassing implementors (Connor, 1983). Implementors frequently decide to modify the direction of a change without gaining the strategists' endorsement. And most often, the impact of the change on the recipients is ignored or underestimated by both strategists and implementors. As one expert said, "[U]nderneath liberal enthusiasm for a more democratic climate of employee participation was impatience and intolerance that discredited those who stood in the way of progress" (Fitzgerald, 1988). Recipients had once again been bypassed and deceived.

TEN COMMANDMENTS FOR EXECUTING CHANGE

Now that we have met the changemakers—all three action roles—we must examine the "script" they are to use. At the outset of this section we introduced the basic model for change. Accompanying this three-step process are a number of tactics that have become standard operating procedures for any organization attempting to achieve significant organizational change. These constitute a kind of "ten commandments" for implementing change (Figure 8.3). While this grouping is our own, the concepts are familiar and have been drawn from a wide range of sources.

1. *Analyze the organization and its need for change.* Managers should understand an organization's operations, how it functions in its environment, what its strengths and weaknesses are, and how it will be affected by proposed changes in order to craft an effective implementation plan (Nadler and Tushman, 1989).

2. *Create a shared vision and common direction.* One of the first steps in engineering change is to unite an organization behind a central vision. The ideal vision is not merely a statement of mission, a philosophy, or a strategic objective. Rather, it is an attempt to articulate what a desired future for a company would be. It can be likened to "an organizational dream—it stretches the imagination and motivates people to rethink what is possible" (Belgard, Fisher, and Rayner, 1988).

3. *Separate from the past.* Disengaging from the past—or pattern breaking (Barczak, Smith, and Wilemon, 1987)—is critical to the "unfreezing" process which Kurt Lewin described back in 1947. It is difficult for an organization to embrace a new vision of the future until it has isolated the structures and routines that no longer work and has vowed to move beyond them.

4. *Create a sense of urgency.* Convincing an organization that change is necessary isn't that difficult when a company is teetering on the edge of bankruptcy or floundering

---

FIGURE 8.3 THE TEN COMMANDMENTS

1. Analyze the organization and its need for change.
2. Create a shared vision and common direction.
3. Separate from the past.
4. Create a sense of urgency.
5. Support a strong leader role.
6. Line up political sponsorship.
7. Craft an implementation plan.
8. Develop enabling structures.
9. Communicate, involve people, and be honest.
10. Reinforce and institutionalize the change.

---

in the marketplace. But when the need for action is not generally understood, a change leader should generate a sense of urgency without appearing to be fabricating an emergency, or "crying wolf." Whether calling this motivating reaction "dissatisfaction" (Beer, 1980; Beer and Walton, 1990) or a "felt need for change" (Tichy and Devanna, 1986), a sense of urgency is critical to rallying an organization behind change.

5. *Support a strong leader role.* An organization should not undertake something as challenging as large-scale change without a leader to guide, drive, and inspire it. These change advocates, or "magic leaders" (Nadler and Tushman, 1989, 1990) play a critical role in creating a company vision, motivating company employees to embrace that vision, and crafting an organizational structure that consistently rewards those who strive toward the realization of the vision.

6. *Line up political sponsorship.* Leadership alone cannot bring about large-scale change. Success depends on a broader base of support built with other individuals who act first as followers, second as helpers, and finally as co-owners of the change (Nadler and Tushman, 1989). This "coalition-building" should include both power sources—"the holders of important supplies necessary to make the change work"—and stakeholders—"those who stand to gain or lose from the change" (Kanter, 1983).

7. *Craft an implementation plan.* While a vision may guide and inspire during the change process, an organization also needs more nuts-and-bolts advice on what to do, and when and how to do it. This change plan is a "road map" for the change effort (Beckhard and Harris, 1987), specifying everything from where the first meetings should be held to the date by which the company hopes to achieve its change goal.

8. *Develop enabling structures.* Altering the status quo and creating new mechanisms for implementing change can be a critical precursor to any organizational transformation. These mechanisms may be part of the existing corporate structure or may be established as a full-fledged parallel organization (Stein and Kanter, 1980). Enabling structures designed to facilitate and spotlight change range from the practical—such as setting up pilot tests, off-site workshops, training programs, and new reward systems—to the symbolic—such as changing the organization's name or physically rearranging space (Lawler, 1989).

9. *Communicate, involve people, and be honest.* When possible, change leaders should communicate openly and seek out the involvement and trust of people throughout their organizations. Full involvement, communication, and disclosure are not called for in every change situation, but these approaches can be potent tools for overcoming resistance and giving employees a personal stake in the outcome of a transformation (Beer, 1980).

10. *Reinforce and institutionalize the change.* Throughout the pursuit of change, managers and leaders should make it a top priority to prove their commitment to the transformation process, reward risk-taking, and incorporate new behaviors into the day-to-day operations of the organization. In their Three-Act model for change, Noel Tichy and Mary Anne Devanna (1986) describe Act III, or the phase for institutionalizing change, as "shaping and reinforcing a new culture that fits with the revitalized organization."

These ten commandments are not the only tactics the planned change literature advocates, but they capture the essence of the advice typically offered. Further, each of the three changemaker groups we've introduced would surely agree that these are sensible and valuable guidelines. But just as surely, they would differ over how these are practiced and interpreted.

For example, let's take Commandment 1—analyzing the organization and its need for change—and imagine how the three groups might comment on this effort.

STRATEGISTS: The competition is at our heels, our product development is lagging, and customers are unsatisfied. We must reorient the troops to meet this challenge—or else.

IMPLEMENTORS: Hey, we're still doing the quality push you guys said was how we'd meet "the challenge"; it's not half implemented.
Do we need to "do" customers just yet?

RECIPIENTS: We haven't mastered statistical process control; already we're pulling apart the line to accommodate that and everyone's confused. We cannot absorb "customers" yet.

This is a highly realistic scenario in light of the fact that most organizations "do" multiple changes. And, if we revisit the point made earlier, that strategists often believe (and want) change to happen more quickly than is perhaps feasible, we realize that they assume that the previous change is in fact "done." To strategists, it is time to introduce another change. Thus, for Commandment 2—create a shared vision and a common direction—strategists may be crafting that vision and direction unaware of the reality facing the two other changemaker groups.

The cascade of potential collisions continues with Commandment 3—separate from the past. Depending on the flurry of change the organization has recently experienced, the immediate "past" may have existed for a short time period indeed. In fact, if multiple changes are in effect, it is unclear what is to be disengaged from. Do we stop working on quality improvements to focus on customers, for example? Separating from the past can generate chaos if the pace of change is too quick.

For the strategists, departing from the past can make a great deal of sense. "Let's start from square one," they say. If, however, implementors are still "doing" the previous change, as implied above, they may not be able to find "square one." Recipients may greet what they perceive to be unnecessary upheaval in their efforts with a yawn, with cynicism, or with outright resistance.

One more commandment shows how different changemaker roles can differ in interpretation and assumptions: Commandment 4—create a sense of urgency. From the strategists' vantage point, urgency originates with need for change in the first place. They might see very real threats that require deep and rapid action. Implementors might believe that the need is not so drastic or that instead of deep change, perhaps more modest alterations will work. Alternatively, implementors might see that the situation is even worse than the strategists have described; hence, they might double the pressure on recipients. Not only are the strategists pushing, the implementors are, too.

Creating a sense of urgency for change recipients needs careful consideration. Is this a threat—do this or the pink slip? Is this crying wolf? Is the organization setting up unnecessary antagonism, or adversarial conditions, where they need not be?

CHARTING A COURSE FOR CHANGE

Some of the collisions described above can be a matter of blatant incompetence, mismanagement, or even ignorance; commandments, after all, can be disregarded or broken. More often, however, such disconnections result from the divergent roles in the change process. Inherent instability and conflict are brought on by these roles as a result of their interdependence. The basic interests, mind sets, experiences, and goals of each group differ fundamentally (Kotter, 1984). Thus, it is not surprising that breakdowns occur and that the ten commandments—as sensible as they may seem—are not "obeyed."

But there are some effective ways to harness and steer an organization's motion even in the midst of instability. By simply being aware of potential disruptions and pitfalls in the change process, organizations will be in a better position to manage change. Change is indeed possible, but it needs to be charted carefully.

Four "rules of the road" are essential in charting a change effort that will end up where it was intended to go. (1) Appreciate the differences inherent in other "changemakers" viewpoints. (2) Respect—but challenge—the ten commandments and their applicability within your own organization. (3) Ensure that the dialogue and communication among the various constituencies has meaning and purpose. And (4) respond flexibly, even opportunistically, not only to what occurs outside of the organization, but also to how the change process is faring within the organization.

There is nothing remarkable in such advice. Like the ten commandments themselves, it reeks of common sense. However, applied within the understanding of the three broad changemaker roles, these four "rules" facilitate any change effort. They are not guarantees, simply enablers.

Appreciating Other Changemakers' Differences

Clearly, an appreciation of the differences among changemakers begins with the acknowledgment that change will not occur unless those who are involved are in harmony. Implementation is more than a mandate given to the "middle" to involve the "bottom" in the bidding of the "top." Once again, this seems like deceptively obvious advice.

But unless a change is predicated on the assumption that "we" are all making the change, it has a slim chance of success. That is, a glance at the three broad implementation roles shows that they, in fact, encompass the entire organization; everyone *ipso facto* is an implementor. This by no means implies that everyone does the same thing or has the same responsibilities. But the differences among the roles cannot be appreciated unless all roles are acknowledged to be a part of the change "play."

The consultant Barry Oshry (1991) examined the dynamics that occur in interactions among "tops," "middles," and "bottoms"—dynamics he considers "predictable." Tops and bottoms have different priorities, he argues, and want different things from one another. When a middle assumes that she or he must resolve these differences, failure is inevitable. He claimed that the experience of being a middle typically leads to "gradual disempowerment in which reasonably healthy, confident, and competent people become transformed into anxious, tense, ineffective, and self-doubting wrecks." This is a familiar description of the experience of change implementors; they not only feel caught in the middle of others' agendas and wishes, they feel obligated—or are told—to resolve those differences. As a result, they internalize the conflicts.

Oshry suggested a series of tactics for minimizing this sense of frustration and disempowerment: be top when you can, and take the responsibility of so doing; be bottom when you should; be coach; facilitate; and integrate with other middles. Thus, to break out of conflict and paralysis, the "middle," our implementor, should take on the viewpoint of the strategist at times and the recipient at other times. This can be called "appreciating" the differences.

Appreciating the differences among the implementation roles is a prerequisite to applying the subsequent "rules of the road" we recommend. The commandments cannot be evaluated, dialogue and communication cannot be meaningful and reactions cannot be flexible unless the effects derived from these "rules" are brought into harmony with the different change roles. That harmony will not be possible unless the roles themselves are understood.

Evaluating the Ten Commandments

Former American President Ronald Reagan and Soviet Premier Mikhail Gorbachev used to refer to an old Russian joke whose punchline was "trust but verify." A similar spirit should be invoked for the ten commandments. Trust the common sense they espouse, but ensure that they are truly applicable to the particular organization and changemaker categories within it. Effective changemakers use the advice embedded in the commandments as a blueprint; while the rough outlines are there, the individual company must fill in the details that bring the drawing to life.

Considering that the ten commandments arose from an earlier era, it is not at all surprising that they appear to fall short in some respects. Most of the planned change efforts of the 1960s and 1970s involved an outside consultant coming in to an isolated plant or division to work on a discrete change program, such as fostering better communication between workers. But most companies in the 1990s find themselves facing large, systemwide changes. These organizations must first put a strong personal imprint on the process. They may follow the commandments, but they also find ways to honor their own specific needs, cultures, and styles. A study of innovation in the Norwegian shipping industry found that "[i]nnovative change efforts . . . that incorporated the spirit and techniques of inquiry, discovery, and invention, produced more significant and lasting innovations and greater understanding of why they do or do not work" (Walton and Gaffney, 1989).

Tailoring the commandments to give them meaning within an organization requires a process similar to the one in which each commandment was considered from each changemaker's perspective. Debate can be triggered through a series of questions, including: Are we addressing the real needs of the company, or following the path of least resistance? How shared is the vision? How do we preserve anchors to the past while moving to the future? Does everyone need to feel the same sense of urgency? Can change recipients, far down in the hierarchy, have an impact? How do we handle those who oppose the change? When should progress be visible? How do we integrate special projects to mainstream operations? When is it wise or best to share bad news? Now that we have gotten this far, is this the direction we still want to go? How much change can the organization absorb?

Posing questions like these helps keep an organization focused and flexible (see Item 4). Moreover, by challenging the particular commandments, managers are reminded that implementing change is an ongoing process of discovery.

Ensuring Meaningful Communication

Experts on organizational development have touted the importance of communication for decades; indeed, the ninth commandment itself advocates open communication. But communication as we use it here goes beyond keeping people informed of change efforts.

Too often, "communication" translates into a unilateral directive. Real communication requires a dialogue among the different changemakers—a give-and-take that allows these different "voices" to express themselves and to be listened to (Ashkenas and Jick, 1990). Consider the list of questions that can challenge the applicability of the ten commandments. Forums should be devised so that the various change constituencies can pose those types of questions—contributing ideas, reactions, and complaints; confronting each other's underlying reasoning and assumptions; and overcoming "defensive routines" (Argyris, 1990). By listing and responding to concerns, resistance, and feedback from all levels, changemakers gain a broader understanding of what the change means to different parts of the organization and how it will affect them.

As with most management techniques, encouraging this kind of give-and-take requires both time and effort, but the results can be all-important. The chairman of Motorola, Bob Galvin, was able to foresee the need for critical changes precisely because he was so well connected with managers farther down in his organization. Galvin created such meaningful dialogues largely by setting the model with his own behavior. In addition to installing participative management programs, he sent out a clear message about his own accessibility by "walking the halls" and sharing lunch with employees from all levels of the corporation. Moreover, he created an opportunity for multiple levels of managers and employees to shape a new direction for the corporation collaboratively. The labor-intensive dialogue at Motorola helped not only to uncover the need for change but also to attack its implementation.

Jack Welch of General Electric is another change leader who has been uncommonly successful at encouraging dialogue between different layers of his company. GE's Work-Out Program has as one of its key goals the regular exposure of corporate leaders to the candid opinion of the workers they oversee. "Real communication takes countless hours of eyeball to eyeball, back and forth," Welch has declared. "It means more listening than talking. . . . It is human beings coming to see and accept things through a constant interactive process aimed at consensus."

Reacting Flexibly and Opportunistically

Advice embedded in the ten commandments places a premium on action—on taking charge. But this focus on action assumes a level of control that simply doesn't exist when large-scale change is being implemented. Those who want to embrace change must be as adept at reacting as they are at acting, and they must be flexible in the way they pursue their goals and implement their strategies.

This flexibility should start with considering the commandments themselves. In addition to challenging their applicability for the particular organization, and examining the advice from the various changemakers' perspectives, the commandments themselves need contemplation. They may have an unintended underside. Seemingly constructive change behaviors such as pattern breaking, experimenting, and visioning each carry their own risks (Barczak, Smith, and Wilemon, 1987). Experimenting, for instance, can cause a company to lose its focus or can paralyze decision-makers who are faced with too many options. And visioning can be inappropriate when it leads to an inflexible adherence to a single goal or points a company in the wrong direction.

Moreover, the commandments could be accused of having a built-in paradox. They are largely designed to help strategists and implementors implement change with fewer risks and more control. And yet change by its very nature requires risk taking and letting go. Thus, while the commandments may serve to minimize failure, maximize control and predictability, and define the end state, a transformation may actually require maximizing experimentation and risk taking, tolerating unknowable consequences, and evolving toward—rather than targeting—an end state.

Thus flexibility, as used here, transcends exploration of tactics; it should challenge, or be prepared for the consequences of, basic strategy. In many cases, this involves wrestling with paradox. Take, for example, the third commandment—separating from the past. As already mentioned, the perception of "the past" can be very different according to the perspectives of strategists, implementors, and recipients. But there is a deeper issue here: while it is unquestionably important to make a break from the past in order to change, it is also important to hang on to and reinforce those aspects of the organization that bring value to the new "vision." That is, some sort of stability—heritage, tradition, or anchor—is needed to provide continuity amid change. As the changes multiply, arguably this past-within-the-future becomes even more essential.

The fifth commandment urges a strong leader role, and yet many organizations of the 1990s do not have just one leader at the helm of their change effort. And the model presented here posits various changemaker roles. Thus, whereas a change effort may seem to demand a leadership role, the fact that there are three implementation roles, all of whose input is vital to success, requires some flexible wrestling with how change is to be managed, and by whom.

Finally, even the apparently elementary advice of the seventh commandment—craft an implementation plan—must be accompanied by an important caveat: Too much planning can lead to paralysis, indecision, and collapse. Organizations that are locked in a rigid change "schedule" of planned goals and events may find themselves following something that no longer meets their evolving needs, much less those of the world around them. Indeed, preprogrammed models may be unrealistic (Beer and Walton, 1987); instead, companies should remain true to the goals of the change, but be flexible about the means. (Of course, there is a paradox embedded in this suggestion as well. Profound change may have to tolerate unknowable consequences, as indicated earlier, which may necessitate evolving goals!)

A way out of these paradoxes within paradoxes (i.e., a way of developing the flexibility to deal with the ramifications of a change effort), is to learn to take (or make) change one step at a time, gauging the effectiveness of each move before going on. For some, this may be a disconcerting approach As alluded to earlier, change implementors have a common sensation of just "muddling along" without making clear progress.

But in fact, properly managed, "muddling along" can be a most effective way of handling multiple changes and complex situations. The theorist James Brian Quinn (1980) has dubbed this piecemeal approach to strategic planning "logical incrementalism"; he suggests this may be the most common way in which well-managed organizations change their strategy. A member of a team trying to introduce design changes at the plant level of an organization observed, "It's stupid to flounder around, but maybe floundering is a necessary period of adjustment" (Hirschhorn, 1988).

According to Quinn, "The most effective strategies of major enterprises tend to emerge step-by-step from an iterative process in which the organization probes the future, experiments, and learns from a series of partial (incremental) commitments rather than through global formulations of total strategies." Others point similarly to a "process of iterative planning, where plans are revised as frequently as new events and opportunities present themselves, bounded only by the intent of the change and how much energy is available" (Nadler and Tushman, 1989).

RESPONDING TO SITUATIONAL REQUIREMENTS

[P]eople assume the end, and consider how they can get it, by what means. Where it seems that the end can be produced by several means, they consider which means does it most easily and best. Where the end is produced by one single means, they examine how that comes about, and what will produce it, until eventually they arrive at the first cause, which in fact is the last in the process of discovery.

—Aristotle, Ethics III.3

The appropriate way of thinking about change implementation has less to do with obeying "commandments" and more to do with responding to the "voices" within the organization, to the requirements of a particular situation, and to the reality that change may never be a discrete phenomenon or a closed book. Managing change today is actually managing a cascade of change; most people are bleary-eyed with their "change agendas."

The new and almost unimaginably complex world facing most organizations today calls for new and, ideally, imaginably—tolerably—complex approaches to managing change. Yet the more we have studied change, and the more we brush up against its effects, the more humble we have become about dictating the "best" way to do it. Behavioral scientists themselves disagree on a number of fundamental implementation issues. A recent book attempting to pull together the best in practice (Mohrman et al., 1989) recognized discord among its own contributors on such basic questions as whether there is a logical sequence to the change process; whether change "agents" can lead an organization through a process that cannot be explained ahead of time; even whether change can be planned at all.

Thus, the ideas presented here have been aimed less at endorsing a particular methodology than at helping people "do" change effectively while in the middle of the change process. At a minimum, there is no such thing as "a change" any longer. There is a sequence of multiple, overlapping changes reflecting constant motion in an activated environment, with each change triggering others. No longer can a single change theme—e.g., quality—presuppose upheavals in the organization. Thus, the basic tenets of implementation can be challenged, but they should not be overturned. Rather, there is a need for more "software" to improve their utility in light of greater complexity.

A more organic approach to change seems the only appropriate way to deal with the reality of most change processes. Institutionalizing change is not the real goal; institutionalizing the journey may be, however. Being able to challenge, react, yes, even act on occasions—that is how we think the flux is "managed." This may be a disheartening conclusion for those who would like change to be engineered as precisely as is a piece of machinery.

In the end, however, this conclusion may cheer the growing number of internal and external changemakers who find dictates from on high insufficient for the real challenges they face. Such leaders are already recognizing the importance of acknowledging the diversity of implementors, the need for challenging and tailoring "commandments," the quintessential value of dialogue, and the need for constant flexibility. Although managing change will never be easy, with the right attitude and approach, it can be a most gratifying adventure.

REFERENCES

Allaire, Y., and M. Firsirotu. 1985. "How to Implement Radical Strategies in Large Organizations." *Sloan Management Review.* Winter, pp. 19–34.

Argyris, Chris. 1985. *Strategy, Change, and Defensive Routines.* Cambridge, MA: Ballinger.

——. 1990. *Overcoming Organizational Defenses.* Boston: Allyn & Bacon.

Ashkenas, Ronald, and Todd Jick. 1990. "Organizational Dialogue." Working paper.

Barczak, Gloria, Charles Smith, and David Wilemon. 1987. "Managing Large-Scale Organizational Change." *Organizational Dynamics.* Autumn, pp. 232–235.

Beckhard, Richard, and R. Harris. 1987. *Organizational Transitions.* Second Edition. Reading, MA: Addison-Wesley.

Beer, Michael. 1980. *Organization Change and Development: A Systems View.* Dallas: Scott Foresman.

——. 1988. "The Critical Path for Change: Keys to Success and Failure in Six Companies." In R. Kilmann and T. J. Covin, eds. *Corporate Transformation.* San Francisco: Jossey-Bass, pp. 17–45.

Beer, Michael, and Elise Walton. 1987. "Organizational Change and Development." In M. Rozenzweig and L. Porter, eds., *Annual Review of Psychology.* Palo Alto, CA: Annual Reviews, pp. 339–368.

——. 1990. "Developing the Competitive Organization: Interventions and Strategies." *American Psychologist.* Vol. 45, no. 2, pp. 154–161.

Belgard, William, K. Kim Fisher, and Steven Rayner. 1988. "Vision, Opportunity, and Tenacity: Three Informal Processes that Influence Formal Transformation." In R. Kilmann and T. J. Covin, eds. *Corporate Transformation.* San Francisco: Jossey-Bass.

Collins, Denis, Ruth Ann Ross, and Timothy Ross. 1989. "Who Wants Participative Management? The Managerial Perspective." *Group and Organizational Studies.* Vol. 14, no. 4 (December), pp. 422–445.

Conner, Daryl. 1983. "Determinants of Successful Organizational Change." O. D. Resources, Inc., Atlanta.

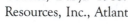

Covin, Teresa, and Ralph Kilmann. 1989. "Critical Issues in Large-Scale Change." *Journal of Organizational Change Management*. Vol. 1, no. 2, pp. 59–72.

Dunphy, Dexter C., and Douglas Stace. 1989. "Evolution or Transformation? Incremental Versus Transformational Ideologies for Organizational Change." *Australian Graduate School of Management* (University of New South Wales).

Fitzgerald, Thomas. 1988. "Can Change in Organizational Culture Really Be Managed?" *Organizational Dynamics*. Autumn, pp. 5–15.

Goodman, Paul S., and associates. 1982. *Change in Organizations*. San Francisco: Jossey-Bass.

Guest, Robert H., Paul Hersey, and Kenneth H. Blanchard. 1977. *Organizational Change Through Effective Leadership*. Englewood Cliffs, NJ: Prentice-Hall.

Hambrick, Donald, and Albert Cannella. 1989. "Strategy Implementation as Substance and Selling." *Academy of Management Executives*. Vol. 3, no. 4, pp. 278–285.

Hirschhorn, Larry. 1988. *The Workplace Within*. Cambridge, MA: MIT Press.

Kanter, Rosabeth Moss. 1983. *The Change Masters*. New York: Simon & Schuster.

——. 1985. "Managing the Human Side of Change." *Management Review*. (April), pp. 5–56. On videotape as *Managing Change, the Human Dimension*. Cambridge, MA: Goodmeasure Inc., One Memorial Drive.

——. 1991. "Improving the Acceptance and Use of New Technology: Organizational and Inter-Organizational Challenges." In National Academy of Engineering ed., *People and Technology in the Workplace*. Washington: National Academy Press, pp. 15–56.

Kilmann, Ralph, and Teresa Covins, eds. 1988. *Corporate Transformation*. San Francisco: Jossey-Bass.

Kirkpatrick, Donald. 1986. *How to Manage Change Effectively*. San Francisco: Jossey-Bass.

Kotter, John. 1984. *Power and Influence*. New York: Free Press.

Lawler, Edward. 1989. "Strategic Choices for Changing Organizations." In A. Mohrman, S. Mohrman, G. Ledford, T. Cummings, and E. Lawler, eds. *Large-Scale Organizational Change*. San Francisco: Jossey-Bass, pp. 255–271.

Lewin, Kurt. 1947. "Frontiers in Group Dynamics." *Human Relations*. Vol. 1, pp. 5–41.

Lippitt, Gordon; Peter Langseth; and Jack Mossop. 1985. *Implementing Organizational Change*. San Francisco: Jossey-Bass.

Mohrman, Susan, Allan Mohrman, and Gerald Ledford. 1989. "Interventions that Change Organizations." In A. Mohrman, S. Mohrman, G. Ledford, T. Cummings, and E. Lawler, eds. *Large-Scale Organizational Change*. San Francisco: Jossey-Bass, pp. 145–153.

Mohrman, Susan, A. S. Mohrman, and G. Ledford, T. Cummings, and E. Lawler, eds. 1989. *Large-Scale Organizational Change*. San Francisco: Jossey-Bass.

Nadler, David, and Michael Tushman. 1989. "Organizational Framebending: Principles for Managing Reorientation." *Academy of Management Executive*. Vol. 3, pp. 194–202.

——. 1990. "Beyond the Charismatic Leader: Leadership and Organizational Change." *California Management Review*. Winter, pp. 77–97.

Neumann, Jean. 1989. "Why People Don't Participate in Organizational Change." In Richard Woodman and William Passmore, eds. *Research in Organizational Change and Development.* Greenwich, CT: JAI Press, pp. 181–212.

Oshry, Barry. 1991. "Conveying Middle Powerlessness to Middle Power: A Systems Approach." *National Productivity Review.*

Quinn, J. B. 1980. "Managing Strategic Change." *Sloan Management Review.* Vol. 21, Summer, pp. 3–20.

Spector, Bert. 1989. "From Bogged Down to Fired Up: Inspired Organizational Change." *Sloan Management Review.* Summer, pp. 29–34.

Stein, Barry, and Rosabeth Kanter. 1980. "Building the Parallel Organization: Creating Mechanisms for Permanent Quality of Work Life." *Journal of Applied Behavioral Science*, pp. 194–210.

Tichy, Noel. 1983. *Managing Strategic Change: Technical, Political, and Cultural Dynamics.* New York: John Wiley.

Tichy, Noel, and Maryanne Devanna. 1986. *The Transformational Leader.* New York: John Wiley.

Walton, Richard, and Michael Gaffney. 1989. "Research, Action, and Participation: The Merchant Shipping Case." *American Behavioral Scientist.* Vol. 32 (May–June), pp. 582–611.

Woodward, Harry, and Steve Buchholz. 1987. *After-Shock: Helping People Through Corporate Change.* New York: John Wiley.

ACADEMIC 30

upon retaining a work force that is motivated, creative, and independent—empowered, in the current jargon. That goal will never be achieved by companies operating with a largely disposable work force, which is yet another reason to believe that in the future, most of us, most of the time, will be holding down permanent jobs. What has changed is that we will likely hold five, six or more full-time posts in our careers, rather than one or two. And as we retool during those transitions, the odds are good that a growing number of us will be forced to find temporary shelter in the uncertain world of contingent work.

MULTIPLE PERSPECTIVES ON ORGANIZATIONAL TRANSFORMATION: THE CASE OF XEROX CORPORATION

INTRODUCTION

The Xerox Corporation is often presented as an example of a company that underwent a major organizational transformation in the 1980s and early 1990s. We use this example to illustrate the multiple models of organizational change, demonstrating how different groups within Xerox perceive this transformation in dramatically different ways.

Xerox is used here not as an example of "best practice," although it indeed has earned a reputation as a benchmark in the area of organizational transformation. We do not suggest (nor do our colleagues at Xerox) that Xerox has arrived at the end point of its efforts to regain market positions lost in prior years or that its various stakeholders—shareholders, employees, managers, union representatives, business partners, contractors, community and government agencies, the societies in which it produces or markets it products, and so forth—are all satisfied with the status quo.

Instead, Xerox serves as an example of a firm that has indeed engaged in multiple change strategies, including a top-down leadership through quality effort, a bottom-up employee participation and labor-management partnership, and an interest group caucus model initiated by the company's African-American managers. Moreover, it is an organization we have studied and worked with in several of these change efforts, and it has been very open to outside analysis and discussion.

For these reasons we present the Xerox story from multiple perspectives and then ask a key question for discussion: What combination of change models will be needed if Xerox is to continue to adapt successfully to the challenges it will encounter in the rest of this century and beyond?

In the following sections we summarize two very different accounts of the company's organizational transformation in the 1980s and early 1990s. One account chronicles the bottom-up model of change involving the partnership that was forged between the company and the union that represented its production workers. The second is an account of change from the top down, as seen by the chief executive office (CEO) and his consultant. As we will see, the two accounts read like ships passing in the night. Indeed, the book written from the perspective of the CEO and his consultant barely mentions the contributions of the bottom-up process. The union-management partnership gets no more than about three paragraphs and three citations in a 300-page book! The account of the bottom-up model, on the other hand, simply notes that the top-down effort created some problems and uncertainty concerning its relationship to the employee participation process that had already been underway for three years.

31

CASE

CHANGE FROM THE BOTTOM UP: EMPLOYEE PARTICIPATION AND UNION–MANAGEMENT PARTNERSHIP[1]

The employee participation process and union-management partnership that Xerox and the Amalgamated Clothing and Textile Workers Union (ACTWU) began in 1980 has become one of the most highly acclaimed and visible examples of the transformation of an organization that began with rank and file workers and their union representatives working with management from "the bottom up."

ACTWU represents all Xerox manufacturing employees in the United States. The bulk of U.S. manufacturing for Xerox is based in Webster, New York, just outside the city of Rochester. This is the city in which Joseph P. Wilson, Sr., transformed the tiny Haloid Corporation into Xerox with the sale of the world's first plain paper copier in 1959. Wilson imprinted on the organization strong community and employee-oriented values. In the 1940s, he recognized, without resistance, ACTWU, the dominant union in Rochester. Since then, the company and the union have enjoyed a generally cooperative and highly professional bargaining relationship, experiencing only one significant strike over its history.

Beginning in 1980, and continuing to the present, a combination of crises and innovations have led to a transformation in the relationship between Xerox Corporation and ACTWU. What began as a narrow experiment to improve the quality of working life of employees and to solve production and quality problems within existing work units, expanded to address more and deeper issues as they arose, and eventually became a company-wide process that fundamentally transformed Xerox's entire labor-management relationship.

Eight key pivotal events occurred over the course of the 1980s that produced this transformation. The following events occurred in sequence beginning in 1980.

1980: Initiation of quality-of-work-life (QWL) effort for greater employee involvement

1983: Confrontation of the wiring harness subcontracting crisis

1983: Establishment of no-layoff policy and joint decision making on all sub-contracting

1984: Transition from QWL to business area work groups

1982–1986: Emergence of autonomous work groups and new work practices

1985–present: Union involvement in strategic decisions (e.g., new plant design, location, etc.)

1985: Bottom-up meets top-down change effort

1994: Seven-year bargaining agreement reached, including extension of no-layoff provision

Each of these periods is briefly described below.

Quality-of-Work-Life (QWL) Program

When local 14A of the ACTWU and Xerox entered into collective bargaining negotiations in 1980, the company had already begun to experience shrinking market share but had not shifted its business strategy in response. During the negotiations the two parties agreed for the first time to experiment with a quality-of-work-life (QWL) effort. The focus was on creating shop-floor problem-solving groups comparable to quality circles.

This program was very successful. Within the first ten months 90 problem-solving groups were established in the four main plants. After two years, about 25% of the 4,000 employees volunteered for QWL training and participated in a problem-solving group. After 30 months, the effort spread throughout the four manufacturing plants.

1 The material in this section is excerpted and adapted from Joel Cutcher-Gershenfeld, "Tracing a Transformation in Industrial Relations," *The Case of Xerox Corporation and the Amalgamated Clothing and Textile Workers Union,* U.S. Department of Labor, 1988.

© 32 CASE

Although much success can be attributed to this effort, dissatisfaction emerged among the workforce for various reasons. Xerox laid off more than 5,000 employees during 1981 and 1982, including 1,200 union members. In addition, there was a growing concern over the amount of time it took to solve a problem and implement a solution—typically a year or more before solutions were considered for implementation. The constraints on the QWL effort—seniority job movement, layoffs, and delays—involved issues that were at the core of the collective-bargaining contract. Thus, about a year after the successful launch of the QWL effort, interest among rank and file workers began to plateau. Ironically, this was just as local union leaders, most of whom were rather skeptical of the QWL effort at the outset, were beginning to see its potential for empowering workers and improving the overall labor-management relationship. What no one foresaw, however, was that the effort was about to confront its first crisis.

The Wiring Harness Crisis

In mid-1982 the union learned that management had decided to outsource its wiring harness operations in its component manufacturing plant. The company stated that it could reduce its costs by $3.2 million by outsourcing this work. This would result in the layoff of 180 people in the wiring harness department—an area that had an active QWL team in place! Employees were outraged because they saw this as a significant break in the trust so essential to the QWL process. After some tough discussions, the union and management agreed to form a study team of employees, supervisors, engineers, and support staff to suggest changes in operations that would allow this work to be done competitively in-house (i.e., result in a $3.2 million, or 28 percent, total cost reduction).

To the astonishment of both company and union leaders, the study team reported back recommendations that exceeded the $3.2 million cost savings targets! Its recommendations ranged from completely revamping the physical layout of the production process, to updating the overhead accounting, to reducing the layers of supervision, to changing job descriptions to include a wider array of maintenance responsibilities. Many of these required changing long-established collective bargaining provisions and closely guarded managerial "rights" to make decisions. This study group served as an object lesson to everyone, showing the power of giving a significant competitive problem to the employees with the most at stake in its resolution and supporting them with the information and technical expertise needed to generate alternative solutions. The company and union therefore not only accepted the study team's recommendations, they agreed to follow a similar process for making outsourcing decisions in the future.

33

CASE

The 1983 Contract Negotiations: Testing Each Other's Commitment

As the time for renegotiation of the collective-bargaining contract approached in 1983, it became clear to both union and management representatives that another crisis for the employee participation process was building. Workers were increasingly frustrated and frightened by continued downsizing and layoffs. Survey data collected by the parties clearly showed that unless job security concerns were addressed by the negotiators, the QWL process was doomed. Workers were simply not going to continue to cooperate in what looked to them as a process of working themselves out of their jobs.

The negotiators reached an impasse over this issue. As a last resort they decided to ask Xerox's chief executive, David Kearns, to visit the negotiating table to share his views of where the QWL process fit into the company's strategy. Coming to the negotiating table for this purpose was a highly symbolic gesture for Kearns; no CEO had ever done so before. He stated his emphatic support for the employee participation process and urged the company and union negotiators to do whatever was necessary to keep it alive and to reinvigorate it. As a result, the negotiators reached an agreement that included a no-layoff commitment for three years in return for a commitment to continue the QWL process, and to follow the precedent of the wiring harness study group when similar issues arose in the future. Thus, this agreement had the effect of getting employees to open up and talk more freely about their jobs and potential cost-cutting suggestions.

Although, this was positive for working in collaboration, three aspects of the contract were actually contrary to the close relationship that was developing between labor and management. First, the contract had no wage increase in the first year. Second, management added a co-pay component to the employee health insurance plan to reduce the cost of health care to the company. The third change was the inclusion of a highly restrictive no-fault absenteeism program. These three changes to the contract were not well received by the rank and file employees, which led to a noticeable decline in the number of volunteers for the QWL program. This tapering off of interest in the QWL program led the union and management to be proactive in finding new ways to increase participation, leading to the next major step in the change process.

Transitions from QWL to Business Area Work Groups

The new contract effectively split the attitudes of employees as to whether it was generally positive for union members or a step in the wrong direction. The split in attitudes was evident in the lack of enthusiasm given to the QWL program and the lack of interest by many employees in participating in the program any longer. By this time, however, both top management and the union had come to value the participative nature of their relationship. Both sides decided to work to find a better solution to build employee participation once again.

An attitude survey was conducted in March 1984 in the Components Manufacturing Operations to better understand employee interest and motivations. From the survey, it was clear that a large number of employees were no longer involved in the QWL program; however, the responses indicated a strong interest in employee participation in other types of programs.

Specifically, employees indicated overwhelming concurrence with statements concerning whether they wanted more say in their work (82.9% said they did), desired more information (86% said they did), and liked the idea of employee involvement (89.8% said they did). Essentially, the employees were saying they valued participative principles but they did not value QWL as the vehicle for this participation.

Both sides worked together to come up with a solution. The parties developed a new system of participation through newly formed functional groupings called business area work groups (BAWGs). Supervisors were designated as BAWG leaders. The first BAWGs went into operation in spring 1985, and soon after the QWL program began to lose focus. However, there was consensus among the parties that this structure would also not be long-lived due to the high variability in the results and potential of each of the work groups. There was also an increasing emphasis on autonomy in group decision making, which led to the next significant step in the process.

Emergence of Autonomous Work Groups and New Work Practices

Autonomous work groups were not a new concept. The first such group started operating in 1982. Autonomous work groups, as their name states, operate without direct supervision. To be successful, however, the autonomous work groups were given one rule of operation—all work must be completed on time and with zero defects. Such groups are more common in brand-new facilities, although in existing operations it is far less common and tends to be far more difficult operating within an established culture.

Autonomous work groups make many decisions on their own. They deal with vendors and sales representatives as a team, and most of the training of new members is on the job. Due to the voluntary nature of the work groups, there was a feeling that such teams can be quite strong in operations and efficiency. What was quite significant about the group decision making was the loss of the importance of seniority that resulted. This would remain as an outstanding issue in the stability of the groups.

CASE

34

Based on the increased prevalence of the autonomous activities, the union brought a demand to the bargaining table in 1986 to institutionalize some of the activities. It proposed that a special classification be created for informal group leaders so that they get an additional pay premium and a dispensation to use 15% of their work time for administrative activities. Agreement was reached that such a classification would be created.

There continued to be uncertainty as to whether it was required to more systematically induce teamwork among engineers and work groups or whether the loss of the seniority system would eventually undermine the work groups' efforts. These issues went unresolved into the next phase of change.

Labor Involvement in Strategic Decisions

While autonomous work groups were still in vogue, the study team concept was also still functioning since 1983. Through the study teams, and the institution of collaboration on issues involving subcontracting grew a series of additional events that increased union involvement in strategic decisions at the plant level.

In late 1983, the degree of union involvement in human resource planning, plant design, product development, and supplier relations expanded considerably. The following is an example from the product development process that illustrates this change in philosophy:

> In the past, hourly workers would only see the new machines during trial production runs late in their development. Now, however, a team of hourly workers has been assigned full-time to work with the engineers in the early stages of product development for the newest Xerox copier—especially around manufacturability issues. Special flexibility has been allowed for in terms of hourly workers' classifications.

This created an even stronger relationship between the parties as the two became more aware of each other's needs up-front, enabling them to meet each other's needs as part of the process rather than as an afterthought.

Bottom-Up Meets Top-Down Change Efforts

David Kearns, then the chairman and CEO of Xerox, embarked in 1983 on an effort to transform the way the entire management structure operated. Termed "Leadership Through Quality" (LTQ), the initiative began with a meeting of Kearns with the senior executives who report directly to him. This cascaded down through the organization as these executives met with the managers who reported to them and instilled in them a sense of ownership for the quality initiative such that each manager would be responsible for meeting the needs of his or her respective customers.

The spreading of the LTQ concepts began to build up tension among employees, who were also being bombarded by the QWL (quality-of-work-life) program. It was feared that top management was building the LTQ program as an alternative to the QWL efforts. Emerging from this tension was the establishment of a core committee with top union leaders, top managers, LTQ trainers, and QWL coordinators. As a result of this committee, the LTQ program concept was modified to fit a unionized setting.

The LTQ program began to show solid results quickly. In the New Build Organization, for example, after the QWL program was credited for a 50% reduction in reject rates from 1982 to 1984, the LTQ program increased the rate of improvement by a factor of seven.

This initiative and the changing of management processes are discussed in the section on transformation from the top down (pages 37–40).

Continuity in the 1986 Negotiations and Beyond

In 1986, management and the unions decided to continue to work on more participatory arrangements arising out of the 1983 negotiations. As part of the new contract negotiations, the union sought to achieve five key objectives: (1) increase tie-in to corporate-wide profit sharing; (2) continue no-layoff guarantee; (3) move compensation to

C

35

CASE

link closer to performance; (4) set up a new classification for leaders of groups; and (5) change the absenteeism control program to be less rigid.

The two parties succeeded in giving the union relief on all the above points. The no-layoff program was seen as a tremendous move forward in providing a solid foundation from which to work on cooperative efforts well into the future.

The 1990s: Downsizing Threats, Expanded Agenda for Partnerships

The labor-management partnership process has continued to the present and expanded to address new problems and opportunities as they arose. In 1992, for example, the company and union jointly studied whether it was feasible to open a new facility in another community in New York to produce components that had been outsourced to Mexico but had not been meeting the company's quality standards. An agreement was reached to do so and that plant is now in operation. In 1993 the company again faced the need to reduce the workforce and entered into negotiations with the union over how to do so without destroying the progress to date in their labor-management partnership. The result was a long-term (seven years) labor agreement that provided employment security for current workers and established a formula for future wage increases in return for an agreement to use attrition and retirements to reduce gradually the overall size of the workforce.

By the early 1990s, the Xerox-ACTWU partnership had gained a reputation as a national model for union-management relations. The company and union representatives were in constant demand to speak to similar labor and/or management groups about how they managed to achieve the transformation at Xerox and to keep the partnership alive and well through some of the difficult times summarized above. In the world of labor-management relations, therefore, it was the union-management partnership, which started at the bottom of the organization by involving rank and file workers, that transformed Xerox in the 1980s from having a market share of 44 percent back to being the dominant force in the market for copiers.

There are many important points to be learned from the above series of events in transforming the relationship between the union and management. Above all is the ability of the company to embrace the concept of employee involvement and participatory management as a distinct concept in itself, rather than as a particular change initiative. This is what enabled management and the union to continuously improve upon their relationship each time difficult issues came up to for resolution. Moreover, this change process incorporated a rich mix of negotiations and cooperative problem solving as the issues warranted. Workers and union representatives retained sufficient independence and power to raise issues of critical concern to them—particularly employment security—as these issues came up. The company representatives likewise were not reluctant to be frank with employees and union representatives about the need to cut costs and remain competitive, even if from time to time this might result in job losses. This ability to maintain trust through a mixture of negotiations and problem solving and to address the issues of critical concern to each party stands out as a key attribute of Xerox and ACTWU's bottom-up partnership model of organizational change.

Building relationships such as this has much to do with the ability to recognize and deal with conflict in such a way that it actually strengthens the relationship rather than impeding it. The early history of concern for employees, as discussed in the beginning of this section, facilitated the initiative of greater employee involvement.

In summary, to hear the union-management specialists tell the story of Xerox's transformation, one would get the impression that all the action started at the grassroots level and gradually, by surviving a set of pivotal events and crises, the change process gained momentum and expanded its focus. From the bottom-up perspective, the real heroes of the Xerox story are the workforce, union-management representatives, and those who facilitated the transformation in labor-management relations.

The next section, however, tells the story as seen from the other perspective.

TRANSFORMATION FROM THE TOP DOWN[2]

For eight years—from 1982 to 1990—the two of us engaged in one of the most exciting undertakings of our careers. We worked together to alter profoundly the course of a major American corporation bloodied by Japanese competition and crippled by its own mistakes.

> This was a partnership, though we assumed very different roles. David Kearns was the corporate leader; David Nadler was the counselor, advisor, and change strategist. . . . Happily, we were successful. In 1982 Xerox was in danger of going out of business. Today it is a vibrant and growing company. We believe that this is due largely to the quality process that we introduced into the corporation. (p. ix)

In 1982, with the help of David Nadler, outside consultant and president of the Delta Consulting Group, David Kearns embarked on a program to introduce dramatic change in the management and operations of Xerox from the top to the bottom of the company. Their strategy was to start with a small team of top executives, work out a shared vision and plan for change, and then to cascade the program down through the rest of the company. Quality provided the focus for the change effort, which became known as Leadership Through Quality (LTQ).

This section describes the evolution of this top-down change process and the LTQ program by drawing on excerpts from a book about this change process written jointly by Kearns and Nadler.

Choosing the Quality Focus: Envisioning a Quality-Driven Organization

The decision to focus on quality as a target and process for change evolved out of evidence that the company's products were no match for their Japanese competitors. This took some effort since the Xerox culture of the 1960s and 1970s stressed growth and quantity. But by the end of the 1970s Japanese competitors were advertising their superior quality compared to Xerox products.

> One of the Japanese manufacturers was running an advertising campaign around this time that hit very close to the truth. The ad showed a closet with a copier repairman inhabiting it. It went on to comment that the repairman had to actually live with you because your machine broke down so much. Nobody was named, but it was pretty clear to everyone in the business that the copier in question was Xerox's. (p. 134)

Shortly after he became CEO in 1982 Kearns decided he needed to get a first-hand understanding of what he considered to be an all-out competitive war with Japanese rivals:

> In May 1982, I took a trip to Japan. . . . I learned some interesting things over there and they stuck with me. On the plane ride back, as usual, I doodled. The thing I kept writing down was the Japanese commitment to quality, something that had come to be labeled Total Quality Control. (p. 134)

Yet few at Xerox really knew much about how to translate the Japanese commitment to quality to a U.S. corporation. Kearns therefore sent two trusted top executives, Norm Rickard and Hal Tragash—individuals he viewed as pioneers in the effort to change the company—off to "come up with a strategy to create a quality company Western-style." (p. 136)

> While Norm Rickard and Hal Tragash sorted out and crystallized their thoughts about bringing total quality to Xerox, they also decided to determine how much of top management of the company was really into this quality idea. Nothing gets very far in a big corporation without a constituency of support in the right places. "The right places" means people in power. Rickard, the astute student of political life in the corporate world, knew

37

CASE

2 The material in this section is adapted from David Kearns and David Nadler. 1992. *Profits in the Dark*, New York: Harper Business Books.

the concept didn't stand a prayer of a chance unless there was a network of support beneath me. (p. 137)

The "Magic Leader" and His Consultant

Rickard and Tragash put together a group of eleven top leaders in the company—kings and princes, as they were called, or as they later became known, the "gang of eleven." This group decided on the need for an outside consultant. Kearns agreed. He described the value of an outside consultant to a CEO as follows:

> . . . it's hard for a CEO to get useful answers from people beneath him in the organization. And so he turns to outsiders with expertise whom he trusts. . . . CEOs like to hear about how other CEOs deal with problems. Consultants can effectively introduce CEOs to other CEOs so they can share thoughts. . . . Consultants serve as sounding boards at minimal cost. Managers are great CEO watchers. They are always looking for signals. So a consultant allows for a private audience in which ideas can be discussed and kept secret from the rest of the organization.
>
> A final, not insignificant factor is that the consultant has no career aspirations or corporate agenda within the company. His only hope is to get more work. And that freedom facilitates the consultant being a source of honest criticism and feedback. (pp. 291–292)

At a meeting with David Nadler, Kearns described his frustration with the situation and why he needed the help of an outside consultant:

> Nadler met with me and I expressed my extreme frustration and gave him my wet noodle spiel. "I'm trying to get a hundred thousand people to act and think differently toward the product, the customer, and each other every hour of every day. . . . All of my senior managers say they agree with me. But I feel that if I leave the company for a couple of days, they will go right back to doing what they were doing. I'm pushing a wet noodle."
>
> Nadler said . . . that if I were really serious about bringing about such extensive upheaval, I would probably have to shoot someone along the way. Unless people get rewarded and punished for how they behave, he said, no one will really believe that this is anything more than lip service. . . . Then he told me that I would have to furnish symbols and signals and create a TDY, an old army term meaning a temporary duty team, and I would have to lead it. (p. 147)

Kearns and Nadler believed that leading change from the top requires a special type of leader. Kearns and Nadler described a "magic" type of leader who must be *envisioning, energizing,* and *enabling.* The CEO must be envisioning to effectively construct and communicate a compelling vision of the future. He or she must be energizing in order to motivate others to act. Many times this means demonstrating one's own excitement and enthusiasm for a particular project. Lastly, the authors indicate the leader must be enabling. The leader must show his or her support and provide assistance to management and members of the organization to enable change to occur. With these three characteristics, the leader has the wherewithal to bring about major change.

Getting Buy-In from Top Management

In February 1983, Kearns and Nadler held an off-site, three-day meeting.

> The first senior management quality meeting . . . was designed to be a high-involvement, participative event. The objective was to involve the twenty-five most senior managers of the corporation in shaping the quality strategy and its implementation. The basic device used to structure the participation was a set of thirty-four questions that the core planning group developed. During the two and a half days, the group of managers worked in various large and small group settings to develop and agree upon answers to these questions. Through that mechanism, they shaped the strategy and developed their own feelings of ownership.
>
> As the Leesburg meeting wrapped up, I felt tremendously encouraged. Nobody argued against our concept, though some of the participants subsequently would prove to be at best halfhearted supporters. It was tough to openly argue against quality. But some of our managers really never did anything to try to implement the project. (p. 184)

In August 1983, Kearns held a second meeting at Leesburg, Virginia, for the same twenty-five executives, plus the 100 members of the quality improvement team (QIT). The final bluebook (goals, objective, project plan) was approved by the full participants in the meeting. Now there were 125 people who had approved the plan.

Educating and Training All Levels of Employees

After the second meeting in Leesburg, each of these managers set out to transform the organization. As Kearns described it: "Each of the people in my own training session went ahead and co-trained his own group, which really helped drill the lessons into his [or her] own head, and the cascade through the company began" (p. 215). This was only the beginning.

> By the summer of 1984, the training cascade had begun in earnest. Each team that went through the training spawned six to ten additional groups that would then be educated as each team member became co-trainer of the family group that he or she led. By 1985, the cascade became a virtual Niagara Falls of training, with literally hundreds of family groups being trained each month. As each one completed the training sequence, it turned its attention to the specific quality improvement project that it initiated during the training and worked it to completion. (p. 216)

Xerox began seeing the results of their efforts almost immediately. Within the first few months of their efforts, Kearns felt that meetings were getting more productive and task forces were getting more done. Rather than waiting for significant events to occur, management felt it was better to communicate small progress to show the continuing momentum. As Kearns and Nadler explained, "When we saw gains from these efforts, we made sure to trumpet them throughout the corporation to inspire and encourage others" (p. 216).

The Failed Product Crisis

More than three years after the launching of the LTQ change effort, Xerox experienced a rude awakening when a major new product, the 5046 mid-range copier, failed in the marketplace because of serious reliability problems. The question was, how could this happen, given the emphasis of the LTQ process?

> After we did some investigation, we learned that our people knew of the shortcomings before the machine was introduced and yet they were covered up, and at the highest levels. The product should not have been announced and shipped. . . . And what caused me so much distress was that this had happened so far in the quality process. It was the sort of thing that the quality process was specifically intended to prevent. But the old culture of our people being afraid to deliver bad news was not yet rinsed from the company. I was plenty mad about the episode, and people were removed from their jobs because of it. (pp. 249–250)

As a result of this experience, the company's president and future CEO Paul Allaire instituted a series of "presidential reviews" to examine what might be learned from this and similar mistakes.

Baldrige Award, Market Share Gains, and Customer Satisfaction Guarantee

Meanwhile, by 1988 one hundred thousand Xerox employees worldwide had been trained in quality improvement tools. By this time, Xerox was also seeing a dramatic improvement in its product quality as well as market share over its Japanese competitors. The company was regaining a reputation for quality, customer service, and organizational innovation. In 1988 it was confident enough to apply for and win the Baldrige Award, a prestigious national award given to companies that have internalized a commitment to quality and have achieved significant market recognition for the quality of its products and services. By 1990, the company was confident enough about its improved quality to offer its customers a total satisfaction guarantee.

CEO Succession: The Quality "Race" Continues

In 1990 Kearns reached the age of 60 and kept his pledge to retire as CEO. Paul Allaire was appointed CEO. Allaire was one of the earliest advocates of the LTQ process, and therefore his appointment as Kearn's successor was a clear signal that the company's commitment to quality as a driving force and focus would continue into the 1990s. Kearns described the future facing Xerox as it entered the 1990s as follows:

> What everyone asks me now is, What next for Xerox? While I was there, I reminded Xerox employees over and over again that the pursuit of quality is a race with no finish line. Nothing ever stands still—not our competitors and not technology. Quality improvement must be a continuous and inexhaustible process. We learned that every time we improved, so did the competition. We also learned that every time we improved, customer expectations increased. And they should. And thus we were part of a never-ending spiral of increasing competition and customer expectations. No matter how good we get, we had to get better. (p. 263)

Kearns also recognized that the change process in the future will have to go beyond the focus on quality.

> As we well know, the Japanese are exceedingly strong in quality themselves. It's doubtful that we can ever do better than to maintain parity with them. So while quality keeps American companies in the game, it doesn't give them the edge that ensures they'll score the most points.
>
> Indeed, the very values embedded in the Japanese culture—traits like discipline, conformity, uniformity—are the values that are fundamental to total quality management. But where American workers shine is entrepreneurism, diversity, and autonomy. . . . So our challenge is to move beyond quality to take advantage of the novel strengths of the American worker. . . .
>
> Right now [circa 1992] Paul [Allaire] is assiduously rethinking the architecture of work and organizations. He foresees the day when Xerox and other big companies will be structured so differently that they will be almost unrecognizable. He wants to rip up the old hierarchical charts, get rid of restrictive ways in which workers are managed, and start afresh. . . . Paul has been promoting empowerment and self-management so that everyone has a greater latitude and gets to do more than routine labor. . . .
>
> And so Xerox is revving up for another thrilling journey. (pp. 263–264)

© CASE 40

ORGANIZATIONAL CHANGE IN THE NEXT ROUND

Efforts at organizational transformation similar to those described at Xerox were typical of the 1980s and first half of the 1990s. By focusing on restructuring, downsizing, teamwork, customer satisfaction, and other innovations, many firms, like Xerox, achieved significant improvements in productivity, quality, cost reduction, and customer satisfaction.

Although most executives were pleased with this progress, an increasing unease began to surface in executive seminars and other discussions about whether the cumulative impact of these efforts was beginning to stress the workforce beyond its limits. At the same time growing voices within the workforce and in public policy circles were beginning to be raised about overwork, burnout, lack of adequate time for family responsibilities, and similar concerns.

Figure 8.4 illustrates how one research group diagrammed both the intended and the unintended second-order consequences of recent change efforts. The effects of innovations spurred on by competitive pressures were improved productivity, cost containment, and quality. These improvements translated directly into improved "bottom-line" results for their firms. But some of the second order, or "below-the-line," consequences were increased pressures on individual time and energy, which in turn were being absorbed largely outside the boundaries of the firm on workers' family and private lives.[3]

When presented with this figure in an executive education program, participants raised a number of questions. Will these pressures reverberate to affect behavior and performance within their firms? Will these pressures produce a backlash or a need for further organizational change now or in the future? Who will initiate the change? How might it be managed?

This led to a vigorous debate among these executives over whether they should be concerned about these issues. The debate was especially intense between managers from countries with different cultural norms about the role of family life and the relationship of work and family. Should the private lives of employees be of any concern to the firm? Shouldn't these issues be left up to each individual? In a global corporation, how do we respect the cultural differences and individual preferences influencing how people balance work and family responsibilities? These questions led some managers to argue that these issues are "outside" the legitimate concerns of organizational leaders. They should be left to employees to sort out in their "private" lives consistent with their cultural norms and personal values. Yet others noted that if this diagram is correct, eventually the effects of the organizational innovations on individuals and families would feed back to negatively affect the bottom line of the firm as employees react to these pressures.

Indeed, there is some evidence that these problems are beginning to surface in different parts of the world. For example, IG Metall, the largest union in Germany representing workers in the metal-working sector, engaged in the longest strike in its history

3 The material in this section is derived from a collaborative project on work-family issues at Xerox Corporation directed by Professor Lotte Bailyn at the MIT Sloan School of Management and Professor Deborah Kolb of the Graduate School of Management, Simmons College. The research team included Susan Eaton, Joyce Fletcher, Maureen Harvey, Robin Johnson, and Leslie Perlow, with Rhonda Rapoport as a consultant. The project is funded by the Ford Foundation.

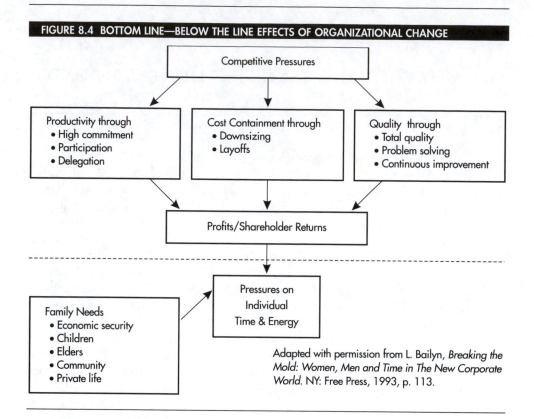

FIGURE 8.4 BOTTOM LINE—BELOW THE LINE EFFECTS OF ORGANIZATIONAL CHANGE

Competitive Pressures

Productivity through
- High commitment
- Participation
- Delegation

Cost Containment through
- Downsizing
- Layoffs

Quality through
- Total quality
- Problem solving
- Continuous improvement

Profits/Shareholder Returns

Pressures on
Individual
Time & Energy

Family Needs
- Economic security
- Children
- Elders
- Community
- Private life

Adapted with permission from L. Bailyn, *Breaking the Mold: Women, Men and Time in The New Corporate World*. NY: Free Press, 1993, p. 113.

in 1984 over its demand to reduce the work week to 37 hours. In 1993 the U.S. Congress signed the Family and Medical Leave Act, which requires employers to grant up to twelve weeks time off for the birth or adoption of a child or care of a sick child or an elder member of one's family. In 1994 General Motors workers in Flint, Michigan, who had been working an average of 50 or more hours per week, went on strike to demand the company hire additional full-time workers to reduce the amount of overtime required of production workers. Even in Japan, the nation with the largest average number of work hours per year, some younger managers are beginning to question the long-established tradition of the "evening office," whereby male managers are expected to socialize with their peers and supervisors after hours before embarking on their commute home.

If these examples are accurate signals of future developments, we might expect that the changes organizations are most likely to experience in the next round are ones that seek to balance or cope with those that sought to make organizations lean and competitive in past years. These reactions are likely to come not from the top of organizations but from within (from employees and their representatives) or from outside (from government agencies, advocacy groups, or other social/political groups). They are likely to challenge and seek change in deeply embedded cultural assumptions and norms, and they are likely, therefore, to meet with strong resistance. They will likely engender more hidden or informal and private discussion among those most affected since in the early stages there may be many who feel it is not "legitimate" to raise these issues openly in their organizations. Thus, pressures for change may be smoldering under the surface long before they are brought out in the open. If so, the potential for explosive conflict over these issues is considerable.

So what should managers do? To explore this question, we can again turn to data from Xerox. In the early 1990s, pilot studies were conducted at several Xerox worksites in the United States to investigate the effects of work patterns on the use of time and their consequences for work and family issues. The results of three of these pilot studies are summarized in Figures 8.5, 8.6, and 8.7 on pages 44–46. Together they suggested that certain work groups were suffering from symptoms of severe time pressures and long hours. Yet the work patterns and norms that produced these symptoms were deeply embedded in the prevailing organizational culture at Xerox.

These pilot studies serve as data for managers to consider whether action on these issues is called for. The data are not conclusive. They come from a small, selected subset of the organization and, therefore, may not be representative of how these issues are being experienced in other parts of the organization. They epitomize the type of preliminary "data" and early "intelligence" that managers might encounter on problems that may grow into significant change issues.

The question to consider, therefore, is how significant a problem are overwork, stress, long hours, and work-family conflicts in organizations in different parts of the world? Should these "data" be taken seriously and acted upon now? If so, how? If not, why not? The Task Force Assignment presented below provides a means for exploring these questions and developing a change model suited to this issue, and perhaps to the types of issues that are most likely to confront organizations in the next round of change.

THE TASK FORCE ASSIGNMENT

Assume you are a middle-level manager in a Xerox manufacturing and sales division in your region of the world. A high-ranking executive in the company who is responsible for your region recently was briefed on the results of the work-family pilot studies conducted in three U.S. units of the company (Figures 8.5–8.6, pages 44–45). He now wonders whether this is a serious problem for employees in the operations in your region for which he is responsible. He has asked you to serve on a task force of middle-level managers and professionals working in the region to examine this issue, assess its importance (or lack of importance) to employees in the region, and, if warranted, to suggest a change strategy for addressing these issues. His only caveat to the group is that any changes proposed should not have a negative effect on the division's bottom line performance.

Specifically, your task force is charged with addressing the following questions:

1. What underlying assumptions are embedded in your culture (national, regional, organizational, etc.) regarding the proper relationship between work and family responsibilities?
2. Are personal and/or work-family stresses serious problems among employees in your region?
3. What steps would you follow to examine and, if needed, change organizational practices and work habits within your division?

Your task force is asked to prepare a 10-minute briefing addressing these questions for the next meeting of the Division's Executive Committee.

© 43

EXERCISE

FIGURE 8.5 MIT/FORD FOUNDATION/XEROX COLLABORATIVE ACTION RESEARCH "WORK-FAMILY AS A CATALYST FOR CHANGE" IN SITE 1

Site Description

This site included an engineering group developing new products for the company on a very tight schedule, with a constant goal of reducing time to market. Most engineers were men, only a few were women. Work-family issues were generally "invisible" to the company, and not commonly discussed, and flexibility was available on an ad hoc personal, emergency basis.

Time and Commitment/Work Culture and Structure

Professionals at this site worked very long hours on their software design. Because of management philosophy and because schedules were so tight, a crisis mentality prevailed—even when the date to market was moved back for other reasons, managers did not tell the engineers because they believed they worked "best" under pressure. Most engineers explained that they had to work before and after hours because they were constantly being "interrupted" during regular hours and could not "get their own work done." One even came to work at 2 a.m. one day a week to have some uninterrupted time.

Intervention and Collaboration

Researchers shadowed, interviewed, and surveyed engineers. The research highlighted a few "lead users," who worked more carefully and steadily to prevent problems rather than racing through first drafts and "fixing" all the problems that resulted. Their work was not recognized as "heroic" because it was more invisible. Many were women who worked with more constrained hours because of family responsibilities.[1]

The researchers identified and gave a name to this practice, thus legitimizing it. After extensive discussion, they also proposed restructuring activities during the normal work day to structure the "interruptions," and to guarantee everyone "quiet time" as well as "interactive time."[2]

Results and Learnings

The software design group achieved the first on-time launch in the division following the intervention to create blocks of uninterrupted and interactive time. The attention to time management forced a clearer understanding of the value of interaction for learning, coordination, and so forth, as well as the problem of interruptions (most of which were by managers). The group did more planning and crisis prevention than crisis management. They realized the importance of time-outs for reflection on their work. They concluded that work structure and culture needs collective thought, not just to be treated as individual problems. Finally, they realized that the ad hoc flexibility they used was only a temporary solution that did not challenge the status quo of their work structure.

1 For an in-depth analysis of this part, see J. Fletcher. 1994. *Toward a Theory of Relational Practice: A Feminist Reconstruction of "Real" Work.* Ph.D. Dissertation, Boston University.

2 For an in-depth analysis of this part, see L. Perlow. 1995. *The Time Famine: The Unintended Consequence of Feeling Success at Work.* Ph.D. Dissertation, MIT.

FIGURE 8.6 MIT/FORD FOUNDATION/XEROX COLLABORATIVE ACTION RESEARCH "WORK-FAMILY AS A CATALYST FOR CHANGE" IN SITE 2

Site Description

The site was a customer administration center with 300 clerical and related workers performing computerized billing, ordering, and credit processing tasks. Most workers were female, hourly-paid employees with children in day care or school, but work-family policies were restricted to using one hour flexibly at either the beginning or end of the day with managerial approval using a narrow definition of "family" as a mother with young children. Employee teams were tightly controlled to ensure coverage. Morale and productivity were moderate.

Time and Commitment/Work Culture and Structure

The "ideal worker" in this site was someone who always showed up, never had problems, and did not ask for flexibility. Although employees (except managers) did not often work long hours, they did not have much ability to switch hours or cover each other. Very few employees had been granted "flextime."

Intervention and Collaboration

Researchers interviewed and shadowed employees, and demonstrated to management that the existing policies created a self-reinforcing dynamic that disempowered workers and teams, and delegitimized various forms of family commitment. Both men and women needed more flexibility.[1] The team worked with the top manager at the site extensively. He responded by opening up work-family policies and flexibility to all employees, regardless of family status or managerial discretion, making "wants" equivalent to "needs" and thus avoiding the backlash of selective flexibility. The researchers proposed and facilitated a team of first-line managers to develop plans to integrate the business and work-family needs of their work groups.

Results and Learnings

Nearly everyone worked out a schedule different from the previous schedule—one that better fit their needs. The site experienced a 30% decrease in absenteeism, as employees could plan for doctors' appointments and other scheduled absences by using their flexible schedules, four-day weeks, and so forth. Once the self-managed teams learned to manage their work-family needs, they further evolved to take control of schedules and work assignments, and also enjoyed greater input into team member selection and evaluation. Customer service improved measurably, and division between employees decreased because apparent favoritism was reduced. The employees and managers realized that work-family issues must be dealt with systematically, not as an individualized accommodation with a manager. As a result, the focus on the "flexible manager" as key to work-family policy implementation and employee satisfaction has been replaced by a focus on "empowered" teams.

© 45

EXERCISE

---

1 For more details on this part, see R. Johnson, *Where's the Power in Empowerment? Definition, Difference, and Dilemmas of Empowerment in the Context of Work-Family Management.* Ph.D. Dissertation, Harvard University.

FIGURE 8.7 MIT/FORD FOUNDATION/XEROX COLLABORATIVE ACTION RESEARCH "WORK-FAMILY AS A CATALYST FOR CHANGE" IN SITE 3.1

Site Description

This site was the largest Sales, Service, and Business Operations District in the country, consisting of a partnership of the three different functions. A total of 600 employees were divided into marketing representatives and analysts; service technicians, trainers, and installers; and business office personnel. Sales people worked long, irregular hours, were paid mostly by commission, and included both men and women, whereas service people were blue-collar, hourly workers, and were mostly men.

Time and Commitment/Work Culture and Structure

Sales people were pushed to keep their "feet on the street" and to stay "in front of the customer," as well as to attend multiple social and "morale" functions. The culture was one of individualistic achievement with constantly increasing budgets. Service people were required to respond to most calls within two hours, sometimes on a 24-hour service schedule, and were seldom included in planning work by sales personnel. A requirement for constant availability, as well as stringent, inflexibly measured results, meant that no part-time or flexible sales jobs were available, nor were service jobs flexible. The "partners" did not really collaborate, often blaming each other for problems.

Intervention and Collaboration

Researchers interviewed and shadowed workers, held roundtable discussions, and surveyed workers. The top sales manager was concerned that "most of his best sales people were women," and he was in danger of losing them. Service managers also wanted to make more effective use of fewer staff, with shifts spread out over more hours. The research team suggested a cross-functional team to include members of all three functions, to increase their ability to leverage their knowledge of customers and their ability to support each other in the "field." The "partners" finally agreed.

Results and Learnings

The cross-functional team met, reluctantly at first, but more and more enthusiastically and successfully. By sharing information, sales was able to identify new marketing opportunities and current problem sites, while service was able to better plan installations, removals, upgrades, software fixes, and so on. Business operations also made better connections across functions. Sales in the printing systems group increased over budget, and service quality improved. In addition, service managers began exploring innovative scheduling for staff (such as weekend 12-hour shifts, 24 for 40 hours' pay) after researcher suggestions. The business partners have decided to implement cross-functional teams for all product lines, to improve communication and collaboration across functions. Learnings included that "systems solutions" are needed to create innovation.[1]

---

1 This work was done by Susan Eaton and Maureen Harvey.

EXERCISE

46

MANAGING FOR THE FUTURE

MASSACHUSETTS INSTITUTE OF TECHNOLOGY

ANCONA, KOCHAN, SCULLY,
VAN MAANEN, WESTNEY

Organizational Behavior & Processes

ORGANIZATIONAL ACTION
IN COMPLEX ENVIRONMENTS

module 9

CONTENTS

MODULE 9 (M-9)

ORGANIZATIONAL ACTION IN COMPLEX ENVIRONMENTS

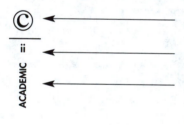

Icon indicates what part you are in, either core Ⓒ or supplemental Ⓢ.

Page number.

Within each part there are sections—Module Overview (OVERVIEW), Academic Perspective (ACADEMIC), Popular Press (PRESS), Case (CASE), Exercise (EXERCISE).

Dedicated to those who have inspired us to try to be better students and teachers.

Special dedications to:
Professor Jack Barbash
Professor Arthur H. Gladstein
Professor Marius B. Jansen
Professor Joanne Martin
Professor Edgar H. Schein

Acquisitions Editor: John R. Szilagyi
Developmental Editor: Jamie Gleich Bryant
Production Editor: Mardell Toomey
Production House: DPS Associates, Inc.
Cover Design: Michael H. Stratton
Marketing Manager: Rob Bloom

Copyright © 1999
by South-Western College Publishing
Cincinnati, Ohio

ISBN: 0-538-87696-4

1 2 3 4 5 6 7 D1 4 3 2 1 0 9 8

Printed in the United States of America

South-Western College Publishing
an International Thomson Publishing company I(T)P®

Cincinnati • Albany • Boston • Detroit • Johannesburg • London • Madrid • Melbourne • Mexico City
New York • Pacific Grove • San Francisco • Scottsdale • Singapore • Tokyo • Toronto

ORGANIZATIONAL ACTION IN COMPLEX ENVIRONMENTS

This module takes us into complex organizational terrain—the organization's environment and how it affects the structures and processes of the organization. The class note applies the three perspectives to the organization's environment. Just as the three "lenses" see the organization itself in different but complementary ways, so each lens provides a different view of the environment. As the case in this module illustrates, the three lenses used together provide a much richer analysis of the complex interactions between an organization and its environment than does any single lens used alone.

The case study in this module takes us into the realm of the organization that has the most complex environment: the multinational firm. A multinational firm is one that owns operations in two or more countries; that is to say, it is an organization that operates in multiple environments. And the case takes us into one of the most complex processes in multinational companies: the cross-border acquisition. In the late 1990s we have seen a surge of cross-border mergers and acquisitions; in the first months of 1998 we have seen major international mergers and acquisitions in autos (Daimler-Benz and Chrysler), in heavy equipment (Volvo and Samsung), publishing (Bertelsmann and Random House), computers (Taiwan's Acer buying the personal computer division of Germany's Siemens-Nixdorf), and even cement (France's LaFarge and Britain's Redland).

Mergers and acquisitions have become a favored means of expanding internationally in industries that are relatively mature, and where buying market share by buying companies is often the fastest way to expand. But cross-border mergers and acquisitions, however strong the strategic logic behind them may be, involve complex organizational processes if the strategic objectives driving the deals are to be met. Companies that have developed in different national environments often differ on many dimensions of their strategic design, their political systems, and their cultures, differences that have developed in response to the different environments in which they emerged and grew. Cross-border acquisitions provide a window on the interactions between organizations and their environments that can be invaluable.

But the organizational processes that unfold as a result of an international acquisition take time to unfold. Where the strategies driving a merger or acquisition can be assessed relatively quickly (and are so assessed by the stock markets, which respond quickly and usually positively to announcements of these cross-border deals), the organizational processes necessary to capture the synergies that are usually so optimistically touted when the deals are announced take years to develop. That is why we have a case study from the 1980s: enough time has passed so that the processes involved can be discussed by the participants with relative openness, and the unanticipated as well as the anticipated challenges of integrating activities in two companies located in very different environments can be analyzed with all the benefits of hindsight. The case presents a cross-border acquisition that is rightly seen as a clear "success story" of international merger and acquisition (M&A). But in such complex organizational processes, even the most successful cases are not without problems and challenges, as the case shows.

The case also spends as much time describing internal organizational processes as it does presenting the organizational environment. The reason is that the case highlights the interactions between the external environment and internal processes, and therefore helps us to develop insights both on the opportunities that the environment can provide and on the constraints that it can impose on effective managerial action.

One element of the case that you should note is the role played by the Swedish and Italian industrial groups. The industrial group is a phenomenon that is often neglected in the strategy and organizations analysis produced in North America, most of which takes the business firm as the highest level of organizational analysis. In most countries of the world, however, the industrial group constitutes an organizational level *above* the individual firm, and many (if not most) major enterprises are part of a larger industrial group: the *chaebol* in Korea, the vertical and horizontal *keiretsu* of Japan, enterprise groups in Taiwan and India, Germany and Italy, France and Sweden. Industrial groups are rapidly emerging in Eastern Europe and Russia. They are important elements of the organizational landscape in most countries outside the Anglo-Saxon economies, and managers neglect their importance in international business at their peril.

This module also contains a supplementary class note on changing models of the multinational corporation. One of the features of the Electrolux-Zanussi case is the organizational change required to achieve greater integration of activities across borders. The 1980s and 1990s have seen a growing tendency for value chains to cross borders (in the words of the strategic design perspective) so that companies can capture greater scale economies. In the case, we can see Electrolux moving not only to integrate Zanussi, but also to change itself to accommodate greater cross-border interactions and a more "transnational" approach to organization. The supplementary class note puts these efforts into the perspective of broader changes in multinationals generally that were occurring at this time and that provided both a model and a justification for organizational change.

ASSIGNMENTS

Come to class prepared to discuss the following questions:

1. How would you map Zanussi's environment, in terms of each of the three lenses? What are the implications of each of the models for Zanussi's internal organization?
2. How does Electrolux deal with the key elements of the environment as it sets up the acquisition, before it signs the final agreement?
3. From the perspective of each of the three lenses, what are the key challenges in managing this acquisition once it is made? What does Electrolux do? How does the external environment reinforce or create problems for these actions?
4. What can Electrolux do to address the remaining challenge of the discontented middle managers in Zanussi?
5. What general "lessons" can you draw from this case?

M-9

core

ORGANIZATIONS AND THEIR ENVIRONMENTS: SETS, STAKEHOLDERS, AND ORGANIZATIONAL FIELDS

For managers, what lies outside their organization is often just as important as what is going on inside—indeed, it is impossible to understand an organization well without understanding the environment in which it operates. Being a manager therefore often involves managing the organization's interactions with its *organizational environment*—that is, with the "social actors" outside the organization, especially other organizations that are important for its survival and success. But just as there are different perspectives on organizations, so there are different but complementary perspectives on the organizational environment.

Each of the three perspectives (lenses) on organizations—strategic design, political, and cultural—has a distinctive way of analyzing the organizational environment. Each highlights different elements of the environment; each provides useful insights on how managers can "manage" the environment—and the limits to managing it—and on how understanding the environment can help in understanding change and the lack of change in the organization.

THE STRATEGIC DESIGN LENS: THE ORGANIZATION SET

As its name suggests, the strategic design lens on the environment has much in common with the strategy field. Both see the organization as an "input/output system" that takes inputs from the environment, adds value to them in some way, and conveys the resulting product or service to clients or customers so that it gains the resources to continue the process. Both the similarity and the differences between the strategy field and the strategic design perspective on organizations emerge clearly if we look at two models of the environment: Michael Porter's Five Forces Model (Porter, 1980), a basic component of most business strategy courses, and the organization-set model that is typical of the strategic design lens.

Porter's *Five Forces* are suppliers, buyers, current competitors, potential competitors, and the threat of substitutes. The *organization-set* model concentrates on the organizations in the environment with which the organization directly interacts: the *input set*—those that supply needed inputs, one part of which is the set of suppliers of materials and components that is one of Porter's Five Forces; the *output set*—those that receive its outputs, including buyers; and the *regulatory set*—those that have formal rights to regulate or restrict its activities (Evan, 1966).

Although the organization-set model has much in common with Porter's Five Forces model, there are several important differences. The Five Forces model is designed to help organizations decide what strategy to follow; the organization-set model is more useful for helping organizations decide whether they are efficiently and effectively organized to carry out their strategies, and for assessing how their organizations might need to change if their strategies change. Therefore, Porter's model of the environment is primarily a map of *opportunities and threats*; the organization-set model is a map of *relationships*. For Porter, competitors—current, potential, and alternative—are critically important. The organization-set model looks at competitors and potential competitors only if they are organizations with which the focal organization develops direct relationships (through industry associations that undertake joint lobbying activities, for example). It also defines its "input-set" more broadly than simply as suppliers of materials and components, to include organizations that supply its people and its technology and know-how. Both models are useful, but they are useful for different things.

Ford Motor Company, for example, has an input-set of suppliers of a vast array of materials (such as sheet metal), components, and subsystems from car seats to air-conditioning systems; of organizations such as universities from which it hires engineers and managers; and of organizations from which it obtains technology or with which it jointly develops technology. Its output set is populated by distributors, through whom it sells its array of vehicles at prices that cover its costs and provide a profit. An array of regulatory agencies interacts with the company in the course of ensuring that its activities conform to requirements and laws, such as the Fair Trade Commission to regulate competitive behavior and the Occupational Health and Safety Administration to oversee worker safety. Ford, like most large U.S. corporations, maintains an office in Washington, D.C., to build relationships with legislators and regulators.

Like Porter's model, the organization-set model looks at the size of the input and output sets: that is, how many organizations there are in the set, and how concentrated they are. It also pays attention to its *diversity*: how many different kinds of organizations there are, and how different they are? Another feature of the set is its *stability* and *predictability*: how quickly the organizations in the set change. The model also pays attention to the *network configuration*: how the members of the organization-set are linked to the firm, to each other, and to the role of *boundary-spanning personnel* who interact with the organization-set members. It identifies the key processes in organization-environment interactions as *exchange* and *resource flows*.

Figure 9.1 portrays a very simple organization set for an organization that sends its products primarily to distributors and to a few large direct-sales customer organizations. There is little overlap between the input and output sets. If we were to look inside such an organization, we would probably find that each relationship is managed by a specialized organizational unit: for example, a Procurement Department deals with suppliers, and a subunit of the Personnel Department deals with relationships with business schools, executive search or "head-hunter" firms, and any other sources of employees with which the organization develops direct relationships. The financial inputs are handled by the corporate Treasurer's Office, and the technology inputs are handled by a department of the Research and Development Laboratory. One of the strategic tasks of each of these

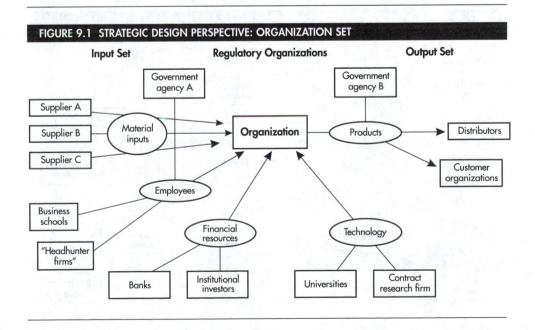

FIGURE 9.1 STRATEGIC DESIGN PERSPECTIVE: ORGANIZATION SET

units is to be alert to changes in the part of the environment with which they deal—e.g., the rise of new organizations, the decline of current members of the set—and to be prepared to respond to such changes. Often regulatory agencies also interact with specialized organizational units: in the exhibit, for example, government agency A, which regulates working conditions and worker safety (such as the U.S. Occupational Health and Safety Agency), may interact with a special department in the company that ensures compliance with regulations; a government agency which sets requirements for products (such as the U.S. Food and Drug Administration, which regulates the approval of all drugs) may interact more broadly with the organization's product development units.

Figure 9.2 provides a slightly more concrete example, the organization set of a research university, although it too is much oversimplified. The output of the university are its graduates and the results of its research activities, embodied in publications, patents, and expertise that is conveyed to the environment in a multitude of other forums, including speeches, consulting activities, and participation in public forums. Both graduates and research outputs are channeled to some organizations that are also providers of inputs, such as companies that fund research projects. In other words, there is considerable overlap among members of the set: government agencies as well as certain industrial companies are members of both the input and the output sets, and certain government agencies also have regulatory authority over certain areas of the university's activities—for example, student tuition support. By and large, these external organizations deal with the university through different departments or subunits of their own: an industrial company, for example, sponsors research at the university through a department of its Research and Development Laboratories, and hires its graduates through its Human Resource Management Department. In cases in which a company has multiple relationships with the university—for example, when companies steadily recruit its technical graduates into the R&D labs and also sponsor research projects, and in addition may make large corporate gifts such as an endowed chair—the university devotes more of its internal resources to its relationship with that company than with organizations with less varied and less dense relationships.

In traditional models of the organization, analysts using this approach assumed that the strategic goal of the organization was to shield itself from uncertainties and instability in its environment. Therefore it tried to protect its core activities by "distancing" mechanisms such as vertical integration, buffering, stockpiling of inventories, and spe-

FIGURE 9.2 EXAMPLE OF AN ORGANIZATION SET: THE RESEARCH UNIVERSITY

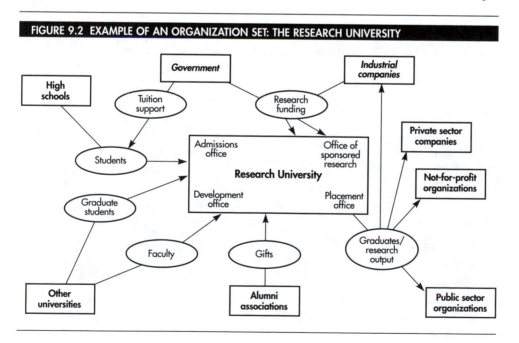

cialized boundary-spanning personnel whose job was to stand between the organization set and the people in the organization carrying out the key functions (see Scott, 1992, Chapter 8). The "new model" of the organization is one whose internal activities are more directly linked to important elements of the organization set—more densely "networked"—as key suppliers are integrated into the manufacturing process, for example, and "lead users" are drawn into product design. The quest for autonomy of the older model gives way to the recognition of interdependence and the challenges of managing interdependent networks effectively.

An organization-set approach to a management issue such as entering a new business or market would ask the following questions: Is the input set already in place? If not, what role should our company play in trying to develop it? Is the output set in place? Can we manage this input set and output set with the same kinds of systems that we use for our current set? What, if any, changes in our design should we make to accommodate differences in the organization set?

For example, if the university finds that its costs are exceeding its revenues and decides to expand the size of its undergraduate body, it will not only need to make internal changes to make this strategy work—such as expanding physical facilities—but it may also need to consider changes in the way it interacts with its organization set. It may need to involve its alumni associations more actively in recruiting promising students; it may need to expand its admissions office and hire people with international experience who can effectively assess and recruit international students. It may need to expand its placement office and reach out to a wider range of potential employers in order in ensure that its graduates find jobs because a university that increases the size of its student body but also in consequence raises the number of its graduates who cannot find jobs will find it more difficult in the future to attract good students. Its reputation may then suffer and its graduates may find it more difficult to get jobs, and over time the number of qualified applicants may fall.

The following example shows how Nissan dealt with its organization set in establishing facilities in the United States.

NISSAN'S ESTABLISHMENT OF AN AUTOMOBILE FACTORY IN THE UNITED STATES
AN ORGANIZATION-SET APPROACH

By the late 1970s, Japanese auto firms faced rising protectionist pressures in the United States, their largest single export market. The Japanese and U.S. governments negotiated a set of so-called Voluntary Export Restrictions, holding Japanese auto manufacturers to the share of the U.S. market that they held at the time of negotiation. Honda, the number-three auto company in Japan in terms of domestic market share, was the first to decide on a strategy of producing automobiles in the United States, and it opened a plant at the site of its existing motorcycle plant in Marysville, Ohio, in 1982. Nissan was the second firm to commit itself to local production, deciding on a site in Tennessee in 1980 and beginning production of trucks in 1983 and autos in 1985 at that location.

Once Nissan decided on a strategy of local U.S. production, it faced several organizational challenges in transferring its production capabilities to a new location so as to maintain the quality and reliability of the vehicles it produced. Several of these involved its organization set. The output set—distribution and sales organizations—had already been built up over two decades of sales in the United States. But it faced challenges in the two other parts of the organization set: the regulatory set, and, especially, the input set.

a. Regulatory Agencies: For Nissan a key set of regulatory agencies was the federal Environmental Protection Agency and related state-level agencies engaged in setting emission standards and pollution control standards.
b. Source of Managers: Nissan needed managers who could understand and transfer the key elements of Nissan's production system to the United States, could work effectively with U.S. suppliers, and could manage a U.S. labor force.

c. Supplier Network: Nissan, like other Japanese producers, produced a relatively low proportion of its components and subsystems in-house. In Japan it relied on a network of suppliers with which it worked closely in new product design (in a system of "simultaneous engineering" whereby suppliers worked on new components simultaneously with Nissan's design of a new model) and in inventory management (suppliers shipped parts to Nissan plants on an "as-needed" or "just-in-time" basis, which contributed both to holding down inventory costs and to ensuring quality).

d. Source of Workers: Nissan's system of building in quality required workers who could analyze problems using fairly sophisticated methods of statistical quality control and who could work in teams, doing a variety of tasks, rather than in an individual position in a factory where quality control was the preserve of engineers.

Nissan chose to deal with these issues as follows:

a. Regulatory Agencies: Nissan set up a research and development organization in 1983 in Michigan to provide Nissan engineers with a better linkage with U.S. regulatory agencies and a better capacity for working with those agencies and finding out what changes were contemplated in U.S. environmental and emissions requirements. It chose to establish this center in Michigan because the concentration of the U.S. auto firms there produced a large number of experienced engineers who understood the industry, had good networks with regulatory authorities, and who, due to the downsizing of U.S. auto firms, were often eager to find good employment in their field.

b. Managers: Nissan hired a former Ford executive who had risen through the manufacturing side of Ford to become its vice-president for body and assembly by the time he retired from the company. He brought with him a number of former Ford executives to form the core of his management team.

c. Supplier Network: Nissan embarked on a major campaign to identify and work with U.S. suppliers who were willing and able to meet Nissan's requirements. In addition, a number of Japanese suppliers to Nissan set up their own branch plants in the United States. Finally, the supplier network of Nissan in the United States stretched across borders to include some suppliers in Japan who shipped components to Tennessee. By the late 1980s, as production expanded in the Tennessee plant, Nissan realized that its U.S. suppliers faced great difficulties in working closely with Nissan design engineers back in Tokyo in order to improve the coordination between component development and new car design. Therefore, in 1988, Nissan expanded the mandate of its Michigan R&D center to include working with U.S. suppliers in the development of components and subsystems. Nissan planned eventually to build an R&D organization in the United States that could design new vehicles for the United States and coordinate the production links with the factory and with suppliers.

d. Workers: Nissan set up a system whereby job applicants had do undergo unpaid pre-employment training in a specially design external training program, funded in cooperation with the state government of Tennessee, before being considered for a job at Nissan. This training was part-time so that it could be combined with other jobs. This training both built up the skills of new recruits before they entered the company and enabled Nissan to be extremely selective in the quality and commitment of its workforce.

Nissan's recognition of the critical role of its organization set in maintaining its competitive advantage in its new setting and its skill in developing the organizational systems for managing that set were critical elements of its management success.

THE POLITICAL LENS: THE STAKEHOLDERS' MODEL

The term "stakeholders," which today has entered the basic vocabulary of businesspeople, lies at the core of a political perspective on the organizational environment. Stakeholders are the social actors (meaning groups of individuals or other organizations) who play a role in the survival and success of the organization and who are affected by an organization's activities—that is, they have a stake in its operations. The stakeholder model of the organizational environment extends the political lens's focus on power, interests, influence, coalition-building and negotiation beyond the formal boundaries of the organization to provide a way to assess the environment's influence—and potential influence—on the organization, and the organization's bargaining power vis-à-vis that environment.

Key stakeholders include employees, unions, customers, suppliers, shareholders, creditors, governments, local communities, and even the general public. Often a distinction is made between internal stakeholders—those who are formally members of the firm—and external stakeholders. But this distinction, while useful in many ways, is difficult to maintain rigorously because many internal stakeholders have multiple stakeholder identities. Employees, for example, are also members of the local community; some may be members of a union, and others (especially top managers) may be shareholders. Some external organizations also play multiple stakeholder roles. In state-owned enterprises (such as Groupe Bull of France, the computer company), government may be simultaneously a customer, a shareholder, and a regulator.

In the stakeholder model, the key variables on which analyses tend to focus are:

- Interests (What does each set of stakeholders want? How clearly defined are those interests? What are the priorities assigned to those interests, and can priorities be altered?)
- Power and influence (What is the basis of power or influence of each set of stakeholders?)

The key processes in organization-environment relations on which this model focuses are *negotiation* between the organization and its stakeholders and *coalition-building*, as internal stakeholders turn to various external stakeholders to build support for their agendas, and vice-versa. Figure 9.3 presents a very simple stakeholders model of an organization.

In the "new" organization, stakeholders are becoming more diverse and often draw the members of the organization more aggressively into recognizing and identifying with their interests: in other words, stakeholders are becoming more densely networked across the boundaries of the organization. They are also crossing boundaries in another sense: as firms become more global, their stakeholders also become more international. In some cases this results in rivalries between parallel sets of stakeholders in different countries (in discussions of which factory gets closed, for example, or which government has jurisdiction over what activities); in other cases, such as environmental and pollution issues, stakeholders are themselves forming global coalitions. For example, in June 1995, Shell UK, a subsidiary of Royal Dutch Shell, one of the world's largest oil companies, announced that it would dispose of one of its obsolete oil rigs in the North Sea by sinking it in deeper waters. Greenpeace and other environmental groups organized large-scale

© 9 ACADEMIC

FIGURE 9.3 THE STAKEHOLDERS' MODEL

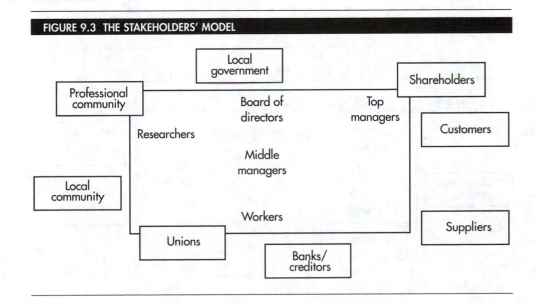

protests in Europe, especially in Germany, where concerns about the pollution of the North Sea were very strong. German consumers began to boycott Shell gas stations, to a point where Shell gas-station owners in that country began to talk of suing Shell for damages in lost business. After insisting for weeks that sinking the oil rig did not threaten the environment, Shell UK suddenly announced that it would instead remove the rig to land and dispose of it there.

Figure 9.4 presents a stakeholders' model of a research university. There are some similarities with the picture of the environment presented by an organization set (see Figure 9.2), and some differences. The stakeholders' model calls attention to groups that are often not formally organized but are potentially important and can be mobilized, such as parents, donors, and alumni(ae). It also includes unions, which organize subsets of the employees (in some universities, for example, graduate students who are teaching assistants have formed a union that is affiliated with similar unions at other universities, or employees charged with the maintenance of the university's physical plant are often members of craft or industrial unions). And it includes the local community, for which the university may be important in a number of ways: as an employer, a source of attraction for industrial companies, and an occupier of land and user of services that pays lower local taxes than a commercial organization of similar scale.

A stakeholders' approach to a management issue such as entering a new business or market or making a major change in the organizational structure would ask questions such as the following: Who are the key stakeholders who will be affected by this decision? What is their reaction likely to be? Can or should we make efforts to increase the involvement of the stakeholders favorably disposed to this move? How will it affect the relative power of current stakeholders?

This model draws attention to the fact that although the interests of various stakeholders may be compatible, they are not identical. The local community may share with the university an interest in the university's maintaining its reputation as a leading center for research in the sciences, for example. But if the university decides that in order to do this it needs additional land to build a new bioscience research laboratory, the local community's interests in maintaining its tax base and in protecting its citizens from the perceived hazards of the by-products of genetic engineering may override the shared interests, and require the university to engage in intensive negotiations with the local community before it can carry out its plans.

The following example shows how Nissan courted stakeholders for its new Tennessee plant.

FIGURE 9.4 STAKEHOLDERS' MODEL OF A RESEARCH UNIVERSITY

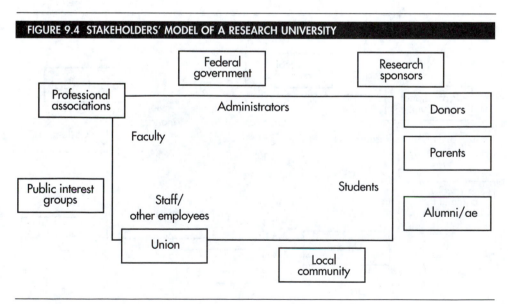

NISSAN'S ESTABLISHMENT OF AN AUTOMOBILE FACTORY IN THE UNITED STATES
A STAKEHOLDERS APPROACH

When Nissan decided to set up manufacturing in the United States in 1980, it was a time of considerable tension between Japan and the United States, especially in the auto industry, given the steady inroads Japanese producers had made on the Big Three (General Motors, Ford, and Chrysler) share of the market and the consequent loss of U.S. jobs.

Nissan therefore set out to cultivate potential stakeholders in the United States. It began this process early in its decision-making process, sending teams of its managers to the United States to negotiate with governors and investment offices in various states to find a favorable setting. It picked Tennessee for a number of reasons, but among them was the strong commitment of the governor to developing a good relationship with Nissan and to providing state support for the plant, and the facts that Tennessee was a state in which the labor force was not strongly unionized and that Tennessee was distant both physically and culturally from the heartland of the auto industry. The "local stakeholders"—the local community, and the local and state governments—had a strong interest in the employment opportunities offered by the plant, the prospect that supporting industries would be attracted to Tennessee as a result of Nissan's location there, and the long-term improvement of the local tax base. They also had no competing direct stakes in U.S. auto plants, which were located in other states.

Nissan stated from the beginning that it did not want to have a unionized workforce, on the grounds that unions introduced rigidities into the organization of work and fostered conflict between management and workers. Its preference for recruiting workers who had no previous auto industry experience was explained by Nissan as the company's desire to have workers with no preconceptions about how work should be carried out, but critics saw it as a way to screen out union members. In 1988, however, the United Automobile Workers (UAW) announced an organizing drive at Nissan in Tennessee, and in a six-month campaign closely watched by the media and by the government's Labor Relations Board, tried to persuade Nissan employees that their interests would be better served with the support of a union that would serve their interests by:

a. ensuring better safety conditions in the plant;
b. protesting against line speed-ups and extended working hours;
c. ensuring orderly promotions and equal opportunities within the plant.

Nissan responded with a vigorous countercampaign, saying that the union was more interested in winning a victory against Nissan than in the interests of the workers themselves, and arguing that with an "open-door" policy whereby workers were encouraged to bring any grievances to management, workers did not need a union. Nissan argued that the union's efforts would lower productivity and make the plant less competitive. At the same time, Nissan announced plans for a major plant expansion. The proposal to join the union was defeated.

Nissan was able to reassure key stakeholders back in Japan that jobs would not be lost there because of production in the United States. Cars would still be exported to North America from Japan, but the limits set by the Voluntary Export Restrictions meant that the only way the company could increase sales in the United States was to produce there. The fact that Japanese workers' interests were not negatively affected by the U.S. plant was significant for getting Japan's cooperation in training U.S. workers, and played a role in the success of the technology transfer from Japan to the United States.

Nissan also made great efforts to ensure that its distributors and customers received vehicles that met all the quality standards to which they were accustomed, with the added appeal of a locally produced vehicle, an appeal that Nissan used in its advertising.

The interests of suppliers were more complicated to handle, and Nissan devoted much attention to negotiating with its suppliers. Nissan demanded a high degree of coordination of suppliers' production schedules with its own and a much greater degree of information-sharing on costs and quality than U.S. auto producers had ever required. However, in exchange, Nissan offered greater stability in the supplier relationship and considerable support in improving quality. Nissan was able to develop a network of local suppliers who felt that their relationship with Nissan had benefits that outweighed the costs in loss of autonomy.

In short, Nissan made great efforts to build and maintain good relations with key external stakeholders, and to ensure that its stakeholders did not include organizations with interests that significantly challenged its own interests.

THE CULTURAL LENS: ORGANIZATIONAL-FIELD APPROACH

A more recently developed way of looking at organization-environment interactions builds on the cultural perspective's fundamental assumption that the shared ways in which people see and interpret their social context is critically important to understanding organizations. It is based on the realization that it is often more difficult than we think to understand a single organization without looking at other organizations that are engaged in the same kinds of activities and occupy similar places in the environment. The organizational-field approach focuses on what people in similarly situated organizations take for granted as "the way things are done" and what they value as intrinsically good and appropriate ways to operate and organize.

This approach asks, "Why are organizations in an industry so similar?" It reminds us that organizations often change in order to look good to other organizations with which they interact, and that when a firm tries to change it tends to reach for "recipes" that are accepted by other organizations. It takes a step away from the individual firm and focuses instead on the "field" of organizations that interact in similar ways with their environments—the "organizational field" being defined as "those organizations that, in the aggregate, constitute a recognized area of institutional life: key suppliers, resource and product consumers, regulatory agencies, and other organizations that produce similar services or products" (DiMaggio and Powell, 1983, p. 147). It also includes professional or trade associations, unions, the business press, and many other elements of the stakeholder model, but it focuses not on their interests and power but on their role in shaping perceptions about what organizational patterns are preferable. Another key difference from the stakeholders' model—and from both the organization set and the Five Forces models—is that the organizational field focuses not on the individual organization but on a group of similar organizations, and looks at the environmental influences that they share and that often make them behave and organize themselves in similar ways. The parallel with the concept of an industry is clear; the difference is that the organizational field is seen as a social rather than an economic structure, in which organizations interact with, observe, and are shaped by what other organizations in their field are doing and how they are organized.

This model is therefore particularly attractive to people who think of organizations as social actors, embedded in a social system of expectations and taken-for-granted ways of doing things. They are interested in how the field affects innovation and change across organizations, such as the spread of total quality control or re-engineering, and how it puts constraints on change (an organization that tries to be particularly innovative in its structures and processes may succeed in convincing its own employees to accept those changes, but it may lose acceptance from other organizations in its field).

The key processes in this approach are *institutionalization* and *isomorphism* (one of the less appealing aspects of this approach is its affinity for code words). Institutionalization is the process by which certain organizational patterns come to be accepted as legitimate—as the correct way to do things or even as the only way to do things (taken for granted). Isomorphism means structural similarity, and refers to the processes by which organizations become similar to others in their field. Organizations adopt prevailing patterns for several reasons: (1) because a powerful organization in their field demands that they do so (coercive isomorphism; for example, when a government imposes certain personnel procedures, or an important customer demands that its suppliers adopt quality control

programs); (2) because professional or interest groups insist that such patterns are the correct way to do things (normative isomorphism; for example, when doctors shape hospital management systems or professors shape research universities); or—most common of the three isomorphic processes in business firms—(3) where organizations take successful organizations as models (mimetic isomorphism). The "imitation" of mimetic isomorphism is most common when organizations really do not know what makes a management system work or fail—that is, under conditions of uncertainty—or when an organization in trouble tries to win credibility by changing its structures and processes to match those used by "successful" organizations. When a CEO comes back from a conference on organizational culture, for example, and calls in his top management team to tell them, "I want a program in place by next week to build a strong corporate culture," we are seeing isomorphism in action.

The organizational field is best understood in the context of a specific type of organization. Figure 9.5 continues the pattern of the two previous perspectives by mapping the organizational field of the research university, that is, the university that defines basic research as one of its key strategic missions, along with education. Although the individual research universities in the United States often emphasize, with much justification, how different they are from each other, they in fact share many basic features of organization and management. This is not surprising, given the extent to which personnel—faculty, graduate students, top administrators—move across them. While U.S. research university faculty have undergraduate degrees from a variety of institutions worldwide, very few have their doctorates from any university other than one of the leading U.S. research universities. As they do their graduate work, they develop an understanding of how a great research university works, an understanding that they carry into their lives as faculty members in one of those universities. The interactions among the faculty, graduate students, and academic administrators (many of whom were faculty members before entering the administration) at the leading research universities, in professional associations, and through the subfield of academic publishing are intense and mutually reinforcing of the established patterns at those institutions.

The research activities in the university are also influenced by—and influence—how research is carried out in other important research settings, such as the research laboratories of leading corporations and government laboratories. For decades after World War

---

FIGURE 9.5 THE ORGANIZATION AS A CULTURAL SYSTEM: THE ORGANIZATIONAL FIELD MODEL

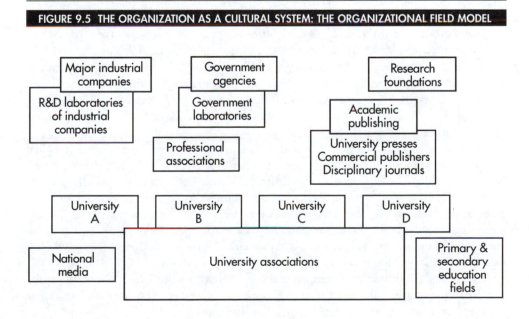

II, the American research university was the model for industrial labs such as IBM's Watson Laboratory and Bell Laboratories. Now that these laboratories have been scaled back considerably and many of their personnel deployed to more applied activities, it is not surprising that universities are beginning to experience similar pressures to demonstrate the value of their research activities in terms of contributions to national competitiveness or the development of new businesses. The pressures on the universities to reorganize to improve their cost structures is not simply a result of the pressures on university finances as the government reduces its spending. Those pressures are reinforced by the current popularity in both industry and government of downsizing and re-engineering, which are seen not only as means to important ends—the reduction of costs—but also as valuable in themselves as demonstrations of a commitment to focus and efficiency. Finally, changes in lower levels of education that affect the educational orientation and skill levels of prospective students have a powerful (although sometimes delayed) effect on the university's educational philosophies and methods.

In the "global" world of today, organizational fields increasingly cross boundaries and involve companies with their "homes" in different countries. The leading companies are increasingly networked with each other in international alliances and cooperative agreements. In the automobile industry, for example, the leading companies include General Motors, Toyota, Ford, Nissan, Honda, Volvo, BMW, Renault, and Fiat—companies from each major region. They are linked in a complex network of alliances with each other and with a number of key, shared suppliers. Each watches carefully what the other is doing, in competitive benchmarking efforts and mutual learning. Powerful isomorphic pressures are operating in these global organizational fields.

An organizational-field approach to a business issue such as entering a new business or market would ask questions such as the following: What other organizations are involved in this field, and what are the established ways of doing business? How different are the expectations from what we are used to? What would the reaction be if we do not follow the established ways? Can we improve our chances of success by following the established (or institutionalized) patterns?

THE MULTIENVIRONMENT FIRM

Large multibusiness firms operate in several environments—each business has a distinct organization set or set of stakeholders, and often has a distinctive organizational field. The most dramatic case of the multienvironment firm is, of course, the multibusiness multinational corporation (MNC). With subsidiaries operating in many countries, the MNC faces enormous challenges in understanding and managing its multiple environments.

A multinational corporation is conventionally defined as a company that produces its product or service at facilities in two or more countries. A company can be global without necessarily being multinational. Boeing, for example, produces its airplanes in the United States only, but works with a worldwide network of suppliers and subcontractors and sells all over the world.

Companies can become multinationals by setting up their own subsidiaries in other countries, by establishing joint ventures in other countries with local partners, or by acquisition. IBM is a company that built its worldwide network of subsidiaries by setting up wholly-owned companies in a large number of countries; Electrolux, the Swedish appliance maker, built its worldwide network by making more than 300 acquisitions in 40 countries between the early 1960s and the mid-1980s. Toyota first entered the United States in a joint venture with General Motors, and then set up a wholly-owned subsidiary three years later.

Traditionally, multinational companies tended to have a multidomestic form of organization and strategy; that is, each country subsidiary was oriented to its own local environment and was organized much like a local company. In the 1980s, however, as international competition intensified and multinational companies wanted to make better use of their extensive geographic reach and internal diversity, these companies moved to more globally integrated strategies and organizations (Bartlett and Ghoshal, 1989). World product organizations, in which a business unit with its headquarters in one country had worldwide responsibility for coordinating the activities of all the company's activities in that business or product, cut across the locally oriented country organizations.

Increasingly, subsidiaries in multinational companies found themselves facing two different kinds of environmental pressures. On the one hand, they continued to face pressures from their local environment to be "local insiders": to design organizations that fit with the local organization set, to deal effectively with local stakeholders, and to follow the patterns accepted as legitimate in the local organization field. On the other hand, they face growing pressures to be "company insiders": to design organizations that ease coordination with company units in other countries, to manage a diverse set of company stakeholders at headquarters and in other key subsidiaries, and to follow patterns seen as appropriate by the parent company. These conflicting pulls can be extremely difficult to manage, but for those interested in understanding organizations, they provide an unequaled arena for studying the interactions between organizations and their environments.

As the following example shows, Japanese automakers were able to move facilities into the United States and gain acceptance, in part, because of the state of the organizational field that existed at the time.

THE JAPANESE AUTO PLANTS IN THE UNITED STATES
AN ORGANIZATIONAL FIELD APPROACH

It is difficult to understand Nissan's entry into the United States—or that of Honda or any of the other Japanese auto firms—without examining what was happening in the organizational field as a whole. Nissan's establishment of production facilities in Tennessee, which we examined in the context of the organization-set model and the stakeholders' model, took place at a time when the organizational field of the U.S. auto industry was being transformed by the entries of a steady stream of Japanese companies. Honda was the first, in 1982; Nissan began production of trucks in 1983 and cars in 1985; Toyota undertook a joint venture (NUMMI) in California with General Motors, which began production in 1984. Mazda followed in 1987 in Flat Rock, Michigan; Toyota built a wholly-owned plant in Kentucky that opened in 1988; and Subaru-Isuzu began production in Lafayette, Indiana, in 1989.

These entries took place at a time when the U.S. auto producers had lost credibility with the American public for being arrogant and unresponsive to customer needs, and for producing high-cost and low-quality vehicles. Their early responses to Japanese export competition had made their image worse: they complained about the low quality of American labor, made large investments in automation to replace that labor, and insisted that the Japanese enjoyed unfair cost advantages because they produced in Japan. By coming to produce vehicles in the United States, the Japanese were saying implicitly as well as explicitly that the problem with the U.S. auto industry was not American labor but American management. The popular and business press picked up this theme and portrayed the early Japanese plants in extremely favorable terms, in part as a way of criticizing the U.S. companies and spurring them to change. Honda, in particular, as the first entrant, was extremely careful to maintain a favorable public image, and it paved the way for later entrants. The Japanese firms all made strong statements about the importance of employment stability and job security, combined with a commitment on the part of workers to work hard, to work in teams, and to use their intelligence as well as their hands—all statements that fit well with the values prevailing in much of the popular press and among academic analysts. The fact that the Japanese were able to produce cars in the United States with an American labor force and maintain their quality and cost advantages seemed to legitimate their organization and management systems. This legitimation was reinforced when U.S. producers themselves began to adopt and adapt several of their systems.

The fact that so many Japanese companies were coming to the United States and the extremely favorable press coverage they received gave legitimacy to the efforts of any one company to change what had been standard practices in the auto industry in labor relations, supplier relations, and customer relations (minimizing the number of options, reducing the amount of bargaining between the distributors and the customers, providing long-term warranties). U.S. management scholars and consultants and the business press contributed to this process by portraying many of these innovations not as "Japanese" but as "post-Fordist," as the next wave of industrial innovation.

The entry of several producers and the move of U.S. producers to emulate such supplier-related practices as just-in-time inventory management and total quality management (shared quality programs undertaken jointly with suppliers) increased the strength of any individual company in convincing suppliers to adopt the new patterns. Moreover, a supplier that could adapt to Japanese transplant demands could expand sales to other Japanese producers, to U.S. producers, and perhaps even to Japanese plants back in Japan. The extensive entry of Japanese producers also attracted leading Japanese supplier companies to the United States: for example, Bridgestone in tires, several Japanese steel companies, and large component producers such as Nippon Denso and Yazaki all entered production in the United States, either by acquisition (Bridgestone acquired Firestone, the Japanese steel companies entered joint ventures with U.S. producers or acquired shares in U.S. companies) or by setting up new plants. These new entrants not only reinforced the competitive pressure on American suppliers to adapt to the new rules of competition; they also provided them with models of those new rules in action in their own territory.

The U.S. auto firms were not alone in losing legitimacy at the time of Japanese entry into the United States. The U.S. labor unions had faced steadily eroding membership and increasing criticism for outdated approaches to labor-management relations and inflexibility. The determination of Honda, Nissan, and Toyota in its wholly-owned plant in Kentucky to build nonunion plants was met with less determined resistance from American workers than might have been the case a decade or so earlier. They also all selected sites that were in nonindustrial, nonunionized communities, where unions had even less legitimacy and acceptance than in the industrial heartland.

The large-scale entry of the Japanese auto producers transformed the field. This transformation smoothed the path for individual firms, and made possible a degree of technology and management transfers from Japan that would have been much more difficult, if not impossible, for any single firm operating alone. When the success of Nissan's establishment of production facilities in the United States is contrasted with Volkswagen's unsuccessful entry in the 1970s, the importance of the field level of analysis is emphasized.

REFERENCES

Bartlett, Christopher A., and Sumantra Ghoshal. 1989. *Managing Across Borders: The Transnational Solution.* Boston: Harvard Business School Press.

DiMaggio, Paul, and Walter W. Powell. 1983. "The Iron Cage Revisited: Institutional Isomorphism and Collective Rationality in Organizational Fields." *American Sociological Review*, 48.

Evan, William M. 1966. "The Organization-Set: Toward a Theory of Interorganizational Relations." In *Approaches to Organization Design*, James D. Thompson, ed. Pittsburgh: University of Pittsburgh Press.

Porter, Michael E. 1980. *Competitive Strategy.* New York: Free Press.

Scott, W. Richard. 1992. *Organizations: Rational, Natural, and Open Systems.* Englewood Cliffs, NJ: Prentice-Hall.

Thompson, James. 1967. *Organizations in Action.* New York: McGraw-Hill.

INTEGRATING ORGANIZATIONS IN DIFFERENT ENVIRONMENTS: THE CASE OF ELECTROLUX AND ZANUSSI[1]

INTRODUCTION

Companies have long used mergers and acquisitions as a major strategic tool. In the United States, Alfred Chandler has identified four waves of mergers and acquisitions in the 20th century. Some would argue that we are seeing a fifth wave in the late 1990s, as banking and financial services are being swept by a wave of mergers, from the Citibank-Travellers mega-merger proposed in April 1998 to the flurry of mergers among local and regional banks. In Europe, the formation of the European market and its expansion to southern and eastern Europe have provided the stimulus for both domestic and international mergers and acquisitions among European companies for nearly two decades; the formation of Mercosur in South America has had similar effects in that region. And in Asia, one of the remedies being proposed for the recent economic crisis is the acquisition of weaker local companies by stronger counterparts, and the acquisition of Asian companies by better-capitalized foreign firms.

Some acquisitions are primarily financial transactions: that is, the acquiring firm spots an opportunity to acquire a company for a price below its market value, and either splits it up and sells off its assets or invests in turning it around and then sells it off. More interesting from both the strategic and the organizational point of view, however, are mergers and acquisitions that are oriented to expanding the company's competitive domain, by adding new organizational capabilities, gaining access to new markets, or exploiting potential synergies in existing or proposed future activities. And from an organizational point of view, the most interesting cases are those that involve companies in different business environments, especially in different countries. These cases highlight the challenges of understanding the organization's business environment and the complex interactions between the environment and internal structures and processes. These challenges are present in all cases, but they are most dramatically evident across borders. The problems of understanding and managing differences in organizational environments and in related aspects of the organizations account for much of the very great difficulty that companies experience in trying to realize the strategic goals of their mergers or acquisitions. Quantitative analyses of U.S. M&A activities have found that in most cases, the benefit accrues to the shareholders of the acquired companies more than to those of the acquiring company, and that the high expectations of strategic benefits from the addition of new capabilities and from synergies across the companies are rarely realized.

One of the most-studied cases of cross-border acquisitions—and therefore one of the few on which we have detailed information about organizational processes—is the acquisition in the mid-1980s of the Italian appliance manufacturer Zanussi by the Swedish

17

CASE

Source: From Sumantra Ghoshal and Philippe Haspeslaugh, "The Acquisition and Integration of Zanussi by Electrolux: A Case Study," *European Management Journal*, December 1990, Vol. 8–4. Reprinted by permission of the author.

1 This case draws heavily on the award-winning case, "Electrolux: The Acquisition And Integration Of Zanussi," developed at INSEAD by Sumantra Ghoshal and Philippe Haspeslaugh, who have graciously given us permission to build on their material. Their case, along with the numerous other sources that have been useful in creating this teaching case, is cited in the references at the end of the case.

company Electrolux. Like most successful acquisitions, it took time and patience. And as is the case in many successful acquisitions, the acquiring company already had extensive acquisitions experience before embarking on the large-scale organizational integration that was required if the ambitious goals of the acquisition were to be achieved.

THE PROTAGONISTS

Electrolux

Electrolux is a Swedish company that traces its origins to 1912, when a Swedish entrepreneur developed a new vacuum cleaner and set up a company with the somewhat forbidding name of Elektromekaniska Aktiebolaget to manufacture and sell it. Fortunately, perhaps, for the longterm success of the company, it merged in 1919 with a firm called AB Lux, and the resulting company adopted the name Electrolux (Solvell et al, 1991, p. 128). By the early 1960s, Electrolux was in serious difficulty: its profitability was eroding rapidly, it had a limited product range (primarily vacuum cleaners and refrigerators), and its old-style absorption-type refrigerators were threatened by the emergence of a more efficient compressor-type technology developed by its competitors. In 1962, in a move that had profound implications for the company's future, Electrolux acquired a Swedish company that had capabilities in the new refrigerator technology. The major shareholder in that company was the electrical equipment company Asea, and Asea sold its interests in the company to Electrolux in exchange for Electrolux shares.

This brought Electrolux under the umbrella of the Wallenbergs, the family at the center of Sweden's leading business group. The Wallenbergs were major shareholders not only in Asea but also in many other leading Swedish companies. These include LM Eriksson in telecommunications, SKF in ball bearings, Saab in automobiles, Alfa-Laval in dairy machinery and industrial systems, Astra in pharmaceuticals, Atlas Copco in industrial products, Stor in pulp and paper, Sandvik in steel and tooling, TV 4 (Sweden's largest commercial television station), and S-E Banken in banking. The Wallenbergs have also been the major benefactors to the Stockholm School of Economics.

The Wallenbergs began their role in the Swedish economy with Oscar Wallenberg's founding of S-E Banken in 1856. Oscar's sons expanded the bank's role from simply making short-term loans and issuing bonds for Sweden's emerging industrial companies to active intervention in turning around troubled enterprises, investing in them on their own account in the process. For five generations the Wallenbergs have been at the top of their diversified industrial group. The key investment vehicle for the Wallenberg group is Investor, the Wallenberg family holding company (which is currently headed by Percy Barnevik, the former CEO of ABB). Investor has taken advantage of Sweden's two-tier shareholding structure, which assigns more votes for "A" class shares than for the "B" class shares sold on the stock market, to deepen its control over the companies in the group without necessarily taking a majority of the shares. Today, for example, the Wallenbergs have 94% of the votes in Electrolux, even though they own only 6.4% of the share capital, through Investor and a few other family foundations (Bartel, 1996, p. 11). Investor usually appoints the chairman of the board of companies in the Wallenberg group, and takes a major role in identifying high-potential managers and moving them across Wallenberg companies (Percy Barnevik, for example, came to the role of CEO of Asea in 1980 from another Wallenberg company, Sandvik).

A recent history of the Wallenberg family asserts that, "Wallenbergs work hard and they expect and demand a full measure of competence and loyalty, both from themselves, their managers and perhaps most of all, from their sons. . . . There is an element of Puritan fatalism in a conviction, passed on from father to son, that duty requires one to uphold the family name, honor, and traditions. If you are a true Wallenberg, then almost from the day you are born, you must do good work, build up and preserve the business, and honor your father." (Bartal, 1996, p. 9). The Wallenbergs are "patient investors," focused on long-term growth. Wallenberg companies share certain organizational features: a very lean corporate headquarters, flat organization designs that group activities into small units with clear performance accountability, and dense vertical and horizontal information flows, both formal and informal.

One of the first results of the Wallenberg involvement in Electrolux was access to investment capital that allowed Electrolux to embark on a wave of acquisitions that over the next twenty years vastly expanded its product range, its geographic markets, and its profitability (Figure 9.6 highlights Electrolux' expansion over two-and-a-half decades of acquisition activity). The early acquisitions were in the Nordic countries, and in fact Electrolux over-expanded in the 1960s; by 1967, it had developed a dominant position in the Swedish market, but a domestic economic slowdown and heavy debt created serious financial problems. The company even sold off its North American vacuum cleaner operations, surrendering the Electrolux brand name in the United States.

In response to these difficulties, the Wallenbergs moved to appoint a new CEO of Electrolux, Hans Werthen, from LM Eriksson (another Wallenberg company). He quickly introduced into Electrolux some of the familiar features of Wallenberg company management: one of his first actions was the drastic reduction of the number of corporate staff, accompanied by the sale of the lavish central Stockholm headquarters and the moving of his trimmed-down office to a converted nineteenth century vacuum cleaner factory on the outskirts (which is still the Electrolux head office building today). He and his top management team decided that Electrolux had to extend its markets beyond Sweden, and they extended the company's acquisition activity into continental Europe and even into North America.

The acquisition strategy was in response to changes in the European appliance industry (or what the Europeans call the "white goods" industry). Until the 1960s, the industry had been segmented by national markets: differences across countries in customer tastes and income levels, distribution channels, high transportation costs in white goods, and government regulations and tariffs all played a part in ensuring that local markets were served by local producers. However, falling tariff barriers, declining transportation costs, and rapidly rising incomes throughout Western Europe opened up opportunities for companies to begin to operate across borders. Italian companies were the first to realize the opportunities: in the late 1960s, a number of Italian entrepreneurial companies (led by Merloni and Zanussi) in northern Italy took advantage of their lower labor costs, the newly formed Common Market's reduction of trade barriers, and their physical proximity to other European markets to export low-priced, standardized appliances throughout Europe. According to Baden-Fuller and Stopford's analysis of the European white goods industry, "by the middle 1970s, the industry seemed to be going fully 'global'; consultants and government agencies such as NEDO in the United Kingdom were advising firms accordingly." (1991, p. 494). The European industry saw steady consolidation:

FIGURE 9.6 THE STORY OF ELECTROLUX: CONDENSED VERSION

LIMITED PRODUCT RANGE	BROAD BUSINESS/PRODUCT RANGE
OUTDATED TECHNOLOGY	TECHNOLOGY LEADER/PARITY
NARROW MARKET NICHE	GLOBAL SCOPE
UNCOMPETITIVE SIZE	LARGEST PRODUCER/MARKET LEADER
NEARLY BANKRUPT	STRONG FINANCIAL POSITION

200 Acquisitions in 40 countries

Mid-1960s → Mid-1980s

---

the top eight producers produced about 40 percent of Europe's output of white goods in 1975, 56 percent in 1986, and 76 percent by the end of 1989. Electrolux was a prime mover in this consolidation, and by the end of the 1980s was Europe's largest appliance maker, thanks to more than 200 acquisitions in 40 countries.

The acquisitions focused on companies in the core appliances industry. But many of the acquired companies also had facilities in other businesses. Many of these were sold off by Electrolux, but others formed the base for new businesses. For example, the Swedish appliance maker Husquvarna, acquired in 1978, had a strong position in chain saws. Electrolux not only kept this business; it added to it by further acquisitions, thereby becoming one of the world's leading chain saw manufacturers, with a global market share of roughly 30 percent (Ghoshal and Haspeslagh, 1990).

Electrolux honed its organizational capabilities in acquisitions in several ways. One was to simulate acquisitions as part of their annual strategic planning processes: to identify what they would do should a company become available. The growing pressures for consolidation in the industry, combined with a fairly mature set of product markets, meant that the opportunities for acquisitions were numerous. Simulating acquisitions during the planning process was a way of preparing to take rapid advantage of opportunities as they emerged. By the early 1980s, Electrolux had developed some routines for managing acquisitions. Ghoshal and Haspeslagh have described the approach as follows:

> Based on their experience, managers at Electrolux believed that there was no standard method for treating acquisitions: each case was unique and had to be dealt with differently. Typically, however, Electrolux moved quickly at the beginning of the integration process. It identified the key action areas and created task forces consisting of managers from both Electrolux and the acquired company in order to address each of the issues on a time-bound basis. Such joint task forces were believed to help foster management confidence and commitment and create avenues for reciprocal information flows. Objectives were clearly specified, milestones were identified, and the first phase of integration was generally completed within 3-6 months so as to create and maintain momentum. The top management of an acquired company was often replaced, but the middle management was kept intact. As explained by Anders Scharp, "The risk of losing general management competence is small when it is a poorly performing company. Electrolux is prepared to take this risk. It is, however, important that we do not change the marketing and sales staff." (Ghoshal and Haspeslagh, 1990, p. 417).

Zanussi

In the early 1980s, Electrolux was looking for acquisition opportunities to expand its European presence. Two acquisition efforts came to naught: a German prospect, AEG's white goods division, was rescued by the German government (it was the seventh largest employer in Germany), and the TI group in the United Kingdom had set its price too high. In 1983, however, an opportunity arose to acquire Zanussi, one of Italy's largest appliance manufacturers.

Founded in 1916, in a small town in northeastern Italy, Zanussi was a privately-owned company that had grown from a small family company manufacturing stoves into a multinational appliance company. In the 1950s and 1960s, Lino Zanussi led a major growth push, expanding the product line both by internal growth and by acquiring complementary Italian producers. Zanussi was one of the leaders of the Italian export surge in the 1960s that began the internationalization of the European appliance industry. It built up an especially strong presence in France, where it established a branch office in 1962, and in Spain, where it became the market leader. Lino Zanussi also engaged in vertical expansion of his company into components, both in Italy and in Germany. By the early 1980s, Zanussi was the second-largest privately-owned company in Italy, and had more than 30,000 employees, 50 factories, and 13 foreign subsidiaries, primarily in sales (Ghoshal and Haspeslagh, 1990, p. 418).

However, in 1968 Lino Zanussi and most of the members of his top management group perished in an airplane crash. Ghoshal and Haspeslagh have succinctly described the ensuing developments at the company:

> Over the next fifteen years the new management carved out a costly programme of unrelated diversification into fields such as colour televisions, prefabricated housing, real estate and community centres. The core business of domestic appliances languished for want of capital, while the new businesses incurred heavy losses. By 1982, the company had amassed debts of over Lit. 1,300 billion and was losing over Lit. 100 billion a year on operations (1990, p. 418).

Zanussi tried to address its problems by selling off some of its subsidiaries and refocusing on its appliance business. However, it desperately needed investment in its long-neglected plant, investment that Italian banks were unwilling to provide.

One of the banks that was heavily committed to Zanussi was Mediobanca, Italy's leading investment bank, dubbed by one writer "the high temple of Italian finance" (Friedman, 1988, p. 92). Founded in 1946 to assist Italy's postwar reconstruction by making medium-term loans to Italian industrial companies, Mediobanca's powerful chief, Enrico Cuccia, expanded his bank's role well beyond what the government had envisioned in establishing the bank. Mediobanca not only lent money to leading Italian enterprises; it also expanded into buying shares in companies and organizing mergers of its client companies, becoming an influential shareholder and power-broker as well as banker to the companies. According to one account, "Mediobanca acquired a far-reaching influence over the destiny of half the Italian economy" (Friedman, 1988, p. 98) Mediobanca was closely linked to some of Italy's most powerful industrialists, including the Agnelli family, which owned the Fiat group, Italy's largest industrial group. Indeed, Fiat actually owned some shares in Mediobanca, through a financial subsidiary. When Zanussi's financial troubles became acute, Mediobanca decided to put together a consortium of companies to rescue the firm, and decided to seek a foreign partner with strong capabilities in the industry.

Electrolux was a natural choice for many reasons: it had built a reputation for successful international acquisition, and it had the capabilities in production and marketing that Zanussi so desperately needed. And there was an Agnelli-Wallenberg connection: Giovanni Agnelli sat on the board of RIV-SKF, the Italian subsidiary of one of the Wallenberg companies, and had developed a great respect for the capabilities of the Wallenberg group companies. Indeed, in 1979 he recruited the top executive for Fiat Auto, Vittoria Ghidella, from the top job at RIV-SKF.

For Electrolux, the strategic arguments for the acquisition of Zanussi were strong. Zanussi complemented Electrolux's product line, being especially strong in washing machines, where Electrolux was quite weak. It also had strong component operations, which Electrolux lacked. And there was a functional complementarity: Zanussi had a strong design and R&D function, where Electrolux was weak, but lacked strong production expertise, where Electrolux excelled. Finally, the geographic market positions were nicely complementary: Zanussi's strength in southern Europe, France, and Germany, which Electrolux had been unable to penetrate, gave the Swedes the market expansion they were seeking. It other words, the acquisition offered *strategic fit.*

But *organizational* fit was another matter. Realizing the potential offered by the strategic fit between the two companies would require a considerable level of integration across the two companies. And in many respects the organizations of the two companies and the environments which had shaped them differed profoundly.

In contrast to the flat organization of Electrolux, with its dense information flows, its collective, team-based management, and its relatively egalitarian and informal patterns of interaction (top managers were known by their first names throughout the organization), Zanussi had a hierarchical, top-down organization, with a large staff and highly formal patterns of interaction, with top managers addressed by their titles. Each

21

CASE

company thus exemplified the business cultures of their respective societies. In Zanussi, the differences from Electrolux were intensified by the legacy of fifteen years of highly politicized company difficulties, in which information was often regarded as a source of power and jealously guarded. Moreover, Electrolux's structure was a "quasi-matrix": operating units were centered on a factory or marketing organization reporting directly to a country manager. However they also had a "dotted line" reporting relationship to a product manager based in Stockholm. The ambiguities of this structure were foreign to Zanussi, which had a clear hierarchy and a long tradition of decisions being handed down from top management (Lorenz, 1989).

Even more striking were the differences in industrial relations in the two countries. Sweden has long had one of the highest rates of unionization in the world: 95 percent of the labor force belonged to a union in the 1980s (Cole 1989, p. 255). A long tradition of cooperative union-management relations rested on both centralized collective bargaining and information sharing between unions and employers' associations at the national level, and strong commitment from both sides to worker participation at the enterprise and shop-floor level. Sweden and Italy had in common an environment in which workers' rights to employment were strongly entrenched in law, and the overhead (i.e., non-wage) costs of labor were very high. But in other respects there were major differences. Labour-management relations had been stormy in Italy throughout the postwar period, and strikes (both official and unofficial) were common. In the 1970s labor had won "cast-iron security of employment in large firms and . . . the right to organize elections in factories and set up factory councils" (Brierly, 1995, p. 182). Employers had resisted this legislation and never fully accepted it; mistrust between labor and management was strong in most large enterprises. Family enterprises like Zanussi often escaped the worst of the labor unrest, but management was seen by workers as heavily paternalistic and autocratic. Labor relations were often highly confrontational, and management and labor were separate camps. It was evident that Zanussi's labor force would have to be reduced if the company was to become profitable, but Electrolux anticipated fierce resistance to headcount reductions if it acquired the company.

Finally, Electrolux had developed considerable capabilities in cross-border acquisition. But the acquisition of Zanussi would be its first major venture into southern Europe, and by far the largest it had ever attempted. With its 30,000 employees, Zanussi had as many employees as Electrolux did in its Swedish homeland.

PRE-ACQUISITION NEGOTIATIONS

The first approach to Electrolux came from the head of Zanussi's major appliance division in France, Mr. Candotti, who had been supplying refrigerators to Electrolux in that market. He approached Leif Johansson, the young (32-year-old) head of Electrolux's major appliance division, with an informal suggestion that Electrolux make a small investment in Zanussi to assure future supplies. Johansson spotted a larger opportunity to acquire all of Zanussi. He talked with his own top management, and so Electrolux was prepared when Cuccia, the head of Mediobanca, was prodded by Giovanni Agnelli into approaching the CEO of Electrolux just over four months later. By that point, Zanussi was facing the prospect of financial disaster. Twelve months of intense negotiations followed, involving the top management of the two companies and key stakeholders in Zanussi. In addition, Gianmario Rossignolo, the Chairman of RIV-SKF, was increasingly involved in the discussions, as the Wallenbergs decided that as an Italian with extensive experience in a Wallenberg company he would be an ideal person to manage Zanussi if the acquisition succeeded.

Electrolux had several problems that it wanted to solve before it committed itself to the acquisition. One was Zanussi's debt. If Electrolux immediately acquired majority ownership, it would be required to consolidate Zanussi's accounts with that of the Electrolux company as a whole, with a decidedly negative impact on Electrolux's bottom line and share price. On the other hand, Electrolux wanted operating control if it was to turn the company around. The issue was resolved by the creation of a consortium of Italian institutions, including Mediobanca, IMI, and a subsidiary of Fiat. This consortium held 40.6 percent of the Zanussi shares. The local government of the Friuli region, anxious to rescue the region's largest employer, took another 10.4 percent. Electrolux took the remaining 49 percent. As Ghoshal and Haspeslagh describe the complex transaction, "While the exact financial transactions were kept confidential since some of the parties opposed any payment to the Zanussi family, it is believed that Electrolux injected slightly under $100 million into Zanussi. One third of that investment secured the 49 percent shareholding, and the remainder went towards debentures that could be converted into shares at any time to give Electrolux a comfortable 75 percent ownership" (1990, p. 420). In addition, Electrolux reached an agreement with over 100 banks to freeze payments on Zanussi's debt until January 1987, and also won some major concessions on interest payments.

Some of the most intense pre-acquisition negotiations took place between Electrolux and the unions.

> At the outset, the powerful unions at Zanussi were against selling the company to the "Vikings from the North." They would have preferred to keep Zanussi independent, with a government subsidy, or to merge with Thomson from France. They also believed that under Electrolux management all important functions would be transferred to Sweden, thereby denuding the skills of the Italian company and also reducing local employment opportunities.
>
> In response to these concerns, Electrolux guaranteed that all Zanussi's important functions would be retained within Italy. Twenty union leaders were sent from Sweden to Italy to reassure the Italians. The same number of Italian union leaders were invited to Sweden to observe Electrolux's production system and labour relations. Initially, Mr. Rossignolo signed a letter of assurance to the unions on behalf of Electrolux confirming that the level of employment prevailing at that time would be maintained. Soon thereafter, however, it became obvious that Zanussi could not be made profitable without workforce reductions. This resulted in difficult renegotiations. It was finally agreed that within three months of the acquisition Electrolux would present to the unions a three-year plan for investments and reduction in personnel. Actual retrenchments would have to follow the plan, subject to its approval by the unions. . . .
>
> One of the most important meetings in the long negotiation process took place in Rome on November 15, 1984, when, after stormy discussions between the top management of Electrolux and the leaders of the Zanussi union, a document confirming Electrolux's intention to acquire Zanussi was jointly signed by both parties. During the most crucial hour of the meeting, Hans Werthen stood up in front of the 50 union leaders and declared: "We are not buying companies in order to close them down, but to turn them into profitable ventures . . . and, we are not the Vikings, who were Norwegians, anyway." (Ghoshal and Haspeslagh, 1990, pp. 419–20)

In addition, Electrolux managed to negotiate with the Italian government to deal with a problem that surfaced relatively late in the process: an audit team from Electrolux discovered that one of Zanussi's previous managing directors had cut a deal with a German company to sell them equipment and machinery and then lease it back, an under-the-table agreement that entailed potentially severe fines and penalties, because it violated Italian foreign exchange and tax laws. When this liability was discovered, Electrolux refused to proceed with the negotiations until the Italian government promised not to take any steps to prosecute in this matter.

In December 1984, the final agreements were signed, and the next stage of the acquisition process began.

Immediate Post-Acquisition Actions

From its previous experience of acquisitions, Electrolux had learned the importance of developing a clear plan for its post-acquisition actions by the time the deal was consummated. Electrolux moved quickly in the first two months after the deal was signed, taking immediate actions to set the course of the subsequent change processes. Among these actions were the following:

1. **Complete Change of Top Management.** Within hours of signing the acquisition agreement, Electrolux announced the dismissal of the entire board of directors of Zanussi. The board that replaced it included the four most senior members of Electrolux's own top management team, including its CEO and its chairman of the board. The new chairman of the Zanussi board, however, was not a Swede but an Italian, Gianmario Rossignolo. He had been chairman of the Italian subsidiary of SKF, the Wallenberg company that had become the world's largest manufacturer of ball bearings, and Electrolux had involved him actively in the pre-acquisition negotiations. RIV-SKF also provided the new managing director (the CEO) for Zanussi: Carlo Verri, who had been its managing director. As Ghoshal and Haspeslagh pointed out, "An Italian, long-experienced in working with Swedish colleagues because of his position as chairman of SKF's Italian subsidiary, Rossignolo was seen as an ideal bridge between the two companies with their vastly different cultures and management styles. . . . Rossignolo and Verri had turned around SKF's Italian operations and had a long history of working together as a team" (Ghoshal and Haspeslagh 1990, p. 421). Below the board level, however, all the former senior managers of Zanussi were retained, except for the industrial relations manager, who was replaced.

2. **Change in Financial Reporting System.** Electrolux moved quickly to introduce its own financial reporting systems into Zanussi, planning to have them in full operation within six months of the acquisition.

3. **Capacity Utilization.** Electrolux announced that it was moving the production of front-loading washing machines from its French subsidiary to Zanussi's plant in Pordenone, while the production of top-loading washers was shifted from Italy to France. In addition, Electrolux announced a plan to source an additional 500,000 units from Zanussi (280,000 household appliances and 7,500 units of commercial appliances for sale throughout its marketing network, and over 200,000 units of components for use in its international network of factories). This plan immediately increased Zanussi's capacity utilization substantially, and the announcement was widely publicized inside and outside the company.

4. **Cost Savings in Sourcing.** As Zanussi's financial situation had worsened in the years prior to the acquisition, some suppliers had feared that the company would go bankrupt, and had begun to charge a risk premium for the parts they supplied to the company. Because nearly 70 percent of the company's production costs were in raw materials and components from external suppliers, Electrolux targeted this area for cost reduction. Arguing that not only was the risk of supplying Zanussi eliminated, but that suppliers should be able to gain greater economies of scale as Zanussi's capacity utilization rose, Electrolux managed to negotiate an immediate saving of 2 percent on external sourcing, and anticipated reaching an eventual target of 17 percent.

5. **Revitalizing Sales.** Zanussi's Italian competitors anticipated that the company would be preoccupied with internal restructuring in the wake of the acquisition, and several launched major efforts to expand their market share at Zanussi's expense during this period. The company responded immediately and aggressively, extending trade credit to retailers and wholesalers from 60 to 360 days (under specified conditions) and embarking on a major marketing campaign, successfully convincing the industry and market that "Zanussi is back!"

CASE
24

6. Formation of Task Force. From the viewpoint of Electrolux, the company faced two closely related organizational challenges: improving Zanussi's performance (its productivity and profitability) and effectively integrating the operations of Electrolux and Zanussi. To initiate the process of organizational change, Electrolux formed eight task forces teaming upper-level Electrolux managers with their counterparts at Zanussi. Two teams were assigned to each of three key areas: components, product development, and commercial appliances, and one each for marketing and management development. Their recommendations provided the basis for subsequent actions to integrate the production and sales activities of the two companies, rationalize component production and leverage Zanussi's capabilities in this area throughout the Electrolux system, and develop specialized capabilities in different sites in both production and product development.

Medium-Term Actions

After these initial actions of the first three months, Electrolux faced complex challenges of organizational change and integration on several fronts. Its actions included the following:

1. Agreement with the Unions. In the pre-acquisition negotiations, Electrolux had promised Zanussi's union leaders that it would present them with a complete restructuring plan for their agreement before undertaking any workforce reductions. The company did so in March, 1985; the discussions were held at the Ministry of Industry in Rome. As Ghoshal and Haspeslagh described the process, "It [the proposed plan] consisted of a broad analysis of the industry and market trends, evaluation of Zanussi's competitive position and future prospects, and a detailed plan for investments and workforce reduction. The meeting was characterized by a high level of openness on the part of management. Such openness, unusual in Italian industrial relations, took the unions by surprise. In the end, after difficult negotiations, the plan was signed by all parties on May 25" (Ghoshal and Haspeslagh, p. 425). The agreement involved a reduction of the workforce by 4,848 employees, phased over the following three years and carried out through early retirement and incentives for voluntary departures.

Ironically, the very success of the turnaround at Zanussi created new industrial relations problems. Even as the planned downsizing was being carried out, several of Zanussi's plants had to increase overtime and even to hire new skilled workers. Management argued that the advanced production technology being introduced into the factories required more highly educated workers of the kind being newly recruited into the company, rather than the retention of older workers. But some of the existing workers were unconvinced. Tensions were particularly high at the Porcia plant, where many of the scheduled departures were concentrated, and the factory experienced a series of localized strikes.

Management decided to hold firm, and turned to the local press to influence both the workforce and public opinion by explaining its point of view and drawing public attention to the issues. The timing was propitious: as one authority on Italy has pointed out, by the 1980s "managers and workers were clearly in search of a new culture for industrial relations to replace the aggressively confrontational culture (on both sides) of the 1970s" (Brierley, 1995, p. 183). Public opinion and government officials were both increasingly concerned that unless Italian labor relations developed greater openness and flexibility, the country would be handicapped in its efforts to become more competitive as it faced the challenges of greater market integration in 1992. Management strategy worked, the strikes ceased, and in 1987 the company reached a new agreement with the unions that linked wage increases to productivity improvements, removed limits on downsizing, and

© 25 CASE

allowed the company to hire almost 1,000 part-time workers (allowing it to take advantage of government subsidies for worker training).

2. **Productivity Improvements.** Electrolux knew when it acquired Zanussi that the company's factories had suffered for years from under-investment. The head of Electrolux's technical research and development organization, who visited the Zanussi plants before the acquisition, had noted that much of the factory technology was two decades old, with very little automation used in the assembly processes and a complete absence of robotics or computerization. Electrolux took two approaches to improving production operations: a program of large-scale capital investment, and a Total Quality (TQ) program. The first included the largest single investment project in Electrolux history: the transformation of the Porcia plant into a highly automated flexible manufacturing system capable of producing 1.5 million washing machines a year, scheduled for completion in 1990. Another 100 million Italian lire were spent on transforming the Susegana plant into a highly automated production system for refrigerators and freezers (with a target date of the end of 1988). The extensive introduction of CAD-CAM systems (computer-aided design and computer-aided manufacturing) was, management insisted, to improve flexibility and quality, not to reduce labor costs. In addition, beginning in May 1986, the managing director, Carlo Verri, took the lead in initiating a major Total Quality program, with guidance and targets set by the technical staff of Electrolux and with education and training programs throughout the company.

3. **Supplier Relations Improvements.** The Total Quality program quickly involved suppliers as well as the company's own organization: raising Zanussi's product quality required major improvements in quality and delivery reliability, as the new plants moved to a flexible production system capable of responding rapidly to shifts in market demand. Zanussi involved key suppliers in its training programs, and made the commitment to quality and to a Just-in-Time delivery system into major factors in its choice of suppliers.

4. **New Product Development.** The development and design of new products was a function in which Zanussi's capabilities were considerably above those of Electrolux, and Zanussi's new top management team moved quickly to counteract the debilitating effects of recent under-investment in R&D, allocating new resources and additional mandates both to the central design and development organization and to the development groups attached to the product divisions. In just over a year, Zanussi's product development organization had validated this strategy with its development of the "Jet-System," a new washing machine design that reduced detergent and water consumption by one-third. It was introduced by Verri himself (via televised link-up from the Pordenone factory) at a Cologne trade show in February 1986. The new product was a market success, and demand threatened to outstrip capacity. The Zanussi R&D organization became the key development center for Electrolux in washing machines and other major appliances, and its product divisions became an important source of product and process improvements.

5. **Staff Reductions.** Unlike Electrolux and most other Swedish companies, Zanussi had a very large number of staff positions at the corporate level, in the business divisions, and in support functions. It also had a very tall organizational hierarchy in staff organizations. Verri reduced the number of staff positions very substantially, reallocating people to line positions wherever possible. He also flattened the hierarchy, making the five remaining staff functions (planning, finance and control, organization and human resources, general administration, and public and legal affairs) report directly to him, along with the four major business divisions.

6. **Cultural Change.** One of the greatest challenges in the post-acquisition period lay in the very great differences in attitudes and management styles between Electrolux and Zanussi. These were exacerbated by the difficulties experienced by

Zanussi in the years preceding the acquisition. In the words of Ghoshal and Haspeslagh,

> During the troubled years the management process at Zanussi had suffered from many aberrations. Conflicts had become a way of life, and information flow within the organization had become severely constrained. Most issues were escalated to the top for arbitration, and the middle management had practically no role in decision making. Front-line managers had become alienated because of direct dealings between the workers and senior managers via the union leaders. Overall, people had lost faith in the integrity of the system, in which seniority and loyalty to individuals were seen as more important than competence or commitment to the company" (1990, p. 423).

Yet many of Zanussi's managers were not convinced of the need for fundamental change. They defined the problems that had nearly brought Zanussi to bankruptcy as a failure of the old top management group, and believed that the investments that Electrolux was making in the company's factories and R&D organization would be all that was needed to turn the company around. Rossignolo and Verri, although Italian, were from outside the company, and their long experience in SKF made them appear more Swedish than Italian to some Zanussi managers.

Verri realized that he faced major challenges in making Zanussi more competitive, more responsive to market opportunities, and better integrated with the rest of the Electrolux organization. He began with a series of team-building sessions with his top management group. One outcome was a statement of the mission, values, and guiding principles of the "new" Zanussi (shown in Figure 9.7). The statement asserted the link between Zanussi's mission and a cultural change in the company, strongly emphasizing the need for improved communications, a more participative management style, and a more international orientation.

A series of management development workshops followed. Verri himself participated in three two-day workshops for the top 60 managers in the company between late 1985 and the middle of 1986. These were followed by a similar set of workshops for 150 managers at the next level.

For the top level of managers, the need for change was reinforced by their constant exposure to the top managers of Electrolux. Three of Electrolux's top managers on the Zanussi board visited Pordenone every two months after the acquisition, to participate in two-day reviews of Zanussi's progress, combining these meetings with tours of the facilities and holding meetings with key managers. Yet, as the top management team at Zanussi recognized, no Swedish managers were imposed on the organization. Instead, the constant involvement of the top Electrolux management signalled that the relationship between Zanussi and Electrolux was a partnership, not a conquest.

Longer-Term Challenges

Electrolux could take great pride in what it had accomplished with Zanussi in the first three years after the acquisition: a stream of new products, greatly improved performance on the part of Zanussi, and the consolidation of Electrolux's position as the leading appliance manufacturer in Europe. But the company could not afford to rest on its laurels. By the end of the 1980s, competition in the European appliance industry was intensifying. Local competitors remained strong in the various national markets, aided by the continuing differences across markets in distribution and sales systems. In many segments of the industry, such as washing machines and cookers, local preferences continued to differ significantly across countries. In the most highly standardized segments, on the other hand (such as microwave ovens and small kitchen appliances), the Japanese and Koreans were able to leverage their global manufacturing scale and expertise in electronics to make major inroads in Europe. And America's leading appliance manufacturer, Whirlpool, had acquired Philips' appliance business and was challenging Electrolux in its home region.

27

CASE

FIGURE 9.7 MISSION, VALUES, AND GUIDING PRINCIPLES OF ZANUSSI

Mission

To become the market leader in Europe, with a significant position in other world areas, in supplying homes, institutions, and industry with systems, appliances, components and after-sales services.

To be successful in this mission, the company and management legitimization must be based on the capability to be near the customer and satisfy his needs; to demonstrate strength, entrepreneurship, and creativity in accepting and winning external challenges; to offer total quality on all dimensions, more than the competition; and to be oriented to an internal vision and engagement.

Values

Our basic values, ranked, are:

1. To be near the customer
2. To accept challenges
3. To deliver total quality
4. With an international perspective

Our central value, underlying all of the above, is transparency, which means that Zanussi will reward behaviour which is based on constantly transparent information and attitudes, safeguarding the interests of the company.

Guiding Principles

1. A management group is legitimized by knowing what we want, pursuing it coherently, and communicating our intent in order to be believable.
2. Shared communication means shared responsibility, not power and status index.
3. The manager's task is managing through information and motivation, not by building "power islands."
4. Time is short: the world will not wait for our "perfect solutions."
5. Strategic management implies:

   - Professional skills
   - Risk-taking attitudes and the skill to spot opportunity
   - Integration with the environment and the organisation, flexibility and attention to change
   - Identification with the mission of the firm, and helping in the evolution of a culture that supports it
   - Team work ability
   - Skill in identifying strengths and weaknesses

Source: Ghoshal and Haspeslagh, 1990, p. 424.

The competitive pressure raised the profile of the remaining integration and coordination challenges in Zanussi. Some of the problems were revealed by the delays in bringing the new automated factory systems into operation. Each major project was carried out by a team of Electrolux and Zanussi engineers. There was considerable friction between the Zanussi engineers and their Swedish counterparts on the teams: the Zanussi people felt that they were quite capable of carrying out the improvements without constant consultations with the Electrolux team members. Top management in Electrolux, however, felt that the expertise of the experienced Electrolux consultants would speed up and improve the process. However, the tensions and resulting problems with information sharing led to serious delays (more than a one-year delay in finalizing the layout of the Susegana factory, for example). This exemplified a larger problem: cooperation and teamwork between the two companies was excellent at the upper management level (approximately the top 60 people in Zanussi), but the middle levels of Zanussi still had not completely bought into the "new" organizational model, and were often unhappy with the changes in their jobs and their company.

Similar problems emerged when the company tried to merge the marketing organizations of the two companies in the many countries in which both had been competing before the acquisition. Electrolux top management laid down the basic principle that in each country, the stronger organization would absorb the weaker one. However, this principle did not mean that the existing top management of the stronger organization would continue to function as the management of the new, combined company. The friction over the amalgamation process was serious, and the head of Zanussi's marketing organization in France, who had been the man who initially approached Electrolux with the possibility of an acquisition of Zanussi, was one of several Zanussi people who resigned over the issue. In fact, Zanussi continued to operate its directly controlled sales companies in Germany, France, Denmark, and Norway, much to the frustration of Electrolux managers.

The international dimensions of the company's operations caused additional frictions around transfer prices. Rationalization of production within Electrolux meant that much of the company's product was being shipped across borders: Zanussi was producing front-loading washing machines for the French market, for example, while the French plants were producing top-loading machines for the Italian market. Zanussi's performance was strongly affected by the transfer price at which they "sold" the washing machines to various international marketing organizations. Transfer pricing therefore became a source of friction in the increasingly integrated production system of the "new" Electrolux.

Both the integration of the marketing organizations and the transfer pricing problems revealed a basic difference between the two companies in their approach to decision-making. Like other Swedish companies in general, and Wallenberg companies in particular, Electrolux made its flat structure and lean headquarters organization work by pushing decision-making down to the operating levels. The company expected operating managers to negotiate and resolve their differences with each other. Zanussi, on the other hand, like many Italian companies, was accustomed to a more authoritative hierarchy, in which operating managers could turn to their superiors to resolve difficult problems and top management was expected, as part of its responsibilities, to resolve disputes at lower levels by fiat. Zanussi managers were frustrated by what they saw as an unwillingness of Electrolux top management to step in and resolve difficult operating issues; Electrolux managers were frustrated by what they saw as the intransigence of the Zanussi managers.

A related difference between the cultures in which the two companies had developed generated further friction. In Italy, one of the "perks" of rising on the corporate ladder was the deference accorded by subordinates. Managers were customarily addressed by their titles, and a corporate etiquette of at least overt deference to rank and adherence to appropriate channels of communication was strictly observed. In Swedish companies, however, and especially in the Wallenberg companies, even top managers were customarily addressed by their first names throughout the company, and an "open-door policy" encouraged frank communications across ranks. Although top managers like Rossignolo and Verri could easily switch back and forth between the two different corporate cultures, others found it more difficult, and even Rossignolo and Verri found it

© 29 CASE

easier to follow the Italian patterns when dealing with their Italian subordinates (Lorenz, 1989, p. 88). As cross-border interpersonal interactions became more intense at lower levels of the organization, the discomfort levels mounted.

Clearly, while the acquisition was on most counts a success, some serious organizational issues remained, and these were concentrated in the middle management levels. Top management at Zanussi saw the importance of building links between Electrolux and Zanussi at the middle management level, but they were unsure about what it might take to do this effectively. Despite the good relationship that had emerged with the three or four top Electrolux managers who constantly visited Zanussi, top Zanussi managers had reservations about what might be required to strengthen ties with the Electrolux mid-level managers. "We don't know them, but our concern is that the next level of Electrolux managers may be more bureaucratic and less open. To them we might be a conquest," said a senior manager of Zanussi. "In the next phase of integration, we must develop bridges at the middle and I frankly do not know how easy or difficult that might be." (Ghoshal and Haspeslagh, 1990, p. 429). Building those bridges might well involve difficult adjustments on both sides. Leif Johansson, who was the prime mover of the acquisition on the Electrolux side and who shortly afterwards was named to head up Electrolux's appliance business worldwide, had stated that, "With the acquisition of Zanussi, the Electrolux group entered a new era. In several respects we were able to adopt a completely new way of thinking." Three years after one of the industry's most successful international acquisitions, he was finding out just how true this might turn out to be.

REFERENCES

Baden-Fuller, Charles, and John Stopford. 1991. "Globalization Frustrated: The Case of White Goods." *Strategic Management Journal* 12, pp. 493–507.

Bartal, David. 1996. *The Empire: The Rise of the House of Wallenberg.* Stockholm: Dagens Industri.

Brierley, William. 1995. "The Business Culture in Italy." In Collin Randlesome, with William Brierley, Kevin Bruton, Colin Gordon, and Peter King, *Business Cultures in Europe*, 2nd edition. London: Butterworth-Heinemann.

Cole, Robert E. 1989. *Strategies for Learning.* Berkeley: University of California Press.

Friedman, Alan. 1988. *Agnelli and the Network of Italian Power.* London: Mandarin.

Ghoshal, Sumantra, and Philippe Haspeslagh. 1990. "The Acquisition and Integration of Zanussi by Electrolux: A Case Study." *European Management Journal*, Vol. 8-4 (December), pp. 414–433.

Lorenz, Christopher. 1989. "The Birth of a 'Transnational'." *The McKinsey Quarterly.* (Autumn), pp. 72–93.

Solvell, Orjan. 1990. "Structural Evolution in the White Goods Industry." Teaching case, Institute of International Business, Stockholm School of Economics.

Solvell, Orjan. 1990. "Electrolux." Teaching case, Institute of International Business, Stockholm School of Economics.

Solvell, Orjan, Ivo Zander, and Michael Porter. 1991. *Advantage Sweden.* Stockholm: Norstedts.

Tully, Shawn. 1986. "Electrolux Wants a Clean Sweep." *Fortune.* August 18, pp. 60–62.

© 30 CASE

ADDITIONAL SUGGESTED READING

Students who are interested in exploring the organizational aspects of mergers and acquisitions will find it rewarding to read the following materials:

Haspeslagh, Philippe, and David Jemison. 1991. *Managing Acquisitions: Creating Value through Corporate Renewal.* New York: The Free Press.

Ⓒ

31

CASE

S

M-9

supplemental

THE MULTINATIONAL CORPORATION AND THE "NEW ORGANIZATION"

The huge multinational corporations (MNCs) that dominate the Fortune International 500 may be global and diverse, but they do not usually spring to mind when we think of the networked, flat, and flexible "new" organization. And yet, since the 1980s, a new model of the multinational corporation has come to dominate both the way many top managers think about their companies and the way management scholars write about them. This new model has many labels; the multi-focal firm, the heterarchy, the integrated network, and the transnational. Underneath the different terms, however, is a consistent image of the "new" multinational that fits to a remarkable degree the model of the "new" organization.

Like the model of the "new" organization, the model of the new MNC, or "transnational" as we shall call it here, emerged in response to changing competitive forces and to technological changes in transportation and communication that have reduced the costs of coordination across distances. And like the model of the "new" organization, the "new" MNC has been defined in part by its contrast with an "old" organizational model. In the case of the MNC, however, there are at least two distinct models of the "old" organization.

THE "OLD" MODELS OF THE MNC

The oldest model of the MNC is now called the *"multidomestic"* model. It developed before World War II, when trade barriers were extremely high and each new country market had to be served not by export but by local production. The main organizational unit was the country subsidiary, which contained most of the value chain, including enough R&D capability not only to adapt the products developed by the parent company to the local market, but also in many cases to develop their own distinctive products. The key linking mechanism was a small cadre of expatriate managers: that is, home country managers sent out to head the various local subsidiaries. They were key "translators" between parent and subsidiary: they served as the main cross-border communication nodes, holders of the parent company's authority, and carriers of the corporate culture. They often spent most of their management careers outside their home country, making their way up the implicit hierarchy of subsidiaries (from the less to the more important). Each country was a separate entity, and its success was defined in terms of success in the local market (a "local-for-local" strategy). The great strength of this model was its ability to respond to the local environment. European firms like Nestle, Philips, and Unilever exemplified this model in the decades before the 1980s. In these firms, the most important environment for each subsidiary was the local environment: the key elements of the input and output sets were local, local stakeholders were very powerful, and the organization adapted to the local business culture.

The U.S. MNCs that dominated international business in the three decades after World War II modified this multidomestic model. The country subsidiary was still the key unit of organization, but the linking mechanisms relied more heavily on the management systems at which U.S. firms excelled, particularly financial control and planning systems. Because these management systems were so central to the control system, U.S. MNCs were more able than their European counterparts to select promising local managers, send them to the United States to learn the systems, and then return them to their countries to run the local units. Another key control mechanism was the U.S. parent company's control of technology development. As the world's lead market in most industries between 1945 and 1970, U.S. MNCs concentrated their development of new products in their home base, and transferred these products to their subsidiaries as local markets for them evolved, maintaining for that purpose a local technology transfer capability in the local units. Over time, this evolved into a more substantial capability for technology development, often pulling the company toward a more traditional multidomestic model. As with the early form of multidomestic firm, the key elements of the organization-set of subsidiaries were local, but the home country organization was a much more important stakeholder, and certain aspects of the organization reflected home country rather than local patterns.

Although there were marked differences between these two models (such as the extent of the home country's power over the country subsidiaries and in the kinds of linking mechanisms on which they relied), they shared certain key design features: the local country subsidiary was the key organizational unit; most of the value chain was located in those country subsidiaries; and communications and interactions were vertical (between each subsidiary and its parent) rather than horizontal (across subsidiaries). And both were faced with serious strategic challenges when they were forced to compete with an alternative model, the so-called "*global*" or home-based company.

In the late 1970s and into the 1980s, rapidly falling transportation costs and diminishing trade barriers made it increasingly feasible to serve a number of markets from a single production base, and thereby realize economies of scale not possible for a company producing on a country-by-country basis. Japanese companies, who began their international expansion much later than most of their European and U.S. counterparts, were especially well-positioned to take advantage of these factors to leverage the organizational capabilities they had built up in their home base and serve markets all over the world by export. They were able to realize very great economies of scale by thus physically concentrating production. This form of the MNC was called the "global" or "home-based" MNC. In this model, the firm's investments in building subsidiaries offshore were initially limited to sales and distribution companies. When they later set up production facilities (which were often assembly plants that, at least initially, put together components and sub-systems imported from Japan), these were linked closely to a "parent" or "sister" plant in Japan, and usually incorporated into a separate local company. Therefore, instead of building a single country subsidiary, most Japanese companies had separate sales and distribution and manufacturing subsidiaries, each more closely linked to their counterpart organizations back in Japan than to each other. Japanese expatriate managers at middle as well as senior levels were rotated into the subsidiaries on a regular basis, playing a key role in transferring technologies and maintaining links with the home country. Japanese MNCs were widely perceived to have a "rice paper ceiling" that limited opportunities for local managers to rise in the company. Key elements of the input-set of each subsidiary were located in the parent country, local stakeholders had relatively little power, and the culture of the organization was profoundly shaped by the home country organization.

For a brief period in the early 1980s, the enormous competitive success of Japanese MNCs in autos and electronics led to projections that this "global MNC" was the model for the future. But it too proved vulnerable. Import restrictions forced many companies to set up local production facilities. More important, the rapid rise in the value of the yen exposed the vulnerability of this geographically concentrated production system to exchange rate fluctuations; the model's economies of scale were increasingly offset by the rising yen. And Japanese companies increasingly felt the need to improve their capabilities to attract able local managers and to be more responsive to local customer needs.

THE "NEW" MODEL OF THE MNC

By the mid-1980s, managers and management scholars were converging on a new model of the MNC that combined the advantages of both of these models (the multidomestic and the global) and added a new capability: learning across borders. In other words, the MNC could simultaneously realize economies of scale by coordinating production and supplier networks across borders, respond effectively to local market and organizational requirements, and—critical to the model—take effective advantage of its internal diversity to be more innovative and agile. According to this model, the chief competitive advantage of the MNC is its internal diversity. One aspect of its diversity is its exposure to a wide range of markets, which ought to enable it to sense various trends and introduce new "hit" products before its purely domestic competitors. Another is its dispersed capacity for innovation and its roots in a variety of national technology systems, which should enable it to put together the capabilities of different centres of excellence in technology (for example, Otis Elevator can produce new elevator models that have the mechanical aspects designed in its German R&D centre, its electronics designed in its Japanese subsidiary, and its overall system designed in the United States). Still another diversity factor is its ability to contain (or have access to) "global best practice," and therefore a superior ability to learn from and disseminate "global best practice" throughout its network.

To realize this potential, the new "transnational" model has developed the following characteristics:

- Strong horizontal links across subsidiaries (in contrast to the vertical links that dominated older models of the MNC), at all levels of the company, not just at the top management level
- Emphasis on the headquarters playing a coordinating role vis-à-vis its various operating units, rather than a controlling role, and a pattern of interdependence replacing both the subsidiary independence of the multidomestic model and the dependence of the global model
- A lean headquarters that is separated organizationally (and often physically) from the home country operating units, so that the home country operations become one subsidiary among many
- Differentiated subsidiary roles, according to the strategic importance of the subsidiary's location and its own organizational capabilities
- A pattern of innovation in which locally-based innovations are leveraged across the MNC network, and in which some innovations are generated through the joint efforts of two or more units
- A balance of functional, geographic, and business perspectives, and clearly differentiated management roles, maintained by a top management team with experience of all three

Many of the companies that aspire to the transnational model have adopted a formal matrix structure; others have developed a "virtual matrix" which, in the words of Bartlett and Ghoshal, "matrixes the minds of the managers" in a strong shared culture. One way to enhance this process is to subdivide country units into a much smaller number of more focused units that are often more densely linked to their counterparts in other countries than to other local units. Both international stakeholders that are common to many of the local units (such as multinational customers) and local stakeholders are important to the transnational MNC, and other subsidiaries often constitute key internal stakeholders of each local unit. The organizational culture tends to be an emergent culture influenced by both local and international organizational fields.

As several of its leading advocates have pointed out, the transnational is an ideal type, rather than a portrayal of any single organization. But companies like ABB, Ford, IBM, and NEC have embraced the ideal and many of the structural features of this new multinational model.

A critic could point out that this model evolved during the mid-1980s, when "Triad" strategies (that is, a focus on the developed country markets of North America, Western Europe, and Japan) dominated international business. The rhetoric of the transnational, with its disavowal of strong central control and direction, smoothed the way in cross-border acquisitions and investments across countries with strong traditions of autonomy and roughly comparable capabilities. In the late 1990s, however, few people are as certain as they were in the late 1980s that the transnational represents the model to which all successful international companies must aspire. Indeed, what is most striking about international business today is not a convergence towards a single model of the MNC but the enormous range of variation in successful cross-border strategy and organization. But the transnational remains a powerful ideal for many companies, especially those that are trying to increase the level of cross-border integration across local units that have been accustomed to high levels of autonomy.

A lingering paradox of the transnational model is that it aspires simultaneously to leverage its internal diversity and to build a strong shared culture that provides all members of the company with a shared "mental map." This is perhaps the most challenging paradox in a model that rejoices in paradoxes (simultaneously "local and global," "big and small," "centralized and decentralized").

ADDITIONAL SUGGESTED READINGS

Students who are interested in pursuing this topic further will find the following materials of interest:

Bartlett, Christopher, and Sumantra Ghoshal. 1989. *Managing Across Borders: The Transnational Solution*. Harvard Business School Press.

Prahalad, C. K. and Yves Doz. 1987. *The Multinational Mission*. Free Press.

Solvell, Orjan, and Ivo Zander, "The Organization of the Dynamic Multinational Enterprise: The Home-Based and the Heterarchical MNE." *International Studies of Management and Organization*. 25½, pp. 17–38.

Ⓢ

37

ACADEMIC

INDEX

MASSACHUSETTS INSTITUTE OF TECHNOLOGY

ANCONA, KOCHAN, SCULLY,
VAN MAANEN, WESTNEY

MANAGING FOR THE FUTURE

Organizational Behavior
& Processes

LEARNING ACROSS
BORDERS: DISNEYLAND
FROM CALIFORNIA TO
PARIS VIA TOKYO

module 10

**LEARNING ACROSS BORDERS: DISNEYLAND
FROM CALIFORNIA TO PARIS VIA TOKYO**

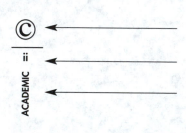

Icon indicates what part you are in, either core Ⓒ or supplemental Ⓢ.

Page number.

Within each part there are sections—Module Overview (OVERVIEW), Academic Perspective (ACADEMIC), Popular Press (PRESS), Case (CASE), Exercise (EXERCISE).

Dedicated to those who have inspired us to try to be better students and teachers. Special dedications to:

Professor Jack Barbash
Professor Arthur H. Gladstein
Professor Marius B. Jansen
Professor Joanne Martin
Professor Edgar H. Schein

Acquisitions Editor: John R. Szilagyi
Developmental Editor: Jamie Gleich Bryant
Production Editor: Mardell Toomey
Production House: DPS Associates, Inc.
Cover Design: Michael H. Stratton
Marketing Manager: Rob Bloom

ISBN 0-538-87697-2

1 2 3 4 5 6 7 D1 4 3 2 1 0 9 8

Printed in the United States of America

South-Western College Publishing
an International Thomson Publishing company IⓉP®

Cincinnati • Albany • Boston • Detroit • Johannesburg • London • Madrid • Melbourne • Mexico City
New York • Pacific Grove • San Francisco • Scottsdale • Singapore • Tokyo • Toronto

CONTENTS

LEARNING ACROSS BORDERS: DISNEYLAND FROM CALIFORNIA TO PARIS VIA TOKYO

When a company takes its operations abroad, it faces an array of conscious decisions about how much of its organizational patterns it will take with it. But it also enters a learning process, because much of what it takes abroad is less the product of conscious choice than a consequence of its organizational culture and its internal political system, and the organizational patterns associated with them often lead to unanticipated problems in the new environment. Moving organizational patterns from the social context in which they were developed to a different context always involves learning and change, if the move is to be successful. Some of the change needed can be anticipated and planned for by managers who have a deep understanding of their organizations and of the similarities and differences across the environments in which they are working, but much is a product of learning by doing in the new environment. Flexibility and fast learning become extremely important in this setting.

This module provides you with a window into these change dynamics through the case of Disneyland. Disneyland has been an outstandingly successful organization in its home environment. It was successful beyond all expectation in its first venture abroad, Tokyo Disneyland. It was troubled beyond all expectations in its second venture in France. Disneyland is a rich case in the study of cross-border learning for several reasons. It is an exemplar of the service industries; organization is not only key to its competitive advantage (in the current language of strategy) but the organization is itself part of the product. Therefore successfully moving key elements of the organization abroad is critical to the success of its internationalization. But service products are usually very much a product of their social context. How do services developed in one particular national context play out in another? Disneyland provides a case where the service seems closely tied to its context: Walt Disney himself said in 1957, "There's an American theme behind the whole park. I believe in emphasizing the story of what made America great and what will keep it great."[1] How does this play out in Japan and France?

The service industry setting has another implication. Disneyland is in what might be called the "feeling business." Its elementary product is emotion—laughter and well being. Its corporate image is one in which the customers are happy, the workers good looking, and the managers all above average. Yet, as the case materials in this module make clear, whatever cheerful services Disney executives believe they are providing to the millions of visitors that flow through the park gates each year, employees at the bottom of the organization are the ones who must provide them. Thus the work-a-day practices that employees adopt to amplify or dampen customer spirits are crucial to the success of the organization. The happiness trade is, like all service-oriented businesses, an interactional one. It rests partly on the symbolic resources put into place by history, other corporate products (notably movies), and park design, but it also rests on an animated workforce more or less eager to greet the guests, pack the trams, push the buttons, deliver the food, dump the garbage, and, in general, marshal the will to meet and perhaps exceed customer expectations. False moves, detected insincerity, rude words or glances, careless disregard for safety, or a sleepy and bored expression on Cinderella can

---

1 Excerpts from *The Magic Kingdom: Walt Disney and the American Way of Life* by Steven Watts. Copyright © 1997 by Steven Watts. Reprinted by permission of Houghton Mifflin Company. All rights reserved.

undermine all the enterprise and ruin a sale. How Disney manages its production and cast of thousands each day is very much a matter of concern in this case.

Like many service companies, but more successfully than most, Disney is widely regarded as addressing this challenge through an extremely strong organizational culture. Although Disney is consistently heralded as one of the best-run companies in the United States, there are a number of instructive anomalies associated with its work policies and practices. For example, visitors to Disneyland are often quite taken by the seemingly effortless courtesy shown them by park operatives, by the energetic ways these operatives take on their work roles, and by their well-scrubbed faces, pleasant smiles, and apparent concern for maintaining order and cleanliness in the park. Yet Disney operatives work at odd times, for minimum wage, on jobs designed for little or no discretion, under omnipresent if not draconian supervision. They have virtually no career opportunities nor is much choice allowed them as to personal appearance, demeanor, type of job, or working hours (which shift from week to week). A standard textbook in the field of organizational behavior would suggest that work designed in such a fashion would be most unattractive and unlikely to generate much employee interest or job commitment. However, Disney attracts an educated, hard-working, loyal, rather charming, and altogether enviable workforce. What is going on here? As suggested in this module, any answer to that question must take into account not only the organizational culture of Disneyland, but its various subcultures as well. Studying Disneyland gives you an opportunity to understand further the action implications of organizational culture, and the strengths and weaknesses of a strong culture.

In addition, Disneyland provides an interesting reversal of the usual internationalization process of U.S. firms. Most U.S. companies set up their first foreign operations in Canada, which is physically and culturally close, and then expand to Europe. Only after being successful there does a company build on its experience in internationalization—what it has learned about crossing borders—to venture to Asia, which is much more distant physically and culturally and often proves to be a much more difficult organizational environment. Disneyland, in contrast, went first to Japan, a notoriously challenging environment for Western companies, where it was an outstanding success, and then, presumably having learned how to "go international," it went to Europe, where it came close to a spectacular failure.

The readings are organized around a running set of class notes that provide you with an overview of Disneyland in each of its three contexts: the United States, Japan, and France. Interspersed between these overviews are more detailed analyses. For example, the class note on Disneyland in the United States is followed by John Van Maanen's **The Smile Factory**, a detailed analysis of the social organization and work culture of ride operators at Disneyland. This is an ethnographic study that focuses on the managerial demands and workers responses at Disneyland. The note on Disneyland in Tokyo is followed by a brief analysis of the Japanese park, also by John Van Maanen, looking at how the Japanese have absorbed, modified, and otherwise made Tokyo Disneyland their own. The note on Disneyland in France is followed by two readings from the business press on Disneyland's problems. These are designated as "optional," because the module is quite lengthy even without them, but they are quite brief and readable, and provide extremely helpful insights for addressing your assignment.

ADDITIONAL SUGGESTED READINGS

On Disneyland

Fjellman, Stephen. 1992. *Vinyl Leaves: Walt Disney's World and America*. Boulder Colorado: Westview Press. A breathless tour of Disney World conducted by a witty anthropologist. The flip side of Steve Birnbaum's Official Disneyland guides.

Grover, Ron. 1997. *The Disney Touch: Disney, ABC, & the Quest for the World's Greatest Media Empire* (revised edition). Chicago: Irwin Professional Publishing. A journalist's account of the Disney corporation, with particular attention to the turn-around of the company in the mid-1980s, which was led by Michael Eisner, and the recent acquisition of ABC.

Kuentz, Jane, Karen Klugman, Sheldon Waldrop, and Susan Willis. (The Project on Disney). 1995. *Inside the Mouse: Work and Play at Disney*. Durham, NC: Duke University Press. A playful but instructive cultural analysis of Disney World's social design and architecture, its consumer practices, and its themes and characters by three literary critics and a photographer.

Watts, Steven. 1997. *The Magic Kingdom: Walt Disney and the American Way of Life*. Boston: Houghton Mifflin Company. A scholarly but very readable account, by an historian, of Walt Disney himself and the evolution of his company and his vision, up to his death in 1966.

On Organizational Culture and Internationalization Processes

Pells, Richard. 1997. *Not Like Us: How Europeans have Loved, Hated, and Transformed American Culture since World War II*. New York: Basic Books. An extremely readable analysis by a cultural historian of the interactions between European and American culture.

Schneider, Susan C., and Jean-Louis Barsoux. 1997. *Managing across Cultures*. New York: Prentice-Hall. An excellent introduction to the comparative analysis of culture and the interaction between culture and cross-border business.

Schein, Edgar. 1992. *Organizational Culture and Leadership*. 2nd edition. San Francisco: Jossey-Bass. A careful, psychologically-oriented look at the role founders and managers play in the creation, maintenance, and alteration of organizational culture.

M-10

core

CLASS NOTE: DISNEYLAND IN THE USA

THE ORIGINAL DISNEYLAND: ANAHEIM, CALIFORNIA

The concept of Disneyland took shape in the early 1950s, when Walt Disney, the creator of Mickey Mouse and the founder of Hollywood's most successful animation studio, decided to construct an amusement park built around the Disney characters. The legends of the Disney company recall how Walt's own brother Roy, the financial director of Walt Disney productions, was one of the many skeptics who thought the idea was ridiculous, and how Walt had to borrow on his life insurance for seed money for his venture (Grover, 1997). There is less inclination to remember that Walt bolstered his famous creative instinct by hiring the Stanford Research Institute to conduct first an economic feasibility study of his plan for the park, and then a follow-up study to analyze demographics, land use, traffic patterns, and so on to come up with a recommendation for the site.

On the basis of SRI's recommendation, Disney acquired 160 acres of orange groves in Anaheim, California, in 1953, and only a few months later signed an agreement with ABC Television that provided the financing to move ahead. All three of America's television networks had been courting Disney, trying to lure him to the emerging medium, but only ABC, then a distant and struggling third among the three major networks, was willing to pay Walt's price: not only generous payments for the weekly show, but also financing for his new "Disneyland" park. ABC became a partner in Disneyland (owning 34.48% of the shares, a proportion equal to that of Walt Disney Productions), and immediately put up half a million dollars to finance construction. It also guaranteed loans for a further $4.5 million.

The premiere of the "Disneyland" TV show on October 27, 1954, drew 52% of the viewing audience, and in its first year had the sixth highest ratings in television; in its second year it rose to fourth (Brooks and Marsh, 1979). It was ABC's first hit show, and the network was delighted when the Disney studios followed it with the weekly "Mickey Mouse Club" (premiering in 1955). From the beginning, the "Disneyland" program was built around the park, whose five "lands" or areas provided the framing for the weekly shows. And in the nine months between the premiere of the show and the opening of the park in July of 1955, there were several programs on the park's construction, ushering viewers behind the scenes of the building process to see the plans taking concrete shape and preparing them for the glories that the finished product would offer. The park's opening took place under the eyes of a platoon of television cameras beaming the opening to a television audience of millions.

The reality of opening day at what some critics dubbed "Walt's Folly" was not as triumphant as it appeared on television. A historian, Steven Watts, has described it as follows:

> While ABC cameras conveyed scenes of bustling joy and announcers pontificated about the historical significance of the event, the behind-the-scenes situation veered dangerously close to total collapse. Construction went on through the night until just moments before the ceremonies began, and Tomorrowland remained muffled in banners and balloons to hide its half-completed state. Near chaos ensued as traffic jams tangled up the Santa Ana freeway and the festivities prompted one disaster after another. A gas leak

forced a temporary shutdown of Fantasyland, the park restaurants ran out of food, a paucity of bathrooms and drinking fountains made many guests grumpy, and the blazing heat melted freshly laid asphalt into sticky black goo that caught and broke many a lady's high heel. Jack Kinney, the studio animator and director, remembered that staff members and their families had been assigned to populate certain areas and they did their duty by smiling and waving when the television cameras turned on them (Watts, 1997, p. 387).

But the same history goes on to say that

After the staff recovered from the opening-day frenzy, worked out the park's kinks, and settled down to business, the seductiveness of the place became clear. Enthusiastic crowds began streaming through the gates day after day, and very quickly attendance far exceeded everyone's expectations. Within six months a million customers had entered the park (Watts, 1997, p. 387).

Disneyland became an American icon, a must-see for foreign visitors (even foreign dignitaries), and the symbol of American culture. It also provided an anchor for the growing Disney empire: the synergies across Disneyland the park, Disneyland the TV show, and Disney movies and other products proved extremely powerful. Excerpts from the movies provided fodder for the TV show and themes for the "rides" in Disneyland, as well as merchandising spin-offs from clothing to records; the television show provided free advertising for the park and the movies. As Steven Watts aptly put it, "Its success quickly became evident. In 1955 [the year the park opened], Walt Disney Productions' gross income more than doubled from the year before, and it continued to grow by leaps and bounds, going from $11.6 million in 1954 to $58.4 million in 1959." (1997, p. 391).

What explains the enduring appeal of Disneyland? In the 1990s, it attracts over ten million visitors a year; Disney World in Florida attracts an even greater number. Disneyland has become an icon of the service industry—a "product" that is completely defined by the customer's interaction with it. In the words of John Van Maanen, "Disneyland . . . has become something of a national institution and treasure. Viewed as a product, Disneyland is part movie center, part tourist site, part shopping mall, part museum, part state fair, part playground, part shrine, part ceremony, part spectacle, part festival, and so on. . . . In contemporary America, Disneyland emerges as an island of calm sanity and safety in troubled times. The forces of decay are arrested, sexual innuendoes are all but banished, liquor is taboo, evil is overcome, the innocent prevail, disorder is tamed, the future is clarified, the past cleaned up, and, in general, the perverse world of doubt, fear, and unfair competition outside the gates is held at bay." (Van Maanen, 1992, pp. 9, 12). One of the most striking features of Disneyland has been its celebration of America. In the remarks he made at the official opening of Disneyland in 1955, Walt Disney explicitly dedicated the park to "the ideals, the dreams, and the hard facts which have created America" (quoted in Watts, 1997, p. 392).

Watts describes Disneyland in similar terms: "The park promoted an unproblematic celebration of the American people and their experience. . . . Functioning as a kind of three-dimensional movie, the park offered guests an ordered sequence of environments that began with the optimistic, nostalgic warmth of Main Street, USA, progressed to the innocent thrills of Adventureland, the patriotic history of Frontierland, the childlike sense of wonder in Fantasyland, and the confident futurism of Tomorrowland. Subtle psychological touches—a carousel where all of the horses are painted white, a haunted house where death is funny, a miniaturized automobile ride where order and safety prevail—combined to encourage feelings of security, harmony, and well-being. . . . Hench [a leading member of the original design team for Disneyland] became convinced that one key was Disney's total control of an environment to create an experience for the visitor" (Watts, 1997, p. 437).

The park was cleverly constructed to conceal this control. "A shrewd design and engineering scheme, for example, manipulated both the movements and emotions of the huge crowds. One essential principle emphasized what Walt liked to call 'weenies,' which caught the eye and drew people along preordained routes so that crowds flowed smoothly. This was augmented by another clever design ploy, which muted the frustration of waiting in long lines for the park's attractions. Disney planners came up with a unique system: first, a snakelike pattern masked the length of a line by running it back and forth in parallel lines; then a variety of visual and audio images kept those in line entertained; and finally, a cleverly engineered schedule kept visitors steadily embarking on the ride so the line would always appear to be moving forward" (Watts, 1997, p. 389).

Three groups of people were responsible for the control that underpinned "the happiest place on earth": the Imagineers, the suits, and the cast (to use Disney-speak). The Imagineers were the designers, located in what in the 1950s and 1960s was a separate Disney subsidiary, WED Enterprises (WED being Walt Disney's initials). An eclectic mix of engineers, artists, landscapers, robotics experts, sculptors, machinists, and model builders, the "Imagineers" designed the park and the rides, scripted the presentations, and shaped the physical and imaginative landscape of the park. Until Walt Disney's death in 1966, they worked directly under him, and they still regard themselves as carrying on his tradition, which included two important values: doing it right, and continuous innovation.

> First, Walt insisted on a genuine commitment to quality. The notion of visitors' getting their money's worth became a kind of gospel at Disneyland. Park designers and managers appreciated Walt's avid commitment to 'plussing,' the term he employed to describe a continuous search for new ideas, new angles, and new additions to make Disneyland more attractive. Marc Davis recalled a revealing experience during a staff meeting when he proposed to rework a park ride, noting that there was a cheap way and an expensive way to accomplish it. Walt, he remembered, got up and walked around the table to lay a hand on his shoulder. 'Marc, you and I do not worry whether anything is cheap or expensive. We only worry whether it's good,' he said. 'I have a theory that if it's good enough, the public will pay you back for it' (Watts, 1997, p. 390).

The "suits" were the finance and marketing people who, among other management tasks, identified and exploited the synergies across Disney's businesses, kept costs in line, and lined up the corporate sponsors whose presence in Disneyland was ubiquitous, from the fast food outlets to corporate-sponsored rides. For example, Monsanto, the American chemical company, sponsored the House of the Future in Tomorrowland, which prominently featured plastics.

But most crucial to the experience and most visible to the customers were the front-line staff at the park, those who welcomed the "guests," as customers were called, operated the rides, staffed the shops and food services, managed and directed the crowds, played the Disney characters that so delighted children, and conveyed the air of spontaneous fun and delight so essential to the Disneyland experience. Carefully selected, trained at Disneyland University, and closely monitored in their jobs, the cast members and their organization are described in detail in the following article in this module, "The Smile Factory."

DISNEYLAND GOES TO FLORIDA

By the 1960s, Walt Disney, while still extremely proud of Disneyland, where he kept an apartment over the firehouse on Main Street, USA, was increasingly unhappy with the kind of uncontrolled development that Disneyland had brought to Anaheim. He saw the motels, restaurants, and tourist shops—often cheap and unattractive buildings—both as an affront to the attractiveness of his park and as a bunch of opportunists making money on his creation. Walt decided to build a second park, this one in the eastern half of the country, and this time, stronger Disney control of the park's environment would be a major criterion for site selection.

In 1964, Walt Disney Productions began buying land around Orlando—surreptitiously, to avoid a run-up in land prices. By 1965, when they went public with their plans, the company had acquired over 27,000 acres. Walt Disney envisioned the creation not only of a bigger Disneyland at the Florida site, but also EPCOT, the Experimental Prototype Community of Tomorrow, a planned urban community complete with industrial park, electric mass transit system, and housing and apartment complexes. Disney's sudden death in December, 1966, meant that his larger vision was never achieved, although EPCOT Center, focusing on technology, provided a pale substitute. Walt's brother Roy presided over the building of Disney World, built on the tried-and-true model of the Disneyland park—but larger in scale—but he, too, died months after its opening in 1971.

The rather conservative top managers that first succeeded the Disney brothers at the top of the company tended to play the role of guardians of the Disney legacy, avoiding risk-taking and excessive expenditures. Contrary to Walt's original plans, they left the development of hotels in the Orlando area to others, and by the early 1980s most of the hotels were not owned by Disney. Attendance was beginning to fall at the parks, just as the audience for "The Wonderful World of Disney" on television (the name had been changed several times over its long run) was steadily falling, with the show eventually being cancelled in the early 1980s. The loss of the free advertising provided by the show was acutely felt, and yet the long tradition of not advertising Disneyland continued until the advent of a new CEO for Walt Disney Productions, Michael Eisner, who came on board in 1984. Eisner brought in a new management team, which raised prices at the two parks, launched an extensive advertising campaign, and made major investments in new rides and in refurbishing the parks, much to the delight of the Imagineers, who had chafed at the penny-pinching ways of the "suits" since the departure of the Disney brothers.

One of the legacies of Walt's planned community that did survive, however, was the Reedy Creek Improvement District, the local government structure devised in 1967 by Disney and the state government of Florida for the governance of the area covered by Disney's considerable land holdings. Disney's virtual control of the District administrative structures meant that its expansion plans over the ensuing decades faced virtually no regulatory hurdles. This was perhaps especially valuable in the case of Pleasure Island, a six-acre district of late-night entertainment spots located on an island, intended to draw the crowd that demanded somewhat livelier entertainment than that provided by Disney World or the futuristic EPCOT Center. Pleasure Island included bars, restaurants, and a disco with 170 video screens. And Disney's control of its local regulatory environment proved invaluable in beating a competitor, the Universal Studios theme park in Orlando, to the completion of the Disney-MGM Studios theme park in 1989 (Grover, 1997, pp. 173-174).

By the late 1980s, attendance was once again thriving at both parks, although the Disney company lamented that the conservatism of Disney management in the 1970s had left only about 14% of the booming hotel business in Orlando in the hands of the Walt Disney Company (as Walt Disney Productions became in 1986). The emergence of the VCR opened up a new market for Disney products and for "free" advertising for Disneyland: most Disney videos opened with "trailers" touting the delights of a visit to "the happiest place on earth." In the 1990s, the synergies across the parks, the movies, the videos, and the merchandising of Disney products were as strong as ever.

REFERENCES

Brooks, Tim, and Earle Marsh. 1979. *The Complete Directory to Prime Time Network TV Shows 1946–present.* New York: Ballantine Books.

Grover, Ron. 1997. *The Disney Touch: Disney, ABC, & the Quest for the World's Greatest Media Empire* (revised edition). Chicago: Irwin Professional Publishing.

Van Maanen, John. 1992. "Displacing Disney: Some Notes on the Flow of Culture." *Qualitative Sociology* 15-1, pp. 5–35.

Watts, Steven. 1997. *The Magic Kingdom: Walt Disney and the American Way of Life.* Boston: Houghton Mifflin Company.

ⒸACADEMIC 10

THE SMILE FACTORY: WORK AT DISNEYLAND

by John Van Maanen

Part of Walt Disney Enterprises includes the theme park Disneyland. In its pioneering form in Anaheim, California, this amusement center has been a consistent money maker since the gates were first opened in 1955. Apart from its sociological charm, it has, of late, become something of an exemplar for culture vultures and has been held up for public acclaim in several best-selling publications as one of America's top companies, most notably by Peters and Waterman (1982). To outsiders, the cheerful demeanor of its employees, the seemingly inexhaustible repeat business it generates from its customers, the immaculate condition of park grounds, and, more generally, the intricate physical and social order of the business itself appear wondrous.

Disneyland, as the self-proclaimed "Happiest Place on Earth," certainly occupies an enviable position in the amusement and entertainment worlds, as well as the commercial work in general. Its product, it seems, is emotion—"laughter and well being." Insiders are not bashful about promoting the product. Bill Ross, a Disneyland executive, summarizes the corporate position nicely by noting that "although we focus our attention on profit and loss, day-in and day-out we can not lose sight of the fact that this is a feeling business and we make our profits from that."[1]

The "feeling business" does not operate, however, by management decree alone. Whatever services Disneyland executives believe they are providing to the 60 to 70 thousand visitors per day that flow through the park during its peak summer season, employees at the bottom of the organization are the ones who must provide them. The work-a-day practices that employees adopt to amplify or dampen customer spirits are therefore a core concern of this feeling business. The happiness trade is an interactional one. It rests partly on the symbolic resources put into place by history and park design but it also rests on an animated workforce that is more or less eager to greet the guests, pack the trams, push the bottoms, deliver the food, dump the garbage, clean the streets, and, in general, marshal the will to meet and perhaps exceed customer expectations. False moves, rude words, careless disregard, detected insincerity, or a sleepy and bored presence can all undermine the enterprise and ruin a sale. The smile factory has its rules.

IT'S A SMALL WORLD

The writing that follows[2] represents Disneyland as a workplace. It is organized roughly as an old-fashioned realist ethnography that tells of a culture in native categories (Van Maanen, 1988). The culture of interest is the Disneyland culture but it

Author's Note: This paper has been cobbled together using three-penny nails of other writings. Parts come from a paper presented to the American Anthropological Association Annual Meetings in Washington D.C. on November 16, 1989 called "Whistle While You Work." Other parts come from Van Maanen and Kunda (1989). In coming to this version, I've had a great deal of help from my friends Steve Barley, Nicloe Biggart, Michael Owen Jones, Rosanna Hertz, Gideon Kunda, Joanne Martin, Maria Lydia Spinelli, Bob Sutton, and Bob Thomas.

Source: John Van Maanen, "The Smile Factory: Work at Disneyland," from *Reframing Organizational Culture*, edited by Peter J. Frost, et al., pp. 58–76. Copyright © 1990 by Sage Publications, Inc. Reprinted by Permission of Sage Publications, Inc.

is not necessarily the same one invented, authorized, codified, or otherwise approved by park management. Thus the culture I portray here is more of an occupational than a strictly organizational one (Van Maanen and Barley, 1985).

This rendition is of course abbreviated and selective. I focus primarily on such matters as the stock appearance (vanilla), status order (rigid), and social life (full), and swiftly learned codes of conduct (formal and informal) that are associated with Disneyland ride operators. These employees comprise the largest category of hourly workers on the payroll. During the summer months, they number close to four thousand and run the 60-odd rides and attractions in the park.

They are also a well-screened bunch. There is—among insiders and outsiders alike—a rather fixed view about the social attributes carried by the standard-make Disneyland ride operator. Single, white males and females in their early twenties, without facial blemish, of above average height and below average weight, with straight teeth, conservative grooming standards, and a chin-up, shoulder-back posture radiating the sort of good health suggestive of a recent history in sports are typical of these social identifiers. There are representative minorities on the payroll but because ethnic displays are sternly discouraged by management, minority employees are rather close copies of the standard model Disneylander, albeit in different colors.

This Disneyland look is often a source of some amusement to employees who delight in pointing out that even the patron saint, Walt himself, could not be hired today without shaving off his trademark pencil-thin mustache. But, to get a job in Disneyland and keep it means conforming to a rather exacting set of appearance rules. These rules are put forth in a handbook on the Disney image in which readers learn, for example, that facial hair or long hair is banned for men as are aviator glasses and earrings and that women must not tease their hair, wear fancy jewelry, or apply more than a modest dab of makeup. Both men and women are to look neat and prim, keep their uniforms fresh, polish their shoes, and maintain an upbeat countenance and light dignity to complement their appearance—no low spirits or cornball raffishness at Disneyland.

The legendary "people skills" of park employees, so often mentioned in Disneyland publicity and training materials, do not amount to very much according to ride operators. Most tasks require little interaction with customers and are physically designed to practically insure that is the case. The contact that does occur typically is fleeting and swift, a matter usually of only a few seconds. In the rare event sustained interaction with customers might be required, employees are taught to deflect potential exchanges to area supervisors or security. A training manual offers the proper procedure: "On misunderstandings, guests should be told to call City Hall. . . . In everything from damaged cameras to physical injuries, don't discuss anything with guests . . . there will always be one of us nearby." Employees learn quickly that security is hidden but everywhere. On Main Street, security cops are Keystone Kops; in Frontierland, they are Town Marshals; on Tom Sawyer's Island, they are Cavalry Officers, and so on.

Occasionally, what employees call "line talk" or "crowd control" is required of them to explain delays, answer direct questions, or provide directions that go beyond the endless stream of recorded messages coming from virtually every nook and cranny of the park. Because such tasks are so simple, consisting of little more than keeping the crowd informed and moving, it is perhaps obvious why management considers the sharp appearance and wide smile of employees so vital to park operations. There is little more they could ask of ride operators whose main interactive task with visitors consist of being, in their own terms, "information booths," "line signs," "pretty props," "shepherds," and "talking statues."

A few employees do go out of their way to initiate contact with Disneyland customers but, as a rule, most do not and consider those who do to be a bit odd. In general, one need do little more than exercise common courtesy while looking reasonably alert and pleasant. Interactive skills that are advanced by the job have less to do with making customers feel warm and welcome than they do with keeping each other amused and happy. This is, of course, a more complex matter.

Employees bring to the job personal badges of status that are of more than passing interest to peers. In rough order, these include: good looks, college affiliation, career aspirations, past achievement, age (directly related to status up to about age 23 or 24 and inversely related thereafter), and assorted other idiosyncratic matters. Nested closely alongside these imported status badges are organizational ones that are also of concern and value to employees.

Where one works in the park carries much social weight. Postings are consequential because the ride and area a person is assigned provide rewards and benefits beyond those of wages. In-the-park stature for ride operators turns partly on whether or not unique skills are required. Disneyland neatly complements labor market theorizing on this dimension because employees with the most differentiated skills find themselves at the top of the internal status ladder, thus making their loyalties to the organization more predictable.

Ride operators, as a large but distinctly middle-class group of hourly employees on the floor of the organization, compete for status not only with each other but also with other employee groupings whose members are hired for the season from the same applicant pool. A loose approximation of the rank ordering among these groups can be constructed as follows:

1. The upper-class prestigious Disneyland Ambassadors and Tour Guides (bilingual young women in charge of ushering—some say rushing—little bands of tourists through the park)
2. Ride operators performing coveted "skilled work" such as live narrations or tricky transportation tasks (like those who symbolically control customer access to the park and drive the costly entry vehicles, such as the antique trains, horse-drawn carriages, and Monorail)
3. All other ride operators
4. The proletarian Sweepers (keepers of the concrete grounds)
5. The sub-prole or peasant status Food and Concession workers (whose park sobriquets reflect their lowly social worth—"pancake ladies," "peanut pushers," "coke blokes," "suds divers," and the seemingly irreplaceable "soda jerks")

Pay differentials are slight among these employee groups. The collective status adheres, as it does internally for ride operators, to assignment or functional distinctions. As the rank order suggests, most employee status goes to these who work jobs that require higher degrees of special skill, relative freedom from constant and direct supervision, and provide the opportunity to organize and direct customer desires and behavior rather than to merely respond to them as spontaneously expressed.

The basis for sorting individuals into these various broad bands of job categories is often unknown to employees—a sort of deep, dark secret of the casting directors in personnel. When prospective employees are interviewed, they interview for "a job at Disneyland," not a specific one. Personnel decides what particular job they will eventually occupy. Personal contacts are considered by employees as crucial in this job-assignment process as they are in the hiring decision. Some employees, especially those who wind up in the lower ranking jobs, are quite disappointed with their assignments as is the case when, for example, a would-be Adventureland guide is posted to a New Orleans Square restaurant as a pot scrubber. Although many of the outside acquaintances of our pot scrubber may know only that he works at Disneyland, rest assured, insiders will know immediately where he works and judge him accordingly.

Uniforms are crucial in this regard for they provide instant communication about the social merits or demerits of the wearer within the little world of Disneyland workers. Uniforms also correspond to a wider

13

PRESS

status ranking that casts a significant shadow on employees of all types. Male ride operators on the Autopia wear, for example, untailored jump suits similar to pit mechanics and consequently generate about as much respect from peers as the grease-stained outfits worn by pump jockeys generate from real motorists in gas stations. The ill-fitting and homogeneous "whites" worn by Sweepers signify lowly institutional work tinged, perhaps, with a reminder of hospital orderlies rather than street cleanup crews. On the other hand, for males, the crisp, officer-like Monorail operator stands alongside the swashbuckling Pirate of the Caribbean, the casual cowpoke of Big Thunder Mountain, or the smartly vested Riverboat pilot as carrier of valued symbols in and outside the park. Employees lust for these higher status positions and the rights to small advantages such uniforms provide. A lively internal labor market exists wherein there is much scheming for the more prestigious assignments.

For women, a similar market exists, although the perceived "sexiness" of uniforms, rather than social rank, seems to play a larger role. To wit, the rather heated antagonisms that developed years ago when the ride "It's a Small World" first opened and began outfitting the ride operators with what were felt to be the shortest skirts and most revealing blouses in the park. Tour Guides, who traditionally headed the fashion vanguard at Disneyland in their above-the-knee kilts, knee socks, tailored vests, black English hats, and smart riding crops were apparently appalled at being upstaged by their social inferiors and lobbied actively (and, judging by the results, successfully) to lower the skirts, raise the necklines, and generally remake their Small World rivals.

Important, also, to ride operators are the break schedules followed on the various rides. The more the better. Work teams develop inventive ways to increase the number of "time-outs" they take during the work day. Most rides are organized on a rotational basis (e.g., the operator moving from a break, to queue monitor, to turnstile overseer, to unit loader, to traffic controller, to driver, and, again, to a break). The number of break men or women on a rotation (or ride) varies by the number of employees on duty and by the number of units on line. Supervisors, foremen, and operators also vary as to what they regard as appropriate break standards (and, more importantly, as to the value of the many situational factors that can enter the calculation of break rituals—crowd size, condition of ride, accidents, breakdowns, heat, operator absences, special occasions, and so forth). Self-monitoring teams with sleepy supervisors and lax (or savvy) foremen can sometimes manage a shift comprised of 15 minutes on and 45 minutes off each hour. They are envied by others and rides that have such a potential are eyed hungrily by others who feel trapped by their more rigid (and observed) circumstances.

Movement across jobs is not encouraged by park management but some does occur (mostly within an area and job category). Employees claim that a sort of "once a sweeper, always a sweeper" rule obtains but all know of at least a few exceptions to prove the rule. The exceptions offer some (not much) hope for those working at the social margins of the park and perhaps keep them on the job longer than might otherwise be expected. Dishwashers can dream of becoming Pirates, and with persistence and a little help from their friends, such dreams just might come true next season (or the next).

These examples are precious, perhaps, but they are also important. There is an intricate pecking order among very similar categories of employees. Attributes of reward and status tend to cluster, and there is intense concern about the cluster to which one belongs (or would like to belong). To a degree, form follows function in Disneyland because the jobs requiring the most abilities and offering the most interest also offer the most status and social reward. Interaction patterns reflect and sustain this order. Few Ambassadors or Tour Guides, for instance, will stoop to speak at length with Sweepers, who speak mostly among themselves, or to Food workers. Ride operators, between the poles, line up in ways referred to above with only ride proximity (i.e., sharing a break area) representing a potentially significant intervening variable in the interaction calculation.

These patterns are of more than slight concern because Disneyland, especially in the summer, can be compared quite usefully to a college mixer where across-sex pairing is of great concern (Schwartz and Lever, 1976). More to the point, what Waller (1937) so accurately called the "rating and dating complex" is in full bloom among park employees. The various modern forms of mating games are valued pastimes among Disneyland employees and are often played with corporate status marker in mind. Thus, when Yvone, the reigning Alice in Wonderland, moved in one summer with Ted, a lowly Sweeper, heads were scratched in puzzlement even though most knew that Yvone was, in her other life, a local junior college student and Ted was in premed at USC. The more general point is that romance flourishes in the park and, at least, if folklore is our guide, marriages made in Disneyland are not uncommon.

Even when not devoted strictly to pairing-off objectives, employee pastimes usually involve other employees. Disneyland's softball and volleyball leagues, its official picnics, canoe races, employee nights at the park, beach parties, and so on provide a busy little social scene for those interested. Areas and rides, too, offer social excitement and bonuses, such as when kegs of beer are rolled out at an off-site party after work crews break turnstile records ("We put 33,147 on the mountain today"). During the summer, some night crews routinely party in the early morning while day shift crews party at night. Sleep is not a commodity greatly valued by many employees caught up in a valued social whirl.

The so-called youth culture is indeed celebrated in and out of the park. Many employees, for example, live together in the large and cheap (by Los Angeles standards) apartment complexes that surround Disneyland. Employees sometimes refer to these sprawling, pastel, and slightly seedy structures as "the projects" or "worker housing." Yet the spirited attractiveness of the collective, low-rent lifestyle for those living it is easily grasped by a few landlords in the area who flatly refuse to rent to Disneyland employees during the summer as a matter of principle, and maybe, sorry experience because these short-term rentals serve as amusement parks for off-duty Disneylanders who, as they say, "know how to party."

A fusion of work and play is notable, however, even when play seems to be the order of the occasion. Certainly no Disneyland get-together would be complete without ride operators launching their special spiels practiced (or heard continuously on tape) at work:

> Welcome aboard the African Queen, folks. My name is John and I'll be your guide and skipper for our trip down these rivers of adventure. As we pull away from the loading dock, turn around and take a last look at the people standing there, it may be the last time you ever see them. . . . Please keep your hands inside the boat as we go past these hungry alligators; they're always looking for a hand-out. . . . And now we return to civilization and the greatest danger of all, the California freeways.

The figurative parallel of this party is, of course, the atmosphere of a most collegial college. It has a literal parallel as well.

Paid employment at Disneyland begins with the much renowned University of Disneyland whose faculty runs a day-long orientation program (Traditions I) as part of a 40-hour apprenticeship program, most of which takes place on the rides. In the classroom, however, newly hired ride operators are given a very thorough introduction to matters of managerial concern and are tested on their absorption of famous Disneyland fact, lore, and procedure. Employee demeanor is governed, for example, by three rules:

> First, we practice the friendly smile.
> Second, we use only friendly and courteous phrases.
> Third, we are not stuffy—the only Misters in Disneyland are Mr. Toad and Mr. Smee.

Employees learn too that the Disneyland culture is officially defined. The employee handbook put it in this format:

Dis·ney Cor·po·rate Cul·ture (diz'ne kor'pr'it kul cher)*n* 1. Of or pertaining to the Disney organization, as a: the philosophy underlying all business decisions; b: the commitment of top leadership and management to that philosophy; c: the actions taken by individual cast members that reinforce the image.

Language is also a central feature of university life and new employees are schooled in its proper use. Customers at Disneyland are, for instance, never referred to as such, they are "guests." There are no rides at Disneyland, only "attractions." Disneyland itself is a "Park," not an amusement center, and it is divided into "back-stage," "on-stage," and "staging" regions. Law enforcement personnel hired by the park are not policemen, but "security hosts." Employees do not wear uniforms but check out fresh "costumes" each working day from "wardrobe." And, of course, there are no accidents at Disneyland, only "incidents."

So successful is such training that Smith and Eisenberg (1987) report that not a single Disneyland employee uttered the taboo and dread words "uniform," "customer," or "amusement park" during the 35 half-hour interviews they conducted as part of a study on organizational communication. *The Los Angeles Times* (July 28, 1988) also gives evidence on this matter, quoting a tour guide's reaction to the employees' annual canoe races. "It's a good release," she says, "it helps you see the other cast members (park employees) go through the same thing you do." Whether or not employees keep to such disciplined talk with one another is, of course, a moot point because the corporate manual is concerned only with how employees talk to customers or outsiders.

The university curriculum also anticipates probable questions ride operators may someday face from customers and they are taught the approved public response. A sample:

Question (posed by trainer): What do you tell a guest who requests a rain check?

Answer (in three parts): We don't offer rain checks at Disneyland because (1) the main attractions are all indoors; (2) we would go broke if we offered passes; and (3) sunny days would be too crowded if we gave passes.

Shrewd trainees readily note that such an answer blissfully disregards the fact that waiting areas of Disneyland are mostly outdoors and that there are no subways in the park to carry guests from land to land. Nor do they miss the economic assumption concerning the apparent frequency of Southern California rains. They discuss such matters together, of course, but rarely raise them in the training classroom. In most respects, these are recruits who easily take the role of good student.

Classes are organized and designed by professional Disneyland trainers who also instruct a well-screened group of representative hourly employees straight from park operations on the approved newcomer training methods and materials. New hires seldom see professional trainers in class but are brought on board by enthusiastic peers who concentrate on those aspects of park procedure thought highly general matters to be learned by all employees. Particular skill training (and "reality shock") is reserved for the second wave of socialization occurring on the rides themselves, as operators are taught, for example, how and when to send a bobsled caroming down the track or, more delicately, the proper ways to stuff an obese adult customer into the midst of children riding the Monkey car on the Casey Jones Circus Train or, most problematically, what exactly to tell an irate customer standing in the rain who, in no uncertain terms, wants his or her money back and wants it back now.

During orientation, considerable concern is placed on particular values the Disney organization considers central to its operations. These values range from the "customer is king" verities to the more or less unique kind, of which "everyone is a child at heart when at Disneyland" is a decent example. This latter piety is one few employees fail to recognize as also attaching to everyone's minds as well after a few months of work experience. Elaborate checklists of appearance standards are learned and gone over in the classroom and great efforts are spent trying to bring employee emotional responses in line with such standards. Employees are told repeatedly that if they are happy and cheerful at work, so, too, will the guests at play. Inspirational films, hearty pep talks, family imagery, and exemplars of corporate performance are all representative of the strong symbolic stuff of these training rites.

Another example, perhaps extreme, concerns the symbolic role of the canonized founder in the corporate mythology. When Walt Disney was alive, newcomers and veterans alike were told how much he enjoyed coming to the park and just how exacting he was about the conditions he observed. For employees, the cautionary whoop, "Walt's in the park," could often bring forth additional energy and care for one's part in the production. Upon his death, trainers at the University were said to be telling recruits to mind their manners because, "Walt's in the park all the time now."

Yet, like employees everywhere, there is a limit to which such overt company propaganda can be effective. Students and trainers both seem to agree on where the line is drawn, for there is much satirical banter, mischievous winking, and playful exaggeration in the classroom. As young seasonal employees note, it is difficult to take seriously an organization that provides its retirees "Golden Ears" instead of gold watches after 20 or more years of service. All newcomers are aware that the label "Disneyland" has both an unserious and artificial connotation and that a full embrace of the Disneyland role would be as deviant as its full rejection. It does seem, however, because of the corporate imagery, the recruiting and selection devices, the goodwill trainees hold toward the organization at entry, the peer-based employment context, and the smooth fit with real student calendars, the job is considered by most ride operators to be a good one. The University of Disneyland,

it appears, graduates students with a modest amount of pride and a considerable amount of fact and faith firmly ingrained as important things to know (if not always accept).

Matters become more interesting as new hires move into the various realms of the Disneyland enterprise. There are real customers "out there" and employees soon learn that these good folks do not always measure up to the typically well mannered and grateful guest of the training classroom. Moreover, ride operators may find it difficult to utter the prescribed "Welcome Voyager" (or its equivalent) when it is to be given to the 20-thousandth human being passing through the Space Mountain turnstile on a crowded day in July. Other difficulties present themselves as well, but operators learn that there are others on-stage to assist or thwart them.

Employees learn quickly that supervisors and, to a lesser degree, foremen are not only on the premises to help them, but also to catch them when they slip over or brazenly violate set procedures or park policies. Because most rides are tightly designed to eliminate human judgment and minimize operational disasters, much of the supervisory monitoring is directed at activities ride operators consider trivial: taking too long a break; not wearing parts of one's official uniform, such as a hat, standard-issue belt, or correct shoes; rushing the ride (although more frequent violations seem to be detected for the provision of longer-than-usual rides for lucky customers); fraternizing with guests beyond the call of duty; talking back to quarrelsome or sometimes merely querisome customers; and so forth. All are matters covered quite explicitly in the codebooks ride operators are to be familiar with, and violations of such codes are often subject to instant and harsh discipline. The firing of what to supervisors are "malcontents," "trouble-makers," "bumblers," "attitude problems," or simply "jerks" is a frequent occasion at Disneyland, and among part-timers, who are most subject to degradation and being fired, the threat is omnipresent. There are

17

PRESS

few workers who have not witnessed first-hand the rapid disappearance of a co-worker for offenses they would regard as "Mickey Mouse." Moreover, there are few employees who themselves have not violated a good number of operational and demeanor standards and anticipate, with just cause, the violation of more in the future.[3]

In part, because of the punitive and what are widely held to be capricious supervisory practices in the park, foremen and ride operators are usually drawn close and shield one another from suspicious area supervisors. Throughout the year, each land is assigned a number of area supervisors who, dressed alike in short-sleeved white shirts and ties with walkie-talkies hitched to their belts, wander about their territories on the lookout for deviations from park procedures (and other signs of disorder). Occasionally, higher level supervisors pose in "plain-clothes" and ghost-ride the various attractions just to be sure everything is up to snuff. Some area supervisors are well-known among park employees for the variety of surreptitious techniques they employ when going about their monitoring duties. Blind observation posts are legendary, almost sacred, sites within the park ("This is where Old Man Weston hangs out. He can see Dumbo, Storybook, the Carousel, and the Tea Cups from here"). Supervisors in Tomorrowland are, for example, famous for their penchant of hiding in the bushes above the submarine caves, timing the arrivals and departures of the supposedly fully loaded boats making the 8½ minute cruise under the polar icecaps. That they might also catch a submarine captain furtively enjoying a cigarette (or worse) while inside the conning tower (his upper body out of view of the crowd on the vessel) might just make a supervisor's day—and unmake the employee's. In short, supervisors, if not firemen, are regarded by ride operators as sneaks and tricksters out to get them and representative of the dark side of park life. Their presence is, of course, an orchestrated one and does more than merely watch over the ride operators. It also draws operators together as cohesive little units who must look out for one another while they work (and shirk).

Supervisors are not the only villains who appear in the park. The treachery of co-workers, while rare, has its moments. Pointing out the code violations of colleagues to foremen and supervisors—usually in secret—provides one avenue of collegial duplicity. Finks, of all sorts, can be found among the peer ranks at Disneyland, and although their dirty deeds are uncommon, work teams on all rides go to some effort to determine just who they might be and, if possible, drive them from their midst. Although there is little overt hazing or playing of pranks on newcomers, they are nonetheless carefully scrutinized on matters of team (and ride) loyalty, and those who fail the test of "member in good standing" are subject to some very uncomfortable treatment. Innuendo and gossip are the primary tools in this regard, with ridicule and ostracism (the good old silent treatment) providing the backup. Since perhaps the greatest rewards working at Disneyland offers its ride operator personnel are those that come from belonging to a tight little network of like-minded and sociable peers where off-duty interaction is at least as vital and pleasurable as the on-duty sort, such mechanisms are quite effective. Here is where some of the most powerful and focused emotion work in the park is found, and those subject to negative sanction, rightly or wrongly, will grieve, but grieve alone.

Employees are also subject to what might be regarded as remote controls. These stem not from supervisors or peers but from thousands of paying guests who parade daily through the park. The public, for the most part, wants Disneyland employees to play only the roles for which they are hired and costumed. If, for instance, Judy of the Jets is feeling tired, grouchy, or bored, few customers want to know about it. Disneyland employees are expected to be sunny and helpful; and the job, with its limited opportunities for sustained interaction, is designed to support such a stance. Thus, if a ride operator's behavior drifts noticeably away from the norm, customers are sure to point it out—"Why aren't you smiling?" "What's wrong with you?" "Having a bad day?" "Did Goofy step on your foot?" Ride operators learn swiftly from constant hints, glances, glares, and tactful (and tactless) cues sent by their audience what their role in the park is to be, and as long as they keep to it, there will be no objections from those passing by.

> I can remember being out on the river looking at the people on the Mark Twain looking down on the people in the Keel Boats who are looking up at them. I'd come by on my raft and they'd all turn and stare at me. If I gave them a little wave and a grin, they'd all wave back and smile; all ten thousand of them. I always wondered what would happen if I gave them the finger? (Ex-ride operator, 1988).

Ride operators also learn how different categories of customers respond to them and the parts they are playing on stage. For example, infants and small children are generally timid, if not frightened, in their presence. School-age children are somewhat curious, aware that the operator is at work playing a role but sometimes in awe of the role itself. Nonetheless, these children can be quite critical of any flaw in the operator's performance. Teenagers, especially males in groups, present problems because they sometimes go to great lengths to embarrass, challenge, ridicule, or outwit an operator. Adults are generally appreciative and approving of an operator's conduct provided it meets their rather minimal standards, but they sometimes overreact to the part an operator is playing (positively) if accompanied by small children. A recent study of the Easter Bunny points out a similar sort of response on the part of adults to fantasy (Hickey, Thompson, and Foster, 1988). It is worth noting too that adults out number children in the park by a wide margin. One count reports an adult-to-children ratio of four-to-one (King, 1981).

The point here is that ride operators learn what the public (or, at least, their idealized version of the public) expects of their role and find it easier to conform to such expectations than not. Moreover, they discover that when they are bright and lively others respond to them in like ways. This Goffmanesque balancing of the emotional exchange is such that ride operators come to expect good treatment. They assume, with good cause, that most people will react to their little waves and smiles with some affection and perhaps joy. When they do not, it can ruin a ride operator's day.

With this interaction formula in mind, it is perhaps less difficult to see why ride operators detest and scorn the ill-mannered or unruly guest. At times, these grumpy, careless, or otherwise unresponsive characters insult the very role the operators play and have come to appreciate—"You can't treat the Captain of the USS Nautilus like that!" Such out-of-line visitors offer breaks from routine, some amusement, consternation, or the occasional job challenge that occurs when remedies are deemed necessary to restore employee and role dignity.

By and large, however, the people-processing tasks of ride operators pass good naturedly and smoothly, with operators hardly noticing much more than the bodies passing in front of view (special bodies, however, merit special attention as when crew members on the subs gather to assist a young lady in a revealing outfit on board and then linger over the hatch to admire the view as she descends the steep steps to take her seat on the boat). Yet, sometimes, more than a body becomes visible, as happens when customers overstep their roles and challenge employees' authority, insult an operator, or otherwise disrupt the routines of the job. In the process, guests become "duffesses," "ducks," and "a__holes" (just three of many derisive terms used by ride operators to label those customers they believe to have gone beyond the pale). Normally, these characters are brought to the attention of park security officers, ride foremen, or area supervisors who, in turn, decide how they are to be disciplined (usually expulsion from the park).

Occasionally, however, the alleged slight is too personal or simply too extraordinary for a ride operator to let it pass unnoticed or merely inform others and allow them to decide what, if anything, is to be done. Restoration of one's respect is called for and routine practices have been developed for these circumstances. For example, common remedies include: the "seatbelt squeeze," a small token of appreciation given to a deviant customer consisting of the rapid cinching-up of a required seatbelt such that the passenger is doubled-over at the point of departure and left gasping for the duration of the trip; the "break-toss," an acrobatic gesture of the Autopia trade whereby operators jump on the outside of a norm violator's car, stealthily unhitching the safety belt, then slamming on the brakes, bringing the car to an almost instant stop while the driver flies on the hood of the car (or beyond); the "seatbelt slap," an equally distinguished (if primitive) gesture by which an offending customer receives a sharp, quick snap of a hard plastic belt across the face (or other parts of the body) when entering or exiting a seat-belted ride; the "break-up-the-party" gambit, a queuing device put to use in officious fashion whereby bothersome pairs are separated at the last minute into different units, thus forcing on them the pain of strange companions for the duration of a ride through the Haunted Mansion or a ramble on Mr. Toad's Wild Ride; the "hatch-cover ploy," a much beloved practice of Submarine pilots who, in collusion with mates on the loading dock, are able to drench offensive guests with water as their units pass under a waterfall; and, lastly, the rather ignoble variants of the "Sorry-I-didn't-see-your-hand" tactic, a savage move designed to crunch a particularly irksome customer's hand (foot, finger, arm, leg, etc.) by bringing a piece of Disneyland property to bear on the appendage, such as the door of a Thunder Mountain railroad car or the starboard side of a Jungle Cruise boat. This latter remedy is, most often, a "near miss" designed to startle the little criminals of Disneyland.

All of these unofficial procedures (and many more) are learned on the job. Although they are used sparingly, they are used. Occasions of use provide a continual stream of sweet revenge talk to enliven and enrich colleague conversation at break time or after work. Too much, of course, can be made of these subversive practices and the rhetoric that surrounds their use. Ride operators are quite aware that there are limits beyond which they dare not pass. If they are caught, they know that restoration of corporate pride will be swift and clean.

In general, Disneyland employees are remarkable for their forbearance and polite good manners even under trying conditions. They are taught, and some come to believe, for a while at least, that they are really "on-stage" at work. And, as noted, surveillance by supervisory personnel certainly fades in light of the unceasing glances an employee receives from the paying guests who tromp daily through the park in the summer. Disneyland employees know well that they are part of the product being sold and learn to check their more discriminating manners in favor of the generalized countenance of a cheerful lad or lassie whose enthusiasm and dedication is obvious to all.

At times, the emotional resources of employees appear awesome. When the going gets tough and the park is jammed, the nerves of all employees are frayed and sorely tested by the crowd, din, sweltering sun, and eyeburning smog. Customers wait in what employees call "bullpens" (and park officials call "reception areas") for up to several hours for a 3½ minute ride that operators are sometimes hell-bent on cutting to 2½ minutes. Surely a monument to the human ability to suppress feelings has been created when both users and providers alike can maintain their composure and seeming regard for one another when in such a fix.

It is in this domain where corporate culture and the order it helps to sustain must be given its due. Perhaps the depth of a culture is visible only when its members are under the gun. The orderliness—a good part of the Disney formula for financial success—is an accomplishment based not only on physical design and elaborate procedures, but also on the low-level, part-time employees who, in the final analysis, must be willing, even eager, to keep the show afloat. The ease with which employees glide into their kindly and smiling roles is, in large measure, a feat of social engineering. Disneyland does not pay well; its supervision is arbitrary and skin-close; its working conditions are chaotic; its jobs require minimal amounts of intelligence or judgment; and it asks a kind of sacrifice and loyalty of its employees that is almost fanatical. Yet, it attracts a particularly able workforce whose personal backgrounds suggest abilities far exceeding those required of a Disneyland traffic cop, people stuffer, queue or line manager, and button pusher. As I have suggested, not all of Disneyland is covered by the culture put forth by management. There are numerous pockets of resistance and various degrees of autonomy maintained by employees. Nonetheless, adherence and support for the organization are remarkable. And, like swallows returning to Capistrano, many part-timers look forward to their migration back to the park for several seasons.

THE DISNEY WAY

Four features alluded to in this unofficial guide to Disneyland seem to account for a good deal of the social order that obtains within the park. First, socialization, although costly, is of a most selective, collective, intensive, serial, sequential, and closed sort.[4] These tactics are notable for their penetration into the private spheres of individual thought and feeling (Van Maanen and Schein, 1979). Incoming identities are not so much dismantled as they are set aside as employees are schooled in the use of new identities of the situational sort. Many of these are symbolically powerful and, for some, laden with social approval. It is hardly surprising that some of the more problematic positions in terms of turnover during the summer occur in the food and concession domains where employees apparently find little to identify with on the job. Cowpokes on Big Thunder Mountain, Jet Pilots, Storybook Princesses, Tour Guides, Space Cadets, Jungle Boat Skippers, or Southern Belles of New Orleans Square have less difficulty on this score. Disneyland, by design, bestows identity through a process carefully set up to strip away the job relevance of other sources of identity and learned response and replace them with others of organizational relevance. It works.

Second, this is a work culture whose designers have left little room for individual experimentation. Supervisors, as apparent in their focused wandering and attentive looks, keep very close tabs on what is going on at any moment in all the lands. Every bush, rock, and tree in Disneyland is numbered and checked continually as to the part it is playing in the park. So too are employees. Discretion of a personal sort is quite limited while employees are "on-stage." Even "backstage" and certain "off-stage" domains have their corporate monitors. Employees are indeed aware that their "off-stage" life beyond the picnics, parties, and softball games is subject to some scrutiny, for police checks are made on potential and current employees. Nor do all employees discount the rumors that park officials make periodic inquiries on their own as to a person's habits concerning sex and drugs. Moreover, the sheer number of rules and regulations is striking, thus making the grounds for dismissal a matter of multiple choice for supervisors who discover a target for the use of such grounds. The feeling of being watched is, unsurprisingly, a rather prevalent complaint among Disneyland people and is one that employees must live with if they are to remain at Disneyland.

Third, emotional management occurs in the park in a number of quite distinct ways. From the instructors at the university who beseech recruits to "wish every guest a pleasant good day," to the foremen who plead with their charges to "say thank you when you herd them through the gate," to the impish customer who seductively licks her lips and asks, "what does Tom Sawyer want for Christmas?" appearance, demeanor, and etiquette have special meanings at Disneyland. Because these are prized personal attributes over which we normally feel in control, making them commodities can be unnerving. Much self-monitoring is involved, of course, but even here self-management has an organizational side. Consider ride operators who may complain of being "too tired to smile" but, at the same time, feel a little guilty for uttering such a confession. Ride operators who have worked an early morning shift on the Matterhorn (or other popular rides) tell of a queasy feeling they get when the park is opened for business and they suddenly feel the ground begin to shake under their feet and hear the low thunder of the hordes of customers coming at them, oblivious of civil restraint and the small children who might be among them. Consider, too, the discomforting pressures of being "on-stage" all day and the cumulative annoyance of having adults ask permission to leave a line to go to the bathroom, whether the water in the lagoon is real, where the well-marked entrances might be, where Walt Disney's cryogenic tomb is to be found,[5] or—the real clincher—whether or not one is "really real."

The mere fact that so much operator discourse concerns the handling of bothersome guests suggests that these little emotional disturbances have costs. There are, for instance, times in all employee careers when they put themselves on "automatic pilot," "go robot," "can't feel a thing," "lapse into a dream," "go into a trance," or otherwise "check out" while still on duty. Despite a crafty supervisor's (or curious visitor's) attempt to measure the glimmer in an employee's eye, this sort of willed emotional numbness is common to many of the "on-stage" Disneyland personnel. Much of this numbness is, of course, beyond the knowledge of supervisors and guests because most employees have little trouble appearing as if they are present even when they are not. It is, in a sense, a passive form of resistance that suggests there is a sacred preserve of individuality left among employees in the park.

Finally, taking these three points together, it seems that even when people are trained, paid, and told to be nice, it is hard for them to do so all of the time. But, when efforts to be nice have succeeded to the degree that is true of Disneyland, it appears as a rather towering (if not always admirable) achievement. It works at the collective level by virtue of elaborate direction. Employees—at all ranks—are stage-managed by higher ranking employees who, having come through themselves, hire, train, and closely supervise those who have replaced them below. Expression rules are laid out in corporate manuals. Employee time-outs intensify work experience. Social exchanges are forced into narrow bands of interacting groups. Training and retraining programs are continual. Hiding places are few. Although little sore spots and irritations remain for each individual, it is difficult to imagine work roles being more defined (and accepted) than those at Disneyland. Here, it seems, is a work culture worthy of the name.

NOTES

1. The quote is drawn from a transcript of a speech made to senior managers of Hurrah's Club by Bill Ross, Vice President for Human Relations at Disneyland, in January, 1988. Elsewhere in this account I draw on other in-house publications to document my tale. Of use in this regard are "Your Role in the Show" (1982), "Disneyland: The First Thirty Years" (1985), "The Disney Approach to Management" (1986), and Steven Birnbaum's semi-official travel guide to Disneyland (1988). The best tourist guide to the park I've read is Sehlinger's (1987) adamantly independent *The Unofficial Guide to Disneyland.*

2. This account is drawn primarily on my three-year work experience as a "permanent part-time" ride operator at Disneyland during the late 1960s. Sporadic contacts have been maintained with a few park employees and periodic visits, even with children in tow, have proved instructive. Also, lengthy, repeated beach interviews of a

most informal sort have been conducted over the past few summers with ride operators (then) at the park. There is a good deal written about Disneyland, and I have drawn from these materials as indicated in the text. I must note finally that this is an unsponsored and unauthorized treatment of the Disneyland culture and is at odds on several points with the views set forth by management.

3. The author serves as a case in point for I was fired from Disneyland for what I still consider a Mickey Mouse offense. The specific violation—one of many possible—involved hair growing over my ears, an offense I had been warned about more than once before the final cut was made. The form my dismissal took, however, deserves comment for it is easy to recall and followed a format familiar to an uncountable number of ex-Disneylanders. Dismissal began by being pulled off the ride after my work shift had begun by an area supervisor in full view of my cohorts. A forced march to the administration building followed where my employee card was turned over and a short statement read to me by a personnel officer as to the formal cause of termination. Security officers then walked me to the employee locker room where my work uniforms and equipment were collected and my personal belongings returned to me while an inspection of my locker was made. The next stop was the time shed where my employee's time card was removed from its slot, marked "terminated" across the top in red ink, and replaced in its customary position (presumably for Disneylanders to see when clocking on or off the job over the next few days). As now an ex-ride operator, I was escorted to the parking lot where two security officers scraped off the employee parking sticker attached to my car. All these little steps of status degradation in the Magic Kingdom were quite public and, as the reader might guess, the process still irks. This may provide the reader with an account for the tone of this narrative,

although it shouldn't since I would also claim I was ready to quit anyway since I had been there far too long. At any rate, it may just be possible that I now derive as much a part of my identify from being fired from Disneyland as I gained from being employed there in the first place.

4. These tactics are covered in some depth in Van Maanen (1976, 1977) and Van Maanen and Schein (1979). When pulled together and used simultaneously, a people processing system of some force is created that tends to produce a good deal of conformity among recruits who, regardless of background, come to share very similar occupational identities, including just how they think and feel on the job. Such socialization practices are common whenever recruits are bunched together and processed as a batch and when role innovation is distinctly unwanted on the part of the agents of such socialization.

5. The unofficial answer to this little gem of a question is: "Under Sleeping Beauty's castle." Nobody knows for sure since the immediate circumstances surrounding Walt Disney's death are vague—even in the most careful accounts (Mosley, 1983; Schickel, 1985). Officially, his ashes are said to be peacefully at rest in Forest Lawn. But the deep freeze myth is too good to let go of because it so neatly complements all those fairy tales Disney expropriated and popularized when alive. What could be more appropriate than thinking of Walt on ice, waiting for technology's kiss to restore him to life in a hidden vault under his own castle in the Magic Kingdom?

REFERENCES

Birnbaum, S. 1988. *Steve Birnbaum Brings You the Best of Disneyland*. Los Angeles, CA: Hearst Publications Magazines.

Hickey, J. V., W. E. Thompson, and D. L. Foster. 1988. "Becoming the Easter Bunny: Socialization into a Fantasy Role."

Journal of Contemporary Ethnography, 17, pp. 67–95.

King, M. J. 1981. "Disneyland and Walt Disney World: Traditional Values in Futuristic Form." *Journal of Popular Culture*, 15, pp. 116–140.

Mosley, L. 1983. *Disney's World.* New York: Stein and Day.

Peters, T. J., and R. H. Waterman. 1982. *In Search of Excellence.* New York: Harper & Row.

Schickel, R. 1985. *The Disney Version* (rev. ed.). New York: Simon & Schuster. (Original work published 1968.)

Schwartz, P., and J. Lever. 1976. "Fear and Loathing at a College Mixer." *Urban Life,* 4, pp. 413–432.

Sehlinger, B. 1987. *The Unofficial Guide to Disneyland.* New York: Prentice-Hall.

Smith, R. C., and E. M. Eisenberg. 1987. "Conflict at Disneyland: A Root Metaphor Analysis." *Communication Monographs*, 54, pp. 367–380.

Van Maanen, J. 1976. *Breaking-in: Socialization to Work.* In R. Dubin, ed. Handbook of Work, Organization, and Society, pp. 67–130. Chicago, IL: Rand McNally.

Van Maanen, J. 1977. "Experiencing Organization." In J. Van Maanen, ed. *Organizational Careers,* pp. 15–45. New York: John Wiley.

Van Maanen, J. 1988. *Tales of the Field: On Writing Ethnography.* Chicago: University of Chicago Press.

Van Maanen, J., and S. R. Barley. 1985. "Cultural Organization: Fragments of a Theory." In P. J. Frost, L. F. Moore, M. R. Louis, C. C. Lundberg, and J. Martin, eds. *Organizational Culture.* Beverly Hills, CA: Sage.

Van Maanen, J., and G. Kunda. 1989. "Real Feelings: Emotional Expressions and Organization Culture." In B. Staw and L. L. Cummings, eds. *Research in Organization Behavior,* Vol. 11, pp. 43–103. Greenwich, CT: JAI Press.

Van Maanen, J., and E. H. Schein. 1979. "Toward a Theory of Organizational Socialization." In B. Staw and L. L. Cummings, eds. *Research in Organization Behavior,* Vol. 1, pp. 209–269. Greenwich, CT: JAI Press.

Waller, W. 1937. "The Rating and Dating Complex." *American Sociological Review,* 2, pp. 727–734.

CLASS NOTE: DISNEY GOES TO TOKYO

In the mid-1970s, the Oriental Land Company, a Japanese development company that owned a large tract of landfill east of Tokyo zoned for public leisure activities, approached Disney with the idea of building a Disneyland in Japan. In that era of conservative management at Walt Disney Productions, Disney management was hesitant about the idea. After all, Japan was far away, very distant in terms of culture, and Tokyo not only had much colder winters than California or Florida but had to endure a lengthy rainy season in June and July. After exploring alternative sites at some length, however, it decided to go ahead. Nevertheless, it insisted on a deal that left Oriental Land with virtually all of the risk: instead of taking an ownership position in Tokyo Disneyland, Disney demanded royalties of 10% of the revenues from admissions and rides, and 5% of the receipts from food, beverages, and souvenirs. Disney also demanded artistic control of the park; its partner, with its experience in development projects in Tokyo, looked after the complex relationships with local planning and regulatory authorities, financing, and adjacent development.

According to most observers, Tokyo Disneyland seems at first glance to be "a physical and social copy of Disneyland in Southern California—a clone created six-thousand miles distant" (John Van Maanen, 1992, p. 8). Disney's Imagineers were at first interested in adapting some of the attractions to the Japanese context—Samurai-land instead of Frontierland, for example. But their Japanese partner resisted strongly efforts to "localize" Disneyland, and persuaded the Imagineers that what would best attract Japanese was a park that replicated as closely as possible the American original (Brannen, 1992). They pointed out that Disney characters were very familiar to Japanese—indeed, Japanese television had carried a highly popular dubbed version of the Mickey Mouse Club for many years, and Disney movies were wildly popular in Japan.

The park opened in April, 1983. The weather was cold, and opening day drew fewer people than anticipated. But by August it drew 93,000 people in a single day, higher than the record one-day attendance records in the U.S. parks (Brannen and Wilson, 1996). By the late 1980s, it was drawing over 15 million people a year, considerably more than either of the U.S. parks. By 1993, ten years after its opening, Tokyo Disneyland had welcomed 125 million visitors, a number, as Brannen and Wilson have pointed out, roughly equal to the population of Japan. Nine out of ten customers were repeat visitors. Tokyo Disneyland has become a favorite destination for the regular school trips that are a feature of Japanese school life. It is also a favorite family vacation in a land of extremely short vacations, and excellent train connections with Tokyo make it an ideal weekend outing for the family. Many young couples prefer it for special dates, and honeymoon packages draw newlyweds from all over Japan. Tokyo Disneyland has even coopted traditional holidays in Japan: "Look, for example, at Tokyo Disneyland's celebration of New Year's Day—perhaps the most serious of Japanese holidays, when people customarily ring out the evils of the old year with 100 rings of a temple bell. Now there's an annual New Year's party at Tokyo Disneyland. This is even so popular that in 1991 it drew in 139,000 people, including a large percentage of young lovebirds who reserved a room at the Tokyo Disneyland Hotel over a year in advance" (Brannen and Wilson 1996, p. 100). And the park's location, relatively close to Narita Airport, Japan's major international gateway, has drawn a growing number of visitors from other Asian countries.

© 25 ACADEMIC

The new management at Walt Disney Company watched as their royalties provided a steadily growing income stream but their Japanese partner, which had borne virtually all of the risk of the venture, enjoyed more of the profits. Oriental Land collected not only the lion's share of the park's revenues but also virtually all the profits from the hotels and adjacent developments around Tokyo Disneyland. The rapid success of the park seemed to prove that Disneyland was a global product that could readily move across national and cultural boundaries. As John Van Maanen puts it, "The company line is that what Japanese customers experience is pure, undiluted Americana. All is a direct copy. This may, of course, be merely an official position, privately scoffed at back at Disney headquarters. But, if so, the public line is pervasive and consistent. Another Disney official, blissfully ignoring the role their partner played in the story, told the New York Times (April 18, 1991): 'We really tried to avoid creating a Japanese version of Disneyland . . . . We wanted to create a real Disneyland" (Van Maanen, 1992, p. 9).

A closer analysis suggests, however, that Tokyo Disneyland has involved more departures from the original model than this indicates. The following article provides you with some of that analysis.

26

ACADEMIC

DISPLACING DISNEY: SOME NOTES ON THE FLOW OF CULTURE

by John Van Maanen

THE TRANSFORMATION

Disneyland went international in 1983 with the opening of its Tokyo operation. As noted on the surface, it claims to be a near perfect replica of the Disneyland production minus a few original attractions. There are some recognized modifications but these are imports selected from the Magic Kingdom instead of Disneyland (e.g., Cinderella's Castle and the Mickey Mouse Theater). In terms of organizational control, it is as decentralized as they come—the Oriental Land Company, a Japanese development and property management firm, took full control shortly after the park was built and now provides Walt Disney Enterprises with a rough ten-percent cut of Tokyo Disneyland's profits from admissions, food, and merchandise sales. A small American management team ("Disnoids") remains in Japan as advisors and consultants to keep the park in tune with Disney doctrine and the firm hires a handful of non-Japanese employees, mainly Americans, as "cast members" (entertainers, crafts people, and characters) strategically scattered throughout the park. The question I now raise concerns the flow of culture from the west to the east. To what extent does Tokyo Disneyland mean the same thing to its new patrons as it means to its old?

In a nutshell, Tokyo Disneyland does not work, indeed, cannot work, in the same way as its American counterpart. The cultural meaning of the park shifts significantly. This is not to say that the symbols and Disney narratives are meaningless in the Japanese context. Such a view could

not begin to explain the popularity of the park which, in 1991, outdrew Disneyland by nearly five million customers (*European Elan*, October 18-20, 1991). But, what does appear to be happening is the recontextualization of the American signs so that the Japanese are able to make them their own. This process may be highly general and something of the norm for cultural transformations.

Most observers of modern Japan note the country's penchant for the importation of things foreign, from public bureaucracies (Westney, 1987) to fashion (Stuart, 1987); to language (Mirua, 1979; Kachru, 1982); to baseball (Whiting, 1977). In fact, Japan's widescale adoption of things American is now something of a universal cliché. The choice of imports is, however massive, highly selective. From this perspective, the consumption of foreign goods in Japan seems less an act of homage than a way of establishing a national identity of making such imports their own through combining them in a composite of all that the Japanese see as the "best" in the world. Some of this conspicuous consumption correlates with significant increases in per capita disposable income and what appears to be a new and more relaxed attitude among the Japanese toward leisure and play (Fallows, 1989; Emmott, 1989). But, whatever the source of this omnivorous appetite, the Japanese seem unworried that their cultural identity is compromised by such importation.

Not to be overlooked, however, are the subtle, sometimes hidden, ways alien forms are not merely imported across cultural boundaries but, in the very process, turned into something else again and the indigenous and foreign are combined into

27

Source: From John Van Maanen, "Displacing Disney: Some Notes on the Flow of Culture," *Qualitative Sociology*, Vol. 15, no. 1, 1992, pp. 5–35. Reprinted by permission of Plenum Publishing Corporation.

an idiom more consistent with the host culture than the home culture. Several features of the way Disneyland has been emulated and incorporated in the Japanese context bear mention. Each suggest that Tokyo Disneyland takes on a rather different meaning for workers and customers alike in its new setting.

Consider the way Tokyo Disneyland is made comfortable for the Japanese in ways that contrast with its California counterpart. In some ways, the fine tuning of the park's character follows a domestication principle familiar to anthropologists, whereby the exotic, alien aspects of foreign objects are set back and de-emphasized, replaced by an intensified concern with the more familiar and culturally sensible aspects (Wallace, 1985; Douglas, 1966). Thus the safe, clean, courteous, efficient aspects of Disneyland fit snugly within the Japanese cultural system and can be highlighted. Disneyland as "the best of America" suits the Japanese customer with its underscored technological wizardry and corporate philosophy emphasizing high quality service. Providing happiness, harmony, and hospitality for guests by a staff that is as well-groomed as the tended gardens is certainly consistent with Japanese practices in other consumer locales (Vogel, 1979; Taylor, 1983; Dore, 1987). The legendary sotto voice, stylized gestures and scripted interaction patterns used by Japanese service providers in department stores, hotels, elevators, and shops is merely a slight step away from the "people specialist" of planned exuberance and deferential manners turned out by the University of Disneyland in the United States—at least in theory if not in practice (Van Maanen, 1990). And, "Imagineering," a smart Disney term used to designate the department responsible for the design of park attractions ("the engineers of imagination"), is used for public purposes in Japan, as in the United States, without a touch of irony or awareness of contradiction.

If anything, the Japanese have intensified the orderly nature of Disneyland. If Disneyland is clean, Tokyo Disneyland is impeccably clean; if Disneyland is efficient,

Tokyo Disneyland puts the original to shame by being absurdly efficient, or, at least, so says *Business Week* (March 12, 1990). While Disneyland is a version of order, sanitized, homogenized, and precise; Tokyo Disneyland is even more so, thus creating, in the words of one observer, "a perfect toy replica of the ideal tinkling, sugarcoated society around it, a perfect box within a box" (Iyer, 1988, p. 333). One of the charms of both Disneyland and Disney World to American visitors is the slight but noticeable friction between the seamless perfection of the place and the intractable, individualistic, irredeemable, and sometimes intolerable character of the crowd. In the midst of its glittering contraptions and mannerly operatives are customers strolling about wearing "shit happens" or "dirty old man" T-shirts. Tourists in enormous tent dresses, double-knit leisure suits and high-prep Brooks Brothers outfits share space in the monkey car of Casey Jones's Circus Train with tattooed bikers, skinheads, and Deadheads. Obese men and women wearing short shorts mingle and queue up with rambunctious teenagers on the make, all to be crammed onto hurling, clockwork bobsleds and sent on their way for a two-minute roller-coaster ride. Park police— dressed as U.S. Marshals or tin-horn cops—chase down the little criminals of Disneyland on Tom Sawyer's Island or Main Street as irate parents screech at their offspring to wipe the chocolate off their faces, keep their hands off the merchandise, and behave themselves. For the Disneyland patron, such contrasts give life to the park and provide a degree of narrative tension.

In Tokyo, the shadow between the ideal and reality is not so apparent. Adults and children bend more easily toward the desired harmonious state and out of order contrasts are few and far between inside (and perhaps, outside) the park. This is a society where the word for different means wrong and "the nail that sticks out is the nail that must be hammered down" (Bayley, 1976; Kamata, 1980, White, 1987). To the extent that there is order in Tokyo Disneyland is expected and largely taken-for-granted such that the park glides effortlessly rather than lurching self-consciously toward its fabled efficiency. Iyer (1988, p. 317–318) summarizes his visit to Tokyo Disneyland in the following way:

> There was no disjunction between the perfect rides and their human riders. Each was as synchronized, as punctual, as clean as the other. Little girls in pretty bonnets, their eyes wide with wonder, stood in lines, as impassive as dolls, while their flawless mothers posed like mannequins under their umbrellas. (They) waited uncomplainingly for a sweet-voiced machine to break the silence and permit them to enter the pavilion—in regimented squads. All the while, another mechanized voice offered tips to ensure that the human element would be just as well planned as the man-made: Do not leave your shopping to the end, and try to leave the park before rush hour, and eat at a sensible hour, and do not, under any circumstances, fail to have a good time.

Such failures to have a good time are rare partly because of the way Tokyo Disneyland has rearranged the model to suit its customers. Despite its claim as a duplicate, a number of quite specific changes have taken place and more are planned. The amusement park itself is considerably larger than Disneyland (124 acres to 74). As a result, it loses some of its uncharacteristic intimacy in a Southern California setting but gives off a feeling of conspicuous spaciousness rather unusual in greater Tokyo, where it seems every square inch is fully utilized. Disneyland's fleet of Nautilus-like submarines is missing perhaps because of Japan's deep sensitivity to all things nuclear. There are a few outdoor food vendors in the park but over forty sit-down restaurants, about twice the number in Disneyland. It is considered rude to eat while walking about in Japan—the munching of popcorn in the park being apparently the only exception.

Several new attractions have been added in Tokyo. Each are quite explicit about what culture is, in the final analysis, to be celebrated in the park. One, incongruously called "Meet the World," offers not only a history of Japan but an elaborate defense of the Japanese way. In this regard, it is not unlike Disneyland's "Meet Mr. Lincoln" where visitors are asked at one point to sing a passionate version of "America the Beautiful" along with the mechanical icon of Honest Abe. In "Meet the World," a sagacious crane guides a young boy and his sister through the past, pausing briefly along the way to make certain points such as the lessons learned by the Japanese cave dwellers ("the importance of banding together") or the significance of the Samurai warrior ("we never became a colony") or the importance of early foreign trade ("to carry the seeds offered from across the sea and cultivate them in our own Japanese garden"). Another site-specific attraction in Tokyo Disneyland is the Magic Journey movie trip across five continents which culminates, dramatically, in the adventure's return to "our beloved Japan where our hearts always remain."

Another singular attraction in Tokyo Disneyland is situated inside Cinderella's Castle and produced as a tightly-packed mystery tour through a maze of dark tunnels, fearsome electronic tableaux, and narrow escapes. Groups of about 15 to 20 persons are escorted through this breathless 13 minute adventure in the castle by lively tour guides. Little passivity is apparent on this attraction as customers whoop and holler to one another and race wildly through the castle trailing their tour guide. The climactic moment of the tour takes place when the guide selects from the group a single representative to do battle with a menacing evil sorcerer. The chosen hero or heroine is provided a laser sword and, backed by nifty special effects and timely coaching from the tour guide, manages to slay the dark lord just in the nick of time. The group is thus spared, free again for further adventures in the park. The attraction ends with a mock-solemn presentation of a medal to the usually bashful group savior who then leads everyone out the exit after passing down an aisle formed by applauding fellow members of the mystery tour.

It is hard to imagine a similar attraction working in either Disneyland or Disney World. Not only would group discipline be lacking such to insure that all members of the tour would start and end together but selecting a sword bearer to do battle with the Evil One would quite likely prove to be a considerable test for the tour guides when meeting with the characteristic American chorus of "Me, Me, Me" coming from children and adults alike. The intimacy, proximity and physical, almost hands-on, interaction between customers and amusement sources found in Tokyo Disneyland are striking to a visitor accustomed to the invisible security and attention given to damage control so prevalent in the U.S. parks. Tokyo Disneyland puts its guests within touching distance of many of its attractions, such that a customer who wished to could easily deface a cheerful robot, steal a Small World doll, or behead the Mad Hatter. This blissful audience respect for the built environment at Tokyo Disneyland allows ride operators to take more of an exhibitory stance to their attraction than a custodial one, which is often the perspective of Disneyland operatives (Van Maanen and Kunda, 1989).

Other distinctly Japanese touches include the white gloves for drivers of the transportation vehicles in the park, a practice drawn from the taxi and bus drivers in Japan; name tags for employees featuring last names rather than first names; a small picnic area just outside the park for families bringing traditional box lunches to the park, a reminder of family customs in Japan and a compromise on the Disney tradition of allowing no food to be brought into the park. All ride soundtracks and spiels are, of course, in Japanese and one American visitor reports considerably more ad-libbing on the part of the Japanese ride operators compared to their American counterparts (Brannen, 1990). The sign boards are dominated by English titles (Romaji) but all have subtitles in Japanese.[11] Such concessions to the Japanese guest contrast with the proclamation of a pure copy. One might argue that such changes are minor adjustments in keeping with the fundamental marketing techniques of both capitalistic societies, namely, tailoring the product to its audience. But, it is also important to keep in mind that even the notion of consumer capitalism in the two contexts varies systematically.

Main Street U.S.A., for example, has become in Tokyo, the World Bazaar. Little remains of the turn-of-the-century midwestern town of Walt's slippery memory. The World Bazaar is quite simply an enormous, modern, up-scale shopping mall where many of the products (and possibilities) of the five continents are brought together in a post-modern Disney collage that is distinctly Japanese. Few modest trinkets are on sale at the World Bazaar but instead costly, high status items are offered, all bearing an official Disney label and wrapped in Tokyo Disneyland paper suitable for the gift giving practices of the Japanese as outlined by Brannen (1990). Frontierland's presentations of the continental expansion of the United States has given way to Westernland, which is apparently understood only through the Japanese familiarity with the Wild West imagery of American movies, television, and pulp fiction. Thus, to the extent that nostalgia, patriotism and historical narratives provide the context of meaning for visitors to Disneyland, visitors to Tokyo Disneyland are made comfortable by devices of their own making. While the structure may appear quite similar, the meaning is not.

Take, for example, something as fundamental as the physical design of Tokyo Disneyland. The very layout of the park seems to be something of a mystery and cultural maze for many Japanese visitors. Far more customers in Tokyo are seen wandering hesitantly through the park with a map in hand than in the United States where customers, by contrast, appear quite confident and determined while strolling about the park. Certain attractions, too, are apparently decoded by the Japanese only with difficulty (and, perhaps, with the help of the guidebook passed out at the front gate). Notoji (1988) quotes some native informants in this regard. One, a middle-age and -class Japanese housewife says:

I went to see the Pirates of the Caribbean at Tokyo Disneyland because the guidebook said it was a must. I had no idea what to expect and I didn't quite understand why they had to have the Pirates of the Caribbean there. The word "the Caribbean" has no meaning to me except for the image of an expensive yacht cruise for some rich folks. I didn't know that pirates once lived there until I saw this attraction at Tokyo Disneyland. Yes, the pirate robots were very well made and their firing of cannon balls at the seaport town was realistic. But so what?

Another, an elderly Japanese woman, remarks:

I didn't understand what the whole thing was trying to say. What impressed me was that the fireflies were computerized. That Americans would go through such trouble to do such things. You know, we used to have Japanese pirates around the Inland Sea, but we are more familiar with those mountain bandits who raided and stripped the travelers naked. I would have understood it if they had these bandits on the show instead of the Caribbean pirates.

In these cases it seems that unless the park visitor is familiar with western-style pirate stories, the ride—as a symbol of exotic adventure, wicked deeds, and the pursuit of treasure and pleasure—simply fails to work. It may of course become something else again. Virtually all of Notoji's informants were taken by the mechanical gimmickry employed on the ride, impressed more by the "movements of the chicken robots and cat robots" than by the narrative. The pirates, to these visitors at least, are simply clever robots doing some incomprehensible things. This may well be the response generated by other attractions in Tokyo Disneyland, such as the Enchanted Tiki Room, the Haunted Mansion, and Bear Country Jamboree; attractions that on the surface at least seem to offer little symbolic worth to the Japanese.

Not all rides fall into this category. Many Japanese children and adults are quite familiar with other western stories and fairy tales. Moreover, Disney editions of some of these stories are so widely circulated that many Japanese children, like their American counterparts, believe Alice in Wonderland, Peter Pan, and Snow White are the products of Walt Disney's imagination. Those who know these tales have little trouble no doubt understanding and enjoying the attractions keyed to them in a way that the ride-designers would appreciate. But, even for the most well-versed of visitors, there remain crucial contextual differences that will not go away and produce for the Japanese in Tokyo Disneyland a rather different cultural experience than what most American expect and take away from their visits to the old parks at home.

This shift in meaning can perhaps best be appreciated by considering some aspects of the emulation process at Tokyo Disneyland that run counter to some of our more benign (or, at least, calming) beliefs about the workings of culture flows. Tokyo Disneyland serves as something of a shrine in Japan to Japan itself, an emblem of the self-validating beliefs as to the cultural values and superiority of the Japanese. Disneyland serves as such a shrine in America, of course, but it is America that is celebrated. How is it that a painstaking near-copy of what is undeniably an American institution—like baseball—can function to heighten the self awareness of the Japanese?

The answer lies in the workings of culture itself, for culture is not only an integrating device, but a differentiating device as well, a way of marking boundaries. Tokyo Disneyland does so in a variety of ways. One already mentioned is the outdoing of Disneyland in the order-keeping domain. The message coming from Japan (for the Japanese) is simply "anything you can do, we can do as well (or better)." If one of the characteristic features of modern Japan is its drive toward perfection, it has built a Disneyland that surpasses its model in terms of courtesy, size, efficiency, cleanliness, and performance. Were the park built more specifically to Japanese tastes and cultural aesthetics, it would undercut any contrast to the original in this regard. While Disneyland is

31

PRESS

reproduced in considerable detail, it is never deferred to entirely, thus making the consumption of this cultural experience a way of marking the boundaries between Japan and the United States. Japan has taken in Disneyland only, it seems, to take it over.

Consider, also, another cultural flow analogous to the way Disneyland itself treats the foreign and exotic. Tokyo Disneyland maintains, indeed amplifies, Self and Other contrasts consistent with Japanese cultural rules. Only Japanese employees wear name tags in the park, the foreign (western) employees do not. Americans hired to play Disney characters such as Snow White, Cinderella, Prince Charming, Alice in Wonderland, Peter Pan, or the Fairy Godmother are nameless, thus merging whatever personalized identities they may project with that of their named character. Other western employees such as craftsmen (e.g., glass blowers, leather workers), dancers, magicians, musicians, and role-playing shopkeepers also remain tag-less. Musicians play only American songs—ranging from the Broadway production numbers put on the large stage settings of the park to the twangy country-western tunes played by a small combo in a fake saloon of Westernland. During the Christmas season, songs such as Rudolf the Red-Nosed Reindeer, Silent Night, and the Hallelujah Chorus of Handel's Messiah are piped throughout the appropriately festooned park as a portly American Santa Claus poses for snapshots with couples and families who wait patiently in long queues for such a photo opportunity. The gaijin (literally "outside person") ordinarily speak only English while in role which furthers their distinctiveness in the setting. Mary Yoki Brannen (1990) writes of these practices:

> . . . rather than functioning as facilitators of the Disneyland experience like their Japanese counterparts, gaijin employees are put on display. Gaijin cast members are displayed daily in a group at the place of honor at the front of the Disneyland parade, and gaijin craftspersons are displayed throughout the day at

their boxed-in work stations not unlike animals in cages at the zoo.

The same general practice is followed at Disneyland where, of course, the roles are reversed and the "Others" are constructed out of different cultural building blocks. Just as blacks are more notable at Disneyland for their absence from the productions and the work force, Koreans are conspicuously absent in Tokyo Disneyland, victims, it seems, of the facial politics of Asia. Villains of the Disney narratives produced in the United States seem often to speak and act with vaguely foreign personae and accents, typically, but not always, Russian or German; evil in Tokyo Disneyland is represented by gaijin witches, goblins, and ghosts whose accents are distinctly non-Japanese. Such a practice of sharply separating gaijin from society mirrors other Japanese cultural productions such as the popular television shows devoted to portraying gaijin stupidities (Stuart, 1987) or the practice of limiting the number of baseball players on professional teams to two gaijin players per team (Whiting, 1989). The outsiders may be accorded respect but they are not to come too close for the culture provides no easy space for them.

CULTURAL EXPERIENCE REVISITED

These contrasts in meaning across the two parks could be extended considerably. The point, however, is not to enumerate all the amplifications, deflations, twists, or reversals in meaning but to note their pervasive presence. The Japanese cultural experience in Tokyo Disneyland is akin to a "foreign vacation" with a number of comforting homey touches built into a visit. The park is seen by the Japanese primarily as a simulated chunk of America put down by the Tokyo Bay. Passports are not required but guide books come in handy.

The perfect copy of Disneyland turns out therefore to be anything but perfect at the level of signification. If Disney is the merchant of nostalgia at home, he is the merchant of gimmickry, glitz, and gaijins in Tokyo. If Disneyland sucks the difference out of differences by presenting an altogether tamed and colonized version of the people of other lands who are, when all is said and done, just like the good folks living in Los Angeles or Des Moines, Tokyo Disneyland celebrates differences by treating the foreign as exotic, its peoples to be understood only in terms of the fact that they are not Japanese and not, most assuredly, like the good people of Osaka or Kyoto.

In this regard, both parks are isolated by a belief in their own cultural superiority. It would be asking too much perhaps of a commercial enterprise to question such a belief since the corporate aim in both settings is, in crude terms, to build and manage an amusement park such that people will come (and come again) to be run assembly-line fashion through its attractions and stripped of their money. But, in the cracks, Tokyo Disneyland offers some intriguing lessons in culture flow beyond the mere fact of its existence. I have three in mind.

First, the presentation of "the best in America" in Japan breaks some new ground and contributes modestly to what might be called post-modernism by combining cultural elements in new ways and then allowing customers and workers alike to develop the logic of the relationship. Thus, Mickey Mouse, a symbol of the infantile and plastic in America, can come to stand for what is fashionable and perky in Japan and used to sell adult apparel and money market accounts. This is not simply a matter of the Japanese appropriating Mickey but rather signals a process by which selected alien imports are reconstituted and given new meaning.

Second, not only are cultural meanings worked out rather differently in a new setting compared to the old and such adaptation takes time; but, as culture flows continue, people on both sides of the border become more aware of their own culture (and its contradictions). The traffic flow is messy but, as cultures move back and forth, people on both sides may discover new ways to do things and new things to do that might not have been apparent within either culture. People are

not passive in relation to culture as if they merely receive it, transmit it, express it. They also create it and new meanings may eventually emerge as cultures interpenetrate one another. The notions of family entertainment, safe thrills, and urban leisure will surely never be the same in Japan since Tokyo Disneyland appeared on the scene.[12] A recent poll in Japan, for example, reported that over fifty per cent of Japanese adults when asked "where they experienced their happiest moment in the last year" responded by saying "Tokyo Disneyland" (Iyer, 1988).

Third, the view that cultural influences move easily along the tracks of massification—mass media, mass production, mass marketing, mass consumerism—ushering in a global culture which spells the eclipse of national and local cultures is certainly discredited by Tokyo Disneyland. This view is I think naive to the point of banality. While our understanding of cultural flows remains woefully inadequate, we do know that cultural acquisition is a slow, highly selective, and contextually-dependent matter. Culture cannot be simply rammed down people's throats. As individual identity and membership distinctions become blurred, culture must be approached more as a rhetorical front than a felt reality. Thus, when a CEO of a multinational corporation refers to his firm as "a family" or when government leaders reach out and try to project the idea of a region as a culture, they may often be regarded as engaging in rhetoric or stating an aspiration that is all too obviously missing in practice. The trick in understanding culture flows would seem to be in finding the level where culture becomes more than an oratorical abstraction and begins to turn on experience, feeling, and consciousness. Here, then, is where meaning will be marked and cultural imports embraced, rejected, or perhaps most commonly, transformed.

All this is to say that cultural flows are loose, on-going matters. Mickey Mouse has been hanging around Japan for along time and his cultural status has a history that is far from closed or complete. Working out the cultural meaning of

Tokyo Disneyland is also a long-term project that is in all respects rather open. Many of the distinctive Japanese characteristics of the park were absent when the gates were first thrown back and more are surely to come.

ENDNOTES

11. English may be as much a graphic code in Japan as a linguistic one (Barthes, 1982). It is perhaps the case that the literal meaning of English phrases (on T-shirts, sweatshirts, merchandise, etc.) is no more important than the pleasant appearance of the script. Full-gibberish seems unacceptable however even if the consumers are indifferent (allegedly) to meaning. How indifferent they may be is always a question when an English-speaking observer spots sweatshirt messages of the following kind in Japan: "Hotscoop," "Always Cherry and Wild," "Action God Speed," and, my favorite, "Post-Modern Boy" (worn by a girl). It may also be that the use of English signs in Tokyo-Disneyland (and Japan itself) is something of a symbol for the modern, international spirit the Japanese seem to savor on occasion. On message shirts, see, Manning (1991).

12. On this point, a global tidal wave is seemingly building in the amusement trade. The number of theme parks is growing rapidly at the moment. Eight parks (not including Euro Disneyland) are scheduled to open in Europe over the next few years. Japan has recently opened Sanrio Puroland ("Hello Kitty"). Sonyland is not far off in the future. Korea's Lotte World opened outside Seoul in March, 1990. The current scramble to break the bank in the theme park business is reminiscent of the amusement boom that struck the United States just after Disneyland first opened. The boom was short-lived. Most of the parks built during that period have long since closed their gates. See, Kyriazi (1981) and Adams (1991).

REFERENCES

Adams, J. 1991. *The American Amusement Park Industry.* Boston: Twayne Publishers.

Barthes, R. 1982. *Empire of Signs.* New York: Hill and Wang.

Bayley, D. 1976. *Forces of Order.* Berkeley: University of California Press.

Birnbaum, S. 1989. *Steve Birnbaum's Guide of Disneyland.* Boston: Houghton Mifflin.

Brannen, M. Y. 1990. "Bwana Mickey": Constructing Cultural Consumption at Tokyo Disneyland. Unpublished paper. School of Management, University of Massachusetts, Amherst.

Britton, D. 1989. The Dark Side of Disneyland. *Art Issues* 4, pp. 3–17.

Dore, R. 1987. *Taking Japan Seriously.* Stanford: Stanford University Press.

Douglas, M. 1966. *Purity and Danger.* London: Routledge and Kegan Paul.

Douglas, M. and B. Isherwood. 1980. *The World of Goods.* London: Penguin.

Eco, U. 1986. *Travels in Hyperreality.* New York: Harcourt Brace Jovanovich.

Emmott, B. 1989. *The Sun Also Sets.* New York: Simon & Schuster.

Fallows, J. 1989. *More Like Us.* Boston: Houghton Mifflin.

Featherstone, M. 1991. *Consumer Culture and Postmodernism.* London: Sage.

Finch, C. 1979. *Walt Disney's America.* New York: Abbeville Press.

Fjellman, S. 1989. It's a Small, Leasable World: Corporate Disney in Florida. Paper presented American Anthropological Association Annual Meetings. Washington D.C. November.

Fjellman, S. 1992. *Vinyl Leaves.* Boulder, Colorado: Westview Press.

Goffman, E. 1969. *Strategic Interaction.* Philadelphia: University of Pennsylvania Press.

Gottdiener, M. 1982. Disneyland: A Utopian Urban Space. *Urban Life* 11, pp. 139-162.

Glover, R. 1991. *The Disney Touch.* Homewood, IL: Irwin.

Gould, S. J. 1979. *The Panda's Thumb.* Boston: Little Brown.

Iyer, P. 1988. *Video Nights in Kathmandu.* New York: Vintage.

Harris, N. 1990. *Cultural Excursions.* Chicago: University of Chicago Press.

Hannerz, U. 1989. Scenarios for peripheral culture. Paper presented at the Symposium on Culture, Globalization and the World-System. State University of New York at Binghampton, April.

Hannerz, U. 1990. Cosmopolitans and locals in world culture. In M. Featherstone ed., *Global Culture.* London: Sage, pp. 237-252.

Irwin, J. 1977. *Scenes.* Newbury Park, CA: Sage.

Kachru, B. ed. 1982. *The Other Tongue: English Across Cultures.* Urbana, IL: University of Illinois Press.

Kamata, S. 1980. *Japan in the Passing Lane.* New York: Random House.

Kasson, J .F. 1978. *Amusing the Millions.* New York: Hill and Wang.

King, M. J. 1981. Disneyland and Walt Disney World: Traditional values in futuristic form. *Journal of Popular Culture* 15, pp. 116-140.

Kyriazi, G. 1981. *The Great American Amusement Parks.* Los Angeles: Castle Books.

Leed, E. 1991. *The Mind of the Traveler.* New York: Basic.

Lowenthal, D. 1985. *The Past is a Foreign Country.* Cambridge: University of Cambridge Press.

Manning, P. K. 1991. Semeiotic ethnographic research. *American Journal of Semiotics* 8, pp. 27-45.

MacCannel, D. 1976. *The Tourist.* New York: Schocken Books.

Marin, L. 1977. Disneyland: A degenerate utopia. Glyph I. Johns Hopkins Textual Studies. Baltimore: Johns Hopkins University Press, pp. 50-66.

Miura, A. 1979. *English Loanwords in Japanese.* Tokyo: Charles Tuttle.

Moore, A. 1980. Walt Disney's World: Bounded ritual and the playful pilgrimage center. *Anthropological Quarterly* 53, pp. 207-218.

Mosley, L. 1983. *Disney's World.* New York: Stein and Day.

Myerhoff, B. 1983. The tamed and colonized imagination in Disneyland. Unpublished paper. Department of Anthropology, University of Southern California.

Notoji, M. 1988. Cultural Boundaries and Magic Kingdom: A comparative symbolic analysis of Disneyland and Tokyo Disneyland. Paper presented at the American Studies Association Annual Meetings, Miami Beach, October 27-30.

Real, M. 1977. *Mass-Mediated Culture.* Englewood Cliffs, New Jersey: Prentice Hall.

Sassen, J. 1989. Mickeymania. *International Management.* November, pp. 32-34.

Schickel, R. 1968. *The Disney Version.* New York: Simon & Schuster (revised, 1985).

Sehlinger, B. 1985. *The Unofficial Guide to Disneyland.* New York: Prentice Hall.

Shearing, C. D. and P. C. Stenning. (1985). From the panopticon to Disney World. In R. Ericson ed. *Perspectives in Criminal Law.* Toronto: University of Toronto Press, pp. 335-349.

Stuart, P. M. 1987. *NihOnsense.* Tokyo: The Japan Times.

Taylor, J. 1983. *Shadows of the Rising Sun.* New York: Morrow.

Urry, J. 1990. *The Tourist Gaze*. London: Sage.

Van Maanen, J. and G. Kunda 1989. Real feelings: emotional expression and organizational culture. B. Staw and L. L. Cummings, eds. *Research in Organization Behavior*, Vol. 11, pp. 43-103.

Van Maanen, J. 1990. The Smile Factory. In P. J. Frost et. al., eds. *Reframing Organizational Culture*. Newbury Park, CA: Sage, pp. 58-76.

Van Maanen, J. 1991. Disney Worlds. *Hallinnon Tutkimus* 3, pp. 227-238.

Van Maanen, J., and A. Laurent (forthcoming). The flow of culture. In E. Westney and S. Ghoshal eds. *Organization Theory and the Multinational Corporation*. London: MacMillan.

Vogel, E. 1979. *Japan as Number One*. Cambridge: Harvard University Press.

Wallace, F. A. C. 1985. Rethinking technology "and" culture. Paper presented for the Mellon Seminar on Technology and Culture. University of Pennsylvania, Department of Anthropology.

Westney, E. 1987. *Imitation and Innovation*. Cambridge: Harvard University Press.

White, M. 1987. *The Japanese Educational Challenge*. New York: Free Press.

Whiting, R. 1977. *The Chrysanthemum and the Bat*. New York: Vintage.

Whiting, R. 1989. *You Gotta Have Wa*. New York: Vintage.

Wolfe, J. C. 1979. Disney World: America's vision of utopia. *Alternative Futures* 2, pp. 72-77.

CLASS NOTE: DISNEYLAND GOES TO EUROPE

The enormous success in Japan led Disney's top managers to decide that Europe offered the next major opportunity for Disneyland. And this time Disney was determined not to let others reap most of the profits. The management team seriously considered two sites: Barcelona in Spain, and Marne-la-Vallee, twenty miles east of Paris. Barcelona had better weather, but it was farther from the affluent population centers of northern Europe, and less easily accessible to major transportation hubs. And the French government, extremely eager to attract the jobs and the development spillovers of Disneyland, offered an extremely attractive deal: 4,800 acres of land at below-market prices, which Disney could re-sell to other developers at any price it could command; low-interest loans from state-owned banks; and plans to extend the high-speed rail network to the park at government expense (Toy et. al., 1990). The French site was chosen in 1985, and after extensive negotiations the final contract for the $2 billion park was signed in 1987 by then-Prime Minister Jacques Chirac and Disney CEO Michael Eisner. In anticipation of the implementation of the Maastricht Treaty, which was to formally change the European Community to the European Union in the year the park was to open, 1992, the park was named Euro Disney.

Although the Walt Disney Company was eager to reap the potential profits from the enterprise, its "suits" were no more enthusiastic than they had ever been about assuming much of the risk. Therefore the structure for the new park was a complicated one. A finance company was set up as the owner of the park, in which Disney took a 17% stake (this is described in greater detail in the article "Mouse Trap," later in this module). A separate company, Euro Disney, was formed to operate the park, of which 49% was owned by the Walt Disney Company. The rest of the shares of Euro Disney were listed on the Paris stock exchange and available to the public, with an opening share price of $11.50. Disney had paid about $1.50 for each of its shares, a fact that, when it became known in the wake of a falling share price in the 1990s, caused considerable public criticism (Solomon, 1994). And Disney made arrangements to collect royalties from Euro Disney on admissions, food, beverages, and souvenirs, similar to those for Tokyo Disneyland.

The business press began to carry stories about possible problems for Euro Disney as early as 1989, when the launch of Euro Disney shares in Paris was met by a group of egg-throwing protesters who managed to pelt Michael Eisner in full view of the press. When Disney began hiring staff for the park, the press carried stories about the demanding conduct and dress code on which Disney insisted, to the dismay of its employees (see the 1991 article below, "France Amazed, Amused by Disney Dress Code," which follows). The company ran into some highly publicized disputes with 16 of its French contractors, which threatened to delay the scheduled opening and were sent to arbitration. Construction costs escalated. And the eagerness of the French government to attract Disney was not matched by French intellectuals. As cultural historian Richard Pells put it:

> "When the park opened in April 1992, writers competed with one another to see whose denunciations were the most hyperbolic. A 'cultural Chernobyl' exclaimed the theater director Ariane Mnouchkine. 'A terrifying giant's step toward world homogenization,' the philosopher Alain Finkielkraut declared. To another commentator, Euro Disney was 'a

37

ACADEMIC

horror made of cardboard, plastic, and appalling colors, a construction of hardened chewing gum and idiotic folklore taken straight out of comic books written for obese Americans.' According to the French intellectuals, Disney commercialized the fairy tales of children everywhere, thereby stifling their dreams and preparing them to become mere spectators and consumers. . . . Worst of all, Disneyland was no longer over *there*, across the ocean, in America, the home of mass culture. Now it was right *here*, in the heart of French civilization, practically within the boundaries of Paris itself" (Pells, 1997, pp. 311–312).

Such criticisms were not abated one whit by Disney's efforts to make the park more "European" than its counterparts elsewhere. In the words of Brannen and Wilson (1996, pp. 99):

"The Walt Disney Company together with the French government decided upon a more locally responsive strategy incorporating many French touches and emphasizing aspects of Disney themes that would be more meaningful to a European clientele. For example, the sources of Disney narratives and fairy tales are attributed back to their European origins, the characters proclaim their roots (Snow White speaks German, Peter Pan is re-situated in London, the Pirates of the Caribbean speak French, and Sleeping Beauty's castle takes back its French name, Le Chateau de la Belle au Bois Dormant—even though the castle is really a diminutive copy of the German castle, Neuschwanstein, built by King Ludwig II), and alcohol is sold on the premises of Disneyland Paris although it is banned at all other Disney locations."

We should note that the serving of alcohol was introduced a year after the park opened, only in response to vociferous visitor complaints.

The problems seemed only to get worse after the opening. Visitors came to the park, but they complained about the lack of restaurant space, the line-ups, and the lack of the friendly service that the park's advertising and their experience of the Disney Parks in the United States had led many of them to expect. One recent commentary noted: "On three out of five visits we noticed bathroom stall doors to be broken and the bathrooms themselves untidy, smiles from service people at restaurants on the park were not only uncommon but in one instance a food server got into a squabble with a customer over whether she had paid or not, and the grounds themselves were littered, with few sidewalk sweepers in sight (a notable fixture at other Disney parks)" (Brannen and Wilson 1996, p. 104).

The relative ease with which the Disney service culture of "the happiest place on earth" was transferred to Tokyo did not prepare the company for the challenges of implementing it in France. One early press story carried the following revealing anecdote: "Disney University, a feature of all company parks, has launched the standard day-and-a-half course in Disney culture, plus job training that can last weeks. 'We have to do more explaining in class,' admits David Kanally, director of the university's Paris branch. Sessions often erupt into debates. One group of French students spent 20 minutes discussing how to define 'efficiency.' Says Kanally: 'That wouldn't happen in Orlando'" (Toy et. al., 1990).

The reaction to the dress and conduct code is covered in detail in the article that follows, and the protests caused Disney to relax some of its limitations. But even so, in 1995 the park was charged with violating French labor law in its efforts to impose its dress code on its French employees (Brannen and Wilson, 1996, pp. 104). French labor law proved to be an unanticipated impediment in other ways as well: it contained far more restrictions on the use of part-time and contingent workers than Disneyland was accustomed to in the United States or Japan. It also saw as illegal some of the major control tools much favored by American managers: the allocation of valued overtime work to the most effervescent and reliable workers, and the speedy dismissal of workers who failed to meet the Disney standards.

Disney's plans for the park were based on meeting fairly ambitious attendance targets. These were indeed met, but the park still lost money. Part of the problem was the accumulated debt, as the article "Mouse Trap" makes clear. But part of the problem was that visitors didn't spend as much as their counterparts in the United States or Japan. They did not stay in the six huge hotels that Disney built next to the park, they spent far less on souvenirs, and many of them were "day-trippers" who spent most of their time in Paris. Americans and Japanese, it turned out, were willing to spend much more on their relatively short vacations than were Europeans, who enjoyed much longer—and cheaper—vacations, and were much less willing to pull their children out of school for a special vacation trip (as in the United States) or to see school trips to Disneyland as an appropriate educational experience (as in Japan). Disney had exacerbated the problems by its pricing policies: staying at one of the Disney hotels was more expensive than staying at a comparable hotel in Paris, souvenirs were very expensive, and admissions charges were higher than in the U.S. parks. The ambitions of Disney to make Euro Disney a primary vacation target (one Disney spokesman proclaimed in 1991 that "We intend to make Paris a sidetrip") proved sadly misplaced (quoted in Van Maanen, 1992).

By 1993, Euro Disney was in very serious trouble (see "Mouse Trap"). Part of the problem was a serious recession in Europe. But the problems went much deeper, and few believed that the recession was the cause of the massive losses that afflicted the park. A new chief executive, Philippe Bourguignon, was appointed to Euro Disney to stem the financial bleeding. The first rescue package proposed by the "suits" from Walt Disney headquarters was indignantly rejected by the most important French stakeholders, the banks. A rescue package was finally approved, one that provided a moratorium on the royalties going to Disney as well as on the interest payments to the banks (*Economist,* 1996). A further step in the turn-around effort was taken in 1994, when the ill-fated name Euro Disney was abandoned in favor of "Disneyland Paris." But as most analysts pointed out, the rescue package and the new name would work only if the park was able to draw more customers, get them to spend more, and at the same time cut its operating costs.

REFERENCES

The Economist. 1996. "The Kingdom Inside a Republic." April 13, pp. 66–67.

Pells, Richard. 1997. *Not Like Us: How Europeans have Loved, Hated, and Transformed American Culture since World War II.* New York: Basic Books.

Solomon, Judy. 1994. "Mickey's Trip To Trouble." *Newsweek* (February 14, 1994), pp. 34–38.

Toy, Stewart, Marc Maremont, and Ronald Grover. 1990. "An American in Paris: Can Disney Work its Magic in Europe?" *Business Week* (March 12, 1990), pp. 34–38.

Van Maanen, John. 1992. "Displacing Disney: Some Notes on the Flow of Culture." *Qualitative Sociology* 15-1, pp. 5–35.

© 39 ACADEMIC

FRANCE AMAZED, AMUSED BY DISNEY DRESS CODE

by Jacques Neher

NOISY-LE-GRAND, FRANCE—Should the French have to shave every day and wear underwear for a Mickey Mouse job? Walt Disney Co., which is in the midst of hiring some 12,000 people to maintain and populate its Euro Disneyland theme park near Paris, thinks so. But in making detailed rules on acceptable clothing, hairstyles, and jewelry, among other things, part of its terms of employment, the company finds itself caught in a legal and cultural dispute.

The controversy has risen above the usual labor squabble as critics in the press, at universities and elsewhere have joined in asking how brash Americans could be so insensitive to French culture, individualism and privacy.

Most of the critics, and many people on the street, seem amazed, if not amused, that Disney found it necessary to put such a subjective and personal hygiene code in writing, and to make its violation a firing offense for everyone, from the actors portraying Mickey and Minnie, who greet visitors, to the chambermaids cleaning hotel rooms.

Disney executives say the planned April 12 opening of the $4.2 billion complex in Marne-La-Vallee, 20 miles (32 kilometers) east of Paris, is unlikely to be delayed by the conflict, which is being investigated by a district court. But they insist that any ruling that bars them from imposing squeaky-clean employment standards could threaten the image and long-term success of the park.

"For us, the appearance code has a great effect from a product identification standpoint," said Thor Degelmann, vice-president for human resources for Euro Disneyland, which has its headquarters in Noisy-Le-Grand. Mr. Degelmann, an American from Los Angeles, is in charge of hiring for the theme park.

"Without it, we wouldn't be presenting the Disney product that people would be expecting." he added. "It would be like going to see a production of 'Hamlet' in which everyone looked different than you expected. Would you ever go again?"

The rules, spelled out in a video presentation for job applicants and detailed in a guidebook, "Le Euro Disneyland Look," go way beyond height and weight standards. They require men's hair to be cut above the collar and ears, with no beards or mustaches. Any tattoos must be covered.

Women must keep their hair in one "natural color" with no frosting or streaking, and they may make only "limited use" of makeup like mascara. False eyelashes, eyeliner and eyebrow pencil are completely off limits. Fingernails can't pass the ends of the fingers.

As for jewelry, women can wear only one earring in each ear, with the earring's diameter no more than two centimeters (about three quarters of an inch). Neither men nor women can wear more than one ring on each hand.

Further, women are required to wear "appropriate undergarments" and only transparent pantyhose, not black or anything with fancy designs. Similar rules are in force at Disney's three other amusement parks in the United States and Japan.

Though a daily bath is not specifically mentioned in the rules, the applicants' video depicts a shower scene and informs applicants that they are expected to show up for work "fresh and clean each day."

In the United States, some unions representing Disney employees have occasionally protested the company's strict appearance code, but with little success.

French labor unions began protesting the regulations in September, when Euro Disneyland opened its "casting center" at its corporate headquarters and began interviewing thousands of applicants who responded to the company's ubiquitous ad campaign, which invited them to "play the role of your life" and to take a "unique opportunity to marry work and magic."

The Communist-led General Confederation of Labor handed out leaflets in front of the center to warn applicants of the appearance code, which represented "an attack on individual liberty," it contended.

A more mainstream union, the French Democratic Confederation of Labor appealed to the Labor Ministry to halt what it termed Disney's violation of "human dignity."

Robert Chabin, an official of the second union, said "no more than 700" employees would be involved in theatrical work at the park—parades, bands and the like—and that for the other positions, the code "cannot be justified by necessity."

French law prohibits employers from restricting individual and collective liberties unless the restrictions can be justified by the nature of the task to be accomplished and are proportional to that end.

But beyond whatever legal prescriptions arise, it is clear that many French people feel stung by the whole episode. Roger Blancpain, a professor of labor law and president of the International Industrial Relations Association, based in Geneva, said Disney's code represented a frontal assault on French and European social standards.

"A certain kind of underwear?" he asked. "There's a limit, and that's going too far."

41

PRESS

M-10

supplemental

MOUSE TRAP

by Peter Gumbel and Richard Turner

PARIS—Europe got its first taste of the management style of Walt Disney Co. when Joe Shapiro started kicking in a door at the luxury Hotel Bristol here.

It was 1986, and Disney was negotiating with the French government on plans to build a big resort and theme park on the outskirts of Paris. To the exasperation of the Disney team, headed by Mr. Shapiro, then the company's general counsel, the talks were taking far longer than expected. Jene-Rene Bernard, the chief French negotiator, says he was astonished when Mr. Shapiro, his patience ebbing, ran to the door of the room and began kicking it repeatedly, shouting, "Get me something else to break!"

Mr. Shapiro says he doesn't remember the incident, though he adds with a laugh, "There were a lot of histrionics at the time." But Disney's kick-down-the-door attitude in the planning, building, and financing of Euro Disney accounts for many of the huge problems that plague the resort, which currently loses $1 million a day because of its sky-high overhead and interest payments on loans. The project is in danger less than two years after opening, as Disney and creditor banks try to work out a costly rescue. The sides are believed to be coming closer to an agreement by a deadline of March 31.

MICKEY'S MISFIRES

The irony is that even though some early French critics called the park an American cultural abomination, public acceptance hasn't been the problem.

European visitors seem to love the place. The Magic Kingdom has attracted an average of just under a million visitors a month, in line with projections, and today it ranks as Europe's biggest paid tourist destination.

Euro Disney's troubles, instead, derive from a different type of culture clash. Europe may have embraced Mickey Mouse, but it hasn't taken to the brash, frequently insensitive and often overbearing style of Mickey's corporate parent. Overly ambitious, Disney made several strategic and financial miscalculations. It relied too heavily on debt—just as interest rates started to rise—and gambled, incorrectly, that the 1980s boom in real estate would continue, letting it sell off assets and pay down the debt quickly. It also made uncharacteristic slips in the park itself, from wrongly thinking Europeans don't eat breakfast to not providing enough toilets for the hundreds of bus drivers.

DISNEY KNOWS BEST

Disney executives declined to comment for this article. In the past, the company has blamed its problems on external factors, including an unexpectedly severe European recession, high interest rates, and the devaluation of several currencies against the French franc. And Disney supporters note that many of the same people now complaining about Disney's aggressiveness were only too happy to sign on with Disney before conditions deteriorated. But Disney's contentious attitude exacerbated the difficulties it encountered by alienating people it needed to work

Source: Peter Gumbel and Richard Turner, "Mouse Trap." *The Wall Street Journal* (March 10, 1994), pp. A1–A12. Reprinted by permission of *The Wall Street Journal*, copyright ©1994, Dow Jones & Company, Inc. All rights reserved worldwide.

with, say many people familiar with the situation. Its answer to doubts or suggestions invariably was: Do as we say, because we know best.

"They were always sure it would work because they were Disney," says Beatrice Descoffre, a French construction-industry official who dealt with the U.S. company.

If Euro Disney had been a financial success, few would have cared. In the project's early days, banks and private investors fell over one another to help finance the deal. S. G. Warburg & Co., a British investment bank that arranged Euro Disney's equity offering in the United Kingdom, put out a brochure describing the project as "relatively low-risk." As of December 31, Euro Disney, which opened in April 1992, had a cumulative loss of 6.04 billion francs, or $1.03 billion.

TARNISHED IMAGE

Now, just when it needs it most, Disney seems to have lost the goodwill it found when it first arrived in Europe—and along with it an unblemished reputation for success. "Tonya Harding just got her first endorsement," comedian Gary Shandling joked at this month's Grammy Awards, referring to the U.S. skater. "They go, `Where are you going?' She says, `I'm going to Euro Disney.'"

In practical terms, Disney's image problem could prove costly. To rescue its 49%-owned affiliate, Disney last October quietly proposed a $2 billion restructuring to the 60 creditor banks, and offered to pick up half the tab. People familiar with the proposal say Disney would have contributed three billion French francs ($520 million) in cash to a rights issue, and waived enough future management fees and royalties to bring its total contribution to $1 billion.

But the banks, feeling they were being steamrolled by Disney, rejected the offer. "They had a formidable image and convinced everyone that if we let them do it their way, we would all have a marvelous adventure," says a top French banker involved in the negotiations. "The Walt Disney group is making a major error in thinking it can impose its will once more."

People familiar with the debt negotiations say Disney and its banks have struck a much more conciliatory tone in just the past couple of weeks, raising hopes that a solution may be at hand.

If an agreement is reached, analysts say, Disney's cash-generating powers are such that it could absorb the blow of spending more than $1 billion in cash and deferred fees to save Euro Disney. More important will be to avoid more write-offs and losses in the future, so Disney can meet the ambitious growth targets it promises its shareholders, and preserve its future fee-earning power if Euro Disney turns around. The alternative for Disney—to walk away—likely would trigger a host of time-consuming lawsuits in France and cause an immeasurable loss of prestige.

Few believe Disney will allow the European resort to fall, even though it has threatened to cut off funding at the end of this month unless it can reach a deal with the banks. Too much rides on the future of Euro Disney for the U.S. company, the creditors, and the French government, which provided $750 million in loans at below-market rates, built road and rail networks to the park, and allowed Disney to buy up huge tracts of land at 1971 prices.

Already, Euro Disney has brought in new management and made other changes to save the project. Even detractors say they have been impressed by the way the company is changing tack, cutting prices, and reducing costs.

CORPORATE HUBRIS

The initial overconfidence of Disney, a company already known for corporate hubris, is perhaps understandable. The current management team of Chairman Michael Eisner and President Frank Wells arrived in late 1984 and immediately began tapping into the theme-park, film, and merchandising riches unmined by their predecessors. In the seven years before Euro Disney opened, they transformed Disney into a company with

45

PRESS

annual revenues of $8.5 billion—up from $1 billion—mainly through internal growth.

"From the time they came on, they had never made a single misstep, never a mistake, never a failure," says a former Disney executive. "There was a tendency to believe that everything they touched would be perfect."

Forged in the go-go culture of California and Florida, where growth seemed limitless, the new Disney team determined it wouldn't repeat two mistakes of years past: letting others build the lucrative hotels surrounding a park, as happened at Disneyland in Southern California, and letting another company own a Disney park, as in Tokyo, where Disney just collects royalties from the immensely profitable attraction.

But this determination exported poorly to Europe, particularly when combined with Mr. Eisner's vow to make Euro Disney the most lavish project Disney had ever built. Though tight with a buck in many ways, Mr. Eisner was almost obsessed with maintaining Disney's reputation for quality. And his designers—the "creative" people with whom he identified—convinced him that in Europe, home of great monuments and elaborate cathedrals, Euro Disney would have to brim with detail. Unlike the Japanese, Europeans wouldn't accept carbon copies of Disneyland and Florida's Walt Disney World, Disney reasoned.

BALLOONING COSTS

In argument after argument, executives say, Mr. Eisner sided with the designers and architects—who had direct access to the chairman's office—and piled on more detail. Even the centerpiece castle in the Magic Kingdom had to be bigger and fancier than in the other parks. So the cost of park construction, estimated at 14 billion francs ($2.37 billion) in 1989, rose by $340 million to 16 billion francs before the opening in April 1992. Construction of the hotels, estimated at 3.4 billion francs, rose to 5.7 billion.

One measure of Disney's overconfidence was a belief that it could predict future living patterns in Paris. Invited to the apartment of French negotiator Mr. Bernard in the western part of the city, where most of the French establishment has long lived, Mr. Eisner one evening boasted, "You live in the west of Paris, as do your friends, but your children and grandchildren will live in the east of Paris" near Euro Disney, Mr. Bernard says. Similarly, Disney executives believed, wrongly, that they could change certain European habits, such as a reluctance to yank their children from school in mid-session as Americans do, or their preference for longer holidays rather than short breaks.

With hindsight, some former executives, bankers, and other say Disney's biggest mistakes were its overambitious plans to develop the site, plus Euro Disney's financial structure itself, which depended on a highly optimistic financial scenario with little room for glitches. Both were creations of Gary Wilson, then the chief financial officer, a man known for his knack for creating financing packages that placed the risk for many Disney projects on outside investors while keeping much of the upside potential for the company. Mr. Wilson, now co-chairman of Northwest Airlines Corp. and still a Disney director, declined comment.

Mr. Wilson set up a finance company to own the park and lease it back to an operating company. This ownership vehicle, in which Disney kept just a 17% stake, was to provide tax losses and borrow huge sums at relatively low rates. Disney would manage the resort for hefty fees and royalties, while owning 49% of the equity in the operating company, Euro Disney SCA. The rest was sold to the public.

The park, moreover, was just the cornerstone of a huge and growing real-estate development by Disney in the area. The initial number of hotel rooms—at 5,200, more than in the entire city of Cannes, was expected to triple in a few years as Euro Disney opened a second theme park to keep visitors at the resort for a longer stay. There would also be office space, which would grow 20 times to a stunning 70,000 square meters, or just slightly smaller than France's biggest office complex, La Defense, in Paris. And the plan called for shopping malls, apartments, golf courses and vacation homes galore. Euro Disney would tightly control the design and build nearly everything itself, selling off the properties in due course at a big profit.

At first, all seemed to work beautifully. Disney's initial equity stake in Euro Disney was acquired for about $150 million, or 10 francs a share, compared with the initial price to investors of 72 francs a share. After the public offering, the value of the company's stake zoomed to $1 billion on the magic of the Disney name, and later to $2.3 billion when the stock peaked just before the park's opening. Today it is worth about $550 million. The company's shares closed at 36.15 francs yesterday on the Paris Stock Exchange.

Dozens of banks, led by France's Banque Nationale de Paris and Banque Indosuez, eagerly signed on to provide construction loans. Euro Disney's total debt stands at about 21 billion francs, or about $3.5 billion. Several European financial institutions, including Lazard Freres—Disney's own adviser—worried that the plan was too clever, according to people familiar with the financing.

"The company was overleveraged. The structure was dangerous," says one banker who saw the figures. The public offering price seemed high, and the proposed financing appeared risky because it relied on capital gains from future real estate transactions, critics charged.

But Disney's attitude, current and former executives say, was that those views reflected the cautious, Old-World thinking of Europeans who didn't understand U.S.-style free-market financing. Those who defend the deal point out that for more than two years after the offering, the stock price continued to swell, and that the initial loans were at a low rate. It was later cost overruns, they say, and the necessity for more borrowing, that handcuffed Euro Disney.

As the European recession started to bite, though, the French real-estate market tumbled, taking with it Disney's hopes that it could quickly sell many of the park's assets, especially the six big hotels. The company also passed up the chance to lessen its burden. "Disney at various points could have had partners to share the risk, or buy the hotels outright," says a Disney executive. "But it didn't want to give up the inside."

GOOD ATTENDANCE

Disney's early worries mainly concerned attendance. If Euro Disney could only meet its target of 11 million visitors in the first year, it reckoned, money would roll in. The target was met, but the reality turned out to be very different And that helps explain why the park is doing reasonably well while Euro Disney is racking up huge losses.

The cost of building was simply too high. In his pursuit of perfection, Mr. Eisner himself ordered several last minute budget-breakers. For example, he removed two steel staircases in Discoveryland because they blocked a view of the Star Tours ride; that cost $200,000 to $300,00, a Disney official estimates. Disney built expensive trams along a lake to take guests from the hotels to the park. People preferred walking. Minibars were placed in economy hotel rooms; they lost money. Disney built an 18-hole golf course, then added nine holes, to adjoin 600 new homes. The homes haven't been built, and the golf courses, which cost $15 million to $20 million, are underused, says a former executive.

Disney and its advisers failed to see signs of the approaching European recession. "We were just trying to keep our heads above water," says one former executive. "Between the glamour and the pressure of opening and the intensity of the project itself, we didn't realize a major recession was coming."

European creditor banks feel they have been victimized by poor communications, too, and resent not being properly appraised of the resort's difficulties, some say. Until last July, Disney continued to say that plans for the development of a second theme park were on track. In November, Euro Disney reported a $905 million loss and Disney itself took a $350 million write-off, covering its initial investment and providing operating capital through March 31. Shortly afterward, Mr. Eisner gave an interview to a French news magazine in which he raised the possibility that Euro Disney could close. Disney advisers, however, say the banks were given regular, detailed financial statements and were just too slow to spot the problems.

Operational errors just made things worse. The policy of serving no alcohol in the park, since reversed, caused astonishment in a country where a glass of wine for lunch is a given. Disney thought Monday would be a light day for visitors, Friday a heavy one, and allocated staff accordingly; the reality was the reverse. The company still is struggling to find the right level of staffing at a park where the number of visitors per day in the high season can be 10 times the number in the low season. Disney, accustomed in Florida to telling an employee, "We don't need you today," has chafed under France's inflexible labor schedules.

The hotel breakfast debacle was another unpleasant surprise. "We were told that Europeans don't take breakfast, so we downsized the restaurants," recalls one executive. "And guess what? Everybody showed up for breakfast. We were trying to serve 2,500 breakfasts in a 350-seat restaurant at [some of the hotels]. The lines were horrendous. And they didn't just want croissants and coffee. They wanted bacon and eggs." Disney reacted quickly, however, with prepackaged breakfasts delivered to rooms and satellite locations.

Another demand, from bus drivers, wasn't anticipated. "The parking space was much too small," says a former executive. "We built restrooms for 50 drivers, and on peak days there were 2,000."

From independent drivers to grumbling bankers, Disney stepped on toe after European toe. Former Disney executives shake their heads when they think about it, because much of Disney's attitude sprang, they say, from a relentless pursuit of quality, the same drive for perfection that has made the company so successful.

"We were arrogant," concedes one executive. "It was like, 'We're building the Taj Mahal and people will come—on our terms.'"

HIGH PRICES

So Disney priced the park and the hotels more to meet revenue targets than to meet demand. Park admission was set at $42.45 for adults, higher than at its U.S. theme parks. A room at the flagship Disneyland Hotel at the park's entrance cost about 2,000 francs, or about $340 a night, the same as a top hotel in Paris. The hotels have been just over half full on average, and guests haven't been staying as long or spending as much as expected on the fairly high-priced food and merchandise.

While visitors to Florida's Disney World tend to stay more than four days, Euro Disney—with one theme park, compared with Florida's three—is a two day experience at most. Many guests arrive early in the morning, rush to the park, come back late at night, then check out the next morning before heading back to the park. There was so much checking-in and checking-out that additional computer stations had to be installed.

Disney executives have frantically lowered most prices in response, but high fixed costs and looming interest payments still are too great a burden without the addition of more development and a second theme park. Euro Disney is, in the words of one senior French banker familiar with the company, "a good theme park married to a bankrupt real-estate company—and the two can't be divorced."

If it didn't foresee all the potential financial pitfalls, Disney clearly realized at the outset that it might encounter cultural problems. It sought to head them off by choosing Robert Fitzpatrick as Euro

Disney's president. He is an American who speaks French, knows Europe well and has a French wife. But he seemed caught in the middle, and quickly came to be regarded with suspicion by some on both sides.

Mr. Fitzpatrick, who was replaced last year by a French native but still does consulting for Disney, declines comment. Officials sympathetic to him say his warnings to Disney management that France shouldn't be approached as if it were Florida were ignored.

While Mr. Fitzpatrick was well acclimated, some of the American managers sent over to start up Euro Disney had their own culture shock. One French manager says he remembers being astonished when an American colleague complained about the cost of Evian bottled water, which is cheaper in France than in the U.S. It turns out the American was going through dozens of bottles per week because he was nervous about using French tap water for anything, including washing. One executive even had his own dog flown over, another manager says.

European executives felt they were in the shadow of Disney corporate types and almost always lost out when the interests of Euro Disney and Disney itself weren't the same. Disney, for example, refused in the early stages of development to renegotiate the management and royalty fees that

it would be paid by Euro Disney; that might have lessened the financial burden on Euro Disney, these executives say.

Unfamiliar with the French market, Disney made mistakes in selecting contractors, French construction-industry officials say. Two general contractors filed for bankruptcy during construction, forcing Disney to pay twice for the work done by subcontractors, once to the failed general contractors and again to the 60 or so smaller firms that carried out the work. Euro Disney won't say how much the double payment cost, but French industry sources peg the amount at about 200 million francs, a number Disney has said is too high.

Bad press has dogged Euro Disney since the opening. Mr. Eisner and his management team dismissed early criticism by scornful French intellectuals as the ravings of an insignificant elite. But the mainstream press, too, described every Disney setback with glee. "There was a perceived arrogance on our part," concedes one former executive. The effect, he adds, was to demoralize the work force and cut down on initial French visitors. "Working for Euro Disney has a very pejorative connotation," says Patrick Roget, a union official at the park. "When I tell people that I work there, they say 'you poor thing.'"

49

PRESS

INDEX

MASSACHUSETTS INSTITUTE OF TECHNOLOGY

ANCONA, KOCHAN, SCULLY,
VAN MAANEN, WESTNEY

MANAGING FOR THE FUTURE

Organizational Behavior & Processes

MANAGING CULTURAL
DIVERSITY

module 11

MODULE 11 (M-11)

MANAGING CULTURAL DIVERSITY

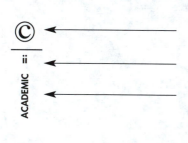

Icon indicates what part you are in, either core © or supplemental ⑤.

Page number.

Within each part there are sections—Module Overview (OVERVIEW), Academic Perspective (ACADEMIC), Popular Press (PRESS), Case (CASE), Exercise (EXERCISE).

Dedicated to those who have inspired us to try to be better students and teachers. Special dedications to

Professor Jack Barbash
Professor Arthur H. Gladstein
Professor Marius B. Jansen
Professor Joanne Martin
Professor Edgar H. Schein

Acquisitions Editor: John R. Szilagyi
Developmental Editor: Jamie Gleich Bryant
Production Editor: Mardell Toomey
Production House: DPS Associates, Inc.
Cover Design: Michael H. Stratton
Marketing Manager: Rob Bloom

ISBN: 0-538-87698-0

1 2 3 4 5 6 7 D1 4 3 2 1 0 9 8

Printed in the United States of America

 South-Western College Publishing
an International Thomson Publishing company I(T)P®

Cincinnati • Albany • Boston • Detroit • Johannesburg • London • Madrid • Melbourne • Mexico City
New York • Pacific Grove • San Francisco • Scottsdale • Singapore • Tokyo • Toronto

CONTENTS

MANAGING CULTURAL DIVERSITY

The diversity of the workforce is a present and future reality. Managers will need to be skilled in managing cultural diversity in order to hire and retain people with a range of talents and to operate in a variety of markets within and across countries. This module helps you to understand the meaning of diversity. Background on the demographic data and the historical context will help you take action from a knowledgeable standpoint, recognizing that everyone has misconceptions and stereotypes when it comes to the complexity of diversity. Because diversity is such a complex topic, your work colleagues will likely have strong feelings. What can you do? The readings and exercises present a way for you to be active in shaping an inclusive, respectful workplace that brings out the best of people's talents. Specific skills in turning around awkward situations will help you create the kind of workplace where you and others want to work.

This module begins with an overview reading on the dimensions of diversity and the multiple levels at which managers need to address diversity (societal, organizational, and interpersonal). Data on changing workforce demographics are presented. This introductory reading also presents the historical context of diversity in the United States and the meaning of affirmative action, often a contentious topic because it is misunderstood and involves conflicting interests. While U.S. organizations may currently give the most attention to diversity, dimensions of diversity exist within every country and are certainly present in managing globally across countries. Challenges remain in increasing diversity in the highest levels of organizations. More deeply, organizations need to tap diversity as a resource for ongoing learning and innovation. A true appreciation of diversity will reveal new ways of handling every aspect of organizational life and operations, from designing products to conducting performance evaluations to managing client relationships.

The next reading, **"Bystander Awareness: Skills for Effective Managers,"** moves from understanding to action. So-called "bystanders" are active participants in the workplace who have a special role in signaling respect for diversity and helping to halt unprofessional behavior. This reading will explain who bystanders are and what they can do. We often admire the person who has the presence of mind to make a difference in a difficult situation and create the space for multiple viewpoints to be heard. With these skills and some opportunities to practice, you can be that person, a valued member of the team. At the same time, these individual actions exist in a broader organizational context that must provide support systems, policies, and resources for organizational level improvements.

In the reading that follows, some specific "scenarios" are presented so you can assess the actions and choices made by some sample bystanders. Finally, a supplementary reading by a noted organizational consultant on diversity introduces organizational level approaches to diversity.

ADDITIONAL EXERCISES

You can expand your learning about these issues in several ways. One way is to go through recent issues of the business press and look for examples of "the business case for diversity" (as summarized in Figure 11.1). How is the case for diversity expressed?

Are there variations on these themes? Are other reasons for valuing diversity expressed (such as "it's the right thing to do" or "it helps us develop as human beings")? Who expresses the case for diversity and with what audience in mind?

Another way to learn more about different approaches is to ask your classmates or teammates about how diversity is understood and managed in their home countries, regions, or companies where they worked. What dimensions of diversity were important? When was diversity valued or ignored and why?

Finally, this module shows you ways to develop specific skills for making a diverse workplace a great place to work. You can practice these skills by doing "role plays" like the scenarios in this module, drawing on your own experiences. Your instructor may direct you to try some specific kinds of role plays.

M-11

core

MANAGING CULTURAL DIVERSITY:
From Understanding to Action

THE MEANING OF DIVERSITY

The term "diversity" is used to describe many different features of contemporary and future organizations. There are many dimensions of diversity. First and foremost, the concept refers to "social identities:" personal characteristics (such as race, gender, nationality, sexual orientation, age, or disability) that are "social" inasmuch as they trigger others to treat people as members of a group rather than as individuals. These groups have layers of stereotypes and history, so the experiences of members and the reactions of others are quite culturally and politically complex.

In addition to these primary social identities, there are important secondary dimensions of diversity, which include additional personal characteristics (marital status, family background, educational level, cognitive style, leadership style, etc.) as well as aspects of organizational role (position, years of service, career employee or temporary worker or consultant, high-level executive or entry-level hourly employee, and so forth). The term "cultural diversity" refers specifically to the primary dimensions of diversity and the opportunities and challenges posed to work teams and departments that represent people from many groups.

Taylor Cox (1993, p. 6), a noted scholar of management science, defines cultural diversity as "the representation, in one social system, of people with distinctly different group affiliations of cultural significance."

Less than ten years ago, diversity was a word used mostly to describe a stock portfolio or to indicate a variety of job functions. Diversity has now become a topic that has catapulted to the forefront of organizational concerns. Organization leaders and management scholars believe that diversity management is an important tool for those organizations that want to achieve a strategic advantage. Consequently, diversity and its management have blossomed into a multi-million-dollar industry.

The diversity of the workforce is a present and future reality. Managers who want to hire and retain people with a range of talents and to tap a variety of markets will need to be skilled in managing diversity. Appendix 1 shows the demographic composition of the U.S. civilian labor force (broken down by sex, by race, and by Hispanic origin).

Diversity Within Nations and Around the Globe

Managers of the global organization of the future will clearly have to be sensitive to and skilled in leveraging the diversity they find in different parts of the world. While cross-cultural diversity across national boundaries is very obvious, there is also much diversity within national boundaries. While it is commonplace to think of diversity as a U.S. phenomenon and preoccupation, most nations have cultural differences, which can be both a source of division and tension as well as a source of creativity, learning, and value.

In the United States, race has historically and currently been the most visible source of conflict. In the 1930s, Swedish observer Gunnar Myrdal dubbed racism "the American dilemma," because racism marred an otherwise exemplary experiment in democracy and equality that could be a worldwide model. The prescient writings of the African-American scholar W. E. B. DuBois (1903, 1968) on not only the hardships, but also the essential talents and distinctly formed perspective, of blacks in America still ring true today.

In Europe, historically and currently, ethnic and religious differences have created the greatest conflicts (for example, the Bosnian, Serb, and Muslim conflicts in the former Yugoslavia or the long-simmering conflicts between Catholics and Protestants in Northern Ireland). Patterns of immigration also create tensions and inequalities (such as Turkish "guest workers" in Germany or Iranians in Sweden). In Asia, differences in national origin and immigration have been sources of division and prejudice (such as Japanese/Korean conflicts and the challenges for Korean workers in Japan or the hardships of Filipino domestic workers in Taiwan). In Latin America, the issues of indigenous peoples and the history of wide class differences continue to create tensions and challenges. Within any nation, there are gender differences that affect the status, health, and opportunities of women.

All these issues will affect how organizations function internally and do business externally, and moreover, they affect whether business can deliver on its implicit promise (dating from Adam Smith) of using profit maximization to improve social welfare (or the "wealth of nations").

What Managers Need to Understand and Do

Whatever the sources, managing diversity requires organizational leaders to be attentive to key stakeholders at three levels. First, at the societal level, citizens and governments expect and/or legally require that organizations will provide equal opportunity and fair treatment to everyone at work. Where inequalities exist, many people believe that it is through work that groups can and should be able to overcome historic injustices and improve their welfare. Also at the societal level, shareholders may expect organizations to engage in diversity programs only to the extent that they improve performance, which is discussed below. There may be conflicts of interest where some regard valuing diversity as a good end in itself or as a longer term source of performance that is worth working patiently toward, while others see attention to diversity as a cost and a short-term drain.

Second, at the organizational level, employees have come to expect fair treatment and equal opportunity as part of the "social contract" (see Module 7) that connects them to their organization and motivates them to contribute their talent and energy.

Third, at the managerial level, it is increasingly every manager's job to translate diversity into positive organizational outcomes. Mission statements from top managers or boards of directors may give broad direction on diversity, while managers enact the vision and may even be formally evaluated on their efforts.

As Lew Platt, CEO of Hewlett Packard puts it, managers are challenged to make the "business case" for diversity in their organizations (see Figure 11.1).

When failures to take diversity seriously are revealed, the consequences—for reputation and for the bottom line—can be disastrous (see Figure 11.2 on the widely publicized Texaco case).

FIGURE 11.1 THE BUSINESS CASE FOR DIVERSITY

"I see three main points to make the business case for diversity:

1. A talent shortage that requires us to seek out and use the full capabilities of all our employees.
2. The need to be like our customers, including the need to understand and communicate with them in terms that reflect their concerns.
3. Diverse teams produce better results.

This last point is not as easy to sell as the first two—especially to engineers who want data. What I need is the data, evidence that diverse groups do better."

Source: Lew Platt, CEO, Hewlett Packard. Informal comments to the Diversity Research Network, Stanford Business School, March, 18, 1998. Reproduced with permission of Hewlett Packard Company.

FIGURE 11.2 THE BUSINESS CASE FOR DIVERSITY

A Lesson in Why It Matters to Take Diversity Seriously

Texaco made headlines when a set of tapes was made public in 1996. The tapes contained demeaning comments made by managers about minorities at the company, secretly recorded by a concerned manager. Public outrage led to boycotts of the oil company and to much debate over whether corporate America had been taking diversity seriously or merely doing some window dressing. Texaco ended up settling a race discrimination case out of court for $176 million. Across corporate America, the case was taken as a serious warning that, even in the 1990s, there was still prejudice even among the top ranks of executives who were supposed to be setting and exemplifying the corporate commitment to diversity. It was a reminder that evidence of discrimination and insensitivity could generate a crisis. The two top executives recorded on the tapes were charged by federal prosecutors with obstructing justice and seeking to destroy evidence relevant to the race discrimination case. They were later acquitted by jurors who worried that the tape quality left open questions about the context of remarks. Civil rights leaders worried that the trial coverage shifted the focus from the moral debate over equal treatment to the technicalities of tape quality. In response to this situation, Texaco has created a program to promote more minorities, a positive step. Inasmuch as Texaco has become a widely cited cautionary tale, this case shows that companies can suffer longer-lasting public relations damage.

This module examines what you as a manager need to know and do to meet these multiple expectations. You will see that there are no single or easy answers. Despite the rhetoric in much of the business press about "valuing diversity" or that "diversity is just good business," the research evidence, accumulated in well over 100 studies conducted over many years, suggests that managers cannot expect that attracting and maintaining a diverse workforce is easy or a natural outgrowth of labor markets (see Williams and O'Reilly, 1997: and Richard, 1997, for reviews of these studies). These researchers explain that diversity does not automatically translate into positive group or organizational performance. Instead, as one comprehensive review recently concluded (Richard, 1997):

> We are not likely to see a simple direct relationship between diversity and performance, at least in the early stages of efforts to increase the representation of minorities in organizations. Instead, the effects are likely to be determined by how organizational leaders and participants respond to and manage diversity. We could posit two contrasting scenarios—a self-reinforcing vicious circle of negative effects, or a reinforcing circle of positive effects, depending on the actions taken as part of efforts to increase minority participation and representation in organizations.

And another set of research experts (Milliken and Martins, 1996) summarized the situation:

> Diversity appears to be a double-edged sword, increasing the opportunity for creativity as well as the likelihood that group members will be dissatisfied and fail to identify with the group.

These observations tell us that, if managed well, diverse groups and organizational units may have greater up-side performance potential; but if managed poorly, there may also be greater down-side performance risk.

Therefore, to capture the benefits of diversity and avoid its potential pitfalls, managers need to understand how increased diversity affects group and organizational processes and how to manage these processes to produce positive results for the different stakeholders. In this module we will discuss the skills you as a manager and organizational participant will need in your organizations.

First, we give some background on the issues so you will understand why people are so passionate about them. Then, we take a zoom lens into the everyday workings of the organization and some skills that can help all employees be part of valuing diversity.

BACKGROUND: THE U.S. SOCIETAL AND POLICY CONTEXT

People bring strong feelings about diversity to the workplace. For you to act in an informed way as a manager and a colleague, you need to appreciate the historic background and the actual definition of currently loaded terms like "affirmative action."

The Civil Rights Movement

Equal opportunity and affirmative action requirements were born in a time of social crisis—in the midst of the upheavals and the civil rights movement of the 1960s led by Martin Luther King, Jr. A broad base of African Americans from all walks of life, and some white allies willing to take a stand against racism, united to contest the separate and unequal treatment of blacks throughout the United States. The legal prohibitions against discrimination and the proactive requirements for affirmative action were born in this time and reflect the U.S. government and American society's expectations for managerial practice and organizational policies.

While modified over time through cases and experience, these policies continue to reflect American commitment to equality as a fundamental belief. Current debates reflect differences of opinion over both the means of achieving equality and the degree to which inequality persists.

The 1960s delivered a wake-up call that social change was desperately needed. It is difficult today to keep in mind the intensity of the change and the need for visionary corporate leaders to play a role. On the one hand, some people believe that much progress has been made since then. On the other hand, some people believe that the problems of racial division persist in the United States and that the clear and courageous language used to discuss racism in the past has been watered down by the contemporary language of "diversity." What do you think? Are there important social issues on which you would take a bold stand today?

Government Policies

Society outlines its broad expectations for managing diversity through the laws and regulations it enacts and the social norms and experiences that employees carry into their organizational roles. In 1964 the U.S. federal government enacted the first comprehensive law requiring firms to provide equal employment opportunities to all people regardless of race, color, religion, sex, or national origin. Later, other protected categories were added to the law, including age and disability. Sexual harassment was specifically prohibited. The law covers essentially all employment practices (hiring, promotion, discharge, and so forth). Moreover, in 1965 President Lyndon Johnson signed an Executive Order requiring all firms doing business with the government (virtually all large corporations and most small to medium size enterprises) to take **affirmative action** to hire and promote minorities and women in numbers proportionate to their availability in the external labor market.

To demonstrate compliance with the Executive Order, firms must have a plan with three components: (1) an analysis of the availability of minorities and women in the relevant labor markets in which the firm operates, (2) statistical data showing the utilization of these affected groups across the different job categories in the firm, and (3) a plan specifying targets and timetables for redressing under-utilization of these covered workers.

Affirmative action does not, however, require hiring unqualified individuals, nor does it require or support choosing less qualified members of a protected group over others who are more qualified. Instead, it requires organizations to make affirmative efforts to hire and promote members of the protected groups who are qualified for the positions involved. It does not require quotas, but does require proactive monitoring of numbers.

These policies have had some positive effects, particularly in their early years as strong enforcement patterns interacted with strong rates of economic growth to expand opportunities. The best empirical studies have shown that the combination of strong economic growth and the pressures of government enforcement improved the status of people of color from the late 1960s through the 1970s. The strongest gains were made by the better educated new entrants to the labor force. The enforcement efforts had their biggest effects on eliminating the most overt sources of discrimination in formal selection, promotion, training, and labor-management policies and practices (Leonard, 1983). These are the features that the strategic design perspective pays the most attention to. Some of the remaining challenges are in resolving conflicts (important from the political perspective) and weaving an appreciation of diversity into the everyday practices of work (important from the cultural perspective).

Remaining Challenges

While there has been progress, the report from the U.S. Department of Labor's Glass Ceiling Commission in 1995 puts these efforts in perspective and illustrates the significant challenges that remain for managers today.

For instance, the report revealed that black men held only 2.3 percent of the executive, administrative, and managerial jobs in all private sector industries; they held 3.9 percent of these jobs in the public and private sectors combined. Black women held 2.2 percent of the executive, administrative, and managerial jobs in all private sector industries; they held 4.6 percent of these jobs in the public and private sectors.

Hispanics are not successfully progressing in the corporate ranks either. The 1990 census data reveal that the percentage of Hispanics who are managers and administrators in both the private and public sectors (Mexican-Americans, 6%; Puerto Ricans, 8%; Cuban-Americans, 7.5%; all other Hispanic-Americans, 7.5%) is far below the percentage of non-Hispanic whites (43%) who are managers and administrators. Eighty-six percent of the Hispanic senior executives were male, and more than 40 percent of these executives had been in their companies 16 years or more. Nationwide, Puerto Ricans account for only 0.7 percent of the managers in the manufacturing industry. Only 0.2 percent of the Cuban-American population is employed in the finance industry.

The story is also not good for Asian-Americans. Although members of this racial/ethnic group (Chinese, Filipino, Japanese, Asian Indian, Korean, Vietnamese, Cambodian, and Hawaiian) are stereotyped as being the "model minority," they lag behind whites in managerial and executive positions. Why? They are perceived as intelligent, hardworking, highly educated, polite, non-confrontational, nonviolent, politically passive, culturally resourceful, and good at science. Consequently, they are perceived as not possessing the leadership skills to be effective managers. They often are trapped in technical jobs and denied access to management positions.

The question facing organizations in the future is not whether government policies promoting and regulating equal employment opportunity are still needed. The majority of Americans continue to support these policies, even while debating the relative merits of different approaches to affirmative action. The real question managers face is how to go beyond legal requirements or fairness arguments and come to a true appreciation of how diversity makes the integral aspects of business work in new and better ways (Thomas and Ely, 1996). We now turn to this question.

ORGANIZATIONAL PROCESSES

Recognition of the limits of government enforcement and legal compliance as a management strategy led throughout the 1980s and 1990s to a flurry of organizational interventions aimed at educating and socializing managers to "value diversity." Figure 11.3 lists the elements frequently included in diversity programs found in large U.S. corporations. The list comes from a survey of Fortune 500 companies published in 1995. Among these companies, fully 72 percent reported having formal diversity policy programs with some or all of the elements shown in this figure.

From a **strategic design perspective**, the focus is on aligning corporate policies to government regulations and other requirements from the corporate environment. The attention to compliance and the monitoring of numbers becomes an element of strategic design. Programs that focus on selecting qualified people, redefining the types of talents the organization needs, and matching people to jobs are all consistent with the concerns of a strategic design approach.

From a **political perspective**, the attention shifts to the underlying tensions and conflicts of interest that affect how diversity programs are perceived and carried out. The above statistics are one indication of why tensions over race and ethnicity continue to be visible in American society and politics. Because organizations are microcosms of the broader society, racial tensions and differences, not surprisingly, spill over into organizational life. On the one hand, some white males believe that affirmative action is a code word meaning incompetent minorities take jobs away from whites. And some people of color are feeling stigmatized from being beneficiaries of special treatment policies. On the other hand, in the face of evidence of persistent inequalities and stereotypes that continue to favor some groups over others in the final outcomes, other people feel strongly that affirmative action is still needed. A political perspective views the organization as an arena in which these political disputes must be mediated by policies and institutions that are updated as interests evolve.

The more recent rise in valuing diversity programs comes at a time when there is a resurgence of resistance from some who feel that people of color are receiving too much preferential treatment in the workplace. As part of a 1995 poll conducted by the *New York Times* and CBS News in 1995, Americans were asked:

> "Do you believe that where there has been job discrimination in the past, preference in hiring or promotion should be given to blacks today?"

FIGURE 11.3 TYPICAL ELEMENTS IN A CORPORATE DIVERSITY PROGRAM

- A formal position or department dedicated to diversity management
- Training programs designed and conducted by employees
- Diversity advisory councils chaired by the CEO
- Mentoring programs open to all high-potential employees
- Participation in benchmarking studies of diversity programs in other companies
- Provision of electronic or printed diversity calendars and schedule of company-sponsored diversity events
- Formal employee networks, support groups, and task forces with direct access to top management that identify issues, explore solutions, and support implementation
- Awareness workshops with follow-up meetings and results
- Global video conferencing supported by a culturally sensitive manual

Source: Survey of Fortune 500 companies reported in *Mosaics*. Society of Human Resource Management, Vol. 1, No. 1, March 1995, p. 5.

ⓒ 9 ACADEMIC

What do you think the responses were? What is your response? How might your classmates respond?

The results were that 58 percent of white people said, "No." In contrast, 24 percent of African Americans answered, "No."

From a **cultural perspective**, the important issues are how employees live out their approach to diversity and what norms they develop. Cultural beliefs about diversity are deeply embedded in the workplace and may even be taken for granted. Who eats lunch together, who golfs together, who invites one another over to their houses for dinner—these are the deep ways in which either exclusion or inclusion get played out. The kinds of jokes that get told, and whether or not people laugh, are important data from the cultural perspective.

In the following sections, we consider three places in the organization where we see the complexities of diversity from a political and cultural perspective. First, we consider top leadership support for diversity. Second, we consider the grassroots efforts of employees who care about and are affected by diversity programs. Finally, we introduce a new approach—bystander awareness—which encourages you to think about how all employees might take ownership for a culture that values diversity.

Top Leadership Commitment

A key feature of diversity programs is that they are top-down, internally motivated initiatives. In the best examples, these efforts have the personal support of the CEO. They focus on education, awareness, and personal attitudes and behavior. Action strategies include one-on-one mentoring, discussion groups, training programs, and support for and exposure to multicultural events. The tone of these programs and the extent of their success reflect the organizational settings in which they are implemented. The reading by R. Roosevelt Thomas outlines the organizational values and strategies needed to support successful diversity programs.

Grassroots Employee Advocacy Groups

Some small groups of concerned employees have taken responsibility for improving their positions in and contributions to their organizations by forming various advocacy or self-help groups, which might be referred to as "networks" or "caucuses." The Black Caucus at Xerox is one of the most well-known and successful examples of this approach. It was created in response to the call from top management for a corporate commitment to social justice. One study finds that the links between top-down espousals of diversity and bottom-up employee efforts to make diversity real are a powerful combination (Scully and Segal, 1997).

Other groups of employees who share a "social identity" (and usually a history of discrimination) have formed networks. It is increasingly common to find a women's group, a Hispanic network, or a gay/lesbian/bisexual/transgender caucus in a corporation. These groups may coordinate their efforts through a Diversity Council, which brings representatives from each group into contact with top managers to address shared and specific concerns. One estimate is that about one-third of Fortune 500 corporations have such groups (Friedman and Carter, 1993). These groups are not motivated by any deep distrust of top management or by a rejection of diversity or affirmative action programs, but by the realization that it is up to them to help themselves and to sustain the commitment to diversity over time. Figure 11.4 provides several excerpts that convey these employees' beliefs.

At a recent meeting of high level executives, there was nearly an even split over whether such groups have been a positive or negative influence in their organizations. Several managers noted that they valued these groups highly for their networking and mentoring roles and indicated that these groups also helped by sharing responsibility for translating diversity into positive organizational results throughout the organization. They also provided a valuable upward communication channel and educated managers

ACADEMIC 10

FIGURE 11.4 GRASSROOTS EMPLOYEE ADVOCACY GROUPS: EXCERPTS FROM INTERVIEWS IN A HIGH-TECH COMPANY

- "We formed because we feel it's important to have a voice, raise issues to senior management and help be proactive in the whole diversity effort."

- "The African-American Caucus evolved with a set of Black individuals coming together and just holding a meeting and saying we need to form an African-American Caucus because we don't feel that these issues are being addressed. To make sure that our agenda is heard and doesn't get swallowed up into this diversity stuff."

- "I see the diversity effort all as having come out of employee initiative, not senior management insight and benevolence . . . that's what gives it life and keeps it alive."

- "Usually there's some grassroots things going on. The people at the top have their heads in the clouds and awareness comes from, 'Oh God, there's an insurgency uprising out there. I mean we should listen to what the peasants are saying.' "

- "My feeling is that there are two routes toward those ends—one is grassroots and the other is sort of HR, top-down. I honestly . . . feel you need the action of grassroots sort of motivated people, who are motivated to make it happen." [Statement of an HR Executive]

- "Well, the grassroots efforts that have happened are certainly all a result of people's frustration at things not happening sooner. They want to keep this whole idea out in front of people's faces."

- "I think it's easier for us now to just push—push to let ourselves be known that we're here to help facilitate the diversity effort, we're here to help support, but we're also going to start holding people accountable and to question the motives."

Source: Maureen Scully and Amy Segal, "Passion with an Umbrella: Grassroots Activists Inside Organizations." Paper presented at the Academy of Management Meetings, Dallas, Texas, August 1994.

11

ACADEMIC

and top level executives as to the real issues facing employees. In doing so, they helped sustain commitment to achieving further progress. Critics, on the other hand, stated their fear that these groups would proliferate in number, thereby making it difficult to integrate their diverse interests and concerns into coherent organizational policies.

What seemed to distinguish those managers with positive from those with negative experiences with employee advocacy groups was largely the organizational culture in which they were situated. Organizational cultures and top management styles that encouraged participation on a wide range of other matters were comfortable with diversity groups and saw them as adding considerable value to their firms. Those with more centralized, formal decision-making structures and cultures in which top executives managed in a more tightly controlled fashion reported more negative experiences. So, the organizational culture and structures have important effects on the viability, success, or failure of this approach to managing diversity. Once again, we are reminded to consider diversity programs—like any program—not as a standalone effort but instead to think holistically about how these programs fit into a broader array of organizational processes.

Bystander Training: A New Method for Broader Involvement
The above sections discuss how top management and the employees most immediately concerned about diversity can play a role. A deep cultural change, however, requires broader involvement. Even where employees bring different political interests to bear,

most want to work in a humanistic and inclusive environment and have to learn to work across differences in their work teams in order to be effective.

The everyday issues that set the tone regarding diversity often pop up suddenly—an insensitive comment, an inappropriate joke, a failure to listen to someone who is "different"—and require quick and informal "interventions."

The remaining readings and cases in this module introduce you to **bystander awareness and skills**, a new approach to enacting diversity in organizations.

A bystander is anyone who is witness to an offensive or inappropriate remark or behavior and faces a choice; is he or she ready, able, and willing to do something about it? One's choices and skills in the moment will set the tone. Will people signal that diversity is valued? Or will they let these moments pass and, perhaps unintentionally, signal that diversity is not a strong, lived value?

What can you do to shape the culture regarding diversity, both as an organizational member and as a manager? The following readings present ideas and ways to practice your skills.

MANAGING DIVERSITY FOR HIGH PERFORMANCE

As a manager today, you will face all these different approaches to managing diversity in your organizations. You are required to comply with legal rules and expected as a responsible citizen to be fair in managing employment relations. Educational programs for valuing diversity and shaping the culture of the workplace will be available to you from outside consultants and often encouraged by senior executives. Employees will speak up individually and sometimes collectively and expect to have input into decisions affecting their work and careers. You will be held accountable for attracting and retaining a diverse workforce and translating diversity into positive performance results. So you will need to apply the tools of the different perspectives presented in the different modules of this book.

Our view of how to meet this challenge grows out of our organizational processes framework and is shared by knowledgeable researchers who have studied the effects of diversity on organizations. Figure 11.5 illustrates how this perspective has been mapped by one research group, the Diversity Research Network, a cross-university and industry consortium that is working together to examine what leading companies are doing to translate diversity into positive business results. As shown in the Figure, this group sees increased diversity affecting—and affected by—a wide array of organizational processes. The net effects of diversity on performance depends on how well teams, business units, and organizational processes respond to increased diversity.

All this suggests that the same skills emphasized throughout this book—aligning formal structures and policies to fit the task and objectives, managing team dynamics, negotiating, resolving conflicts, assessing culture, and managing change—are also essential to managing diversity. In short, the future of managing diversity lies in working with legal and social pressures and expectations, ensuring that formal human resource and organizational policies are designed and implemented fairly, nurturing a culture that values differences, and supporting and managing self-help groups or caucuses if and when employees choose to form them. By doing so, you will manage in ways that produce the virtuous circle all stakeholders are looking for in organizations today and in the future.

REFERENCES AND ADDITIONAL READINGS

Cox, T. 1993. *Cultural Diversity in Organizations*. San Francisco: Berrett-Koehler Publishers.

DuBois, W. E. B. 1903. *The Souls of Black Folk*. Chicago: A. C. McClurg & Co.

DuBois, W. E. B. 1968. *The Gift of Black Folk: The Negros in the Making of America*. New York: Johnson Reprints.

FIGURE 11.5 SITUATING DIVERSITY WITHIN MULTIPLE ORGANIZATIONAL PROCESSES

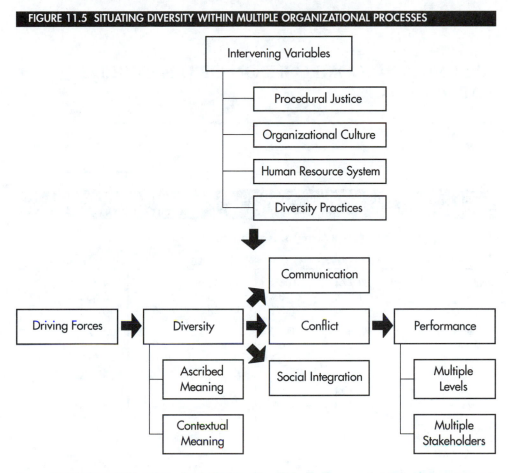

Source: From Maureen Scully and Amy Segal, "Passion with an Umbrella: Grassroots Activists Inside Organizations." Paper presented at the Academy of Management Meetings, Dallas, Texas, August 1994. Reprinted by permission.

The Glass Ceiling Commission. 1995. "Good for Business: Making Full Use of the Nation's Human Capital." A Fact-Finding Report of the Federal Glass Ceiling Commission, Washington, D.C.

Milliken, F. and L. Martins. 1996. "Searching for Common Threads: Understanding the Multiple Effects of Diversity in Organizational Groups." *Academy of Management Review*, 21, pp. 402–433.

Myrdal, Gunnar. 1962. *The Negro Problem and Modern Democracy* (20th anniversary edition). New York: Harper and Row.

Offerman, L. and M. Gowing. 1990. "Organizations of the Future: Changes and Challenges." *American Psychologist*, 45, pp. 95–108.

Richard, O. 1997. "Understanding the Impact of Cultural Diversity on Firm Outcomes." Report to the Alfred P. Sloan Foundation.

Scully, M. and A. Segal. 1997. "Passion with an Umbrella: Grassroots Activists in Organizations." Working Paper, MIT Sloan School of Management.

Thomas, D. and R. Ely. 1996. "Making Differences Matter: A New Paradigm for Managing Diversity." *Harvard Business Review*. September–October, pp. 79–91.

Williams, K. and C. O'Reilly. 1997. "Demography and Diversity: A Review of 40 Years of Research." Unpublished paper, Stanford University Graduate School of Business.

APPENDIX 1—COMPOSITION OF U.S. CIVILIAN LABOR FORCE

TABLE 11.1 COMPOSITION OF THE U.S. CIVILIAN LABOR FORCE BY SEX, RACE, AND HISPANIC ORIGIN

Annual Averages, Selected Years, 1970–2005*

	1970		1980		1990	
Total	82,774	100%	106,940	100%	124,787	100%
Men	51,228	61.8%	61,453	57.5%	56,554	54.7%
Women	31,543	38.2%	45,487	42.5%	56,554	45.3%
White	73,556	88.9%	93,600	87.5%	107,177	85.9%
Men	46,035	55.6%	54,473	50.9%	59,298	47.5%
Women	27,521	33.3%	39,127	36.6%	47,879	38.4%
Black & Other**	9,218	11.2%	10,863	10.0%	13,493	10.8%
Men	5,194	6.2%	5,612	5.1%	6,708	5.4%
Women	4,024	4.8%	5,253	4.9%	6,785	5.4%
Asian & Other***	—		—		—	
Men	—		—		—	
Women	—		—		—	
American Indian	—		—		—	
Men	—		—		—	
Women	—		—		—	
Hispanic****	—		6,146	5.7%	9,576	7.7%
Men	—		3,818	3.6%	5,755	4.6%
Women	—		2,328	2.2%	3,821	3.1%

Civilian Labor Force (Bureau of Statistics)—The civilian labor force comprises all civilians classified as employed or unemployed 16 years of age or older.

* Figures for the Years 2000 and 2005 are Bureau of Labor Statistics Civilian Labor Force Projections.

** Black and other figures for 1970 *only* includes blacks, Hispanics, and the Asian and other group.

*** Asian and other group consists of Asian and Pacific Islanders, American Indians, and Alaskan Natives.

Percents do not always add up to 100.

Detail for Hispanic-origin groups will not sum to civilian workforce totals because data for Hispanics are included in white, black, and other population groups.

— = Data not available.

Source: Bureau of Labor Statistics Current Population Survey—Annual Averages, Selected Years 1970–1990; Bureau of Labor Statistics-Office of Employment Projections, April 1994.

Ⓒ

14

ACADEMIC

TABLE 11.1 COMPOSITION OF THE U.S. CIVILIAN LABOR FORCE BY SEX, RACE, AND HISPANIC ORIGIN (CONTINUED)

Annual Averages, Selected Years, 1970–2005*

	2000 (Projection)		2005 (Projection)	
Total	142,596	100%	152,154	100%
Men	76,041	53.3%	80,356	52.8%
Women	66,555	46.7%	71,798	47.2%
White	119,604	83.9%	126,485	83.1%
Men	64,523	45.2%	67,645	44.4%
Women	55,080	38.6%	58,840	38.7%
Black & Other**	16,046	11.3%	17,395	11.4%
Men	7,815	5.5%	8,355	5.5%
Women	8,231	5.8%	9,040	5.9%
Asian & Other***	6,947	4.9%	8,274	5.4%
Men	3,703	2.6%	4,356	2.9%
Women	3,244	2.3%	3,918	2.6%
American Indian	—		—	
Men	—		—	
Women	—		—	
Hispanic****	14,271	10.0%	16,581	10.9%
Men	8,434	5.9%	9,626	6.3%
Women	5,837	4.1%	6,963	4.6%

15
ACADEMIC

M-11

supplemental

BYSTANDER AWARENESS:
Skills for Effective Managers[1]

A team calls for a break after a productive morning of work. Someone tells an offensive joke. Everyone is silent. A few people laugh quietly but nervously. One or two people may feel the sting of the joke especially sharply. Others worry about what to do and how to get back on track. The team's momentum is broken.

In this scenario, the "bystanders," those who witness offensive talk or inappropriate actions, could play a crucial role in signaling that the group values diversity and that offensive jokes are not appreciated. At best, they can help those who are offended understand that they are not alone and those who have given offense, intentionally or unintentionally, to back up, reconsider, and apologize and perhaps still save face. At least, bystanders can call for a halt and break the downward spiral of tension and misunderstanding that can destroy team cohesion.

Bystanders can uphold norms about the importance of valuing diversity. From the cultural perspective, we recognize the importance of norms in the workplace and the ways in which behavior over time can reinforce or erode a norm. If a norm is deeply held, its violation should provoke reactions. What sense can we make, then, of the silence of the bystanders?

Bystanders may very well appreciate that valuing diversity creates the kind of inclusive and culturally rich work world that they want to inhabit and that it encourages the contribution of talent from all people. They just may not know what to do.

FROM VALUING DIVERSITY TO TAKING ACTION

Valuing diversity is an easy goal to espouse. But how do we practice and realize that goal? Diversity training is quite common in companies in the United States and has helped many organizations to find the "positive spiral" of diversity referenced in the Module Overview. However, there has also been significant backlash against diversity training. White men complain that they are demonized and misunderstood. Women and people of color complain that they are set up to speak for their entire group or to reveal their difficulties, only to have their candor come back to haunt them when the trainer goes away.

Diversity training too often delivers lectures to would-be "perpetrators," offers assertiveness hints for would-be "victims," or gives legal advice to worried managers. A new, alternative training approach has been designed at the MIT Sloan School of Management. A number of companies and other departments at MIT have approached Sloan to learn more about this new approach. Instead of focusing on perpetrators, victims, or managers, we focus on another crucial and often overlooked party: the bystander. A bystander is anyone who witnesses offensive or unprofessional behavior. With training, bystanders can have the presence of mind, the understanding of how norms get shaped, and the needed skills to intervene.

1 **Acknowledgments:** The bystander training program at the MIT Sloan School relied upon the research, expertise, and energy of many people. In particular, thanks for the material that informs this reading go to: Laura Moorehead (of Joppa Consulting Partners), Bill Qualls, Rochelle Weichman, and especially Mary Rowe, who has observed the importance of bystanders in her experience as ombudsperson at MIT.

It is easy to fall silent in an awkward situation. People rarely have a chance to rehearse how they might intervene effectively in a tense and awkward situation. But the actions of bystanders are often the most crucial for signaling that the norms of respect and inclusivity are to be taken seriously. A norm is empty if no one challenges its violation. Bystanders are concerned parties who take ownership for setting the tone.

The lack of support from bystanders often worsens the strains in work groups. Team members who are upset about mistreatment in a team setting do not just complain about the person who was offensive; they may expect that "there is one in every crowd." Instead, the real hurt often comes from the silence of others, which appears to be consent or indifference. People who are upset by stinging, prejudicial remarks will say things like "I can't believe no one jumped in to say anything—everyone just sat there," or "I was left out there alone without any support," or "Sure Joe is insensitive, but does everyone else agree?"

Practicing in advance helps bystanders know what to do; the word, gesture, or approach that turns around the situation and reinforces a shared commitment to inclusivity and respect.

HISTORICAL AND CONCEPTUAL BACKGROUND

Research on bystanders comes from a number of areas of social science: the effects on children of watching someone getting hurt in abusive family settings, the motives of Good Samaritans in stopping to help someone in trouble, the reasons why some people join a social movement to improve conditions while others "free ride" on the collective benefits that may result, as a few examples.

Social psychologists in the United States addressed apparent bystander apathy following a disturbing and much-reported event. In 1965, a woman named Kitty Genovese was murdered on a street in New York at night, while many people from adjacent apartment buildings watched. No one called the police or intervened. Why?

The first reaction of the press and the American public was that New York was a heartless place and New Yorkers were cold and uncaring. But some researchers thought it was not quite so simple. The witnesses were horrified and upset. What is it that causes bystanders not to react?

They focused on two factors: uncertainty about what to do (people freeze when they do not have a well-rehearsed script in an unfamiliar situation) and diffusion of responsibility (everyone thinks that the situation is so serious that surely someone else, perhaps someone better qualified, will do something).

Other factors may affect bystander's reluctance. Mary Rowe has characterized reasons why complainants do not come forward or request that no further action be taken, reasons that apply as well to bystanders: fear of loss, including the loss of respect, ease, and comradeship with fellow employees; fear of silent disapproval; fear of vulnerability or invaded privacy in speaking from one's personal perspective; the risks of getting in the middle of things; the belief that they lack sufficient information about the situation; and concern they may be overreacting, as a few examples.

These insights about bystanders can be incorporated into diversity training. Bystander inaction can be reduced if people:

- Practice some interventions in a safe space so they feel more ready.
- Think through various scenarios in advance.
- Expand their menu of possible responses.
- Understand cultural differences in appropriate interventions.
- Learn from others' experiments and discover new ways to act.
- Take personal ownership for the situation, instead of just sitting back.
- Become self aware and understand the norms they want to uphold.
- Discuss options with one another and make bystander action more open, expected, and legitimate.

Consider emergency medical technicians, who have to respond quickly in crises. They play out many scenarios in their training so they will have the "situational awareness" they need to size up what is happening and intervene effectively.

THE BYSTANDER IN THE WORKPLACE

A bystander reacts immediately in the moment. The first step is to be good enough at reading the political and cultural dynamics to know that trouble is brewing. Often the most important thing a bystander can do is just stop the situation from escalating. A simple call for a pause or clarification can help.

A bystander is not charged with dealing justice on the spot. It might be more appropriate to give feedback to individuals at a later time. Calling on institutional resources—such as a mediator or ombudsperson—can help.

To clarify the nature of the bystander, some images of what the bystander is and is not were generated. These are summarized in Table 11.2.

THE COURAGE OF ONE'S CONVICTIONS

Speaking up rather than remaining quiet requires some moral courage. You can speak from your own vantage point, about how uncomfortable the situation is making you or about your concern that the tone does not reflect the kind of organization in which you want to work. Or you can speak on behalf of another, which is more complex. In general, it is best to intervene just enough to let others have the chance to speak for themselves.

Speaking on behalf of another requires:

- *Tactfulness.* Quite simply, a bystander should not drown out or embarrass the person they're supporting or make them feel helpless or pathetic by jumping in too strongly.
- *Willingness to take risks.* There can be group backlash against the bystander. Bystanders can become the target of the escalating anger in the group. They might be called "Pollyanna" or "bleeding heart liberal" or "knight in shining armor." They might be asked, "Who are you to say?" A bystander has to be prepared to take some heat.
- *Awareness of one's own power or privilege.* Diversity training tends to focus on the experience of disadvantage by people who occupy solo roles in a group (e.g., the only older person in a young start-up) or who belong to historically

---

TABLE 11.2 WHAT A BYSTANDER IS . . . AND IS *NOT* . . .

A Bystander Is . . .

Witness	Observer	Onlooker	Eavesdropper
Concerned Party	Stakeholder	Advocate	
Listener	Colleague	Peer	Audience
Mediator	Helper	Friend	
Facilitator	Peace-Maker	Humble Questioner	Learner

A Bystander Is *Not* . . .

Judge	Avenger	Enforcer	Fixer	Know-It-All
Rescuer		Hero/Heroine	Final Authority	

---

oppressed social groups (e.g., African Americans in the United States). A true understanding of diversity adds the dynamics of privilege (what does it mean to be one of the "young fast-trackers?" What does it mean to be white in the United States?). It is emotionally exhausting for people in disadvantaged positions to keep presenting their perspective and advocating for their rights. Members of a privileged group can develop a sense of empathy and spend some of their "political capital" to speak out when they see injustice. It is powerful when white people speak out against racism, when men speak out against sexism, when straight people speak out against homophobia, etc.

Given the delicacy and risks, why should bystanders do anything? Aren't they giving away more than they're getting? Are the costs too great?

One benefit of playing an active bystander role is that you get to help create the kind of climate that you want in your organization and of which you may someday be a beneficiary. You can crystallize norms by exemplifying and defending them. Some bystanders who have taken heat from others say it is worth it to be true to themselves and what they believe. Another benefit is that you can demonstrate your group dynamics skills, which are increasingly listed as a factor in performance appraisals.

COLLUSION

Despite the advantages of playing an active bystander role, sometimes it is reasonable not to jump in. What are the costs and benefits of silence? One cost is a feeling of collusion with the offense. For example, sometimes women laugh at sexist jokes to signal that they're good sports, but afterwards they may wonder if they're just perpetuating a negative climate of sexism.

At the same time, there can be some benefits to holding back. Sometimes it is necessary to "pick one's battles." Timing is important; waiting for "teachable moments" can make an important point. Speaking out too much can dilute one's message.

Another benefit of not speaking out in the moment is that sometimes it is best to pull people aside afterwards, to reduce embarrassment and wait until tempers have cooled to the point where feedback can be heard and absorbed.

CULTURAL VARIATION IN INTERVENTION STYLES

Whether bystanders act in the moment or wait, both the style and content of the intervention must be considered in cultural context. Cultures vary, for example, on one of the most delicate questions of intervention: whether to reprimand someone else's children when you see them misbehaving. It might be considered out of line to say something in one culture, or negligent *not* to say anything in another culture.

Survey your team members to see what kinds of interventions might work or fail in the countries or companies they come from. For example, is it better to stand up and leave than to say something? Is that considered dignified? Or would it be considered rude and awkward?

Bystanders just throw fuel on the fire if they fight one stereotype by invoking another. For example, a bystander intervenes on behalf of a woman on a team by saying, "You men from <wherever> are all so chauvinistic!" and potentially makes the situation worse.

IDEAS FOR BYSTANDERS

Some general types of interventions suggested by a range of participants in bystander training sessions are summarized in Table 11.3.

TABLE 11.3 SOME TACTICS FOR BYSTANDERS: IDEAS FROM WORKSHOP PARTICIPANTS

Inclusion:

Invite someone into the conversation
Solicit the opinions of people who have been quiet
Be an ally for someone taking a risk
Be gracious, help others save face

Discovery:

Ask questions
Give people a chance to clarify
Check assumptions
Consider the big picture, the broader context

Cooling things down:

Ask for a break
Use humor (but with care)
Suggest next steps, another meeting, off-line conversations

Heating things up:

Surface emotions
Say how the situation makes you feel
Point to the "unspeakable" issues that may be lurking

Body language/signaling:

Stand up
Turn away
Raise your hand
Bang the table
Say "ouch"
Laugh
Leave the room

Source: Reprinted by permission of *Harvard Business Review*. From "Making Differences Matter: A New Paradigm for Managing Diversity" by David A. Thomas and Robin J. Ely, Sept/Oct 1996. Copyright © by the President and Fellows of Harvard College. All rights reserved.

STRUCTURAL SOLUTIONS

The bystander's role during or just after an incident is important and can help shape cultural norms. However, it is an *ad hoc* response to issues that often require structural solutions. A successful bystander will interrupt unprofessional behavior, but there must be systems in place that back up the norms and provide any subsequent support or action that is needed to prevent future incidents. Some examples of structural solutions, at both the local and corporate level, include:

- An organizational policy on harassment, distributed to everyone, periodically reviewed, systematically enforced
- A third party (mediator, ombudsperson, employee advocate) who can counsel individuals or groups, whose services are supported and publicized, and who keeps track of aggregate data on incidents
- Clear policies governing promotions, a mentoring program, and a review board that keeps track of who is promoted (or not) and why
- Regular sessions to discuss and consider the alternative ways in which people from different cultural backgrounds might approach the process and product of work, especially helpful for breaking free of taken-for-granted assumptions and "thinking outside the box"

Ⓢ

22

ACADEMIC

- Training sessions on a variety of issues, such as giving culturally sensitive feedback, curbing sexual harassment, recognizing different leadership styles, etc.
- Celebrations of diversity, to recognize accomplishments and best practices from different teams or departments, to celebrate different heritages (for example, a speaker or film during Black History Month in February)

Structural solutions should align with the organizational vision of how to embrace diversity. Organizations that plan to fundamentally reshape how work is done, based on more diverse inputs, will need more innovative structures to support that approach. Table 11.4 shows an evolution of three approaches.

A CLOSING THOUGHT

Jewish tradition gives us a Talmudic story that is relevant:

In the book of Proverbs, King Solomon said:
"A tongue can bring either life or death."
[Proverbs 18.21]

Why is a tongue mightier than a sword?
A sword can only kill one person at a time.

Hurtful words kill three people at once:
They hurt the one about whom they are spoken.
They hurt the one who said them.
They hurt the one who listened to them.
(Bereshit Rabbah 98)

TABLE 11.4 MANAGING DIVERSITY—THREE PARADIGMS

Paradigm 1 Discrimination and Fairness	Paradigm 2 Access and Legitimacy	Emerging Paradigm 3 Connecting Diversity to Work Perspectives
Philosophy: tolerate differences	value differences	learn from differences
Rationale: increase numbers	access market niches	work in new ways
Sample action: mentoring program	employee networks	new processes

Source: David Thomas and Robin Ely, *Making Differences Matter, Harvard Business Review,* Sept–Oct 1996.

SOME BYSTANDER SCENARIOS:
What Would *You* Do?

This reading describes some scenarios in which a bystander might want to take action. The scenarios have been videotaped. The video features real personnel, from the management department of a major university, role-playing the different parts. All the scenarios are based on real incidents that people from the school contributed. You'll read a brief introduction to the premise of each scenario. A few questions are included for you to think about when you view the videotape. Your instructor might ask you to view the videotape as a basis for discussion, either in your class or within your team, or might ask you to make up, and even videotape, some scenarios of your own, based upon your own experiences and using the video as a model.

In each scenario, you'll see three to five individuals in settings that should be familiar to you from everyday life in the university and in the workplace. You'll notice that there's a bystander (or two) who might remain silent or who might step in and try to do or say something.

Each of these scenarios has one to four "takes." Typically in Take One, the scene is set. Some offensive remark or behavior escalates unchecked. If there are subsequent takes, various more-or-less effective styles and strategies for bystanders are role-played. You can consider which of these strategies you like, as well as other approaches that you might try in a similar situation. In some cases, all the action happens in one take.

All the "actors" are real people from the management department, including faculty, administrators, staff, and students from different programs (MBA, Ph.D., and mid-career).

Note: IMPORTANT: The "actors" are role-playing. Their behaviors and remarks DO NOT reflect their real identities or beliefs.

The actors agreed in discussions before each role-play who would act—or overreact—in different ways, and then they let the role-play unfold improvisationally. The scenarios are not scripted. They allowed for some spontaneity. As a result, you'll hear some laughing sometimes at the end of a scenario, as the actors react to a surprising turn in the scene or just let out their nervous energy. The laughter is retained in the final edit, because it shows how intense, but enlightening, it was to do the role-playing. All the actors were incredibly good sports and willing to experiment and take risks. In our editing, we purposely left a bit of raw "MTV" feeling, which we think makes the scenarios more real and fun. You'll see the actors warm up a bit, hear the countdown, see the actual take, hear the "cut" instruction, and then some quips and unwinding.

As you read about the scenarios and watch the videotapes, be thinking at two levels. First of all, as a participant on a team or in an organization, you might encounter situations in which you could be an effective bystander. Think about approaches that might be comfortable for you.

Second, as a manager, you will need to find ways to signal to your employees that diversity is valued and to teach them the skills they need to advocate effectively for diversity. Being a bystander is one such way that employees can help uphold norms about diversity that you would like to see reinforced. These scenarios were used for training workshops at the university where they were created and were generally

TABLE 11.5 EIGHT SCENARIOS	
Scenario Name	**Some Dimensions of Diversity That Are Addressed**
1. "Introducing the Invisible Colleague"	gender
2. "Is It Really About Race?"	race
3. "The Awkward Invitation"	sexual orientation
4. "Is It the Nature of the Project?"	nationality, language
5. "Counting On a Colleague"	invisible disability
6. "I Was Just Trying To Be Sensitive"	nationality, language, gender
7. "You Just Weren't Listening"	nationality, language, status
8. "The Stapler"	class/status/hierarchical level

Special thanks to all the "actors" in the role-plays, for being bold and creative and willing to experiment and learn in order to help teach others.

received quite positively. A mix of faculty, students, administrators, and staff participated in the training, and many commented on the special opportunity to discuss diversity issues with a mix of people from different positions and levels. The focus on everyday skills provided participants a way to really relate to the issues. A number of other universities and companies have become interested in these bystander training materials. As a manager, what kind of training programs will you sponsor?

In total, 16 scenarios were videotaped, representing many issues, dimensions of diversity, and approaches for a bystander. In the videotape for this Module, eight scenarios are selected. Your instructor might have you view all or just a few.

SCENARIO 1: INTRODUCING THE INVISIBLE COLLEAGUE

Role-Players: Gil, Ph.D. student
Jean, MBA student
Jim, MBA Program administrator
Nils, Ph.D. student

Synopsis
A recruiter approaches a group of three students, two men and a woman. He pays attention only to the two men, even though the woman has the most interest in the company and the most relevant experience. How will she join the conversation?

Take One:
Jean, Gil, and Nils talk about the company presentation they just heard from Jim. Nils and Gil are lukewarm about it, confused about the issues, not really interested. Jean is clear, has experience in the area, and very interested. This is an important set-up for their differential treatment by Jim. Jim approaches the group and pays attention to Gil and Nils, while ignoring the enthusiastic Jean.

Gil interrupts Jean as she begins to ask questions of the recruiter. Nils takes Gil's lead to jump in with questions. Jean is rendered invisible to Jim as the men's excitement and enthusiasm develops.

Jean manages to give Jim her business card, but has not had a chance to talk about herself, so Jim pays no attention to her. Although he acknowledges that the two men don't have the background, he devotes his time and attention to them as potential candidates. Jean becomes increasingly frustrated.

Discussion Questions

- What are the issues here?
- Who stands to gain or lose?
- How is Jean responding to being rendered invisible? What other responses might we have seen in this situation?

Take Two:

In this replay of the situation, Nils tries to bring Jim's attention to Jean, however awkwardly. Gil takes over by asking about "Clone Corp.," the (fictitious) company where Jean had spent a summer. Nils is prodded by Jean to introduce her, and he does so by touching her shoulder and saying awkwardly, "She also has some background," but not introducing Jean by name. Jim is not interested yet.

Take Three:

Nils now recognizes that Jean should be in the conversation and does what he can to have Jim speak with Jean, rather than focus on Gil and Nils.

Take Four:

This time, Nils tries to tell Jim about Jean's experience, but Gil interrupts. Jean intervenes by suggesting that they all introduce themselves first as a way to be inclusive.

Discussion Questions

- What seemed like the best option among the multiple "takes?" Why?
- How did it feel when Jean was able to intervene successfully for herself? What does this say for the role the bystander can play? What does it feel like when this doesn't happen?

SCENARIO 2: IS IT REALLY ABOUT RACE?

Role-Players: Fred, Mid-Career Program student
John, MBA student
Wendy, Ph.D. student

Synopsis

Three students are discussing a class they've just attended. John is enthusiastic. Fred is less so, explaining that the problem with the class was that all the cases of business failures were about African-American-owned businesses. He fears this pattern reinforces negative stereotypes about blacks in business. He wants to have a discussion about how race is a factor, but the others shut down the topic.

In the first take, Wendy is silent. In the second take, she jumps in and agrees that the choice of cases is a problem. In the third take, John and Wendy reverse roles.

Take One:

John is very excited about the class, and is unwilling to accept that Fred has a differing opinion. John denies vigorously that race is a factor and attempts to argue Fred out of his opinion. Fred quietly asserts himself, trying different ways to get through to John, but ends up discouraged. Wendy remains silent.

Discussion Questions

- What's going on for Fred?
- How could Fred have shifted the conversation?
- Is Wendy's silence awkward? Why?
- What strategies is John using?

Take Two:

Wendy now nods her head in agreement with Fred and joins in the discussion. With her support, Fred shows more energy. Their non-verbal cues and the rhythm of their conversation show connection and support.

Discussion Questions

- What does it mean for a bystander to be an ally versus taking over?

Take Three:

In this replay of the situation, Wendy and John switch roles. Now, Wendy is the person who is resistant to Fred's opinion, and John intervenes. Wendy struggles to find a reason why the professor may have selected these cases, as an alternative to the possibility that race is a factor. John supports Fred's disappointment, using a logical argument rather than responding to the emotion behind Fred's experience. Wendy comes around, Fred begins to take an educational stance, and John suggests they talk with the professor about the issue. The group moves to a proactive and collective action plan.

Discussion Questions

- How do the two bystander strategies differ?
- Are there some gender dynamics that distinguish the bystander approaches in takes two and three?
- Why do white people seek attributions other than race when such incidents happen?

SCENARIO 3: THE AWKWARD INVITATION

Role-Players: Jean, MBA student
John, MBA student
Maureen, professor
Nils, Ph.D. student

Synopsis

The research team is having a final meeting after a successful presentation. The professor proposes a celebratory dinner. She invites people to bring their spouses, boyfriends, or girlfriends. The students all know that John would want to bring his partner, Mike, and they try to help him let the professor know about his partner, while also trying to help her recover from her awkwardness.

Take One:

The professor is very enthusiastic about her idea, and misinterprets John's reluctance to join them for dinner. Jean tries to provide an alternative for the group, that the four of them go to lunch instead.

Discussion Questions

- What is the dimension of diversity here?
- What is John's strategy? Why is Jean evasive?

Take Two:

Here Nils and Jean attempt casually to let the professor know about Mike, by telling her why she'll enjoy meeting him, and by speaking in glowing terms about him. However, they aren't direct, and because the professor is unprepared, she stumbles and is confused until John explains that Mike is his partner.

Discussion Questions

- What do the bystanders do? What is the effect of having two people share a bystander role?

Take Three:

In this take, Nils talks about Mike. The professor catches on quickly and bluntly blurts, "Oh, you're gay. . . ." She proceeds to make light of it, saying it's "no problem." However, she is so awkward that everyone becomes uncomfortable.

Discussion Questions

• What options do they have to reduce the awkwardness in the room?

Notice how the professor's pre-emptive assertion that there's no problem (when she clearly has one) makes it hard to find a wedge into the discussion.

SCENARIO 4: IS IT THE NATURE OF THE PROJECT?

Role-Players: Benjamin (Yoong Il), MBA student
Hyun, Ph.D. student
Michael, professor
Roy, MBA student
Stephen, MBA student

Synopsis

The professor is concerned about the Staples team project. He has asked the team to meet with him after reading the last progress report. He asks what is going on, turning to the white, American men to respond first. Roy begins by complaining about Benjamin and Hyun's activities on the project. Stephen attempts to bring in another, more balanced perspective. The professor listens closely.

Hyun defends their contribution and says that the problem is that Stephen and Roy run the show without eliciting input from Benjamin and him. When Benjamin gets a chance to speak, he responds to Roy and Stephen's concerns, proposing that they try to understand the time pressure. He suggests that this may be less about culture differences than about the nature of the project. He proposes that they slow down and try to understand each other's strengths and weaknesses, and that they in essence "retreat from battle for awhile" to do so.

Stephen agrees to Benjamin's proposal. Roy goes along, but does not respond enthusiastically. The Professor says to Roy, "Well, you say 'sure', but do you mean 'sure'?" Roy is able to explain himself.

[*Note:* The layers of issues and the shifting bystander roles here are somewhat more complex than in preceding scenarios, but representative of the dynamics of cross-cultural teams at school and in the workplace.]

Discussion Questions

• Who plays the roles of the bystanders in this scenario? How do they intervene, and how are they effective?
• What types of effective mediation skills does the professor use?
• What else could the professor have done in this role? Does having a position of authority help or hinder a bystander?
• Where did you see cultural insensitivities?

SCENARIO 5: COUNTING ON A COLLEAGUE

Role-Players: Maura, Career Office administrator
Maureen, professor
Meg, Marketing administrator

Synopsis

Maura, Meg, and Maureen are planning the logistics for a student educational trip to Cuba over spring break. All the details are in order, except for the concern that Maura has just raised. It seems that the co-leader, Josephine, has told Maura that she has epilepsy. Maura is unsettled about Josephine's ability to successfully lead the trip without a medical emergency.

Take One:

The discussion, starting with a straightforward concern, escalates. Their conversation conveys all their fantasies and fears about the trip being much more difficult to manage because of Josephine, not to mention that she might embarrass them in a public place or on a company visit. No one halts the heaping up of stereotypes.

Discussion Questions

- What are the issues here?
- Does Josephine have a responsibility to tell Maura, Meg, and Maureen?

Take Two:

Meg intervenes effectively, but Maura and Maureen nonetheless gang up on her for being sentimental and impractical. Meg experiences backlash against her intervention as a bystander.

Discussions Questions

- What are some of the risks for a bystander? How can they be handled?

Take Three:

Meg brings a sense of calm and logic to the conversation, in spite of the resistance, helping them understand how they can manage their concerns. The group resolves to talk to Josephine and hear her concerns directly.

Discussion Questions

- What works about Meg's intervention?
- How will the group rebuild its trust of Josephine?

SCENARIO 6: I WAS JUST TRYING TO BE SENSITIVE!

Role-Players: Danielle, MBA student
Karen, Master's Program administrator
Ken, Master's Program staff member
Miguel, MBA student

Synopsis

The planning for the students' educational trip to Japan trip is going well. As they work into the evening on the final details, Miguel expresses concern that Danielle may need to leave, hinting at family obligations. With his question, the team interactions become stormy and confusing. Danielle is offended by Miguel's question, attributing his comments to chauvinism ("It's just like you Latin Americans. . . ."). Ken attempts to assist Miguel, but cannot quite turn the conversation around and adds new issues. Karen and Danielle resort to sarcasm to express their anger, exacerbating Miguel's embarrassment and confusion. Miguel, who was "just trying to be sensitive," doesn't understand their reactions, but apologizes.

Discussion Questions

- What are the various cross-cultural issues that arise?
- What do you think was Miguel's intent?
- How might Danielle have reacted differently?
- What role does Karen play in the scenario?
- What about Ken's attempt to intervene as a bystander?
- Danielle suggests they "get back to work"—is this going to be possible at this point?

SCENARIO 7: YOU JUST WEREN'T LISTENING

Role-Players: Benjamin (Yoong Il), MBA student
Devra, MBA student
Hyun, Ph.D. student
Pete, professor
Stephen, MBA student

Synopsis

Devra and her team are meeting with their professor to convey the team's confusion about an accounting problem they are working on together. Benjamin attempts to clarify how they should be thinking about the problem, but the professor does not respond to him. Instead, he asks Stephen to translate ("Is that what he said?"). When Stephen repeats the same message, Benjamin insists that that was what he was saying. The professor responds by saying, "I didn't hear that." Benjamin tries to save face by muttering, "OK, sometimes that happens."

Discussion Questions

*   Was Benjamin unclear? What was in the way of the professor's hearing Benjamin?
*   Who took the bystander role?
*   Why might Hyun have chosen not to intervene for Benjamin?
*   How do you suppose Benjamin was feeling when he said, "OK, sometimes that happens"?

SCENARIO 8: THE STAPLER

Role-Players: Molly, MBA Program staff member
Stephen, MBA student
Tony, MBA Program staff member

Synopsis

Molly and Tony are working on a scheduling issue, when Stephen, an MBA student shows up requesting to use Tony's stapler, a typical interruption in a day in the life of an administrative assistant. Stephen feels overworked and is anxious to get his paper turned in on time. Molly and Tony have a long list of tasks to handle that day.

Take One:

The interaction gets out of hand as the frustration level rises for everyone. How might it have been different if there had been another, less involved person who was willing to mediate?

Discussion Questions

*   Have you seen this happen? What are the issues?

Take Two:

Molly intervenes, attempting to get Stephen to calm down and understand what might be happening for Tony. When Tony explains how he has to do his job, Stephen is more willing to step back and wait.

Discussion Questions

*   In what ways did Molly successfully stop the interaction from spiraling further out of control?
*   In what ways are class and power asserted?

FROM AFFIRMATIVE ACTION TO AFFIRMING DIVERSITY

by R. Roosevelt Thomas, Jr.

Sooner or later, affirmative action will die a natural death. Its achievements have been stupendous, but if we look at the premises that underlie it, we find assumptions and priorities that look increasingly shopworn. Thirty years ago, affirmative action was invented on the basis of these five appropriate premises:

1. Adult, white males make up something called the U.S. business mainstream.
2. The U.S. economic edifice is a solid, unchanging institution with more than enough space for everyone.
3. Women, blacks, immigrants, and other minorities should be allowed in as a matter of public policy and common decency.
4. Widespread racial, ethnic, and sexual prejudice keeps them out.
5. Legal and social coercion are necessary to bring about the change.

Today all five of these premises need revising. Over the past six years, I have tried to help some 15 companies learn how to achieve and manage diversity, and I have seen that the realities facing us are no longer the realities affirmative action was designed to fix.

To begin with, more than half the U.S. workforce now consists of minorities, immigrants, and women, so white, native-born males, though undoubtedly still dominant, are themselves a statistical minority. In addition, white males will make up only 15 percent of the increase in the workforce over the next ten years. The so-called mainstream is now almost as diverse as the society at large.

Second, while the edifice is still big enough for all, it no longer seems stable, massive, and invulnerable. In fact, American corporations are scrambling, doing their best to become more adaptable, to compete more successfully for markets and labor, foreign and domestic, and to attract all the talent they can find. (See the inserts for what a number of U.S. companies are doing to manage diversity.)

Third, women and minorities no longer need a boarding pass, they need an upgrade. The problem is not getting them in at the entry level; the problem is making better use of their potential at every level, especially in middle-management and leadership positions. This is no longer simply a question of common decency, it is a question of business survival.

Fourth, although prejudice is hardly dead, it has suffered some wounds that may eventually prove fatal. In the meantime, American businesses are now filled with progressive people—many of them minorities and women themselves—whose prejudices, where they still exist, are much too deeply suppressed to interfere with recruitment. The reason many companies are still wary of minorities and women has much more to do with education and perceived qualifications than with color or gender. Companies are worried about productivity and well aware that minorities and women represent a disproportionate share of the undertrained and undereducated.

Fifth, coercion is rarely needed at the recruitment stage. There are very few

Source: Reprinted by permission of *Harvard Business Review*, "From Affirmative Action to Affirming Diversity," by R. Roosevelt Thomas, Jr., March–April 1990. Copyright 1990 by the President and Fellows of Harvard College; all rights reserved.

places in the United States today where you could dip a recruitment net and come up with nothing but white males. Getting hired is not the problem—women and blacks who are seen as having the necessary skills and energy can get into the workforce relatively easily. It's later on that many of them plateau and lose their drive and quit or get fired. It's later on that their managers' inability to manage diversity hobbles them and the companies they work for.

In creating these changes, affirmative action had an essential role to play and played it very well. In many companies and communities it still plays that role. But affirmative action is an artificial, transitional intervention intended to give managers a chance to correct an imbalance, an injustice, a mistake. Once the numbers mistake has been corrected, I don't think affirmative action alone can cope with the remaining long-term task of creating a work setting geared to the upward mobility of *all* kinds of people, including white males. It is difficult for affirmative action to influence upward mobility even in the short run, primarily because it is perceived to conflict with the meritocracy we favor. For this reason, affirmative action is a red flag to every individual who feels unfairly passed over and a stigma for those who appear to be its beneficiaries.

Moreover, I doubt very much that individuals who reach top positions through affirmative action are effective models for younger members of their race or sex. What, after all, do they model? A black vice president who got her job through affirmative action is not necessarily a model of how to rise through the corporate meritocracy. She may be a model of how affirmative action can work for the people who find or put themselves in the right place at the right time.

OUT OF THE NUMBERS GAME AND INTO DECISION MAKING

Like many other companies, Avon practiced affirmative action in the 1970s and was not pleased with the results. The company worked with employment agencies that specialized in finding qualified minority hires, and it cultivated contacts with black and minority organizations on college campuses. Avon wanted to see its customer base reflected in its work force, especially at the decision-making level. But while women moved up the corporate ladder fairly briskly—not so surprising in a company whose work force is mostly female—minorities did not. So in 1984, the company began to change its policies and practices.

"We really wanted to get out of the numbers game," says Marcia Worthing, the corporate vice president for human resources. "We felt it was more important to have five minority people tied into the decision-making process than ten who were just heads to count."

First, Avon initiated awareness training at all levels. "The key to recruiting, retaining, and promoting minorities is not the human resource department," says Worthing. "It's getting line management to buy into the idea. We had to do more than change behavior. We had to change attitudes."

Second, the company formed a Multicultural Participation Council that meets regularly to oversee the process of managing diversity. The group includes Avon's CEO and high-level employees from throughout the company.

Third, in conjunction with the American Institute for Managing Diversity, Avon developed a diversity training program. For several years, the company has sent racially and ethnically diverse groups of 25 managers at a time to Institute headquarters at Morehouse College in Atlanta, where they spend three weeks confronting their differences and learning to hear and avail themselves of viewpoints they initially disagreed with. "We came away disciples of diversity," says one company executive.

Fourth, the company helped three minority groups—blacks, Hispanics, and Asians—form networks that crisscrossed the corporation in all 50 states. Each network elects its own leaders and has an adviser from senior management. In addition, the networks have representatives on the Multicultural Participation Council, where they serve as a conduit for employee views on diversity issues facing management.

If affirmative action in upward mobility meant that no person's competence and character would ever be overlooked or undervalued on account of race, sex, ethnicity, origins, or physical disability, then affirmative action would be the very thing we need to let every corporate talent find its niche. But what affirmative action means in practice is an unnatural focus on one group, and what it means too often to too many employees is that someone is playing fast and loose with standards in order to favor that group. Unless we are to compromise our standards, a thing no competitive company can even contemplate, upward mobility for minorities and women should always be a question of pure competence and character unmuddled by accidents of birth.

And that is precisely why we have to learn to manage diversity—to move beyond affirmative action, not to repudiate it. Some of what I have to say may strike some readers—mostly those with an ax to grind—as directed at the majority white males who hold most of the decision-making posts in our economy. But I am speaking to all managers, not just white males, and I certainly don't mean to suggest that white males somehow stand outside diversity. White males are as odd and as normal as anyone else.

THE AFFIRMATIVE ACTION CYCLE

If you are managing diverse employees, you should ask yourself this question: Am I fully tapping the potential capacities of everyone in my department? If the answer is no, you should ask yourself this follow-up: Is this failure hampering my ability to meet performance standards? The answer to this question will undoubtedly be yes.

Think of corporate management for a moment as an engine burning pure gasoline. What's now going into the tank is no longer just gas, it has an increasing percentage of, let's say, methanol. In the beginning, the engine will still work pretty well, but by and by it will start to sputter, and eventually it will stall. Unless we rebuild the engine, it will no longer burn the fuel we're feeding it. As the workforce grows more and more diverse at the intake level, the talent pool we have to draw on for supervision and management will also grow increasingly diverse. So the question is: Can we burn this fuel? Can we get maximum corporate power from the diverse workforce we're now drawing into the system?

Affirmative action gets blamed for failing to do things it never could do. Affirmative action gets the new fuel into the tank, the new people through the front door. Something else will have to get them into the driver's seat. That something else consists of enabling people, in this case minorities and women, to perform to their potential. This is what we now call managing diversity. Not appreciating or leveraging diversity, not even necessarily understanding it. Just managing diversity in such a way as to get from a heterogeneous workforce the same productivity, commitment, quality, and profit that we got from the old homogeneous workforce.

The correct question today is not "How are we doing on race relations?" or "Are we promoting enough minority people and women?" but rather "Given the diverse workforce I've got, am I getting the productivity, does it work as smoothly, is morale as high, as if every person in the company was the same sex and race nationality?" Most answers will be, "Well, no, of course not!" But why shouldn't the answer be, "You bet!"?

When we ask how we're doing on race relations, we inadvertently put our finger on what's wrong with the question and with the attitude that underlies affirmative action. So long as racial and gender equality is something we grant to minorities and women, there will be no racial and gender equality. What we must do is create an environment where no one is advantaged or disadvantaged, an environment where "we" is everyone. What the traditional approach to diversity did was to create a cycle of crisis, action, relaxation, and disappointment that companies repeated over and over again without ever achieving more than the barest particle of what they were after.

Affirmative action pictures the workforce as a pipeline and reasons as follows: "If we can fill the pipeline with *qualified* minorities and women, we can solve our upward mobility problem. Once recruited, they will perform in accordance with our promotional criteria and move naturally up our regular developmental ladder. In the past, where minorities and women have failed to progress, they were simply unable to meet our performance standards. Recruiting qualified people will enable us to avoid special programs and reverse discrimination."

This pipeline perspective generates a self-perpetuating, self-defeating, recruitment-oriented cycle with six stages:

1. *Problem Recognition.* The first time through the cycle, the problem takes this form—We need more minorities and women in the pipeline. In later iterations, the problem is more likely to be defined as a need to retain and promote minorities and women.

2. *Intervention.* Management puts the company into what we may call an Affirmative Action Recruitment Mode. During the first cycle, the goal is to recruit minorities and women. Later, when the cycle is repeated a second or third time and the challenge has shifted to retention, development, and promotion, the goal is to recruit qualified minorities and women. Sometimes, managers indifferent or blind to possible accusations of reverse discrimination will institute special training, tracking, incentive, mentoring, or sponsoring programs for minorities and women.

3. *Great Expectations.* Large numbers of minorities and women have been recruited, and a select group has been promoted or recruited at a higher level to serve as highly visible role models for the newly recruited masses. The stage seems set for the natural progression of minorities and women up through the pipeline. Management leans back to enjoy the fruits of its labor.

4. *Frustration.* The anticipated natural progression fails to occur. Minorities and women see themselves plateauing prematurely. Management is upset (and embarrassed) by the failure of its affirmative action initiative and begins to resent the impatience of the new recruits and their unwillingness to give the company credit for trying to do the right thing. Depending on how high in the hierarchy they have plateaued, alienated minorities and women either leave the company or stagnate.

5. *Dormancy.* All remaining participants conspire tacitly to present a silent front to the outside world. Executives say nothing because they have no solutions. As for those women and minorities who stayed on, calling attention to affirmative action's failures might raise doubts about their qualifications. Do they deserve their jobs, or did they just happen to be in the right place at the time of an affirmative action push? So no one complains, and if the company has a good public relations department, it may even wind up with a reputation as a good place for women and minorities to work.

   If questioned publicly, management will say things like "Frankly, affirmative action is not currently an issue," or "Our numbers are okay," or "With respect to minority representation at the upper levels, management is aware of this remaining challenge."

   In private and off the record, however, people say things like "Premature plateauing is a problem, and we don't know what to do," and "Our top people don't seem to be interested in finding a solution," and "There's plenty of racism and sexism around this place—whatever you may hear."

6. *Crisis.* Dormancy can continue indefinitely, but it is usually broken by a crisis of competitive pressure, governmental intervention, external pressure from a special interest group, or internal unrest. One company found that its pursuit of a Total Quality program was hampered by the alienation of minorities and women. Senior management at another corporation saw the growing importance of minorities in

their customer base and decided they needed minority participation in their managerial ranks. In another case, growing expressions of discontent forced a break in the conspiracy of silence even after the company had received national recognition as a good place for minorities and women to work.

Whatever its cause, the crisis fosters a return to the Problem Recognition phase, and the cycle begins again. This time, management seeks to explain the shortcomings of the previous affirmative action push and usually concludes that the problem is recruitment. This assessment by a top executive is typical: "The managers I know are decent people. While they give priority to performance, I do not believe any of them deliberately block minorities or women who are qualified for promotion. On the contrary, I suspect they bend over backward to promote women and minorities who give some indication of being qualified.

"However, they believe we simply do not have the necessary talent within those groups, but because of the constant

---

"IT SIMPLY MAKES GOOD BUSINESS SENSE"

Corning characterizes its 1970s affirmative action program as a form of legal compliance. The law dictated affirmative action and morality required it, so the company did its best to hire minorities and women.

The ensuing cycle was classic: recruitment, confidence, disappointment, embarrassment, crisis, more recruitment. Talented women and blacks joined the company only to plateau or resign. Few reached upper management levels, and no one could say exactly why.

Then James R. Houghton took over as CEO in 1983 and made the diverse work force one of Corning's three top priorities, alongside Total Quality and a higher return on equity. His logic was twofold:

First of all, the company had higher attrition rates for minorities and women than for white males, which meant that investments in training and development were being wasted. Second, he believed that the Corning work force should more closely mirror the Corning customer base.

In order to break the cycle of recruitment and subsequent frustration, the company established two quality improvement teams headed by senior executives, one for black progress and one for women's progress. Mandatory awareness training was introduced for some 7,000 salaried employees—a day and a half for gender awareness, two-and-a-half days for racial awareness. One goal of the training is to identify unconscious company values that work against minorities and women. For example, a number of awareness groups reached the conclusion that working late had so much symbolic value that managers tended to look more at the quantity than at the quality of time spent on the job, with predictably negative effects on employees with dependent-care responsibilities.

The company also made an effort to improve communications by printing regular stories and articles about the diverse work force in its in-house newspaper and by publicizing employee success stories that emphasize diversity. It worked hard to identify and publicize promotion criteria. Career planning systems were introduced for all employees.

With regard to recruitment, Corning set up a nationwide scholarship program that provides renewable grants of $5,000 per year of college in exchange for a summer of paid work at some Corning installation. A majority of program participants have come to work for Corning full-time after graduation, and very few have left the company so far, though the program has been in place only four years.

The company also expanded its summer intern program, with an emphasis on minorities and women, and established formal recruiting contacts with campus groups like the Society of Women Engineers and the National Black MBA Association.

Corning sees its efforts to manage diversity not only as a social and moral issue but also as a question of efficiency and competitiveness. In the words of Mr. Houghton, "It simply makes good business sense."

complaints they have heard about their deficiencies in affirmative action, they feel they face a no-win situation. If they do not promote, they are obstructionists. But if they promote people who are unqualified, they hurt performance and deny promotion to other employees unfairly. They can't win. The answer, in my mind, must be an ambitious new recruitment effort to bring in quality people."

And so the cycle repeats. Once again blacks, Hispanics, women, and immigrants are dropped into a previously homogeneous, all-white, all-Anglo, all-male, all native-born environment, and the burden of cultural change is placed on the newcomers. There will be new expectations and a new round of frustration, dormancy, crisis, and recruitment.

TEN GUIDELINES FOR LEARNING TO MANAGE DIVERSITY

The traditional American image of diversity has been assimilation: the melting pot, where ethnic and racial differences were standardized into a kind of American puree. Of course, the melting pot is only a metaphor. In real life, many ethnic and most racial groups retain their individuality and express it energetically. What we have is perhaps some kind of American mulligan stew; it is certainly no puree.

At the workplace, however, the melting pot has been more than a metaphor. Corporate success has demanded a good deal of conformity, and employees have voluntarily abandoned most of their ethnic distinctions at the company door.

Now those days are over. Today the melting pot is the wrong metaphor even in business, for three good reasons. First, if it ever was possible to melt down Scotsmen and Dutchmen and Frenchmen into an indistinguishable broth, you can't do the same with blacks, Asians, and women. Their differences don't melt so easily. Second, most people are no longer willing to be melted down, not even for eight hours a day—and it's a seller's market for skills. Third, the thrust of today's non-hierarchical, flexible, collaborative management requires a ten- or twentyfold increase in our tolerance for individuality.

So companies are faced with the problem of surviving in a fiercely competitive world with a workforce that consists and will continue to consist of *unassimilated diversity*. And the engine will take a great deal of tinkering to burn that fuel.

What managers fear from diversity is a lowering of standards, a sense that "anything goes." Of course, standards must not suffer. In fact, competence counts more than ever. The goal is to manage diversity in such a way as to get from a diverse workforce the same productivity we once got from a homogeneous workforce, and to do it without artificial programs, standards—or barriers.

Managing diversity does not mean controlling or containing diversity, it means enabling every member of your workforce to perform to his or her potential. It means getting from employees, first, everything we have a right to expect, and, second—if we do it well—everything they have to give. If the old homogeneous workforce performed dependably at 80% of its capacity, then the first result means getting 80% from the new heterogeneous workforce too. But the second result, the icing on the cake, the unexpected upside that diversity can perhaps give as a bonus, means 85% to 90% from everyone in the organization.

For the moment, however, let's concentrate on the basics of how to get satisfactory performance from the new diverse workforce. There are few adequate models. So far, no large company I know of has succeeded in managing diversity to its own satisfaction. But any number have begun to try.

On the basis of their experience, here are my ten guidelines:

1. *Clarify Your Motivation*. A lot of executives are not sure why they should want to learn to manage diversity. Legal compliance seems like a good reason. So does community relations. Many executives believe they have a social and moral responsibility to employ minorities and women. Others want to placate an internal group or pacify an outside organization. None

TURNING SOCIAL PRESSURES INTO COMPETITIVE ADVANTAGE

Like most other companies trying to respond to the federal legislation of the 1970s, Digital started off by focusing on numbers. By the early 1980s, however, company leaders could see it would take more than recruitment to make Digital the diverse workplace they wanted it to be. Equal Employment Opportunity (EEO) and affirmative action seemed too exclusive—too much "white males doing good deeds for minorities and women." The company wanted to move beyond these programs to the kind of environment where every employee could realize his or her potential, and Digital decided that meant an environment where individual differences were not tolerated but valued, even celebrated.

The resulting program and philosophy, called Valuing Differences, has two components:

First, the company helps people get in touch with their stereotypes and false assumptions through what Digital calls Core Groups. These voluntary groupings of eight to ten people work with company-trained facilitators whose job is to encourage discussion and self-development and, in the company's words, "to keep people safe" as they struggle with their prejudices. Digital also runs a voluntary two-day training program called "Understanding the Dynamics of Diversity," which thousands of Digital employees have now taken.

Second, the company had named a number of senior managers to various Cultural Boards of Directors and Valuing Differences Boards of Directors. These bodies promote openness to individual differences, encourage younger managers committed to the goal of diversity, and sponsor frequent celebrations of racial, gender, and ethnic differences such as Hispanic Heritage Week and Black History Month.

In addition to the Valuing Differences program, the company preserved its EEO and affirmative action functions. Valuing Differences focuses on personal and group development, EEO on legal issues, and affirmative action on systemic change. According to Alan Zimmerle, head of the Valuing Differences program, EEO and Valuing Differences are like two circles that touch but don't overlap—the first representing the legal need for diversity, the second the corporate desire for diversity. Affirmative action is a third circle that overlaps the other two and holds them together with policies and procedures.

Together, these three circles can transform legal and social pressures into the competitive advantage of a more effective work force, higher morale, and the reputation of being a better place to work. As Zimmerle puts it, "Digital wants to be the employer of choice. We want our pick of the talent that's out there."

of these are bad reasons, but none of them are business reasons, and given the nature and scope of today's competitive challenges, I believe only business reasons will supply the necessary long-term motivation. In any case, it is the business reasons I want to focus on here.

In business terms, a diverse workforce is not something your company ought to have; it's something your company does have, or soon will have. Learning to manage that diversity will make you more competitive.

2. *Clarify Your Vision.* When managers think about a diverse workforce, what do they picture? Not publicly, but in the privacy of their minds?

One popular image is of minorities and women clustering on a relatively low plateau, with a few of them trickling up as they become assimilated into the prevailing culture. Of course, they enjoy good salaries and benefits, and most of them accept their status, appreciate the fact that they are doing better than they could do somewhere else, and are proud of the achievements of their race or sex. This is reactionary thinking, but it's a lot more common than you might suppose.

Another image is what we might call "heightened sensitivity." Members of the majority culture are sensitive to the demands of minorities and women for upward mobility and recognize the advantages of fully utilizing them. Minorities and women work at all levels of the corporation, but they are the recipients of generosity and know it. A few years of this second-class status drives most of them away and compromises the effectiveness of those that remain. Turnover is high.

Then there is the coexistence-compromise image. In the interests of corporate viability, white males agree to recognize minorities and women as equals. They bargain and negotiate their differences. But the win-lose aspect of the relationship preserves tensions, and the compromises reached are not always to the company's competitive advantage.

"Diversity and equal opportunity" is a big step up. It presupposes that the white male culture has given way to one that respects difference and individuality. The problem is that minorities and women will accept it readily as their operating image, but many white males, consciously or unconsciously, are likely to cling to a vision that leaves them in the driver's seat. A vision gap of this kind can be a difficulty.

In my view, the vision to hold in your own imagination and to try to communicate to all your managers and employees is an image of fully tapping the human resource potential of every member of the workforce. This vision sidesteps the question of equality, ignores the tensions of coexistence, plays down the uncomfortable realities of difference, and focuses instead on individual enablement. It doesn't say, "Let *us* give *them* a chance." It assumes a diverse

---

DISCOVERING COMPLEXITY AND VALUE IN P&G'S DIVERSITY

Because Procter & Gamble fills its upper level management positions only from within the company, it places a premium on recruiting the best available entry-level employees. Campus recruiting is pursued nationwide and year-round by line managers from all levels of the company. Among other things, the company has made a concerted—and successful—effort to find and hire talented minorities and women.

Finding first-rate hires is only one piece of the effort, however. There is still the challenge of moving diversity upward. As one top executive put it, "We know that we can only succeed as a company if we have an environment that makes it easy for all of us, not just some of us, to work to our potential."

In May 1988, P&G formed a Corporate Diversity Strategy Task Force to clarify the concept of diversity, define its importance for the company, and identify strategies for making progress toward successfully managing a diverse work force.

The task force, composed of men and women from every corner of the company, made two discoveries: First, diversity at P&G was far more complex than most people had supposed. In addition to race and gender, it included factors such as cultural heritage, personal background, and functional experience. Second, the company needed to expand its view of the value of differences.

The task force helped the company to see that learning to manage diversity would be a long-term process of organizational change. For example, P&G has offered voluntary diversity training at all levels since the 1970s, but the program has gradually broadened its emphasis on race and gender awareness to include the value of self-realization in a diverse environment. As retiring board chairman John Smale put it, "If we can tap the total contribution that everybody in our company has to offer, we will be better and more competitive in everything we do."

P&G is now conducting a thorough, continuing evaluation of all management programs to be sure that systems are working well for everyone. It has also carried out a corporate survey to get a better picture of the problems facing P&G employees who are balancing work and family responsibilities and to improve company programs in such areas as dependent care.

workforce that includes us and them. It says, "Let's create an environment where everyone will do their best work."

Several years ago, an industrial plant in Atlanta with a highly diverse workforce was threatened with closing unless productivity improved. To save their jobs, everyone put their shoulders to the wheel and achieved the results they needed to stay open. The senior operating manager was amazed.

For years he had seen minorities and women plateauing disproportionately at the lower levels of the organization, and he explained that fact away with two rationalizations. "They haven't been here that long," he told himself. And "This is the price we pay for being in compliance with the law."

When the threat of closure energized this whole group of people into a level of performance he had not imagined possible, he got one fleeting glimpse of people working up to their capacity. Once the crisis was over, everyone went back to the earlier status quo—white males driving and everyone else sitting back, looking on—but now there was a difference. Now, as he put it himself, he had been to the mountaintop. He knew that what he was getting from minorities and women was nowhere near what they were capable of giving. And he wanted it, crisis or no crisis, all the time.

3. *Expand Your Focus.* Managers usually see affirmative action and equal employment opportunity as centering on minorities and women, with very little to offer white males. The diversity I'm talking about includes not only race, gender, creed, and ethnicity but also age, background, education, function, and personality differences. The objective is not to assimilate minorities and women into a dominant white male culture but to create a dominant heterogeneous culture.

The culture that dominates the United States socially and politically is heterogeneous, and it works by giving its citizens the liberty to achieve their potential. Channeling that potential, once achieved, is an individual right but still a national concern. Something similar applies in the workplace, where the keys to success are individual ability and a corporate destination. Managing disparate talents to achieve common goals is what companies learned to do when they set their sights on, say, Total Quality. The secrets of managing diversity are much the same.

4. *Audit Your Corporate Culture.* If the goal is not to assimilate diversity into the dominant culture but rather to build a culture that can digest unassimilated diversity, then you had better start by figuring out what your present culture looks like. Since what we're talking about here is the body of unspoken and unexamined assumptions, values, and mythologies that make your world go around, this kind of cultural audit is impossible to conduct without outside help. It's a research activity, done mostly with in-depth interviews and a lot of listening at the water cooler.

The operative corporate assumptions you have to identify and deal with are often inherited from the company's founder. "If we treat everyone as a member of the family, we will be successful" is not uncommon. Nor is its corollary "Father Knows Best."

Another widespread assumption, probably absorbed from American culture in general, is that "cream will rise to the top." In most companies, what passes for cream rising to the top is actually cream being pulled or pushed to the top by an informal system of mentoring and sponsorship.

Corporate culture is a kind of tree. Its roots are assumptions about the company and about the world. Its branches, leaves, and seeds are behavior. You can't change the leaves without changing the roots, and you can't grow peaches on an oak. Or rather, with the proper grafting, you *can* grow peaches on an oak, but they come out an awful lot like acorns—small and hard and not much fun to eat. So if you want to grow peaches, you have to make sure the tree's roots are peach friendly.

5. *Modify Your Assumptions.* The real problem with this corporate culture tree is that every time you go to make changes in the roots, you run into terrible opposition. Every culture, including corporate culture, has root guards that turn out in force every time you threaten a basic assumption.

Take the family assumption as an example. Viewing the corporation as a family suggests not only that father knows best; it also suggests that sons will inherit the business, that daughters should stick to doing the company dishes, and that if Uncle Deadwood doesn't perform, we'll put him in the chimney corner and feed him for another 30 years regardless. Each assumption has its constituency and its defenders. If we say to Uncle Deadwood, "Yes, you did good work for 10 years, but years 11 and 12 look pretty bleak; we think it's time we helped you find another chimney," shock waves will travel through the company as every family-oriented employee draws a sword to defend the sacred concept of guaranteed jobs.

But you have to try. A corporation that wants to create an environment with no advantages or disadvantages for any group cannot allow the family assumption to remain in place. It must be labeled dishonest mythology.

Sometimes the dishonesties are more blatant. When I asked a white male middle manager how promotions were handled in his company, he said, "You need leadership capability, bottom-line results, the ability to work with people, and compassion." Then he paused and smiled. "That's what they say. But down the hall there's a guy we call Captain Kickass. He's ruthless, mean-spirited, and he steps on people. That's the behavior they really value. Forget what they say."

In addition to the obvious issue of hypocrisy, this example also raises a question of equal opportunity. When I asked this young middle manager if he thought minorities and women could meet the Captain Kickass standard, he thought they probably could. But the opposite argument can certainly be made. Whether we're talking about blacks in an environment that is predominantly white, whites in one predominantly black, or women in one predominantly male, the majority culture will not readily condone such tactics from a member of a minority. So the corporation with the unspoken kickass performance standard has at least one criterion that will hamper the upward mobility of minorities and women.

Another destructive assumption is the melting pot I referred to earlier. The organization I'm arguing for respects differences rather than seeking to smooth them out. It is multicultural rather than culture blind, which has an important consequence: When we no longer force people to "belong" to a common ethnicity or culture, then the organization's leaders must work all the harder to define belonging in terms of a set of values and a sense of purpose that transcend the interests, desires, and preferences of any one group.

6. *Modify Your Systems.* The first purpose of examining and modifying assumptions is to modify systems. Promotion, mentoring, and sponsorship comprise one such system, and the unexamined cream-to-the-top assumption I mentioned earlier can tend to keep minorities and women from climbing the corporate ladder. After all, in many companies it is difficult to secure a promotion above a certain level without a personal advocate or sponsor. In the context of managing diversity, the question is not whether this system is maximally efficient but whether it works for all employees. Executives who sponsor only people like themselves are not

making much of a contribution to the cause of getting the best from every employee.

Performance appraisal is another system where unexamined practices and patterns can have pernicious effects. For example, there are companies where official performance appraisals differ substantially from what is said informally, with the result that employees get their most accurate performance feedback throughout the grapevine. So if the grapevine is closed to minorities and women, they are left at a severe disadvantage. As one white manager observed, "If the blacks around here knew how they were really per-ceived, there would be a revolt." Maybe so. More important to your business, however, is the fact that without an accurate appraisal of per-formance, minority and women employees will find it difficult to cor-rect or defend their alleged short-comings.

7. *Modify Your Models.* The second purpose of modifying assumptions is to modify models of managerial and employee behavior. My own per-sonal hobgoblin is one I call the Doer Model, often an outgrowth of the family assumption and of unchal-lenged paternalism. I have found the Doer Model alive and thriving in a dozen companies. It works like this:

THE DAILY EXPERIENCE OF GENUINE WORKPLACE DIVERSITY

Chairman David T. Kearns believes that a firm and resolute commitment to affirmative action is the first and most important step to work force diversity. "Xerox is committed to affirmative action," he says. "It is a corporate value, a management priority, and a formal business objective."

Xerox began recruiting minorities and women systematically as far back as the mid-1960s, and it pioneered such concepts as pivotal jobs (described later). The company's approach emphasizes behavior expectations as opposed to formal consciousness-raising programs because, as one Xerox executive put it, "It's just not realistic to think that a day and a half of training will change a person's thinking after 30 or 40 years."

On the assumption that attitude changes will grow from the daily experience of gen-uine workplace diversity, the Xerox Balanced Work Force Strategy sets goals for the num-ber of minorities and women in each division and at every level. (For example, the goal for the top 300 executive-level jobs in one large division is 35% women by 1995, com-pared with 15% today.) "You *must* have a laboratory to work in," says Ted Payne, head of Xerox's Office of Affirmative Action and Equal Opportunity.

Minority and women's employee support groups have grown up in more than a dozen locations with the company's encouragement. But Xerox depends mainly on the three pieces of its balanced strategy to make diversity work.

First are the goals. Xerox sets recruitment and representation goals in accordance with federal guidelines and reviews them constantly to make sure they reflect work force demo-graphics. Any company with a federal contract is required to make this effort. But Xerox then extends the guidelines by setting diversity goals for its upper level jobs and holding division and group managers accountable for reaching them.

The second piece is a focus on pivotal jobs, a policy Xerox adopted in the 1970s when it first noticed that minorities and women did not have the upward mobility the company wanted to see. By examining the backgrounds of top executives, Xerox was able to iden-tify the key positions that all successful managers had held at lower levels and to set goals for getting minorities and women assigned to such jobs.

The third piece is an effort to concentrate managerial training not so much on man-aging diversity as on just plain managing people. What the company discovered when it began looking at managerial behavior toward minorities and women was that all too many managers didn't know enough about how to manage anyone, let alone people quite different from themselves.

Since father knows best, managers seek subordinates who will follow their lead and do as they do. If they can't find people exactly like themselves, they try to find people who aspire to be exactly like themselves. The goal is predictability and immediate responsiveness because the doer manager is not there to manage people but to do the business. In accounting departments, for example, doer managers do accounting, and subordinates are simply extensions of their hands and minds, sensitive to every signal and suggestion of managerial intent.

Doer managers take pride in this identity of purpose. "I wouldn't ask my people to do anything I wouldn't do myself," they say. "I roll up my sleeves and get in the trenches." Doer managers love to be in the trenches. It keeps them out of the line of fire.

But managers aren't supposed to be in the trenches, and accounting managers aren't supposed to do accounting. What they are supposed to do is create systems and a climate that allow accountants to do accounting, a climate that enables people to do what they've been charged to do. The right goal is doer subordinates, supported and empowered by managers who manage.

8. *Help Your People Pioneer.* Learning to manage diversity is a change process, and the managers involved are change agents. There is no single tried and tested "solution" to diversity and no fixed right way to manage it. Assuming the existence of a single or even a dominant barrier undervalues the importance of all the other barriers that face any company, including, potentially, prejudice, personality, community dynamics, culture, and the ups and downs of business itself.

While top executives articulate the new company policy and their commitment to it, middle managers—most or all of them still white males,

remember—are placed in the tough position of having to cope with a forest of problems and simultaneously develop the minorities and women who represent their own competition for an increasingly limited number of promotions. What's more, every time they stumble they will themselves be labeled the major barriers to progress. These managers need help, they need a certain amount of sympathy, and, most of all, perhaps, they need to be told that they are pioneers and judged accordingly.

In one case, an ambitious young black woman was assigned to a white male manager, at his request, on the basis of her excellent company record. They looked forward to working together, and for the first three months, everything went well. But then their relationship began to deteriorate, and the harder they worked at patching it up, the worse it got. Both of them, along with their superiors, were surprised by the conflict and seemed puzzled as to its causes. Eventually, the black woman requested and obtained reassignment. But even though they escaped each other, both suffered a sense of failure severe enough to threaten their careers.

What could have been done to assist them? Well, empathy would not have hurt. But perspective would have been better yet. In their particular company and situation, these two people had placed themselves at the cutting edge of race and gender relations. They needed to know that mistakes at the cutting edge are different—and potentially more valuable—than mistakes elsewhere. Maybe they needed some kind of pioneer training. But at the very least they needed to be told that they were pioneers, that conflicts and failures came with the territory, and that they would be judged accordingly.

9. *Apply the Special Consideration Test.* I said earlier that affirmative action was an artificial, transitional, but necessary stage on the road to a truly

diverse workforce. Because of its artificial nature, affirmative action requires constant attention and drive to make it work. The point of learning once and for all how to manage diversity is that all that energy can be focused somewhere else.

There is a simple test to help you spot the diversity programs that are going to eat up enormous quantities of time and effort. Surprisingly, perhaps, it is the same test you might use to identify the programs and policies that created your problem in the first place. The test consists of one question: Does this program, policy, or principle give special consideration to one group? Will it contribute to everyone's success, or will it produce an advantage for only blacks or whites or women or men? Is it designed for *them* as opposed to *us?* Whenever the answer is yes, you're not yet on the road to managing diversity.

This does not rule out the possibility of addressing issues that relate to a single group. It only underlines the importance of determining that the issue you're addressing does not relate to other groups as well. For example, management in one company noticed that blacks were not moving up in the organization. Before instituting a special program to bring them along, managers conducted interviews to see if they could find the reason for the impasse. What blacks themselves reported was a problem with the quality of supervision. Further interviews showed that other employees too—including white

males—were concerned about the quality of supervision and felt that little was being done to foster professional development. Correcting the situation eliminated a problem that affected everyone. In this case, a solution that focused only on blacks would have been out of place.

Had the problem consisted of prejudice, on the other hand, or some other barrier to blacks or minorities alone, a solution based on affirmative action would have been perfectly appropriate.

10. *Continue Affirmative Action.* Let me come full circle. The ability to manage diversity is the ability to manage your company without unnatural advantage or disadvantage for any member of your diverse workforce. The fact remains that you must first have a workforce that is diverse at every level, and if you don't, you're going to need affirmative action to get from here to there.

The reason you then want to move beyond affirmative action to managing diversity is because affirmative action fails to deal with the root causes of prejudice and inequality and does little to develop the full potential of every man and woman in the company. In a country seeking competitive advantage in a global economy, the goal of managing diversity is to develop our capacity to accept, incorporate, and empower the diverse human talents of the most diverse nation on earth. It's our reality. We need to make it our strength.

43

INDEX

MASSACHUSETTS INSTITUTE OF TECHNOLOGY

ANCONA, KOCHAN, SCULLY,
VAN MAANEN, WESTNEY

Prepared by Deborah M. Kolb

Organizational Behavior & Processes

NEGOTIATION AND
CONFLICT RESOLUTION

module 12

CONTENTS

MODULE 12 (M-12)

NEGOTIATION AND CONFLICT RESOLUTION

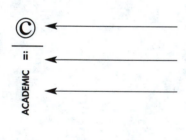

Icon indicates what part you are in, either core Ⓒ or supplemental Ⓢ.

Page number.

Within each part there are sections—Module Overview
(OVERVIEW), Academic Perspective (ACADEMIC),
Popular Press (PRESS), Case (CASE), Exercise
(EXERCISE).

Dedicated to those who have inspired us to try
to be better students and teachers.

Special dedications to:
Professor Jack Barbash
Professor Arthur H. Gladstein
Professor Marius B. Jansen
Professor Joanne Martin
Professor Edgar H. Schein

Acquisitions Editor: John R. Szilagyi
Developmental Editor: Jamie Gleich Bryant
Production Editor: Mardell Toomey
Production House: DPS Associates, Inc.
Cover Design: Michael H. Stratton
Marketing Manager: Rob Bloom

ISBN 0-538-87699-9

1 2 3 4 5 6 7 D1 4 3 2 1 0 9 8

Printed in the United States of America

 South-Western College Publishing

an International Thomson Publishing company I(T)P®

Cincinnati · Albany · Boston · Detroit · Johannesburg · London · Madrid · Melbourne · Mexico City
New York · Pacific Grove · San Francisco · Scottsdale · Singapore · Tokyo · Toronto

NEGOTIATION AND CONFLICT RESOLUTION

The Negotiation and Conflict Resolution module is designed to help you become a more effective negotiator. In the past, you probably would need negotiation and conflict resolution skills only if your job entailed formal dealings with unions, suppliers, and customers. In other words, negotiation was a skill needed only by people who did it for a living. All that has changed in the new organization.

When viewed through a political lens, all interactions both internal and external to the new organization, are basically negotiations. That means that as a manager, you are frequently operating in a situation where your responsibility exceeds your authority. You will need to negotiate with a range of internal and external stakeholders in order to get your job done. In network and team structures, you are but one voice among many. To get your agenda accomplished, you will need to negotiate to build coalitions among different stakeholders and constituencies. As organizations become more diverse demographically and culturally, the potential for conflict increases, requiring even more attention to how we deal with it.

To be an effective negotiator in the new organization requires an understanding of the basic building blocks of the process. These include: developing a stakeholder map of the parties; framing the issues; analyzing relative bargaining power; considering different models of negotiation; and planning and carrying through the process of agreement making. The core material presents these building blocks conceptually, and then translates them into a series of pragmatic preparation questions that can be used to get ready for a negotiation. At the same time as you are working out the substantive issues in a negotiation, you are also working out the terms of your relationship. In these shadow negotiations, you are simultaneously positioning yourself to be an effective advocate for your interests at the same time as you strive to get buy in from others parties. It is in the shadow negotiations, where gender, race, and cultural issues are most likely to surface. When an impasse is reached in negotiations, a person not directly involved in the process, a third party, can often assist. There are a variety of functions a third party can play, but there are challenges in taking on this role in organizations.

The module is structured around a complex negotiation role play—**Mango Systems**. Two senior managers from different divisions—Casey Roberts and Chris Mahoney—are under pressure from their respective bosses to work out an agreement on a significant organization change. Each has different personal and organizational issues that play a part in the goals they set for the negotiation. The fact that the case is set in an organization means that the cultural, political, and strategic issues that inevitably influence negotiations play an important role in how the negotiations are framed and conducted.

Two readings supplement the core materials. In **Some Wise and Mistaken Assumptions about Conflict and Negotiation**, Jeffrey Rubin challenges conventional wisdom that negotiations are either cooperative or competitive. He introduces the concept of "enlightened self-interest," to show how an effective process includes both a focus on ourselves and the other party. With many examples from the international realm, Rubin shows how effective negotiation practice is similar across very different domains. In **Interests: The Measure of Negotiation**, David Lax and James Sebenius provide a thorough analysis of what is meant by interests in negotiation, the various types of interests parties have, and how they can be analyzed to promote creative deal making.

To be an effective negotiator requires practice and reflection. The materials in this module are only a beginning. The more you negotiate, the better you will become at it. But just negotiating is not enough. On a regular basis, you will want to reflect on your emerging expertise. Where are your areas of strength? Of weakness? What skills do you need to work on to become more effective? Becoming a reflective negotiator is a sure way to become more effective at this critical skill.

M-12

core

INTRODUCTION

Being able to deal with conflict effectively is a requirement for survival in the new organization. While conflict is certainly nothing new in organizations, in the past it was channeled into hierarchical structures, formal rules and procedures, and ideologies of cooperation that kept it more or less hidden. In times of stability, negotiation and conflict resolution are the primary responsibility of certain individuals (corporate counsel, labor negotiators, senior managers, among others). In the new organization, all of this has changed. Conflict is built into the very structure and fabric of the new organization, and the capacity to deal with it is key to getting things done on an individual, managerial, and organizational level.

Consider the story of Sandy Max. Sandy is a marketing manager at a medical diagnostics firm. Her day began at 6 a.m. with a phone call from another mother in her car pool. The other mother was ill and wanted Sandy to pick up the children after school to take them to music lessons. Today is not the day for this. The division president has invited Sandy to an important meeting this afternoon on new product design. She turns to her husband and asks what his day is like, and whether he can take over. His day is busy too, and so they negotiate over who will do what and when. The result is that he'll do the pickup at school but Sandy will have to break away from her meeting early so she can take over after the music lesson, while he finishes the report due that day.

Sandy arrives at work at 8 a.m. for a meeting with the engineering group, which is developing a new product. She needs to get changes made in this product, based on trials with the customer. The engineers are already under pressure to get the project completed. She has taken one of the engineers to the customer site, and he now understands the issue and is willing to support her. They will stand together on the need for changes in the design, and hence a revised schedule. The outcome is that they agree to go to the Vice-President for Research and Development to see what can be done.

Her next meeting is with the Division President and his other direct reports. They are doing their twice-yearly ranking of individual performance. It's one of those meetings (that used to be smoke filled) where the managers put forth their people and argue for the rank they want. Although it's supposed to be based on objective criteria, it's a game of hanging tough and making trades.

Finally she returns to her office. The consultant she wants to bring in for negotiation training is on the phone to hear Sandy's reaction to her proposal. Sandy makes a few suggestions and they agree on the price and deliverables. Her friend Laura comes in next for a brown bag lunch. Laura has just returned from maternity leave (her second child) and realizes that she needs to drop back to part-time. But her boss is not supportive and so she wants Sandy's advice on how to negotiate an agreement that will work for her but won't jeopardize her standing in the company. During lunch, Sandy gets a call from the Director of Marketing, who has just gotten off the phone with a distributor in Asia. The Asian distributor complained that the company must not value him as a strategic partner; if it did, he claimed, then the company would have sent a more senior person, and not a woman, to work out the agreement. It was a pretty standard contract, one that Sandy had negotiated all over the world. Under the circumstances, Sandy agrees that she and the director will handle this one together.

After lunch, Sandy prepares for an upcoming negotiation with Joe Green, an important customer. Last week, they had reached a tentative agreement on the level of services and the costs, with everything set to go. Yesterday, Joe called and told her he had just received the last quarter's results and a freeze on new spending was instigated company-wide. He wants her to come back with a different proposal that is much lower than their tentative agreement. But Sandy is also under pressure to produce and tries to see what kind of deal she can put together, one that won't be too expensive but won't hurt her group's performance.

Some quiet time, and then it's off to the meeting to talk about the new product design process. This turns out to be an interesting meeting with lots of good ideas. The division president asks Sandy to head the task force. Flattered, she agrees. But now she has to convince people to join the task force, and help them find time and resources to do the work. And that's only the beginning; resistance to changing the process will be considerable. So she'll have to plan out a strategy to build support for whatever proposal the group pulls together.

Sandy says she'll be in touch with all members of the task force via e-mail later that day to plan a meeting schedule, then excuses herself so she can pick up the children from music class at 5 p.m. After driving the other child home, she starts dinner, then gets on her home computer to send out e-mail messages regarding the meeting schedule and agenda for the first session. Her husband takes over dinner preparations at around 6 p.m., leaving Sandy time to continue working at her computer. The family eats together at 6:30. At 7 o'clock, Sandy's seven-year-old is glued to the television and homework is yet to be done. The 12-year-old wants to go to a party on a school night. Negotiations ensue. Her husband, as he heads into their shared home office to go back to work, points out some brochures for the camping trip in the mountains he wants to take for summer vacation. All Sandy wants to think about right now is lying on the beach at a wonderful resort somewhere. This, too, will come up for discussion.

A day in the life of Sandy in the new organization and in the new economy shows how much negotiation is required just to get through the day. In the flat organization in which Sandy works, her responsibility inevitably exceeds her authority to get things done so she must negotiate with the engineers and other groups in order to achieve her objectives. Sandy's function is networked both internally and externally: She carries out formal negotiations with key stakeholders (suppliers, customers, strategic partners) and informal ones with colleagues over compensation and commitment. Her organization is always changing and responding to meet the needs of individuals and of key stakeholders; negotiating is a way to deal with the resistances that inevitably accompany change. Her firm is diverse and learns from its diversity as individuals and groups negotiate for changes that make the company more inclusive and more sensitive to the blurred boundaries between work and family. Finally, the global nature of her function means that all negotiations take place in a context of cultural difference and diversity.

At one level, it is easy to distinguish negotiation from normal, everyday interactions. Certain negotiations are clearly demarcated events—for example, negotiating a contract with a supplier or customer, collective bargaining between union and management representatives, negotiating the terms and conditions of a potential job. While these events are common enough, they represent only a small segment of the negotiations that take place in the new organization. To recognize these other negotiations—and they are ubiquitous—we need to consider negotiation as an ongoing activity of social decision making where two or more interdependent people with some interests in common and some in conflict (mixed motive) engage in back- and-forth communication aimed at reaching a settlement (Strauss, 1978; Firth, 1995). In the new organization, we negotiate for resources, authority, time, products and services. We negotiate to improve performance, solve problems, strive for equity and fairness, and foster learning and innovation.

NEGOTIATION AS A FORM OF CONFLICT MANAGEMENT

In the new organization, conflict is ubiquitous, but negotiation is only one of the many ways we have to deal with difference. Take a simple example from Sandy's organization. On a task force of engineers and marketers, conflicts erupt over the design of the prototype—Sandy wants the product that gives her customers flexibility while the engineers complain that what marketing wants will cost more and delay the product launch. Here are a few of the ways this situation could be handled:

- *Forcing behavior.* The division vice president could direct the squabbling groups to produce the flexible system and instruct the engineers to do it in a timely fashion. If she's feeling generous, maybe she'll provide extra human or financial resources to help.
- Sandy and the engineers could smooth over their differences. In the meetings they appear collaborative. The engineers promise to make the changes and agree to keep to the schedule—it's no problem. But when they get to the next meeting the changes have not been made and the schedule has slipped.
- They can directly avoid each other and skip the meeting entirely.
- If they decide to negotiate, each party (the marketers and engineers) can put its issues on the table and work through a process to see if they can come to an agreement. That agreement may involve engineering capitulating or maybe marketing will cave and bear the consequences with their customers; or maybe the two sides will creatively work together to fashion an agreement that meets both their interests.
- Finally, they could ask an impartial outside person, a *third* party, to help them figure out what to do. The plant manager, with an interest in moving the product into production, could help facilitate the process.

THE BUILDING BLOCKS OF NEGOTIATION

Parties, issues, and interests, all in varying combinations, are the building blocks that structure the negotiation process. That process can resemble the prototypical market transaction where parties exclusively pursue their individual gain at the expense of the other. For example, Laura insists on a part-time schedule to accommodate family needs but her boss rejects her proposal. Laura threatens to quit, and the boss gives in. Or the process can be one where parties pursue mutual gain, looking to *expand the pie*, so that both can obtain more of what each wants—Laura figures out what she needs to deal with family issues and the boss determines his needs vis à vis the business. Together, they come up with a plan where Laura gets a part-time office schedule but agrees to provisions that will ensure that her customers continue to receive good service. Or the process can have elements of both individual and mutual gain in it. Although Laura is able to get the part-time office schedule and her boss gets what he needs to justify this arrangement to his boss, Laura has to make a significant compromise to attend regular staff meetings at a time she would not necessarily be there.

Sometimes the process leads to a new framing of the problem with a different set of outcomes. As Laura pursues her negotiations over a flexible schedule, others in the group begin to think about how such an arrangement would help them integrate their work and personal life, and also start to see how telecommuting might actually make the total group effort more efficient. So other parties become part of the discussion and the negotiation shifts from being about one person's schedule to one about how the group can pursue a dual agenda of increasing business effectiveness and enabling people to integrate their work and family lives. It is in these multiple ways that parties deal with issues and interests in a particular context that shapes what the negotiation process is like.

Parties

Negotiation takes place between and among parties. Parties can be two people negotiating on their own behalf. I sell my used car to you. Or parties can also be agents acting on behalf of somebody else—a client—or some institution—my department or group. When we negotiate on our own behalf for a salary, for example, psychological issues, considerations of self-esteem and self-worth become part of the picture. When we negotiate on behalf of others as an agent, these issues may be more or less prominent. But as agents, we need to worry not only about what happens across the table, but also how we deal with constituent expectations; the challenge of intraorganizational negotiation or the "second table" problem (Walton and McKersie, 1965). As an example, my group asks me to negotiate with the facilities manager over office space. As is usually the case, I am likely to come back with somewhat less than my group wants. Then I face the challenge of lowering their expectations so that I am not scapegoated for the deal I bring back.

Relationships Parties have different relationships with each other. In the prototypic market, we are strangers. What we negotiate and how we negotiate are seen as having little consequence in these encounters. However, most negotiations in the new organization, and across its boundaries, take place among parties who have ongoing relationships. There are three primary consequences of this new fact of organizational life. First, matters of relationship may be as important to the outcome we negotiate as the substantive issues that give rise to the process in the first place. Second, in ongoing relationships, negotiators develop their own norms which constrain behavior on the one hand, but also help parties interpret and make sense of strategic moves of each other. In labor negotiations, for example, a tendency to act adversarial and denounce the other party is not an indicator of how one feels about the issues, but rather is interpreted as a symbolic gesture, a performance for a constituent audience (Friedman, 1994). Finally, in ongoing relationships, there are possibilities for linkage between a current negotiation and ones in the future. So I might be willing to give you some slack at the moment, with the understanding that you will repay me as part of our next deal.

Number of Parties Although we tend to think about negotiations as taking place between two parties, negotiations may involve multiple parties. Working on a team or task force, mobilizing an organization change effort, or pulling together an industry consortium are tasks that involve multiple parties. Once there are more than two parties, the opportunities and possibilities for coalition formation become a key consideration. Coalition building entails mapping key stakeholders and their interests and concerns, and then building a strategy that sequences bringing them on board (Lax and Sebenius, 1986). Orchestrating decisions at meetings often involves building coalitions prior to the actual meeting.

Negotiator Characteristics Part of the skill in negotiations is being able to read the other party, or to make sense of their strategies and tactics. We can type negotiators by style and membership in particular groups. We all know negotiators with certain styles they have honed over the years which they believe serve them well. First, there is the *thug*, the negotiator who takes a position (and has the wherewithal to back it up) and never departs from it. His or her intransigence means that others must organize their agreements with the thug's position as a constraint. Then there is *conciliator*, the negotiator who wants to make sure that everybody feels good about the agreement and looks for ways to make that happen. Contemporary negotiation theory would have us become *rational analysts*, neither hard nor soft in our tactics. This third type of negotiator has constructed her decision trees before every making a move. Last there are the *intuitive* types, who simply let their experience be their guides. However, research tends not to bear out our everyday experience. Consistent styles are more anecdotal than matters of empirical proof (Rubin and Brown, 1975).

Certain characteristics such as gender, race, and national culture are thought to influence how parties negotiate. There is a tendency to see these characteristics as invariant qualities of a person; that is, men will negotiate competitively, women collaboratively. Westerners will emphasize the terms of agreement, Asians will be more concerned with the relationship. Not surprisingly, research is equivocal on these issues. The belief, for example, that women are more collaborative than men is borne out in some studies but not in others (see Kolb and Coolidge, 1992). While the wish to categorize parties in these terms is understandable, it ignores the importance of background, experience and context in influencing how a negotiator negotiates. For example, a person whose negotiating experience occurs primarily in situations where he or she lacks power and influence will more likely be attentive to relationships and more collaborative, because that is the posture that has served him or her well in the past. Identifying that approach as more feminine than masculine appears to have more to do with how we code behaviors (Kolb and Williams, forthcoming) than what the approach actually is. Similarly, a negotiator new to the international business arena is more likely to display the characteristics of his or her national culture than an international negotiator who has done many deals. The professional and business culture, one that is shared across national boundaries, is more likely to minimize national differences (Rubin and Faure, 1993).

Expectations and stereotypes of others can influence how parties interpret action and the course of the negotiations. In studies of car buying, for example, women and minorities fare considerably worse than white men did because of dealers' beliefs about the relative skill and knowledge about cars of these groups. Under these circumstances, the expectations of the dealers act as a hidden constraint in the negotiations. Similarly, cross-cultural stereotypes impact how we interpret tactics in negotiation. If we believe that a particular culture is exemplified by trustworthiness and honor and another by shady dealing and manipulation, we will hear what parties say differently. Once into the negotiations, these expectations more often than not become self-fulfilling prophecies, where we find evidence to reinforce our expectations, but ignore cues that would disprove them (Rubin and Faure, 1994). In a sense, we create gender and cultural differences in negotiation more than we discover them.

Rather than see a negotiator's actions as individual attributes that mark him or her as a certain kind of person or reminding ourselves of our cognitive limitations, another approach is to focus on the interaction itself where these expectations and behaviors are enacted. In this interaction, negotiators can be *positioned* in a number of different ways. For example, we can pursue our goals by trying to undermine and challenge another party. Predictably, under these circumstances, where parties are in negative subject positions, they will respond in kind, defensively arguing from that one-down position (Cobb, 1985). Positioning another in a positive manner, however, means appreciating and looking for good intentions behind what that person says and does. It means making objections legitimate, acknowledging the other's situation, holding open multiple interpretations of a situation and talking in ways that foster interdependence. These kinds of *connected* practices do not necessarily turn negotiation thugs into collaborators, but they do create a space for others to participate on terms that preserve their sense of themselves and the legitimacy of their issues (Kolb and Williams, forthcoming).

Organization Context Organizational and other incentives can also shape parties' actions. Reward systems can set up competitive dynamics that encourage parties to act solely in their own interests. In collective bargaining, for example, one company evaluated its plant managers on how minimal a wage increase they could achieve in negotiating with the local union representatives. Despite a rhetoric of "win-win" negotiations, the plant managers understandably took a hard line, and the union negotiators responded in kind. Where incentives promote interdependence, then parties often act more collaboratively. For example, in Sandy's organization, performance is judged on the product's performance, rather than on individual functional contribution. Thus, it is more likely for members of her organization to negotiate to solve problems that, under other conditions, they might avoid.

Similarly, culture in an organization can influence how parties negotiate. In cultures that promote competition among individuals and groups, negotiations will tend to be more distributive. In one organization, for example, groups were given similar assignments and encouraged to fight it out, the idea being that truth would come through conflict. On occasions when these groups had to work together and negotiate their differences, they found it difficult to come to agreements. In another organization, where a culture of individualism and individual heroics reigned, even getting a sales group to sit down to negotiate over how to coordinate its customer promises with the operational realities was next to impossible. In sum, how parties act in negotiation is a complex combination of their individual styles, their experiences, others expectations and interactions with them, and the context in which the negotiations take place.

Preparation Questions

1. Who are the relevant parties? Who makes the decisions? Who will actually negotiate? Who are their relevant constituencies?

2. What do I want from the other party(ies)? How do they see their choices? What problems will meeting my needs create for them? Their boss(es)? Their colleagues? Other constituencies?

3. What organizational considerations are relevant? What negotiating behaviors are rewarded? How does the culture view negotiations? What organization constraints exist for them? For me?

4. What kinds of behaviors should I expect? How do they usually negotiate? How do I react to their negotiating style? What should I do to prepare myself? Should I expect that gender, race and/or culture will be issues in the negotiation?

Issues

Issues are the matters over which parties disagree and seek to reach agreement on. The most common distinction people make about issues concerns the number of them. When we negotiate over a single issue, such as price, negotiations inevitably become distributive, or zero sum (Raiffa, 1982). That is, what one party gains comes at the expense of another, the so-called *fixed pie*, where we are splitting up shares or *claiming value.* When there are multiple issues on the table, the possibilities for integrative, or joint gain bargaining increase because parties can make tradeoffs among them. Under these circumstances, we are *creating value* (Lax and Sebenius, 1986).

While the number of issues bears important relations to the type of negotiation process, it is not the only dimension that affects it. Issues can differ in terms of their specificity and clarity. Some issues are pretty straightforward; what price I will pay for the red sports car I covet. In these situations, negotiations are a matter of finding an agreement that meets both parties' needs. But within organizations, issues are often more complex; how will we fulfill the mandate to reduce costs without loss in productivity. In these situations, defining the issues—how to structure a procedure for layoffs or figure out how to streamline processes—in many ways prefigures the agreement. The power to define the issues is a critical, yet often unrecognized, source of influence in negotiations.

Finally, issues are not etched in stone. When we sit down to negotiate, we may think we are pretty clear on what the issues are, but find that the issues change and/or new ones emerge through the process. The manager of a major task force sits down to negotiate with her boss about the schedule for the final report. As they negotiate over the project, its charge changes, as does its members, all factors that impact the deadline. The fact that issues change during a negotiation means that we are never really in a domain where one form of negotiation is inevitable.

© 9 ACADEMIC

Preparation Questions

1. What are the issues we need to negotiate? Try to be as clear as possible.
2. Are the issues separate or can they be linked in the current situation or over time?
3. Are there other ways to frame the issues?

Interests

Interests are what parties seek to advance in negotiations. If the issues are the matters over which parties disagree, then interests are the wants, needs, goals, and desires parties have relative to the issues. In *Getting to YES* (Fisher, Ury, and Patton, 1991), an important distinction is drawn between positions and interests. Positions are the stands we take about an issue; I demand a 10 percent salary increase this year. Interests are the reasons we take a position. The idea is that if we focus on interests, there is more bargaining room to find agreement than if we just stick with positions. I might not be able to get that 10 percent increase in salary, but if we explore my interests—I want credit for a job well done; I feel I am not equitably compensated for my work; I need more child care for my children—there are ways my firm can satisfy some of my interests even if they do not exactly meet my demands. I can get a bonus for a recent project, stock options, a new title and office, more time off, etc. What happens when one focuses on interests is that they provide the means to convert single-issue negotiations with constrained definitions of the issues into the possibilities for joint gain. Knowing your own interests and learning about those of the other party, and distinguishing them from positions, can potentially lead to more integrative outcomes. Whereas positions might be in direct conflict, interests offer the possibilities of compatibility and complementarity.

Types of Interests   We tend to think of interests primarily in monetary or substantive terms; i.e., self-interest equates to selfish, economic interests. However, within organizations, interests are considerably more complex. Consider a negotiation between a systems group and a user group over a new system. Assume the parties have agreed on the scope of the project and are now negotiating over the cost and time frame. Substantive interests are those that relate directly to the issues being negotiated. They can cover the costs of a project (in human and financial terms), and the time and timing, among others. The systems group's substantive interests are in developing a good system and not being constrained too much in terms of cost and time. The user group is desperate for the system, wants it up and running as soon as possible, and does not want to pay too much for it.

Both groups have interests relative to the relationship. They want to maintain a good relationship, especially important to the systems group who sees this project as the first of many. If they can get it done in a reasonable amount of time and for reasonable cost, they feel it is more likely that they will get a follow-up project. On a personal note, the two negotiators are attentive to the fact that they have to sell their agreements to their bosses and so they have to be defensible. Were one to have a potential agreement overturned, it would have negative consequences to both parties.

There are organizational interests as well. Both parties want to do what is best for their particular departments but recognize that, by pursuing this aim exclusively, there might be consequences for the total organization or for others who are not directly at the table. So, the systems group has an interest in not setting a precedent that they underprice their services. At the same time, they do not want to price their services too high, else the user group might prefer an outside vendor, which would have negative consequences to the organization. Both negotiators might have career issues at stake—a successful negotiation (and a successful project) can help both parties and the opposite can hold true as well. When these interests "kick in," they suggest that any agreement must be implementable if the parties are to realize the benefits of their negotiation.

ACADEMIC 10

Finally, each negotiator has personal interests at stake. Each wants to be seen by the other as competent and skilled. So there is often a mutual interest in saving the face of the other; that is, trying to find agreements that make each look good. The user group negotiator, for example, has not had much experience negotiating about systems, at least as compared with his counterpart who negotiates them both internally and externally. So the user has an interest in being seen as a person who got a good deal and was not exploited. Reputation is also important in this regard. If the systems negotiator develops a reputation for inflexibility or exploitation, this will have negative consequences for her, her career, and her group.

There are several important points to make about this process. First, it is helpful to be as specific as one can in articulating one's interests. Often people start with an interest like ". . . we want to do what is best for the organization." Such broad generalizations are of little help, and may actually work against understanding what each side really needs. One can start more generally and then continually unpack interests, pushing back on what people really think and feel they want or need. So in our systems example, the user group wants the project done yesterday and the systems group needs time. Unpacking the interests, it may be that the users need certain functions quickly but have more flexibility on others. The systems group, it turns out, is very worried about resources, because it is currently stretched by other projects. So its interests concerning time have to do with side issues to the negotiation. Understanding these different interests can lead to solutions that would work to the benefit of both.

Second, parties value interests and, indeed, issues differently. Understanding these differences constitutes the core of thinking about integrative and mutual gains negotiations. Since time is crucial to the user group and resources are crucial to the systems group, there are multiple opportunities to make creative deals. The user group might be willing to pay more in order to get the job done on time. These extra resources might be used either to put more engineers on this project or on the others the group is engaged in and/or to enable overtime work. Alternatively, the user group may be able to devote some of its human resources to the project to alleviate the burden on the systems group. The key is that once parties move away from their positions on time and money, they open up possibilities. Other priority interests that are less tangible (such as reputation and relationship) influence the degree to which the groups want to probe and unbundle interests.

How does one learn about interests? There is much we can do ahead of time in preparing for a negotiation. Identifying interests is an important part of negotiation strategy. It begins with an analysis of one's own and the other negotiators' interests relative to a given set of issues, and by working with the information one has to think through the consequences to each party of agreeing to different proposals. However, there is a limit to what one can ultimately know about the other in the absence of interaction.

Talking About Interests One of the major challenges in negotiation is to find ways to talk about interests. At one level, it is a pretty simple matter—one asks. Questions about people's wants and needs can be directly posed: *What are your major areas of concern? What are the key things you need from an agreement? Why are you interested in this issue?* Indeed, research suggests that if you seek information about others' preferences and provide information, you are more likely to achieve mutual gain agreements (Thompson, 1997). However, learning about interests is considerably more complex for a number of reasons.

First, the naive ways that people frame negotiations, as a competitive, zero-sum game, means that they fear that revealing information will jeopardize their positions. It will be used to exploit them, to push for more concessions. So they tend to play their cards close to the vest and reveal information about their interests only reluctantly. If you ask directly about interests, you may be met with a hostile response: what business is it of yours?

Second, the structure of negotiation, where there are possibilities to both create value in terms of joint gain and to claim the value that is created, creates incentives to withhold information. This phenomenon is referred to as the ==negotiator's dilemma== (Lax and Sebenius, 1986; Walton and McKersie, 1965). In practice, what it means is that if negotiators are open and truthful about their interests, the opportunities to discover joint gains are increased. However, in sharing that information, they may cede advantage to the other side who may be in a position to claim more of the value created. When both sides recognize this dilemma and act on it, then they conceal information about interests which forecloses the possibility of joint gains. Further, when a negotiators acts from a value-claiming position, they often interpret the other's sharing of information about interests as a claiming tactic.

Third, in organizations, ==issues and interests are rarely clear-cut and fixed.== In contrast to the clarity of our interests when we buy a car, our interests in complex negotiations are likely to be multiple and not always immediately obvious. Interests emerge and get constructed through the negotiation process itself (Kolb and Putnam, 1992). Thus, we want to create a space where parties can individually and collectively discover their interests, where they differ and where they dovetail. One way to do that is to help each other construct stories about our issues and interests. What we want to do is learn more about the context that produced the issues and how they emerged. So we want to ask questions about history, or how we got to this point. We want to learn more about the conditions under which the issues arose. So rather than general questions about interests and what a person wants and why, we are more likely to elicit useful information by asking specific questions about causes, context, time, and conditions. Other indirect methods can also help elicit interests in complex situations. ==We can propose different scenarios and see how the other side responds.== We can propose specific possibilities as a starting point. We can make multiple equivalent proposals and learn from their reactions. This kind of participative process can help strengthen relationships, and possibly lead to different formulations of a problem that parties have a commitment to solve.

Preparatory Questions

1. Why are the parties at the table?
2. What are my underlying concerns? What are theirs? What are their goals? Mine?
3. What interests are of higher priority? Are their differences in priorities?
4. What would they consider a good outcome? What would it be for me?
5. What kinds of questions can I ask to learn about interests?

Bargaining Power

Henry Kissinger once said that best one can ever hope to get in negotiations is the offer you open with, and it is generally downhill from there (Lax and Sebenius, 1986). The path from that opening offer to a place where agreement is reached involves the use of bargaining power. ==Bargaining power,== in this sense, ==is the capacity to achieve agreement on one's own terms== (Bacharach and Lawler, 1981). While negotiators may come to the table with different sources of potential power, it is in how that power is mobilized to shape perceptions and expectations that ultimately affect what kinds of agreements are reached.

Sources of Power   There are a number of potential sources of power. One of these would be ==my ability to reward or coerce you to make particular concessions.== If I am your boss or occupy a position of legitimate authority, you may be more likely to see things on my terms. Similarly, if you identify with me or somehow see me as admirable, you may be more likely to agree with me. If I have information or expertise that you credit, I might be able to use that to persuade you of a deal I want. If I have others who support me, strategic allies, they may intervene to convince you to go along with me.

Another important source of bargaining power is one's "best alternative to a negotiated agreement," or BATNA (Fisher, Ury, and Patton, 1991). Your BATNA is the answer to the questions, "What will I do if I cannot reach agreement? Do I have other courses of action?" BATNA is an indicator of dependence of one party on another. The more I need an agreement, because I have few alternatives, the more potential power you will have over me and vice versa. If I have other viable alternatives, I might be able to take a stronger position in negotiation because I can walk away from the deal. Without such alternatives, I may be forced to accept terms that are not much to my liking.

Developing a BATNA Evaluating one's BATNA can be pretty straightforward when the issues are simple—I can get prices on the same car from two dealers, for example. The currency is the same. More often, however, evaluating one's BATNA is more complicated. First, it may be difficult to compare two alternatives. For example, I have two job offers, each with its own combination of desirable attributes and limiting drawbacks. Second, it may be difficult to identify an alternative: If the engineers simply will not agree to switch the schedule, identifying a substitute course of action is not easy. Third, one's BATNA can involve escalating to difficult courses of action that might have high costs, such as going to court, quitting one's job. Fourth, one's BATNA can be a combination of actions that involve other parties whose impact is difficult to analyze precisely. Finally, it is rarely the case that one's BATNA is as good as one might hope to get from the agreement one is negotiating. If it were, you would not be negotiating, so it may be difficult to keep in your mind as a viable alternative.

Even when it is difficult to develop a BATNA and evaluate it, doing so is a useful exercise for several reasons. In simple negotiations, it sets the reservation price or bottom line in a defensible way. If I know what price I can get for the car I covet down the street, I know then the maximum I am willing to pay. But even in the more common situations where one's BATNA is not exactly comparable, it makes sense to consider it because it helps put you in a better position when you negotiate. It does so for two reasons. First, it helps you distinguish situations where you have potential bargaining power from those where you are lacking. If you have another job offer (even if it is not your first choice), you are not quite as dependent on the outcome of your negotiation than you would be if you were in a desperate situation with no other possibilities. Desperate situations; e.g., you're out of work, the mortgage and all the other bills are due, and you have no other job offers, generally mean that you go into negotiations in a weaker position than would be the case if you had a BATNA. Second, if you feel you have other choices, you are likely to be a more effective negotiator than if you see yourself in a weak, one-down situation. That is why it makes sense to try to improve one's BATNA going into a negotiation. Indeed, the research shows that negotiators who have alternatives do better at both creating value in negotiations and in claiming it (Thompson, 1997). It is also important to learn as much as you can about the other party's BATNA.

Mobilizing Power and Influence Potential bargaining power is only part of the story. If power mattered absolutely, outcomes in a negotiation could be predicted by assessing the differential power and influence of the parties. But that is not always the case. Less powerful parties can often do very well in negotiations. The key is how negotiators manage and manipulate impressions of power to their advantage, or how they use their influence to shape perceptions of agreement possibilities. Persuasion is perhaps what we think of first. We use our skill and knowledge to marshal facts and figures to convince you of the merits of our sense of the deal. We let you know subtly that we have a good BATNA. If you know our user group has entertained an offer from an outside vender, then you may be more flexible in giving us what we want. We let you know that other influential people support our ideas. We use our authority (and your acceptance of it) to convince you that we know best what kind of deal will work. We use your feelings of respect for us to suggest that what we want has merit. We can flatter and ingratiate ourselves and you might be more tempted to go along with us.

In all these examples, mobilizing the power we have in the situations is directed toward our getting what we want and doing so in a tactical and somewhat manipulative way. There are two important points we need to raise here. First, when our sources of power are mobilized in a negotiation, we are sending messages about how tough we are. At least some parity of toughness is required for parties to discover joint gains. If I come across as too weak, you are unlikely to want to accommodate my concerns. Likewise if I see you as weak relative to me, I have little incentive to work with you to create value. Thus, negotiators must engage in some mutual posturing in order to move to a place where they can work toward joint gains.

Second, there are always ethical issues when we talk about managing impressions in the kinds of opportunistic situations that negotiations typically entail. While the structure of negotiations sometimes creates incentives to exaggerate, distort, and otherwise misrepresent the situation, there are often consequences to doing so. One's reputation can be irreparably harmed by engaging in tactics that might lead to brief short-term gains at the expense of long-term relationships. In judging what is ethical or not, one scholar in the field uses the "mother" test: Would I be happy telling my mother I did this?

Since negotiation is a two-way street, you are using influence tactics at the same time they are being used on you. One way to view negotiations is as an information game. Through moves and countermoves, through arguments and counter arguments, through proposals and counterproposals, negotiators struggle to define the situation in terms that will advantage them.

Preparatory Questions

1. What sources of power/influence does each party have?
2. What is your BATNA? Theirs? What ways exist to improve yours? Worsen theirs?
3. Does each party perceive negotiations as in their best interests?
4. What resources do you have to influence perceptions? How will you mobilize them in the negotiations?

Process

Process is the means by which parties work out their differences over issues and pursue their interests. It is typical in the field of negotiations to describe two basic processes: distributive and integrative negotiations. Each has a set of tactics, particularly around communication, associated with it that in some ways stand in marked contrast to each other. These contrasts capture the *mixed motive* quality of most negotiations; in other words, the distributive and integrative potential are both present.

Distributive Negotiations Bargainers in distributive (or win-lose) negotiations view each other as adversaries with interests that are in direct conflict over a single issue like price.[1] These negotiations are called zero sum because what one party achieves comes directly at the expense of the other. The tactics used in distributive bargaining are intended to claim as much value as you can for yourself. Value claimers analyze their BATNAs and those of their opponents, seeking to enhance theirs and make the others worse. Claiming tactics begin with extreme opening offers that reveal as little information about true preferences as possible. One argues persuasively for one's own position and minimizes those made by the other side. Concessions are made slowly and grudgingly, all the time exaggerating the value of any concessions made. Concessions made by the other side tend to be devalued and demeaned. Power tactics, such as bluffs and threats to leave the negotiation or commitments to accept only certain deals, are common. Information about preferences is closely held.

---

1 For excellent discussions of distributive bargaining and claiming tactics, see Lax and Sebenius (1986).

Introduction

The concessionary dance that marks these negotiations moves along a bargaining zone called the "Zone of Possible Agreements," or ZOPA. The ZOPA is bounded by the reservation price (the least you'd be willing to accept or most you'd be willing to pay) of each party.[2] Parties make opening offers that anchor the negotiations and often become the focal point around which the negotiations pivot. There is no reliable advantage to making opening offers unless you possess good information about the reservation price or bottom line of the other party. Absent such information, there is the risk that you will give away too much information. Advice from the experts cautions one to avoid opening offers without good information but, if forced to do so, make an offer that reveals as little as possible about one's bottom line. Opening offers lead to counter offers and a series of concessions that typically get smaller as parties approach the point of a compromise agreement (Raiffa, 1982).

The communication tactics that mark these negotiations are intended to shape people's perceptions of what the bargaining zone is and where a likely agreement will be. The symbolic management of issues, alternatives to agreement, positions, and interests are critical elements in distributive negotiations. Think about purchasing a car. As a buyer, you might want to dress in something other than your designer suit and mention good offers you have from another dealer, among other tactics. Such tactics are signals to suggest that you will not pay as much as the dealer might like. The salesperson likewise might ignore you for awhile, signaling her presumed lack of interest in a sale, then have trouble locating the model you want, and then make you wait while she checks with the dealer about price. These moves, in addition to the offers and counteroffers made are intended to make you think again about how much this car will cost you.

Integrative Negotiations In integrative negotiations, the process is intended to be more open, making these symbolic and strategic communication gestures less prominent. Integrative negotiations are based on the premise (and observation) that it is possible, using a certain kind of problem solving process, to find synergies and mutual gains in situations that look distributive. The way to do that is to focus on interests, not positions and then to be creative in searching for options that meet these interests (Fisher, Ury, and Patton, 1991). A story that is frequently used to describe this phenomenon deals with two sisters who both need the last orange in the house to bake a cake. One sister wants the orange for a fruit cake and the other for a chiffon cake. Neither sister can bake her cake with half an orange and so they appear at a stalemate. Through further dialogue, they discover that the first sister, who is making a fruitcake, needs the rind of the orange while the second sister needs the juice to make the chiffon cake. Both can get what they want from the single orange. The process operates based on a notion of *enlightened self-interest* (Breslin and Rubin, 1991): I can get what I want if I can find ways to help you get what you want.

Sources of Joint Gains Identifying joint gains is a process that requires some open sharing of interests, then a search for agreements that meet both parties needs. There are a number of ways to meet these mutual needs—finding new resources, logrolling, nonspecific compensation, cost cutting, and bridging (Pruitt, 1981). In the systems group example, parties can expand the pie by *acquiring more resources*. Perhaps other interested groups could benefit from the system and might be willing to contribute to its development. *Logrolling* involves making tradeoffs and exchanges based on differences. Since the user group is concerned about time and the developers about costs, they could make agreements that capitalize on these differences. The systems group would be willing to put more engineers on the project if the user group is willing to pay

2 Establishing one's reservation price can be a simple matter or a complex process of assessing alternatives to agreement and the probabilities of reaching various outcomes. See Raiffa (1982) and Lax and Sebenius (1986).

for overtime. Other dimensions along which parties can differ relative to their interests include differences in priority of issues; in expectations of uncertain events; in the amount of acceptable risk; and in time preferences, among others. These differences can lead to tradeoffs and contingent agreements that can leave both parties better off (Lax and Sebenius, 1986). *Nonspecific compensation* means that one party gets what it wants and the other is paid in some unrelated coin. For example, the developers get the additional funds and, in return, offer a training program at some later date. *Cost cutting* is when one party gets what it wants and the other side's costs are reduced. In order to get the project done on time, the user group devotes some of its human resources to the project to alleviate the burden on the systems group. *Bridging* means coming up with a totally new option nobody else had thought about. In scoping out this project, both parties see that this project is really a template for others in the firm and so sell it to the executive committee as a means of developing more integration across units.

There are several important points to make about these approaches. First, the key to mutual gains agreements is to work from interests to find new issues, and to expand the range of possibilities for making tradeoffs. Using *what if. . . ?* questions gets people to think more expansively about the possibilities for joint gain. Joint gains can also come from defining a joint problem that both have a stake in solving and that minimizes conflict of interests and emphasizes those that are shared.

The key issue in mutual gains negotiation is to understand as much as you can about the situation of the other negotiator at ever-deeper levels and continue to float options that will meet mutual needs. There are a number of barriers to this creative process. They include: seeing the negotiation exclusively as a distributive and adversarial process; focusing only on one's needs and interests; failing to take into account others' needs, or failing to assert one's interests effectively; working under a tight deadline; and lacking authority, among other issues (Bazerman and Neale, 1992; Mnookin, 1993). Overcoming these barriers to creativity requires challenging assumptions, suspending judgment and evaluation about particular ideas, looking at the problem from different perspectives, and continuing to offer new options and/or alternative package deals if the first one is not a fit.

Negotiator's Dilemma No matter how creative one becomes, there is still the dilemma that is based in the mixed-motive structure of most negotiations. The *negotiator's dilemma* is inevitable in most situations. If we pursue distributive negotiation tactics—tactics to claim value for ourselves—we will be unlikely to move to a process of option creation that leads to mutual gain. If we pursue integrative negotiation tactics; that is, we try to create value, there is still going to be the issue of how we distribute the new value we have created. How much time for what level of compensation will always be an issue. Some argue that one can use objective, fair, or independent criteria to solve the distribution issue, but one side's objective criteria may be seen as merely another bargaining position by the other (Fisher, Ury, and Patton, 1991).

While it is theoretically possible to negotiate an agreement that maximizes potential value created with parties claiming equitable shares, that is typically not what happens in the real world. But the degree to which it matters is variable. To the degree that the communicative contradictions of claiming and creating (described above) happen, and so possible mutual gains are left on the table, there is a problem. To the degree that, in the interests of creating value, one party cedes all to another, that is also probably less than desirable. Working around the negotiator's dilemma (one cannot really eliminate it) is best achieved in relationships that build over time, in situations where the value of creating outweighs incentives to claim, where creating is functionally separated from claiming (e.g., by separating the inventing process from the actual decisions), and in situations where parties can achieve small wins and then build on them either with the help of a third party or through improving them after the fact with post-settlement settlements (Lax and Sebenius, 1986; Raiffa, 1982).

Preparatory Questions

1. What assumptions does each party make about the type of negotiations? Is this likely to be distributive or integrative?
2. What arguments and tactics will I use to handle the distributive parts of the negotiation?
3. What options exist to satisfy mutual interests in the integrative parts of the negotiation? What tradeoffs are possible based on differences in views regarding time, risk, resources, responsibilities, needs?
4. What kind of process should we agree to in order to come up with options that satisfy out mutual needs?
5. How will we manage the negotiator's dilemma?

Shadow Negotiations   Up to this point, we have described the negotiation process primarily in terms of the substantive issues parties negotiate. But there is another parallel, a shadow negotiation also going on. That negotiation is also about the norms that will govern the interaction (Kolb and Williams, forthcoming). When parties negotiate with each other, they are doing more than arguing for their proposals; they are presenting themselves. The shadow negotiation is where negotiators work out the personal dynamic of their exchange. It is where they vie for control over who will set the terms of the discussion, or whose interests will be heard. It's where they size each other up, where they check for flexibility. The relational by-play in the shadow negotiations affect how issues and interests are seen, and what kind of agreement is reached. Parties enter negotiations with certain predispositions and expectations about the other. These get played out as parties test and size each other up, looking for weakness or opportunity, to determine what kind of process will ensue. It makes a difference whether one side believes the other is speaking for the CEO or just itself.

In this shadow negotiation, one can see the equivalents of claiming and creating. Moves to position oneself advantageously are the tough side of negotiation. In these moves, negotiators seek to establish the legitimacy of themselves and their positions, to present themselves as parties the other side needs to negotiate seriously with. Managing these impressions is one of the ways we convince others to attend to us and our interests. When we negotiate a salary increase, it helps if we have just come off a big and successful project and start the conversation there. Moves by the other to challenge our presentations need to be met head on, else they begin to define the situation in ways that can be undermining. When the Asian distributor called Sandy's boss to complain about the partnership negotiations, for example, Sandy and her boss made a countermove intended to reinforce her legitimacy as the spokesperson for the firm. When they met with the distributor, Sandy's boss deferred to her regarding all questions. In this way, he demonstrated that Sandy has the authority to speak for the firm.

Sometimes in a negotiation, moves will be made that seriously undermine you. These are the *dirty tricks* of negotiation (Fisher, Ury, and Patton, 1991). These moves, such as giving you a seat with the sun directly in your eyes, the "good-cop-bad cop" routine, or changing an agreement at the last minute, are intended to place a negotiator in a one-down position. Sometimes, just recognizing these behaviors and the purpose they are intended to serve is sufficient. You can just ignore them. At other times, you can interrupt the moves, either by taking a break or shifting the conversation back to your issues. (Fisher, Ury, and Patton, 1991; Kolb and Williams, forthcoming).

All these moves and countermoves are intended to preserve your image as a legitimate and savvy negotiator, so that the other side resists the temptation to take advantage. But the parallel negotiation also involves gambits to build a more collaborative relationship. These are efforts to connect to the other person in order to build bridges to create relationships that foster norms of collaboration. Among other techniques, these include engaging in shared rituals; emphasizing the interests held in common—

golf, football, children; exploring a common background; making references to mutual acquaintances and associations; demonstrating respect for status; and reinforcing each other's self-concept (Kolb and Williams, forthcoming; Walton and McKersie, 1965). These efforts are intended to foster impressions of interdependence and common fate, which are more likely to lead to norms of collaboration.

Preparatory Questions

1. How am I positioned in the organization to negotiate?
2. Whose support do I need?
3. What kinds of moves can I expect that might fluster or confuse me? How will I respond?
4. What can I do to foster interdependence and problem solving in these negotiations?
5. What would be good mutual outcomes that we can work toward?

Just as creating and claiming on the substantive issues creates a dilemma, so too does the need to present oneself as tough and, simultaneously, connected (Kolb and Williams, forthcoming). Both impressions are critical and need to work together. Good agreements are more likely to be reached when both sides recognize the toughness of the other. That provides the incentives to negotiate seriously. However, the process requires connection so that parties can recognize their mutual needs. Too much emphasis on one can drive out the other. If I signal a great deal of concern for you and your situation but fail to push my own agenda, then you may not feel any compulsion to meet my needs. On the other side, if I act too tough, you may see me as someone who is only out for myself and respond in kind, and we will not develop the kind of working relationship that would encourage collaboration.

Blending toughness and connection can play out in different ways. If legitimacy is seen as a problem, for example, then tough moves to establish it will be a precondition for connected overtures. In established relationships, such moves may be superfluous and connection will dominate. These are not linear processes nor is there jumping back-and-forth between the two qualities. Rather, the blending of toughness and connection occurs throughout a negotiation as both deliberate action and responsive turns.

Assisted Negotiations

Negotiations do not always yield agreements. Sometimes, negotiations just stalemate or come to an impasse. Claiming tactics might have driven out creating or even obscured potential areas of agreement. The issues may be difficult or of such a technical nature that it is hard to figure out where agreement might lie. Emotions may be running high, making it difficult for people to negotiate with each other. Power differentials might inhibit the kind of toughness and advocacy that is needed to engage in serious negotiations. Maybe relationships have deteriorated so much that even the most basic of communication is impossible. In the waning days of Lehman Brothers, the two executive partners could not even be in the same room with each other. An administrative partner served as go-between to run the firm by assisting their negotiations on a one-on-one basis (Auletta, 1986). Sometimes parties avoid conflict and need somebody to help make negotiations happen.

Third-Party Roles Third parties can sometimes help. They can play many roles, from process consultant to a binding decision maker, such as an arbitrator or judge. Assisted negotiation is more akin to mediation, a process that emphasizes intervention into the dispute but without the formal authority to render a decision. Mediators assist negotiators by helping the parties manage some of the dilemmas and difficulties of bilateral negotiations. In organizations, mediation is often employed as part of a formal complaint or grievance procedure and informally when managers and peers, from the same or different departments, become involved in some capacity.

Who plays this kind of role in organizations? Potentially, many people. Some are in positions where they are likely to be drawn into disputes. In one organization, continual blaming behind the scenes but reluctance to confront differences openly kept the firm from moving ahead on a life-saving strategy. All sides took a human resource executive into their confidence and, based on the information she had, she was able to force issues out into the open, thereby creating the possibilities for confronting the issues directly through negotiation (Kolb and Bartunek, 1992). Other people develop a reputation for being good at it and so are sought out by colleagues. People come to their offices to discuss their situations and ask for help. Sometimes another person is indirectly affected by a failure to resolve differences and so finds it in her best interests to assist the negotiations. Failure of engineering and operations, for example, to deal with a quality problem has negative implications for a marketing manager and so he decides to intervene. While managers can assist negotiations with their subordinates, research suggests that they favor making decisions themselves over taking the time to assist the negotiations (Sheppard, 1984).

Functions   There are a number of functions that informal mediators can perform. Because they are not directly involved, they can cool things down and keep the other parties focused on the issues. They can do this by building agendas and orchestrating the meetings. The structure of third-party involvement where a mediator can meet separately with each party means that she can explore for areas of flexibility without causing a party to make a public commitment to a deal that might be exploited. She might be able to be quite creative and invent options that the two parties have not been able to see. In other words, the presence of a third party might allow for public claiming but private creating and so contribute to finding a mutual gains agreement that had eluded the parties. Finally, the third party can help those directly involved explore the consequences of no agreement. Mediators call this the *dose of reality*. Do you really want this disagreement to be aired to senior management? Do you really want the outside vendor to get this project? Have you considered the costs to your career of opting out of this project?

Challenges   While the potential contribution of a third party is significant, it is not an easy role to fulfill. There are a number of challenges that informal mediators face. First, is the tendency to want to tell people what to do rather than assist them to resolve their own differences. Not surprisingly, such telling tends to breed resistance. While parties in the beginning might look to the mediator to suggest ideas, once those ideas are suggested, their open stance often shifts to finding reasons to reject what is offered. After all, any solution will be less than the parties might actually prefer. Thus, any agreement that parties can accept requires some time for them to adjust. And of course, time is a rare commodity in the new organization.

A second key issue centers on the question of neutrality. Neutrality is basic to the ethic of most mediators; they need to keep their preferences under wraps. While this advice might fit the role of professional mediators (and even this is disputed), absolute neutrality as the concept is generally understood is virtually impossible in organizations. Given their knowledge of the organization and their own interests (no matter how tangential), informal mediators are rarely unbiased about outcomes. Typically, there are outcomes they would prefer over others. Existing relationships and career aspirations means that it is typically difficult to be absolutely indifferent among parties. However, even without being unbiased and impartial, it is still possible to be neutral, if one thinks about neutrality as a practice and not a state of being or individual characteristic (Cobb, 1993). A neutral practice means providing the space for each party to tell its story, and to argue its position on its own terms, not defensively in reaction to the first account of the situation. When mediators are neutral, parties feel heard, and are more likely to feel that the outcome is fair; hence, they are more committed to the outcome (Shapiro and Kolb, 1994).

Finally, when parties are at an impasse in negotiations, it is often difficult to help them come to an agreement. Not only might the problems themselves be difficult, but the parties may find it difficult to make concessions for a variety of reasons they think have merit. The informal third party has a number of ways she can help. The first is to help the parties shift the way that they talk about the issues. Rather than blaming the other, for example, it helps to talk about the problem. Rather than dwelling on what happened, it helps to talk about the future, or what could be. Rather than make demands, it helps to talk about interests, to talk about what people want and are looking for from an agreement. Rather than make unilateral proposals, it helps to talk in terms of exchange, posing the "what if. . ." and "if then. . ." questions. A third party can help shift the conversation by restating what people say and/or asking questions that help the parties talk about the problem differently. If they talk about it differently, they may begin to see it differently (Kolb and Associates, 1994).

The second approach is to help the parties by framing the outlines of a possible agreement. Listening carefully and meeting in separate caucuses with them, the mediators begin to piece together elements of an agreement that might work. There might be obvious tradeoffs they can see or they may come up with a creative idea to break a deadlock. Interestingly, however, it is as important how one introduces such ideas as what the ideas are. It is often useful to introduce them as questions. Would this be possible? How would you improve on this idea? It is also important, research suggests, that mediators not become too vested in what they propose, because it will likely undergo many changes before a final agreement is reached.

Finally, mediators can create explicit situations of choice. They can ask people to compare the current agreement to their BATNA, the alternative they would have to consider if agreement is not reached. One mediator describes this as the *iron fist in the velvet glove* (Kolb and Associates, 1994). It is often difficult for people to make concessions or even to agree to deals that involve mutual gains. People tend to compare what is currently on the table with what they most want rather than what they will have to settle for if agreement isn't reached. Pointing out the costs of delay, of costs to one's career and image, or of costs to the organization, can often provide the extra push for parties to reconsider. It encourages parties to think more clearly about what would work for them and what they would be willing to accept.

IN CONCLUSION

The new organization is built on the capacity to deal with conflicts more productively, efficiently, and as close to the nexus of problems as possible. Forcing, smoothing, and avoiding, while still common responses to conflict, can undermine the very virtues the new organization is meant to promote. Being able to confront differences productively through negotiation and/or with the assistance of a third party can turn conflict into a creative and innovative force.

REFERENCES

Auletta, Ken. 1986. *Greed and Glory on Wall Street.* New York: Random House.

Bacharach, Samuel, and Edward Lawler. 1981. *Bargaining.* San Francisco: Jossey-Bass.

Bazerman, Max, and Margaret Neale. 1992. *Negotiating Rationally.* New York: Free Press.

Breslin, J. William, and Jeffrey Z. Rubin. 1991. *Negotiation Theory and Practice.* Cambridge, Mass.: PON Books (The Program on Negotiation at Harvard Law School).

Cobb, Sara. 1993. "Empowerment and Mediation: A Narrative Perspective." *Negotiation Journal*, 9 (3), pp. 245–259.

Firth, Alan. 1995. *The Discourse of Negotiation*. New York: Elsevier.

Fisher, Roger, William Ury, and Bruce Patton. 1991. *Getting to YES: Negotiating Agreement Without Giving In*. 2nd ed. New York: Penguin.

Friedman, Raymond. 1994. *Front Stage, Backstage: The Dramatic Structure of Labor Negotiations*, Cambridge, Mass.: MIT Press.

Kolb, Deborah and Judith Williams. Forthcoming. *Her Place at the Table: Managing Toughness and Connection in Negotiation*. New York: Simon and Schuster.

Kolb, Deborah M. and Associates. 1994. *When Talk Works: Profiles of Mediators*, San Francisco: Jossey-Bass.

Kolb, Deborah M. and Jean Bartunek, eds. 1992. *Hidden Conflict in Organizations*, Newbury Park, Calif.: Sage.

Kolb, Deborah M., and Linda L. Putnam. 1992. "The Dialectics of Disputing." In Deborah M. Kolb and Jean Bartunek, eds. *Hidden Conflict in Organization*. Newbury Park, Calif.: Sage.

Lax, David A. and James K. Sebenius. 1986. *The Manager as Negotiator*. New York: Basic Books.

Mnookin, Robert M. 1993. "Why Negotiations Fail: An Exploration of Barriers to the Resolution of Conflict." *Ohio State Journal of Dispute Resolution* 8 (2), pp. 235–249.

Pruitt, Dean. 1981. *Negotiation Behavior*. New York: Academic Press.

Raiffa, Howard. 1982. *The Art and Science of Negotiation*. Cambridge, Mass.: Harvard University Press.

Rubin, Jeffrey Z., and Bert R. Brown. 1975. *The Social Psychology of Bargaining and Negotiation*. New York: Academic Press.

Rubin, Jeffrey Z., and Guy Olivier Faure. 1993. *Culture and Negotiation*. Newbury Park, Calif.: Sage.

Shapiro, Debra, and Deborah Kolb. 1994. "Reducing the 'Litigious Mentality' by Increasing Employees' Desire to Communicate Grievances." In S. Sitkin and B. Bies, eds., *The Litigious Organization*. Newbury Park, Calif.: Sage.

Sheppard, Blair. 1984. "Third Party Conflict Intervention: A Procedural Framework." In B. M. Staw and L. L. Cummings, eds. *Research in Organizational Behavior*, Vol. 6. Greenwich, Conn.: JAI Press.

Strauss, Anselm. 1978. *Negotiations*. San Francisco: Jossey-Bass.

Thompson, Leigh. 1997. *The Mind and Heart of the Negotiator*. Upper Saddle River, N.J.: Prentice-Hall.

Walton, Richard, and Robert B. McKersie. 1965. *A Behavioral Theory of Labor Negotiations*. New York: MGraw-Hill.

21 ACADEMIC ©

M-12

supplemental

SOME WISE AND MISTAKEN ASSUMPTIONS ABOUT CONFLICT AND NEGOTIATION

by Jeffrey Z. Rubin

For many years the attention of conflict researchers and theorists was directed to the laudable objective of conflict *resolution*. This term denotes as an outcome a state of attitude change that effectively brings an end to the conflict in question. In contrast, conflict *settlement* denotes outcomes in which the overt conflict has been brought to an end, even though the underlying bases may or may not have been addressed. The difference here is akin to Herbert Kelman's (1958) useful distinction among the three consequences of social influence: compliance, identification, and internalization. If conflict settlement implies the consequence of compliance (a change in behavior), then conflict resolution instead implies internalization (a more profound change, of underlying attitudes as well as behavior). The third consequence, *identification*, denotes a change in behavior that is based on the target of influence valuing his or her relationship with the source, and it serves as a bridge between behavior change and attitude change.

In keeping with the flourishing research in the 1950s on attitudes and attitude change, social psychological research on conflict in the 1950s and 1960s focused on conflict *resolution*. Only recently has there been a subtle shift in focus from attitude change to behavior change. Underlying this shift is the view that, while it is necessary that attitudes change if conflict is to be eliminated, such elimination is often simply not possible. Merely getting Iran and

Iraq, Turkish and Greek Cypriots, Contras and Sandinistas to lay down their weapons—even temporarily—is a great accomplishment in its own right, even if the parties continue to hate each other. And this simple act of cessation, when coupled with other such acts, may eventually generate the momentum necessary to move antagonists out of stalemate toward a settlement of their differences. Just as "stateways" can change "folkways" (Deutsch and Collins, 1951), so too can a string of behavioral changes produce the basis for subsequent attitude change.

The gradual shift over the last years from a focus on resolution to a focus on settlement has had an important implication for the conflict field: It has increased the importance of understanding *negotiation*—which, after all, is a method of settling conflict rather than resolving it. The focus of negotiation is not attitude change per se, but an agreement to change behavior in ways that make settlement possible. Two people with underlying differences of beliefs or values (for example, over the issue of a woman's right to abortion or the existence of a higher deity) may come to change their views through discussion and an exchange of views, but it would be inappropriate and inaccurate to describe such an exchange as "negotiation."

Similarly, the shift from resolution to settlement of conflict has also increased the attention directed to the role of *third parties* in the conflict settlement process—individuals who are in some way external to a dispute and who, through

Jeffrey Z. Rubin was Professor of Psychology at Tufts University, Medford, MA and former Executive Director of the Program on Negotiation at Harvard Law School.

Source: Jeffrey Z. Rubin, "Some Wise and Mistaken Assumptions About Conflict and Negotiation" from *Negotiation Theory and Practice* edited by J. William Breslin and Jeffrey Z. Rubin. Reprinted by permission of Plenum Publishing Corporation.

identification of issues and judicious intervention, attempt to make it more likely that a conflict can be moved to settlement.

Finally, the shift in favor of techniques of conflict settlement has piqued the interest and attention of practitioners in a great many fields, ranging from divorce mediators and couples' counselors to negotiators operating in environmental, business, labor, community, or international disputes. Attitude change may not be possible in these settings, but behavior change—as the result of skillful negotiation or third-party intervention—is something else entirely. Witness the effective mediation by the Algerians during the so-called Iranian hostage crisis in the late 1970s; as a result of Algerian intervention, the Iranian government came to dislike the American Satan no less than before, but the basis for a *quid pro quo* had been worked out.

COOPERATION, COMPETITION, AND ENLIGHTENED SELF-INTEREST

Required for effective conflict settlement is neither cooperation nor competition, but what may be referred to as "enlightened self-interest." By this I simply mean a variation on what several conflict theorists have previously described as an "individualistic orientation" (Deutsch, 1960)—an outlook in which the disputant is simply interested in doing well for himself or herself, without regard for anyone else, out neither to help nor hinder the other's efforts to obtain his or her goal. The added word "enlightened" refers to the acknowledgment by each side that the other is also likely to be pursuing a path of self-interest—and that it may be possible for *both* to do well in the exchange. If there are ways in which I can move toward my objective in negotiation, while at the same time making it possible for you to approach your goal, then why not behave in ways that make both possible?

Notice that what I am describing here is neither pure individualism (where one side does not care at all about how the other is doing) nor pure cooperation (where each side cares deeply about helping the other to do well, likes and values the other side, etc.)—but an amalgam of the two.

Trivial though this distinction may seem, it has made it possible in recent years for work to develop that, paradoxically, creates a pattern of *inter*dependence out of the assumption of *in*dependence. Earlier work, focusing as it did on the perils of competition and the virtues of cooperation, made an important contribution to the field of conflict studies. However, in doing so, it also shifted attention away from the path of individualism—a path that is likely to provide a way out of stalemate and toward a settlement of differences. I do not have to like or trust you in order to negotiate wisely with you. Nor do I have to be driven by the passion of a competitive desire to beat you. All that is necessary is for me to find some way of getting what I want—perhaps even *more* than I considered possible—by leaving the door open for you too to do well. "Trust" and "trustworthiness," concepts central to the development of cooperation, are no longer necessary—only the understanding of what the other person may want or need.

A number of anecdotes have emerged to make this point; perhaps the most popular is the tale of two sisters who argue over the division of an orange between them (Fisher and Ury, 1981; Follett, 1940). Each would like the entire orange, and only reluctantly do the sisters move from extreme demands to a 50-50 split. While such a solution is eminently fair, it is not necessarily wise: one sister proceeds to peel the orange, discard the peel, and eat her half of the fruit; the other peels the orange, discards the fruit, and uses her 50% of the peel to bake a cake! If only the two sisters had understood what each wanted the orange for—not each side's "position," but rather each side's underlying "interest"—an agreement would have been possible that would have allowed each to get everything that she wanted.

Similarly, Jack Sprat and his wife—one preferring lean, the other fat—can lick the platter clean if they understand their respective interests. The interesting thing about this conjugal pair is that, married though they may be, when it comes to dining preferences they are hardly interdependent at all. For Jack and his wife to "lick the platter clean" requires neither that the two love each other nor care about helping each other in every way possible; nor does it require that each be determined to get more of the platter's contents than the other. Instead, it is enlightened self-interest that makes possible an optimal solution to the problem of resource distribution.

The lesson for international relations is instructive. For the United States and the Soviet Union, Israel and its Arab neighbors, Iran and Iraq, the Soviet Union and Afghanistan, the United States and Nicaragua to do well, neither cooperation nor competition is required, but rather an arrangement that acknowledges the possibility of a more complex mixture of these two motivational states—enlightened individualism. While the United States and Soviet Union will continue to have many arenas of conflict in which their interests are clearly and directly opposed, and will also continue to find new opportunities for cooperation (as in the management of nuclear proliferation, hazardous waste disposal, or international political terrorism), there are also arenas in which each side is not at all as dependent on the other for obtaining what it wants (e.g., the formulation of domestic economic or political policy). The world is a very big place; the pie is big enough for both of us, and for many others, (as my grandmother might have said) to live and be well![1]

A COMMON PROCESS SUBSTRATE

It has been fashionable for several years now to observe that conflicts are fundamentally alike, whether they take place between individuals, or within or between groups, communities, or nations. Nevertheless, conflict analysts in each of these domains have tended not to listen closely to one another, and have largely proceeded as if international conflict, labor disputes, and family spats are distinct and unrelated phenomena.

Within the last decade or so, with the advent of conflict and negotiation programs around the United States, a different point of view has begun to emerge: one that argues for a common set of processes that underlie all forms of con-

flict and their settlement.[2] Third-party intervention—whether in divorce, international business and trade negotiations, a labor dispute, a conflict over nuclear siting or hazardous waste disposal, or an international border dispute—follows certain principles that dictate its likely effectiveness. Similarly, the principles of negotiation apply with equal vigor to conflicts at all levels of complexity, whether two or more than two parties are involved, negotiating one issue or many issues, with problems varying in difficulty, etc.

Acceptance of this bit of ideology has had an extremely important effect on the field of conflict studies, for it has made it possible for conversations to take place among theorists and practitioners, at work in an extraordinarily rich and varied set of fields. Anthropologists, sociologists, lawyers, psychologists, economists, business men and women, community activists, labor experts, to name but a few, have now started to come together to exchange ideas, and to map areas of overlap and divergence. This, in turn, has made it possible for the development of conflict theory and practice to take shape under a larger umbrella than ever before. In fact, the symbolic location of these conversations is more like a circus tent than an umbrella, with beasts of different stripe, size, and coloring all finding a place under the big top.

Most recently, yet another twist has appeared. Having emerged in fruitful preliminary conversations about the nature of conflict and negotiation in their respective fields and disciplines, scholars and practitioners are now turning to areas of *divergence* rather than *similarity*. Instead of homogenizing theory and practice in the different social sciences, analysts are now beginning to look beyond the areas of process similarity to the distinguishing features that characterize dispute management in different arenas.

At another but related level, conflict analysts are at last beginning to acknowledge that our pet formulations have been devised by, and are directed to, a community that is predominantly white, western, male, and upper-middle class. Now that fruitful conversations have begun to take place among members of our own intellectual community, it is becoming clear that some of our most cherished ideas may be limited in their applicability and generalizability. Other societies—indeed, other people within our own society—may not always "play the conflict game" by the set of rules that scholars and researchers have deduced on the basis of American paradigms.

As one example of what I mean, "face saving" has been an extremely important element of most conflict/negotiation formulations: the idea that people in conflict will go out of their way to avoid being made to look weak or foolish in the eyes of others and themselves. While face saving seems important in the United States and in countries such as Japan or Korea, less obvious is the extent to which this issue is of *universal* significance. Do Pacific Islanders, Native Americans, or South Asians experience "face," and therefore the possibility of "loss of face?" It is not clear. Do women experience face saving and face loss, or is this a phenomenon that is largely restricted to the XY genetic portion of the population?

Similarly, what does it mean to set a "time limit" in negotiations in different cultures? Do other cultures measure a successful negotiation outcome the same way we tend to in this country? Are coalitions considered equally acceptable, and are they likely to form in much the same way, from one country to the next? Do different countries structure the negotiating environment—everything from the shape of the negotiating table to the presence of observing audiences and various constituencies—in the same way? The answers to questions such as these are not yet in, and we must therefore learn to be cautious in our propensity to advance a set of "universal" principles.

THE IMPORTANCE OF "RELATIONSHIP" IN NEGOTIATION

Much of the negotiation analysis that has taken place over the last 25 years has focused on the "bottom line": who gets how much once an agreement has been reached. The emphasis has thus largely been an *economic* one, and this emphasis has been strengthened by the significant role of game theory and other mathematical or economic formulations.

This economic focus is being supplanted by a richer, and more accurate, portrayal of negotiation in terms not only of economic, but also of relational, considerations. As any visitor to the Turkish Bazaar in Istanbul will tell you, the purchase of an oriental carpet involves a great deal more than the exchange of money for an old rug. The emerging relationship between shopkeeper and customer is far more significant, weaving ever so naturally into the economic aspects of the transaction. An initial conversation about the selling price of some item is quickly transformed into an exchange of a more personal nature: Who one is, where one is from, stories about one's family and friends, impressions of the host country, and lots more. When my wife and I purchased several rugs in Turkey some years ago, we spent three days in conversation with the merchant—not because that is how long it took to "cut the best deal," but because we were clearly having a fine time getting to know one another over Turkish coffee, Turkish delight, and Turkish taffy. When, at the end of our three-day marathon transaction, the shopkeeper invited us to consider opening a carpet store in Boston that could be used to distribute his wares, I was convinced that this invitation was extended primarily to sustain an emerging relationship—rather than to make a financial "killing" in the United States.

Psychologists, sociologists, and anthropologists have long understood the importance of "relationship" in any interpersonal transaction, but only recently have conflict analysts begun to take this as seriously as it deserves. Although it seems convenient to distinguish negotiation in one-time-only exchanges (ones where you have no history of contact with the other party, come together for a "quickie," and then expect never to see the other again) from negotiation in ongoing relationships, this distinction is more illusory than real.

Rarely does one negotiate in the absence of future consequences. Even if you and I meet once and once only, our reputations have a way of surviving the exchange, coloring the expectations that others will have of us in the future.

NEGOTIATION IN A TEMPORAL CONTEXT

For too long, analysts have considered only the negotiations proper, rather than the sequence of events preceding negotiation and the events that must transpire if a concluded agreement is to be implemented successfully. Only recently, as analysts have become more confident in their appraisal of the factors that influence effective negotiation, has attention been directed to the past and future, as anchors of the negotiating present.

Analysts of international negotiation (e.g., Saunders, 1985) have observed that some of the most important work takes place *before the parties ever come to the table*. Indeed, once they get to the table, all that typically remains is a matter of crossing the *t*'s and dotting the *i*'s in an agreement hammered out beforehand. It is during *prenegotiation* that the pertinent parties to the conflict are identified and invited to participate, that a listing of issues is developed and prioritized as an agenda, and that the formula by which a general agreement is to be reached is first outlined. Without such a set of preliminary understandings, international negotiators may well refuse to sit down at the same table with one another.

Prenegotiation is important in other contexts as well, something I discovered in conversation with a successful Thai businessman. He observed that Thais are extremely reluctant to confront an adversary in negotiation, or to show any sign whatsoever of disagreement, let alone conflict. Yet many Thais have succeeded admirably in negotiating agreements that are to their advantage. The key to their success is prenegotiation, making sure beforehand that there really *is* an agreement before labeling the process "negotiation," before ever sitting down with that other person. In effect, they use prenegotiation to arrange matters to their own advantage, and they do so without ever identifying the relationship with the other party as conflictual, or signaling in any way that concessions or demands are being made.

At the other end of the temporal continuum lies the matter of follow-up and implementation. To reach an agreement through negotiation is not enough. Those parties who are in a position to sabotage this agreement, unless their advice is solicited and incorporated, must be taken into account if a negotiated agreement is to succeed. (Witness the failure of the Michael Dukakis campaign to consult sufficiently with Jesse Jackson and his supporters, prior to the 1988 Democratic Party convention in Atlanta.) Note the tradeoff here: The greater number of parties to a negotiation, the more difficult it will be to reach any agreement at all. But only if the relevant parties and interests are included in the negotiations is the agreement reached likely to "stick."

As negotiation analysts have broadened the temporal spectrum to include pre- and post-negotiation processes, more work has been done toward devising creative options for improving upon the proceedings. To cite but one example, Howard Raiffa (1985) has proposed a procedure known as "post-settlement settlement" by which parties who have already concluded an agreement are given an opportunity—with the assistance of a third party—to improve upon their agreement. The third party examines the facts and figures that each side has used in reaching a settlement; based on this information, which is kept in strict confidence, the third party proposes a settlement that improves upon the agreement reached. Either side can veto this post-settlement settlement, in which case the *status quo ante* remains in effect. However, if both sides endorse the proposed improvement on the existing contract, then each stands to benefit from this proposal—and the third party, in turn, is guaranteed a percentage of the "added value" of the contract.

NEGOTIATING FROM THE INSIDE OUT

Conventional wisdom regarding effective negotiation calls for the parties to start by making extreme opening offers, then conceding stepwise until an agreement is reached. If you want to sell a used car, purchase a rug, secure a new wage package or settle a territorial dispute with a neighboring country, you begin by asking for more than you expect to settle for, then gradually move inward until you and the other side overlap; at that point you have a negotiated settlement.

A large body of negotiation analysis has proceeded in accordance with this conventional wisdom. Moreover, this way of negotiating "from the outside in" makes good sense for several reasons: It allows each negotiator to explore various possible agreements before settling, and to obtain as much information as possible about the other negotiator and his or her preferences, before closing off discussion (Kelley, 1966). It also allows each party to give its respective constituency some sense of the degree to which the other side has already been "moved" thereby maintaining constituency support for the positions taken in negotiation.

On the other hand, this "traditional" way of conducting the business of negotiation ignores an important and creative alternative: working "from the inside out." Instead of beginning with extreme opening offers, then moving slowly and inexorably from this stance until agreement is reached, it often makes sense to start with an exchange of views about underlying needs and interests—and on the basis of such an exchange, to build an agreement that both parties find acceptable. The key to such an approach is, as negotiation analysts have observed (e.g., Fisher and Ury, 1981), to work at the level of interests rather than positions—what one really needs and wants (and why), rather than what one states that one would like to have.

This was precisely what happened in October of 1978 at Camp David where, with the mediation of President Jimmy Carter and his subordinates, President Anwar Sadat of Egypt and Prime Minister Menachem Begin of Israel were able to settle the disposition of the Sinai Peninsula. The Sinai had been taken by the Israelis in 1967, and its complete and immediate return had been demanded by the Egyptians ever since. Had the discussions about the fate of the Sinai been conducted solely at the level of positions—with each side demanding total control of the land in question, then making step-wise concessions from these extreme opening offers— *no* agreement would have been possible. Instead, with assistance from President Carter, the Egyptians and Israelis identified their own respective underlying interests—and were able to move to an agreement that allowed the Israelis to obtain the security they required, while the Egyptians obtained the territory they required. "Security in exchange for territory" was the formula used here, and it was a formula devised not by moving from the outside in, but by building up an agreement from the inside out.

A useful variation on this inside-out idea is the "one-text" negotiation procedures (Fisher, 1981), whereby a mediator develops a single negotiating text that is critiqued and improved by each side until a final draft is developed for approval by the interested parties. Instead of starting with demands that are gradually abandoned, the negotiators criticize a single document that is rewritten to take these criticisms into account, and eventually— through this sort of inside-out procedure— a proposal is developed for which both sides have some sense of ownership.

THE ROLE OF "RIPENESS"

Although it is comforting to assume people can start negotiating any time they want, such is not the case. First of all, just as it takes two hands to clap, it takes two to negotiate. *You* may be ready to come to the table for serious discussion, but your counterpart may not. Unless you are both at the table (or connected by a telephone line or cable link), no agreement is possible.

Second, even if both of you are present at the same place, at the same time, one or both of you may not be sufficiently motivated to take the conflict seriously. It is tempting to sit back, do nothing, and hope that the mere passage of time will turn events to your advantage. People typically do not sit down to negotiate unless and until they have reached a point of "stalemate," where each no longer believes it possible to obtain what he or she wants through efforts at domination or coercion (Kriesberg, 1987). It is only at this point, when the two sides grudgingly acknowledge the need for joint work if any agreement is to be reached, that negotiation can take place.

By "ripeness" then, I mean a stage of conflict in which all parties are ready to take their conflict seriously, and are willing to do whatever may be necessary to bring the conflict to a close. To pluck fruit from a tree before it is ripe is as problematic as waiting too long. There is a *right* time to negotiate, and the wise negotiator will attempt to seek out this point.

It is also possible, of course, to help "create" such a right time. One way of doing so entails the use of threat and coercion, as the two sides (either with or without the assistance of an outside intervenor) walk (or are led) to the edge of "lover's leap," stare into the abyss below, and contemplate the consequences of failing to reach an agreement. The farther the drop—that is, the more terrible the consequences of failing to settle—the greater the pressure on each side to take the conflict seriously. There are at least two serious problems with such "coercive" means of creating a ripe conflict: First, as can be seen in the history of the arms race between the United States and the Soviet Union, it encourages further conflict escalation, as each side tries to "motivate" the other to settle by upping the ante a little bit at a time. Second, such escalatory moves invite a game of "chicken," in which each hopes that the other will be the first to succumb to coercion.

There is a second—and far *better*—way to create a situation that is ripe for settlement: namely, through the introduction of new opportunities for joint gain. If each side can be persuaded that there is more to

gain than to lose through collaboration— that by working jointly, rewards can be harvested that stand to advance each side's respective agenda—then a basis for agreement can be established. In the era of *glasnost*, the United States and Soviet Union are currently learning this lesson—namely, that by working together they can better address problems of joint interest, the solution of which advances their respective self-interest. Arms control stands to save billions of dollars and rubles in the strained budgets of both nations, while advancing the credibility of each country in the eyes of the larger world community. The same is true of joint efforts to slow the consequences of the "greenhouse effect" on the atmosphere, to explore outer space, and to preserve and protect our precious natural resources in the seas.

A "RESIDUE" THAT CHANGES THINGS

It is tempting for parties to a conflict to begin by experimenting with a set of adversarial, confrontational moves in the hope that these will work. Why not give hard bargaining a try at first, since if moves such as threat, bluff, or intimidation work as intended, the other side may give up without much of a fight? Moreover, even if such tactics fail, one can always shift to a more benign stance. The problem with such a sticks-to-carrots approach is that once one has left the path of joint problem solving, it may be very difficult to return again. It takes two people to cooperate, but only one person is usually required to make a mess of a relationship. The two extremes of cooperation and competition, collaboration and confrontation, are thus *not* equally balanced; it is far easier to move from cooperation to competition than the other way around.

In the course of hard bargaining, things are often said and done that change the climate of relations in ways that do not easily allow for a return to a less confrontational stance. A "residue" is left behind (Pruitt and Rubin, 1986), in the form of words spoken or acts committed, which cannot be denied and which may well change the relationship. The words, "I've never really liked or respected you," spoken in the throes of an angry exchange, may linger like a bad taste in the mouth, even when the conflict has apparently been settled. Similarly, a brandished fist or some other threatening gesture may leave scars that long outlive the heat of the moment. Thus, the escalation of conflict often carries with it moves and maneuvers that alter a relationship in ways that the parties do not anticipate.

The implication of this point for conflict and negotiation studies is clear: Insufficient attention has been directed to the lasting consequences of confrontational tactics. Too often scholars, researchers, and practitioners have assumed cooperation and competition are equally weighted, when in fact cooperation is a slippery slope; once left, the path leading to return is difficult indeed. Required for such a return journey is a combination of cooperation and persistence—the willingness to make a unilateral collaborative overture, and then to couple this with the tenacity necessary to persuade the other side that this collaborative overture is to be taken seriously (Axelrod, 1984; Fisher and Brown, 1988).

NOTES

1. Two recent books (Lax and Sebenius, 1986; Susskind and Cruickshank, 1987) treat rather extensively the topic of enlightened self-interest, pointing out the ways of expanding the resource pie, or finding uses for it that satisfy the interest of each side.

2. See, for example, the draft curriculum developed in cooperation with the Program on Negotiation for use in universities outside the United States.

REFERENCES

Axelrod, R. 1984. *The Evolution of Cooperation.* New York, Basic Books.

Deutsch, M. 1960. "The Effect of Motivational Orientation Upon Trust and Suspicion." *Human Relations* 13, pp. 123–139.

————, and M. E. Collins. 1951. *Interracial Housing: A Psychological Evaluation of a Social Experiment.* Minneapolis: University of Minnesota Press.

Fisher, R. 1981. "Playing the Wrong Game?" In J. Z. Rubin, ed. *Dynamics of Third Party Intervention: Kissinger in the Middle East.* New York: Praeger.

————, and W. L. Ury. 1981. *Getting to YES: Negotiating Agreement Without Giving In.* Boston: Houghton Mifflin.

Follett, M. P. 1940. "Constructive Conflict." In H. C. Metcalf and L. Urwick, eds. *Dynamic Administration: The Collected Papers of Mary Parker Follett.* New York: Harper.

Kelley, H. H. 1966. "A Classroom Study of the Dilemmas in Interpersonal Negotiations." In K. Archibald, ed. *Strategic Interaction and Conflict: Original Papers and Discussion.* Berkeley, Calif.: Institute of International Studies.

Kelman, H. C. 1958. "Compliance, Identification, and Internalization: Three Processes of Attitude Change." *Journal of Conflict Resolution* 2, pp. 51–60.

Kriesberg, L. 1987. "Timing and the Initiation of De-escalation Moves." *Negotiation Journal* 3, pp. 375–384

Lax, D. A., and J. Sebenius, 1986. *The Manager as Negotiator.* New York: Free Press.

Pruitt, D. G., and J. Z. Rubin. 1986. *Social Conflict: Escalation, Stalemate, and Settlement.* New York: Random House.

Raiffa, H. 1985. "Post-settlement Settlements." *Negotiation Journal* 1, pp. 9–12.

Russell, R. W., ed. 1961. "Psychology and Policy in a Nuclear Age." *Journal of Social Issues* 17(3).

Saunders, H. H. 1985. "We Need a Larger Theory of Negotiation: The Importance of Prenegotiating Phases." *Negotiation Journal* 2, pp. 249–262.

Susskind, L. and J. Cruickshank, 1987. *Breaking the Impasse.* New York: Basic Books.

Ⓢ
31
PRESS

INTERESTS: THE MEASURE OF NEGOTIATION

by David A. Lax and James K. Sebenius

People negotiate to further their interests. And negotiation advisers urge attention to interests—often solemnly, as if the suggestion were original and surprising. Yet Socrates' admonition to "Know Thyself" surely scoops any late twentieth century advice of this sort. So, academic compulsiveness aside, why write an article on interests or, more to the point, why read one?

The answer, in part, is that negotiators often focus on interests, but conceive of them too narrowly. We will argue for a more expansive conception of negotiator's interests. Moreover, interests often conflict, and simply listing them without understanding the tradeoffs among them is a bit like writing out a recipe without including the proportions. In addition to determining interests, negotiators need ways to assess the relative importance of those various interests. We will try to clarify the logic of assessing tradeoffs.

As hard as it may be to sort out one's own interests, understanding how others see theirs—*their* subjective scheme of values as perceived through *their* peculiar psychological filters—can be extraordinarily difficult. Obviously, suggesting a stretch "in the other person's shoes" is good advice; equally obviously, it is only a starting point. In this article we will try to further.

AN EXPANSIVE CONCEPTION OF A NEGOTIATOR'S INTERESTS

In evaluating the interests at stake, a typical negotiator might focus on commodities that can be bought and sold or on concrete terms that can be written into a contract or treaty. And negotiators definitely have such interests: the crippled plaintiff desperately wants compensation; a sales manager cares intensely about prices, profit margins, return on investment, and personal compensation; managers may derive value from seeing their particular product sweep the market or furthering some vision of the public interest.

Throughout this article, we assume that negotiators want to do well for themselves. Of course, "doing well" is only measured with respect to the things they care about, whether out of direct self-interest or concern for the welfare of others. Thus, doing "better" in a negotiation need not imply pressing for more money or a bigger share; rather, it means advancing the totality of one's interests, which may include money and other tangibles as well as fairness, the well-being of one's counterparts, and the collegiality of the process. For instance, furthering Robert's interests may mean taking less money to obtain a fair settlement by a friendly process; by the same token, Helen may want only to publicly humiliate her counterpart and extract from him the very biggest check.

It is especially common in business negotiations, however, to assume that interests extend only to the bottom line. Yet imagine holding rigidly to this assumption when negotiating with the number two executive of a technical products company from the upper half of the Fortune 500. He echoed his firm's philosophy when he stated:

David A. Lax is managing director and general partner in ECO Management, New York City. James K. Sebenius is a Professor at the Harvard Business School, Cambridge, MA 02138.

Source: David A. Lax and James K. Sebenius, "Interests: The Measure of Negotiation" from *Negotiation Theory and Practice*, edited by J. William Breslin and Jeffrey Z. Rubin. Reprinted by permission of Plenum Publishing Corporation and the authors.

Our most important goal is to do a good job. We don't have a specific growth target, but what we want to do is make a contribution. Not just a "me too" thing, but to develop technically superior products. Another goal is to earn our way, to grow from our own resources. A third goal is to make this an interesting and satisfactory place to work. The fourth goal . . . there must be a fourth goal. I mentioned it also in a speech at [a nearby university]. Oh yes, the fourth goal is to make a profit (Donaldson and Lorsch, 1984, p. 85).

Negotiators' interests can go beyond the obvious and tangible. Take for example the almost universal quest for social approval or the simple pleasure one derives from being treated with respect, even in a one-time encounter A stockbroker may want to build a relationship with a customer because of the future business it may bring; or a plaintiff, anxious at the thought of a trial, may be willing to take a reduced settlement to avoid courtroom trauma. Negotiators have good reasons to be concerned with their reputations. A person who is widely known never to recede from a position may rarely be called on for concessions. Fisher and Ury (1981) argue that a negotiator should seek to be known for reaching agreements only by means of "objective" principles; once achieved, among other effects, such a "principled" reputation may reduce the need to haggle.

Beyond concerns about reputation relationship, and process, negotiators often care about subtle aspects of precedent. For example, Luther—a product manager in a fast-growing medical devices firm—confronted his colleague Francoise for the second time with a vigorous demand for priority use of the firm's advertising department—even though Francoise had informally "reserved" this block of the ad department's time for her people. After analyzing her interests in this unexpected negotiation, Francoise balked at a few seemingly reasonable settlements that Luther suggested. Why? Francoise sought to avoid two undesirable, precedents: first, in the *substance* of the issue (*her* division needed to count absolutely on future ad

department reservations); and second, in the *procedure* set for raising a whole range of similar matters (she wanted to bolster the use of established policies). Concern with both types of precedent abounds in organizations and elsewhere.

Strategic interests are often at stake for managers. By this, we refer to the alignment of a particular decision with the manager's long-term personal or institutional strategy. Suppose that a prompt investment in the capacity to manage mutual funds appears likely to have high short term potential for a firm whose long-term plan has been to develop expertise in real estate investments. Would a key manager's proposal now to devote substantial energy to mutual funds research and investment be wise? Recourse to strategic rather than short-term financial analysis may unravel the firm's best interests in this case.

Through actions in one negotiation, a manager may have an interest in reducing the cost of later encounters and in affecting their outcomes. A manager may thus strive to create in subordinates the impression that explicit bargaining is impossible and that commands must be obeyed. Perhaps the back-and-forth process has become too costly and inefficient for the task at hand. In such cases, paradoxically, a prime managerial interest in routine dealings may actually be to drive out future overt bargaining. It is exceedingly ironic that a powerful interest to be achieved through a determined pattern of negotiation may be to establish an impregnable image of rigid hierarchy, potent command, and iron control—that brooks *no* conscious negotiation. Especially in early encounters, say, between a freshly hired vice-president and others in the firm, the new officer may regard the establishment of a favorable pattern of others automatic deference to "suggestions" as of central interest. Or the new officer may strongly weigh the effects on his or her perceived track record or esteem as an expert so that others may be more likely to show deference in the future.

Comparing obvious "bottom line" interests with "others"—reputation, precedent, relationships and the like—a very

33

PRESS

detailed study of corporate resource allocation in a multidivisional chemical company noted:

> These are the dimensions a manager takes into account when he makes his decisions. In some instances they far outweigh the importance of the substantive issues in his assessment of decision-making priorities.
>
> It is worth pausing to emphasize this point. There is a very strong tendency in financial or decision-making treatments of capital budgeting to regard the personal status of managers as noise, "a source of bias.". . . Theoreticians do not consider the problem a rational manager faces as he considers committing himself to a project over time. He has made other commitments in the past, other projects are competing for funds and engineering at the division level, and other managers are competing for the jobs he seeks. At the same time those same managers are his peers and friends. Whatever he does, he is more than likely going to have to live with those same men for a decade or more. While only some projects are technically or economically independent, all are organizationally interdependent (Bower, 1972, p. 302).

It is not always easy to know how to evaluate interests; sometimes they may derive from interactions too complex to understand directly. In such cases, carefully chosen *proxy interests* may help. For example, the President of the United States cannot possibly predict the effects of any particular negotiated outcome on all of his substantive interests over the course of his term or beyond. Taking account of this, Richard Neustadt, in his classic bargaining manual, *Presidential Power* (1990), counsels him to evaluate his dealings in terms of three particular interests. The first is obvious: his interest in the *substance* of the immediate issue.

Second, however, the president's *professional reputation* can heavily affect the reactions of important Washingtonians to his later concerns and actions. The president needs the resources and cooperation of these Washingtonians to carry out his programs. Thus, beyond the substance of the issue, Neustadt suggests, the effect of the current negotiation on the president's professional reputation among Washingtonians should be a proxy interest reflecting, in part, his ability to get the Washingtonians to act in accord with his subsequent desires.

Third, Neustadt argues that the president should evaluate the effect of his actions on his *popular prestige*. High prestige reflects the strength of his mandate and influences Washingtonians. It is, in part, a proxy interest; actions that enhance his public prestige improve his chances favorably to influence subsequent outcomes of direct concern. A president may also value popular prestige for its own sake. As negotiator, the president may well have to trade these interests off against each other; for example, he may yield somewhat on his substantive interest in the immediate issue to enhance his reputation and prestige elsewhere. In many positions less complex than that of the president, negotiators' interests are difficult to enumerate because the link between actions and eventual outcomes is hazy. In such cases, a negotiator may benefit by finding simplified proxy interests that predict outcomes either directly or indirectly, by predicting the negotiator's subsequent influence on outcomes of concern.

In short, interests include anything that the negotiator cares about; concerns that are evoked by the issues discussed. Clarifying interests, however, can sometimes be difficult. We have often found that two distinctions can help.

TWO HELPFUL DISTINCTIONS

Interests, Issues and Positions

Negotiators seek to reach agreement on specific *positions* on a specific set of *issues*. For example, a potential employee may initially demand $36,000 (the position) for salary (the issue). The job seeker's underlying *interests* may be in financial security, enhanced lifestyle, organizational status, and advanced career prospects. Or, the desire of a Midwestern utility company to build a dam may collide with farmers' needs for water and environmentalists' concern for the downstream habitat of endangered whooping cranes. Increased economic return, irrigated crops, and preserved species are the relevant *interests*; they conflict over the *issue* of the dam's construction, *positions* on which are pro and con.

Negotiators often assume that issues directly express underlying interests. Of course, many different sets of issues may reflect the same interests: a country might seek to serve its interest in mineral development through negotiations over *issues* as varied as simple royalty concessions, joint ventures, or service contracts. Conceivably, the country's interest could be equally satisfied by different terms on each of these alternative issues. The issue at hand, however, may be only a proxy for imperfectly related interests. For example, the United States in the Paris Peace talks may have insisted on a round table and the North Vietnamese a rectangular one. The relevant compromise would hardly have been oval. The real interests were far from the rectangular versus round issue.

Many negotiators retard creativity by failing to distinguish the issues under discussion from their underlying interests. When the issues under discussion poorly match the interests at stake, modifications of the issues sometimes enable all parties to satisfy their interests better. For example, recall the conflict between the Midwestern utility company, the farmers, and the environmentalists. After several years of costly and embittering litigation, the parties came to a resolution by a shift to issues that matched their underlying interests in a more fruitful manner. By moving from positions ("yes" and "no") on the issue of the dam's construction to discussions about the nature of downstream water guarantees, the amount of a trust fund to protect the whooping crane habitat, and the size of the dam, the parties reached an agreement that left all of them better off.

Negotiators who mistakenly see their interests as perfectly aligned with their positions on issues may be less likely to shift issues creatively. They might even suspiciously oppose proposals to modify the issues. Indeed, in attempting to protect their perceived interests, such negotiators may dig their heels in hard to avoid budging from their desired positions. In the "dam versus no dam" conflict, positions could have hardened to a point where the grim determination of each side to prevail over the other—whatever the cost—would have ruled out any real search for preferable options. At a minimum, such rigid dealings can be frustrating and time-consuming: impasses or poor agreements often result.

The prevalence of hard-fought, time-consuming, unimaginative "positional" negotiations led Fisher and Ury (1981, p. 11) to propose a general rule: "Focus on interests, not positions." While we think that negotiators should always keep the distinction clearly in mind, focusing exclusively on interests may not always be wise. When parties have deep and conflicting ideological differences, for example, satisfactory agreements on "smaller" issues any only be possible if ideological concerns do not arise. In such cases, the negotiations should focus on the issues or on a much narrower set of interests, not the full set of underlying interests. Two hostile but neighboring countries embroiled in tribal, religious, or ideological conflict may be best off handling a sewage problem on their common border by dealing only with this more limited issue. Or leftist guerrilla leaders, each with an underlying interest in ruling the country, might unite on the issue of overthrowing the rightist dictator; an agreement that attempted to reconcile their underlying interests would likely be more difficult to achieve. Moreover, a negotiator may choose to focus on an issue that, for legal or other reasons, provides greater leverage than do discussions of underlying interests. The nature-loving group that has an abiding interest in preventing development may develop a sudden attachment to the issue of wetlands protection if the Wetlands Preservation Act provides the strongest grounds for negotiating with and deterring developers.

At times, a tenacious focus on positions may yield desirable results. With a group of landowners, the CEO of a major mining company had negotiated the general outlines of a contract along with a few critical particulars. Then the CEO turned the rest of the negotiations over to a company lawyer to finish in short order—before a hard-to-obtain environmental permit expired. One provision that the second group of negotiators inherited had not been extensively debated before. Yet, its tentative resolution, while barely acceptable to the landowners, clearly would confer great benefits on the company. Though the landowners' representatives sought to focus on "interests" and "fairness" in order to undo the provision, the company's lawyer made a powerful commitment to it and turned a completely deaf ear to all argument, urging instead that they get on with "unresolved" matters. Though this tactic risked negative repercussions on the other issues, the lawyer's firm commitment to a position was an effective means of claiming value in this instance.

Thus interests should be distinguished from issues and positions.[1] Focusing on interests can help one develop a better understanding of mutual problems and invent creative solutions. But such a focus may not always be desirable when, for example, underlying interests are diametrically opposed or when a focus on particular issues or positions provides leverage. Whatever the focus, however, interests measure the value of any position or agreement.

Intrinsic and Instrumental Interests

It should be clear that negotiators may have many kinds of interests: money and financial security, a particular conception of the public interest, the quality of products, enhancing a reputation as a skilled bargainer, maintaining a working relationship, precedents, and so on. However, one distinction—between intrinsic and instrumental interests—can provide an economical way to capture some important qualities of interests, call negotiators' attention to often-overlooked, sometimes subtle interests, and lead to improved agreements.

One's interest in an issue is *instrumental* if favorable terms on the issue are val-

ued because of their effect on subsequent dealings. One's interest in an issue is *intrinsic* if one values favorable terms of settlement on the issue independent of any subsequent dealings. Thus, a divorcing parent's interest in gaining custody of his or her child, the farmer's interest in water rights, or a country's interest in secure borders can usefully be thought of as intrinsic interests. Such interests need not have any obvious or agreed-upon economic value. For example, Charles, a 60-year-old venture capitalist, was negotiating the dissolution of a strikingly successful technology partnership with Marie, a young, somewhat standoffish woman whom he had brought on as a partner two years before. At first Charles bargained very hard over the financial terms because he viewed them as indicating who had really contributed important ideas and skills to the venture's success. When Marie belatedly acknowledged her genuine respect for his ideas and contributions, Charles became much less demanding on the financial issues. In this instance, it happened that the venture capitalist also had a strong intrinsic interest in psychic gratification from acknowledgement of his role as mentor and father-figure.

Most issues affect both intrinsic and instrumental interests. Dealings with a subordinate who wants to hire an assistant can arouse an intrinsic interest in the overall size of the budget as well as a concern with the perceived precedent the hiring will set in the eyes of the subordinate's peers—an instrumental interest. Recognizing the distinction may lead to improved agreements; the subordinate who can create a justifiable device to prevent decisions about his or her staff support from setting precedents may well receive authorization to hire a new assistant.

One of the main reasons we focus on the intrinsic-instrumental distinction is for the light it sheds on three often-misunderstood aspects of negotiation, interests in the process, in relationships, and in principles.

"Process" Interests—Intrinsic and Instrumental Analysts often assume that negotiators evaluate agreements by measuring the value obtained from the outcome. Yet, negotiators may care about the *process* of bargaining as well. Even with no prospect of further interaction, some would prefer a negotiated outcome reached by pleasant, cooperative discussion to the same outcome reached by abusive, threat-filled dealings. Others might even derive value from a strident process that gives them the satisfied feeling of having extracted something from their opponents. Either way, negotiators can have intrinsic interests in the character of the negotiation process itself.

Beyond such intrinsic valuation, an unpleasant process can dramatically affect future dealings; the supplier who is berated and threatened may be unresponsive when cooperation at a later point would help. Indeed, negotiators often have strong instrumental interests in building trust and confidence early in the negotiation process in order to facilitate jointly beneficial agreements.

"Relationship" Interests—Intrinsic and Instrumental Negotiators often stress the value of their relationships; this interest sometimes achieves an almost transcendent status. For example, Fisher and Ury (1981, p. 20) say that "every negotiator has two kinds of interests: in the substance and in the relationship." Many negotiators derive intrinsic value from developing or furthering a pleasant relationship. Moreover, when repeated dealings are likely, most negotiators perceive the instrumental value of developing an effective working relationship. After studying hundreds of managers in many settings, John Kotter (1985, p. 40) sensibly concluded:

> Good working relationships based on some combination of respect, admiration, perceived need, obligation, and friendship are a critical source of power in helping to get things done. Without these relationships, even the best possible idea could be rejected or resisted in an environment where diversity breeds suspicion and precludes giving orders to most of the relevant players. Futhermore, since these relationships

serve as important information channels, without them one may never be able to establish the information one needs to operate effectively.

Of course, in the dissolution of a partnership or the divorce of a childless couple with few assets, the parties may find no instrumental value in furthering their relationship; that is, the parties would not be willing to trade substantive gains on, say, financial terms, to enhance their future dealings. In fact, a bitter divorcing couple may actually prefer a financial outcome that requires absolutely no future contact over another that is better for both in tax term but requires them to deal with each other in the future. Similarly, a division head with two valuable but constantly warring employees may have a keen interest in separating them organizationally to prevent *any* active relationship between them. And, when dealing with an obnoxious salesperson who has come to the door or by the office, one's interest in the "relationship" may mainly be to terminate it.

Interest in "Principles"—Intrinsic and Instrumental Negotiators may discover shared norms or principles relevant to their bargaining problem. Such norms may include equal division, more complex distributive judgments, historical or ethical rationales, and objective or accepted standards, as well as notions that simply seem fair or are represented as such (Gulliver, 1979; Fisher and Ury, 1981). Acting in accord with such a norm or principle may be of intrinsic interest to one or more of the parties; for example, a settlement of $532—arrived at in accord with the mutually acknowledged principle that each party should be paid in proportion to time worked—may be valued quite differently than the same dollar figure reached by haggling. Of course, an acknowledged norm need not be an absolute value in a negotiation: it may be partly or fully traded off against other interests.

Even when none of the parties derive intrinsic value from acting in accord with a particular principle, it may still guide agreement. Principles and simple notions often serve as naturally prominent focal points for choosing one settlement within the range of possible outcomes (Schelling, 1960). For example, equal division of a windfall may seem so irresistibly natural to the partners in a small firm that they would scarcely consider negotiation over who should get more.

The principles that guide agreement in the first of many related disputes may set a powerful precedent. Thus, negotiators may work hard to settle the first dispute on the basis of principles that they believe will yield favorable outcomes in subsequent disputes. They may take a loss with respect to intrinsic interests in the first negotiation in order to satisfy their instrumental interests in the principles used to guide the agreement.

In short, with many less tangible interests—such as process, relationships, or fairness—a negotiator should ask why they are valued. Distinguishing between their instrumental and intrinsic components can help. But even with these components sorted out, how can a negotiator go about assessing their "relative importance?" More generally, what logic guides setting priorities among conflicting interests?

THINKING ABOUT TRADEOFFS

Listing one's own interests as well as a best guess at those of other parties is certainly useful. But difficult questions tend to arise in negotiations that force one to make sacrifices on some interests in order to gain on others: How much of a trade is desirable? In buying a seller-financed house, how should Ralph evaluate higher purchase prices compared to lower mortgage interest rates? How much more should a manufacturer be willing to pay for the next quality grade of components? How much should a sales manager trade on price for the prospects of a better relationship? How much should a manager be willing to give up on substance to secure a favorable precedent?

Thinking about tradeoffs is often excruciatingly difficult and badly done. Yet, whether or not negotiators choose to ponder priorities, they effectively make tradeoffs by their choices and agreements in negotiation. Because we believe that negotiators benefit by being self-conscious and reflective about their interests and the tradeoffs they are willing to make, we propose several methods to illuminate tradeoffs. These methods draw primarily on judgment about interests, not about negotiating. The methods we consider help to convert developed substantive judgments into forms useful for analysis and practice (e.g., Raiffa, 1982; Keeney and Raiffa, 1976; Barclay and Peterson, 1976; or Greenhalgh and Neslin, 1981). Finally, although these techniques have formal origins rooted in management science and technical economics, we find that their prime value comes in their contribution to clear thinking rather than from their potential for quantification. While negotiators may often choose not to quantify their tradeoffs, they may benefit greatly by employing the same style of thought in comparing interests.

Certain tradeoffs are easy to specify. The present value or total cost of a loan is a well-known mathematical function of the amount and duration of the loan and the interest rate. Thus, beginning with a given price and interest rate for the seller-financed home, Ralph can calculate precisely the benefit of a one percent decrease in interest rate and how much of a price increase he would be willing to accept before he became indifferent to the original price and interest rate. Yet other tradeoffs may seem much harder to think about, especially ones that involve "intangibles" like principles, anxiety about a process, or the relationship.

Assembling Tradeoffs Among Seemingly Intangible Interests. Seemingly intangible tradeoffs can also be dealt with in analogous ways. For instance, consider Joan, a plaintiff crippled in a car accident who wishes to negotiate an out-of-court settlement with an insurance company that is better than her alternative of a full court trial. Suppose that, only taking trial uncertainties and legal fees into account, Joan would be willing to accept a settlement of $300,000. But this analysis leaves her uncomfortable. The trial would cause her great anxiety, and her analysis so far does not take this anxiety into account. How should she consider the anxiety factor in her preparation for negotiation? Perhaps she should lower her minimum requirements, but by how much? How can she even think about this?

After several anxious, inconclusive struggles with this assessment, a friend asks Joan to imagine the anxiety she would feel during a trial. The friend then asks her to imagine that a pharmacist offered to *sell* her a magic potion that would completely eliminate the feeling of anxiety from court proceedings. What would be the most she would pay for the potion before the trial? Would she pay $10? "That's silly. Of course." Would she pay $100? "Sure." $100,000? "Certainly not, that's one-third of my minimum settlement!" What about $50,000? "Probably not." $1,000? "I think so." $10,000? "Well, that's a tough one. But, if push came to shove, the trial would be an awful experience. So probably yes." $25,000? "Maybe not, but I'm not sure." . . . And so on.

We want to stress our opinion that the important point in making such assessments is not quantitative precision. An absolutely precise cutoff would seem artificial. What is important is to get a sense of the order of magnitude of the value Joan places on avoiding anxiety. Here we see that she would pay between $10,000 and $25,000 or a little more to eliminate the anxiety. Thus, she should be willing to reduce her minimum settlement requirements by that amount because a negotiated settlement would avoid the anxiety. She should, of course, strive for more, but she can feel more comfortable knowing that her minimum requirements now roughly reflect her interest in avoiding trial anxiety.

Similarly, Mr. Acton, the insurance company executive, may feel that going to trial against a plaintiff who evokes such sympathy will harm his firm's reputation. How should he value this reputation damage and how should it affect his approach to the negotiation? As described in this thumbnail sketch, in comparing the court alternative to possible negotiated agreements, the executive sees two interests at stake: money and reputation. Acton could try to value the reputation damage directly by estimating the number of present and future customers he would lose and the financial loss this would create. If he finds such direct assessment difficult, he could attempt, like the plaintiff, to place a monetary value on the "intangible" interest. What is the most he would be willing to pay a public relations firm to completely undo the reputation damage? If the most he would be willing to pay is $20,000, Acton could modify his maximum acceptable settlement and take this into account when negotiating with the plaintiff.

In some instances, concerns with precedent, prestige, anxiety, reputation, and similar interests loom large; negotiators focus on them and, because such interests are difficult to weigh, feel paralyzed with respect to their choices as a negotiator. After fretting inconclusively, the negotiators may ask themselves how much they would be willing to pay to have the prestige conferred upon them by other means. They might discover that they value the prestige possibilities little relative to possible substantive gains. Or, by similar analytical introspection, they might discover that they would be willing to pay only a small sum to avoid an undesirable precedent. In such cases, the negotiators would have learned a great deal. First, the intangible interest is a second or third order concern rather than a first order one as they originally feared; they can now feel freer to make concessions on the less important interest if necessary. Second, unless the choice between packages becomes close, they may need to pay little attention to this interest. In short, much of the purpose of such assessments is more to discover the relative importance of different interests rather than to be painstakingly precise about monetary or other valuations.

In other instances, interests in precedent or reputation overwhelm the possible improvements in substantive outcome.

S
39
PRESS

Suppose that Jeff, a lawyer working on a highly publicized class action suit against a corporation, has an interest in his financial compensation and in the reputation he might develop by exceeding expectations for how favorable a settlement he can get for his clients. Even if Jeff finds the range of possible financial compensation paltry, he may see that his interest in enhancing his reputation and political ambitions is extremely well-served by every increment he can obtain in the settlement. Thus, he may bargain tenaciously on his client's behalf. In this case, the interest was the first order concern. In other instances, simple self-assessment may suggest that the monetary and non-monetary issues are roughly comparable concerns or that the monetary aspects predominate.

A More General Approach for Assessing Tradeoffs. The judgment that one "cares more about quality than price" cannot be made independently of the *range* of possible values of quality and price. That is, in the abstract, a manufacturer may say that it cares more about quality than about price. However, while the total increment in technologically feasible quality may be small, the price differential necessary to achieve it may be undesirably high. Relative to the feasible range of qualities, the manufacturer actually places greater weight on price. Similarly, the management negotiator who professes to care more about obtaining productivity-enhancing changes in work rules than about wages must analyze the ranges of work rules and wages that are possible outcomes from this negotiation. Wages might range from a minimum of $10 an hour to a maximum of $13 an hour—and this increment would have a significant impact on the competitiveness of the negotiator's firm. Yet if the increment from the worst to best possible work rules was small and would only marginally affect the firm's competitiveness, the negotiator should give greater weight or importance to wages. The tradeoff rate should result from comparing the valuation of the wage increment between $10 and $13 with the valuation of the benefit of moving from the worst to best work rules—not on the judgment that the negotiator "cares more" about one or the other issue in general.

This leads to a straightforward method for such assessments. Like the preceding examples, the purpose of this method is to help organize one's subjective judgments to get a clearer sense of the relative importance of various interests. Again, we are concerned with orders of magnitude rather than precise quantification. To illustrate the central elements of this approach, we shall work through the thought process in a highly stylized, simplified example and then discuss the more general lessons for thinking about tradeoffs.

Assessing Lisa's Interests

Consider Lisa, a 34-year-old second level manager who has been offered a position in another division of her firm as the supervisor of a soon-to-be created department. She must soon negotiate with William, a long-time engineer who moved into senior management ranks seven years ago and has cautiously but steadily improved his division's results. Lisa has narrowed the issues she will have to negotiate to three: the salary, vacation time, and the number of staff for the new department. We will ask her to analyze her interests and then draw on her subjective judgment to assign 100 points to the issues in a way that reflects their relative importance to her. To begin, she should assess the range of possibilities for each issue. Based on a variety of discussions with William, with others in the firm, and on the results of numerous feelers, Lisa has concluded that the salary could plausibly run from $32,000 to $40,000, the vacation from two to four weeks, and the staff size from 10 to 20. Suppose that her current job pays her $32,000, gives her four weeks of vacation, and assigns her a staff of 10 (See Table 12.1).

Lisa should start by imagining the least appealing scenario: $32,000, two weeks of vacation, and a staff of 10. Her next task is to assess her relative preferences on each issue. To do this, she must decide

TABLE 12.1 LISA'S NEGOTIATION: ISSUES AND RANGES

Issues	Range
Salary	$32–40,000
Vacation	2–4 weeks
Staff	10–20 people

which one of the three incremental improvements she values most. That is, would she feel best with (a) $40,000 salary but only two weeks vacation and 10 subordinates; (b) four weeks vacation but only $32,000 salary and 10 subordinates; or (c) 20 subordinates but only $32,000 salary and two weeks of vacation? In making this evaluation, she examines her interests in money and the effects of a higher salary on her satisfaction, as well as the peace of mind and pleasure from longer vacations. On further reflection, Lisa realizes that she must also consider her ability to do her job effectively and thus to improve her subsequent career prospects. A bigger staff could help her effectiveness directly; enhanced organizational status from a big staff and high salary may independently bolster her job prospects as well as add to her effectiveness. Suppose that after contemplating her interests in this way, Lisa decides that she prefers the salary increment to the other two increments, and, of the other two, she prefers the staff increment to the vacation possibilities.

Now comes a harder part. She must allocate 100 points—importance weights—among the three increments in a way that reflects her underlying subjective feelings. Would she prefer the package with the largest salary increment but minimum vacation and staff to the package with the lowest salary but maximum staff and vacation? If so, she should allocate more than 50 points to the salary increment. If she is indifferent between the two packages, she should allocate exactly 50 points to the salary increment.

Lisa decides that she slightly prefers the salary increment and assigns an importance weight of 60 points to the salary increment. Now, she can either assign importance weights to the staff and vacation increments or she can think about the relative value she places on each of the possible salaries. She begins with the latter and again compares ranges. How does she compare the salary increment from $32,000 to $35,000 with the increment between $35,000 and $40,000? The first increment would improve her housing and thus enhance her life in direct and important ways; the second increment although larger, would go toward luxuries and saving. She thus feels indifferent between the first, smaller increment and the second, larger increment. In other words, she gives 30 of the 60 importance points to the increment between $32,000 and $35,000 and 30 to the remaining increment.

Table 12.2 presents importance scores that reflect Lisa's preferences for salary; Figure 12.11 shows a plot of them. Interpreting this assessment, Lisa would get 0 points if she receives a salary of $32,000, 30 points if she manages to receive $35,000, 60 points if she is able to get a salary of $40,000. She must now assign points reflecting her comparative valuations of the vacation and staff increments. Naturally, making an assessment like this can feel like comparing apples and oranges—but Lisa will end up doing it either explicitly or implicitly.

She can assess her valuations of the other two issues by comparing their

TABLE 12.2 LISA'S ASSESSMENT OF THE VALUE OF DIFFERENT SALARIES

Salary	Importance Points Assigned
$32,000	0
$33,000	10
$34,000	20
$35,000	30
$36,000	36
$37,000	42
$38,000	48
$39,000	54
$40,000	60

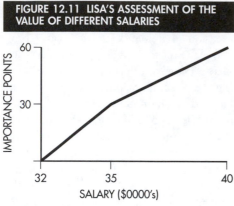

FIGURE 12.11 LISA'S ASSESSMENT OF THE VALUE OF DIFFERENT SALARIES

increments directly, or by comparing one of the increments with her salary assessments. For example, how does the increment from 10 to 20 subordinates compare with the salary increment from $32,000 to $35,000? If Lisa is indifferent, she should assign 30 importance points to the staff increment and, thus, the remaining 10 points to the vacation increment. She decides and continues in this manner, finishing the assessment by assigning 20 of the 30 importance points to the increment between 10 and 15 subordinates and 10 points to the remaining increment. Lastly, she assigns eight of the 10 vacation points to getting the third week of vacation and two points to the remaining week.

Table 12.3 shows a scoring system that reflects this assessment. From the table, a $35,000 salary, three weeks of vacation, and 15 subordinates would be valued at

58 points (30 + 8 + 20) whereas a salary of $37,500, two weeks of vacation and 16 subordinates would be valued at 67 points (45 + 0 + 22). It is worth noting that all the scoring is relative to an arbitrarily chosen zero point. That is, the "worst" agreement—$32,000, two weeks of vacation and 10 subordinates, the bottom of the range for each issue—receives a score of zero. All other possible agreements are scored relative to this "worst" agreement. The important comparison, though, is with Lisa's current job which, at a salary of $32,000, four weeks of vacation, and 10 subordinates is valued at 10 points. Although any such scoring system is necessarily rough, Lisa can use it to evaluate possible agreements and to understand the tradeoffs she may have to make.

Comparing different increments can be difficult, but a few tricks can sometimes facilitate the process. For example, Lisa might construct one package of $32,000, two weeks of vacation, and 20 subordinates and another of $32,000, four weeks of vacation, and 10 subordinates. But, to compare them? Lisa might imagine that the phone rings and the call eliminates one of the options. Which option would feel worse to lose? Or, suppose that a coin flip will determine the choice of packages. Is a fifty–fifty chance of losing each appropriate? Or, would she prefer sixty-forty chances favoring one of the packages?

In helping Lisa construct this scoring system, we assumed that the value of an

Salary ($000)	Importance Points	Weeks of Vacation	Importance Points	Staff Size	Importance Points
32	0	2	0	10	0
33	10	3	8	15	20
34	20	4	10	20	30
35	30				
36	36				
37	42				
38	48				
39	54				
40	60				

TABLE 12.3 LISA'S ASSESSMENT OF THE IMPORTANCE OF SALARY, VACATION, AND STAFF SIZE

increment on one issue did not depend on how other issues were resolved; thus, scoring a package simply involves adding the points obtained on each issue. In some situations, though, the value of the outcome on one issue depends on how other issues are resolved.[2] For example, suppose that with a high salary Lisa would like a larger number of subordinates. With a low salary, however, she might feel aggrieved; a larger staff would mean more responsibility for which she was not compensated. Thus, how she values staff size could depend on her salary level. Such interdependent preferences could be assessed using more elaborate techniques, but the general logic of defining and comparing increments would remain roughly analogous.

Assessing William's Interests

Lisa, in addition to assessing her own interests, must also do the same for her negotiating counterpart and potential supervisor, William. Her preliminary investigations had fairly confidently bounded the ranges of the issues, but now the question becomes how *he* sees *his* real interests in them. Tentative discussions with William left Lisa little doubt that he would prefer to pay less, allow shorter vacations, and get by with as few new staff as possible. In fact, during a meeting in which he enthusiastically offered her the job "in principle," William sketched the terms he felt were appropriate: "a bit over $30,000, a few weeks vacation, and only the staff you really need." More than a little daunted by this less than forthcoming stance, Lisa feels a strong need to develop a much deeper understanding of William's interests.

Asking around, she discovers that William is generally not at ease with "personnel" matters and that he tends to seek out whatever firm "policy" he can find for guidance. Fortunately for Lisa, little in the firm would be directly comparable to the new department she would head. But a few discreet inquiries turn up the fact that the supervisor of the firm's largest department makes around $39,000. Since the new department is an important endeavor, Lisa feels fairly certain that salary money will not be too tight, but that the other supervisor's compensation will make any salary above $39,000 very uncomfortable for William to consider.

In trying to ferret out William's feelings about vacation, Lisa discovers that he has been a hard worker, seldom taking more than a few days or a week each year. Also he has mentioned the extreme importance of dedication and long hours during the uncertain start-up of this new organizational unit. Lisa infers that the prospect of her taking extended vacations early on, while not at all uncommon elsewhere in the firm, would not sit at all well with William.

Finally, on the matter of staffing, Lisa recalls some comments William made during a long lunch they had together to explore the possibilities of her heading the new department. In the course of their conversation, he had mentioned two significant incidents from his career. First, he recalled extreme pressure on the engineering group some years ago to come up with a new design. The group was simply too small to produce the needed results in time. Quality of work and quality of life "needlessly suffered" and, to William's mind, that kind of "economizing" makes no business or personal sense. Yet William also recounted an agonizing experience some years later when the engineering group had greatly expanded. A mild economic downturn and the loss of a major customer had forced him to lay off nearly a quarter of the group's engineers. Recalling the pain of that experience, he noted that things would have been much better if most of those let go had never been hired in the first place; instead, others already in the department should have worked somewhat longer hours. To Lisa, the implications of these incidents seemed obvious: William would have little problem giving her the staff that he believed she really needed, but would be allergic to any perceived excess.

Lisa could then make this assessment much more precise, estimating importance weights for William. Already, however, the contours of a possible approach have begun to emerge as she considers her interests (recall Table 3) together with her insights into William's concerns. Lisa expects to press fairly hard for a salary in the $39,000 range, perhaps conceding a few weeks of vacation time for the last few thousand dollars. Money, she reasons, is most valuable to her and relatively "cheap" to William; in addition, he cares a great deal about avoiding too much time off and two extra weeks of vacation are not crucial to her. From her analysis of the new department's mission so far, Lisa has become increasingly sure that the job can be done with 15 people, though 20 would certainly be nice. She plans to devote a great deal of time to developing and presenting justification of the need for 15.

We will not go further in exploring how William's interests might be more formally assessed or how his and Lisa's preferences could be better dovetailed.[3] And, of course, this rough assessment of an artificially simplified set of issues only starts the process. As Lisa learns more, relative valuations may be revised, issues may be reformulated, and new options invented. For example, her interests in "salary" could be expanded to include stock options, bonuses, fringe and in-kind benefits. "Vacation" might encompass time to be taken in later years, a generous policy of accumulating unused vacation or turning it into salary, or leaves for various purposes like education. "Staff" may mean direct employees of various backgrounds and levels, "loans" from other departments, consultants, temporary help, or equipment to enhance the productivity of a given number of staff. But throughout, constant probing of each party's interests is the sine qua non of creating value by designing good negotiated agreements.

General Lessons for Assessing Interests

The most important lessons from this kind of assessment are those that help one think more clearly about the qualitative judgments that negotiators implicitly make all the time. Such evaluations are often made with respect to nominal issues rather than directly on underlying interests. Lisa's interests in money, lifestyle,

peace of mind, career prospects, and organizational status are not perfectly aligned with the issues of salary, vacation limits, and staff size. When thinking about how well different packages satisfy her interests, the negotiator may discover reformulations that align more closely with her interests. If some of these "new" issues are easier to grant, they may form the basis for a better agreement.

During the process, the negotiator may learn about and change her perceptions about how well different positions on the issues serve her interests As she learns, the relative importance of the increments on the issues may shift. If so, she should modify her assessments.

In contrast to the apparent crispness of the issues, interests are often vaguer. There may be no apparent scale with which to measure, for example, precedent or organizational status. Yet, the same logic that is useful for making issue trade-offs can apply to assuring the relative impact of interests. The generic steps are as follows:

- Identify the interests that may be at stake.
- For each interest, imagine the possible packages that serve it best and worst; for example, imagine the range of precedents that might follow from the negotiation. This roughly defines the *increment*.
- As with Lisa's job negotiations, the importance of each interest depends on the relative importance of its *increment* compared to those of the other interests; how does the gain from the worst to the best possible precedent compare with the gain from the worst to the best possible monetary outcome?

The currency of negotiation generally involves *positions* on *issues* but the results are measured by how well underlying *interests* are furthered. As such, it is helpful to shuttle constantly between often abstract interests and more specific issues, both to check for consistency and to keep real concerns uppermost in mind.

Assessing the Interests of Others

Finally, it goes almost without saying that negotiators should constantly assess their counterparts' interests and preferences. Obviously, careful listening and clear communication help this process. Uninvolved third parties can render insights not suspected by partisans wrapped up in the negotiation. And some negotiators find that, as part of preparing for the process, actually playing the other party's role can offer deepened perspectives. In various management programs at Harvard, for example, senior industrialists have been assigned the parts of environmentalists and vice versa. To simulate arms talks, high-level U.S. military officers and diplomats have been assigned to play Russian negotiators in intensive simulations. Palestinians and Israelis have had to swap places. After some initial discomfort and reluctance, the most common reaction of participants in these exercises is surprise at how greatly such role-playing enhances their understanding of each side's interests, of why others may seem intransigent, and of unexpected possibilities for agreement.

Beyond various ways of trying to put oneself in the other's shoes, assessment of another's interest may be improved by investigating:

- Their past behavior in related settings, both in style and substance.
- Their training and professional affiliation. Engineers and financial analysts will often have quite different modes of perception and approaches to potential conflict from, say, lawyers and insurance adjusters.
- Their organizational position and affiliation. Those in the production department will often see long, predictable manufacturing runs as the company's dominant interest while marketers will opt for individual tailoring to customer specs and deep inventories for rapid deliveries. This is but one example of the old and wise expression "where you stand depends on where you sit."

- Whom they admire, whose advice carries weight, and to whom they tend to defer on the kind of issues at stake.

In the end, interests are bound up with psychology and culture. Some settings breed rivalry; others esteem the group. Some people are altruists; others sociopaths. To some, ego looms large; to others, substance is all. Airport bookstore wisdom names Jungle Fighters, Appeasers, Win-Winners, and Win-Losers. Professionals diagnose personality Types A and B and victims of cathected libido. Others have developed such classes, sometimes wisely, but for now we stress that *perceived* interests matter, that perceptions are subjective. Thus, to assess interests is to probe psyches.

INTERESTS AND ISSUES ARE VARIABLE

Many academic treatments of negotiation take the issues and interests at stake as unchanging over the course of the negotiation. Yet both the issues under discussion and the interests perceived to be at stake can change.

The link between issues and interests is often unclear; the negotiator faced with a set of issues must figure out which of his or her interests are at stake. For example, getting a corner office might enhance prestige and status, but how much would this affect various dealings and decisions?

Because these links are often vague and complex, perception of the links can be influenced or manipulated. One may shape the "face" that an issue wears (Neustadt, 1980); presenting Food Stamps as a means to increase demand for agricultural products rather than as a welfare program may win agricultural state representatives' support for the program. Similarly, by portraying a new project that in reality departs sharply from a firm's past strategy as a direct extension of current projects, a subordinate may both obtain funding and avoid a review of the project's fit with broader strategic goals.

One may attempt less drastic changes in an individual's perception of the relationship between the issue at hand and the underlying interest. Thus, the mining company negotiator may attempt to persuade a small country's finance minister that high royalty rates, although they appear to further the country's interest in revenues, will actually be worse than lower royalty rates. The mining company might argue, "once rates reach a certain level, we will invest less, other companies will be scared off, and you will end up losing in term of your monetary interests." If persuaded, the country's evaluation of how its interests would be satisfied by different potential agreements would change.

Certain other tactics may effectively expand or contract the interests evoked, often in ways not intended by the negotiator. "Take-it-or-leave-it" offers, forced linkages, commitment moves, threats, and preemptive actions all have potential to elicit strong negative reactions that may overwhelm the original issues at stake. Concern for one's reputation or self-esteem may predominate. A trade union's motivation for strikes, for instance, may shift over time from the strictly economic to a desire for revenge. Likewise, wars can escalate out of all proportion to the possible substantive gains for either side. The sudden Argentine occupation of the Falkland Islands in 1982 and the British response quickly came to involve weighty, irreconcilable interests such as national "honor" and the "right" response to aggression.

In many circumstances threats, commitments, and deterrent moves are effective and can be analyzed in terms of values for the immediate issues involved (Tedeschi, Schlenker, and Bonoma, 1973). In other cases, such tactics can induce anger, loss of "face," and aggression (Deutsch and Kraus, 1962; Rubin and Brown, 1975). That is, the tactics bring new and often unhelpful interests into the negotiation. Counter-tactics may well bring in additional interests and a spiral begins. Conflicts are more likely to escalate when disputants attribute their concessions to their own weakness; similarly, escalation is less likely when concessions can be attributed to something impersonal, such as a budgeting system, a formal procedure, or a widely accepted norm (Bachararch and Lawler, 1981).

The essence of some tactics is to add new interests. For example, one may make a commitment to a position by invoking an interest that the other negotiator cannot satisfy and that would not otherwise be part of the process; in holding to a position, the insurance claim adjuster may invoke a strong interest in maintaining a reputation as a tough bargainer for subsequent claims negotiations. The potential house buyer who announces that one's spouse would be tremendously angry if the purchase price were to exceed $150,000 adds a new interest to the negotiation: the relationship between husband and wife.

Other tactics, in contrast, may eliminate interests. Flipping a coin or submitting a dispute to arbitration may remove implications of weakness, strength, coercion, or tactical advantage.

Thus, interests can change even when issues remain fixed. The reverse is also true. Because the relation between issues and interests may be unclear, negotiators may reformulate the issues During negotiations over deep seabed mining in the Law of the Sea negotiations, for example, many of the different nations' underlying interests remained fairly constant. However, as the negotiations evolved, the issues changed dramatically—from whether mining should be done by private firms at all or by an international mining entity to the nitty-gritty aspects of mining contracts for private firms and the financing mechanism for the first operation of a new international mining entity. Trying to pin down the precise nature of the final issues at stake occupied a great deal of the negotiators' time, perhaps more than it took ultimately to resolve the issues (Sebenius, 1984).

PRESCRIPTIVE SUMMARY

As a summary for analysts and practitioners, we have converted the main observations of this paper into the following prescriptive checklist:

Assessing Which Interests Are At Stake

- Beyond the obvious tangible interests that may be affected by issues to be discussed, consider subtler interests in reputation, precedent, relationships, strategy, fairness, and the like.

- Distinguish underlying interests from the issues under discussion and the positions taken on them.

- Distinguish between intrinsic and instrumental reasons for valuing interests, especially some of the subtler ones.

- In seeking to understand others' interests, remember that interests depend on perceptions, that perceptions are subjective, and thus that to assess interests is to probe psyches. This process can be aided by clear communication, the advice of third parties, role-playing, and taking into account past behavior, training, professional affiliation, and organizational position, as well as those to whom the other defers.

- Keep in mind that interests and issues can change on purpose or accidentally as the parties learn, events occur, or certain tactics are employed.

Assessing Tradeoffs

- Tradeoffs are as important to interests as proportions are to recipes.

- To assess tradeoffs among intangible interests, it is sometimes helpful to imagine services one could buy otherwise to satisfy the same interests.

- To assess tradeoffs among issues:

  - Specify the worst and best possible outcomes on each issue to define the possible increments.

  - Compare the increments by thinking hard about underlying interests and which increments are most valued.

  - Break the increments into smaller pieces and similarly compare their relative evaluation.

  - Change assessments with learning about how different positions on the issues affect interests.

  - Assess interest tradeoffs using the same logic.

When to Focus on Interests and When on Issues

- Focus the negotiation on interests to enhance creativity and break impasses by reformulating issues to align better with underlying interests.

- Focus the negotiation on positions, issues, or a narrower set of interests when underlying conflicts of ideology make agreement difficult or when a restricted focus is more advantageous for claiming value.

Negotiation is a process of potentially opportunistic interaction in which two or more parties with some conflicting interests seek to do better by jointly decided action than they could otherwise. The alternatives to negotiated agreement or what the parties could do alone define the threshold of value that any agreement must exceed. The potential of negotiation is bounded only by the quality of agreement that can be devised. But, for evaluating alternatives and creating agreements, interests are the measure and raw material of negotiation.

NOTES

We would to thank Arthur Applbaum, Mark Moore, Howard Raiffa, Lawrence Susskind, and Thomas Weeks for helpful and friendly comments. A number of the ideas in this paper have been stimulated by the work of, and discussions with, Roger Fisher and William Ury, whom we also thank. Support from the Division of Research at the Harvard Business School and the Sloan Foundation Program of Research in Public Management is gratefully acknowledged. Much of this article is drawn from material prepared for a chapter of our book, *The Manager as Negotiator* (New York: The Free Press, forthcoming).

1. More technically-minded readers may find the following formulation helpful: Let u represent a negotiator's multi-attribute utility function; the attributes of u are the negotiator's interests. Let p be a vector of positions taken on the issue vector i(.). Let f be a vector-valued function that reflects the negotiator's beliefs about how well an agreement with position p on issues i advances his interests. Thus, an agreement p gives the negotiator utility $u(f(i(p)))$. Typically, of course, the negotiator will be uncertain about the relationship between issues and interests, which we might model by letting w represent the random variable reflecting relevant uncertain events and letting $f(i(p),w)$ reflect the negotiator's beliefs about the relationship between issues and interests conditional on w. Thus, we might say that the negotiator wants to choose p to maximize $E_w[u(f(i(p),w))]$, where E_w is the expectation over the negotiator's subjective beliefs about w.

2. The "additive scoring rule" constructed in this example is a simple case of a multi-attribute value or utility function. When interdependencies exist, non-additive, multi-attribute utility functions (see Keeney and Raiffa, 1976) can be used in this assessment.

3. Or for that matter, how to take the twin scoring systems for Lisa and William's values to produce a Pareto frontier. For a discussion of how to do this, see Raiffa (1982) or Barclay and Peterson (1976).

REFERENCES

Barclay, S. B. and C. Peterson. 1976. "Multi-Attribute Utility Models for Negotiators," *Technical Report* 76-1, McLean, Virginia: Decisions and Designs. Inc.

Bower, J. L. 1972. *Managing the Resource Allocation Process*. Homewood, Ill.: Irwin.

Deutsch, H. and R. M. Kraus. 1962. "Studies of Interpersonal Bargaining," *Journal of Conflict Resolution* 6, pp. 52–76.

Donaldson, G. and J. W. Lorsch. 1984. *Decision Making at the Top*. New York: Basic Books.

Fisher, R. and W. L. Ury. 1981. *Getting to YES: Negotiating Agreement Without Giving In*. Boston: Houghton-Mifflin.

Greenhalgh, L. and S. A. Neslin. 1981. "Conjoint Analysis of Negotiator Preferences." *Journal of Conflict Resolution* 25, pp. 301–327.

Gulliver, P. M. 1979. *Disputes and Negotiations: A Cross Cultural Perspective*. New York: Academic Press.

Keeney, R. and H. Raiffa. 1976. *Decisions With Multiple Objectives*. New York: Wiley.

Kotler, J. 1985. *Power and Influence*. New York: Free Press.

Neustadt, R. E. 1990. *Presidential Power*, 4th ed. New York: Wiley.

Raiffa, H. 1982. *The Art and Science of Negotiation*. Cambridge, Mass.: Harvard University Press.

Rubin, J. Z. and B. R. Brown. 1975. *The Social Psychology of Bargaining and Negotiation*. New York: Academic Press.

Schelling, T. C. 1960. *The Strategy of Conflict*. Cambridge. Mass.: Harvard University Press.

Sebenius, J. K. 1984. *Negotiating the Law of the Sea*. Cambridge. Mass.: Harvard University Press.

Tedeschi, J. T., B. R. Schlenker, and T. V. Bonoma. 1973. *Conflict, Power, and Games*. Chicago: Aldine.

INDEX

MASSACHUSETTS INSTITUTE OF TECHNOLOGY

ANCONA, KOCHAN, SCULLY,
VAN MAANEN, WESTNEY

Prepared by Susan J. Ashford
and Jane E. Dutton

MANAGING FOR THE FUTURE

Organizational Behavior & Processes

CHANGE FROM WITHIN:
ROADS TO SUCCESSFUL
ISSUE SELLING

module 13

CONTENTS

MODULE 13 (M-13)

CHANGE FROM WITHIN:
ROADS TO SUCCESSFUL ISSUE SELLING

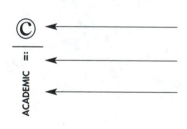

Icon indicates what part you are in, either core Ⓒ or supplemental Ⓢ.

Page number.

Within each part there are sections—Module Overview (OVERVIEW), Academic Perspective (ACADEMIC), Popular Press (PRESS), Case (CASE), Exercise (EXERCISE).

Dedicated to those who have inspired us to try to be better students and teachers. Special dedications to

Professor Jack Barbash
Professor Arthur H. Gladstein
Professor Marius B. Jansen
Professor Joanne Martin
Professor Edgar H. Schein

Acquisitions Editor: John R. Szilagyi
Developmental Editor: Jamie Gleich Bryant
Production Editor: Mardell Toomey
Production House: DPS Associates, Inc.
Cover Design: Michael H. Stratton
Marketing Manager: Rob Bloom

ISBN: 0-538-87700-6

1 2 3 4 5 6 7 D1 4 3 2 1 0 9 8

Printed in the United States of America

South-Western College Publishing
an International Thomson Publishing company I(T)P®

Cincinnati • Albany • Boston • Detroit • Johannesburg • London • Madrid • Melbourne • Mexico City
New York • Pacific Grove • San Francisco • Scottsdale • Singapore • Tokyo • Toronto

This module is designed to increase your skills in influencing change from the middle of an organization. We propose that long before business professionals reach the tops of their organizational hierarchies, they want to make change. They do so through a variety of processes. One of these is what we call issue selling. Issue selling involves the manager's active steps to get issues on the organization's agenda. Issue selling is important for both the employee manager and the organization. In today's organizations, hierarchy is being de-emphasized and speedy responses to a very complex environment are required. Consequently, being able to get ideas and surface issues from within the organization's own management ranks is critical. Employees also are becoming increasingly impatient with organizational settings that can't be responsive to new ideas. Given these two trends, it is in the organization's best interest to create a context in which issues can be surfaced and communicated.

For the individual employee, the ability to make a difference is becoming an important talent differentiator. Employees who are able to affect change are highly valued in today's organization. It is important, therefore, that new management professionals develop skills not only in managing change when they are the leader in charge, but also in suggesting and promoting changes from below.

This module gives you insights into both how organizations can be better managed to promote change from within and how employees can effectively use this skill. The goal is to give you the capability to make change in the contexts you enter and, perhaps later, better to create a context as an organizational leader that promotes change from within.

This module is divided into three parts consisting of some academic input on the topic and then both a case and exercise to get you more directly involved in using these new skills. The academic perspective serves as an introduction and overview of this critical managerial skill. The **Inex** case then asks you to assess the issue-selling efforts of a particular case character and to evaluate the context that exists at Inex. Is it one that facilitates change? The exercise asks you to put yourself into a situation and evaluate whether and how you would raise a particular issue. We provide citations at the end of the module to help you find additional materials if you are interested in following up on this topic. Finally, students have found an article by Steve Floyd and Bill Wooldridge so useful in the past that we have included it as a supplemental reading.

M-13

1

OVERVIEW

M-13

core

CHANGE FROM WITHIN: ROADS TO SUCCESSFUL ISSUE SELLING

Issue selling is important to both organizations and managers in today's newer, flatter, more dynamic organizational settings. Recent research evidence suggests that organizations gain from finding ways to foster input and involvement from below— organizations that involved middle managers in the strategy process outperformed organizations that did not. A simple argument may explain why. First, the world is getting increasingly complex. Organizations have to respond to environments that are themselves changing rapidly. New firms are entering the industry, and industries themselves are changing and evolving (consider, for example, the phone industry which now competes with computer companies which are in turn being bought up by entertainment companies). Relationships with suppliers and distributors are becoming more complicated and diverse (especially when we consider global companies). Companies' customer bases are also becoming more complex as they court new customers and respond to more individualized tastes and demands.

In the face of all of this complexity, it is increasingly difficult for one small group at the top of any organization to cope! Top managers' cognitive capacity is limited, to say nothing of their time. These realities make it advantageous for an organization to have *multiple* avenues for importing critical environmental information into the organization and simple pathways for getting it into the hands of the appropriate decision maker(s). Issue selling is one of those potential pathways. Organizations that open pathways for managers to raise issues of importance to those above them should reap two benefits. First, they direct *many* minds to consider what is most important for the organization's future. Second, they have minds closer to the problem (customers, suppliers, and technological developments) providing input into important priorities. Such firms should be more adaptable—they should learn quickly about new market opportunities and problems and be able to react faster than other firms without these pathways. Middle managers in this view are an important source of change and renewal from within the firm (see work by Nonaka, 1988, for a similar view).[1] Clearly in order to make this work, top management teams (TMTs) need the ability to sort and process issues quickly, but recent research suggests that fast decision-makers use more rather than less information.[2] Access to an use of more information may make the TMT susceptible to information overload. However, in the long run, information overload may be less damaging to the firm than isolation from the marketplace. Issue selling is a critical process that prevents this form of isolation.

Organizations exist to get things done. They make cars, develop software and market shoes. Action is coordinated, in part, by a strategic agenda that specifies what goals are important to the organization and what issues are "on the table" for organizational consideration. In some organizations, the strategic agenda is transparent; everyone knows

1 Nonaka, Ikujiro. 1988. "Toward Middle-Up-Down Management: Accelerating Information Creation." *Sloan Management Review.* (Spring), pp. 9–18.

2 Eisenhardt, K. M. 1989. "Making Fast Strategic Decisions in High-Velocity Environments." *Academy of Management Journal.* 32, 3, pp. 543–576.

the dominant goals and the top issues are recognized and shared by all. In other organizations, the strategic agenda is operating, but it is hidden, tacit, and generally difficult to sense. Whether explicit or implicit, the strategic agenda directs action in organizations.[3] For example, the agenda may indicate that the firm is most interested in increasing market share and that issues of product positioning, distribution and advertising are directing action. The prominence of these issues focuses action. In our example, marketing departments will be busy and powerful while financial and human resource issues may have a more difficult time being heard. In this way, the strategic agenda helps to direct which decisions get attention in organizations. Issues that make it onto the organizational agenda are the ones that get attended to by important decision-makers in the organization, while other issues fall by the wayside. However, organizational decision-makers can't attend to everything.[4] When key organizational members choose to focus on some issues, they are also choosing not to focus on others.

Who sets the organization's agenda? Common wisdom is that the top management team (TMT) sets the organization's goals and identifies the issues relevant to those goals. The top management team is a small group at the top of the organization, typically including the CEO, the COO, various subsidiary presidents, and/or functional vice-presidents. The team or group can be formally named or may operate informally. They are the group with the formal authority to get resources allocated. Once the top group has set goals and priorities, marching orders are then sent down the organization so that the top management's goals can be realized. Top management groups clearly do play this role in some organizations.

Recently, however, researchers have begun to question the completeness of this portrayal. They have argued that in addition to this "top down" picture of how strategy works, there are significant "bottom up" processes also at play. A new picture has emerged that portrays middle-level managers as important participants in the strategy process.[5] These managers take active steps to get issues on the organization's agenda. They do so either because they believe that the issue in question is important for the organization and/or because they think it is in their own or their department's interest to have the firm address the issue. The TMT is still centrally involved. Indeed they play two critical roles. First, they are the recipients of influence attempts (often-called **issue selling**) from the managers below them. Given that the TMT has limited time and attention, lower-level managers compete to get the ear of the TMT. Thus, the first important role of the TMT lies in its judgment regarding which issues are worthy of attention and which are not. In addition to simply reacting to ideas brought to them by middle managers, TMTs play an important second role. They can take active steps to create an organizational context that stimulates middle managers to participate in the strategy setting process. Essentially, TMTs can invite middle managers into the strategy process or signal to them that their input is not wanted.

For managers too, issue selling is an important activity and skill. Managers need to be able to sell their ideas within a firm if they are to be successful. Managers who can articulate why the firm ought to attend to issues that they think are critical to the firm's survival will be seen as having the leadership skills necessary to fill top roles within the company. All managers must manage down, but managers at the middle levels also need to manage up, and issue selling is part of that upward management. Managerial careers can be "made" or "broken" by associations with certain issues. For example, a manager who brought a firm's attention to an important, transformational

3 Dutton, J. E. and R. B. Duncan. 1987. "The Influence of Strategic Planning on Strategic Change." *Strategic Management Journal*. 8, 3, pp. 279–295.

4 Ocasio, W. 1997. "Toward an Attention-Based View of the Firm." *Strategic Management Journal*. 18, pp. 187–206.

5. Floyd, S. W. and B. J. Wooldridge. 1996. *The Strategic Middle Manager*. Jossey-Bass: San Francisco.

technological development, would likely be seen in a very positive light due to your association with this issue. At the same time, bringing issues that are perceived as unimportant or inappropriate to the attention of top management can have derailing effects, hurting rather than helping a manager's career.

THE CHOICE TO SELL ISSUES IN ORGANIZATIONS

If issue selling can have positive consequences for both the firm and for the managers who undertake it, then it is important to understand middle managers' choice processes. What motivates them to participate in the strategy process in this way? What makes them choose to stay silent? Our research suggests that situational assessments drive this choice, but in ways that rely on individual psychology. People appear to be more willing to speak up for issues in contexts where they perceive that management will listen and where the context is experienced as supportive.[6] That support may come from a supportive culture in general, or from supportive relationships that middle managers have with those above them. Both of these conditions increase the sense of safety that managers feel in raising potential controversial issues to those above them.

The context may enhance issue selling. For example, managers are sensitive to the presence of change in the organization. In one organization, managers told us that the time was ripe for them to raise issues because the organization itself was going through a lot of change. With so much in flux, these managers felt that they could easily raise another issue to consider. By implication, staid, tradition-bound organizations may shut off the very input that they need to adapt and change, while organizations that are good at change (or at least who are changing) invite even more input and ideas! Managers also see the context as more favorable for issue selling when top management is seen as open.

At the same time, the context may inhibit issue selling. For example, sellers see a conflict-avoiding culture as a barrier to effective issue selling. They also note that politics that are very complex make selling more difficult. In these types of cultures, managers do not raise issues either because it is not normative to do so or because they are unable to figure out how to go about it.

Woven throughout most of the stories that managers told us about their choices to sell issues or stay silent were concerns about damaging their reputations or images in the eyes of others. Sellers worried about how it might look if they were to raise particular issues in their organization. They expressed concerns that they might look critical, naïve, or weak. Many of the context factors that discouraged issue selling seemed to do so by heightening concerns about possible image damage. Not surprisingly, much of the advice sellers gave regarding how to raise issues effectively had to do with how to protect their own images.

Top managers play an important role in prompting issue selling. They set the context for initiatives of those below them. Understanding sellers' choice processes gives top management some insight into how to intervene to make the choice to speak up and raise issues more likely. Early indications suggest that top managers can enhance the likelihood of issue selling by reducing the perceived image costs of the act. Image costs can be reduced, in turn, by creating a supportive context, signaling openness, and creating norms supporting issue selling.[7] Top managers can reinforce their openness and create such norms by celebrating early issue sellers and initiating conversations about potential issues. Top managers can also institute forums in which possibilities, half-baked ideas, and preliminary analyses could be presented. In one

6 Dutton, J. E., S. J. Ashford, L. Wierba, R. M. O'Neill and E. Hayes. 1997. "Reading the Wind: How Middle Managers Assess the Context for Selling Issues to Top Managers." *Strategic Management Journal.* 18, 5, pp. 407–425.

7 Ashford, S. J., N. Rothbard, S. Piderit and J. Dutton. 1998. "Out On A Limb: The Role of Context and Impression Management in Selling Gender-Equity Issues." *Administrative Science Quarterly.* June.

conservative hospital we studied, they entertained issue discussions when only a full-blown analysis, along with recommendations, had been conducted and prepared. Such sessions are hardly the venue for raising ideas that are unattached to solutions (and yet are important for the firm) or for which a better solution might be reached if it was worked on collectively.

Tactical Choices in the Issue-Selling Process

The question for managers lower down in the organization is not how to promote issue selling, but how to engage in it successfully. There are two aspects of success for these managers. First, the managers must actually get the TMT to give some time and attention to the issues raised. Second, the manager must proceed in such a way that he or she "lives to sell another day." That is, their images can't be so badly damaged in this selling effort that they lose all credibility for subsequent efforts. Our research suggests that managers have a variety of choices to make regarding how to sell an issue. These choices have to do with how the issue is bundled, framed, and moved throughout the organization. Table 13.1 identifies critical issue selling choices.

Bundling. The first basic selling choice is whether to try to tie a new issue to other issues currently circulating within the organization. A seller might, for example, propose that a new technology issue is really a part of a bigger issue considered previously or another issue currently on the agenda. The advantages of bundling a new issue with others are several. By doing so, a seller taps into resources and communication currency the other issue may have. If the new issue is linked to an issue that is seen as important by others, then the new issue gains by association. There may also be some established routines or mechanisms for talking about the other issue from which the new issue might benefit. For example, if a new technology issue becomes linked to a larger product-development issue, then there may exist a cross-functional team designated to address the company's problems in getting new products up and running. The seller's new technology issue can then be channeled through this structure as a means of getting this issue a hearing.

© 7

ACADEMIC

TABLE 13.1 ISSUE SELLING PROCESS CHOICES

Connect issue to other issue	**Bundling**	Sell issue as an isolated concern
Business frame No implied TMT responsibility	**Framing**	Moral frame Implied TMT responsibility
Universal	**Language**	Particularistic
Go Solo	**Involvement**	Involve others as co-sellers
Formal Public	**Approach**	Informal Private
Early Connected to waves of change	**Timing**	Late

Of course, there is also a potential cost of bundling an issue with other issues. If the old issue comes to be seen in a negative way, for example, the new issue that the seller has carefully linked to it may be tainted with the same brush. It will be seen negatively as well. Ties to an "old issue" that has political enemies may activate conditions or political resistance that dampen enthusiasm for the new issue. In addition, links to an old issue may limit the range of solutions and participants connected to the neighborhood of the old issues. Thus, bundling needs to be a measured tactic used with care in the selling process.

Framing. Sellers implicitly or explicitly choose a framing for their issue by the ways that they describe and present an issue. For example, they can choose to frame an issue as an opportunity for the company or as a threat that the company faces. If they frame the issue as an opportunity, this frame may induce greater participation in the issue,[8] more commitment to taking action,[9] and changes of lesser magnitude,[10] than if the issue is framed as a threat. To frame an issue effectively as an opportunity, managers must work hard to help others to see the issue as controllable, involving gain, and as positive in impact.

Another basic choice that any seller has to make is whether to frame the issue to imply that the top group has a responsibility or obligation to address it. For example, managers interested in having their organizations become more environmentally responsive can push this issue as a moral obligation for the firm. In this approach, managers would emphasize the communal obligation of all parties and the morality of an affirmative response. Such framing makes getting the ear of the top more likely (in that they exert more pressure on this group). However, it may have attendant image costs. TMTs may not like feeling pushed and may think poorly of managers who take this kind of stand. Most sellers appear to prefer a business frame to such a "hard sell" approach. With a business frame, managers use facts and figures to suggest the financial costs of, for example, not attending to the environment. With this framing, managers appeal to their target's "heads" and a concern for their instrumental outcomes. With a moral appeal, managers appeal to their targets' "hearts" and their sense of what is right. Both frames are powerful and each may be useful in certain situations.

Language. Closely tied to tactics surrounding issue framing are choices regarding the use of language to describe an issue. Managers make language choices in their issue-selling attempts. For example, choosing a business frame for an issue requires one kind of language and a moral frame implies another. In choosing language to use, issue sellers need to be mindful of what a particular target is interested in hearing. Issue sellers chose whether to speak similarly about their issues to everyone or whether to customize language use to a specific target. Issue sellers often credited their success to an attempt to communicate flexibly about their issues. Effective sellers are able to speak "numbers to the numbers person and morality with the idealists." These managers effectively become multi-lingual! By tailoring their approaches to particular targets, sellers appeal to the targets' different zones of acceptance for an issue, making them more likely to be effective.

A second language choice involves sellers' attempts to link an issue to important organizational goals (e.g., this issue fits well with our plans to . . .). Managers can also cast the issue as a solution to current organizational issues and problems. For example, closely aligning a potential issue with an organization's strategic targets of increasing customer

8 Ashmos, D. P., D. Duchon, and W. D. Bodensteiner. 1990. "Swords into Plowshares: Strategic Decision Making and Response to 'Crisis' Issues in the Defense Industry." Working paper at University of Texas at San Antonio.

9 Ginsberg, A. and N. Venkatraman. 1992. "Investing in New Information Technology: The Role of Competitive Posture and Issue Diagnosis." *Strategic Management Journal.* 13, (Summer), pp. 37–53.

10 Dutton, J. E. and S. Jackson. 1987. "Categorizing Strategic Issues: Links to Organizational Action." *Academy of Management Review.* 12, pp. 76–90.

satisfaction, energy costs, or reducing waste may motivate targets to invest more attention in an issue. Both connecting strategies make the language used consistent with what decision-makers are ready to hear and to what has already been collectively affirmed as important in the organization. Sellers can thus more easily get an ear for their issues.

Involvement. Managers must decide whether to push their issues alone or to involve others in any selling effort. Though sometimes managers have little choice (e.g., when no one wants to get involved with the issue), our sellers indicate that often they are faced with deciding whom to involve. Many managers gave the advice that sellers should involve others who have a stake in the issue. Sellers might consider who might be affected by their issue and try to include them in the selling attempt. This strategy co-opts people who might object to the issue being raised or who might have a stake in how it gets implemented. The advantage here is that it gets these voices working "for" the issue rather than, potentially, speaking out against it. The disadvantage is that by including those with additional and perhaps unique concerns, it can dilute the selling effort as the seller adds sub-issues or deletes central messages to appease the new "co-sellers."

A second group to be targeted for involvement are those who stand to gain from the issue being raised. Here the seller invites additional issue champions on board his or her selling effort. The advantages of such an invitation are two-fold. First, more sellers mean a greater potential of being heard, as there is strength in numbers. Second, if the issue is badly received, the seller who has involved others in his or her selling effort risks less image damage. Any negative reactions may be attributed to the group. There is a cost to a high involvement strategy too, however. If the issue is welcomed, no one particular seller stands out as the champion.

Approach. Sellers also have to make choices about their selling approach. Here two decisions stand out. First, sellers have to decide whether to make a formal or informal appeal and second whether to make a public or private pitch for their issues. Our research indicates that rather than make these selling choices independently, sellers tend to follow the dominant organizational recipe for this activity. For example, if people tend to raise issues in private forums using informal means, then issue sellers would be better off if they sold the issue using a similar approach. In contrast, if a firm had a formal presentation norm, then sellers would be better off customizing their efforts to this type of approach. By following the prescriptive routines, issue sellers would be more likely to get a hearing for their issue. This "recipe following" tendency suggests that organizations might want to take a look at the prescribed routines in their settings. For example, remember the conservative hospital? A factor seen as blocking issue selling there was that there was no room in the organization to "think out loud." One of the changes contemplated by senior management as a result of our study was to institute a "not ready for prime time" issue-discussion forum. In this forum, managers could raise issues that were not yet thoroughly worked out. By this mechanism, senior management hoped to get an earlier read on emerging issues than they had been able to previously.

Timing. Managers in several different organizational settings have given us lots of advice for how issues can be raised effectively. For example, managers emphasize the importance of being opportunistic about timing. One seller, for example, talked about an issue that she, "kept in her desk drawer," ready to raise when the time was right. More effective managers may pay attention to "waves" of thought, opinion and political momentum when deciding whether to sell a particular issue. Researchers who have studied politicians who effectively get issues on the congressional docket liken them to surfers.[11] Good docket setters (or good issue sellers) are able to sense the waves of

---

11 Kingdon, J. W. "How do Issues Get on Public Policy Agendas?" Paper presented at the annual meeting of the American Sociological Association.

changing sentiment in an organization. They capitalize on the momentum created by the changing tides of openness and opportunity that exist in an organization. Getting in front of one of those waves with one's issue may help to propel that issue onto the organizational agenda. On the other hand, a selling attempt that is poorly timed may have little chance of getting on the agenda given the existing currents in the organization no matter how meritorious it is! Savvy managers learn how to read the context effectively and to initiate their selling at the right time.

Other Tactics

In addition, many sellers have emphasized the importance of doing one's homework as part of the work of effective issue selling. Homework has two elements. First, sellers need to become experts in the content of what they are promoting. This might involve gathering external evidence on a new technology, articles from industry publications about a proposed practice or anecdotes from senior colleagues about a new technique. The goal is to not only have one's facts straight about the issue one is promoting, but also to gather evidence that will be seen as credible by those one is selling to. In addition to homework about the topic, there is also the need to do one's political homework. This involves assessing the organizational history around an issue. Has it been brought up before? What happened then? The seller should also assess other people's agendas related to the issue. Who is likely to be for or against it? This knowledge will be crucial in tailoring the selling approach.

Doing one's political homework can also include informally testing the waters by stimulating early conversations about the issue of interest. In this way the seller can obtain valuable information about the issue and how others might view it. From these early, informal discussions, the seller can draw better inferences about how others higher up in the organization might respond and can modify his or her approach to better ensure obtaining their support. These early informal conversations are also crucial for assessing whether and how much image cost there may be in pushing this issue. This assessment can be crucial in making decisions about both whether and how to proceed.

THE CHALLENGE OF CHARGED ISSUES

The discussion to this point has ignored the *nature* of the issue that sellers might be considering. Sellers, however, appear to think carefully about the content of the issue that they are selling. Certain issues seem to be more worrisome in the minds of potential issue sellers. These issues have a characteristic nature. Sellers are reluctant to raise them in all different contexts. We have called these issues "charged." By charged, we mean that the issue is tough. These are what some authors have labeled "undiscussables" in organizations. Our research suggests that charged issues are evaluated negatively, emotion laden, politically hot in that they are seen as having a divisive quality, and complex. We have studied gender-equity concerns (whether men and women are treated equitably in organizations) as one example of a charged issue. Other such issues might be the treatment of employees with AIDS, the treatment of racial minorities, the treatment of the natural environment or other social issues. These issues are often scary ones for managers to raise. There are several concerns. Managers wonder whether they will be seen as rocking the boat. They worry too about being shunned by the group for bringing up issues that cause controversy. They also worry about being labeled. For the gender-equity issue, for example, managers worried about being labeled a troublemaker.

How do organizations handle such issues? A typical way is that top management creates defensive routines that reduce the likelihood that such issues will be expressed. For example, aggressive statements from the top regarding how wonderfully the organization is addressing the issue in question can send strong signals to those below that

messages to the contrary are not wanted. The top thereby protects itself from hearing that all is not well. Our research suggests that middle managers collude in this protection. Out of an interest in remaining accepted by the group and maintaining their team player image, managers restrain themselves from going out on a limb for an issue that they think will be controversial or emotional. Over time and by behaviors such as these, certain issues become undiscussable within an organization. One manager described his setting as a conflict-avoiding culture. Other managers would agree with him in private that an issue needed to be addressed, but there would be no support in public settings. Many managers suggested that risk taking is not rewarded in their settings. Given these beliefs, such managers are unlikely to raise issues that entail risk.

Should organizations care that certain issues take on the quality of undiscussables? There is reason to believe that they should. If the issue that causes concern continues, it will fester within the organization. Women feeling inequitably treated, for example, will continue to experience this. If they have no place to talk about this issue within the organization, they are more likely to leave. There is a cost attached to such a talent drain. In addition, if looming concerns (say over the need to be more environmentally responsive) are undiscussables, then the organization loses valuable time in formulating a response. The organization may have to respond to the concern more in a crisis mode (say when a lawsuit is brought against the firm) than it would if there had been avenues for discussion earlier.

Firms interested in opening up the corporate conversation to include discussion of charged issues such as the treatment of employees (in all its various guises) need to work hard to make the context supportive and to establish communication avenues that put issue sellers less at personal risk. For example, GE holds a town meeting forum in which managers from all over the world can anonymously call in their information and concerns about a variety of topics. The call is heard simultaneously by their top managers worldwide. Often these calls raise issues along the lines of "our competitor in Brazil appears to be coming out with a new product." An alternative way to use this management practice (which is also used by Wal-Mart) is to have people surface these more troubling concerns too (e.g., "our competitors are taking significant steps to address the environmental impact of their production processes, should we?"). If managers can create a supportive atmosphere, charged issues can more easily enter the broad-based "discussion" created by this use of computer technology. What was undiscussable becomes discussable—and by a broad range of folks simultaneously.

CONCLUSION

Survival in an increasingly changing environment demands that organizations develop effective engines for change that work inside the organization. Our research indicates that a vital source for change from within is created and perfected through the effective identification and selling of critical organizational issues. Issue selling is a skilled activity. It takes a mindset and a competence that can be developed. Effective issue sellers have a good sense of the full range of issue-selling choices and they customize issue-selling efforts to the contexts in which they find themselves. Over time, they learn to make these choices thoughtfully and enact them with skill. The best issue sellers undertake this activity as a natural part of their middle managerial jobs. These are the managers who are seen as influential and able to get things done in the organization. In this way issue selling is an important political skill in fostering managerial success.

© 11 ACADEMIC

THE ISSUE WITH INEX

Nestled in California's "Silicon Valley" is a middle-sized firm called Inex, a minor player in what has recently been a booming computer industry. While generally considered a "clean" industry, many computer companies had been coming under increasing attack during the past decade, from environmentalists, public groups, and politicians for emitting sulfuric and hydrochloric acid into the atmosphere.

These groups have not yet targeted Inex, given its size. However, their presence caused Inex's president, Sara Lightwood, concern. Sara Lightwood worried that Inex's turn in the spotlight might soon be coming. Lightwood worried that her company's carefully created image as a new-age, enlightened workplace might be damaged if Inex was cited for harming the environment. In addition, it was also possible that the government might get involved. Congress recently passed new, special regulations that would control pollution from computer companies. Lightwood faced a tough choice. She could do nothing and face potential penalties for non-compliance, or she could spend enormous sums to tackle the problem. Her long-run strategy for the firm might change if the penalties were a certainty—but right now she couldn't be sure.

President Lightwood's concerns were not without reason. Recently she learned that LTX in Tucson's "Silicon Desert" had undertaken a $330 million dollar program to install somewhat low-tech scrubbers in their production facilities. LTX spent nearly six years in legal battles with the state of Arizona over their air emissions. While Inex was near LTX's size, Inex had been listed in the EPA's toxic release inventory system as a noted air pollutant contributor. There had also been increasing publicity in recent months about air quality in the valley, allegedly caused by computer manufacturers.

In January, Lightwood met with Brad Jones, a young engineer who has worked at Inex for three years. He was hired based on Sara Lightwood's recommendation. A faculty member at the University of Michigan's School of Information recommended Jones highly to Lightwood. Jones had combined training in computer science with training in environmental engineering through Michigan's Corporate Environmental Management Program. Lightwood herself was a Michigan graduate and when Jones was hired, the two had a long meeting. They discussed Lightwood's vision for Inex, her management style, and the plans she had for Jones and other young computer-savvy engineers. As Jones remembered the conversation, Lightwood's message centered on personal initiative and the interconnectedness of organizational life. She said:

> Even if you have the best ideas, your insights in Inex, or indeed in any organization, will only have power and real impact if you are able to "work" the organization. Managing well involves reading the context and managing up. Power and influence are not dirty words! They are the essence of managerial success!

Jones and Lightwood met at 2 p.m. on January 11 for a regularly scheduled meeting. After initial pleasantries, Jones explained that he had begun the process of looking for another job. Jones noted that he asked for the meeting because he didn't want Lightwood to hear it from others. According to Jones, new ideas didn't appear to be welcome within Inex. "Even top level line and staff personnel resist change," Jones said. Jones then described a recent experience in which he tried to convince Janet Brown, the sector manager of the company's CPU Division, to support an idea that

This case is based on a prior case, Pegasus Chemical Company.

Jones had for reducing toxic air emissions. Jones felt he had a process that could essentially eliminate toxic sulfuric and hydrochloric acid from the smoke going up Inex's stacks.

Lightwood had many contacts in the field. She had already heard about Jones' recent activities. She knew that Jones, with Brown's approval, had just completed a $60,000 pilot project in designed to reduce toxic emissions. The project was apparently successful. Jones now recommended that the company spend $3.4 million dollars to purchase and install special filtered smokestack "scrubbers" able to do the job for the entire company for at least the next 11 years. Lightwood probed a bit regarding Brown's reaction. Jones summarized Janet Browns' concerns.

1. Why this much? Brown thought that Jones' scrubbers were more than what was needed and, therefore, too costly! The EPA didn't require the reduction of toxins to such an extreme level. So why should they do it?

2. Why now? The company was experiencing little pressure from community groups. The media and public groups hadn't yet focused on pollution in Silicon Valley. When they did, Brown argued, they would focus on firms much larger than Inex first.

3. Can we afford it? $3.4 million was a lot of money. There were other company priorities that required resources in the immediate future.

Sara Lightwood was most interested in Jones' personal opinion of the process he had invented—was it really good? Jones said he was convinced that it was. Jones also argued that the money required to install the scrubbers was inexpensive when you looked at what the same equipment would likely cost in even just a few years.

Lightwood listened carefully to Jones. After sitting in silence for a moment, Lightwood reminded Jones of their conversation just after he was hired. Lightwood noted that if the equipment was as good as Jones said, then he should be able to convince others of his plan. She wanted Jones to understand, though, that a convincing idea wasn't enough. In Lightwood's mind, new ideas rarely make it on pure merit. Ideas sell because the seller knows the political landscape of the organization and works the idea with sensitivity to the organization's power sources. In Lightwood's mind, it was this knowledge that separated mere ideas from ultimate organizational changes.

Lightwood told Jones that as president, she wouldn't decide on her own to spend the $3.4 million even if she were certain it would benefit the company. She said, "Personally, I like your idea. Your task now is to make it happen. If you believe in this idea put the heat on me! Pressure me through the organization. Have the organization convince me, the president, now that you've convinced me, the individual."

Lightwood encouraged Jones to stay on, stay with it, and work the context to make his idea a reality. Lightwood then hit Jones with the big one. She said that if he decided to stay and push for what he believed in, that he shouldn't tell anyone of their conversation. She said that if she were to hear that he did, he wouldn't work for Inex any longer. Lightwood supported her strong stand by noting that she didn't believe in management by command and that orders from the top never created effective change.

Their conversation that day was brief, and Jones remembered leaving feeling angry. It didn't make sense to him that the company wouldn't adopt his process right now! In Jones' mind, Inex had a societal responsibility to cease polluting the atmosphere. It didn't matter what bigger companies were doing or whether regulatory agencies were focused on Silicon Valley or not! Sara Lightwood seemed unwilling to back her words with action!

Jones took the next several days off and traveled to the Alexander Valley north of Sonoma. In the beauty of the vineyards and hills he sought some perspective. What would he gain by quitting? He would certainly lose credit for all the work done thus far. He saw that Lightwood had boxed him in—he would have to work the project through

CASE 13

the organization. So he decided to go for it—to try to get the organization to pressure Lightwood to accept the value of the scrubbers. Jones figured he had two things going for him. First, he was known as an excellent engineer. He was recognized as having great potential to advance within the company. Second, his pilot was acknowledged by technically competent people to be effective. The filtered scrubbers were a good idea. In fact, the company was seeking patents for them. Other companies had also expressed interest in purchasing the rights even at this early stage.

INEX COMPANY

Inex was a medium-sized computer company. It competed successfully with both small start-ups and with the giants in the industry. Inex's competitive advantages were competitive prices and a somewhat faster and more reliable delivery to regional customers.

The company had three major operating Units. They were the Central Processing Unit (CPU) sector, the Peripherals/Processors sector, and the Storage Devices sector. Each sector was run as a profit center. Each had its own manufacturing, developmental research, and marketing operations. The sector managers reported to Lightwood. They were rewarded with a salary plus a bonus based on sector profits. In good years, bonuses for sector managers would amount to 35 to 49 percent of their base salaries.

Top and mid-level operating managers at Inex tended to be moved around a lot. Young, ambitious managers who desired top operating positions were especially likely to move. In Jones' opinion, the rapid movement of management along with the method the firm used to evaluate and pay managers was responsible for a general resistance to try out new ideas. Such ideas often had long-term profit potential and required managers to spend money in the short run. Line managers at Inex became so concerned with short-term results that they sometimes ignored important longer run concerns like preventative maintenance. On occasion, managers also concealed safety violations as well as environmental issues. The hope seemed to be that by the time the consequences of such violations became obvious the manager would have moved on to another job. Movement into and out of Inex, both from and to other companies in the industry was also frequent. As a result, good ideas from one company could easily be picked up in others. Consequently, managers tended to be less-than-open with others in the organization.

COMPANY STRUCTURE

In addition to the three operating sectors, there were several small staff groups. President Lightwood had a particular view of staff groups. She didn't like them. She felt that they tended to begin masterminding things. She wanted the operating sectors left to the sector managers (with small staff groups within each sector). Corporate staff groups were there to assist. Inex had five staff groups: marketing, production, research, finance, and personnel. Marketing and personnel were quite small (two staff assistants reporting to a VP), but research was much larger. Lightwood picked staff VPs for their knowledge. She saw their major responsibilities as keeping her and her Management Committee (MC) up-to-date as to major market and technological issues facing the business. The MC used this information in setting long-range strategy for the sectors. A second staff VP responsibility was to review one- and five-year plans submitted by the sectors and to review annual sector performance. Lightwood counted on these staff groups for the expertise to evaluate the specifics of sector goals and performance. Finally, the staff groups were charged with being helpful to the sector managers and sector staff personnel. They were to give them needed information on changes in their fields of expertise.

To ensure that staff personnel were responsive to line managers, staff vice presidents at Inex were paid a set salary. They were not eligible for bonuses. The president evaluated the vice presidents based on how well the line functions they supported performed. In making her evaluation, Lightwood placed a great weight on how line managers viewed the performance of corporate staff employees. Their division managers also evaluated staff managers working in the divisions.

When President Lightwood discussed staff personnel, she often placed them into four categories. There were those who were approaching senility. They tried to compete with line personnel to try to support their own existence. The second group were those who had been "kicked upstairs" to a position where they couldn't hurt the firm too badly. A third group contained the activity creators. These folks felt the need to have others see that they are busy "doing" something. These employees tended to put out volumes of paper and sought to put responsibility for decisions on others. When they send memos, they often contained "fudge factors" that made responsibility for a decision ambiguous. For example, they might say, "I am in agreement with the proposal broadly, however, I have concerns about the chance that. . . ." Sometimes they would refer in public to a memo that they never had sent. If the idea were seen as meritorious, then they would take the photocopy out of their file! In Sara's mind these folks were the "hiders" in the organization.

There was a fourth group, however. These were the "well balanced." These folks recognized that line employees drive the decisions. Staff groups can advise, but it was the line manager's right to say "take a hike!" In Lightwood's view, staff people would do well to remember that line managers really want acknowledgement. Well-balanced staff personnel find ways to put the line managers center stage and to stay out of the spotlights themselves.

Brad Jones's first position at Inex was as a section staff engineer in the CPU sector. He worked in the sector's largest plant.[1] Brad had worked in the plant less than eight months when his performance drew the attention of the sector's manager, Janet Brown. Brown felt that Jones was one of the smartest and one of the most hard-working young engineers she had ever met. Brown noted that Brad got along well with everyone. He could not only talk to professionals, but could relate well to hourly production workers. Brown tapped Brad for a special assignment, a project that the sector had been trying to get going for over two years. Brown was impressed because in four months Brad had gotten it in shape! Brown kept an eye on him and soon tapped Jones to be her special assistant. He worked as a point person on the important problems facing the sector. Brown commented that, "Brad handled them like a pro!" Brown was impressed that despite Brads lack of experience, he had the sensitivity and the good sense to know when he doesn't have all the answers and where to go to get them. With Brad's talent, Brown was not surprised when Jim Sands soon "stole" Brad from her.

Jim Sands was the staff VP heading up production. He was viewed by opinion leaders in the company as the most knowledgeable person in the production area. Sara Lightwood had appointed him to the vice-presidency two years prior to Brad Jones's arrival in the firm. When one of his two subordinates was stolen away to another computer company, Sands asked Brown if he could approach Jones about working in the production staff group for a year of two. His rationale was that he needed his talents and that this move would broaden Jones by giving him experience in the work of Inex's other two divisions.

> "I didn't want to lose Brad," said Brown, "but this seemed like an opportunity too good for me to stand in his way. I predict that Brad Jones will be running one of our divisions before too long if we are lucky enough to keep him."

C

15

CASE

---

1 Exhibit 1 at the end of this case contains an Inex organization chart.

When he was offered the job, Jones was working on his filtered scrubber pilot program. He wasn't sure he was ready to move. He asked Sands for time to consider the offer. He explained that he wanted to complete the pilot before moving. Sands understood and offered Jones a six-month extension on the offer. That conversation took place this past August.

During the six months Jones wrote a detailed proposal for the incorporation of the scrubbers. Chris Davis, Plant Manager of the CPU Sector's Fremont, California facility, helped Brad in his efforts. The proposal went into great detail. It contained drawings and a 1/3-inch scale mock-up of the facility showing the smokestacks with the filter scrubbers. Jones had obtained four different construction estimates and had looked into a couple of different plans for financing. Jones was enthusiastic when he went to Brown in January to show her the plan. Brown, to Jones's surprise, did not share the enthusiasm.

She did concede that Jones made several good points, but she feared that he put too much stock on the pollution question. She commented that what Inex sent into the atmosphere was a pittance compared to what other companies in the industry were doing. She continued:

> Sure, in time we'll have to act, but there hasn't been any recent pressure since the Silicon Desert incident. I believe it will be four years, at minimum, before the pressure on big companies really will get hot. Only then will they take real action. Our efforts now will not make any difference! We alone can't affect air quality. The costs of action are significant. The filter scrubbers would add hundreds of thousands of dollars to our sector's operating costs over the next several years. In addition, I worry about the indirect costs. It will be disruptive to install these new scrubbers. It could upset our whole production flow for a week or more if there are problems. The total expense, when you take disruption into account might be much more than what Brad was estimating.

Beyond these concerns, Brown also thought that the system was too much—that Inex could get by with other measures, perhaps that did only less than a top job, for far less money.

It was after this discussion that Jones seriously thought about quitting Inex. However, he felt then that he ought to try one more time. That try involved seeking out Sara Lightwood, and the two met on January 11.

Jones continued to be unhappy after the Lightwood meeting. After spending time in the wine country thinking things over, he called Jim Sands and asked if he might still take the staff assistant's job that Sands had extended more than six months earlier. Sands asked about how the filter scrubber project was going. Jones said he had stopped working on it for the present.

Jones went to work for Sands on March 20th. Sands asked him to evaluate the CPU sector's plans for production. These reviews were undertaken annually. They gave Sands the information that he needed to be able to question the specific sector managers prior to the bringing the total plan to President Lightwood and the Management Committee for evaluation. The staff review and the talks between staff and division personnel that they engendered often resulted in the issues being resolved without taking the time and attention of the president and other Management Committee members.

As Jones began his staff work with Sands, he remembered what Lightwood always said about the four types of staff personnel. He aspired to the "well balanced" group. In fact, Brad Jones, aspired to a top-level position. Given that, Lightwood's views of staff managers challenged him. He would like to have recognition himself, but if he were going to be successful in **this** organization, he would have to set his own recognition aside as long as he worked in a staff area. If he didn't, he wouldn't have much chance of ever getting back to a line position. Jones did question if Lightwood's ideas about staff actually worked. He worried that if staff managers gave away the limelight all the time, they might not be considered when promotions came up. They wouldn't be visible! It may be, too, that if they were really good at standing at the side and feeding the line managers ego needs, the line manager might never want them to stop!

In his ruminations about staff roles at Inex, Jones' idea for the filtered scrubbers was never far from his mind. He knew that to get action on this issue, ultimately, the Management Committee would have to give it some attention. He needed to figure out how to work it through the organization to get it to the Management Committee. To get it there he would have to work both the line and the staff sides of the organization. The key, though, was the Management Committee.

THE MANAGEMENT COMMITTEE

Sara Lightwood headed up the Management Committee. The committee consisted of the three sector managers, and the five staff vice-presidents. It met once every two months to assess sector performance relative to the sector plans (one- and five-year plans) that the MC approved each year. Lightwood also used the committee for advice on cross-sector issues, issues that might influence the overall corporate direction, and on all requests for major capital investments (over $2 million). The tradition in Inex was that Lightwood approved proposals if she was satisfied that the proposal wouldn't "take the company under" or mean a significant new strategic direction and if the relevant sector manager and at least two staff vice-presidents supported it. When the proposal involved two or more sectors, Lightwood also considered whether all who had a stake in the proposal had given their approval.

If all of these conditions were met, then Lightwood generally approved. When Lightwood approved, the MC tended to go along. Sometimes Lightwood asked for a straw vote at MC meetings, but formal paper ballot votes weren't done.

Often, there were "intense" discussions in MC meetings, but lingering conflicts were not the norm. Usually the pertinent staff and line people worked beforehand to build a consensus. In this process, many compromises and side deals were cut. Often managers traded off support for each other's proposals.

17

CASE

JONES'S DILEMMA

Jones didn't know how the MC members felt about his issue. He knew Lightwood liked it, but he wasn't allowed to mention this important fact. He had to build consensus among MC members. Of these, Janet Brown had already "trashed" the idea. Jones had to get Brown to change her mind! He also had to convince Sands, his current boss and Lee Crandall, the head of the Storage Devices sector.

Sands was taken by Jones's data. The pilot data were particularly impressive! The government fines that Jones cited as possible were also daunting. Sands knew that he could push the project through given what he knew about Lightwood's stand on pollution. Unfortunately, he could not take the issue up. He was currently involved in a dispute with another sector manager. He would have to take that one to the MC too. He did not feel he could also bring Jones's issue.

Sands did agree to get together with Brown to see if Brown would be willing to raise the issue herself in July. Sands reported back to Jones days later, however, that Brown was still reluctant. He said that he was sorry, but Brown wouldn't go along. Sands still felt the proposal had merit, but asked Jones to back off and to try again the following year.

Jones was let down. He didn't say much to Sands at the time but it bugged him. It was the principle that bothered him. It seemed like the managers all wanted someone else to take action. And meanwhile time was wasting! "They find all sorts of reasons not to 'make a big deal' out of something that *is* a big deal." "I don't know what to do. I know compromise is needed, but where do I draw the line!?" "How do I proceed in my job of 'trying again next year'."

EXHIBIT 1 PARTIAL ORGANIZATION CHART FOR INEX COMPANY

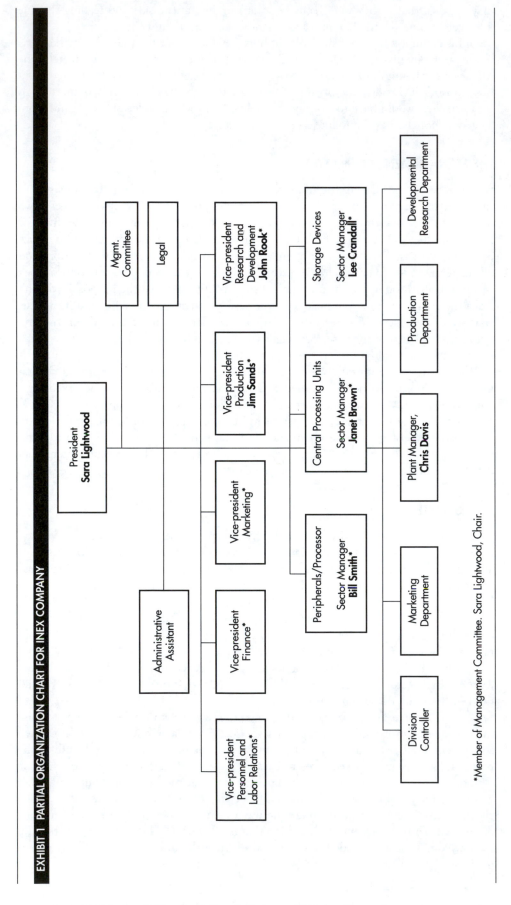

*Member of Management Committee. Sara Lightwood, Chair.

ISSUE-SELLING EXERCISE

INSTRUCTIONS

Read the attached case situation.[1] The case describes an issue experienced by a manager. Assume that this manager works at "your firm." For "your firm," think of a firm with which you are most familiar. It may be the firm in which you have done most of your full-time work or the firm that you worked in most recently (e.g., your summer internship firm). Give the manager described in the case advice on how to "sell" this issue within your firm.

Please give the case some thought, answer the questions that follow, and then attach your issue-selling plan. In your plan, use bullet points, be brief, but be sure to describe the complete set of steps that you think Chris Peters should follow in raising this issue. Draw upon your understanding of Chris Peters's issue, as well as your own experience of how things get done in organizations.

Remember: This is an individual assignment.

CHRIS PETERS AND THE "PEOPLE" ISSUE

After a wonderful dinner at a fancy seafood restaurant, your friend, Chris Peters, pushes the attached memo across the dinner table. "Take a look at this and tell me what I should do," Chris asks. "I really need your advice." You have known Chris since your early college days and have followed Chris' career proudly. Chris has worked at your firm for ten years in the marketing department.

Chris wrote the attached memo because she thought it was time that someone at the top really knew what was going on at the company. Chris believes that the message is important, but does not know how it will be received. She really wants your advice.

19

EXERCISE

1 Reardon, Kathleen. 1993. "The Memo Every Woman Keeps in her Desk." *Harvard Business Review*, March–April, pp. 3–8.

TO: MR. PETER JONES, CEO
FROM: Chris R. Peters
         Director of Product Marketing
DATE: February 5, 1998

I've been working in the marketing department for ten years. I have been stretched and have grown in this department, but have also had challenges. I've enjoyed being part of this dynamic and interesting company. Despite my general enthusiasm about the company and my job, however, I was taken aback when I received your memo announcing the resignations of Jan Sims and Lee Chambers, two of our firm's high ranking people. Just nine months ago, Noel Fredrickson resigned, and a year before that, it was Pat Hayes. The reasons that they gave seem surprisingly similar, they wanted to "spend more time with their families" or "explore new career directions."

I wonder if there is a pattern here? Why do such able, conscientious people who seem to be committed to their careers suddenly want to change course or spend more time with families? It's a question I've been thinking about and one that I want to raise with you.

Despite our firm's policies to hire and promote good people and your own efforts to recognize and reward people's contributions, the overall atmosphere in this company is one that seems to slowly erode people's sense of worth. I believe that top-level people are leaving our firm not because they are drawn to other pursuits but because they are tired of struggling against a climate of failure. Little things that happen daily send subtle messages that people are less important, less talented, less likely to make a difference than they really could.

Let me try to describe what I mean. I'll start with meetings, which happen all the time at our firm and seem devaluing for people. People are often talked over and interrupted; their ideas never seem to be heard. Last week, I attended a meeting with eleven people. As soon as the two started their presentation, several side conversations began. Their presentation skills were excellent, but they couldn't seem to get people's attention. When it was time to take questions, one man said dismissively, "We did something like this a couple of years ago, and it didn't work." They explained how their ideas differed, but the explanation fell on deaf ears. When I tried to give them support by expressing interest, I was interrupted.

But it's not just meetings. There are many things that make people feel unwelcome or unimportant. One department holds its biannual retreats at a country club where some don't feel welcomed. At the end of the sessions, some typically hang around at the bar and talk, while others quietly disappear. Needless to say, important information is often shared during those casual conversations.

Almost every formal meeting is followed by a series of informal ones behind closed doors. Some are rarely invited. Nor are they privy to the discussions before the formal meetings. As a result, they are often less likely to know what the boss has on his or her mind and therefore less prepared to react.

Any of these incidents on its own is a small thing. But together and in repetition, they are quite powerful. The people here fight to get their ideas heard and to crack the informal channels of information. Their energy goes into keeping up, not getting ahead, until they just don't have any more to give.

I can assure you that my observations are shared by many in the company. I can only speculate that Jan Sims and Lee Chambers shared them.

Our firm needs people if it is to become preeminent. We need to send stronger, clearer signals that people matter. And this kind of change can work only if it starts with strong commitment at the top. That's why I'm writing to you. If I can be of help, please let me know.

PART ONE

Now that you've read the memo and thought about Chris's situation, we are interested in whether or not you would raise (or sell) this issue to the top management team. **Assume that Chris has not yet sent this memo to the CEO when you answer the questions below.**
   Can Chris sell this issue successfully to the top management team (where success is indicated by the top management team giving the issue their time and attention to it)? To what extent do you agree or disagree with the following (Please circle one number on the scales for the questions below):

1. I am confident that Chris could get the top levels of my firm to pay attention to this issue.

1	2	3	4	5	6	7
Strongly Disagree			Neither Agree or Disagree			Strongly Agree

2. Based on the scenario, how willing should Chris be to try to sell this issue to the top management team (using whatever approach or style that you think best)?

1	2	3	4	5	6	7
Not at all Willing						Extremely Willing

3. Please explain below the rationale for the rating that you provided in question 4.

_____
_____
_____
_____

4. How much effort should Chris be willing to put into selling this issue to the TMT?

1	2	3	4	5	6	7
None at all						A great deal of effort

5. How much *time* should Chris be willing to spend in selling this issue?

1	2	3	4	5	6	7
Not at all Willing						Extremely Willing

6. What are the different steps that Chris might consider taking in selling this issue to the top management team? (What is your issue-selling plan?) List below.

_____
_____
_____
_____

© 21 EXERCISE

M-13

supplemental

DINOSAURS OR DYNAMOS? RECOGNIZING MIDDLE MANAGEMENT'S STRATEGIC ROLE

by Steven W. Floyd and Bill Wooldridge

EXECUTIVE OVERVIEW

Reengineering has automated and obliterated middle management, and has diminished their number dramatically. What have also been lost in many delayering efforts, however, are the benefits of the strategic roles of middle managers.

This article describes how certain middle management behavior is crucial to developing organizational capability. This is a learning process which calls on organizations to interpret the world, uncover new market opportunities, focus existing resources, and accumulate new resources. In our research, we identified a middle management role with each of these elements and uncovered a strong relationship between the roles and organizational performance. Therefore, rethinking middle management's strategic role is a necessary part of the delayering process. The article closes by illustrating how to encourage strategic behavior in the reengineered organization.

Are middle managers becoming the dinosaurs of the business world? They once dominated the corporate landscape with salaries and perks that were the envy (and career goal) of every MBA. Now, like prehistoric reptiles, these behemoths of bureaucracy appear likely to succumb to a hostile environment.

In the past, when a company needed to grow, management simply added workers to the bottom and then filled in management layers above. This focused managers' attention on planning and control and provided the rationale for legions of middle managers. Growth slowed dramatically in the late 1980s, however, and today's priorities are higher quality, lower cost, flexibility, and, most important, speed.

People in the middle slow things down, increasing the distance between the customer and the corporate response. The current wave of reengineering is aimed at removing this obstacle by rethinking the division of work and reorganizing around "horizontal" processes. As part of this, "delayering" has entered the management jargon to represent the expected reduction in hierarchical levels.[1] Thus, for middle managers, the shift in emphasis from planning and control to speed and flexibility may mean the end of an epoch. Roughly twenty percent of the job losses since 1988 have come from middle management positions.[2]

There is growing evidence, however, that delayering often has unanticipated, adverse consequences. The consulting firm of Towers Perrin asked 350 senior managers in 275 major firms whether hoped-for cost reductions had been achieved, and half said "no."[3] Some firms lose valuable skills in the delayering process. Kodak, for example, slashed 12,000 positions between 1988 and 1992—many of them middle managers—

but failed to achieve lasting performance improvement. Instead, innovation and creativity declined, and the company fell behind in the crucial race for new products.[4] Why doesn't delayering always work?

There are many things that can undermine successful organizational restructuring. But, at the heart of the problem in delayering seems to be the stereotypical "plan and control" view of middle management work. Seeing all middle managers from an operational viewpoint, top managers often fail to make distinctions about the variety of contributions made by middle managers, and, in particular, overlook the possibility that middle managers play strategic roles. Across-the-board or random influences (like attrition) become the *de facto* criteria for eliminating positions. As a result, delayering has the effect of "throwing the baby out with the bath water"—curtailing vital strategic capability while eliminating middle management layers.

In this article, we take a fresh look at the contribution of middle managers and provide a framework for differentiating the baby from the bath water. We argue that sustaining an adaptive balance between industry forces and organizational resources depends on the *strategic* roles of middle management. The recognition of these roles fosters a discriminating approach to delayering that increases the organizational influence of surviving middle managers. More like the Phoenix bird than the dinosaur, a new breed of middle managers—whose roles are more strategic than operational—should be rising from the ashes of the delayered corporation.

THE MISUNDERSTOOD MIDDLE MANAGER

Typically, middle managers have been seen as part of an organization's control system. Middle management does things which translate strategies defined at higher levels into actions at operating levels. This involves (1) defining tactics and developing budgets for achieving a strat-

egy, (2) monitoring the performance of individuals and subunits, and (3) taking corrective action when behavior falls outside expectations. This description, or major elements of it, has applied for decades to the organization members we call middle managers, including functional department heads, project or product managers, brand managers, regional managers, and the like. In the language of strategic management, their role has been defined as "implementation."

In the reengineered organization, however, senior managers rely less and less on middle managers. Information and communications technologies make it easier for those at the top to monitor and control activities directly. In addition, empowerment and cross-functional teams allow operators to take responsibility for defining their own roles. The emphasis on business processes vastly reduces the relevance of functional departments and the accompanying managerial hierarchies. Such "stove pipes" gave rise to middle management in the first place, and as the layers disappear, so does the rationale for middle managers.

The withering of middle management's *operating* responsibilities undeniably justifies reductions in the number of middle managers. But our research shows that performance of middle managers' *strategic* roles remains as a crucial factor in organizational success. In a study of twenty companies, for example, we found that middle manager involvement in the *formulation* of strategic decisions was associated with higher financial performance.[5] This is not to say that implementation is unimportant. Strategies that lack middle management commitment suffer serious implementation problems.[6] What differentiated higher performing organizations in this study, however, was an arrangement in which middle managers actively participated in the "thinking" as well as the "doing" of strategy. Involvement is an important stimulus to strategic thinking, so that strategies formulated with middle management input are likely to be superior to those designed solely by top managers.

In short, middle managers are frequently misunderstood by corporate America. Typically, they are seen in strictly operational terms, and their potential for enhancing the quality of firm strategy is discounted or ignored. Yet, research shows that middle management's strategic contributions directly affect the bottom line. What are these strategic contributions, and how do they sustain competitive advantage? Further, which middle management positions are likely to be most important in strategy? To answer these questions, we initiated a second study of 259 middle managers within a diverse set of companies and industry circumstances. Before presenting the results, the following section details middle management's strategic roles and explains why they are related to an organization's economic performance.

COMPETITIVE ADVANTAGE AND MIDDLE MANAGEMENT STRATEGIC ROLES

In a number of widely read papers, Jay Barney, Gary Hamel, C. K. Prahalad, David Teece, and others have argued that competitive advantage results from unique organizational resources. According to this view, the most important strategic resources are the knowledge and skills accumulated collectively over time by organization members. The organizational capabilities associated with such human assets cannot be bought on an open market. They are acquired over an extended period and as part of complex interpersonal processes, and this makes capabilities difficult or impossible to imitate. When they effectively differentiate a firm from its competitors, they are called "core capabilities." In comparison with specific products or technologies which can be copied, capabilities provide the potential for a more sustainable advantage. In principle, therefore, *dynamic capability*, or the ability to develop new capabilities, is the feature of organizations most likely to be associated with long-term economic performance.[7]

The striking correspondence between the nature of dynamic capability and our sense of how middle managers influence the quality of strategy provided impetus for our second study. Dynamic capability is a learning process which calls on organization members to interpret the world around them, to uncover new opportunities, to focus existing resources efficiently, and to accumulate new resources when existing ones become obsolete. Put simply, capabilities develop as the organization learns how to deliver what customers want and how to create new combinations of assets and skills. In other words, capabilities develop through the brains and nervous systems of middle managers.

After talking with dozens of middle managers and weaving our impressions from these interviews with the threads of prior research,[8] we developed a theoretical framework which captures the roles of middle managers in dynamic capability. Two principle dimensions underlie the roles. Each can be described as a dichotomy. Shown in Figure 1, the model combines upward and downward influence with integrative and divergent thinking to describe four roles: championing alternatives, synthesizing information, facilitating adaptability, and implementing deliberate strategy.[9]

CHAMPIONING STRATEGIC ALTERNATIVES

Sometimes, middle managers play an important part in bringing entrepreneurial and innovative proposals to top management's attention. Championing involves a complex sequence of activities. First, middle managers act as an initial screen, selecting from the broad array of business opportunities, new processes proposals, and administrative innovations suggested at operating levels. Living in the organizational space between strategy and operations, middle managers are uniquely qualified to make such judgments. Once committed, managers begin to nurture the idea, providing "seed" resources that allow experimentation. At this stage, the endeavor lacks formal sanction, and managers' effectiveness depends greatly on their ability to get informal cooperation

FIGURE 1 A TYPOLOGY OF MIDDLE MANAGEMENT ROLES IN STRATEGY

Behavioral Activity

		Upward Influence	Downward Influence
Cognitive Influences	Divergent	Championing Strategic Alternatives	Facilitating Adaptability
	Integrative	Synthesizing Information	Implementing Deliberate Strategy

and support. After gaining experience and building a credible proposal, middle managers take the initiative forward.

SYNTHESIZING INFORMATION

Not all the ideas brought upward by middle managers are full-blown strategic proposals. Frequently, their role is to supply information to top management concerning internal and external events. Inevitably, middle managers are not objective channels of data, however. They saturate information with meaning through personal evaluation and explicit advice. Events are likely to be reported as "threats" or "opportunities," and these seemingly innocent labels are a powerful influence on how superiors come to see their situation.[10]

In conveying "facts," middle managers may be laying the foundation for a future agenda. An opportunity can be championed successfully only when all agree the "timing is right," and usually this requires a considerable amount of prior discussion. Accordingly, middle managers are often able to control, or at least influence, top management perceptions by framing information in certain ways. This role can be crucial in encouraging overly cautious top management teams to take needed risks.

FACILITATING ADAPTABILITY

In her clinical analysis of a large computer manufacturer, Rosabeth Kanter describes the efforts of middle managers who sheltered and encouraged an employee involvement program in the midst of an emotional, top-down redesign of production processes.[11] Their efforts created an environment in which fears about the change could be brought into the discussion. Though participation helped the organization adopt the new work processes, the process diverged completely from top management's original intention. Without middle management's efforts to facilitate change, however, the reengineering would have met with considerably more resistance and could have failed.

Thus, while middle managers are often called change resisters, Kanter describes them as "change *masters*." We compare this role with the flexible, accordion-like structure between the two sections of a reticulated passenger bus. The shape and composition of the accordion overcomes the rigidities of the vehicle, while at the same time assuring that the front and back head in the same direction.

IMPLEMENTING DELIBERATE STRATEGY

In championing, synthesizing, and facilitating, middle managers go beyond, or even ignore, the plans embedded in top management's deliberate strategy. The most commonly recognized strategic role, however, is the implementation of top management's intentions. Here, the strategic contribution rests on middle managers' efforts to deploy existing resources efficiently and effectively. Reports suggest a widening gap between intentions and implementations,[12] however, and the cause is often attributed to middle manager obstinacy. Our research suggests another reason.

Implementation is commonly perceived as a mechanical process where action plans are deduced and carried out from a master strategy conceived by top management. The reality is more complex. Even in fairly stable situations, priorities must be revised as conditions evolve and new information unfolds. Implementation, therefore, is best characterized as an ongoing series of interventions which are only partly anticipated in top management plans and which adjust strategic directions to suit emergent events.

In summary, the conception that top managers formulate strategy while middle managers carry it out is not only unrealistic, it is also self-defeating. Effective implementation requires that middle managers understand the strategic rationale behind the plan, in addition to the specific directives. Such understanding appears to result from broad participation in the strategic process,[13] and middle management's effectiveness in implementing strategy is thus directly related to their involvement in other roles. The "implementation gap" reflects a broader chasm between senior management's perception of implementation and what middle managers must know to get the job done. In an earlier *AME* article, we described the problem as lack of *strategic consensus* and outlined a process for narrowing the gap.[14]

LINKING STRATEGIC ROLES TO CORE CAPABILITY

Seen through our own conceptual lens, anecdotal evidence suggested links between middle management and core capability. Because the argument countered prevailing wisdom, however, we wanted to go beyond logic and case study to examine the issue more systematically. Thus, we developed a questionnaire that would measure middle manager behavior in a large-scale, statistical survey. The

research design called for observation of hundreds of middle managers across many organizations and drew from a combination of objective and subjective data. Because different strategies rely on different capabilities, we expected to tie the middle manager roles to the success of particular organizational strategies.

The results uncovered three convincing patterns.[15] First, in organizations whose strategy depended on product innovation and exploiting new market opportunities, we found significantly higher levels of middle management championing and facilitating. Since core capability in innovating firms is related to the discovery of new business opportunity and operational flexibility, these results suggested the centrality of middle management.

Second, certain middle managers within the innovating firms were greater champions than others, and in particular, the involvement of those in "boundary spanning" functions (i.e., marketing, sales, purchasing, and R&D) was highest overall. Ideas arose most often from interactions with customers, suppliers, and technologies, and we found championing highest where such exposure was most likely. Not only was innovative capability in the firm related to middle management championing and facilitating, then, but these behaviors were concentrated in certain positions. In other words, boundary-spanning middle managers appeared to use strategically important knowledge in ways that fostered the development of core capabilities.

These results supported our argument that middle management was important to strategy and that some middle management positions were more important than others. To establish a link to core capability, we needed to determine whether such behavior actually led to improved economic performance. We did not expect a simple linear relationship, however. In fact, this appeared to be a case where "more is not always better."

Rather than simply *more* of the strategic role behaviors, the successful development of core capability demands variety. A similar hypothesis was suggested by

Stuart Hart and Catherine Banbury, who showed in a survey of top managers that firms who combined a diverse mix of strategy-making skills enjoyed enhanced capability and organizational performance. These skills included everything from formal planning procedures to informal experimentation, and even creating a "dream" about the company future.[16] Such skills and the behaviors associated with them are not likely to be distributed evenly throughout organizations. The successful formal planner, for example, is not likely to be the best dreamer. Similarly, middle managers are likely to differ widely in their ability and willingness to assume a strategic role at a particular point in time. As a result, one would expect considerable diversity in the levels of middle management strategic behavior within organizations that were successful in developing core capability.

Consistent with this, we asked top managers in each of the 25 companies we studied to assess the financial performance of their organization. Then we examined whether performance was associated with a statistical measure of diversity in middle management behavior. We found strong relationships between variation in the performance of the strategic roles and economic performance. This provided the first scientific evidence to support the proposition that middle managers are potential reservoirs of core capability.[17] But how does this change the way one thinks of middle managers in a world of flatter, reengineered organizations?

MIDDLE MANAGEMENT'S ROLE IN THE REENGINEERED ORGANIZATION

At the beginning of this article we noted that middle managers in hierarchical organizations have been seen as the implementers of top management strategies. Thus, as organizations have been reengineered around horizontal processes, it is not surprising that the perceived need for middle managers has diminished. Unfortunately, the dominant, operational stereotype of middle managers has led to the diminution of their strategic contributions.

Conversations with top and middle level managers reveal that the strategic roles we describe are misunderstood, considered secondary, almost always nonsanctioned, and often discouraged. Yet, reengineering's emphasis on responsiveness, flexibility, and speed puts a premium on the middle manager behavior associated with the development of new capabilities. In this section we first illustrate how organizations unwittingly discourage strategic behavior. The paper closes, then, with a set of guidelines for senior managers who want to encourage effective behavior in the reengineered organization.

The behavior associated with facilitating adaptability is often seen as risky and somewhat subversive. In his study of resource allocation, Joseph Bower describes how middle managers diverted resources and hid experimental programs from top management scrutiny in order to gain experience and acquire new capabilities. Not surprisingly, our interviews suggest that some top managers often view this role cynically. One CEO commented, "Oh, they've all got their own pet projects; I guess that's part of the price you pay." This view discourages the learning gained from experimentation and thereby lowers the level of dynamic capability.

Championing is generally recognized as a middle management activity, but its potential contribution is not always appreciated. One top manager described middle management championing as an "earned right," reserved only for a few in recognition of many years of "credible service." Similarly, many middle managers in our interviews observed that championing meant "spending currency" with top managers. It was pursued sparingly, as "an exception." Just as telling, some middle managers felt their real influence was minimal.

The role of middle managers as channels of communication and sources of information is well recognized. However, middle managers are often criticized for "putting their own spin on it." Senior managers use elaborate systems such as formal planning to objectify and rationalize middle management input. Unfortunately, formal, bureaucratic processes make the ongoing re-interpretation of events less likely and introduce undesirable rigidity into the decision-making process. Subjective interpretation is inevitable, and need not be considered pernicious.[18]

REALIZING MIDDLE MANAGEMENT'S STRATEGIC VALUE

In sum, our ongoing research on middle management's role in strategy suggests that as organizations move away from hierarchical toward more horizontal business structures, the importance of middle managers in achieving competitive advantage is likely to increase. While often unrecognized, their contributions in interpreting, nurturing, developing, and promoting new capabilities take on new importance as organizations strive to achieve increased levels of adaptability and responsiveness. Thus, the reengineered organization is likely to be delayered and certain to have fewer middle managers, but those remaining will be crucial to the firm's ongoing success. Senior managers interested in leveraging these human assets should reexamine middle management according to the following set of principles:

- **Recognize the link between middle management, core capability, and competitive advantage.** Most fundamentally, reengineering should occur with an awareness of the link between middle management and firm competitiveness. Effective delayering can be guided by an understanding of the contributions required of surviving middle managers. The goal is to cut cost and increase responsiveness, not cripple dynamic capability.
- **Identify middle managers with the appropriate skills, experiences, and potential to thrive within the new organization.** Not all middle managers are created equally, and certain middle managers are better equipped than others to thrive within the reengineered organization. Our research shows the importance of boundary spanning experience as one criterion

for discriminating among middle managers. Another consideration is that middle management in the reengineered organization requires strategy and teaming skills. In the long run, developmental experiences that foster teamwork and a strategic mind set can be avoided only at the cost of eroding core capability.

- **Develop a better understanding of desired roles within the organization.** Few top- or middle-level managers fully understand the strategic roles described here. How many top managers have articulated their expectations along these lines to middle management? For reengineering to pay off, top managers need to analyze the changed role of middle management and begin to develop it within the organization. Interventions with middle managers can clarify expectations and encourage appropriate behavior.
- **Redesign the organization to leverage the knowledge and skills of a selected set of middle managers and encourage their influence on strategic priorities.** Delayering should be accompanied by reorganizing according to a process-oriented, horizontal logic. Though most top managers understand the idea of horizontal design, few appreciate the redistribution of power called for in the new arrangements.

Organizational boundaries are becoming increasingly fuzzy as networks of suppliers, customers, and competitors are formed to cope with enormously complex and demanding circumstances. Organizations want to capture the influence of middle managers who relate to the market and technological environments. In order to open up the organization to environmental influence, boundary-spanning middle managers should become the owners of product development, order fulfillment, and other key business processes.

The need for power shifts—from functional to process leadership, for example—is often lost on those considering or undergoing a reengineering effort. Sometimes, senior managers expect middle managers to take charge of a process but give them very little real authority. Without the freedom to experiment, middle managers quickly become frustrated and cynical about top management's intent. "Slack" has become a dirty word, but the flexibility, experimentation, and learning which is the goal of horizontal organization does require resources.

- Renegotiate the "psychological contract" by committing to the ongoing involvement of middle management in the strategy-making process.

Restructuring is often seen as destroying a time-honored employment contract and ". . . many companies have given no indication of what the new psychological contract is."[19] Most managers want to be loyal, but if the old vision is simply thrown out with nothing to replace it, management loyalty goes out the window, too. An unknown future does not inspire confidence. Instead, it encourages talented managers to leave, thereby draining the reservoirs of core capability and eroding competitive position. Disloyalty also contributes to foot dragging and even sabotage of a reengineering strategy.

RECOGNIZING MIDDLE MANAGEMENT'S STRATEGIC VALUE

The key to broadening middle management's participation beyond the implementation role is to bring them into the strategic communications loop. Unfortunately, most senior managers think of communicating strategy "to the troops" as an annual or quarterly effort handled in large auditoriums or in a video conference. The idea of discussing strategy eye to eye with middle managers, much less engaging in an ongoing strategic dialogue, seems like an unnatural act.

The restructuring effort of a large insurance firm provides an example. An early step involved assembling district managers at corporate headquarters for a week-long planning session. In prior years, the agenda had been limited to financial reporting and budgeting. Since the company hoped to decentralize as a part of the delayering, some of the week was set aside to "do strategic planning." When it was suggested that the regional managers were likely to generate ideas for new products and market opportunities, however, the reaction of top management went beyond skepticism. One of the executives commented "These people don't even understand the basics . . . and we're going to get new ideas about our strategy from *that* bunch?"

Much of the initial problem in this firm, as in most, was that upper and middle managers had lived wholly different realities in the organization and spoke a different language. Bridging this kind of communications chasm meant translating the strategy into a vision that could be interpreted across diverse perspectives.

This company was facing declining premium revenues as rivals chipped away at what had been a very comfortable niche. Senior management saw the problem as a need for new technical services that would differentiate them from rivals, retain customers, and build new business. It was far less clear, however, which particular services would appeal to customers or which ones the organization could deliver. These initiatives could have come from the field. But how do you solicit strategic initiatives when you really do not know what you want?

The answer came in creating a dialogue with regional managers about a strategic vision. The basis of the vision was captured by this admonition: to chart your own competitive future get to know the future of your customer's business. By communicating this simple idea, and more important, by talking about its implications one-on-one over a period of time, top management began getting substantive input from its middle management. These ideas provided the basis for reorganizing, redeploying managerial talent, and reinvigorating the competitive edge.

In many of our conversations with middle- as well as senior-level managers, this set of consequences seems to be inevitable. One thing becoming clear where delayering has succeeded, however, is that surviving middle managers enjoy a renewed sense of power and contribution. This results from an acknowledgment by company executives that middle managers have strategic value. Delayering can enlist middle managers in new strategic roles, but this requires a vision, organizational redesign, and new power relationships. The insert on the previous page details one company's experience in realigning middle management's roles.

EVERYONE A MIDDLE MANAGER?

The growth of the ranks of middle management during the post-war period allowed many Western companies to expand. Middle management provided the consistency and control so necessary to enterprise. While the resulting bureaucratic hierarchy may no longer fit today's demand for flexibility, wholesale elimination of the middle management role may be short-sighted. Some suggest middle management is a dying breed, but Tom Peters writes that everyone is becoming a middle manager.[20] This outlook is grounded in his customer- and change-dominated view of organization. There will be fewer layers and fewer managers overall, but the strategic roles of middle managers are likely to become more, rather than less, important in the organizations of tomorrow.

REFERENCES

1 A host of terms related to organizational restructuring have entered the lexicon. For our purposes, restructuring is the most general, referring to all efforts aimed at radical reorganization. Consistent with Michael Hammer and James Champy's book, *Reengineering the Corporation* (Harper Business, 1993), we use reengineering to refer to the process-driven style of organizing. Delayering is one aspect of reengineering and refers to the reduction of managerial levels.

2 Touby, Laurel. 1993. "The Business of America is Jobs." *Journal of Business Strategy*, pp. 21–31.

3 Fisher, Anne B. 1991. "Morale Crisis," *Fortune.* (November 18).

4 Burrus, Daniel. 1994. Technotrends: *How You can Go Beyond Your Competition by Applying Tomorrow's Technology Today.* New York, NY: Harper-Collins.

5 Wooldridge, Bill, and Steven W. Floyd. 1990. "The Strategy Process, Middle Management Involvement, and Organizational Performance," *Strategic Management Journal*, 11. pp, 213–241.

6 Guth, W. D., and Ian C. MacMillan. 1986. "Strategy Implementation Versus Middle Management Self-Interest." *Strategic Management Journal*, 7, pp. 313–327.

7 Few managers would dispute the importance of core capabilities in competitive strategy, and numerous examples suggest a strong relationship to organizational performance. A widely circulated working paper by David Teece, Gary Pisano, and Amy Shuen summarizes the scholarly literature on the resource-based view of strategy and core capabilities: "Dynamic Capabilities and Strategic Management," University of California at Berkeley working paper, 1992.

8 The principal studies we relied on for an initial definition of middle managers' roles in strategy included: J. L. Bower. 1970. *Managing the Resource Allocation Process* (Boston, MA: Harvard Business School); R. A. Burgelman. 1983. "A Process Model of Internal Corporate Venturing in the Diversified Major Firm," *Administrative Science Quarterly*, 28, pp. 223–244; R. M. Kanter. 1983. *The Change Masters* (New York, NY: Basic Books); T. Kidder. 1981. *The Soul of a New Machine* (Boston, MA: Little, Brown); I. Nonaka. 1988. "Toward Middle-Up-Down Management: Accelerating Information Creation," *Sloan Management Review*, Spring, pp. 9–18; and P. C. Nutt. 1987. "Identifying and Appraising How Managers Install

Strategy," *Strategic Management Journal*, 8, pp. 1–14.

9 This model was first described in our article: S. W. Floyd and Bill Wooldridge. 1992. "Middle Management Involvement in Strategy and its Association with Strategic Type," *Strategic Management Journal*, 13 (special issue), pp. 153–167.

10 See Jane E. Dutton and Susan E. Jackson. 1987. "Categorizing Strategic Issues: Links to Organization Action," *Academy of Management Review*, 12, pp. 76–90, for a more elaborate discussion. More recently, Jane E. Dutton and Susan J. Ashford published an article related directly to middle managers: "Selling Issues to Top Management," *Academy of Management Review*, 18, 1993, pp. 397–428.

11 Kanter, *op. cit.*

12 A study by Booz-Allen and Hamilton, Inc., "Making Strategy Work: The Challenge of the 1990s," was published in 1990. It is particularly articulate on this point and is available from their New York Office.

13 In this study cited under reference number 5, we found that middle managers who were involved in formulating as well as implementing strategy tended to understand the strategy better.

14 Floyd, Steven W., and Bill Wooldridge. 1992. "Managing Strategic Consensus: The Key to Effective Implementation," *Academy of Management Executive*, 6, pp. 27–39.

15 These results were first described in the study cited in endnote number 9.

16 Hart, S., and C. Banbury. 1994. "How Strategy-Making Processes Can Make a Difference," *Strategic Management Journal*, 15, 251–269.

17 The results on boundary-spanning middle managers and organized performance are reported in a working paper: S. W. Floyd and Bill Wooldridge. 1994. "Middle Management Behavior, Dynamic Capability, and Organizational Performance."

18 The reader interested in pursuing this idea could begin by reading Richard Daft and Karl Weick's article, "Toward a Model of Organizations as Interpretation Systems," *Academy of Management Review*, 9, pp. 284–296.

19 The fading expectations of middle managers were expressed eloquently in an article titled "The Death of Corporate Loyalty," in *The Economist*, April 3, 1993, 63, which quoted David A. Nadler on this particular point.

20 See Tom Peters' book, *Thriving on Chaos* (New York, NY: The Free Press, 1987).

ABOUT THE AUTHORS

Steven W. Floyd and Bill Wooldridge are associate professors of strategic management at the University of Connecticut and University of Massachusetts at Amherst, respectively. Their recent research focuses on middle managers and the behaviors associated with developing and sustaining competitive advantage. In addition, the authors study the processes related to strategy formation and emergent adaptation within top management teams. Their work on strategic consensus and middle managers has been published previously in the *Academy of Management Executive*, and appeared frequently in the *Strategic Management Journal*. Jointly or independently, they have also published in the *Academy of Management Journal*, *Journal of Management Information Systems*, and the *Handbook of Business Strategy*. Currently, they are writing a book on the strategic roles of middle managers. As consultants, the authors apply a high-involvement approach to strategy making that helps organizations appreciate and elicit contributions from all managers.

PRESS

INDEX